The Song of the Sun: Collected Writings

In Lausanne, Switzerland, 1 August 1961

The Song of the Sun
✥ Collected Writings

Leah Bodine Drake

Edited by David E. Schultz

Illustrations by Jason C. Eckhardt

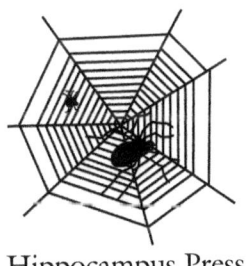

Hippocampus Press

New York

Copyright © 2020 by Hippocampus Press. Introduction and editorial matter copyright © 2020 by David E. Schultz. Joshi. Interior artwork copyright © 2020 by Jason C. Eckhardt.

Published by Hippocampus Press, P.O. Box 641, New York, NY 10156
www.hippocampuspress.com

All rights reserved. No part of this work may be reproduced in any form or by any means without the written permission of the publisher.

Grateful acknowledgment is made to the following institutions and parties for permission to publish material in their possession: Leah Bodine Drake papers, 1918–1968, undated, University of Kentucky Special Collections Research Center, 68m100, for unpublished poems by and photographs of Leah Bodine Drake; Wisconsin Historical Society, Library–Archives Division, for Drake's letters to August Derleth and the Stuart Art Gallery, a letter by Derleth to Drake, and a passage from Derleth's Sauk Prairie Journal; David L. Rice Library University Archives & Special Collections at the University of Southern Indiana, for unpublished poems and an essay by and a photograph of Leah Bodine Drake, as well as a drawing by Cornelia B. Drake; Yale Collection of American Literature, Beinecke Rare Book and Manuscript Library, for letters by Leah Bodine Drake to William Rose Benét and the *Saturday Review*; Mercury Press Records, Special Collections Research Center, Syracuse University Libraries, for letters by Leah Bodine Drake to Anthony Boucher and *The Magazine of Fantasy and Science Fiction*; John Hay Library, Brown University, for letters by Leah Bodine Drake to Joseph Payne Brennan; L. Tom Perry Special Collections, Brigham Young University, Provo, UT, MSS 391, for a letter by Leah Bodine Drake to August Derleth laid in with the typescript of *A Hornbook for Witches*; Library Special Collections, Western Kentucky University, collection number SC 1575, for letters by Leah Bodine Drake to Grace and Fletcher Stewart; August Derleth estate for a letter by Derleth to Leah Bodine Drake and an extract from his Sac Prairie Journal.

Cover illustration by Cornelia B. Drake. Interior illustrations by Jason C. Eckhardt. Cover design and map on p. 27 by Dan Sauer, dansauerdesign.com.
Hippocampus Press logo designed by Anastasia Damianakos.

First Edition
1 3 5 7 9 8 6 4 2
ISBN 978-1-61498-266-1 hardcover
ISBN 978-1-61498-267-8 paperback

Contents

INTRODUCTION	19
PHOTOGRAPHS	71
COLLECTED POEMS	93
A Dream of Samarkand (1919–1934)	97
On a Chinese Screen	99
I. Lady Writing a Letter	99
II. Moon Festival	99
III. The Deserted Courtyard	100
IV. By the River	100
V. A Lady of the Emperor's Palace	101
VI. One Intoxicated	101
Mombāsa	101
To a Lost Sweetheart	103
Song at Sunrise	103
Words After Wisdom	104
The Ballad of Fair Elspeth	105
Gazelles in a Zoo	108
Apple	109
The Land of the Japanese Prints	110
Burma: Moulmein Bazaar	111
The Country Lover	112
Belle and Beau	113
The Belle	113
The Beau	114
The Sailorman (1690)	115
A Dream of Samarkand	116
Our Lady's Song	118
The Pixy Fair	119
Turn of Year	119
The Croon of the Mer-Mother	120
Jilly and the Elf	123
The Saints of Four-Mile-Water	124
The Haunted Hour	125
Mad Jenny	126
Little Things	129
"There Are Fairies"	129

The Little Piper 130
Peddler's Pack 131
"My Help Cometh from the Hills" 134
Descent of Angels (1935–1936) 135
   In the Shadows 137
   The Man Who Married a Swan-Maiden 137
   High Renaissance 138
   India: In the Garden of Spices 139
   He Dreams of Barbary 140
   The Assyrian Lion 141
   A Sigh in Spring 142
   The Fairies in Autumn 142
   The Giant's Garden 143
   Unhappy Ending 145
   Winter Harvests 146
      Frozen Heart 146
      Owl's Cry 147
      "Peace on Earth" 147
      Winter Harvest 149
   Explanation 150
   Figures in a Nightmare 150
   The Witch Walks in Her Garden 151
   Descent of Angels 152
   Terror by Night 153
   Old Wives' Tale 155
   A Hornbook for Witches 157
      I. The Covenant 157
      II. The Besom 157
      III. The Coven 157
      IV. The Hell-Broth 157
      V. The Magic Circle 158
      VI. The Conjuration 158
      VII. The Pentagram 158
      VIII. The Spells 158
      IX. Magician's Hat 159
      X. Witch's Wheel 159
      XI. The Familiar 159
      XII. Enchanted Sleep 159
   The Nixie's Pool 160
   The Wind and the Leaves 161

CONTENTS

    All-Saints' Eve 161
    Witches on the Heath 162
    Curious Story... 163
    The Girl in the Glass 164
    Goat-Song 165
Fantasy in a Forest (1937–1941).. 169
    The Path through the Marsh... 171
    Tiger.. 172
    Crocodile 173
    Japan: The Persimmon Gatherers 174
    The Old Khan and His Falcon 175
    'Round and 'Round 176
    Midsummer Night.. 177
    Ducks and Pigs 178
    Puss-in-Boots and the Three Mice 179
    The Journey of the Queen of Sheba.. 181
    Serpent-Ring 184
    The Seven Sons of the King of Thule 185
    Conversation in an Oak-Tree 186
    The Last Faun 187
    The Naughty Fairy 188
    The Three Green Ladies of Greenwich 190
    Born under Capricorn... 192
    The Bittern 192
    The Centaurs 193
    Rabbit-Dance 194
    The Old Granny's Story... 195
    Sea-Shell 196
    The Stranger.. 197
    "What Are Little Girls Made Of?" 198
    The Tenants... 199
    Bad Company.. 199
    "Run with the Fox" 201
    Encounter in Broceliande 202
    A Star Came Out... 203
    The Daughter of the Grand Turk Loses Her Ball......................... 204
    "Apples and Apricots, Peaches and Plums" 206
    The Steps in the Field 207
    Mouse Heaven... 208
    Protective Colouring 210

They Run Again 210
The Wood-Wife 211
House Accursed 214
The Minotaur 215
Rhymes without Reason; or, History Made Difficult 215
From Nonsensical Rhymes 217
I Met a Lion 218
Fantasy in a Forest 219
Full Moon, 1940 220
The Girl on the Saw-Backed Mountain 221
Lost Heritage 222
King Gog and King Magog 223
Gold from a Kettle 224
Drake of Devon 226
Griffon's Gold 227
On a Night of Stars 228
Man in Winter 229
The Hen-Wife's Chickens 230

Honey from the Lion (1942–1948) 233
Vestal 235
The Singer from the Waste 236
The Fruit Uneaten 237
Gage to a Lover 238
A Vase from Araby 240
The Window on the Stair 240
The Phoenix Egg 241
Changeling 242
Retrogression 243
Bread of Solitude 244
Music for Sun and Moon 245
Enchanted Honey 246
Luna 247
Ballad of the Seal-Woman's Daughter 248
Fairy Cider 249
King Solomon 250
Turning Point 253
Nativities 253
The Comet 254
Bird's-Eye View 255
December Stars 255

CONTENTS

Cold Orchard 256
Bats 257
The Unclimbed Hill 257
The House in the Hollow 258
The Black Peacock 259
Snowy Night 260
Cinder-Jewels 261
Birds in a Barn 262
A Country Grave 263
No Refuge 264
Earth: Atomic Age 265
Daphne 266
To an Atheist 267
Cold Comfort 267
The Beaches Beyond Oblivion 268
Ballad of the Jabberwock 269
To One Who Fears Poetry Is Useless 273
Design for a Tapestry: 14th Century 273
To Elinor Wylie 274
Legend 276
Beyond Eden 277
Heard on the Roof at Midnight 278
Help Wanted 279
A Likely Story! 280
Leonardo Before His Canvas 281
Dark Memory 282
Snow Crystals 283
The Vision 284
Minor Poet 285
Old Daphne 286
Wild Geese in Spring 286
Moment at Sunset 287
Poplar-Wind 287
The Fur Coat 288
Honey from the Lion 288
The Heads on Easter Island 289
The Return 290
Song against Smallness 291
Willow-Women 292
Mad Woman's Song 293

Song of the Sun.. 294
The Old World of Green 295
Currier and Ives Prints... 296
The False Messiah... 296
The Unknown Land 297
The Green Door 298
After the Green Star Dies 300
"Like Breath upon a Glass".. 301
The Pool... 301
Precarious Ground (1949–1952) 303
The Windows of Chartres... 305
The Lariat: 6000 B.C. 305
Gifts for Christ 306
The Darkened Glass.. 307
Atavism 308
Dirge for a Doomed Planet 309
To Certain Poetry Critics.. 310
The Undine 310
Sunset Apocalypse 311
Kingfisher Lake 311
The Revenant 313
Cave Paintings, Altamira 314
The Unploughed Field 315
We Come Out of the Forest, Fearing Stars................... 316
The Vision of Jenghiz-Khan 317
Precarious Ground.. 317
Love Song 318
The Mermaid... 319
Cobra 321
Six Merry Farmers 322
The Wind in the Chimney 323
Out!.. 324
Bookworm 325
A Warning to Skeptics.. 325
The Final Green.. 326
The Foam-Born... 327
Red Ghosts in Kentucky... 329

Contents

An Unlikely Noah's Ark 330
    Wyvern 330
    Satyr 331
    Centaur 331
    Pooka 331
    Minotaur 331
    Werewolf 332
    Fury 332
    Cockatrice 332
    Chimaera 332
    Spirit-Fox 333
    Salamander 333
    Ghoul 333
    Roc 334
    Sphinx 334
Overheard in Baghdad 334
Atlantis 336
The Four 337
The Birth of Beauty 337
We Move on Turning Stone (1953–1956) 339
    Powers of the Air 341
    The Web 341
    Fool's Paradise 342
    The Enchanted Swans 343
    Gipsies 344
    Solar 345
    Cat Mummy 345
    The Jannigogs 347
    The Middle Ages: Two Views 348
    Semele 349
    Childhood Summers 350
    Railroad Tracks 351
    The Web of Living 352
    Air 352
    Flemish Artists 353
    Through-Train 354
    The Unicorn Wounded 355

Incoming Tide 356
Drone 356
We Move on Turning Stone 358
The Gods of the Dana 358
Ark 359
Rock and Bramble 360
Fairy-Tale: Twentieth Century 361
The Lazy Prince 362
The Storks 363
Old Man on the Seashore 365
Zanzibar 365
The Woods Grow Darker 366
The Crows 367
The Rain on the Stone 367
The Weeds and the Wilderness 369
The Well 371
Under Funereal Lilies 371
The Good-Advisors 372
The Crying of the Grass 372
Noon Light 373
High Wire 374
The Word of Willow 374
The Harvest 376
The Fawn 376
Moment in Paradise 378
Comment on Man 379
A Memory 379
The Forerunner 380
The Nail 381
Multiple Clay 382
The Hand 383
The Prisoner 384

The Face in the Water (1957–1964) 385
The Rider 387
The Robin 387
The Hellenic World 388
"In the Night I Awoke" 390
"Brightness Falls from the Air" 391
Alone 391
"I Dreamed That You Took My Arm." 392

CONTENTS

Uncle Jay 392
Folk-Tale 394
The Tale of Tannhauser 395
Lullaby After Death 396
With Her Death 397
To Mother 398
Ariadne on Naxos 398
A Voice 398
The Convent Bell 399
"Only a Little Dust" 400
That Summer 400
Lying Awake 401
What the Devil Said 402
The Cry 403
[Untitled] 404
The Spray 404
On the Night-Wind 404
The Growing Tree 405
The Wasp in the Window 405
The Witches 406
A Meeting on a Northern Moor 409
Tarascon 409
Little Song 410
Orchids 411
The Snake 411
In the Night 412
The Terrible Meek 412
The Morning 413
All-Hallows 414
Royal 414
Circe 414
The Presence 415
The Face in the Water 415
The Eve of St. Tib 416
At Alise Sainte-Reine 417
Fairy Tale 417
Ask the Trees 419
A Back-Country Road in God's Country 420
The Gossip 420
Okio's Geese 421

ॐ 13

Alternate Readings and Unfinished Poems 423
   Evening in Late Summer 425
   Unicorn 425
   Coming Back to the House 426
   Nativities 427
   Gothic 427
   Cold Orchard 429
   Unlikely Story 429
   Poplar Wind 430
   Landscape with Horses: 6000 B.C. 431
   Dirge for a Doomed Planet 432
   Reincarnation 433
   This Side of Oblivion 435
   The Under-Seas 435
   The Under-Seas 436
   The Cytherean 436
   Air 437
   Adam's Hand 439
   With Every Death 439
   That Summer 440
   From a destroyed early poem 440
   "Hunter" 441
   Adam the First Poet 442
   From a poem to Mother 442
   The Five Angels 442
   A Charm for the New Year 443
   [Untitled] 444
   Coral Reef at Calico Key 444
   Switzerland 447
   in the woods of the Vaud 448

FICTION 449
   Time and the Sphinx 451
   Whisper Water 454
   Foxy's Hollow 470
   Mop-Head 477

NONFICTION 493
   Frederic Prokosch 495
   [Untitled judge's report] 499
   Gremlins 500

Contents

Whimsy and Whamsy 501
The Devil and Miss Barker 502
Abracadabra 504
Miscellaneous Reviews 505
[On "We Come Out of the Forest . . ."] 516
New Voices in Poetry 524
The New Poetry 533
Books and Pictures Which Influenced My Poems 542
Magic Casements 542
A Poem Should Have 544
To Be a Poet 544
Life in These United States 545
[For *The Living Voice*] 546
    What Poetry Means to Me 546
    The Web 546
    Precarious Ground 548
    Old Man on the Sea Shore: Morning 548
    The Undine 549
    The Birth of Beauty 549
    Final Green 550
Foreword [to *The Various Light*] 551

Letters **553**
    Published Letters 555
        To the *Chicago Sunday Tribune* 555
        To *Hearst's International* 555
        To *Photoplay*, "Brickbats & Bouquets" 556
        To *Weird Tales* 556
        Letter to *Sight and Sound* 561
        Letter to *American Mercury* 562
    Unpublished Letters 563
        To August Derleth 563
        To Anthony Boucher 621
        To William Rose Benét 635
        To Joseph Payne Brennan 638
        To Grace and Fletcher Stewart 643
        With Lawrence S. Thompson 647
        To the Stuart Art Gallery 654

The Song of the Sun ❧ Leah Bodine Drake

APPENDIX 657
   [Announcement of Award] 659
   Leah Bodine Drake Writes Volume of "Macabre" Poems 660
   Possible Earnings on *A Hornbook for Witches* 662
   A Hornbook for Witches [Jacket Blurb] 663
   The Lineaments of Faerie 664
   [From *The International Who's Who in Poetry*] 667
   [From *The Supplement to Who's Who*, March–May 1959] 668
   [Death Announcement] 668
BIBLIOGRAPHY 673
INDEX OF TITLES OF POEMS 745
INDEX OF FIRST LINES OF POEMS 757

PHOTOGRAPHS
In Lausanne, Switzerland, 1 August 1961 2
Leah Bodine Drake, December 1949 73
Drake as an infant and toddler 74
Drake and her father 74
Location and date unknown 75
Lexington, Kentucky, 1923 75
Artesia, New Mexico, 1926 75
Philadelphia, March 1928 76
Brownwood, Texas, June 1928 76
"Mrs. Leslie MacAllister," Jackson, Mississippi 77
"Mac," Jackson, Mississippi, August 1929 77
August 1930, location unknown 77
1931, location unknown 77
"Queen," Dallas Centennial, 1936 78
Drake on float, "Spirit of Dallas" 78
Miss Leah Bodine Drake, 5 November 1941 78
Drake looking jubilant, date unknown 79
Thomas Hulbert Drake, 1947 80
Date unknown, possibly 1947 80
421 W. 2nd, Lexington, KY 81
1023 First St. Henderson, KY 81
3115 E. Mulberry St., Evansville, IN 81
1219 S.E. 1st Street, Evansville, IN 81
The Poet's House, New Harmony, Indiana, December 1958 81

CONTENTS

"The Pool" (1955) by Cornelia B. Drake 82
Unidentified drawing (1896) by J. J. Waugh. 82
Drake c. 1944 83
Drake, date unknown.. 83
Drake December 1950, Evansville 83
Drake and Wanda M. Rogers tending to a stray dog, 1952 83
Jim Carey and Drake flanking Pat Dean Smith, September 1941........ 84
Drake c. 1954 84
Wallace Stevens, Lenora Speyer, and Drake, 24 January 1951 84
Paul S. Nickerson, Drake, and Dr. Robert T. Moore at a
    dinner of the Poetry Society of America... 85
Drake with Dr. Robert T. Moore, February 1954 85
Evansville, c. 1955 86
A typical page from one of Drake's "illuminated" scrapbooks 87
Drake c. 1953 88
Drake, Parkersburg, 1957 88
Drake and Dr. Alfred J. Niedermayer, 1958. 88
Drake c. 1958, Parkersburg... 89
"En Route to Europe," 29 May 1960 89
Drake c. 1961, Parkersburg... 89
"Myself and Sabrina" (unidentified), Lausanne, Christmas 1961 89
1801 Avery Street, Parkersburg 90
1316 Market Street, Parkersburg, Drake's last residence 90
Trinity Episcopal Church, 430 Juliana St., Parkersburg 90
Charles A. Musès 91
Leah Bodine Drake, 1 August 1961, Lausanne, Suisse........................ 91
The grave marker of Leah Bodine Drake... 92

DRAWINGS
. . . with her black eyes wild a-glitter and her grey hair all askew 127
Soft, ghostly calls across the midnight come....................................... 148
The plush sides quiver and the jade eyes gleam 154
O there's no doubt! a witch I must be... 200
A bit more than human and much less than good. 212
And snug in the gloom, emptied jug after jug, ... 251
Then folk began to see it . . . clinging to the steeple 270
A lean shadow now obliquely moves across her rippled roof............. 320
Skeins of her hair in tapestry are wound, in Persian rug and
    Byzantine brocade.. 328

The Song of the Sun ❧ Leah Bodine Drake

You walked softly once to little bells 346
To a crow kinship means Crow, ... 368
The tiny creature . . . gave a little bound, frantic with joy, ... 377
"Who are you, flimsy ghost on a ghost-horse riding the
   night-wind?" 408
He sings to her, the flaxen-haired, compassionate king's daughter 418
Don't nobody live around here except you-all and Old Man Tuttle ... 457

Introduction

When the muse sits on my shoulder, I must write.[1]

Leah Bodine Drake has long had the dubious distinction of being the little-known author of one of the rarest (and therefore now most expensive) books that appeared from Arkham House, a specialty publisher of weird and fantasy fiction. Lately she has gained a reputation as a pioneering female science fiction writer,[2] although little of her work is truly science fiction, and she was no pioneer in the genre. A scant handful of her works have been reprinted recently, but the vast bulk of it has long been unavailable—out of print, uncollected, unpublished. But in her day, Drake was a well-known and much-admired mainstream poet. Who was this elusive figure?

Leah Bodine Drake was the only child of oilman Thomas Hulbert Drake (24 September 1881–17 May 1963) of Parkersburg, West Virginia, and Cornelia Woodward (Bodine) Drake (21 May 1869–28 December 1956) of Williamstown, New Jersey.[3] Thomas was the son of Sedgwick S. Drake (10 April 1846–25 September 1912) of Parkersburg, also an oilman, and Cornelia Martha (Gale) Drake (6 February 1847–1 July 1921) of New York. Cornelia Gale was the daughter of E. L. Gale and Mary Gale. Gale drilled for oil in West Virginia at Volcano and Burning Springs in the 1860s. (Burning Springs sold petroleum many years before the Edwin L. Drake well struck oil at Titusville, PA.) Both his son-in-law and grandson went into the oil business. Leah's mother was the daughter

---

1. Attributed to LBD, as related by Bethel D. Swint (Wood 2).
2. See Eric L. Davin, *Partners in Wonder*, and Lisa Yaszek and Patrick B. Sharp, *Sisters of Tomorrow*.
3. One version of LBD's poem "That Summer," drafted in 1959 completed in 1964, concludes with the line "That was the summer when my brother drowned." In an earlier version, the identity of the drowning victim is unknown. LBD once told AD (11 September 1960), "I *had* a mother who died, I never had a brother or a sister who even lived. (Only Child.)" What she meant by "who even lived" is uncertain, but it seems to imply that a sibling may have been stillborn or died in infancy.

The Song of the Sun ❧ Leah Bodine Drake

of William Henry Bodine (9 January 1824–17 December 1908) of Tuckerton, New Jersey, and Mary Virginia (Slacum) Bodine (16 April 1833–10 February 1913) of Dorchester County, Maryland. Her father was a prominent businessman retired from the glass business.

Thomas Drake and Cornelia Bodine met on 4 July 1902, while he was attending the U.S. Naval Academy. Cornelia had visited Annapolis with friends to observe various drills and exercises. The newspapers said theirs was "love at first sight." Midshipman Drake did not graduate, and instead left the academy to work at the Oil Well Supply company in Chanute, Kansas. Cornelia's parents had consented to her being married at home around Christmas 1903, but the couple could not wait, and so Drake traveled several hundred miles from Chanute, ostensibly on business, and Cornelia 1500 miles from Williamstown, New Jersey, ostensibly to meet a girlfriend in St. Louis, where they were married on 21 August 1903 at the Planters Hotel. Thomas was twenty-three; Cornelia gave her age as twenty-seven (she was actually thirty-four). One newspaper account said the couple would make Chanute their home permanently. That proved to be anything but the case.

Their daughter Leah was born Thursday, 22 December 1904, in Chanute, where her father was "a personable oil speculator."[4] The birth record gives her father's age as twenty-five and her mother's as twenty-six, and Leah's middle name not as Bodine but Virginia. Perhaps Cornelia, who "was artistic, and known for both her beautiful etchings and some of the finest needlework imaginable,"[5] had named her daughter Leah Virginia, selecting her mother's own middle name, which her mother apparently used as her preferred praenomen. The reason Leah adopted Bodine as her middle name is unknown, but she did so prior to 1920, before she turned fifteen. She may have done it in recognition of Leah Bodine (1809–1879), second wife of Joel Bodine (1794–1879), who was father of William Henry Bodine, and so her great-grandfather. Or perhaps she wanted to recognize the overall lineage of her mother's family. Drake, who had a lifelong interest in witches, enjoyed pointing out that Jean

---

4. Wood 3.
5. As related by Louise Helm (Wood 3).

Introduction

Bodin (1530–1596), a French jurist, political philosopher, and witch-hunter, was a distant relative to whom she dedicated her first book.

Three months after Leah was born, the family moved to Philadelphia. Drake once quipped, "true to the old saying, 'Thursday's child has far to go,'"[6] and indeed she did, for her father spent his entire life crossing the country with his wife and daughter in pursuit of oil. The earliest surviving photographs of Leah, as a baby and a toddler, were taken in Philadelphia. When Leah's grandfather William Henry Bodine made his will on 28 August 1908, it noted that his daughter Cornelia B. Drake resided in Coffeyville, Kansas, some 50 miles south of Chanute, and so the Drakes had headed west again. The obituary of M. Virginia Slacum Bodine, Leah's grandmother, mentions in 1913 Mrs. T. Hulbert Drake as living in Gallup, New Mexico,[7] near the border with Arizona. Leah was nine then. Of this time in her life, Drake said: "I once lived near the Navajo Indian reservation in New Mexico . . . The majestic and lonely desert country made a lasting impression on me—I was about eight years old at the time—and I'm sure it inspired the poem . . . 'The Lariat.'"[8]

Cornelia, who was eleven years older than her husband, routinely took about ten years off her age and, in later years, off her daughter's as well. Consider these census statistics:

> From Kentucky Federal Census Records: 1920 (5 January) Lexington, Fayette County: Thomas H. DRAKE 40 WV Drilling Contractor, Cornelia B. 40 NJ wife, Leah B. 15 KS dau.

> From Indiana Federal Census Records: 1940 (22 April) Evansville, Vanderburgh County: Thomas H. DRAKE 60 WV Oil Operator, Cornelia 60 NJ wife, Leah 24 KS dau.[9]

---

6. *Kaleidograph* (May 1946): 15.
7. *Christian Advocate* (13 March 1913): 375.
8. "Miss Drake, the Poet and the Critic, Joins Us in Henderson," *Henderson Gleaner and Journal* (25 October 1953): 1.
9. The census for 1920 gives Leah's age correctly, but that for 1940 cuts eleven years from her age.

The Song of the Sun ~ Leah Bodine Drake

Leah herself regularly trimmed at least ten years off her age, in part to make her mother's own adjusted age seem more credible but also because of vanity. (She wore glasses but never for photographs and rarely in public.) Her letter to *Weird Tales* of 1935 says that she had read Algernon Blackwood's "The Wendigo" "as a child ten years ago." Ten years previous, she was twenty—hardly a child. Rolfe Humphries's *New Poems by American Poets* and August Derleth's *Dark of the Moon* give her birth year as 1914. When Drake submitted poems for *Dark of the Moon*, she provided some biographical background, but wrote: "I make no mention of my birth-date [and] I don't intend to." When Derleth met the Drakes at his home later that year, Leah coyly avoided telling him her age, which he wanted to know for the purpose of placing her chronologically by birth among the other poets in the anthology he was compiling; he noted that Cornelia was quick to state that Leah was born in 1914. Drake appeared in the *Atlantic Monthly* in its "Young Poet Series" when she was in her forties. Newspaper columns about Drake (probably written by her) describe her consistently and somewhat insistently as a "young poet." A notice about Drake winning an award for *This Tilting Dust* states that she is "about 32."[10] She was actually fifty-three. But the entry in the *Who's Who* supplement of 1959, at which time Drake was in her mid-fifties, accurately gives her birth year as 1904. Because Cornelia had died two years previous, there was no reason to keep up the charade, and photographs from that time show she would be hard pressed to convince anyone she was in her forties. Even so, her birth year is still often given as 1914.

Drake observed in later years, "As a child, I spent all my summers at Ocean City, N.J., where my mother's parents had a summer home."[11] The area was near the location where supposed sightings of the "Jersey Devil" occurred in 1909, recounted in Drake's "The Ballad of the Jabberwock." Her maternal grandparents lived in Williamstown, New Jersey, less than 45 miles from Ocean City. A few years later, the Drake

---

10. "Kentucky Poet Is Awarded High Honor," [Louisville, KY] *Courier-Journal* (29 January 1954): 26.
11. As related in her essay "Old Man on the Sea Shore: Morning."

INTRODUCTION

family lived near her paternal grandparents. It was at their place that she underwent a poetic awakening: "'I was sitting in a cave formed by overgrown honeysuckle in the backyard of my grandparents' home in Parkersburg when I had my first feeling of the poetic world, a world apart,' she told her friend and nurse Betty Callahan in recalling her breakthrough into that realm of ethereal things that she loved so well."[12] At a reading of her poetry, Drake told auditors that her poem "The Green Door" was inspired by real memories of childhood. She said she picked up her poetic technique ("cadence" she called it) from Amy Lowell and that her literary influences were the Bible, the fiction of Lord Dunsany, and the poems of Walter de la Mare, Edith Sitwell, and Elinor Wylie. She once stated: "I taught myself to write by reading my scrapbooks,"[13] which contained clippings of poems by others that she had collected and preserved. Drake once observed, "being the child of an oil man [. . .] close and yearly acquaintances with deserts, prairies, the sea every Summer, the hills and the painted Indian mountains, has influenced my poetry, giving me a sense of the marvelous and supernatural that is in all solitudes."[14]

An article in the *Parkersburg News* that appeared the year after Drake's mother died, when she and her father were visiting his sister, stated that Drake had once lived there and that she had attended the 13th Street elementary school. This would have been around 1914. The paper also noted that the family had moved from Parkersburg to Marietta, Ohio, only 12 miles to the north. The city directory for Marietta lists her parents living in that city at 315 5th Street in 1916, so the Drakes lived in Marietta from around 1915 to 1917. Drake would have been eleven to thirteen.

Thomas Drake's draft registration, dated 10 September 1918, gives his address as 421 W. Second, Lexington, Kentucky.[15] It was there, presumably, that Leah at fourteen wrote what she believed to be her first

---

12. Wood 4.
13. Wood 5.
14. [Unsigned, untitled biographical sketch,] *Southern Literary Messenger* 6, No. 3 (July–August 1944): 325.
15. He also registered in 1942, at the age of 61.

The Song of the Sun ❧ Leah Bodine Drake

poem, "The Deserted Courtyard," part of the group she called "On a Chinese Screen." A late article about her (possibly written by her) states that "her verses have been attracting attention ever since she ticked off her first rhyme at the age of seven." At first she was interested in theater, but she ultimately realized that writing would be her life's work. Her parents and teachers showed avid interest in her writing and encouraged her. Few early poems survive. Drake's scrapbooks contain some early poems, such as "Mombāsa" (1920), "To a Lost Sweetheart" and "Song at Sunrise" (both 1924), and "Words after Wisdom" (1926). She may have destroyed her early efforts, but it seems more likely that she did not begin writing poetry in earnest until she left college and her family moved to Texas, for it is in the early to mid-1930s that the number of poems she wrote increases significantly. Seventeen years after she wrote her "first poem" she sold "A Sigh in Spring" to the *New York American* for $2.50, her first sale.

Most of what is known of Drake's life comes from her own pen, such as brief statements provided to poetry magazines to accompany her poems, and these few sketchy lines, provided for the dust jacket of her first book:

> HORNBOOK FOR WITCHES......Leah Bodine Drake
> Born, Chanute, Kansas, daughter of an oilman, moved to Lexington, Kentucky, as a child, lived all over the South and Southwest, summers spent on the Jersey coast. Earliest memories are of trains, the ocean, the tremendous silences of the Navajo country, the woods and swamps of the South, tales of han'ts by "Aunt Coopie", a Negro member of the household.
> Attended Hamilton College for Women in Lexington.
> Ancestral background is English, Irish, Welsh and French, and family-tree includes Sir Francis Drake, Davy Crocket and Jean Bodin.[16] [OK = no final "e" at that date (1550)]
> At present living in Evansville, Ind., where (she) is movie, dramatic and music critic for the *Evansville Courier*.
> Main interests, beside poetry, are collecting books illustrated by Dulac

---

16. The dust jacket of *TD* also claims Admiral John Drake Sloat (1781–1867), who claimed California for the U.S., as an ancestor.

INTRODUCTION

and Rackham, walking in the woods, the works of C. S. Lewis, Dixieland jazz, D.A.R. work, and, as vice-president of the local humane society, rescuing dogs, cats and horses from what E. E. Cummings calls 'manunkind'.

When Drake provided this "bare outline," she said, "I left out a lot,—about being married and divorced, a showgirl, Miss Dallas,—all that. It seemed irrelevant."[17] This brief sentence gives tantalizing hints about her early years. The highly compressed narrative provided much of the scant information known about Drake at the time, but even so, the published version left out much—about her moving to Lexington, her childhood summers, her memories of trains and the ocean, her belonging to the D.A.R.—so that Derleth would have room to declare on the printed dust jacket of *A Hornbook for Witches*, "Her choice of the macabre in poetry comes naturally"; to describe the "swamps of the South" as "deep"; and somewhat fatuously to add to the list of her ancestors, "—all names with which the student of history will be familiar." Of course, that was all meant to give the proper slant for promoting a book of macabre verse. Drake's specific mention of memories of trains pertains to the frequent moves the Drake family made across the country, and trains figure in several of her poems.

When Derleth mistakenly declared in the *Arkham Sampler* (before he had received Drake's short autobiography) that she was a native of Indiana, she was quick to correct him, with mock dudgeon: "You'll say that Kansas, my real birth-state, is no better,—I can't dispute you there, as I know nothing about it, having left there at the ripe old age of three months. I'm Kentucky-reared and Kentucky-schooled, boy, and don't you ever forget it!"[18] Her allegiance to Chanute is unseemly, for she had no vivid memory of living there; yet brief biographies of her usually note correctly that she was born in Kansas.

The peregrinations of the Drakes are not known with certainty. Drake says she "lived all over the South and Southwest," and mentions

17. LBD to AD, 26 January 1950.
18. 29 October 1948. AD did not repeat the error in the brief author biography in *Fire and Sleet and Candlelight* (1961), but he erroneously stated there that LBD was a native Kentuckian.

The Song of the Sun ❧ Leah Bodine Drake

"Navaho country" and "the woods and swamps of the South." She also mentions living along the Atlantic seaboard. One imagines that she lived anywhere from Pennsylvania to the Carolinas, from Georgia to Arizona.

The U.S. Census for 1920 has the family living at 193 N. Mill Street in Lexington. From 1920 to 1922, Drake attended Helen F. Kendrick's Collegiate School for Girls (i.e., Oakhurst, Walnut Hills, Cincinnati), for only a year by her account. This probably was Drake's first time on her own, although she was not living all that far from her parents. Drake's obituary[19] and another newspaper account state that she attended Sayre College in Lexington.[20] She herself stated vaguely that she attended Sayre College "for a time."[21] One article, possibly by Drake, lists Oakhurst, Hamilton, and Sayre in that order, presumably reflecting the order in which she attended the schools. It would seem that she would have gotten a degree from Sayre, but an article about her in the *Parkersburg Sentinel* of 5 July 1961 states: "She is a graduate of Hamilton College, Lexington, Ky.," majoring in history. Drake acknowledged in her *Who's Who* entry that she attended Hamilton College for Girls from 1923 to 1924, but tellingly her entry, unlike those of other notables in the publication, does not give a degree earned, only years of attendance (which are shorter than the usual college term).[22] Most published accounts about Drake stated only that she "attended" Hamilton. Perhaps she did not actually graduate.

An article announcing publication of her first book noted that "she's lived in Lexington, Ky., Shreveport, La., Dallas and Ft Worth, Tex., Cincinnati, O., New Mexico, Jackson, Miss. and Philadelphia, Pa."[23] Another item repeats many of these locations but also adds New Jersey. Drake once wrote that she lived in "about" fifteen states by 1946, but only eleven can be named with certainty. Notes on photographs of Drake indicate that she lived in or visited Artesia, New Mexico (June 1926), Philadelphia again (March 1928; only 21 miles from William-

---

19. In the *Evansville Press* (23 November 1964).
20. *Evansville Courier* (?) (15 November 1950).
21. *Kaleidograph* 18, No. 1 (May 1946): 16.
22. College records from the time no longer survive.
23. See Appendix.

INTRODUCTION

ston), and Brownwood, Texas (June 1928). Drake made her formal debut into society in 1926 in Philadelphia. Of her residence in New Jersey (just across the Delaware River from Philadelphia), all we know is that she witnessed a gun battle between mob gangs in Camden, where her aunt Anne lived. The duration of her stay in these places is unknown, and there may have been other short-term residences in between. Presumably she always dwelt with her parents with few exceptions. A letter to *Photoplay* magazine dating to late 1930 is addressed from Coleman, Texas. That was the start of "8 horrible years" spent in Texas.[24] The city directory (1931) for Fort Worth has Thomas and Cornelia Drake living at 4809 El Campo Avenue. Letters to *Weird Tales* from 1935 to 1941 emerge from Fort Worth (October 1935), Dallas (June 1937), Shreveport, Louisiana (September 1938), Owensboro, Kentucky (January, March, August, and October 1939), and Evansville, Indiana (March 1941). The appearance of Drake's poem "'My Help Cometh from the Hills'" in the *Louisville Courier-Journal* in May 1935 gives her location as Fort Worth. When the Drakes lived in Dallas, Leah was the "Spirit of Dallas" in the parade for the Centennial Exposition of 1936–37 and also a dancer (among some 200 others) in the showgirl line at Billy Rose's Casa Ma-

24. LBD to Stuart Art Gallery, 25 November 1956.

The Song of the Sun ~ Leah Bodine Drake

ñana in Fort Worth. Of that time she said, "I was a very corn-fed showgirl—swished around in gorgeous satins and spangles twice a night, and loved it, for a while."[25] Not long after, the Drakes were back in Kentucky, first in Owensboro (1939), then again in Lexington (1940).[26] Census records for 1940 (22 April) and Drake's letter to *Weird Tales* in the March 1941 issue indicate the Drakes as living in Evansville, Indiana. A clipping from the Evansville paper gives her address as 901 Southeast Sixth Street. (Another clipping states that Drake had moved to Evansville from Elkton, Kentucky.) She spent the next seventeen years living in the Tri-State area—if not in Evansville, then in nearby cities in Kentucky.

It is not known what Drake did following college. As noted, she was in Artesia, New Mexico, in June 1926; in the Philadelphia–Camden area 1926–28; and in Brownwood, Texas, in June 1928. There were oil companies in all those locations, and so her father probably was pursuing work there. Her mother had family in the Philadelphia area, where Drake lived as a child, which was 21 miles from Williamstown and 56 miles from Ocean City, where Drake spent summers. Because she moved so frequently, it is surprising that she had time to meet Lewis Leslie McAllister,[27] a traveling salesman headquartered in Jackson, Mississippi, much less to marry him on Thursday evening, 29 November 1928. Leah and her mother went to Texas following the wedding, but she soon returned to Jackson to be with her new husband. The time between her apparent arrival in Brownwood and her marriage was not long. Neither was the marriage, for the McAllisters divorced in 1930. It is surprising that she provided these details about her marriage in her *Who's Who* entry, nearly thirty years after the fact. Her marriage is men-

---

25. "Miss Drake, the Poet and the Critic, Joins Us in Henderson," *Henderson Gleaner and Journal* (25 October 1953): 1.
26. Lexington is about 143 miles northeast of Owensboro. Once the Drakes moved to Evansville, Indiana, they stayed in that area, moving back and forth between Evansville and Henderson, Kentucky, less than 10 miles apart over the oxbow in the Ohio River, which was the border between the two states.
27. The Find a Grave website lists a Lewis Leslie McAllister, Sr. (21 December 1903, Caldwell County TX–[no day] February 1978), buried in Meridian, MS, at the Magnolia Cemetery. The page for him states: "2. DEATH: SS DEATH INDEX #5097. In 1929, the obit for Lewis's father states that Lewis is in Jackson, Mississippi."

INTRODUCTION

tioned only in *Who's Who,* in letters to August Derleth, on two photographs among her papers, and a brief newspaper notice. In a later letter to Derleth, Drake hints at something momentous that she intends to tell him, adding, "No, I am NOT getting married again!" as though she knew with certainty that marriage definitely was not for her.

Lewis Leslie McAllister (1903–1978) was a graduate of Howard Payne University (1923–26) in Brownwood. The writer Robert E. Howard, who like Drake was a contributor to *Weird Tales* years later, took a bookkeeping class at the university in 1926–27. Presumably he and McAllister did not attend Payne at the same time. One wonders if Howard and Drake might have met, or even passed each other on the street. It is not known how McAllister and Drake met. A newspaper notice of the marriage said that Leah and her mother were visiting Jackson "when the young people made their plans which were soon carried into effect."[28] A studio photograph of Drake, probably her bridal portrait—undated, but identifying her as "Mrs. Leslie MacAllister [*sic*] [/] Jackson, Mississippi"— shows a pretty but lugubrious young woman who appears to be sad about the prospect of married life. A photograph of McAllister from August 1929 shows a stern, unsmiling "Mac." Someone other than Drake noted on the back of that photograph that he was "Leah's husband of app. 1 yr." The U.S. Census for 1930 states that "Louis L. McAllister" was boarding in Talladega, Alabama, and working as an athletic goods salesman, that he was twenty-six, and that he had married at age twenty-four.

Drake described her married life as short and hectic, but the reason for its termination is unknown. Divorce must have occurred after the census date of 15 April 1930.[29] The fact that McAllister was boarding in Talladega suggests that his wife was not with him. She may have been living in Talladega, or in Jackson while her husband was working away from home, or possibly with her parents. Drake's death certificate states incorrectly that she "never married," but this error (and several others) is probably an assumption by the people with whom she spent her last days and whom she had known for only four years. After all, Drake had no close

28. [Jackson, MS] *Clarion-Ledger* (1 December 1928): 8.
29. McAllister was soon remarried by 1931, to Annie (Payne) McAllister (1910–2011).

living relatives at the time who could have informed authorities otherwise. Her brief, early marriage probably never arose in discussion. When the marriage dissolved, Drake apparently went to live with her parents in Texas, and she then lived with them her entire adult life.

Besides joining the Billy Rose dancers, Drake engaged in some modeling. As a dancer, she was required to wear revealing costumes. A clipping from the Evansville paper (January 1941) shows her sporting a red, white, and blue jersey play suit. Presumably that photo shoot was not an isolated occurrence. A late newspaper article stated that she had modeled in hat shows and fashion shows not only when she was living in Parkersburg late in life, but also years before in Fort Worth and Dallas. A photograph of Drake from 1960, taken as she was preparing to leave for Europe, shows her striking a model's pose, wearing a smart dress suit, wide-brimmed hat, and gloves.

The byline that appeared on Drake's first published poem was given as "Lea." She spelled her name thus from at least 1934 until June 1937, when she resumed the conventional spelling. In October 1935, her first poem in *Weird Tales*, "In the Shadows," was published, along with a letter to the editor. The fantaisiste H. P. Lovecraft surely read both, although he made no mention of it. He may also have seen her poem in the March 1936 *Driftwind*. He was a correspondent and friend of its editor, Walter J. Coates, and himself had a poem in the December issue that year. He probably did not live to see her second poem in *Weird Tales*, "The Witch Walks in Her Garden," which appeared in April 1937. Drake had a poem published in the book *Contemporary American Woman Poets* in 1936—her first appearance in a book and one of the very earliest published appearances of her work, at a time when she had only a very few poems previously published.[30] Initially her work appeared in newspapers and other conventional publications.

Drake had an early interest in fantasy. She read fairy tales in illustrated

---

30. The book was published by the vanity publisher Henry Harrison. LBD probably responded to an advertisement calling for submittals to the book, the subtitle of which describes it as containing "verse by 1311 Living Poets," all women.

Introduction

children's books, *Weird Tales* magazine, and the work of Algernon Blackwood. She published twenty-four poems in *Weird Tales* between 1935 and the magazine's demise in 1954, trailing behind only H. P. Lovecraft (forty-three), Clark Ashton Smith (forty), and Robert E. Howard (thirty-five), and tying Dorothy Quick. However, Lovecraft published only eighteen poems in the magazine in his lifetime, the remainder being submitted by August Derleth following his death. Howard had only twenty-one poems published there in his lifetime. *Weird Tales* had accepted Drake's poem "The Old World of Green," but the poem was published in its sister publication *Short Stories*.[31] If not for these exceptions, Drake would have been the woman with the most poems in *Weird Tales* and the poet with the second greatest number of poems published during the poet's lifetime, behind only Clark Ashton Smith. After *Weird Tales* folded, Drake published her outré verses in the *Magazine of Fantasy and Science Fiction*, persuading the editors, who had been only reprinting poetry, to publish original poems. She was not successful at first and had poems returned for revision or rejected outright. *Fantasy and Science Fiction* published eight of her poems from 1954 to 1964.

Drake wrote some short fantasy fiction but not much. Her first, "Time and the Sphinx," dedicated to Lord Dunsany, with whom she corresponded briefly, appeared in 1947 in Lilith Lorraine's little magazine *Different*. *Weird Tales* published two of her short stories in the 1950s. "Whisper Water" is in part about a man in the oil business, and the terminology of the trade as used in the story surely was obtained from her father or from secondhand familiarity with the business through him. "Foxy's Hollow" (*Fantasy Fiction*) is a saucy tale about a woman who can change into a fox—a theme explored in her poem "Spirit Fox." The female character in "Foxy's Hollow," Clarinda Foxer, seems to be much like Drake herself: good-looking (although redheaded), flirtatious (and more), headstrong, and independent. A friend described Drake as having "wonderful joie de vivre and vitality," stating

---

31. Dorothy McIlwraith was editor of *Short Stories* from 1936 onward. In 1940 she succeeded Farnsworth Wright as editor of *Weird Tales* and edited both magazines. As such, she could shift content between them.

The Song of the Sun 🙠 Leah Bodine Drake

she had a "marvelous, almost Elizabethan baudiness [sic] which contrasted sharply with a deep and unexpected spirituality."[32] The photographs presented herein show Drake in her later years in mostly reserved poses, but some early photos display vivacity and joy.

Most of Drake's early poems were not published, or were published years after they were first written. Besides *Weird Tales*, early publications that took her work were *Driftwind*, *L'Alouette*,[33] *Silver Star*, and *Country Bard*. In time she appeared in the more notable poetry journals of the day: *Cornhill Magazine*, *Kaleidograph*, *Talaria*, *Lyric*, *Poetry Chap-book*, *Wings*, and many others. The work of Clark Ashton Smith and August Derleth also appeared in some of these little magazines. Eventually she broke into the bigger magazines, such as *Southern Literary Messenger*, *Prairie Schooner*, *Saturday Evening Post*, *Atlantic Monthly*, *Saturday Review*, *Poetry*, *Commonweal*, and the *New Yorker*, while continuing to appear in *Weird Tales*. Her poems were reprinted in syndicated newspapers and thus seen by readers across the country. Drake was frequently represented in the annual Borestone Mountain best poetry volumes, other "best of" collections, and other anthologies, including textbooks. She also received many honors (and monetary recognition) for her poems: the Borestone Mountain award, various Poetry Society of America awards, the Arthur David Ficke Memorial Award, and others.

One of Drake's favorite topics and areas of study was witches and witchcraft. Her interest in witches was rather benign: she was no practicing witch, although she joked about casting spells and making potions; she was merely interested in the historical folklore about witches. Among her papers is a notebook called *Notes on Witchcraft*, in which she recorded information obtained through her reading, sometimes in question-and-answer format; e.g., "What is the difference between a witch and a magician?" (She similarly kept a notebook of *Notes on Folklore and Art*, which she consulted from time to time when writing verse on certain topics.) She once observed, "Of all states (in the present day,) Kentucky has more

---

32. Josephine Elliott to John Herring, 17 April 1965 (TLS, Rice University).
33. LBD's papers indicate one poem as having appeared in the magazine, and another as to be published, but neither appearance has been found.

Introduction

witches and belief in witchcraft than any other," and so she was familiar with Kentucky folklore. In 1956, she hoped to appear on the television show, *The $64,000 Question,* which was later embroiled in the infamous quiz show scandal, competing on the subject of witches. The question-and-answer format of her witchcraft notebook seems to have served as a guide for her to study in order to answer questions she might be asked. Drake hoped to write an article for the *American Mercury* on witch-hunts in the past and present, but that did not come to pass. She also hoped to do articles on survivals of witchcraft in modern times for *Weird Tales* and *Fantasy and Science Fiction,* but that also did not occur. She jokingly signed herself in letters "The Witch of the Wabash" and "The Hag of the Hollow," and even included a tiny drawing of a witch riding a broom in her correspondence. But all this was for her own amusement.

Drake realized she was a "minor poet." She philosophically recognized that her poems were not great—she compared them to common, not noble, hunting trophies.

> My walls are not without their heads
> Of deer; there's meat upon the board.
> But still I seek the golden prides,
> The burning lions of the Lord! ("Minor Poet," ll. 21–24)

In frank recognition of her limited skills, she wrote:

> I've watched the strange
> Dance of the lonely hippogriff,
> Wings folded—still beyond the range
>
> Of my crude weapons! ("Minor Poet," ll. 14–17)

When she was dying, she still acknowledged her stature, for she included "Minor Poet" in a scrapbook containing her "selected poems."

As a minor poet in a crowded market, Drake did not stand to make big earnings. Little magazines such as *Driftwind, Kaleidograph, Poetry Chap-book, Talaria, Voices,* and *Wings* paid only a few dollars for a poem or a small per-line amount, or nothing but a copy or two of the publication in which it appeared. Stanton Coblentz of *Wings* published a comment she had made to him: "she has a rare feeling of altruism toward her fellow poets, for her ambition is 'to run a poetry magazine and pay the poor, underdog race of poets about two hundred dollars for each poem!'"[34] Still, she did win sizable monetary awards for some of her poems.

When Drake's father was successful, she could afford to be a poet. When his fortunes changed, she needed more remunerative work to help support the family, and so she took a position as the drama, music, and cinema critic for the *Evansville Courier*, for which she worked from 1941 to 1951. It does not appear to be a job she relished, merely one she was capable of doing—and one that paid.

Drake was active socially throughout her life. She was vice president (1950–54) of the Vanderburgh County (Ind.) Humane Society, and a member of the Wilderness Society and the Wood County Humane Society in Parkersburg. During her years in Evansville, she was an active member of the Vanderburgh Chapter of the Daughters of the American Revolution, for which she did a radio program, vice president of Evansville's Animal Refuge, Inc., and press relations chairman. She was a board member of the Women's Association of the Philharmonic Orchestra, for which she edited the monthly newsletter, the *Baton*, and a member of the Tyro-Press Club. She taught dancing. She was a member of the Poetry Society of America from May 1942 onward (aside from a few brief lapses), the Catholic Poetry Society of America, and the League to Support Poetry. She was a member of the Evansville chapter of the American Association of University Women, Creative Poetry section, to the archives of which she provided more than 100 typescripts of her poems, including some after she moved to Parkersburg. She attended their meetings, at which she read her poetry, and she also read her work at many other events. Her interests included reading, jazz music, dancing, conversation, and walking in the country. In Parkersburg, she was influential in forming a local chapter of the Zonta Club, an international service organization with the mission of advancing the status of women, and was herself a charter member. The guest book from her funeral was signed by many members of the Zonta Club, and also the James Wood Chapter of the D.A.R.

34. Stanton A. Coblentz, *The Music Makers* 53.

Introduction

In late 1945, Drake was doing "movie work in California"—presumably not acting or writing screenplays, but perhaps interviewing people in the movie business for the Evansville paper in her role as its film critic. She announced to August Derleth in September 1947 that she was leaving the paper: "If I'd stayed there seeing six and seven movies a week for *another* six years I'd have gone blind. I'm now at what is classically called a loose end. Writing lots of poetry, though."[35] By her reckoning, she had seen (and reviewed?) anywhere from 260 to 364 movies annually, or some 1,560 to 2,184 movies over a six-year period, perhaps a bit of an exaggeration.

In the late 1940s, the Drakes alternated between Evansville, Indiana, and Henderson, Kentucky, which were less than ten miles apart. The reason for moving probably was not her father's pursuit of work, nor her own. One need not move in order to take a new job nearby within a small geographic area. The reason likely was financial—to seek better lodging in up times, less costly lodging in down times. Drake does not appear to have been gone long from the *Courier,* and she remained associated with the paper until 1951. The Drakes landed in Henderson again in 1953, and Leah soon was writing special features for the *Henderson Gleaner and Journal.* In April 1955 she became the paper's society editor. By November, she was back in Evansville.

Drake wrote to August Derleth in September 1943 to inquire if his publishing company, Arkham House, might consider publishing a book of her poetry, noting that "possibly the same readers who buy your Lovecraft and Smith volumes would like my poems."[36] This would be for her first book. Even at that early date, she knew she wanted to call her book *A Hornbook for Witches.* Her request was bold. Derleth and Donald Wandrei had founded Arkham House in 1939 for the sole purpose of publishing the work of H. P. Lovecraft in three volumes—nothing more. The first was *The Outsider and Others.* Derleth decided only in

---

35. In another letter, LBD claims she saw five to six movies a week, all in only two days' time.
36. LBD to AD, 13 September 1943.

The Song of the Sun ❧ Leah Bodine Drake

1942, the year before Drake's letter of inquiry, to expand its publishing program to include other authors. At the time Drake wrote to Arkham House, it had published only four books in four years: two by Lovecraft, one by Derleth, and one by Clark Ashton Smith. The second Lovecraft volume, *Beyond the Wall of Sleep* (1943), included a selection of his poetry. Unknown to Drake, Arkham House early on was nurturing the idea of publishing weird poetry. In 1942, Wandrei began coaxing Smith to prepare an omnibus of his poetry. To be sure, Smith's work was much more suited to Arkham House than Drake's was at the time, and he was well known among the publisher's clientele. His *Selected Poems* was an ambitious effort, taking Smith five years (1944–49) to prepare the text of the large book, and it took about another twenty-five years for the book to see print—indeed, ten years after the poet's demise. In time, Arkham House published books by both poets, with Drake, not Smith, blazing the trail.

Derleth had seen Drake's work over the past eight years, not only in *Weird Tales* but also in the various little magazines where their work regularly appeared. There is no record of Derleth's response to Drake's inquiry, but two years later he requested a brief selection of her poems for another project. In January 1946 she submitted seven poems for inclusion in a book Derleth was editing, *Dark of the Moon: Poems of Fantasy and the Macabre*, a large collection of weird verse both historic and contemporary. Five of her poems had appeared in *Weird Tales* and two in the *Southern Literary Messenger*. In July she inquired whether it was too late to include yet another poem, "The Ballad of the Jabberwock." It had won first prize (from among more than 100 entries) in the 1946 Stephen Vincent Benét Ballad Contest, conducted by the Word Weavers of Los Angeles. Derleth took the new ballad, which had not been published, as it was too long for *Weird Tales* and *Atlantic Monthly* and Drake was not willing to cut it.

As *Dark of the Moon* was being prepared, Drake asked if she could stop by to visit Derleth at his home in Sauk City, Wisconsin, because she had an appointment at the Mayo Clinic (Rochester, Minn.) on 9 August for a check-up following a "serious" but unspecified operation performed there in the summer of 1945. The trip was delayed several times, but Derleth noted in his journal that the Drakes finally arrived on 11 October 1946:

INTRODUCTION

In the course of today Leah Bodine Drake and her parents stopped to visit briefly. Found her not quite what her poetry suggested—a [. . .] shapely-enough young woman circa thirty, very coy about her age, which she would not reveal even for the purpose of my anthology of poetry in which she is represented, though I gathered from comments of her mother that she was born in 1914. Given somewhat to exaggerated speech and a typically Kentucky accent, though this was too in large part affected.[37]

On 28 February 1947, Drake wrote to notify Derleth the Drakes were "moving back over to Evansville," where they lived until 1953, then moved to Henderson, Kentucky, only to return to Evansville in 1955. The Drakes lived there until the death of Cornelia in 1956.

Following publication of *Dark of the Moon* in March 1947, Derleth started gathering material for a new journal, the *Arkham Sampler*. The first issue contains Drake's "A Hornbook for Witches." She wrote: "I'll admit that I sent 'A Hornbook for Witches' to WEIRD TALES, and they sent it back, said it was too long. Also, (although they didn't say so) I suspect that the rather tongue-in-the-cheek attitude toward my subject put them off: WT allows no ironic attitude towards magic, witchcraft and spooks!"[38] Drake is correct in her assessment of her "spookers": many have a note of whimsicality rather than pure horror or fantasy.

Drake submitted five more poems to the *Arkham Sampler*, a brief article, and three book reviews during its two-year run. In 1948, the *Sampler* began to publish oblique references to a book of her poetry. First, "Leah Bodine Drake is best known for her delightful fantastic poetry, which has appeared in *Weird Tales* and other magazines for many years. While she has as yet published no book collection of her verse, she has every right to look forward to such publication ultimately,"[39] followed in the next issue by "Leah Bodine Drake is an Indiana-born [*sic*] poet whose verse ranks high in the annals of fantasy. A contributor to *Weird Tales, Voices*, and many other magazines, she is currently preparing a collection of her fine fantastic poems for book publication."[40] Derleth does not say that

37. *Sac Prairie Journal* (T.Ms., WHS). LBD was forty-one at the time.
38. LBD to AD, 26 September 1947.
39. *Arkham Sampler* 1, No. 3 (Summer 1948): 99–100.
40. *Arkham Sampler* 1, No. 4 (Autumn 1948): 98.

The Song of the Sun ❧ Leah Bodine Drake

Drake was preparing her book for Arkham House, probably because he was not certain he could publish it, at least any time soon. The 1950s proved to be a lean period, during which Arkham House published only fourteen books, four of which were thin poetry volumes. Nevertheless, in September 1948 Derleth requested a typescript for a book of Drake's poetry. Her letter to Derleth of 4 September 1948 sheds light on the matter:

> I think your proposition about a book of my "spookers" sounds fine—and I'll be *delighted* to get together that first and well-known "slim volumn" [*sic*]. I think, with you, that a whole book of weird poems *should* be on the thin side, as too many weirdies are a little hard to take.
>
> I'll look over my published and unpublished stuff, & get a list compiled, and see how large a book-manuscript it would make. I should think thirty-five to forty poems should be enough, don't you? Anyway, I'll get busy & type them off in the next few weeks. [. . .]
>
> Thanks awfully for your offer—I'm honored to be one of the *Arkham House* gang.

The five years following Drake's initial inquiry served to make her more familiar to Arkham House patrons, and so in 1948 the prospect of a book of her verse was more feasible.

Drake mentioned having to make another trip to Rochester and hoped to visit Derleth again. The trip was postponed until December, and by the following April they still had not made the trip. "There's no great need for me to go, but they like to check up on all their patients, and of course with what I had, it's the best thing."[41] The reason for checkups at the clinic is not known, nor how often Drake was required to have them done. One wonders if the condition for which she had been treated returned and ultimately took her life.

On 7 October 1948, Drake mailed the typescript of the book, which contained forty-seven poems, ten of which had not been previously published. She and Derleth executed a memorandum of agreement regarding her book on 14 October 1948. Derleth wanted to omit "The Journey of the Queen of Sheba," intended as the last poem. Drake admitted that it "really isn't so *very* spooky—altho it does border on the

41. LBD to AD, 17 April 1948.

Introduction

fantastical: her method of traveling, for instance."[42] (Drake's observation is an accurate assessment of much of her poetry: it is borderline fantastical.) The poem was removed, and she substituted "Encounter in Broceliande" and "Mad Woman's Song," poems she had wanted to include initially but had been unable to get into proper shape.[43] Drake gave specific instruction as to where they were to be placed—most definitely not merely at the end, where "The Journey of the Queen of Sheba" had been.

The oft-repeated story about *A Hornbook for Witches* is that Drake subsidized its publication. For example:

> [. . .] Ms. Drake approached Derleth and requested that a book of her poetry be published by Arkham House [. . .] Derleth refused except on the condition that she bear the cost, to which she agreed. After publication of *A Hornbook for Witches*, Drake received back about 300 copies as her share of the enterprise. Thus, the rarity of the book is explained, as only 253 were available for distribution by Arkham House directly to its dealers and subscribers. It's uncertain what became of Drake's 300 copies, although many may have been given or sold to her friends and neighbors.[44]

Again:

> The cost of printing this slim volume of poetry was subsidized by the author, who, in turn, received 300 copies of the 553 copies printed. Thus, Arkham House had only 253 copies for sale, making this title one of the scarcest books published by Arkham House. One may speculate what happened to the 300 copies given to the author, who died in 1964, but with the passing of time, some may find their way back into the rare book market.[45]

Although we have no direct evidence as to how Drake was compensated for her book—Arkham House's papers for the period no longer

---

42. LBD to AD, 11 October 1948.
43. LBD to AD, 6 November 1948 (TLS, Brigham Young University). Note that on 10 February 1954, LBD wrote AD that "Lawrence Thompson, Director of libraries at the U. of Ky., wants the typescript of HORNBOOK FOR WITCHES very much for the library's collection of Drake. [. . .] Could you dig it out of the attic and send it to him?" It is not known how the T.Ms. came to Brigham Young University.
44. Jaffery 39.
45. Nielsen 73.

The Song of the Sun ~ Leah Bodine Drake

exist—we have her testimony for the plan for the book, about which she gushed when she mentioned it to William Rose Benét:

> You may be interested in knowing that August Derleth of ARKHAM HOUSE [. . .] is bringing out a book (my first!) of my weird poems. [. . .] The best thing about MY BOOK (you can just hear me say it in capitals!) is, that August [. . .] wrote me and suggested the whole idea to me, and is going to finance the job and pay me 10% royalties. I had a horrible idea that poets always had to put up the money for their own first book,—but I must have been wonderfully wrong![46]

Drake did not realize it was possible for a relatively unknown poet to be paid royalties per usual industry practice.

The fact is, Derleth himself requested a book from Drake, one he envisioned as the first in a line of poetry volumes, and he intended to finance it in the usual fashion. Because Drake's book was Arkham House's first poetry collection by a single author, it was something of a test case. More than a year after he first proposed the book, Derleth balanced production cost and royalties against his ability to sell copies at a reasonable price. He wrote Drake on the matter on 23 January 1950, telling her that the production cost per copy (he estimated $1.00), coupled with the highest price he felt readers could be asked to pay for the book ($2.00), the discount he would have to allow dealers (40% maximum), and the royalties he would pay Drake (10%, or 20¢ per copy) would lose money for Arkham House. Instead of paying 10% royalties on all copies, he offered to give Drake fifty copies of the finished book (which she was free to sell herself) against the royalties for the first 250 books sold, and then pay 10% royalties on the balance. Her royalties would, in this case, be reduced by $50.00, but if she sold fifty copies of the book herself, she could double the money those books would have earned in royalties. In response, Drake wrote: "It's all right about taking part of the royalties in books. I never expect to make money out of poetry anyway! Who does? I'm glad to have the book published,—any profit on it will just be lagniappe!"[47] Ultimately, Arkham House charged $2.10 per copy.[48]

46. LBD to William Rose Benét, 24 November 1948. Benét had one poem in *DM*.
47. LBD to AD, 26 January 1950.

Introduction

In January 1950, Drake provided to Arkham House an image of a wyvern, which she wanted to see on the dust jacket along with a drawing of Pan or a centaur. Frank Utpatel, who had done illustrations for *Weird Tales* and dust jackets of Arkham House books and had long designed Derleth's ever-changing stationery, devised a cover with both images being small and repeated sixteen times (though sometimes obscured by panels containing type). This white-on-black motif was repeated on two poetry books by Clark Ashton Smith (*The Dark Chateau and Other Poems* [1951] and *Spells and Philtres* [1958]) and one by Robert E. Howard (*Always Comes Evening* [1957]). Donald Wandrei's *Poems for Midnight* (1964), similar in size and format to the other poetry volumes, had a dust jacket with a different sort of design. In February and March, Drake submitted lists of names and addresses for persons to whom to send Arkham House's March catalogue. It is unlikely that Arkham House mailed catalogues or bulletins to the more than 100 individuals who were not among its regular patrons. Perhaps a simple postcard notice may have been sent. Drake herself had postcards printed locally that she mailed to associates.

On 3 October 1950, Drake said she had read "this" over—presumably her contract. She wrote: "I'm mighty pleased that you think enough of the book to venture *600* copies, instead of the proposed 500."[49] She also mentions that she hopes Arkham House would not be stuck with unsold copies, thus indicating that she did not expect to have to sell them on her own. On 15 November, she returned the corrected proofs with a brief listing of her corrections. She wrote: "I'm sending the proofs back tomorrow, with a very few corrections. [. . .] I don't see why it won't sell. I think I can dispose of the fifty copies right here in town, and I have lots of interested friends elsewhere. My own paper, the COURIER, will give me a good write-up (even if I have to write it my ownself! [*sic*])."[50]

A Hornbook for Witches was published in December 1950 in an edi-

---

48. See Appendix for a breakdown of probable earnings on *HW*.
49. LBD to AD, 13 October 1950.
50. LBD to AD, 14 November 1950. LBD's galley proofs, and an itemized list of corrections (very few) are held at WHS.

The Song of the Sun ~ Leah Bodine Drake

tion of 553 copies. It was Arkham House's forty-third book. Smith & Butterfield's, the office supply store in Evansville, initially took fifty copies and perhaps another 100,[51] to sell at an autograph party on 29 November 1950. Arkham House would have had to sell 173 copies in about three months' time in order for it to be in the clear by February, and so the book sold fairly well as Derleth told Smith. August Derleth sent Drake six author's copies, fifty more as part of her "payment," and fourteen for her to autograph or inscribe and return to him. She inscribed Derleth's copy "To August Derleth, one of the best friends a witch could have!—Leah Bodine Drake. 1950." Clark Ashton Smith bought two copies and told Derleth: "I'm glad the book has sold so well."[52] When Derleth proposed doing a similar book of verse by Smith, he told Smith: "The way we are now operating is this: each book must pay for itself before we publish another. Miss Drake's book of poems has done that, or will have done it in another month."[53]

Drake sold eighteen of her own copies in less than a week and the remainder by early January 1951. In other words, Drake and Smith & Butterfield's combined sold at least 150 copies in less than a month. It is not known exactly when the book when out of print, but in a letter to Drake Derleth wrote, "since it is a practise [sic] of Arkham House [. . .] to relinquish all rights to a book once it has been six months out of print with us, all rights to A HORNBOOK FOR WITCHES are surely yours."[54] That being the case, the book must have sold out around June 1955. In "The Future of Arkham House," Derleth mentioned patrons "now belatedly [are] asking for earlier books they scorned, like Leah Bodine Drake's A

---

51. LBD told the poet Joseph Payne Brennan: "I had an autograph party, given me by the local bookstore in Evansville (Ind.) & sold over 150 copies." It is not certain whether the 150 books sold included any of LBD's own. If so, the store acquired another allotment of fifty copies on top of the fifty ordered initially. If not, it must have ordered another 100.
52. 15 April 1951; *Eccentric, Impractical Devils* 318.
53. AD to Smith, 26 February 1951; *Eccentric, Impractical Devils* 413.
54. AD to LBD, 9 December 1955, TLS, University of Kentucky. See letter 51.

Introduction

HORNBOOK FOR WITCHES and some others in small editions."[55] Drake asked Derleth on 18 September 1959 if any copies remained, even though *Arkham House: The First 20 Years*, which she had received not long before, said the book was indeed out of print. He remarked by letter that it was out of print, and so the *Parkersburg News*, at which Drake was then assistant society editor, proclaimed a week later that her book was now a collector's item.

No documentary evidence has been found to support the claim that Derleth "refused" to publish Drake's book unless she bore the cost herself. To the contrary, Derleth himself requested a book from her. Nor is there evidence that Drake herself received 300 copies of *Hornbook* as opined. The claimants may have had access to documentation indicating this, but the story of the book's publication smacks of repeated gossip as though it were common knowledge; more likely these claimants did not realize that Drake moved in much larger circles than the narrow field of fantasy literature. Drake's correspondence with Derleth indicates that she herself received fifty-six copies and Smith & Butterfield fifty, at least initially. She and the store may have received as many as a combined 206 copies (as suggested by her comment to Joseph Payne Brennan), of which all apparently were sold except for a few presentation copies. We may never know the exact number of copies Smith & Butterfield obtained—perhaps as many as 150—but if so, Arkham House still had at least 347 copies to sell, much more than the 253 various writers claim, and possibly as many as 397.

Drake did not, unlike Clark Ashton Smith in the case of his two poetry books, request more cartons of her book for her to dispose of personally to inquirers. Smith had obtained at least sixty-six copies of *The Dark Chateau* and seventy-five of *Spells and Philtres*—more copies than Drake herself obtained of her own book—for which he had to pay out of his royalties, but which he was free to sell at cover price (*and* still earn royalties). Aside from purchasing a single copy, Drake merely inquired from time to time if copies remained. She doubtless referred inquirers directly to Arkham House.

---

55. AD, "The Future of Arkham House" (*Outré* No. 3 [1956]: 16–18); rpt. in S. T. Joshi, *Eighty Years of Arkham House* (Seattle: Sarnath Press, 2019), 209.

The Song of the Sun ~ Leah Bodine Drake

The book was well received. Orville Prescott, the main and influential book reviewer for the *New York Times* for twenty-four years, wrote that "a little book of ghastly poems was published two weeks ago which is certainly about as far from the beaten track as poetry can go. . . . Miss Drake goes her own original and fanciful way. Her poems may not be contributions to the great art of poetry, but they are rather fun in a grisly fashion." Not a resounding recommendation, but Drake was elated to see that Prescott had deigned to review her book at all, and favorably at that.

The lesson Derleth learned from this experiment was that he could sell a poetry book at a reasonable price and make a little money, and so in December 1951 he brought out Smith's *The Dark Chateau*, a book slightly smaller than *Hornbook* (63 versus 70 pages) in a slightly larger edition (563 versus 553) at a slightly higher cost ($2.50 versus $2.10).

In October 1951, the *Poetry Society of America Bulletin* announced (p. 19) that Drake had won a $100 prize for her book-length manuscript *Honey from the Lion* in a recent poetry contest conducted by the Midwestern Writers' Conference. No other reference to such a manuscript, in print or among Drake's papers, has been found. In November 1951, less than a year after *Hornbook* appeared, Drake queried of August Derleth: "When do you want me to get a new weird poems book together?" A second book seems to have been Drake's idea, not Derleth's, but perhaps not. She wrote to Anthony Boucher in April 1952 of her "second book of fantasy verse for ARKHAM HOUSE. (No title, as yet.) . . . Derleth will publish my new spooker whenever I can get it ready,—maybe next year." This implies some interest on Derleth's part. Drake said she didn't have enough verse on hand to fill a book similar to *A Hornbook for Witches* and that she would have to write some new poems for it. She repeated her inquiry to Derleth in February 1953, but a second book of Drake's poetry for Arkham house never came to be. Derleth did take six of her poems for *Ghosts and Marvels*, published as *Fire and Sleet and Candlelight* (1961). Twelve of the poets in *Fire and Sleet and Candlelight* contributed to the anthology of poetry that Drake herself was editing at the time, and more than twenty of the contributing poets belonged to the PSA. *Honey from the Lion* does not appear to be the book Drake had in

INTRODUCTION

mind for Arkham House. No book of that title was ever published, and no manuscript exists.[56]

Drake was a guest speaker at the Poetry Society of America's annual dinner meeting at Sherry's Restaurant in New York on 24 January 1951, where she read "The Lariat: 6000 B.C.," which had won a second place prize on one of the regular PSA contests. She shared the speakers' table with Wallace Stevens, who himself was presented with a gold medal.

Drake did publish another book of poetry, but the history of *This Tilting Dust* is even more sketchily documented than that of *A Hornbook for Witches*. The book is quite unlike her first, in that its content is mostly mainstream, containing poems that had appeared in the *New Yorker, Atlantic Monthly, Saturday Review,* and numerous little poetry magazines. An Evansville newspaper described *This Tilting Dust* as a "collection of love songs." Drake submitted the manuscript for the annual Borestone Mountain Poetry Award contest. She won first place honors and a cash prize of $1250 for an unpublished book-length manuscript, and it was eligible for publication by the Book Club for Poetry, through which it appeared as its fourth title. Other Book Club publications included such titles as *This Rowdy Heart* (1954) by Frances Frost, *Three Stones* (1955) by Cloyed Mann Criswell, and *Dance without Shoes* by William Pillin (1956). The Borestone Mountain awards were not exclusively for lesser-known poets. In 1955, Robinson Jeffers won the $250 Borestone Mountain Poetry Award for his published book *Hungerfield*. Drake's friend Eric Barker won $625 for his unpublished *Directions in the Sun*. Paul S. Nickerson won the $1,000 second prize for his book *The Edge of Light* (Kaleidograph Press), and Robert Hillyer won the $300 third prize for best poem (magazine verse) for his poem "The Bats." The year Drake won the grand prize, Eric Barker took second place for his book manuscript *Lazarus*. Drake was in good company.

Drake's Borestone Mountain award was not without controversy. In his article "They Called Him 'Cal,'" Louis Simpson (1923–2012) wrote that he, too, had submitted a manuscript, *Good News of Death,* to the contest. Simpson had joined the PSA in October 1949, winning first

---

56. "Possible Titles for Books" (S5.4) lists *Honey from the Lion* as the very first.

The Song of the Sun ❧ Leah Bodine Drake

prize for his poem "Epitaph." Gustav Davidson, secretary of the PSA, telegraphed him that he had won the coveted prize and the opportunity to have *Good News of Death* published. Davidson had previously published Simpson's *The Arrivistes* (1949) through his Fine Editions Press. A few days later, Davidson contacted Simpson again:

> He had some bad news for me. The judge of the Borestone Mountain Award had telephoned to say that there had been an error . . . a "miscount." I was not to have the award . . . it was to go to someone else. A lady named Leah Bodine Drake.
>
> Davidson was mumbling . . . he sounded nervous as well he might. The story about a "miscount" was absurd. What was there to be counted? The judge had given me the prize and then days later, changed his mind for some reason. The judge was Robert Lowell. Davidson asked me please not to tell anyone what had happened—it would bring the Borestone Mountain Award into disrepute.
>
> It is hard to believe but I didn't run into the street shouting "I've been robbed!" I was stunned. It is one thing to have your work rejected—a writer has to be able to accept that. But to be given an award and have it taken back! In the nights and days that followed I walked, sat, or lay down with a sick feeling. I was as close to despair as I have ever been in my life. I obliged Gustav Davidson. I did not make the story public. I had been brought up to behave and not make a spectacle of myself. This was wrong. I should have protested vigorously, I should have raised the roof.[57]

Simpson repeated the story in an interview in 2001.[58]

There is, however, an alternate version of this story. The *Evansville Press* published an article on 23 June 1955, "Miss Drake Writes Book." In noting that the Book Club for Poetry would publish Drake's award-winning *This Tilting Dust,* it stated that the editors and judges involved in selecting her book were Gustav Davidson, secretary of the PSA, George Abbe, a board member of *Poetry Public Letter* (for which Drake was an "advisory editor"), and Loring Williams, editor of *Poetry Weave*. This is also stated on the book's dust jacket. But they may have been in-

---

57. Louis Simpson, "They Called Him 'Cal,'" *Harvard Review* No. 12 (Spring 1997): 123.
58. "The Sound That Comes from Character: An Interview with Louis Simpson on the Life and Poetry of James Wright," *Georgia Review* 55, No. 3 (Fall 2001): 449–74; see pp. 461–62.

INTRODUCTION

volved only in selecting the book for publication by the Book Club, not in the Borestone Mountain judging. No mention is made of the well-known poet Robert Lowell. In fact, there seems to be no evidence whatsoever that Lowell had anything to do with the contest, so one is at a loss as to how to reconcile the two contradictory accounts of the judging.

Lowell was one of five poetry judges for the National Book Award in 1956, but there is no record of him ever being involved with the Borestone Mountain awards, and in any case, the Borestone outfit used panels of volunteer judges, not only one individual. If there were instead a panel of judges, there may well have been a miscount. Davidson and Abbe were great champions of Drake's work, but one hopes that did not contribute to the alleged miscount that ultimately gave her the award. Simpson was awarded the Pulitzer Prize in 1964 for his book *At the End of the Open Road*. Ironically, he, Davidson, and Drake all had poems in Derleth's *Fire and Sleet and Candlelight*, and Simpson also contributed to Drake's anthology, *The Various Light*. It is not known if Drake was aware that she supposedly had received the award amid controversy. *This Tilting Dust*, dedicated to her parents, was published in 1955 by Golden Quill Press,[59] and it was a selection of the Book Club for Poetry. Smith & Butterfield once again held an autograph party when the book appeared.

This Tilting Dust was one of fifteen finalists for the 1957 National Book Award in the poetry category, along with books by Kenneth Fearing, Robert Fitzgerald, Rolfe Humphries, Anne Morrow Lindbergh, W. S. Merwin, Marianne Moore, Ezra Pound, Kenneth Rexroth, and other eminent poets. Again, it is clear that Drake was a recognized poet, not merely a dabbler in the weird genre. The award went to Richard Wilbur for *Things of This World*.[60] The judges that year were Louise Bogan, Edward Davison, Horace Gregory, Yvor Winters, and none other than Louis Simpson. Edelene Wood stated that *This Tilting Dust* was reprinted in 1965, and Drake herself said she wished to make a correction in a

---

59. In 1960, the press published AD's book *West of Morning*.
60. Lin Carter erroneously stated in his editorial to the revived *Weird Tales* magazine (as a paperback book) that LBD had won a Pulitzer Prize and claimed that Farnsworth Wright, editor of the original magazine, "discovered" her (*Weird Tales* 48, No. 1 [Spring 1981]: 257).

The Song of the Sun ❧ Leah Bodine Drake

probable second printing, but this does not seem to be the case.

Drake received her cash award at the forty-fourth annual dinner of the PSA on 28 January 1954 at the Ambassador Hotel. She shared a table with Major Paul S. Nickerson and Prince and Princess Alexis Droutzkoy. Drake's mother had traveled to New York for the event, but it does not appear she attended the banquet. Lord Dunsany, whom Drake admired and with whom she had exchanged a few letters, attended the meeting the following month, but Drake did not.

The November–December 1954 issue of *Poetry Public Letter* listed Drake as an advisory editor, in which position she served until the magazine folded with the issue for October–December 1958. She was pleased to inform others that she was, initially, the only woman in that position. Other advisory editors for the magazine over time included John Ciardi, May Sarton, Alan Swallow, George Abbe, and Lawrence Lipton among others. Lawrence R. Holmes, assistant professor of English literature at Chadron College and editor of the *Letter*, considered Drake the "foremost woman poet writing in the English language today, and one who gets better and better."[61]

Drake was a speaker again at the PSA's annual dinner meeting in New York on 17 November 1955, where she read selections from *This Tilting Dust*.

> Miss Drake read a dozen and more short pieces [. . .] all of them bearing the special hallmark of the poet's metrical style—a style which clothed ordinary objects of the workaday world with a strange imagery, or transformed them into arresting, other-world symbols. There was witchery in the Speaker's voice, and incantation, with eerie creatures emerging out of the realm of myth, magic and demonology. One got the feeling, at times, that Miss Drake was a priestess of a pagan cult assisting at forbidden rites, into which the audience was gradually drawn, willy-nilly, to participate as votaries.[62]

About her performance, the president of the Society, Edward Davison, a professor at Hunter College, said: "I haven't heard anyone read poetry

---

61. Quotation in clipping from an undated, unidentified paper.
62. [Unsigned.] "Leah Bodine Drake," *PSA Bulletin* (December 1955): 4–5.

INTRODUCTION

like that since Dylan Thomas."⁶³ Drake appeared at a gathering at Hunter with W. H. Auden, Archibald MacLeish, and Cardinal Spellman.

The *PSA Bulletin* announced, in February 1957, that Drake was one of four recipients of the 1956 Arthur Davison Ficke Memorial Award for a brace of sonnets titled "The Hand." The award was established and funded by the poet Witter Bynner. Drake, along with Margaret Haley Carpenter, Frances Minturn Howard, and Ulrich Troubetzkoy, shared the $400 prize. The poems were submitted anonymously for judging.

Drake had always been very close to her parents; indeed, she lived nearly her entire life with them. When her mother died shortly after Christmas in 1956 at the age of eighty-seven of acute coronary thrombosis, Drake was devastated and inconsolable. She wrote numerous poems in the next two years dedicated or addressed to her mother. In October 1957, she and her father went to Parkersburg, West Virginia, ostensibly to visit her aunt Mary, her father's sister. Such was Drake's love for her deceased mother that she could not bear the thought of leaving her behind in Indiana, and she assumed the visit to Parkersburg was only that. The Drakes returned to Indiana for a time, though where they lived is not known. Drake spent three weeks in July 1958 in New Harmony at a kind of writer's retreat, where she wrote more than a dozen poems, including "With Her Death," a poem to her mother that Drake struggled through many drafts to get on paper. Drake's friend Josephine Elliot, an archivist at Indiana State University, Evansville, who used to drive her home from Evansville when she lived in Henderson, later lived in New Harmony. Elliott (1912–2002) wrote several papers on the history of New Harmony and may have helped arrange Drake's stay. Her father presumably resided at the family homestead in Evansville. The Drakes eventually moved permanently to Parkersburg, where her father had been born and where his sister Mary Gale Drake (26 December 1878–29 March 1962) still lived. Drake informed a correspondent in 1960 that her books were still all in storage in Evansville. It is unlikely that she ever retrieved them.

---

63. From the back panel of the dust jacket for *TD*.

The Song of the Sun ❦ Leah Bodine Drake

The Parkersburg paper stated that Thomas Drake was retired.[64] He was seventy-seven years old at the time. Leah, however, said that the reason the Drakes were in Parkersburg in October 1957 was that there was a small oil boom there and that her father was having success, but she noted that she still needed to work to help make ends meet.[65] Not long after arriving in Parkersburg for good in 1958, Leah took a position at the *Parkersburg News* c. 28 September as associate society news editor. The title sounds glamorous, but Drake described her job as a "rock-crusher," noting that she and another editor often worked more than twelve hours a day two days a week, doing all the writing, editing, paste-up, and other work readying the society pages for the Sunday edition of the paper. Bethel Doyle Swint (1907–1983), the society news editor, said that Drake disliked working for the newspaper because she wanted to write poetry and her job prevented her from doing so.[66] In October Drake joined the Parkersburg Civic Woman's Club. Around that time she became a charter member of the Kentucky University Libraries Associates.

Drake applied for a Guggenheim fellowship so that she could write more poems for a third book. Among her papers is notification (26 November 1958) of receipt of a report from Dr. Robert T. Moore, professor at Occidental College, Los Angeles, editor of the annual Borestone Mountain poetry anthologies in which Drake was represented many times. The poet George Abbe, assistant professor of English at Russell Sage College (Troy, New York), and Laurence S. Thompson, head librarian of the University of Kentucky, also submitted very favorable reports. However, Drake was not awarded a fellowship. She resigned from the *News* in July 1960 to take a job in "hat salon management" at Broida, Stone & Thomas, with the hope of being transferred to the firm's store in Lexington, Kentucky. She found the work unsatisfactory and resigned that position after a few months.

In July 1960, Drake informed August Derleth that she was helping edit a book for Falcon's Wing Press. She described the project as "per-

---

64. "Leah Bodine Drake Noted Poet," *Parkersburg News* (26 October 1957): 6.
65. AD 55.
66. Wood 5.

fect," for it was literary in nature, not journalism or sales. She worked briefly for the *Mid-Ohio Valley Observer* from 23 September (first issue) to 7 October 1962 (when the paper folded), but remained engaged on the book. Her father had an operation for prostate cancer on 18 November.

It is not known with certainty how Drake came to be associated with Charles Arthur Musès (28 April 1919–26 August 2000), an esoteric philosopher who held unusual and controversial views relating to mathematics, physics, philosophy, and other fields. He earned his master's degree (1947) and doctorate (1951) at Columbia University. Musès published articles, books, and poems under various pseudonyms, including Musaios, Kyril Demys, Arthur Fontaine, Kenneth Demarest, and Carl von Balmadis.[67] With Joseph Campbell, he coedited *In All Her Names: Explorations of the Feminine in Divinity* (1991). Under the name Kyril Demys, he published *Wings of Myrahi* (Falcon's Wing Press, 1960). He founded the Lion Path, a shamanistic movement.[68]

In 1952, Musès and his fiancée, Charlotte Barth Howell (1895–1977), former wife of the diplomat Williamson S. Howell, Jr. (1893–1947), purchased 640 acres in Indian Hills, Colorado. Howell, granddaughter of William Barth, a leading Denver resident and philanthropist, owned considerable real estate holdings in Denver, selling the Equitable Building at 730 17th Street in 1956 for $2 million. The Indian Hills property became known as Falcon Wing Ranch. Howell founded the Falcon's Wing Press in 1954 for the purpose of publishing fine editions of nonfiction. Dr. Musès was editor-in-chief and a Mrs. Beardslee was associate editor. The first work published was Musès's edition of the *Septuagint Bible*. Musès and Howell married on 4 June 1954 in Fairfax County, Virginia. He was thirty-five, she fifty-nine.

Promotional copy from Falcon's Wing Press said Musès was the

---

67. Among his books are *Illumination on Jacob Boehme: The Work of Dionysius Andreas Freher* (1951); *The Septuagint Bible: The Oldest Version of the Old Testament in the Translation of Charles Thomson, Secretary of the Continental Congress of the United States of America, 1774–1789* (1954); *Esoteric Teachings of the Tibetan Tantra* (1961); and *Destiny and Control in Human Systems: Studies in the Interactive Connectedness of Time* (1985).
68. See *The Lion Path: You Can Take It with You: A Manual of the Short Path to Regeneration for Our Times* (1990), as by Musaios.

The Song of the Sun ❧ Leah Bodine Drake

firm's "Editor and Field Research Director." In 1957, he led a "successful archaeological expedition in the Middle East, resulting in the discovery of a hitherto unknown Pharaoh, Ameny'aum [sic] of ancient Egypt."[69] Musès was arrested in March 1957 in Egypt when he tried to remove valuable artifacts from the country. He claimed he did not realize that a license was required. Nevertheless, he was convicted in August 1957 but later allowed to return to the United States. Drake probably did not know of this.

Drake's association with Musès began in 1957 or so, when he contacted her for poems to include in a poetry anthology he was editing, and lasted through 1964. In 1958, Musès published a 711-page collection of poetry he edited called *Prismatic Voices: An International Anthology of Distinctive New Poets*. The hefty collection contained the work of only nineteen poets, several of whom were PSA members. It included twenty-one poems by Drake and twenty-nine by Musès himself as Kyril Demys. It was published in Colorado by Falcon's Wing Press but printed in Switzerland.

It is not known how Musès came to know the work of Leah Bodine Drake, but he clearly admired it. Perhaps he had encountered her poetry in such magazines as the *Atlantic* and the *New Yorker*. As *Prismatic Voices* was being prepared, Drake had informed a staff member at Falcon's Wing Press about the appearance of her poetry review "The New Poetry" in the July 1958 issue of the *Atlantic,* and so Musès requested to see a copy of it. Perhaps he was impressed enough with her acumen to feel that she could be a helpful co-editor for a future project. How he came to team up with her to edit and publish *The Various Light* also is unknown. Musès had told Alfred Dorn that he was planning a sequel to *Prismatic Voices*. But in a letter to Drake clarifying the significance of the subtitle of *Prismatic Voices* Musès writes: "As to your suggestion of collaboration, I believe I would enjoy it. In early June I shall be in New York. Is there any possibility of seeing you there and talking the matter out vis-à-vis? Please keep this information *completely* confidential, even from mutual acquaintances like Dorn and George Abbe."[70]

---

69. Ameny-Qemau was a king of the early Thirteenth Dynasty and ruled c. 1775–1750 B.C.E. Musès found his pyramid at Dahshur, but no excavation report was made.
70. 15 May 1959 (ALS, University of Kentucky).

INTRODUCTION

Both Abbe and Dorn were represented in *Prismatic Voices*. Possibly one or both, ardent admirers of Drake, had spoken favorably of her to Musès. It would appear that the idea for the new anthology was Drake's—the title of the book appears to have been suggested by her, for it appears in one of her notebooks as number three on a list of "Possible Titles for Books," where it is prominently checked off in red pencil with the note "used in F.W. anthology." It derives from "The Garden" by Andrew Marvell:

> My Soul into the boughs does glide;
> There like a Bird it sits, and sings,
> Then whets, and combs its silver Wings;
> And, till prepar'd for longer flight,
> Waves in its Plumes the various Light. (ll. 52–56)

But Musès appears to have exerted the chief editorial hand, for Drake told correspondents that she was working for him. In a form letter to poets she wrote: "Dr. C. A. Muses, editor, has asked me to select the poets, and to help him choose the poems, which will be used in this volume."[71] In another form letter she described herself as "only a guest-editor."[72] She handled the administrative duties, but she also assisted in selecting poems.

Drake was required to make several trips to Switzerland to work on the project. Her partner must have felt that both of them needed to be in the same location to work effectively on the book. Initially she sent form letters with general guidelines for submission, but later, in personal letters to poets, she often specified certain titles that she wished to include, indicating that she had familiarity with the work of at least some of the poets. The poets represented in Musès's previous *Prismatic Voices* are somewhat esoteric, with few recognizable names. Even Drake herself does not seem a likely inclusion in a book described as "an international anthology of distinctive new poets," since her work had been appearing since 1935, and thus she was not a "new" poet, and she had been appearing in publications unlikely to be recognized internationally. *The*

---

71. 12 March 1960 (TLS, May Swenson papers, Washington University).
72. 6 March 1961 (TLS, May Swenson papers, Washington University).

The Song of the Sun ❧ Leah Bodine Drake

Various Light includes the work of Drake's poet and publisher friends whose work she admired, including many members of the PSA: Eric Barker, Joseph Payne Brennan, August Derleth, and Joseph Joel Keith. Her work and theirs appeared in the little poetry magazines of the day. Drake had written of or reviewed the work of eleven of the contributors, most of them in her reviews in the *Atlantic*. George Abbe, Bernice Ames, Kyril Demys (i.e., Musès), Alfred Dorn, Drake, Patrick Galvin, William Milne, William Pillin, Ruth Forbes Sherry, and Mary Woodlee were Musès's own choices, for their work was included in his other anthology, although Drake was in touch with Abbe and Dorn. Many of the other poets were quite well known for their work: Sylvia Plath, Ted Hughes, Alastair Reid, Howard Nemerov, Richard Wilbur (whose book won the National Book Award over Drake's), W. S. Merwin, C. S. Lewis, Thomas Burnett Swann, Robert Graves, Dan Berrigan, Loren Eisley, Donald Hall, Louis Simpson, and others.

As many of the other contributors were members of the PSA, they readily saw Drake's call for poems published in the *Bulletin* for March 1960, requesting that submissions arrive in Locarno no later than 15 May. Drake described the poets contributing to the book as a "first-class flight of talent" and felt, when naming some of them, that giving their last names only indicated that they were recognizable figures. The editors did not pore over poetry books or journals in order to select poems; rather, Drake made the single announcement in the *PSA Bulletin* and sent a few inquiries to personal acquaintances who were not PSA members. Her published notice asked for American, British, and Canadian poets to submit up to twenty-five poems for consideration. They would not, of course, use that many from any individual, though even half that amount would be in line with the number of poems given to individual poets in Musès's *Prismatic Voices*. Since *The Various Light* contains poems by ninety-one poets, the editors could not use more than a few poems by each, and so when Drake approached August Derleth, who did not respond to her initial notice, she wrote: "Will you send me about 10 of your poems, old & new, published or not, for me to consider?"[73] When

---

73. 2 July 1960.

Introduction

the poems were received, she passed them on to Musès. Drake was embarrassed that he wanted to use eight of her poems. In the end they used only four, three of which, oddly enough, had appeared in *Prismatic Voices*.

Drake was primarily doing the administrative work required to obtain material from potential contributors, and yet her name appears ahead of Musès's own on the title page, a practice usually indicating that the first-named editor had the leading role in the project; but then, alphabetically her name would precede his, or perhaps Musès thought "Ladies first."

Drake likely expressed certain preferences as to content, but all final decisions were made by Musès, who often was traveling and difficult to reach, leaving Drake awkwardly to fend for herself in dealing with authors. Musès's work methods frustrated Drake ("I don't dig that cat at times"), but overall she seems to have been pleased to have the work. Musès also wanted her to catalogue his library, and she was glad to get the assignment, since she had no other employment, but the failing health of her family members and then her own derailed the project. The headnote to a story by Drake published in *Fantasy and Science Fiction* in February 1965 said she was acting "as confidential secretary and editorial assistant to cybernetic[74] expert, Dr. C. A. Muses, of Lausanne, Switzerland (with whom she has just finished editing an anthology of contemporary British and American verse THE VARIOUS LIGHT)," but Drake had died the previous November.

Musès spent Easter 1961 with the Drakes in Parkersburg on his way from Los Angeles to Washington, then to Locarno, Switzerland. Drake's first trip there was in June 1960. Charlotte Howell resided in Locarno, presumably as Musès's wife. An unspecified problem arose with Falcon's Wing Press in early 1961, and there was a dispute with the publisher as to whether the book would be published. Drake issued a form letter to contributors attempting to forestall adverse communication from Falcon's

---

74. Cybernetics is a transdisciplinary approach for exploring regulatory systems—their structures, constraints, and possibilities. Norbert Wiener defined cybernetics in 1948 as "the scientific study of control and communication in the animal and the machine." In other words, it is the scientific study of how humans, animals, and machines control and communicate with each other. LBD believed that animals attempted to communicate with humans.

The Song of the Sun ~ Leah Bodine Drake

Wing, stating: "There is some kind of misunderstanding out in the Colorado office of the Barth Foundation (Falcon's Wing Press), and the word seems to be going around that the book has been abandoned. [¶] This simply is not so—and if you get any word to that effect from ANYONE other than Dr. Muses or myself, just ignore it. It will carry no weight at all."[75] As she expected, contributors to the book were notified, in a form letter, by C. M. Spicher of Indian Hills, manager of the press, that "due to circumstances beyond our control" publication of the book was being cancelled."[76] The letter also stated that Dr. Musès had resigned from the Barth Foundation. It appears that her letter reached the poets well ahead of the notification that came from Falcon's Wing. Further work to be conducted with Musès in Switzerland was done in Lausanne. Some sort of rift must have developed between Musès and Howell. Why would there have been difficulty in Musès's dealing with his own company, unless friction developed between him and his partner—his wife?

Drake clearly admired Musès. She presented to him a copy of *A Hornbook for Witches* (recycled, apparently, as its front flyleaf had been removed) with her inscription on the half-title, "To my favorite Sorcerer and White Magician, Charles A. Muses, with affection and admiration, L.B.D. January, 1962, Lausanne, Switzerland." On the back flyleaf she pasted in a clipping from the Summer 1963 issue of *Fiddlehead* of "Two Poems by Leah Bodine Drake": "Cold Orchard" and "In the Night," inscribed "For Charles—". Drake had written both poems in Lausanne in 1961, and the message of "In the Night" is quite transparent:

> Lie on my breast a moment, so—
> As gently as the moon's cool glow
> Lies on the sleeping poplar-lands;
> Touch me with undemanding hands.
> As softly as a windless shower

---

75. LBD to May Swenson, 6 March 1961 (TLS, Washington University). LBD wrote to Joseph Payne Brennan on 21 February 1961 telling him to ignore any communique that the book was being cancelled.
76. C. M. Spicher, "To all contributing authors," 27 March 1961 (May Swenson papers, Washington University).

INTRODUCTION

> Touches the petals of a flower—
> Oh, lie still, lie so—
> Before the winds of passion start
> And the great storms shake the heart.

None of her previous poems are quite so bold as this, although "The Snake," also from this time, reflects similar passion. Another poem written in Lausanne, "The Terrible Meek," has as its unusual subject (for Drake) a wife who torments her husband psychologically. Was it a reflection of the relationship between Musès and his wife? A brief note from Musès among Drake's papers states "Lonely! Again, much love," but that could be a simple pleasantry. Musès and his wife eventually divorced. Musès remarried, though particulars are unknown. Among books found in Musès's library was one of Drake's scrapbooks, which her will specified was to go to him.[77]

There is no way to know for certain, but there seems to have been a romance between Drake and Musès. This could account for the rift between Musès and Falcon's Wing Press, and the shift of his work base from Locarno to Lausanne. The words of Griffin and Betty Callahan make one wonder about Drake's relationship with Dr. Musès: "Leah Bodine Drake had a kind of mystery. Her ability to inspire attracted all who have the slightest shred of mystic understanding . . . especially men!"

Upon her return from Switzerland in early 1962, Drake wrote to August Derleth telling him that she had been job-hunting in New York; she had landed two jobs and noted that her acceptance of the positions depended on the health of her father. Her aunt Mary Gale Drake died on 29 March, about a week after falling down the stairs and suffering a grave injury. Her father's health, which had been declining since 1961, did not allow a move to New York, and so Drake remained in Parkersburg for the rest of her life save for brief stints spent in Lausanne working for Musès. In those cases, her father and aunt "Nancy" (i.e., "Nanna," or Anne Bodine) stayed with Mary Gale Drake at 828 Murdoch. Leah otherwise provided care as she could, aided by her elderly

---

77. Benjamin J. Parker (1923–1970) of Hiteshew, Cather, Renner & Parker, Attorneys at Law in Parkersburg, acted as administrator of LBD's estate in early 1965.

The Song of the Sun ❧ Leah Bodine Drake

aunt Anne, who had come from Camden, New Jersey, to help.

Thomas Drake died on 17 May 1963. His death certificate says he died of uremia, partial urinary obstruction, and cancer of the prostate, although Leah told a correspondent he had long had bone and stomach cancer and kidney trouble. Leah's aunt Anne, her mother's twin sister, died on 20 May 1964, one day shy of her ninety-fifth birthday, of arteriosclerotic heart disease. The settling of Anne's estate fell to Leah, and she soon realized that she was unable to resolve her relatives' debts. She meant to do right, but her own health was so poor that she simply could not manage, and she found herself in dire poverty. Despite the need to care for her family, Drake continued to write poetry during the summer of 1964. Drake herself had become quite ill in late August 1963 and underwent surgery for "gastric malignancy." She was well enough to return to Lausanne in January 1964 to resume work on *The Various Light*, but she had to return to the U.S. in March to attend to her aunt Anne. Drake's death certificate states that she had had carcinomatosis for the fourteen months before her death, a condition presumably resulting from the ailment that had prompted the need for surgery. Not long afterward she entered the hospital, where she stayed for two weeks, learning that she herself was dying of terminal gastric carcinoma, which apparently returned despite the previous year's surgery. Her doctor, Delmer Jencks Brown (1907–1973), stated that he last saw Drake alive on 7 November.

Around that time, Drake undertook in earnest the preparation of what was to be her final book, conceived three years previous. In 1961, she requested permission from August Derleth to use two of her poems that he had published in his periodical *Hawk and Whippoorwill* for "a book I'm planning of new & old poems of mine[.] The project is still tenuous—I haven't even titled the collection yet."[78] Clarence Farrar, publisher of *This Tilting Dust*, wrote Drake: "While the new manuscript that you propose does have a large portion from *This Tilting Dust*, the present rate of sale of the Book Club selection would not warrant any objection from us. So go ahead and use them as you please."[79] And so

78. 23 February 1961.
79. 10 March 1961 (TLS, University of Kentucky).

Introduction

early on, she knew her final book would consist in large part of poems from the previous volume. She first named the manuscript *Airs, Waters, and Places,* a title taken from the work of that name around 400 B.C.E. by Hippocrates, in which he sought to show a connection between local climate and the diseases plaguing an area. Eventually Drake changed the title to *Multiple Clay,* after a poem she published in 1957, perhaps because her own words spoke best to her reflection on her failing health:

> What multiple clay fused to the single grain
> That is myself, no family-tree can tell,
> Or what fires lit my senses' heaven and hell.
> These limbs are but a momentary loan
>
> That I'll repay before I even know
> What ends they've served.

The typescript has two parts: I. New Poems, comprising twenty-five poems, most dating from the mid-1950s onward, including two poems apparently unpublished, and one that appeared in the July 1964 number of the *Magazine of Fantasy and Science Fiction;* and II. Selected Poems, comprising twenty-four poems, all from *This Tilting Dust* save one from *A Hornbook for Witches.* It seems odd that Drake would assemble a book of which roughly half was culled from her previous book, when she had 200 other uncollected or unpublished poems on hand, but her selection constituted what she felt was her absolute best work. It is telling that she selected only one poem from her first book. The typescript bears the dedication "To the Memory of Mother, Father, and Nanna 1956, 1963, 1964," the dates being the years each died, respectively. It also bears the handwritten address, 1316 Market St., Parkersburg, West Va., the address of Griffin and Betty Callahan with whom Drake spent her last days. Mrs. Callahan said that two days before Drake died, the completed typescript was sent to a publisher who asked to see it, following an inquiry made on her behalf by Gustav Davidson.

Griffin Clay Callahan (31 October 1919–25 October 2013) graduated from Bluefield Junior College in 1938 and then from the College of William and Mary and Virginia Theological Seminary. In 1944 he was

The Song of the Sun ❧ Leah Bodine Drake

ordained to the priesthood in the Episcopal Church. He began his ministry in Greenbrier and Monroe counties, serving as rector of six parishes during the mid-1940s. He served many congregations in West Virginia and was also assistant rector at Calvary Church in Pittsburgh. In 1960 he became rector of Trinity Episcopal Church in Parkersburg, where he served until he retired in 1974. Drake was a parishioner at Trinity. Her *Who's Who* entry states her religion as Episcopalian.[80] Elizabeth (Boykin) Callahan (17 May 1920–28 January 2006) was Griffin's first wife. The Callahans and others in Parkersburg knew Leah as a parishioner and formerly a writer for the local paper. In the form letter the Callahans circulated following her death, they wrote: "She has left a wealth of wonderful creative writing. We have just begun to discover how great a quantity of her published poems Leah has collected in scrapbooks, and in the hand written illustrated manuscripts which she has kept of all her poems."

A word must be said about those scrapbooks. Drake had scrapbooks in which she kept clippings of her published poems, articles about her from the newspapers, letters from friends, publishers, and appreciative readers, and other miscellany. She also had scrapbooks in which she preserved poetry by others, but these do not survive. The books to which the Callahans refer, however, are twenty-four scrapbooks in which she wrote out her poems by hand, from as few as eight to as many as twenty-one, averaging about twelve in each. These scrapbooks consist of loose leaves bound into detachable covers, as would be expected. For the most part the poems are what could be called fair copies, though Drake revised some texts. She noted that she had rewritten or revised poems that had been published previously. All the books have titles and tables of contents, just like real books, though the list and the pages themselves have no page numbers. Their contents are grouped more or less thematically (e.g., *Magic Casements. Children's Poems by Leah Bodine Drake. 1935–37*) rather than chronologically. Despite the date ranges sometimes indicated on the title pages, as in the title above, poems separated very far in time may appear in the same scrapbook, sometimes outside the range specified. Besides published poems, she also recorded roughly 100 un-

---

80. In Evansville, she had attended St. Paul's Episcopal Church.

Introduction

published poems.

Many readers will misconstrue Elizabeth Callahan's term "illustrated manuscripts." Drake did not do her own illustrations, nor did the images necessarily illustrate any given poem; they were included because of loose thematic resemblance. She obtained them from books, magazines, greeting cards, and other sources, leaning heavily on art by Arthur Rackham, Edmund Dulac, J. J. Lankes, Denys James Watkins-Pitchford, Gertrude Alice Kay, and other of her favorite illustrators of children's books, and also clippings of random spot illustrations, and ornamented capitals and borders. A friend called them "illuminated manuscripts," and in a crude way they do resemble mediaeval texts (see, e.g., p. 87). Some of the books were prepared late in life, but the practice extended back to her youth:

> I haven't even tried to write fiction since I was a child and wrote innumerable fairytales, illustrated beautifully by Rackham, Dulac and Pogany: I tore their pictures out of my books, AND my family's. I remember a copy we had of Omar's RUBAIYAT illustrated by Dulac. Almost every picture in it came out, to illustrate my own almost-exclusively Oriental fairytales.[81]

She even preserved in her scrapbooks a drawing by her mother and another by Frank Utpatel (obtained from the dust jacket of her copy of William Hope Hodgson's *Carnacki, the Ghost Finder*), who illustrated the dust jacket of *A Hornbook for Witches*. The term "illuminated manuscripts" suggests careful, deliberate, painstaking ornamentation. Nearly all the pages in Drake's scrapbooks are decorated somehow, with large ornamental capitals and ornate little drawings, but the books are rather sloppily prepared. The pictures are somewhat battered—as Drake noted, she "tore" pictures from books—and many pages bear evidence that pictures once pasted on them had been removed, and not very carefully, perhaps to be pasted on other pages. Some pages are wrinkled or thinned from application and subsequent removal of pasted material. In some cases, removal of images resulted in holes in the pages, on which Drake pasted crude patches to make repairs. The books themselves are covered, again somewhat carelessly, in what appears to be shelf paper.

---

81. LBD to AD, 6 November 1952.

The Song of the Sun ❧ Leah Bodine Drake

The fact that Drake had twenty-four decorated scrapbooks of her poetry indicates that she considered them to be precious, but the exact purpose of the books is not known. They seem to be an extension of a cherished childhood ritual. Because the poems have few written revisions, the scrapbooks may have served as repositories for file copies of her poems, an unusual practice because most writers would have kept either clean typed copies or carbons for their files. In comparing the poems recorded in her scrapbooks against published versions, the scrapbook texts contain readings that generally (but not always) are slightly superior to published appearances. She provided dates for most poems—usually by year only—sometimes noting that they either took a long time to be considered complete or that she had rewritten some at a later date, often long after publication.

Drake sometimes typed copies of her poems, but very few are found among her own papers. The David L. Rice Library of the University of Southern Indiana in Evansville, Indiana, holds 100 typescripts of her poems. Drake was a member of the Evansville chapter of the American Association of University Women. The typescripts held at the Rice Library are clean for the most part, although Drake signed or initialed many and sometimes wrote dates of composition or notes about impending publication. Again, the purpose is uncertain. It seems that upon completion of a new poem, she sent a copy to the AAUW for archiving or some other purpose. Among the typescripts are several poems written or revised when she was living in West Virginia. Poems in Drake's scrapbooks that are also at Rice seem to be final versions, whereas the Rice texts seem to have been initial impressions that she later revised. The Rice Library holds nearly thirty unpublished poems not found among Drake's own scrapbooks.

Besides preparing *Multiple Clay,* Drake completed one other project before she died. She assembled yet one more scrapbook in her fashion, but it differs significantly from the others. She titled it *Goblin Market: Selected Poems of Leah Bodine Drake,* comprising fifty-eight pages. As with her other scrapbooks, *Goblin Market* (the title taken from a famous weird poem by Christina Rossetti) was illustrated with the usual images taken from books, but for this book they are all neatly cut. A circular print is trimmed very carefully as a neat circle. The various ornaments—capitals, decorative borders, and other illustrations—also are cut very carefully and unbroken, unlike the illustrations in her other scrapbooks. Unlike the other books, the ornamented title of this special book is set up on a verso page with a large full-page illustration on the facing recto page, to make a large, dramatic spread. Most significantly, the texts of the twenty-two poems included therein are typed, each poem cut neatly and pasted squarely on the page. The book contained a note laid into it by its owner, Dr. Charles A. Musès. It reads "GOBLIN MARKET—Leah Bodine Drake Rec–d. Feb 20, 1964, [sic] by Leah's Will." Presumably the date is meant to read "1965," since it was presented to Musès per instruction in Drake's will, which would not have been acted upon until after she had died. It is unknown exactly when Drake prepared the scrapbook. The book was lovingly and painstakingly assembled, but like her personal scrapbooks, it still is somewhat amateurish in appearance. Since Drake fancied her own notebooks as special, personal keepsakes, it is fitting that she wanted to make a special memento for Musès.

The *PSA Bulletin* of October 1964 welcomed Drake as a reinstated member (again). Her membership must have lapsed during the period when she was caring for three elderly relatives and having her own health problems. But that reinstatement was short-lived.

According to the Callahans, when Drake left the hospital after a two-week stay, she returned home, alone, to care for herself. A neighbor, Opal E. Cariens (1902–1986), looked in on Drake every day and performed various tasks for her. The Callahans state that "a variety of Parkersburg landlords cut the rent or charged none during times of her greatest financial stress" and that she did not even have a telephone. Her last known address before living with the Callahans was 812½ West Virginia Avenue, where she lived with her aunt Anne at least until 20 May. It is not known where Drake dwelt after that. It is sobering to think that the dying woman may have been shunted several times from one dwelling to another, unable to afford the rent and faced with complete poverty in the last six months of her life. The Callahans finally took Drake into their own home, the church rectory. Elizabeth, a registered nurse, cared for Drake.

Leah Bodine Drake died at 4:30 A.M., Saturday, 21 November 1964, at the age of fifty-nine. The funeral director who tended to her was Stanley Norris Vaughan, Sr. (1902–1998), who performed the same

The Song of the Sun ❧ Leah Bodine Drake

duties following the deaths of her father and aunts. Drake's death certificate states that her "Length of Stay in City or Town" was "2 wks," but she had been living in Parkersburg since 1958. The period "2 wks" must have referred to her stay with the Callahans, for Drake was last seen alive by her doctor on 7 November. Griffin Callahan is named the "informant" on Drake's death certificate. Drake completed *Multiple Clay* (although she did not prepare a neat, final typescript) but was unable to submit it to a publisher herself. The Callahans contacted Gustav Davidson, PSA secretary, to see if he could find a publisher for the book. John C. Farrar of Farrar, Straus & Giroux wrote on 18 November, stating that he would read the typescript, which was mailed to him two days before Drake died. On 31 December 1964 Farrar wrote regretfully to say he was going to pass on the book, and that he thought Wesleyan University Press might be a suitable publisher. It does not seem that any other publisher was approached, and the book was never published.

At her funeral on 23 November, Griffin Callahan read aloud "Multiple Clay," the title poem of her intended final book. Gustav Davidson stated that he intended to publish "Multiple Clay" in the *PSA Bulletin*, but only a brief, unsigned obituary (probably by Davidson) was published. It claimed that *Multiple Clay* was "a manuscript highly regarded in New York publishing circles,"[82] but it does not seem that anyone other than John C. Farrar saw the manuscript. In early December, Callahan and his wife sent a mimeographed letter to Drake's friends and relatives, telling of her final days in their care. John Ashton Herring (1924–1982), a distant cousin and a professor at the University of Virginia–Charlottesville, who had met Drake only once previously, acquired her papers, which he donated in 1968 per Drake's wishes to the University of Kentucky–Lexington,[83] to which she had previously sent some manuscripts at the request of Lawrence S. Thompson, the library director. Josephine Elliott, a friend of

---

82. *PSA Bulletin* (February 1965): 41.
83. Herring said he had her papers photocopied at the University of Virginia Library's Manuscripts Division in 1965, but it is not known what became of those copies. Probably they were merely for his own personal use. He told Edelene Wood that he intended to publish *Multiple Clay* himself, but that did not occur.

INTRODUCTION

Drake in Indiana and a librarian, who drove her home from time to time, sent money to Herring for a grave marker for Drake, and the two alone saw that one was obtained and placed.

Drake shouldered the debts of her father, his sister Mary, and ultimately her aunt Anne, along with her own. Except for working as Musès's assistant (probably an intermittent post and possibly at no pay), Drake was last employed by Broida's, from which she resigned, and briefly at the short-lived *Mid-Ohio Valley Observer* in 1962. She did not have a steady income the last four years of her life. She sold few poems, and they reaped very little in terms of payment. The Callahans stated that "Nan[n]a died and left Leah one half of the trust fund, (the other half going to her cousin, Mrs. C. E. Downs)."[84] That was only $75. Drake was interred near her father's grave in Parkersburg Memorial Gardens. The Creative Poetry Section of the American Association of University Women held an open meeting on 15 November 1965 as a memorial to Drake. Her friend Vardine Moore led the program, at which some of Drake's poems were read.

Drake died without seeing publication of the book on which she had worked intermittently for five years through many hardships, both personal and project-related. Because of the break with Falcon's Wing Press, Musès needed to find another publisher. Ultimately the book was printed in Portugal, but the address of the publisher, Aurora Press, was Musès's own in Lausanne, and so the book was self-published in an edition of 500 copies. It seems to have gone unnoticed, for no reviews of it have been found. The fact that the collection of poems by American and British authors was published in Switzerland, and that nearly 100 copies went to contributors, may account for its lack of impact, though the book seems to be a competent compilation of poems by established poets.

August Derleth had not forgotten about publishing a second book of Drake's poems. In June 1968, fifteen years after Drake had broached the subject to him, he inquired with the Margaret I. King Library in Lexington about obtaining photocopies of Drake's papers. Jacqueline Bell, Head of Special Collections, somewhat exasperatedly informed Derleth that the library was not about to copy the material, consisting mainly of twenty-

---

84. This was Virginia Bodine (1903–1968), wife of Charles E. Downs (1902–1973).

The Song of the Sun ~ Leah Bodine Drake

four scrapbooks. The tightly bound books would have been very difficult to handle on a copier, and there were many pages to copy. Perhaps they could have been unbound to facilitate copying, but the unbinding, copying, and rebinding of twenty-four scrapbooks would have been a significant undertaking. Bell suggested that someone come to Lexington to consult the scrapbooks at first hand, which would have meant transcribing select content from the scrapbooks, a task that would have taken weeks if one were to transcribe everything. Even if only a selection were made, it would still take time for someone to read the totality of her poems and then to transcribe selected items. Derleth could not afford the time to travel there himself, or the expense to have someone else do the work. And so a second Arkham House book of Drake's poetry never came to be.

How do we define the literary legacy of Leah Bodine Drake? She is virtually forgotten today, but in her time she was a well-regarded poet. She published only 200 or so poems, gathering about half of those into two thin books now difficult to find, four short stories, and a scattering of essays and reviews. All this was overshadowed in volume by the ephemeral articles or reviews she wrote for various newspapers. The time she spent working for newspapers encroached on creative pursuits. But her poems appeared in some of the country's more notable periodicals, and she was a prominent figure in the culture of the "little magazine." Her "spookers" were divertissements with macabre themes written mostly for her own amusement. She is known more for the "spookers" than anything—but not because people have enjoyed reading them, for they are in a book and in other publications that have long been difficult to obtain. Her celebrity comes instead from the rarity of her book among Arkham House completists, not from actual acquaintance with her work. Drake is held these days by some as a pioneering female writer of science fiction, but hefty reference works such as *The Encyclopedia of Fantasy*, *The Encyclopedia of Science Fiction*, and *The Penguin Encyclopedia of Horror and the Supernatural* take no notice of her. She was not really a writer of fantasy or science fiction, although her work sometimes appeared in publications devoted to those genres. Even if one will grant that she did write pieces with fantastic themes, she is hardly a pioneer in

INTRODUCTION

the genres. She did not break new ground; she merely published in outlets for the most part dominated by men.

But Drake was a poet well recognized for her work outside the science fiction and fantasy arenas. Awards may be largely meaningless, but she received many for her work—sometimes monetary, sometimes merely in recognition, sometimes for work merely regarded as superior to that by others in the previous month's issue of a magazine, as determined by a guest judge. Her poetry appeared in numerous annual anthologies of "best poems"—no mean feat. Like the work of George Sterling, Clark Ashton Smith, and Samuel Loveman, her verse is largely unknown because she tended to work in fixed or formal forms and disdained "obscure" poetry, as evinced in her tart comments in "To Certain Poetry Critics." Her work appeared not only in the little poetry magazines of her time, but also in major magazines that received hundreds of submissions a week but which accepted and published very few items. In an milieu in which the likelihood of publication is small, it is an achievement to have one's work appear at all. The *Atlantic Monthly* published seven of her poems, assigned her to write essays on recent books of poetry, and included her work in a book celebrating 100 years of the magazine's publication—a book that included the work of only eighteen poets, including Longfellow, Yeats, MacLeish, Dunsany, Robinson, Wallace Stevens, Dylan Thomas, and other august figures.

It is hoped that those approaching this book because of interest in or curiosity about Leah Bodine Drake's rare first book, or because they wish to explore the work of a "pioneer," will find themselves rewarded with a wealth of poetry of all kinds: poems for children, poems with mythological or historical subjects, sometimes treated with whimsy, more often not, poems about the perils of the modern age, and other, unclassifiable works. Her themes emerge from her lifelong fascination with nature, mythology, folklore, witchcraft, the dignity of animals, and even strange couplings of humans with gods or animals (as in "The Ballad of the Seal-Woman's Daughter" and "Foxy's Hollow").

Drake seemed intent on infusing a depth of meaning in her poems far beyond the surface signification of the deceptively simple words and phrases she customarily used; even in her weird poetry she was not in-

The Song of the Sun ❧ Leah Bodine Drake

clined merely to produce a shudder. Each poem stands as a slender facet of her understanding of the world and the place of humanity within it, and as such her work will bear repeated re-reading as the product of a keenly sensitive mind and heart fully aware of the legacy of myth and history that has made us who we are.

A Note on the Text

The poems in this edition derive primarily from Leah Bodine Drake's scrapbooks. They were clearly prepared over a long period of time as evidenced by gradual changes in handwriting; but comparison of the readings in them against those in her published books, *A Hornbook for Witches* (1950) and *This Tilting Dust* (1955), and also to magazine appearances, seems to indicate that the texts written out by hand (and two typescripts therein) are her preferred readings of most poems and thus constitute her permanent file copies. Drake tinkered extensively with her work, mostly adjusting punctuation. The surviving drafts of "With Her Death" and "Honey from the Lion" may or may not be indicative of the degree of effort she expended in writing a single poem. The readings in her scrapbooks generally seem to be for the better, and so I have followed them. A key exception in my method is that I have followed the typescript of *Multiple Clay*, the book she prepared very late in life but which never saw publication, since the texts of the poems therein probably represent her final preferences. The bibliography lists the contents of that typescript. The scrapbook *Goblin Market: Selected Poems*, also prepared late in life and containing typescripts of poems, could not be consulted.

The poems are arranged herein in approximate chronological order, based primarily on Drake's own notes. At times, she somewhat confusingly gave several dates for individual poems. Her intent seems to have been to indicate a date of initial composition, with any later date representing the time of a later revision, sometimes indicating final completion after a false start, sometimes indicating second thoughts after publication. For the purpose of chronological arrangement, the earlier date is used and the later date ignored. The intent is to indicate her first inspiration for the piece. When she has not noted a date of composition, the date of publication is used, allowing for a slight lag between presumed composition and publication. There are fourteen poems, all unpublished, for which the

INTRODUCTION

date of composition is not known. All these, held at the David L. Rice Library, exist as fair copies only; none are found in her scrapbooks. Their placement among the dated poems is entirely conjectural and based upon style and content. Drake's poems in *Prismatic Voices* have dates (year only) for the individual poems. They do not always agree with dates in scrapbooks and may represent the dates of final touchup. In the bibliography, these dates are provided in parentheses after the citation.

In the listing of items in the bibliography, an asterisk indicates the copy text when multiple readings are available. ($*^a$ indicates copy text for an alternate reading.) When only one source is listed, it is the copy text and has no asterisk. Because the poems in the scrapbooks seem to indicate Drake's final wishes for them, the scrapbooks are the source of the text of most poems herein. If the rewritten poem is greatly changed from the original, both are provided, the latter in the section of alternate readings. I have altered the texts very slightly, in order to ensure consistency and in keeping with Drake's usual practices. Minor spelling errors and slips of the pen have been corrected in her formal writing, but not in her letters. Footnotes in the text proper are Drake's own.

Acknowledgments

I wish to thank Daniel Weddington, Matt Harris, and the staff at the Margaret I. King Library of the University of Kentucky–Lexington; Jennifer Greene and James Wethington of the David L. Rice Library, University of Southern Indiana; Nicole Westerdahl of the Special Collections Research Center, Syracuse University Libraries; Alison Fraser, assistant curator of the Poetry Collection, University at Buffalo; Susan Stravinsky and the staff in Special Collections at the University of Wisconsin–Madison Memorial Library; Katherine Marschall of the Cushwa-Leighton Library, Saint Mary's College (South Bend, Indiana); Lee C. Grady and the staff of the Wisconsin Historical Society; and Robin Wheelwright Ness of the John Hay Library, Brown University (Providence, Rhode Island). They provided assistance in obtaining copies and providing other services, for which I am truly grateful. S. T. Joshi provided invaluable assistance in shaping the book, composing many items previously published, and preparing the bibliography. Kenneth W. Faig, Jr. unearthed much of the genealogical and census data about Drake and

The Song of the Sun ~ Leah Bodine Drake

her family included herein. Martin Andersson, Leigh Blackmore, David Bodine, Ashley Dioses, Michael Dirda, Stefan Dziemianowicz, Derrick Hussey, Gary Morris, K. A. Opperman, and Michael John Thompson assisted in various ways, often providing copies of published appearances and biographic or bibliographic data. Jordan Douglas Smith spent many hours in the New York Public library seeking published poems, often with only the most tenuous of leads. David Rajchel provided copies of three letters by Drake to August Derleth not held by the Wisconsin Historical Society and the photograph of Drake from her Christmas card. And lastly, Torin Mizenko assited in proofreading the book.

Abbreviations
AD   August Derleth
ALS   autograph letter, signed
A.Ms.   autograph manuscript
ANS   autograph note, signed
LBD   Leah Bodine Drake
MIK   Margaret I. King Library, University of Kentucky–Lexington
PSA   Poetry Society of America
R   Drake's T.Mss. held by David L. Rice Library, University of Southern Indiana
S   Drake's scrapbooks held by the University of Kentucky–Lexington
T.Ms.   typescript
TLS   typed letter, signed
TNS   typed note, signed
WHS   Wisconsin Historical Society

DM   *Dark of the Moon* (ed. August Derleth)
FSC   *Fire and Sleet and Candlelight* (ed. August Derleth)
F&SF   *Magazine of Fantasy and Science Fiction*
GM   *Goblin Market: Selected Poems* (T.Ms.)
HW   *A Hornbook for Witches*
MC   *Multiple Clay* (T.Ms.)
PV   *Prismatic Voices* (ed. Charles A. Musès)
TD   *This Tilting Dust*
VL   *The Various Light* (ed. Leah Bodine Drake and Charles A. Musès)

Photographs

Leah Bodine Drake, c. December 1949, from her Christmas card

Drake as an infant and toddler;
lower right: Drake and her father

Location and date unknown

Lexington, Kentucky, 1923, around the time Drake was attending Hamilton College for Girls

Artesia, New Mexico, 1926

Philadelphia, March 1928

Brownwood, Texas, June 1928

"Mrs. Leslie MacAllister," Jackson, Mississippi

"Mac," Jackson, Mississippi, August 1929

August 1930, location unknown

1931, location unknown

"Queen," Dallas Centennial, 1936

"Me, on float, 'Spirit of Dallas.'"
"Miss Dallas welcomes the world—
June 6, 1936"

Sunday Courier 5 November 1941,
Miss Leah Bodine Drake,
901 South East Sixth-st.

Drake looking jubilant, date unknown;
in *Kaleidograph*, May 1946

Thomas Hulbert Drake, 1947   Date unknown, possibly same setting (i.e., Evansville, Indiana)

421 W. 2nd, Lexington, KY   1023 First St. Henderson, KY

3115 E. Mulberry St., Evansville, IN

1219 S.E. 1st Street, Evansville, IN

The Poet's House, New Harmony, Indiana, December 1958. (not known if Drake resided in this particular house during her stay)

"The Pool" (1955) by Cornelia B. Drake. In Drake's scrapbook *The Woods Grow Darker*, to illustrate "Okio's Geese."

Unidentified drawing (1896) by J. J. Waugh. Drake has embellished the drawing with a title in her hand, as found in her scrapbook.

c. 1944

Date unknown

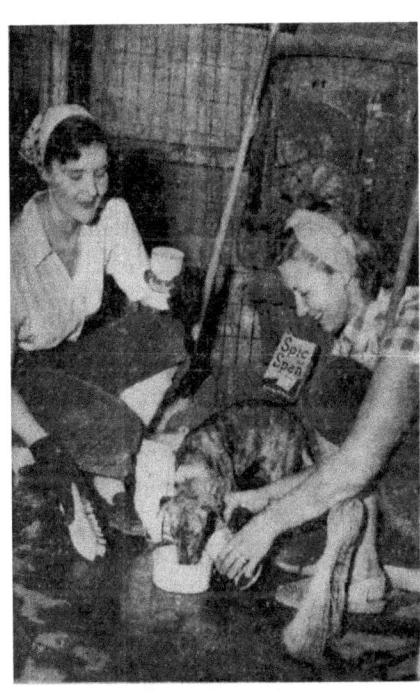

Evansville, December 1950, c. the release of *A Hornbook for Witches*

Drake (left) and Wanda M. Rogers tending to a stray dog at the Animal Refuge, 1952

Jim Carey (manager of Loew Theater in Evansville) and Drake flank Pat Dean Smith, showgirl in *An American in Paris*, September 1941

c. 1954

Wallace Stevens, Lenora Speyer, and Drake (reading her poem "The Lariat: 6000 B.C."), Sherry's Restaurant, New York City, 24 January 1951

c. 1955

"Paul S. Nickerson, of Charleston, South Carolina, and Leah Bodine Drake of Henderson, Kentucky, congratulating each other after being named winners of the Borestone Mountain poetry awards at the annual dinner of the Poetry Society of America. Dr. Robert T. Moore (right) of Pasadena, California, announced the awards." Nickerson (b. 1894) died 15 May 1955, not long after receiving his award.

Leah with Dr. Robert T. Moore
February 1954

Evansville, c. 1955

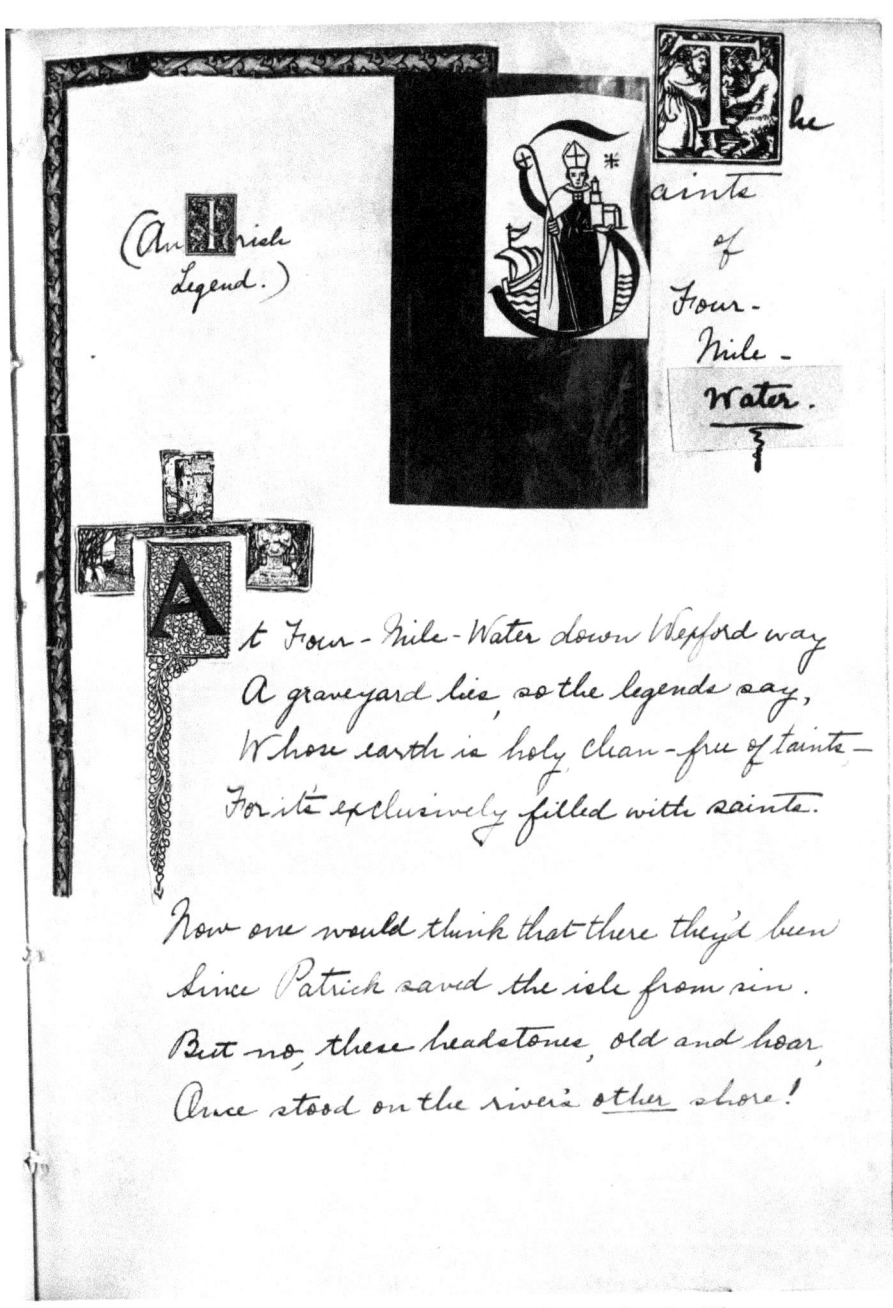

A typical page from one of Drake's "illuminated" scrapbooks. There are ten items pasted on the page. The L-shaped border is broken into several parts. Even the word "Water" in the title is a separate piece.

c. 1953

Parkersburg, 1957, during visit with father to his sister Mary

Dr. Alfred J. Niedermayer and Leah Bodine Drake (in New Harmony?), 1958.

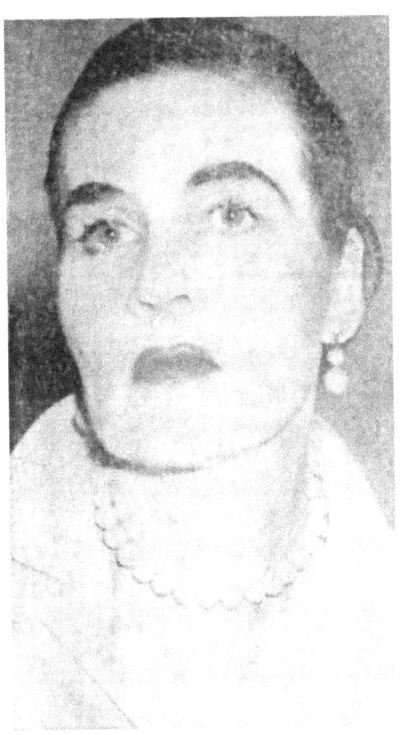

c. 1958, Parkersburg

"En Route to Europe."
Parkersburg News, 29 May 1960

c. 1961, Parkersburg

"Myself and Sabina" (unidentified),
Lausanne, Christmas 1961

1801 Avery Street, Parkersburg

1316 Market Street, Parkersburg, Drake's last residence with Griffin C. and Mary Elizabeth Callahan

Trinity Episcopal Church, 430 Juliana St., Parkersburg

Charles A. Musès

Leah Bodine Drake, 1 August 1961, Lausanne, Suisse

Collected Poems

. . . my hope it is, that something I may say,
some verse or rhyme,
might wash up on that shore like a drifted spar
from the drowned ship that was I.

from "The Beaches Beyond Oblivion"

A Dream of Samarkand

1919–1934

A Dream of Samarkand ❧ 1919–1934

On a Chinese Screen

I. Lady Writing a Letter

Lord, when will you return to us?
When will we behold again the dragon-banners?
It is now the time of scarlet maple leaves,
It is the season of slate-grey skies,
When cranes drift like smoke across a misty moon.

In robes of orange silk lined with lamb's wool
The small-wives crouch over the fire-bowl.
They chatter of ghosts and demons and ask me,
"When will our lord return, O High Wife?"

I reply, "In the Season of Greater Cold;
Or when Those-Who-Sleep-Through-The-Winter awaken, perhaps."
But they shiver over the fire-bowl
And whisper behind their wide, padded sleeves.

Thinking of you far off in a place of battles,
Tears fall like dew upon the purple asters of my sleeve;
My lute is silent in the chest of cinnabar,
And my mirror has forgotten my face.

II. Moon Festival

Since beholding your peach-bloom countenance
Framed by the black-satin loops of hair,
When you stood idly beneath a flowering acacia,
My brain has become dizzy with the tinkling of jade ear-drops,
My heart beats time to the fluttering of a little painted fan.
I see an orange-silk girdle in every persimmon-tree;
I hear the sound of dainty feet in every falling leaf.

The Song of the Sun ~ Leah Bodine Drake

* * *

Surely our feet were tied together at birth
By the Old Worthy in the moon!

III. The Deserted Courtyard

Upon the grey flags of the courtyard
The moss trails a jade-green scarf;
The lotus-pool is dry, and blown leaves fill its basin.
At night there is only the lantern of the moon
To light the deserted walks.

Autumn has struck upon her deep-toned gong,
Frightening away the birds
From beneath the yellow eaves of the pavilion.
She has woven her red brocade of maple-leaves,
And hidden somewhere the frayed green gauze of Summer.

A bleak wind tugs at the padded sleeves of my plum-coloured robe,
As I pass sorrowfully from the courtyard:
I shall not linger in this place
Shadowy with the ghosts of all dead Summers.

IV. By the River

From the damp earth rise the scents of Spring;
The western sky still remembers the sun.
For the first time the little, thin new moon
Beholds herself in the mirror of the water.
River-mists like purple veils float upward;
Birds call sleepily to one another from tall trees.
Boatmen are going home to the brushwood fires,
Where scanty fare and troubled rest await them;
But the dew is cool beneath their tired feet,
And hark! in the willow-tree a nightingale is singing!

A Dream of Samarkand ❧ 1919–1934

V. A Lady of the Emperor's Palace

There's a warm wind rustling my green-gauze canopy;
There's a whispering among the wisteria-vines.
The breeze that sets the painted lamps to swinging
Is like a voice heard long ago
In the village of my youth.

I have donned a robe of fuchsia-coloured satin
Embroidered with yellow butterflies;
I have placed in both my ears the drops of amethyst and amber.
Soon I will hear footsteps approaching from the dragon-palace;
But now I hear only the crying of lost voices in the wind.

VI. One Intoxicated

When I gaze into my wine-cup
I see your face smiling up at me
From a garden of lotus-pools and porcelain pagodas.
Your hair falls down across your shoulders
And swirls in a dark mist about your feet.
With a needle of gold set with pearls you loop up your tresses;
With bashful coquetry, hide your moon-flower face
Behind the folds of your azalea-pink sleeve.

What is it your lips are saying from the depths of my wine-cup?
Could I hear you more plainly
If I emptied a few more cups of wine?

Mombāsa

Sunk deep in night Mombāsa lies.
    The jeweled stars hang low.
  Upon the blue-black tropic tide

The Song of the Sun ❧ Leah Bodine Drake

Like ghosts the tall ships anchored ride,
To silent ebb and flow.

Silver and blue Mombāsa sleeps.
    The lamps gleam dim and cold
In houses still as mystery,
And on the dusky boats at sea
Like swinging stars of gold.

Softly the Afric breezes croon
    Tales of fiery loves and tears,
Passions that flame beneath the moon
    As wildly as those of yesteryears.

For years may pass, the old laws die,
The conquerors come and blood run free;
But down in the south Mombāsa will lie
An old, dark city beside the sea.

Sinning, and sinned against, she sleeps.
    Her strange sins are the same
As when for gold and ivory,
And pearls and slaves and ebony,
    The Arab raiders came.

Silent the palm-trees stand by palaces sad and white,
Where once delirious tom-toms beat
A tune for painted, dancing feet
On many a barbarous night.

But down in the spicy, hot bazaars
In many a shadowy, small café,
Ouled Naïl women beneath the stars
Danced desert dances of yesterday:

A Dream of Samarkand ❧ 1919–1934

For years may pass, new cities rise,
Kings may to new kings bend the knee—
But down in the south Mombāsa lies,
An old, dark city beside the sea.

To a Lost Sweetheart

O, when I walked abroad with you
    I held my head up high
And was no girl the country through
    More proud and gay than I.

And now I'm always gay and proud,
    And walk abroad alone;
And when I pass you in the crowd
    I feel my heart turn stone.

Song at Sunrise

The sky grows pale with the morning light,
    The dawn rides up the sea,—
And it might just as well be night
    For aught it means to me.

Now I must rise and don my dress,
    And comb and bind my hair,—
And it might just as well hang down
    For all you'll know or care.

I'll do the old things day by day,
    From sunrise to sunset,
As if you'd never gone away
    Or we had never met.

The Song of the Sun ❧ Leah Bodine Drake

If I could run away and hide
    Where none could come to see,
I'd let my heart break deep and wide
    And ease this misery.

But I must rise, and sweep and sew,
    Through days as long as years,—
For woman's work that is to do
    Can't wait on woman's tears.

I still must tend my beasts, and bake,
    And still be clothed and fed,
And see the endless mornings break—
    When I might as well be dead!

Words After Wisdom

When I was but a young thing
    And did but little know,
I thought love would be lasting
    And wept to see it go.

The years have taught me wisdom,
    Two bitter things and true:
Weeping butters little bread
    And little's worth the rue.

Now I can see love wither
    And mute and quiet keep,
For long ago I found that I'd
    Forgotten how to weep.

A Dream of Samarkand ～ 1919–1934

The Ballad of Fair Elspeth

Who calls beyond the garden? . . . . .
    Fair Elspeth in her bed
Wakes from her sleep and listens,
    And lifts her flaxen head.

She hears the placid murmur
    Of the beck beside the door;
She hears the tiny scamper
    Of a mouse across the floor.

The slow hushed moon is rising
    Beyond the hawthorn bloom . . . .
Fair Elspeth leaves her pillow
    And steps across the room.

She opens the leaden casement
    And listens in the gloom.
(Full fair and tall, the maiden,
    With hair like honeycomb.)

Who calls so clearly, sweetly,
    Beyond the hawthorn tree?—
"Fair Elspeth, wake from dreaming,
    And come you down to me!"

The curtains at her window
    Blow in the trembling air;
Her sentinel candle flickers
    Like firefly caught there.

Then down beyond the garden,
    Behind the quicken wall,
She sees a beckoning finger,
    She hears that magical call.

The Song of the Sun ~ Leah Bodine Drake

She listens, lingers, gazes,—
    Clasps hands and tries to pray,
But the spell has 'round her gathered
    And the words she cannot say.

She dons her gown, she binds her hair,
    She tiptoes like a mouse
Across the room and down the stair
    And leaves the sleeping house . . . . .

He comes between the hawthorns
    White as their blooming boughs;
But dark, oh dark, the elf-locks
    That cluster 'round his brows!

And dark, oh darkly burning
    His strange and lovely eyes!
And rich his outland garments,
    Green with the woodlands' dyes!

Son of no mortal woman
    Fairer than mortals all,
'Tis a Green Man of the Shian*
    Hath Fair Elspeth in thrall!

Part II.
Tall Alain in the village
    Wakes sudden in his bed:
He dreamed he saw his Elspeth
    Upon a bier, dead.

He starts up in a terror,
    And runs to Elspeth's farm;
He bursts upon the sleepers
    Like one the Fiend would harm.

*Shian = the Faëry host or tribes.

A Dream of Samarkand ❧ 1919–1934

"Some danger threatens Elspeth,
    My promised one, my bride,—
O waken, Goodman! Waken, Wife!
    And haste to Elspeth's side!"

Her door is wide, her bed is bare;
    Gone are her gown and shoon.
The candle gutters out and leaves
    Her chamber to the moon.

Call, Alain, and call, Father!
    Rouse, village, and rouse, farm!
Ring out the bells, call out the dogs,
    And raise the loud alarm!

To no avail, sad parents;
    To no avail, Alain—
You never will see Elspeth
    By sun or moon again.

Part III.

Through meadows deep in moonlight,
    By dreaming hazel-cover,
Hand in hand Fair Elspeth walks
    With more than mortal lover.

Beyond the farms, beyond the fields,
    The little fields of man
To where the hills of Faërie
    Rise magical and wan,

To lands beyond the moonrise,
    Farther than evening-star,
Where the smiling Secret People
    And the hidden towers are;

The Song of the Sun 🙿 Leah Bodine Drake

Where age and grief come never
    That timeless folk among,
Who pluck the golden apples
    In the Country of the Young.

Gazelles in a Zoo

Here in their man-made dells
    Of careful rock and sand,
    Far from their fierce land
Live the lightfoot gazelles.

Brown velvet flanks, each vein
    Cloisoned upon the skin;
    Antennae-horns, and thin
Strong legs, whose nerves disdain

The pull of Earth's old leash—
    Some element of heaven
    To all gazelles is given
And kneaded in their flesh.

On tiny elfin feet
    They race their narrow pen,
    Around and back again—
What swallow is so fleet?

Born in these tended plots
    They hardly guess the speed
    Their kind commands at need
To flee the desert-cats!

Once on an Asian plain
    I saw gazelles escape

A Dream of Samarkand ⁓ 1919–1934

>Death in his lion-shape,
>Couched in the river-cane.

>Arced like a golden bow
>>The lion sprang . . . . and fell
>>Too short of his gazelle!
>I watched the whole herd go

>In an eye's blinking, shot
>>Like stones from unseen slings—
>>As though they had the wings
>Life planned, and then forgot.

Apple

>Bride of small, humble orchards,
>Goal of old kingly quests,
>Bane of an Eastern city,
>Treasure that was the West's;

>Youth-Bringer of the Northings
>Cause of an Eden fled . . . .
>Hail to the queen-fruit, Apple!
>Hail to her gold and red!

>Symbol of good and evil,
>The Tree's twi-natured fruit—
>The Dove perched in her branches,
>The Serpent at her root.

>Bitter and sweet, the Apple!
>Beauty's prize; Dead Sea dross;
>Heart-warming ale—and vinegar
>Held, mocking, to a Cross . . . . .

The Song of the Sun ❧ Leah Bodine Drake

The Land of the Japanese Prints

I.

There's a curious land in a faïrytale clime
That's unbounded by space and unmeasured by time,
More remote than the snow-cap on high Fuji-San . . . .
It's the rice-paper country of painted Japan!

II.

There tinkling pagodas of lacquer and pearl
Rise by jade-coloured seas where the lacy waves curl;
Where white herons wing when the grey twilight mints
A new silver moon, in the Japanese prints.

III.

There lie the gardens of iris and plum,
Where no buds are shaken and no harsh winds come;
Where rainbow-arched bridges fantastically span
The lily-decked fish-pools of pictured Japan.

IV.

There come the slim ladies with butterfly hair,
In swirling kimonos as fragile as air,
To gather the blossoms of cherry and quince
That bloom on forever in Japanese prints.

V.

The two-sworded knights are their lovers, you know,
Who stand by their windows and sigh in the snow,
And send them small verses neat-writ on a fan
In the dignified courtship of painted Japan.

VI.

And when the snow falls there it's not cold at all,
But just an excuse for a gay parasol;

A Dream of Samarkand ~ 1919–1934

And lady and gallant forth daintily mince
Through the warm faëry snow of the Japanese prints.

VII.
On firefly rivers a-sailing they go
In cockle-shell boats with their lanterns a-glow;
And samisens tinkle and lantern-light glints
On the moon-haunted landscape of Japanese prints.

VIII.
The fox is a demon both wicked and fair;
The willow's a witch-wife with gauzy green hair;
And the Sea Princess marries the brown fisher-man—
For all things come true in the prints of Japan!

IX.
O, the butterfly ladies! The dragonfly knights!
They bow and they smile through a life of delights;
And I wish I could walk through the paper and tints
Right into that land of the Japanese Prints!

Burma: Moulmein Bazaar

In the hot shadows of the old bazaar
Silks glow like forgotten sunsets, pile on pile—
Nasturtium, orange and flamingo-rose,
And gold-shot gauzes blue as river-mist.
Here sit *thanaka**-sellers with the scented bark
That, ground, will turn to pale camellia-flowers
The faces of the little golden ladies.
Stacked like heaps of jade are watermelons
Lined cunningly with coral,

---

*A bark used as face-powder.

The Song of the Sun ❧ Leah Bodine Drake

And rose-apples that a shaft of sun
Turns to jewel-fruits out of Faërie;
And everywhere, on platters, in rushy baskets and in jars,
Rice, the life of Asia . . . . .

Outside the darkling sheds, against a topaz sky,
Brown boatmen shout and chatter like wild parrots,
Unloading pumpkins like great goblin moons
From sampans on the mist-hung river.
The sun goes down in one last burst of flame
And all the little boats turn suddenly
To carven cinnabar.
Lights blossom on the shore, ships'-lanterns twinkle,
Long purple shadows encroach upon the glimmering colours.
Lost overboard, forgotten, great amber fruits
Drift seaward under a copper moon
Upon a river of flowing amethyst.

The Country Lover

My young Lord walks with Lady Anne
    Within her garden-close,
And maybe she will smile at him
    And give him one red rose.

I meet my sweeting on the hills,
    Her flock agraze with mine,
And she will weave a crown for me
    Of honey-sweet wood-bine.

My young Lord foots it in the Hall
    In coat of velvet grand;
With Lady Anne he leads the maze
    And kisses her white hand.

A Dream of Samarkand ~ 1919–1934

I swing my Bess to "Money Musk"
    When low the full moon dips
And in the thickest of the press
    I kiss her rosy lips.

My young Lord makes the serenade
    With fiddlers out of France;
Beneath Milady's casement high
    He sings a plaintive stance.

But down along the river-road
    Where sleepy waters croon,
My arm about sweet Bessie's waist
    I'm singing to the moon!

My young Lord's cheek is wan wi' grief,
    His eye is e'er cast down:
His Lady Anne has spurned his suit
    For a Money-Bag's in town.

Oh, wear your silks, my poor young Lord,
    And woo cold Lady Annes,—
My bonny's given me her word
    And Parson's read the banns!

Belle and Beau

(18th Century)

The Belle.

Like stately ship upon the Main
    Comes Lady Arabella;
Black Sambo follows with her train
    And Ayah with umbrella.

The Song of the Sun ❧ Leah Bodine Drake

With wide-spread hoops and powdered hair
    Forth Arabella sallies,
To take the pleasant summer air
    Along the garden's alleys.

She sniffs a rose but lets it stay
    A-bloom, (thorns scratch one's fingers;)
She views (not near) the fountain's spray,
    And by the sun-dial lingers.

She faints! . . . . . Ayah, her salts, her fan,
    A bench—ah, help her to it!
She's talked a full five minutes' span!—
    Good lack, how *did* she do it?

The Beau.

Valentine's took to his bed,
    His face is pale with care, O.
With sigh and curse he knocks his head
    With fist clenched in despair, O.

With towels and possets, up and down
    The servants beat a path, O;
The doctor leaves some pills (dark brown)
    And orders, "Trip to Bath, O."

What horrid crime has found him out
    That Grief and Shame should sport so?—
His waistcoat worn at last night's rout
    Was half an inch too short, O!

A Dream of Samarkand ❧ 1919–1934

The Sailorman (1690)

Where have you been, O Sailorman,
    Back from the deep blue sea?
On the Spanish Main, my pretty lass,
    And the coasts of Barbary.

Oh, how, did you get your skin so brown,
    And your eyes so keen and bright?
From scaling masts in tropic noons,
    And watching stars by night.

And how did you get such brawny arms,
    And lips so hard and level?
From pulling Spanish galley-oar,
    And cursing God and Devil!

And where did you get that heathen charm
    That hangs on your breast a-down?
Two soft brown hands once placed it there,
    In a garden in Sallee-Town.

And where did you get that wicked scar
    That slashes your cheek athwart?
From a knife in a hand that missed its goal
    And sheathed in a maiden's heart.

And what have you brought from far-away?
    And what is your fortune's whole?
A handful of gold and a rolling gait,
    And a Moor's curse on my soul.

And what will you give to a pretty lass
    From out of your seaman's loot?
A topaz ring and a talking bird,
    And a sailor's kiss, to boot!

The Song of the Sun ⁊ Leah Bodine Drake

Ah, sailorman, so gallant and bold!—
   Was your heart in that kiss you gave?
Hush, lass! Don't ask for a broken thing! . . . .
   It lies deep in a Moorish grave!

A Dream of Samarkand

"Hai-ai! Uu-aah-ai!"
           O camel-man,
  What song singeth thy caravan?
"We sing of Golden Samarkand
     And the Tartar King who will rule the land!"

A rusty sword, a conquered throne,
Samarkand, are you today:
Stormy Timur's limped away
Into dust and time: remain
Only songs and crumbling stone
To tell us of your golden reign.

Once the fabled Eastern lands
Saw your captains go and come,
Loud with trumpet and with drum:
Proud men riding, sword on thigh,
Down the hills, across the sands,
While the war-drums shook the sky.

Pearls and perfumes, furs and jade,
Once your hot bazaars could show,
Wines of Shiraz chilled with snow,
Slaves and gold and white macaws;
While beneath the plane-trees' shade
Scholars taught the Koran's laws.

A Dream of Samarkand ❧ 1919–1934

Once the palace, "Heart's Delight,"
Like Aladdin's cavern shone;
There the gold and ivory throne
Stood where walls with jewels blazed,—
Beryl, turquoise, topaz bright,
Spoils of proudest cities razed.

There the Tartar warriors knew
Splendid nights of revelry;
There the stolen wine ran free,
And the slaves brought gems and gold
At the heroes' feet to strew
While the drums of victory rolled.

In the gardens where the rose
Blushed beside the lily pale,
Walked the queens of faërytale!—
Golden Mongol, Persian gay,
And, on tiny tripping toes,
Porcelain ladies of Cathay.

These have passed . . . . . The flags of war
Droop above the Conqueror's tomb.
Alien in the sunlight loom
Shadows out of Moscovy.
All the queens are dead. No more
Rides your thundering cavalry.

Yet I've heard the camel-train
Singing of an ancient tale:
How once more the earth shall quail
As the horse-tail banners come
From the highlands . . . . . hear again
The roar of Timur's kettle-drum!

The Song of the Sun ❧ Leah Bodine Drake

"Oua-ai! Uu-aah-ai!"
    O camel-man,
  What song singeth thy caravan?
  "We sing of Golden Samarkand
    And the Tartar King who will rule the land!"

Our Lady's Song

Little Babe, how strange a thing:
I can hold Thee in my arms.
Yet Thou art a mighty king;
Shaking Herod with alarms!

See, Thy tiny fingers twine
'Round my thumb as though it were
Dearer thing than caskets fine,
Holding frankincense and myrrh.

What the angel showed to me
On that night of awe and pride,
I am trying not to see:
Piercèd hands and bleeding side.

I am trying not to see
Tired feet that climb a hill
To a promised agony
It is glory to fulfil.

For a little longer while
I'll pretend that Thou art just
Mortal babe with angel smile,
Dust of dear, familiar dust.

For a little longer space
I will sing a foolish tune,

A Dream of Samarkand ᚛ 1919–1934

Laugh, and kiss Thy baby face!
Thou will be crowned King so soon.

The Pixy Fair

O what do they sell at the Pixy Fair
In the markets of Toadstool Lane?
Bonnets of pease-blossom, lilac and blue,
Kerchiefs of cobwebs, earrings of dew,
Swords for the gallants, of thorns sharpened fine,
Acorn-cups brimming with moon-honey wine,
    And glow-worms in cages
    For elf-ladies' pages
To light their way home again!

What do they use at the Pixy Fair
    To buy each delectable thing?
Worn-out moons that they fish from wells,
Bright red berries and fluted shells;
And they trade-in buckets of milkweed milk
For beautiful dresses of poppy-silk!
    And if there are any
    Without price or penny,
The stall-keeper asks them to sing, to sing.
    They're only requested to sing!

Turn of Year

Now in the slyly-lengthening dark
The firefly blinks a lonely spark,
The beetle wings with his tiny thunder.
Now summer's stars are turning under,
And up from tremendous depths of space

The Song of the Sun ~ Leah Bodine Drake

Remote, cold figures take their place:
Pegasus plunges overhead,
The Chair wheels higher. Lonely, red,
Out of the south Fomalhaut soars;
And out of his urn the Waterer pours
White frozen fire through the root
Of orchards heavy-boughed with fruit;
And brooks forsense a freedom lost,
Remembering the feel of frost.

Now apple-ripe, the huge moon comes
Over the fields where the cricket drums.
On browning fern the dew lies cold,
And the heart of the rose on her stem feels old;
And all night, while slow hours pass,
The apples fall into the grass.

The Croon of the Mer-Mother

By-low, little mer-babe,
    The horned moon hangs low
Over the green seas'
    Thunder and flow,

The mer-folk are gathering
    In the curve of the bay,
Their sea-songs to sing,
    Their gold harps to play.

In the little white village
    Upon the dim shore
The lamplight twinkles
    From casement and door.

A Dream of Samarkand ✥ 1919–1934

No lamplight for thee
    When the dark cometh down,
No snug little house
    In the little white town.

But for thee are the caverns
    Of coral and pearl,
Where the old wrecks lie
    And the sea-weeds curl,

And fishes glide
    Like jewels a-light,
And the Sea-Serpent dreams
    In his house of night.

For thee are the coffers
    Of tiaras and rings
Lost from the galleons
    Of ancient kings;

Bracelets shall deck thee
    Of opals and gold,
Wreaths of red coral
    And sea-flowers cold.

Thou wilt sit on the rocks
    When the red sun dips,
And sing sea-spells
    To the passing ships!

Sleep, little mer-babe,
    The moon rides high;
The town lies darkling
    Beneath the sky.

The Song of the Sun ❧ Leah Bodine Drake

The mortal childer
    Are safe in bed;
Holy prayers hover
    'Round each loved head.

No prayers for the mer-babe!
    Outcast is she,
With the rest of the outcast
    Folk of the sea.

For we are the Soulless,
    We are the Torn—
No Babe in a manger
    For us was born;

For us was no Calvary
    Nor Easter Day:
Our life is as sea-foam
    That bloweth away!

Oh, sleep, little mer-child
    On mother's chill breast,—
Thy mer-mother loves thee,
    Though her love is unblest!

Thy mother will love thee,
    Soulless and faï,
Till the seas shrink up
    On Christ's Judgement Day;

When Christ born of Mary
    (Oh, merciful, He!)
May ransom and save
    The Folk of the Sea.

A Dream of Samarkand ❧ 1919–1934

Jilly and the Elf

"Will you come away with me?" said the Elf,
  Grinning down at Jilly from the garden wall;
"I will weave a wild-grape crown
  For your lovely locks of brown,
    And we'll foot it when the fairy dancers call."

"Will you come away today?" said the Elf,
  Skipping after Jilly to the well-house door;
"I will bring you sweet red cherries,
  Oak-leaves heaped with wild strawberries,
    And honey stolen from the bee-folks' store."

"Won't you leave your stuffy house?" said the Elf.
  Peering through the window as Jilly skimmed the cream;
"There are woodlands good for roaming,
  And tree-houses in the gloaming
    Where I'll sing a pretty tune while you dream."

Will you *kindly* go away?" Jilly said,
    Dimpled arms a-kimbo and dainty brows drawn down;
"Do you really think I'd ramble
  Over stick and stone and bramble
  With a raggle, taggle Elf?
  Wet my slippers, scratch myself
  In your thorny, lorny wood?
  Tear my apron, lose my snood?
  Leave my bed to lie in grass?
  Never see a looking-glass?
    Go away! Don't bother me,—I'm busy, silly Clown!"

The Song of the Sun ❧ Leah Bodine Drake

The Saints of Four-Mile-Water

(An Irish Legend)

At Four-Mile-Water down Wexford way
A graveyard lies, so the legends say,
Whose earth is holy, clean-free of taints—
For it's exclusively filled with saints.

Now one would think that there they'd been
Since Patrick saved the isle from sin.
But no, these head-stones, old and hoar,
Once stood on the river's *other* shore!

None among them but was of God
First slept in its green and gracious sod,
Till on a day (which St. Patrick condemn!)
A thief was buried to rest with them.

A rogue, a tipster, a roaring blade
In that sanctified ground unkindly laid,
To sleep by his betters,—that pious throng,—
And molder his bones with theirs along!

The goodly worships (and faith, 'tis true!)
Turned in their graves the whole night through:
What saint could hope to sleep on in bliss
In Devil-owned company such as this?

So the very next night they all arose
And shook the dust from their burial-clothes;
And the staring moon, as she trundled low,
Saw the blessèd fathers a-moving go.

Their haloes shining against the sky,
They lifted their tombstones. Mounting high,
Over the river the whole band flew
To settle their bones in pastures new!

A Dream of Samarkand ❧ 1919–1934

The wide-eyed moon stopped in her flight
To look again at that wondrous sight,—
Each displaced corpse, with his hand to chin,
Pond'ring the place to bury him in!

Then when the rosy morning broke
What a view met the eyes of the village folk!—
A new graveyard o'er the river made,
While one lone grave in the other stayed!

A graveyard left with but one green mound
Where an acre of wasteland stretched around;
While over the river the grass grew tall,
And never a thistle at all, at all!

And some folks swear that a mortal wight,
Passing the place on All Souls' Night,
Will hear a humming—the peaceful sound
Of the good saints snoring beneath the ground.

Now let no skeptic the legend doubt,
Nor Christian's word let the godless flout;
For there lie the graveyards, say what you may,
At Four-Mile-Water down Wexford way!

The Haunted Hour

The sky is coloured like a peacock's breast;
There lingers yet one thin, chill line of gold
Down where the woods their somber branches hold
In silhouette against the fading West.
Dark leaves, dark earth, slow-breathing and at rest,
Whence frail scents rise of dew-wet grass and mold.
A single star gleams diamond-clear and cold
Like one sharp note from lute of angel wrest.

The Song of the Sun ❧ Leah Bodine Drake

* * *

This is the haunted hour—such woods surround
    Grey Merlin in his oak, adrouse with dwale;
In such a gloaming once the lorn knight found
    The faëry woman in the river-vale;
And underneath this star long, long ago
The Dark Tower heard a lonely slug-horn blow!

Mad Jenny

Have ye seen the old witch-woman who lives on the edge o' town?
Hush, lads, she's a-comin', in her red and tattered gown,
With her black eyes wild a-glitter and her grey hair all askew;
Hear her mutter as she wanders,—oh, we dare not guess to *Who!*

Keep down low behind the hedgerow, or she'll see ye in a trice,
And sure, a witch's curses can change lads to toads and mice!
For she hates all lads and men-folk, and I've heard my Granny say,
That of all men it is Squire that she hates the most of a'y.

Granny says she can remember when the witch was young and fair,
When she was a buxom lassie, pink o' cheek and brown o' hair;
And she says her eyes were smilin', and she had a sweetsome tongue,—
Oh, isn't it the queer thing, for a witch to have been young?

She can put a spell on butter quicker than you can nod your head,
And 'tis woe to them as cross her, for they'll find them sick-abed;
She bewitched the mooley Kerry that Pat Dawson bought at Fair,
And 'tis known all over County that she rode to death his mare!

Tommy Regan said he saw her once within the haunted wood,
Where the Wishy Pool lies gleamin', and he says that there she stood
In the water to her knee-caps, with the water-lilies there,
And she a-pickin' o' them, and a-puttin' in her hair;

And she smilin', like to someone that might be there standin' by;
And Tommy says he heard her say, "Oh, sir, you wouldn't lie

. . . with her black eyes wild a-glitter and her grey hair all askew

The Song of the Sun ❧ Leah Bodine Drake

To a poor girl, oh my darlin', when you say you love her true,
And that none but Jenny Daly should be lady-wife o' you?

"Oh, I know you're high-born gentry and I must your oath believe;
And faith, *you* know *I* love you, for my heart's upon my sleeve!
And though I'm low-born Jenny, yet you crowned me your 'Heart's
     Queen'
With these dripping water-lilies and their leaves of glossy green."

And Tommy said she laughed and laughed, and then began to cry,
And Tommy thought the time had come when he had better fly;
For when an old witch-woman starts to talkin' to the air,
Sure, you know she's gone *clean* crazy,—or the Devil's standin' there!

And once I passed her cottage when the night had just begun,
With a bag o' rabbit I had snared that day upon the dun;
And I heard a low voice croonin', and 'twas high and sweet and thin,
And I crept up to her window, and I dared to peep within.

And lads, she was a-sittin' by her fire, dim and low,
All huddled in her rushy-chair and rocking to and fro,
And cuddlin' of her arms, and bendin' down and smilin' glad,
Singin', "Hush, my wee white babby, hushee now, my little lad."

But there wasn't any babby in her arms at all, at all,
And the room was still and empty,—ye could hear a feather fall;
And I turned and ran so swiftly I lost bag and hares and cap,
For *what* was she a-singin' to, with *nothin'* in her lap?

So hide, lads, when Mad Jenny comes a-hobblin' down the street;
She hates the townsfolk and wee boys, and curses when they meet;
And folks say, when she dies her heart must be pierced with a stake,—
But Granny says, they needn't fear,—her heart long past was brake!

   In the old days, witches were buried at a cross-roads with a stake of ashen wood through their hearts,—that was to lay their ghost, and prevent them from doing any harm after they were dead.

A Dream of Samarkand ～ 1919–1934

Little Things

I like little, fragile things,
Fireflies and toadstool-rings,
Painted fans and midget trees,
Tiny verses Japanese.

A dandelion's silver ghost,
Spiderwebs, and lace of frost,
Jeweled clocks with elfin chimes,
Fairy-tales and nursery rhymes.

Little lies that soften life,
Heal the wounds of truth's blunt knife,
Little loves that ease the heart
Torn by one too-piercing dart!

"There Are Fairies"

Never let them tell you
    That all the elves are gone:
See the cobweb robes they've spun
    All night upon the lawn!
Do not let them tell you
    All the dwarves have died:
You may see their mushroom hats
    On the dark hill-side.

Never let them whisper
    How Lob is just a fable:
I have put a bowl of cream
    On the kitchen table,
When it's Midsummer Eve,
    And found in the dawn

The Song of the Sun 🙣 Leah Bodine Drake

A neat and tidied kitchen—
    And the cream all gone!

Never heed the folk who say
    Pan is just a myth . . . .
On any sunny meadow,
    On any forest path,
You may hear a piping—
    Never bird or breeze!—
And see a merry slanting eye
    Peering through the trees.

Oh, run away and hide from
    Pompous, scoffing fools
Who've never heard of leprechauns,
    Or nixies in the pools!
For sometimes in the summer dusk,
    A moth whose wings are green
Will softly flutter by . . . . . . O, *then*
    You've seen the Fairy Queen!

The Little Piper

Where is the tune we heard one day
    A while and a while agone?
Where is the sound of the little feet
Capering over the cobbled street,
    And the piper who played on us?

Out of the gardens and through the square,
    By the church upon the hill—
Jinny and Robin and Rose-Marie,
Alice and Hugh and little shy me!—
    We danced to the piper's trill.

A Dream of Samarkand ❧ 1919–1934

Where did he come from? Nobody knew;
   But his eye was fey and wild,
And his clothes were green as the elfin rings,
And his ears were peaked like a woodsy thing's—
   Like none on a human child.

But oh, the sweet tune that he played
   There in the sunset light!
Sweeter than even thrush's call
Or the dripping notes of the water-fall
   Or the sigh of the wind at night.

He piped us up and down the street
   He danced us all over town:
A wreath of children wild and gay;—
Happy were we on that far-off day
   As the dusk came creeping down.

Now the years are many, the years are long,
   A score and a score they be
Since I walked the streets that the dancers knew;
Jinny is wed and Rose-Marie, too,
   And Hugh's gone over the sea;

And Alice ran off with a sailor,
   And Robin lies quiet and still;
And the piper's gone (for folk somehow
Never seem to hear his piping now)
   Back to his faïry hill.

Peddler's Pack

A peddling fellow came our way.
He cried his wares and he doffed his pack
In our busy square. We heard him say:
"What d' ye lack? What d' ye lack?

The Song of the Sun ❧ Leah Bodine Drake

I've a Phoenix for sale with a fiery tale
   only the size of a finger-nail!
Here's the face of Helen in a glass,
And kerchiefs woven by pixy-maids
Under the moon in elfin glades.
      Come, dame and goodman, lad and lass!
The missing star
From the Pleiad's throng;
The opening bar
Of the sirens' song;
A lamp to employ
A willing jinn
Owned by the boy
Ala-ad-din;
And aubergine-
Coloured wine
Pressed from the mer-folks' deep-sea vine;
A penny's the price—come buy!"

But although we listened none of us bought—
We were too knowing to ever be caught
By such fiddledeedee from a foreign knave
Exchanging good coppers we'd schemed to save
   For a song, indeed.
   Or a useless bird—
   We didn't need
   One thing we'd heard!—
Such a hugger-mugger of foolish truck!

So he went as he came with his curious pack,
That silly-gillie from far away,
And some of us thought we heard him say:
   "Good men, good wives,
     You were given the chance
   Of your dull, fat lives
     For joy and romance;
   But you closed your breast

A Dream of Samarkand ✢ 1919–1934

And shut your purse . . . . .
If you won't take the best
You shall take the worst,—
I'll come one day with another pack
And you'll buy with gold, and I won't trade back."

Alas for our village! A year, a day,
To the very hour, he came our way
With a clattering cart and a one-eyed mare,
And he cried his goods in the market-square:
  "Cobwebs for sale!
  Cobwebs for sale!
  Here is the hammer used by Jael.
  Here's a book whose words
  Run widder-shin;
  Here's a crook which herds
  Only black sheep in;
  Church-bells wrought
  By Satan's crafts,
  Poems thought
  By Bedlam's dafts;
  A weed from Bluebeard's funeral-wreath
  Roots of mandrake, dragons'-teeth;
  A clock unsprung,
  A witch's pot,
  The rope that hung
  Iscariot . . . . .
  The price is high.
    But you'll buy, you'll buy!"

Alack, we never found out his spell,
But it must have come from the pits of Hell,
For we bought and bought from that cheating knave!
All the gold we had sinned to save
Poured from strong-box, purse and till.
Goodman, goodwife, Jack and Jill,

The Song of the Sun ~ Leah Bodine Drake

Wept in rage, while he laughed in scorn
To see us so busy and so forlorn.

He pouched our money and drove away,
And some of us near him heard him say:
    "You got what you measure,
      You have what you should
      Who turn down treasure
      And spurn the good."

And there we were with our filthy buys,
Our pots of poison and devils' eyes,
With cockatrice roosting on Deacon's stile
And a wyvern crouched on the town-hall's tile!

And a mocking tune, fading far away
As the Peddler passed at the end of day.

"My Help Cometh from the Hills"

Oh, take me to my native hills again!
My cool green mountains—for I am so tired
Of level lands, the cactus-prickled plain,
The dry creek-beds by suns unceasing fired!
Too long my eyes have mirrored alien things.
I am made wise in desert, heat and glare,
But still unloving, for my spirit sings
Only where green hills are, and rain-wet air.

Oh, take me back once more unto my hills!
Oh, let me see the laurels veiled in mist,
And smell snow-water swelling countless rills
On woody uplands that the Spring has kissed,

And see once more the stately, tall trees rise,
Like mountain-folk, their foreheads near the skies.

Descent of Angels
1935–1936

DESCENT OF ANGELS ❧ 1935–1936

In the Shadows

As we went up the narrow stair,
    My candle slim and I,
From the crouching shadows came
    A little, tired sigh.

And there was nothing on the stair
    Or in my garret room
But cobwebs on the rafters
    And corners filled with gloom.

And still and silent was the house,
    And dark and still the air . . . . .
But where the shadows wavered
    In the candle-flare,
Something small, unearthly, sighed
    Out of some strange despair.

The Man Who Married a Swan-Maiden

Say what more, what more can I do, O wild swan's daughter,
To magic away your memories of storm-grey skies?
Of lakes like agates shining where tall pines rise,
And the sound in your ears of wild white wings
        Beating above black water?

Under a holy thorn lies your robe of feathers
That I buried deep when the moon pressed a wizened chin
On the Old Hill's shoulder. There I bound it in
With seven spells to guard against the lure of wild swan-weather.

The Song of the Sun ❧ Leah Bodine Drake

But can one be content beside the drousy fire
Who has felt the Polar Lights aflame on her wings?
Does the cloak you wear of sables caught in my springs
Feel as soft to the touch as the plumes of your old desire?

You smile as you take my gifts in your thin, webbed fingers
That are yet so deft at the distaff and the loom;
And when you press my lips in the curtained room
I dare to hope that no wild dream, nor memory lingers,

Behind your wide, black eyes, of that strange sky-faring.
I say: She is well content with her mortal life;
The white swan-maid is lost in the human wife
Who sings as she goes about on her calm house-caring.

But, Autumn and Spring, returns the wild swan's-daughter....
At night by my side I feel you move and sigh,
As the veils of sleep are torn by a haunting cry
And the sound of great white wings in the dark,
    Rushing above black water.

High Renaissance

Yes, madonna! I have some curious treasures!
    What might be your gracious ladyship's wishes?
Here is a cup most pleasantly wrought
With Leda's amours—the Duca himself bought
    One very similar, with two matching dishes.

Here is a lute of pearl and amber for soft measures
    To wake from, when two dainty, noble feet
Would trip it at the hour when day is done,
In scented chamber with some favored one!
    De Pavia himself made the strings most sweet.

Descent of Angels ~ 1935–1936

Or here, a casket splendidly enamelled,
    Blue as madonna's eyes!—with beads
Of lapis lazuli set in lock and key of gold;
Madonna's jewels it would so-jealously hold—
    And secret bottom for more private needs.

Madonna's need *is* private? . . . . . She may speak untrammeled
    To her most humble servant—he is dumb
Alas, and has no memory! . . . . She desires
A ring, to hold a thing more fierce than gem's fires,
    That could be given to grace a thicker thumb

That is Duchessa's own? Perhaps for cavalier
    Somewhat my lord the Duca's size? . . . . .
I have the very one—a band where serpents twist—
Golden, about a hollowed amethyst;
    One light, unconscious pressure, and it flies

Open . . . . . If one had secretly concealed in here
    (Madonna knows, of course, we do but jest!)
Some fluid of malign and terrible power
That penetrates the skin, within the hour
    That one would know my craftsmanship the best.

My price is high! . . . . madonna's sure to see
I must charge *twice,* for jewel and—*secrecy!*

India: In the Garden of Spices

Now with flute and little drum my skilled musicians
    Play sweetly beside the lotus-pool
        In the garden of spices.

Come, my belovèd!
I have put on a robe of yellow gauze

The Song of the Sun ~ Leah Bodine Drake

Spangled with silver,
I have plaited my hair with pearls and perfumed it with nard,
My hands are delectable with henna.

The sun is westering,
The air drousy with sandalwood,
The lotus-pool sends up incense
Into the sky of hyacinth.

Come, my belovèd, from your lofty chamber,
Down to the garden of spices . . . .
My maidens shall fan us with the tails of peacocks
And my musicians shall play softly
Songs that were made for the sunset and the lotus,
Songs that are sung to the loved one by the lover.

He Dreams of Barbary

"The terns that feed among these dunes
 Have flown up from that shore," said he,
 Gazing with distance-hungry eyes
 Across the grey, bird-haunted sea.

"Down there the white-walled towns that flow
 Like music to the flame-blue bays,
 When a more intimate sunlight falls
 In arabesques on reed-thatched ways.

"Down there are sloe-eyed women, and men
 Fierce as panthers, many a dark band
 Riding with strange calls stranger beasts
 From mirage-cities in the sand.

"There the deep nights are broken when
 Slim turrets beckon with pious cries,

DESCENT OF ANGELS ❧ 1935–1936

Or curious drums are drummed by fires
Ringed where the black djinn-mountains rise.

"And there are the trees of fantastic fruits,
And crystal fruit upon a vine
Filled with a sweeter juice than ours,
That makes a more passionate wine."

"Here are green fields, your own," I said,
"And orchards shining in the rain:
Those hard blue landscapes hold their wealth
In the closed fist of parching pain;

"And deep in this soil, like your trees,
Burrow and cling your ancient roots."

Still he gazed southward, still he cried
"Those burning bays! Those fiery fruits!"

The Assyrian Lion

We see him sculptured in each ruined hall,
The hunted lion!—
               Side transfixed by spear,
Wide, anguished jaws, the body strained to rear
Upon the merciless princes but to fall.
Slaughter unceasing!
               Thus the lions all
Perished in stone, once symbols of the fear
That haunted man: the Desert crouching near,
Lashing his tail beyond their hard-won wall.

And yet the Lion triumphed in the land: . . . . .
Time is a foe that does not warn nor wait:
The conquered cities of the hunters saw

The Song of the Sun ~ Leah Bodine Drake

The waste-land come with lion-coloured sand
Springing at last through every crumbling gate
To swallow them in one vast, golden maw!

A Sigh in Spring

The year comes 'round to Spring again,
    The primrose blooms anew;
The skylark soars to sing again
    Up flights of rain-washed blue.

The face of earth grows young and fair
    In every wood and lane;
But no new Spring turns woman's hair
    From grey to brown again!

The Fairies in Autumn

Through the rusty brambles,
    Down along a hill,
I saw fairies trooping
    When the dusk was chill.

Wings of gauzy rainbows
    Trembled in the cold;
All their cobweb dresses
    Now were torn and old.

Their feet went pitter-patter
    Like fieldmice in the sheaves;
Their teeth went chitter-chatter
    Like crickets in the leaves.

DESCENT OF ANGELS ❧ 1935–1936

Holding persimmon lanterns
    And toadstools shining red,
The elfin clans were going
    The road where Summer fled,

To curl in oak-tree hollows,
    And in the roots below,
Leaving their dancing-places
    To silence and the snow.

The Giant's Garden

Oh, me!
    How awful to be
    Caught stealing plums
    In a Giant's plum-tree!
    Oh, what a plight!
    The crows take flight
    From such a doomed wight
        As Dickory Dee!

Oh, my!
    He climbed so high—
    No other laddie
    So daring and spry!
    Now he's held by his smock
    As tight as a lock,
    Like a thief in the dock
        For the Giant to spy.

"*Fi, fo fums!*"
(Here the Giant comes!)
"*Who's up there,
    With my juicy fat plums?*"
(His tread is a 'quake—

The Song of the Sun 🙢 Leah Bodine Drake

O Dickory, shake!
'Tis your bones he will break
     To crumbledy crumbs!)

Whist, hear!—
What words of cheer
Are these that fall
On Dickory's ear?—
"Thank you, macree,
You've frightened, I see,
Those crows from my tree
    That were jabbering here.

"Good luck!
Such clatter and clack
As they did be making!—
'Twould turn one's ears black!
But a *living* scare-crow—
That's the trick, I trow,
That has made them all go,
    And they'll never come back!

"Take some plums—take a capful;
Take some more—take a lapful!
    And if that's not enough
    I will get you a sack."

    (Ah,
        what
            a
                relief!)

DESCENT OF ANGELS ~ 1935–1936

Unhappy Ending

The wood was lonely and grey,
The wood was misty and cold,
The wood was unspeakably old.

The four who journeyed that way
Were lost, for their lantern had died
And the map they'd consulted had lied,—

For the path did not turn where it should,
And dead leaves lay deep on the ground
While brambles grew thick all around.

Now the four were alone in the wood;
And a fear of which none of them spoke
Had settled on each like a cloak,

For night had darkened the sky,
And the wood was so silent and cold,
The wood was so terribly old . . . . . .

Then did the travelers spy
A little, squat round-tower loom
Ahead in the lowering gloom:

A tower, set deep in the wood
With a light from a high, broken slat
Like the stare of an old, one-eyed cat.

Then the four had visions of food,
Warm fires, and beds in a house;
And they halloo'd the dwellers to rouse!

And They who lived in that tower
Listened . . . . and each crouching Thing eyed
His brother, and nudged furry side.

The Song of the Sun ~ Leah Bodine Drake

Like coals did their lidless eyes glower,
As with mouths that driveled and slobbered
They quietly mewed and gobbered.

Then one padded slyly downstair
And drew back the double-barred lock,
And waited . . . . All was still. Then a knock

Thundered: "Is there anyone there?
We are four honest, lost journeymen,"
Cried the first of the wayfarers. Then

He opened that dubious door
And the four followed hopefully after,
Those plump, tender journeymen four! . . .

In the tower was horrible laughter.

Winter Harvests

Frozen Heart

After the storm of sorrow with its wrack,
Comes the slow freeze, layer on whitening layer,
Building protective cover from the black
Of the soul's night and harrowing, cruel air,

Soothing, with glassy calm, once-turbulent
Waters within my breast. Now, henceforth, such
As seek my brittle pool must be content
To skim its surface with a glancing touch.

O skater on this ice! Who treads too bold
On such unsure placidity will hear
The thin crust crackle, and dark depths behold
Chill as old grief and bitter as a tear.

Descent of Angels ~ 1935–1936

Owl's Cry

Listen!.....
          Where sleeping pasture-lands of white
Meet the high woods, etched darker on the dark,
And branches like witch-tapers hold alight
The chilly stars, dripping ice-tallow—Hark!
Dropping down forested height and frosty air
Soft, ghostly calls across the midnight come,
Lonely and strange as meadows stark and bare,
Mournful as song the winter tree-harps strum!

Hush seems unbroken where these long notes go,
The silence is made yet more manifest:
They fall on quiet as snow falls on snow
Or water thickening on a cold pool's breast.

The owl's cry.....
                 This, the essence turned to sound
Of frozen stars, and hollows deep snow-piled,
Of brittle moon, and streams by black ice bound:
The soul made vocal of the winter wild!

"Peace on Earth"

Now that the tumult of the Spring has fled,
And Summer has slaked desire, and the wail
Of Autumn's stilled in snow, the jealous dead
Can rest again. Now nothing can assail

Faint, ghostly senses with a scent or sound
Of lovely life above them going by,
While they lie rigid in unyielding ground!
At last the earth has hushed each troubling cry

Soft, ghostly calls across the midnight come

Descent of Angels ~ 1935–1936

With snow that muffles and calm ice that binds.
They are at peace, they can rest quiet now,
Dead in a world of dead, where only winds
The horn of Winter in the naked bough.

These waters stiffened by his icy breath,
These meadows whitened where his flags unfurled,
Cold comfort give—for all the lands of death
Are not more barren than this Winter world.

Winter Harvest

Where apple-trees drift down a hill
Deep-carpeted with snow, I hear
Through the white twilight, cold and still,
The faëry footfalls of the deer.

Beneath low branches antler-crown
Thrusts warily, and tentative foot
Paws through the glassy ice-crust down
To wet, black earth and iron root,

Where frozen withered apples lie
Ungathered of the autumn's store,
Waiting the creatures wild and shy
That hunger brings to mankind's door.

With quivering nostril, cautious air
And eye alert, a buck and doe
Feed where the branches black and bare
Bloom with the flowers of the snow.

This is the harvest winter brings
To orchards barren for a span:
Food for the need of wilding things,
Stark beauty for the soul of man.

The Song of the Sun ❧ Leah Bodine Drake

Explanation

High on the wires across the land
Little birds sit in the sun and rest.
Along the tracks where the tall poles stand—
That's the place the birds like best!
They cock their heads in a listening way
To the news that runs on the wires below,
And *that's* the reason that grown-ups say,
"My dear, a little bird told me so!"

Figures in a Nightmare

"Is this the road to the City?" I said
    To a man I met on the way.
The wind in the gnarled thorns was chill;
The sky was pale as a grey-goose quill;
And over the brow of the stony hill
    I knew that the sea rolled grey.—
    And the man was gnarled and grey.

"Does the City lie yonder beside the sea?"
    I asked of the man in my dream;
"The City squared upon every side
 With the jasper walls where the bright ones bide,
 And scarlet trumpets salute the tide,
    And the golden towers gleam?—
    In glory eternal they gleam!"

"There is no City beside the sea!"
    Wildly he laughed and shrill:
"That City lies not 'round any bend
 Of any road that your feet might wend.—
 Why, you can't go further—you've come to the end

When you cross the crest of the hill!"
And he howled in the wind on the hill.

"But someone waits in that town for me!"
   I wept; and wilder cried he:
"I, too, have searched for that jasper wall;
The rams of scarlet, they seemed to call—
But there's nobody, nothing there—nothing at all,
   There's nothing down there but the sea!" he shrieked,
"There's nothing down there but The Sea!"

The Witch Walks in Her Garden

"I have spells to cast tomorrow," says the witch,
   Walking in her garden in the twilight gloom;
"There's to bog the Squire's sorrel,
Brew for Meg a lover's quarrel
'Twixt her Ned and Gipsy Kate,
Curse two stiles and bailie's gate;
   And I'll mend my riding-broom," says the witch.

II.
"I must track my foe tomorrow," says the witch,
   Bowing to the moon arise above the Druid stones;
"Where he wanders I will follow;
Loam that bears his footprint hollow
I will lift with rune-carved shell,
Toss it down a secret well:
There he'll drown e'er even-bell . . . .
   He'll mock no more my old bones!" says the witch.

III.
"I will change my skin tomorrow," says the witch,
   Peering in her pocket-glass, afrown at what she sees;

The Song of the Sun ❧ Leah Bodine Drake

"There's a milkmaid young and fair
  Whom I'll catch in subtle snare,
  Hurl her silly soul to space,
  Don her form and wild-rose face:
    Then the lordly lads I'll please!" says the witch.

  IV.
"Oh, I'll break their hearts tomorrow," says the witch,
    Whistling up her demon-cat and tying on its bells;
"While a twelve-month circles by
  I'll be young and jimp and spry!
  'Till One comes to claim his own
  Sweet revenge I will have known—
    Then let me burn in all his hells!" says the witch.

Descent of Angels

  "When the sons of God came in unto the daughters of men and they bare children to them, the same became mighty men which were of old."
      —*Genesis 6:4.*

Time was when maidens in the Lebanon groves
Drew down from Heaven their stupendous loves.

First came the sound of air furiously riven
    By unseen monstrous wings
    Humming like zither-strings.
Then she to whom this dubious boon was given

Saw blaze before her in the primitive dusk
    Intense unwavering light
    Flame-shaped and diamond-white,
And breathed a scent like sandal-tree or musk.

Descent of Angels ❧ 1935–1936

Then she would see the great wings, opal and chrysoprase,
 Over the wool-white shoulders fold,
  See hair like living gold
And meet for one moment the unbearable, bright gaze

Of eyes immortal . . . . . before her senses fled
 She would see the man-form hover,
  Feel those jeweled pinions cover
Her breast like fire, where pressed that fiery head!

Now maidens may walk lonely upon any shore
 With face innocent of veil,
  Unfearful that cheeks will pale
At sound of terrible wings: the angels come no more,

Dropping like stars beside dark earthly waters
To get the giants upon mankind's daughters.

Terror by Night

Deep in the gold forests of that dream,
 Beyond the ivory gates,
  The snow-white Leopard waits.

The plush sides quiver and the jade eyes gleam,
 Biding their evil time
  In that outlandish clime.

And there it lurks, dream after dream, for me!
 A night at last will come
  When I, defenseless, numb,

Facing once more that curious wood, will see
 The topaz blossoms shake
  And the bright thicket break,

The plush sides quiver and the jade eyes gleam

Descent of Angels ⁂ 1935–1936

Loosing at last, like arrow from a bow,
    The terrible, sure pounce
    Of that unearthly Ounce!

I may awaken to the world I know,
    Or rigid in my bed
    The dawn may find me dead.

Therefore by night I call on every Name
    Holy and puissant; tell beads
    Of all remembered creeds,

Hoping to hold by spell and candle-flame
    My soul from those too-deep
    And perilous vales of sleep.

But farther and farther in that alien land
    My unjessed spirit roves
    Toward those unfriendly groves;

And hidden, alert, where the dream-jungles stand,
    With tail lashing to and fro
    Waits that implacable foe.

Old Wives' Tale

She went to the moor in the honey-coloured twilight
To pick wild rushes under a rising moon.
But she had forgotten that the elfin-rings
Were green on the Ancient Mound
And that goat-hooved things
Piped by the marshy pool.

When we told her what night it was
And what herd-girls had seen

The Song of the Sun ~ Leah Bodine Drake

Up on that moor of old, at moonrise,
She said: Still, one must pull certain herbs
In the moon's hour
When roots fill with sleep-inducing power
From that white fiery orb.
She said there was nothing to fear.
She would walk undaunted
By any sound she might hear,
For the clever ones tell that now the moor is unhaunted
And no enchantment lingers
On upland or fell,
Even on Walburga's Eve. She said
That silen and troll have fled
And night is shriven of all unnatural dangers.

So we let her go,
Small and dark against the afterglow,
Away from our warning talk,
And some of us felt like fools
As we turned our faces
Toward the farms and the paths we know
And the unwitched places.

In the dawn a herd with her flock
Found a basket tumbled
On the slope of the Ancient Mound,
And a rabbiting boy stumbled home
And told in a voice that was hoarse with fear,
How he'd seen a torn shoe lying in
A patch of gorse,
And beside the marsh
The prints of enormous hooves in the swart, wet loam.

DESCENT OF ANGELS ❧ 1935–1936

A Hornbook for Witches

I. The Covenant

Writ on scroll of felon's skin
With her blood, for evil's sake,
Is her name. Now she is kin
To Pamphiles, Endor, Bork!
Lucifer will bless her work
And reward her—with the stake.

II. The Besom

When full gallop they would speed
To a coven far away
Thrifty witches use a steed
Economical, the broom.
This asks neither stall nor groom,
Never runs a bill for hay.

III. The Coven

Cross-legged on the Sarsen Stone
Satan sits, with stag-horn crown.
Witches kneeling by his throne
Wonder at his mask in fear:
Is it Sin in person here?
(Likely just a clerk from town!)

IV. The Hell-Broth

Vervain, henbane, lizard's leg,
In a pot as black as Hell;
Brains of flittermouse and frog,
Moldy bones and aconite:
Fumes from this give second sight!
But it has a dreadful smell.

The Song of the Sun ~ Leah Bodine Drake

V. The Magic Circle

Here within this potent round,
Witch secure from fiends may stay.
Safety lies in circles: bound
In such mystic cypher goes
Earth and all the worlds . . . . . Who knows
What grim shapes it keeps at bay?

VI. The Conjuration

Bring the black cock and the knife,
Stir the screaming mandrake brew,
Draw the signs of death and life,
'Round the brazier's smoking cup . . .
She can raise the Devil up!
Or at least, an imp or two.

VII. The Pentagram

Hosts of Mazikeen and Djinn
To the twin-triangles bow.
By it Solomon could win
Lordship over every race;
And the dullest witch can trace
This, to cure a farmer's cow.

VIII. The Spells

There are words of awful might
That each witch-wife must be learning.
If the runes are spoken right
Fiends will hasten to obey.
Let the tongue slip—neighbors may
Suddenly smell something burning!

DESCENT OF ANGELS ❧ 1935–1936

IX. Magician's Hat

Like a steeple to the skies
Soared the occult headdress, once
Worn with pride by adept wise.
'Round the brim the Zodiac
Whirled in scarlet thread.
      Alack,
Now this cap denotes the dunce!

X. Witch's Wheel

By the turning of this wheel,
Faithfulness in hearts of men
Young enchantresses can seal.
Circe long ago did hold
Such a wheel. (Yet we are told
Ulysses never came again.)

XI. The Familiar

Mangy, lean, of evil fame,
Subject to her own dark laws,
Old Grimalkin tells her dame
Ancient lore that all cats know,
And their secret: how to show
Friendship,—while you flex your claws!

XII. Enchanted Sleep

Vivien, the limmer lass,
Stepping from the faëry lake,
Bound Merlin in tree of glass
With her magic cup of dwale.
Now she lies (so ends each tale)
In sleep of death no spell can break.

The Song of the Sun ❧ Leah Bodine Drake

The Nixie's Pool

Oh, go not to the Nixie's pool!
In those waters dim and cool
Gleams a pale and lovely face
Framed in hair like green fern-lace,
Arms of more than mortal grace
Smooth as lily, and as cool.

By all that's holy, all that's good,
Shun the hollow in the wood
Where the giant beech-trees grow
And the water-lilies glow,
And the rushes, parting, show
Wet limbs white as birchen-wood.

Knight-at-arms with blazoned shield,
Ploughboy homing from the field,
Never heed what you may hear—
Song that rises wild and clear,
From the little hidden mere,
Like bird in no man's field.

If you harken, if you follow
To her water-haunted hollow,
Bid farewell to tilting-ground,
Plodding ox or faithful hound,
For deep in Faërie you'll be bound
With the Nixie of the hollow!

DESCENT OF ANGELS ❧ 1935–1936

The Wind and the Leaves

Where is the place that the wind is going
When he hustles the yellow leaves along?
What is the cry that his horn is blowing
That lures the leaves in a hurrying throng?

The wild leaves whirl in the frosty hollows;
They fly to the arms of the boisterous breeze;
They are bundled along and the old wind follows,
Over the fields and the desolate trees.

Over the fields where the sad, dry stubble
Gripped by the bitter, withered ground,
Looks up and sees all that spangled rabble
In the arms of the wind, to a far place bound,—

To the far-off place where the wind is going,
And no one knows where that place may be
But Wind, who forever and ever is blowing
The leaf that leaps from the wintry tree.

And comes the time when I, too, am going,
My soul like a leaf from an old, lorn tree,
Will leap and follow the wind a-blowing,
And find the place that is meant for me.

All-Saints' Eve

Look! . . . .
                There,—beyond the window-pane!
Through the withered and rattling vine!—
A wee face, spangled with silver rain,
Lovely and wan, stares in at mine!

The Song of the Sun ❧ Leah Bodine Drake

White as a shell upon the sands
Where the black billows break and pass,
Something is pressing tiny hands
Against the barrier of the glass.

Something eerie and fay and pale
Is peering in from the haunted night,
At our small room snug from the angry gale,
Where faces glow in the firelight.

Slant, strange eyes under seagreen hair
Look wistfully in through the window-pane!
Quick, open the casement! . . . . . .
                        What is there
That cries in the wind and the streaming rain?

It has gone, it has gone! There is nothing there,
Blown by the storm to our window-pane;
Only the night and the chill sea-air
And the voice of the sorrowful rain.

Witches on the Heath

Three witches danced on the heath last night,
    Dancing widdershins round a tree.
    Wildly widdershins whirled the three
Under a wild and cloud-swept sky,
While a goblin moon rode high
Over the hill where the Old Stones lie;
    And their hats were peaked,
    And they twittered and squeaked
As they danced in the green moonlight.

And out of the boughs of the twisted thorn
    Came the wail of a violin,

Descent of Angels ❧ 1935–1936

    Queer and evil and sad and thin . . . . .
And though there was nobody one could see,
Somebody played in the twisted tree
Queer, sad tunes for the witches three,
       Till a lost wind crept
       From the hills and wept,
And the farm-cocks crowed up the morn.

Curious Story

"Yes . . . yes . . . I saw the sirens once,"
       The ancient seaman said,
Staring beyond the driftwood blaze
Into a past of nights and days,
       Incredible, and dead.

"We saw them sitting on their rock
       In that blue, alien sea;
The tales men told of them are true,
For none save I, of all our crew,
       Won home alive and free.

"Bird-winged, bird-breasted, with calm eyes
       That knew not right or wrong,
They looked at us—I saw them smile,
I saw their girl lips part, the while
       They sang their deadly song.

"It must have been a marvelous song!
       It drew men o'er the side
Of our stout ship like a lodestone, even,
Plunging like souls in hope of Heaven!
       They listened, and they died."

The Song of the Sun ❧ Leah Bodine Drake

"And what song did the sirens sing?"
    He turned his trembling head,
Watching me closely as I spoke:
"I am alive of all that folk:
    For I am deaf," he said.

    He gazed beyond the cottage door
        To where the harbour slept,
Each small ship folded like a bird:
"Deaf! Deaf! Alas, I never heard
        That song!" he said, and wept.

The Girl in the Glass

I found a curious looking-glass
Up in a dusty attic room,
Quivering with a greenish glaze,
Half hidden in the gloom.

Deep in those cobwebbed, misty depths
(Veiled like a door to the Other Land),
My image, queerly different, peeped,
Smiled and waved a shadowy hand.

"Who are you in the mirror? Who?"
Who was that strange, blurred double there
Worlds away from the self I knew,
With elfin face and luminous hair?

Eyes I know are a cloudless blue
Gazed into mirrored eyes of green,
Mooney, unhumanly wise and faë . . . . .
"Who is the girl that has lived unseen

Descent of Angels ~ 1935–1936

But sister-near in this lonely place?"
Green eyes mocked into eyes of blue . . . . .
Close to my lips, in the glimmering glass
Those twin-lips mimicked *"Who?"*

Goat-Song

Part I.
Young wives and blossoming maidens
    Would hear the satyr-men
Piping in laurel thickets
    In the high mountain glen.

Gathering mint and gentians
    Beside the shadowed brook
Girls heard the goat-cry, listened,
    But dared not turn and look

At peering, uncouth faces
    Grinning in grotesque mirth:
The shagged and cloven races
    Old as the wrinkled earth!

Lutie in upland pastures
    Had heard the goat-song, heard
Pipes in a wild-rose cover
    Sob like a hidden bird.

Lutie had paused and harkened
    Amid her maddened sheep
To music that mocked and beckoned,
    Feeling her young blood leap

The Song of the Sun ~ Leah Bodine Drake

Wild with the antique terror;
    Then with her flock had fled,
Glimpsing through leaf and briar
    The horned, half-human head.

Lying o' nights by Peter,
    Lutie would dream of eyes
Green as the green fox-fire,
    And of brown, furry thighs.

Where curls like black grapes clustered
    She'd see the curved horns prick,
Feel swart lips press and blister—
    And waken half sick,

Longing for monstrous wooings
    Beneath the laurel shade . . . . .
Then pray, and fall to weeping,
    And greet the dawn afraid.

Part II.

Winter is time left fallow
    When green blood does not burn:
Crouched in beech-tree hollows
    Sleep the people of the fern.

Winter is time turned craven
    When red blood does not flame
Bold in the veins of humans:
    Or not the same.

Under their snow-thatched rafters
    Lutie sang and wove,
Content with stolid Peter
    And Peter's homespun love;

DESCENT OF ANGELS ❧ 1935–1936

Giving a curious welcome
    To snowdrifts thickly piled
Against their hillward windows,
    Walling out the Wild.

Only the north wind wandered
    On uplands grown remote,
Only the hearthfire whispered
    Its low, untroubled note.

Yet under the fire's purring
    Or in sleep too deep for dream,
She'd feel a cold thought stirring
    Like a fish in placid stream:

That the wise birds wing back ever,
    Green lives and red awake,
Earth's children stretch and quiver,
    And leap within the brake,

And from the thawing ridges
    The wild wet breeze would bring
The sound of satyrish stamping
    And the perilous pipes of Spring!

Fantasy in a Forest

1937–1941

FANTASY IN A FOREST ❧ 1937–1941

The Path through the Marsh

There is a path through a marsh
    That I must take to go home.
    Mallows and thick black loam,
Alder and bog-grass harsh,

And the marsh-pools glinting with light
    Of the sunset that stains the sky:
    That is all to the eye,
Yet something is there that affrights.

Something which I never see
    Though I feel its eyes on my back
    As I cross on that narrow track—
Something that watches me.

It is never bittern, who thumps
    At his hidden churn in the reeds.
    It is never heron, who feeds
In the shallows beside old stumps,

Or spotted bull-frog, who eyes
    Me passing his tiny lake
    Where the great green bubbles break
And the veils of the bog-mist rise.

But deeper than long-drowned log
    Something that never sleeps
    Lies crouched in those oozy deeps,
Something as old as the bog . . . .

They say that there was a time
    When Indians called this sod
    "The place of the evil god,"
And prayed to the quivering slime.

The Song of the Sun ~ Leah Bodine Drake

They say that a Face would appear
    In the mists that the night-winds brew,
    And would ask for Its ancient due:
One human heart a year.

All that is a long-closed book . . . . .
    But still, as I pass on that track,
    I feel something's eyes on my back
And I never dare turn to look,

For fear that the mists should spread
    And curdle to mouth and eyes
    Malefic and old and wise,
Demanding its terrible bread!

Tiger

Now this is the way of the tiger . . . . . He goes
Through the jungle on velvet toes,
Through golden moonlight and ebon shade,
Himself of moonlight and shadow made.

Great lilies coloured like his pelt
Stir not beside him: unseen, unfelt
As a shadow slips into shadow, so
A shade among shades does the tiger go.

As moonbeam drifts into gold moonbeam
He drifts 'neath the night to the jungle-stream.
The jungle-doe, she takes no fright
From moonbeam drifting into moonlight.

But the moonlight leaps! The shadow flames!
Bold and rampant and free from shames,

FANTASY IN A FOREST ❧ 1937–1941

Tiger is here by the water-flow,
And feasts himself on the jungle-doe!

For this is the way of the tiger: he goes
The secret way that the tiger knows,
Moonlight and ebon shade by turn—
And always too late the jungli learn
That *both* are Tiger as he goes
Through the jungle on velvet toes!

Crocodile

Away down on the River Nile
Dozes the armored crocodile.
His back is jasper, huge his size,
And he has bubbles for his eyes.
He does not toil, he does not spin;
All he does is sleep and grin.

All he does is grin and sleep
(And eat, of course) supinely deep
Among the green papyri rods.
He was the first of Egypt's gods
And centuries have held him fast
Like a fossil, in her past.

Asprawl within his rushy groves
He seldom wakes, he seldom moves.
He hardly seems to live at all . . . .
Yet he will see great Memnon fall
And pyramids crumble.
                    Afterwhile,
The Sphinx may weary of her smile
And sink her head between her claws

The Song of the Sun ❧ Leah Bodine Drake

And sleep; and even Nile may pause
In his ceaseless ebb and flow.

But somewhere oozy banks will show
The tall papyri, file on file,—
And there will be the Crocodile
Lolling in his bed of slime
And grinning in the face of Time!

Japan: The Persimmon Gatherers

The orchard has been invaded
By a swarm of butterfly-ladies.
In gold-orange kimonos,
In black-and-mauve kimonos,
In sashes of silver brocade and with hairpins of lacquer
They pull out the branches with sticks of bamboo
To reach the ripe persimmons.
One climbs upon the shoulders of her maid,
Another is handed a heavy-weighed spray
By her gallant wearing the two swords.
Laughing, they strip the elfin fruit from the branches,
Filling little baskets with the spoils.
All this happened a long time ago
In a gold-screen faëryland, on an autumn day.
But the persimmon-trees still light their goblin lanterns
In that enchanted orchard,
The ravishing people, blown long ago away
Like the dust of butterflies,
Are there in Utamaro's picture,
In robes of gold-orange and lilac,
In robes like purple iris and rose peonies,
Plucking fruit from branches,
Happy, frivolous, and eternal . . . . .

Fantasy in a Forest ❧ 1937–1941

The Old Khan and His Falcon

Upon his ivory throne the old Khan is weeping;
Down his revered beard the weak, salt tears are creeping;
He rests his worn old brow on his trembling hand
And the little flames in his culgee are set a-leaping.

II.
Tired and bored and sad, the Khan is crying
For pity of Shaykhah, his falcon of golden flying:
There is no lure worth her invincible stoop,
No quarry fit for such magnificent dying!

III.
Alas for Shaykhah! She should have birds from Faërie,
Loosed in their glittering flights from a jinni's eyrie
To battle her matchless wings in the steeps of sky . . . . .
Of heron they both are more than a little weary.

IV.
Where is the Rukh, that bird of the diamond mountains?
Where the white swan-maids who bathed in the glacial fountains?
And where is pious Simurgh, feathered with flame?
Gone from the ken of man, to the world's-end's mountains.

V.
They only are worth the loosing of jess and varvel;
They only are worthy of death from this hawk of marvel:
What's heron, what's fox, and what's the fleet gazelle
That Shaykhah the huntress should slip one golden varvel?

VI.
The courtiers speak of black storks in the valleys,
Of peacocks burning like gems in the jungle-alleys;
And hunters whisper of wolf . . . . . . and on her perch
Shaykhah the chieftess stirs, and the old Khan rallies.

The Song of the Sun ❧ Leah Bodine Drake

VII.
But always, again, the old slow thoughts come, bringing
The word that nothing is worth the terrible winging
Of Shaykhah the Proud, Shaykhah the Angry-Souled!
And his tears on the marble floor make a delicate ringing.

'Round and 'Round

'Round and 'round an elder-tree
Dances the fairy Tillywee.

Wings a-flutter, pansy gown
Torn and rumpled, hair blown down
Dancing widdershins goes she
'Round and 'round the elder-tree

Tillywee must foot it spry
'Til a mortal year goes by.
She must trip it, ring-around
In a magic circle bound,
As a punishment, they say
For dancing on a Sabbath Day,
When a saint we will not name
Caught her at her fairy game!

In full mid-whirl he chanced to behold her
Then with bell and book he told her
There to dance (if dance she would
On holy days) to dance for good.

Saints are kindly men at heart.
So he cut his judgement short:
"Dance," he said, "my naughty dear,
For a twelve-month human year."

Fantasy in a Forest ❧ 1937–1941

* * *

So by sun and star and moon
Skip the little walnut shoon,
Elder-bloom and elder-berry:
To the flutes of wren and veery.
To the sighing of the snow,
Whirl and dip and point a toe.

What the good Saint did not guess
Was, that this is happiness
To an elf or sprite or fairy!
So, delighted, lone and merry,
'Round about the elder-tree
Dances the Fairy Tillywee!

Midsummer Night

Now from the spray of the branching briar
    The cobweb trembles, adroop with dew;
The white moth seeks the foxglove's spire,
    The witch-owl cries "Tu-whoo, tu-whoo,"
        And from the gloom
        Of her pine-tree room
            Her silent wings dip low.

Now from the banks of the reedy pool
    The fireflies dance in a golden reel.
Where the toadstool-tapers burn green and cool
    The spider spins at her busy wheel;
        And through the ferns
        Where the cricket churns
            The thin young foxes go.

The brown bee sleeps in the thistle's house
    But the bull-frog blows on his deep bassoon.

The Song of the Sun 🙢 Leah Bodine Drake

On some secret journey goes flittermouse;
   The faraway hills await the moon.
      The shadows brim
      The valley's rim
         And deeper the twilight falls.

And over the hills the round moon rolls;
   She reaches a white and summoning hand
And taps on the silver beech-trees boles,
   And strange doors open to her command:
      The bark swings free,
      And from tree to tree
         Dryad to dryad calls.

Ducks and Pigs

I met an old woman down in a valley
   When I was leading my ducks to the mere;
She said, "Tell me, where are thy ducks' little bonnets
Tied with blue ribbons, my pretty, sweet dear?"
I told her, "Good gammer, ducks *never* wear bonnets."
"Hoity toity!" says she, "Now what do I hear?
   No duck with a bonnet
   With blue ribbons on it?
I must say *thy* country's remarkably queer!
Tee hee,
Oh me,
Ye're remarkably queer!"

I met an old man on the hills in the heather,
   As I was driving my pigs to the Fair;
He said, "Are thee selling thy pretty pink piglets
To hitch to the carriage of squire or mayor?"
I told him, "Good gaffer, pigs *never* pull coaches."

Fantasy in a Forest ⁓ 1937–1941

"Hoity toity!" says he, "In my land over there,
    Fleet, neat-harnessed pigs
    Draw our coaches and gigs.
This country's a queer one, I vow and declare!
Ho ho!
I trow
Ye're remarkably queer!"

Oh, pigs in harness,
And ducks in bows!
Now where is their country,
Do you suppose?
Oh, riddle me this;—
Of all the three,
Are *they* the daffies,
Or do *I* be?

Puss-in-Boots and the Three Mice

Three little mice sat down to spin,
    Tippet, Snippet and Snap.
In their wee little house in Blackberry Wood
They spun and they sewed for their livelihood,
And were no seamstresses quite so good
    As Tippet, Snippet and Snap.

Now who peers in through their casement-glass,
    And who knocks Rap-a-tap-tap?
It's Puss-in-Boots from Carabas!
Oh, what can *he* want with the spinners?—Ah,
Great is the fear! "Alas! Ala!"
    Cry Tippet, Snippet and Snap.

"Be not afraid, my good little dames,
    Miss Tippet, Miss Snippet, Miss Snap!"

The Song of the Sun 〜 Leah Bodine Drake

Says Master Boots: "I wish some new clothes,
Doublet and breeches and silken hose,
For a wedding draws near, as the whole world knows
    That lies on a Christian map."

"Oh, pardon us, sir," cry the three little mice,
    Tippet, and Snippet and Snap;
"But claws and whiskers *do* give us a fright!
Sir Puss-in-Boots, we will work day and night
To make you a wonderful lordly sight
    If we never take sup or nap!"

So they cut him a doublet of pansy plush,
    Those little mice, One, Two, Three,
Breeches of green moss, spiderweb hose,
A vest embroidered in petals of rose,
From the bow on his tail to the boots on his toes
    He'd shine like a Christmas tree.

So they spun and they cut and they stitched and they sewed,
    Those little mice, Three, Two, One;
They dyed his coat in a tulip-vat.
Their shears and needles went clatterty-clat;
O never such clothes had a kit or a cat
    In any land under the sun!

The Marquis of Carabas gave a ball.
    The feet went tap-a-tap tap;
And Puss-in-Boots was his master's pride,
He raised the toast and he swung the bride;
And dancing their merriest by his side
    Were Tippet and Snippet and Snap!

FANTASY IN A FOREST ❧ 1937–1941

The Journey of the Queen of Sheba

Balkis the Wise, the Ethiops' Queen,
Came riding up from the faëry south.
She came with all her fabulous train
To hear the words of Solomon's mouth.

(Over the desert and over the water
Rode Queen Balkis, the White Doe's daughter.)

She sat in a peacock-shaded throne
On a grey beast out of myth, whose walk
Woke the thunder beneath the ground,
And whose tusks were inlaid with orichalch.

Cloaked with lion her spearmen trod,
Tall black panther-men who bore
Shields made out of Behemoth's hide,
Silent as panthers, four by four.

Then came chattering slaves with jars
Holding opals and tourmalines,
Vases of red-gold filled with myrrh,
Baskets of melons and muscadines

From slopes of the Mountains of the Moon
Where rivers are born and dragons hiss;
Plumes of ostrich, and ivory horns
Heaped with spices and ambergris.

On snow-white camels, in curtained chairs
Perched her ladies with comb and fan,
Laughing behind their spangled scarves
At scribe and jester and wizard-man

Kicking their tasselled donkeys—mage
In steep hat starred with the Zodiac;

The Song of the Sun ~ Leah Bodine Drake

From lanterned Chin, cat-whiskered sage;
Conjure-king from the Congo's track.

Then in their squealing, clattering hordes
Came the zebras and small red apes,
Cameleopards in silver cords,
Ibises daintily pecking grapes

Thrust from the toppling, reed-work bales
Which asses bore in a tinkling band,
As over the lamia-haunted fells
The Queen's host trundled toward Judah's land.

(Over the desert and over the water
 Rode Queen Balkis, the White Doe's daughter.)

PART II.
She passed through Ham, she passed through Khem
Shadowed with hawks like ghosts of pride.
She crossed the Red Sea into Shem,
She faced the doors of Jerusalem;
Her horns gave tongue: their horns replied.

Straight to the lion-carven throne,
To Solomon's feet went Balkis, Queen.
(Her face was pale as a small moonstone,
Her mouth was the reddest ever seen.)

David's son reached down his hand,
He lifted her to a golden chair;
And so they talked of wars and men,
Of bees and honey and sea and air.

They talked of seasons and love and fate,
Of pentagrams and the fiery Jinn.
The sun went down, and the moon rose late,
And Solomon talked to the beautiful Queen.

Fantasy in a Forest ᓚ 1937–1941

Part III.
Out of the desert-facing gate
Of Solomon's city in Judah's land,
Balkis rides with her ambassade
Over the cinnamon-coloured sand.

What were the secrets Solomon spoke?
What is the wisdom she learned from him?
What is the news she is bringing back
From a king who talks with the Seraphim?

Her magi question the stars, and fight
Wordy battles for various things
That queens could study by day or night
All alone at the side of kings.

Her ladies whisper, the slave-girls wink,
The jester trolls an impudent song;
Nobody cares what the spearmen think,
Padding like pards along.

But the Queen sits straight in her peacock chair
And her lips are tender and proud and grave,
And her eyes are wise with an ancient lore
Shared by empress and sunburnt slave.

"O garden of spices! O Little dove!" . . . . .
Flooding up from her soul's deep well,
Hoarse and shaken with love, the words
Echo like tones of a living bell.

"O fountain sealed!" . . . .
      Through glassy airs
Relentlessly the hawk-sun flies;
But Balkis dreams of the stranger-stars
That blazed in the black Judean skies.

The Song of the Sun ~ Leah Bodine Drake

(Over the desert and over the water
  Rode Queen Balkis, the White Doe's daughter.)

The satyrs peer from the dry ravines,
The lizards scatter, the antelopes run;
And into Sheba comes Sheba's queen,
Bringing them Solomon's son.

Serpent-Ring

This flexible, bright, foolish thing
I wear upon my hand, this ring
That seems by arachnean goldsmith wrought,
(So cobweb-fine the mesh is caught)
Is more than gaudy toy or charm
To please the sight or shield from harm:

For I bear on my finger here
In ribboned gold, the symbol clear
Of sudden death and healing rod,
Of floods that quicken Egypt's sod,
The woes of Han and the waters beneath,
The sign of fire's living breath;
The sun at noon, the moon at even,
The scarlet Worm whose heads are seven;
The sign of good, the stamp of evil,
The shape of seraphim and devil,—
Most holy Serpent! He who holds
Eternity within his folds . . . . .
Thus life and death relentless swing
Within the confines of my ring.

And just as I so lightly wear
This awful sign on finger bare
Of all but impotent human clay,

FANTASY IN A FOREST ❧ 1937–1941

Thus God, perhaps, some destined day
Upon His mighty hand will place
Our universe of time and space;
And with half-sad, half-smiling air
Sometimes may contemplate it there,
Rigid as metal, cold and numb,
An outworn bauble on His thumb.

The Seven Sons of the King of Thule

The seven sons of the King of Thule,
They all rode out on a morning cool,
A bride to win (as was the rule),
    Sing Tra-la-la and a folderay.

The first Prince journeyed across the sea
To the pearl-domed cities of Heathenry
And he stole the Princess of Araby!
    Tra-la-la and a folderay.

The second followed a water-queen
To her island palace, and there he's been
Held by spells of silver and green,
    Tra-la-la and a folderay.

The third son wandered across the Down
Where the gipsy-folk have their trundling town;
And he found a strange bride, wild and brown,
    Tra-la-la and a folderay.

The fourth sought the fabled Fay de Lune
In her ice-bound castle and magic swoon.
He kissed her . . . . but could not break the rune
For he'd come a hundred years too soon!
    Tra-la-la and a folderay.

The Song of the Sun ~ Leah Bodine Drake

The fifth wooed the child of the Golden Khan:
He failed in the quest he was set upon
So they cut off his head with a yataghan!
    Tra-la-la and a folderay.

The sixth Prince traveled the whole world through,
But never found maid he wished to woo;
So he's wandering yet, if the tale be true,
    Tra-la-la and a folderay.

But the *youngest* sought Princess Far-Away
There were trolls to fight and a dragon to slay,
But he killed them all with a sword from Faï
And rescued her from the tower grey,
And their wedding-feast was a year and a day—
So my story ends in the good old way
    With a tra-la-la
        and a folderay!

Conversation in an Oak-Tree

"Ho! Hob-in-the-Oak! Are you there?"
"Who calls?"
          "'Tis Fly-by-Night—I call!
We are flitting tonight through the upper air
Over to Zealand, to the troll-king's ball."

"Dancing, is it? Why ask me?
  I'm too old and knotty to leap!"

"Well, the truth is, Hob . . . . you see,
  We need your lantern to light the deep."

"Where's Jack-with-the-Candle?"

Fantasy in a Forest ❧ 1937–1941

                "He caught cold—
He was reaching for moon-bubbles in the marsh
And the nixies doused him."

                "I'm too old
To wander about on a night so harsh;
And marsh-wife's brewing a fog. Go home!"

"*Do* come, Hob! We *must* have a lamp."

"Cannot Queen Mab use her wand-tip's gleam?
I'm a sleepy hobgoblin and fogs are damp."

"But Leprechaun's made us new slippers, Hob!"

                        "Well when do you host?"

"When the crickets drum
    At noon-o'-the-night on Wayland's Knob—
Ah, those beautiful troll-girls!"

                      "Weep not—I'll come!"

The Last Faun

I saw him! I saw him!—just yesterday,
    Curled up on my misty lawn—
The small snub nose and the amber horns—
    I saw him, the last faun!

The last of the prick-eared, joyous folk
    That startled brake and wood
In the timeless days when the Earth was young
    And the dreams of men were good.

The Song of the Sun ❧ Leah Bodine Drake

They have all passed down to the Hollow Land
　　That lies back of the rising moon—
The leaf-brown nymphs and the centaurs wise,
　　And Pan and the Panic tune.

And here was the world's last, lonely myth
　　Asleep in the early dew
Beneath my window! . . . Then shrill and clear
　　The cock his bugle blew.

The Wild Thing leapt! With a flash of fur
　　And a clatter of hooves he fled,
And nothing to show where he had been
　　But the crushed grass of his bed.

He had gone! He had gone! The final faun,
　　Searching the lands we know
For that ancient path to the secret land
　　Where his kind passed long ago.

The Naughty Fairy

The Fairy who lives
　　In the spindle-tree
Morning and evening
　　Teases me!

When I put on the kettle,
　　When I sweep out the room,
She pokes at the fire,
　　She plucks at the broom.

She drums on the bee-hive
　　And frightens the bees;
She teaches the rabbits
　　How to steal peas.

FANTASY IN A FOREST ❧ 1937–1941

When I sit down to knit,
   My skein's all undone
And Pussy gets scolded
    For that bad fay's fun.

When I draw up the bucket
    Out of the well,
Perhaps there'll be naught in it
    But a cockle-shell,

And there's Mistress Fairy
   In the spindle-tree
Swinging and sniggering,
    "You can't catch me!"

When I dress in my muslin
    To go to the Fair,
My caps will be crumpled,
    My combs not there.

When I look in the glass
    She mocks from my shoulder!
She's turning my hair grey,
    As she gets bolder!

Beware, limmer Fairy!
    Someday I'll get
A charmed spider-web
    From the Wise-Wife, and set

A soft, wicked snare
    In bee-close or dairy:
And when you flit thither,
    Sly-handed, airy,

The Song of the Sun ❧ Leah Bodine Drake

There you will blunder,
   And there you must cling—
Thieving hand, mocking tongue,
   Naughty, bright wing—

Until you have promised
   By Oak, Ash and Thorn,
To give over plaguing me
   Evening and morn!

The Three Green Ladies of Greenwich

The Three Green Ladies of Greenwich
   Were a wonderful pea-green hue!
   In eighteen hundred and thirty-two
They came to Greenwich from far away
In a coach piled high with band-boxes gay.
Why they chose our village, who can say?
   But with elegant muffs
   And their sleeves all puffs,
The ladies descended on Greenwich.

II.
The Three Green Ladies of Greenwich
   Took a house as green as cheese
   In which they gave fashionable green-tea teas.
There came the ladies from the manor and manse
To sit on the sofas of Louis Quinze,
In an awestruck, admiring, envious trance,
   To sample the flavors
   Of China, from Sèvres,
With those hoity-toit ladies of Greenwich.

Fantasy in a Forest ❧ 1937–1941

III.
The Three Green Ladies of Greenwich
    Over a dish of Bohea,
    Would express their sympathy
(By inference subtle) for dame and maid
Who had not been born with the noble shade
Of bank-notes, seaweed, lettuce and jade,
    Till each visitor vowed
    She would lie in her shroud
If she couldn't find dye-pots in Greenwich.

IV.
The Three Green Ladies of Greenwich
    Set the style the country 'round.
    Their extremely unusual appearance was found
To be most *bon-ton*. Complexions of green
Became the thing. Each village queen
Covered her roses with aquamarine;
    And faces once pallid
    Soon looked like a salad,
And green paint was sold out in Greenwich.

V.
Once came a tinker to Greenwich
    From somewhere over the Down:
He said he came from the very town
Of the Three Green Ladies. We heard him say
"That they weren't called Beauties up along *his* way,
But such terrible freaks they had run away!"
    He was heard with scorn
    And run off next morn
By our modish green ladies,
Our chic, unique ladies,
By all the green ladies of Greenwich!

The Song of the Sun ~ Leah Bodine Drake

Born under Capricorn

When I am dead, when I am still
Let me lie in the heart of a hill.
Let me sleep in the timeless sod—
The ancient, wrinkled, beloved of God,
Holy mother of flesh and flower,
The man in his strength, the bloom of an hour,
The fox in the thicket, the owl on the bough,
The corn that leaps in the wake of the plough!
All of us by the old dark earth
Were made and molded and given birth;
And man and beast, when our work is over,
Lie with the corn and the wild white clover.

But I am twice an earth-child, born
Under the stars of Capricorn,—
The earth-sign, whose dominion brings
Kinship with dark and the roots of things.
The mole's my sister, the tree's my brother
That clings to the breast of the great brown Mother:
And there's no fear of the green hill-grave
For one who loved what the warm earth gave,
For one she fashioned out of her loam:
It is only a going-home.

The Bittern

Where red cranberries light the dusk
    Upon the reaches of the bog,
Beyond a rotting cedar's husk,
    The bittern mourns within the fog.

FANTASY IN A FOREST ❧ 1937–1941

Disconsolate, remote from man,
    He tells his few remembered words—
Echo of some old sorrow, born
    Back in an age when all were birds.

The Centaurs

Once in my youth I saw the centaurs drinking
Up where the pines are fur on the mountain's flank.
They stood to their girths in the hazel-coloured water;
Monstrous, they drank.

Under their glossy sides the water rippled
In widening rings of amber and gold.
Their eyes
Were golden with rings of jet; and tawny-amber,
I saw the close-curled heads from their man-necks rise.

Under the pines and the thin, sun-dappled birches
They cupped the water to lips that were dark and thick.
Beneath my hesitant foot a dry branch crackled . . . . .
Furred ears a-prick,

Startled, they whinnied, gold eyes rolling in fury;
The water churned topaz and crystal between their knees.
Crashing, they gained the bank and the ferny thickets;
They vanished among the trees.

Then I said: When I am tall, when I am older,
I shall come again upon centaurs.
One I shall chase
And catch and bind for my own, whip, saddle and halter,
To go at *my* pace!

The Song of the Sun ❧ Leah Bodine Drake

But never again have I seen the proud, wise creatures.
No mark of a hoof in the turf nor a god-like head.
None of those whom I ask have heard that thunderous passing:
From the woods and over the last blue ridges
The centaurs have fled.

Rabbit-Dance

Out in the woods where the snow lies white
A rabbit is dancing, dancing tonight.

The world is hushed and the wind is still;
The woodchucks sleep within the hill.
Muffled in snow, tall cedars loom
Like white-cloaked wizards in the gloom;
And with delicate capers and curious prances
On the frozen snow a rabbit dances.

The moon comes up with a questioning face,
And leans and looks in that woodland place
At the snow-white rabbit who stamps and leaps
On his dancing-ground, while the white world sleeps.
She leans and looks with a wondering eye,
Then trundles higher into the sky.

But with hind-legs beating the glistening snow
And forepaws wavering to and fro,
All by his lone to a secret song
The rabbit dances the whole night long.

FANTASY IN A FOREST ≈ 1937–1941

The Old Granny's Story

Yestere'en, as ever was,
    While I dozed on the settle,
The Liddle Folk came trooping in
    By ways of thorn and nettle.

They led me out with bobbing lights
    And voices thin and cheery.
They led me down the hilly path
    And through the witch-wood eerie.

And O, they sang about their land
    That lay in Fox's Hollow,
And how they'd make me rich therein,
    If I would only follow.

I clean forgot my helpless hens,
    The kettle on the fire;
I only thought on fairy gold
    And all my heart's desire.

How their lanterns twinkled!
    How their wee hands beckoned!
All the wildwood ways we went
    I no' cared nor reckoned.

Och, the tree-roots tripped me!
    O, the brambles prickled!
How I slipped and stumbled!
    How the fern-blades tickled!

Then off through a limmer bog
    And up a wee hill—
Where did I walk but o'er
    My own door-sill!

The Song of the Sun ⁊ Leah Bodine Drake

And where were all the Liddle Folk?
    Gone away!—and I
A-muddying up my kitchen
    Like a foul pig-sty!

But off in Fox's Hollow
    I heard them laugh and shout
Of how they'd fooled a mortal
    And run her round about!

Sea-Shell

    Stranded upon the sand,
    Here is a twisted shell:
    Lift it within your hand,
    Press it against your ear,
    Listen . . . . . . and you will hear
    Echo of deep-sea bell
Ringing in belfry beneath the brine,
Where mermaidens scaled with tourmaline
    Toll a dolorous knell . . . .
It's the voice of a city beneath the sea!
Gold-eyed fishes stare endlessly
At turrets and ramparts of porphyry
    Drowned in a gold-green well.

    Who built that city forlorn?
    What was its perilous fame
    That tymbal and gong and horn
    Blared from the torch-lit wall?
    When did its doom befall?
    What was the reason it came
Crashing down over palace and keep,—
A sea that rose like a mountain's steep

Fantasy in a Forest ⇒ 1937–1941

 Quenching the living flame?
Hark! ..... Do the sea-shell's echoes tell
The name of that city before she fell?
*Ah, no! I can hear its cry, its bell,
 But never its fabulous name!*

The Stranger

(For Lord Dunsany)

The stranger, the proud-headed man who sat
 With us by the inn's fire,
Spoke all that day of gusty rain
 Of the land of his desire:

It is a land of apple-trees (he said)
 On islands watered by many a spring,
The boughs bearing both bloom and fruit
 Wherein white birds sing.

White towers they have there, scarlet-roofed,
 Circled with rivers, windowed with amethyst,
Where dwell the beautiful, smiling folk
 Who doeth as they list,

And little of that is evil. Love and death
 Trouble also that land with their old story,
But set in loftier halls and under sunnier skies,
 And rainbowed with glory.

And there are quests for alien grails; and sea-maids walk
 At sunset on the desolate sunken sands.
There is no sorrow less than the fall of kings,
 And the winged sphinx is the terror of the land.

The Song of the Sun 〜 Leah Bodine Drake

Up the jagged mountains, over the cold plateaus
    Curious bugles ring from thunderous cliffs
Where, furred with otter and belted with peridots,
    Queens and young princes hunt the hippogriffs.

And those are the perilous mountains of the trolls
    Who hoard the rubies that the witches fear . . . .
That is the country whence I came (he said):
    It is not here, not here.

"What Are Little Girls Made Of?"

Old Jingle

This block of hexagons carved out of topaz comes
From the dark secret city of the bees;
And here are satin pears with crystal-dripping gums,
Fur-coated peaches, and from distant trees
Where the gilt wasp-army clings and sips,
These balls of red carnelian—these small delicious plums!

And here is creamy milk that meadows wear
Awhile upon their breasts as clover. Here are sun
And rain along the wind and azure air,
All here to eat!
These sweets make fruity flesh, Sweet One!—
Peach-soft and peach-furred cheeks, ripe lips
And honey-smooth and honey-yellow hair.

FANTASY IN A FOREST ❧ 1937–1941

The Tenants

Among the black trees spider-webbed
    Against a red and wintry dusk,
I leaned upon the sagging gate
    And looked up at the evil husk

Of that old house, remote from town
    And haunted—so the farm-folk said—
By brother ghosts: the elder stabbed,
    The killer hanged till he was dead.

"How does it feel," I asked the pair
    Of farmers slouching in the door,
"To live within a haunted house?
    You must have nerves of steel and more!"

A hoot-owl cried within the wood;
    The sky above was red as sin;
The shadows deepened: side by side,
    Each figure eyed me with a grin.

Then one replied "We have to stay—
    This is our home, the land we tilled—
For I'm the one they hanged," he said,
    "And *he's* the one I killed."

Bad Company

The owl, the bat, and the twisted tree:
I wonder why they are dear to me?
    The owl is eerie,
    The owl is evil,
And everyone knows that the bat's of the Devil!
And a tree that's gnarled and leans awry

O there's no doubt! a witch I must be

Fantasy in a Forest ❧ 1937–1941

And bears wild fruit that is puckered and dry,
Is surely one that the most pass by—
    Afraid of its goblinry.

There's something wrong with a human wight
Who likes to be out in the windy night . . . .
    I love the night and the wild wind over;
    The wind to me is a sky-born lover!
But the night is black and so is sin,
And witches ride while the good stay in;
And the owl and the bat are the witches' kin—
    So look at my fearful plight:

I love the things that the most pass by,
The tree on the heath that leans awry,
    The wild black night and the lanterned owl,
    The bat that goes in a velvet cowl . . . .
O there's no doubt! a witch I must be
Who love with unholy ecstasy
The owl and the bat and the twisted tree
    And wind in a midnight sky!

"Run with the Fox"

    I started with the hunt,
    The jolly, jolly hunt
With its rosy coats, and faces all as rosy-pink as they;
    With its hounds, and its noise
    Of the laughing men and boys,
And each pretty girl so dashing on her sorrel or her grey.

    Joy of living then we knew
    When the sky was fresh and blue,
To be off across the dewy fields in tides of belling song!
    It was splendid, it was gay

The Song of the Sun ~ Leah Bodine Drake

    To see Robert far away
Like a tawny arrow from a bow, that shot the hills along!

    It was splendid, it was fun,
      Thus to see our Robert run,
Too far, too far as yet for any hound to cross his trail!
    It was grand to watch him go!
    Till his pace began to slow,
And the thrusters saw how eyes grew wild and breath began to fail.

    Oh, it didn't seem so gay
      When at last he turned at bay
At the little rocky hole he knew, and found it stoppered tight;
    Oh, it wasn't quite the fun
    It had been, when just begun,—
For it wasn't "joy of living" that had made *those* eyes so bright!

    It was cruel it was cruel
      To see the tongues a-drool
Of the leaping dogs, and how *his* mouth was open, hot and dry!
    It was very like to sin
    To see how the hounds closed in,
And how the people on their mounts laughed down to see him die!

    Oh, I started with the hunt!
      The jolly, jolly hunt,
With its rosy coats and rosy cheeks above the tidy stocks . . . .
    It had lover, kin and friend,—
      But it found me at the end,
In my shaken soul, all muddy, torn and dying with the fox!

Encounter in Broceliande

I knew that shape the instant seen
Approaching through the fabled wood;

FANTASY IN A FOREST ❧ 1937–1941

I saw the wreath of helleborine
Beneath the shadow of her hood.

Stepping between two oak-tree boles
On light feet shod in miniver,
No dry leaf stirred beneath her soles,
The bracken did not bend for her.

The cup of dwale within her hand
I saw sly Vivien at last,
Moving remotely through the land
In some queer mirage of the past!

So did she pass behind the trees,
Smiling sidewise beneath her cowl . . . . .
The white mist billowed to my knees,
The dusk swooped downward like an owl,

And hid was that malevolent face,
And lost the secret of her sin:
Of where in that enchanted place
Her sorceries had bound Merlin!

A Star Came Out

A star came out, the first!—so small
It shivered in the sky so tall,
The sky so wide—no other star
To keep it company, near or far.

So small a star, none other by—
So I cried "Oh, here am I!
I'm here with you! Don't be afraid!"
So it wasn't, and it stayed.

The Song of the Sun ❧ Leah Bodine Drake

The Daughter of the Grand Turk Loses Her Ball

The Princess of Turkey has lost her ball!
It bounced right over the garden wall,
Right off the ground—
And it cannot be found
In garden or palace at all, at all.

Her ladies trip on their tinkling feet
To climb up ladders and peer down the street,
But it isn't there,
It has flown through the air
Like a scarlet swallow so fleet, so fleet.

The little black page-boys scuttle like mice;
They swarm up the trees of flowers and spice.
They shinny up poles
And peep down holes,
And boast they will find it in a trice.*

The Mage in his tower casts many a spell;
He questions the planets, he squints down the well.
The Djinn and the Peris
Can't answer his queries:
Where is the royal ball? No one can tell.

The mincing Princes in rose-coloured coats
Scramble up balconies just like goats.
They search kennels and mews
And dirty their shoes,
And mutter curses deep down in their throats.

---

*Nobody has ever found out *what* or *where* a trice is!

Fantasy in a Forest ~ 1937–1941

Pashas and Mullahs bustle about;
They fish in the pool of the golden trout,
And make a fine din;
And one falls in
And it takes three soldiers to pull him out:
(He is so very remarkably stout!)

Now the First Vizier, turbaned and grave,
Crawls under the tables like any slave.
He bumps his head
On an ivory bed,
And yells for potions his pate to lave.

Even the dread Grand Turk himself
Searches from throne to the pantry shelf;
He opens each cupboard
Like old Mother Hubbard
And claws through his treasures of rubies and pelf.

Now from crescented turret to dungeon's gloom,
From kitchen-midden to Carpet-Room,
In the pomegranate grove
Where the peacocks rove,
The household hunts while the kettle-drums boom!

Each royal hawk has her jess untied;
The wolfhound runs by the cheetah's side.
The horns are blown
And the standards flown
As over the meadows the huntsmen ride!

So in aigrette, scimitar, pantaloons,
The Sultan hunts with the Court Buffoon.
Mameluke, mage,
Princess and page,
They search by the light of the sun and moon!

The Song of the Sun ~ Leah Bodine Drake

. . . .
This happened a long, long time ago . . . .
But "They say" (and They almost always know.)
That her darling pet
Is bouncing yet,
From Turkey to Texas to Tokyo.

If you should find it, Jill or Jack,
Remember the Princess and send it back
As fast as you can
By caravan,
Or the flying horse or a pedlar's pack,

Addressed to "The Princess of Old Turkee,
Care of the Grand Turk, R. O. D.,*"—
But how find a way
Into yesterday?
My story is ended, so don't ask *me!*

"Apples and Apricots, Peaches and Plums"

What are Earth's gifts to a child of Spring?
The curious note that the hylas sing,
The light that shines in a daffodil,
A white lamb gamboling on a hill,
A meadow pool that a warm rain dapples—
Sing peaches and apricots, plums and apples!

Summer will bring you a dog-rose petal,
A moon carved out of some genie-metal,
Queen-Anne's-Lace for fairies' dresses,
Wild strawberries and cool green cresses,

*"Reward On Delivery."

FANTASY IN A FOREST ❧ 1937–1941

And pink sea-shells from the mermaids' grots—
Sing apples, plums, peaches and apricots!

What has Autumn for daughter or son?
Gossamer scarfs that the pixies spun,
Milkweed puffs and a wild goose feather,
Persimmons lanterning story weather,
The golden glow in a grove of beeches—
Sing apples and apricots, plums and peaches!

Now tell me the gifts of the Wintertide:
A frozen pond on which to slide,
A crystal star that a snowflake made,
A wreath of mistletoe for your head,
A midnight carol, and the Elf who comes
With a sleigh-load of toys and sugar-plums!
Sing apples and apricots, peaches and plums!

The Steps in the Field

Out in a field that no one weeds
A flight of stone steps upward leads
From the grasses and Queen-Anne's-Lace:
It is a still and lonely place.

There is no house there any more;
The steps go mounting to no door:
They lead the way but to the sky
Where the hawks are hovering high.

If trespassers climbed that stair
What would happen to them there?
Would they merely stand, and see
Where the portals used to be?

The Song of the Sun ❧ Leah Bodine Drake

Maybe when they reached the top
They would find they could not stop—
Go on climbing, foot and shoe,
Secret stairways in the blue!

They might vanish, boot or dress,
Into sunny emptiness,
Leaving field and Queen-Anne's-Lace
For some very different place . . . . . .

Though we know it's just a game
Children play there, just the same
Do not venture . . . . what if you
Climbed those steps and found it true?

Mouse Heaven

Heaven is a great House
    Paneled thick with oak;
Terrier nor cat will rouse
    Fear in little folk.

Heaven is the Quiet
    And the deep, deep dark;
Never comes nigh it
    Lamp nor candle's spark,

Only the shadowed glancing
    Of Mother Moon bright,
On floors bare for dancing
    Of feet wee and light.

Fantasy in a Forest ❧ 1937–1941

There are the cheeses
    Yellow as moons,
And rare bacon-greases,
    And sausage-festoons,

On low shelves flaunted
    In reach of tiny paws,
In pantries unhaunted
    By traps or claws.

There little hearts may beat
    Calmly in bed,
Shaken by no giants' feet
    Thundering overhead.

None need to flee the feasts
    Nor die in the snares,—
All of us helpless beasts
    Will live without cares.

For up where the shadows drouse
    In His holy hall,
Abides the Very-Mouse
    Watching over all.

Obey the ancient law,
    (Hear ye, O Folk!)
Which is to run and gnaw
    And housewife-provoke,

And death will not deny
    The long-promised House,
The good Mansion-in-the-Sky
    Of the Tribe of Mouse!

The Song of the Sun ❧ Leah Bodine Drake

Protective Colouring

The hare in the stubbled meadow
    Is the colour of ground;
Hunched beneath the hawk's shadow
    She cannot be found:
While the wings poise she is furrow
    And the husks around.

The doe in the golden glade
    Is speckled with sun;
Her sides and the flickering shade
    Are suddenly one:
The hunter abroad in the wood
    Sees shadow alone.

The snake is son to the rock.
    He is still dark root
That coils itself at the shock
    Of approaching boot.
He is sand that was sleeping, awake
    To slip by the foot.

Forest and field and hill
    Shield the pad, the wing;
But alien now to the wild
    Goes the pale man-thing:
And death can stalk him at will
    And leisurely spring.

They Run Again

Beyond the black and naked wood
In frosty gold has set the sun,
And dusk glides forth in cobweb hood . . . .
Sister, tonight the werewolves run!

Fantasy in a Forest ❧ 1937–1941

With white teeth gleaming and eyes aflame,
The werewolves gather upon the howe,
Country churl and village dame—
They have forgotten the wheel and plough,

They have forgotten the speech of men,
Their throats are dry with a dreadful thirst,
And woe to the traveler in the glen
Who meets tonight with that band accurst!

Now up from the hollows creeps the dark;
The moon like a yellow owl takes flight;
Good people on their house-doors mark
A cross, and hug their hearths in fright.

Sister, listen! . . . . .
     the King-Wolf howls!
The pack is running! . . . .
       Drink down the brew,
Don the unearthly, shaggy cowls—
We must be running, too!

The Wood-Wife

In a hollow oak-tree
 I live by the wood,
A bit more than human
 And much less than good.

I've queer spells, potent spells,
 That I went to learn
From the goat-hooved and shaggy ones
 Who hide in the fern.

A bit more than human and much less than good.

Fantasy in a Forest 1937–1941

Down the brambly hedgerows
    You may see me pass,
Gathering berries for a wine
    Not for mortals' glass.

The good-wives, the house-wives,
    They shudder at my sin:
But much they'd give to learn to weave
    Cloth of spiders'-spin!

My pet-fox, my russet fox,
    He ravishes their geese,
Yet none dare call out the hounds
    If they would know peace!

On a day of falling leaves
    I met the young Squire;
I gave him a sidelong look
    That set his face a-fire.

The bonny young Squire,
    He dreams in his bed;
But not of golden curlylocks
    Nor round cheeks of red,

Nor of blue eyes, the gentle eyes
    Of Parson Jones' Nell—
But of red hair, and green eyes
    That have looked on Hell!

Dream, pretty Squirekin!
    It's small use to burn!
For when the moon is up
    The wood-wife will turn

The Song of the Sun ❧ Leah Bodine Drake

Three times widdershins,
    And greet where ye stood
The shagged men, the satyr men
    Who creep from the wood!

House Accursed

"A curse upon this house!" cried he,
    Slamming the door behind,
Turning to shake a furious fist
    At windows closed and blind.

"A curse upon it, night and day,
    From north unto the south,
And east and west, and in and out,
    I curse it with my mouth!

"Down with the house of treachery,
    And down with all within!"
While those who listened gave no sign
    Or answer to his din.

But as the lengthening shadows fell
    Of dark hills all around,
From that day forward fell the curse
    On all that house and ground.

For panes grew cloudy with greenish film,
    That once had been clear as air;
Doors stuck fast and a mirror cracked
    And the newell fell from the stair.

Fungi gleamed from the dairy's flags
    And walls grew dark with damp;
The chimney fouled and would not draw
    And the flame burned low in the lamp.

Fantasy in a Forest ❧ 1937–1941

Then up from the cellars swarmed the rats
    In frightened and frantic gangs!
They slew the cat on the kitchen floor
    And the dog howled under their fangs.

Tails and whiskers and bloodshot eyes,
    They hurried away in the dark.—
That was the night the well went dry
    And the lamp would not show a spark.

Quietly, steadily sank the house . . . . .
    Of those who huddled here,
One went mad, but nobody fled,
    Bound in a spell of fear.

Then came the night when the earth beneath
    Cracked with a stealthy sound,
And a huge mouth opened . . . . and all that house
    Vanished into the ground!

The Minotaur

The Minotaur
Did nothing but roar:
He'd had nothing for weeks
But 'teen-age Greeks.

Rhymes without Reason; or, History Made Difficult

First lesson:
Egypt's king, the Pharaoh,
Was glad to let the Israelites go;
He frankly told Moses
"I don't like their noses."

The Song of the Sun ~ Leah Bodine Drake

Second lesson:
Eric the Red
Ate crackers in bed.
He said crumbs felt nice,
And it was kindness to mice.

Third lesson:
Catherine the Great of Russia
Called all her lovers "Macushla."
When told it was Irish,
She said "It sounds stylish."

Fourth lesson:
The sun-god of the Nile
Had horns and a smile.
His real name was Ra,
But his kids called him "pa."

Fifth lesson:
Leonardo da Vinci
Never lived in Cinci-
nnati or Buffalo,—
At least, as far as I know.

Sixth lesson:
Anne of Cleves
Chewed tobacco leaves.
When her friends protested.
She had them arrested.

Seventh lesson:
Philip of Spain
Liked to sit in the rain;
He would use no umbrella,—
What a deuce of a fellow!

FANTASY IN A FOREST ~ 1937–1941

Eighth lesson:
Messer Marco Polo
Had a pup named Rollo.
It could speak Chinese,
Had a gold collar and fleas.

Ninth lesson:
James the Pretender
Put his feet on the fender;
When kicked from the settle
He put them in the kettle.

Tenth lesson:
Buckingham's duke
Found mice in his peruke.
He knew it was messy,
But said wigs were dressy.

From Nonsensical Rhymes*

A bersark was one
who killed bears for fun.
As bear-killers
bersarkers were killer-dillers.

Hereward the Wake
loved carraway-cake.
He went thisaway and thataway
looking for carraway.

The Emperor Baber
cut off heads with his sabre.

*Clerihews.

The Song of the Sun ~ Leah Bodine Drake

He said it killed time
and didn't cost a dime.

William Shakespeare
lived on skittles and beer.
He swore the only vittles
were beer and skittles.

I Met a Lion

I met a lion in the sands.
He came and fawned upon my hands,
He came and lay across my door.
I cannot hunt him anymore.

He was the shape beyond the light,
The voice that thundered in the night
That roused my fear and cruelty:
I thought he was my enemy!

But he is good and he is mild,
An innocent, huge and golden child.
No fear of me he seems to know:
I broke my arrows and my bow.
Now days are long and sleep comes late
With nothing left to hunt or hate.

Go back, good Lion, to your sands,
To your own tawny, outlawed bands
And leave my ancient hate to me—
I will not have your charity,
I will not have my foe my friend!
Such peace between our kinds would end
That darling fiction I embrace:
The over-lordship of my race.

FANTASY IN A FOREST ❧ 1937–1941

Fantasy in a Forest

> ... *"And it is well known that the Unicorn, by touching the Water with his Horn, doth render it free from Poison; and each Creature of the Wild putteth his Trust in him and doth Drink thereof."*
> —BESTIARY OF AMELIUS OF GAULT

Between two unknown trees I stood
Within an Abyssinian wood.

Unseen beside a cold pool's brink
I saw the beasts come down to drink—
The elephant, the shy gazelle,
The leopard in his painted fell,
The camel coloured like the sand,
The serpent like a burning brand,
The horse, giraffe, the red baboon
Down from the Mountains of the Moon,
The zebra striped with light and shade
Beside the lion, unafraid.

Around the pool they took their stand:
I could have touched them with my hand!
No creature moved, no creature leapt,
But all a curious silence kept,
And nothing in the forest stirred:
They waited as if for a word.

Then stepping lonely from the wild
He came, the white, the undefiled,
With ivory hoof and pearly horn—
The one immaculate unicorn!
Moving serenely to the pond,
Bending no blade nor ferny frond
Beneath the quiet of his tread,

The Song of the Sun ❧ Leah Bodine Drake

He dipped his proud and lovely head
And that dark fountain's veil was torn
By the sharp splendour of his horn.

Around the circle went a sigh
As if a breeze were passing by;
And then beside the curving brink
I watched the creatures crouched to drink
Those waters cleansed and strangely blessed
By that unhuman exorcist.
They drank together, shy gazelle,
The leopard in his painted fell . . .

I saw these things the day I stood
Lost in that Abyssinian wood.

Full Moon, 1940

Now up from Hades creeps the moon:
Among the trees her shadows wake,
The lean wolf trembles in the brake,
The long tide seeks the silver dune.

The cities crouched in gothic dark
Regret their proud, reflective spires,
And lovers curse her classic fires
And village dogs forbear to bark.

Destruction comes upon her flood:
The bombers find their human prey,
And through her bright unnatural day
Perish the beautiful and good.

Sink down, O Luna! from our sky
To some black under-pit of space:

FANTASY IN A FOREST ❧ 1937–1941

Beneath your bland benignant face
The ancient civilizations die.

Ungild the dome, withdraw your light
From mirroring fountain in the square;
Give back the highroads of the air
To the unmapped, deluding night!

The Girl on the Saw-Backed Mountain

Flatland fields grow tall tobacco,
    Corn-rows stretch where the rivers glide;
Lean and lorn lie the hill-folks' acres,
    Clinging tight to a mounting's side.
Rocks jut out of the old hill's shoulder,
    Might near jarring the plow from hand:
Hard's the life on the saw-backed mounting;
    Easy's the life in the level land.

Flatland men are kind and handsome,
    Build big barns and plow with a team;
Hill-born men are cruel and careless,
    Wild and troublous as a mounting-stream.
Shooting, fighting, allus in a ruckus,—
    But talking sweet as the whippoorwills!
Heavy's the heart of the foolish maiden
    Who loves a man from the saw-backed hills.

I could have a house where the lands are level,
    Porch and parlor and a broad front hall.
Hill-shack's old and bald and chinky,
    Grey as a 'possum, and going-for to fall;
Muddy ol' hound-dog messing up the cabin;
    Fire on the hearth, and snow blowing in the door . . . . .
Hard come-by is a hill-shack's plunder;
    Rich are the houses on the valley floor!

The Song of the Sun ❧ Leah Bodine Drake

I'd don my gown with the rosy ribbons,
    Put on my shoes when I got to town,
And find me a lowland man tomorrow
    To wed me and bed me in silk and down—
But I'm feared I'd hone for my bony mounting,
    The wind and the stars and the sourwood's flame,
And the sweet, sweet sound of a hill-boy's hailing,
    Coming 'long the branch side, calling me by name.

Lost Heritage

Adam sitting at his ease
    When the work was done;
To his right hand, left hand,
    Came a small son.

Abel cried, "Daddy,
    Come down to the pond!—
Make me a whistle
    From a willow-wand!"

"I never made a whistle
    From any kind of stick,—
I didn't have a father
    To show me such a trick;

"So I can't make willow-whistles,"
    Adam shook his head.
"Then find me a woodchuck's hole!"
    Son Cain said.

"I can hunt the lion,"
    Said Adam, "And the deer.
I never had time enough
    For woodchucks, I fear."

FANTASY IN A FOREST ✿ 1937–1941

Cain said, "Daddy,
    I know what let's do!—
Tell us about the time
    You were little, too!"

Adam looked upon his sons
    With a wistful eye;
Then he gazed upward
    At the silent sky:

"God," said Adam,
    "That you made me live
Without having been a boy
    I just can't forgive.

"I don't know a boyhood thing
    To hand to a son . . . . .
That's my lost heritage
    When all's said and done!

"I'm used now to Eden lost,
    To fighting thorn and thistle;
But oh, that I never had"—
    He sighed—"a willow whistle!"

King Gog and King Magog

Gog, he was a heathen king and Magog was his brother;
A fiery Genie was their Pa, and Sheba's queen their Mother.

The heavens split with lightnings the night that they were born,
And each babe grew a flaming beard before the break of morn!

They gobbled twenty cows a day and twenty tons of bread;
And forty slaves with forty drums would drum them up to bed.

The Song of the Sun ~ Leah Bodine Drake

These twins slept on an ivory couch
Carved from a mammoth's tooth,
And they wore dragon's scales for mail, they were a pair, forsooth!

Their steeds were zebras, ten abreast, that drew their cars of gold,
And all the jewels of Ala-ed-din were nothing to their hold.

O, Gog and Magog loved to fight! They fought the sly Chinese;
They fought the Huns, they fought the Tsar
And brought him to his knees.

They fought the King of all the Bears,
They killed his demon brother—
And when there was none left to fight, they fought each other.

And when they fell to earth, the crash was like a thunder-clap!
The tide ran inland for a week, and Hind slid down the map!

When Gog and Magog breathed their last a mountain opened wide,
And both were buried in its depths of emeralds, side by side:

It was the holy mountain Kâf that tombed those mighty men.
They were the giant-kings—their like will ne'er be seen again.

Gold from a Kettle

There was an old wizard who tried
    To make gold in a kettle, heigh-ho!
      Soapsuds and dew
      And red pepper, too,
The recipe said must go into the brew,—
    All must go into the kettle.

The hour was growing late
    And the wizard was old, heigh-ho;

Fantasy in a Forest ❧ 1937–1941

So the words he read
And the runes he said
Got all mixed up in his crazy head,
   And he put the Wrong Things in the kettle!

He put in a rainbow's arc,
   And a peacock's tail, heigh-ho!
   And a powdered wig
   (where the book said "Pig")
And a pearl or two and a musty fig—
   It all went into the kettle.

Abracadabra, whiz-bang!
   The brew boiled over heigh-ho!
   And out came a flight
   Of creatures of light,
Elf and sylphin and fairy sprite,—
   All flew out of the kettle!

They shimmered around the room,
   They swarmed o'er the wizard, heigh-ho!
   They plucked at his clothes,
   And tickled his toes,
And twitched the spectacles off his nose,
   And upset the magical kettle!

Then the wizard picked up his gown
   And he danced with a heigh-hi-ho!
   And he flew away
   With pixie and fay,
And nobody's found him to this day!
   Now wasn't *that* gold from a kettle?
      Heigh-ho!
The best kind of gold from a kettle!

The Song of the Sun ❧ Leah Bodine Drake

Drake of Devon

A.D. 1573

"Who is this sailing on our Main?" the ruffled Señors say,
  Peering seaward from their fort on Nombre de Dios Bay;
"And who's it thieves our Indian gold and fills our hearts with fear?"
"It's El Draque!" their soldiers cry, "the Devon men are here!"

> For the Dons can't keep young Frankie Drake
>   In Devon, safe and dry,
> Since first he saw in Panama
>   The gold-trains go by.

"Drake! Drake! Drake!" the waves sing this refrain,
  "On the high seas and the narrow seas he's sailing once again!"

A.D. 1577

"Whose ship is beating through the storm?" the whales and mermen say,
"The hard ice weighs the rigging down, the sails with sleet are grey.
And what's that lusty shouting for that cracks the frosty morn?
It's Drake and his bully-boys, roaring 'round the Horn!"

> For where no man has steered a ship
>   The Devon man can make
> Through wind and rain and hurricane
>   A road for England's sake.

"Drake! Drake! Drake!" the stars sing this refrain,
  "On the high seas and the narrow seas he's sailing once again!"

A.D. 1588

"Whose guns are these that thunder on our fleet, from Plymouth Town?
Whose are these flaming boats that ride our great Armada down?"
The dark Dons curse into their beards,—"El Draque is here again!
He's called the tempest from the Pole to drive us back to Spain!"

FANTASY IN A FOREST ❧ 1937–1941

> For none can challenge England's Drake
> And live to tell the tale,—
> When Devon gun and arm are done
> The good Lord sends a gale!

"*Drake! Drake! Drake!*" the winds sing this refrain,
"*On the high seas and the narrow seas he's sailing once again!*"

A.D. 1940

"What ship is this that guides our craft through waters dark with death?"
The Tommies out in Dunkirk Road* question with bated breath;
"*Their* wings of steel benight the sky, *their* mines befoul the sea!"
A ghostly figure on the deck makes answer cheerily,

> "Ahoy, my hearties, follow me
> And scorn *their* grisly sport!
> Ye'll always find my Golden Hind
> Will steer ye straight to port!"

"*Drake! Drake! Drake! Brave souls may see him plain
On the high seas and the narrow seas, till England's safe again!*"

Griffon's Gold

Men told him:
Do not hunt the griffon
guarding his secret gold!
There is no griffon—in all sooth,
we tell you there is naught of truth
in that hoar myth—
'tis but an old-wives'-tale once told:

* * *

*Dunkirk Road is the sea-lane off the French coast.

The Song of the Sun ❧ Leah Bodine Drake

Thus did they speak, the wise ones and the old.
So he turned his back
on those glittering peaks
and gave over
dreams of a prize that no man can discover.
And though he feels a lack
of something jeopardous and bright
to salt his days, he never now
climbs higher than his plough
climbs a low hill's brow
from dawn to night.

But up in the fabulous mountains,
past the pines and the pebbled fountains,
a mighty shape lies crouched
in the blaze of sun.
Over the tawny fur
the great wings fold,
where, on the last red scar,
at the door of his rocky dun,
the griffon keeps his ancient ward
over that immemorial hoard
of gold!

On a Night of Stars

The air revealed a glimmering form
Whose flesh was mist, whose blood was fire,
Blown by some inter-stellar storm
From lands beyond the Swan and Lyre.

In speech that was unlipped but heard
He told me of his outpost shore,
Whose cloudless noons are never scarred
By death's long shadow on the door.

Fantasy in a Forest ❧ 1937–1941

My soul cried out, "How happy he
Whose planet has no myth of pain!
Where that which is will ever be
And neither flesh nor seasons change."

Our hearts speed on from sun to sun
To make at last the grasses' bread,
And those we love we see undone:
"But what is love?" the spirit said.

His eyes told all their alien truth:
No pity welled from springs of grief;
His race had not found beauty's mouth
As tender as her time is brief.

Our double wicks of birth and loss
(The old immutable gemini)
Burn in life's lamp, and through its glass
Shines one unriven lucency.

Then did I know how blest we are
Who, in our span of transient breath
Upon a dusty, twy-lit star,
Can clasp the ways of love and death.

Man in Winter

This is the season when the earth grows small
And crouches in herself without a cry.
This is the season when all men look tall
Against a landscape tightened by a sky

That leans upon the hills, by woods that press
Their branches on the grey, low-lying cloud;
And over fields once peopled by the grass,
Unrivaled now man walks unique and proud.

The Song of the Sun ~ Leah Bodine Drake

Four-sided to the sight his houses rise
That summer's trees held in a long green spell,
And chimneys take possession of the skies
That the lost larks have left an empty shell:

For earth has shed her voices bird by bird,
And all her songs pursue the flying sun;
Her cold breast trembles at the briefest word
Flung into quiet by the hunter's gun.

This is the time of man: now he alone
Looms giant in the earth, his alien light
Stares from his windows like a challenge thrown
Into the face of old, advancing night.

The Hen-Wife's Chickens

The Hen-Wife in the valley
    Is a witch!
See her chickens scratching
    In the ditch?

Oh, *they* look all right,—
    But I know
She has others that
    She'll never show!

One is purple
    With a golden tail;
One can sing
    Like a nightingale.

Fantasy in a Forest ❧ 1937–1941

One wears a ruff,
    One's striped like a kit,
And one can turn
    The Hen-Wife's spit.

One has a little crown
    Just like a queen,
And one can play the
    Tambourine!

Jilly the Herd-Girl
    Swears and vows
A hen came walking
    And made a bow

Just like a Christian!
    And Jilly will swear
That the chicken asked her
    The way to the Fair!

Here comes the Hen-Wife
    Leaning on her stick!
Her eyes are gleaming . . . .
    Come away, quick,

Before she changes *you* to a chick!

Honey from the Lion
1942–1948

HONEY FROM THE LION ❧ 1942–1948

Vestal

Confess that in your secret wood
The season stands forever winter;
The suns of summer cannot enter
A place of such implastic mood.

No hunter's loud halloo will crack
The calm that coats these prismed aisles,
No whisper sways these icy bells:
A word would splinter to a flake.

Your world's the snowscape in its globe
Caught in a mignon glassy trance,
Too small for passion's lordly dance,
Too locked for sorrow's knife to probe.

But once, they say, a satyr came
Curious, shy, from outer lands;
The wind-bells clashed beneath his hands,
He stamped the astonished snow to flame!

Creeping into a hollow place
He found a frozen heart-shaped pond
Armoured with crusted reed and wand.
He stooped: he saw no Pannish face

Answer his own, no horn-pricked head
Mirrored in waters blanked with ice!
Amazement held him till a pulse
Of terror shook him, and he fled.

Your woods no other vagrants know—
Only this one this little lust.
The aisles are bare, yet never lost
Are prints of savage hooves in snow.

The Song of the Sun ❧ Leah Bodine Drake

The Singer from the Waste

I made the wilderness my home
And seven ravens fed me there.
I tamed the lion in his lair
And shared with him a honey-comb.

On such precarious meats I throve,
The wells from which I drank were salt,
And I grew wise and free from fault
And there was none for me to love.

But demons sang to me by night
And angels walked with me at noon;
The face of God to me was shown
Thorned in a bush of living light.

Then from the waste I journeyed forth
Girded with hunger, pride and pain,
Down to the cities of the plain
And fire tethered on the hearth.

I hastened in on bleeding feet
For I had goodly words to say:
But all the towns were rich and gay
And all the waters there were sweet.

I drank my fill, I sleeked my hair,
I bleached with subtle herbs my brown;
I took a lover from the town
And he for words had little care.

I said: Tomorrow I must rise
And tell men all that I have learned
And how the holy visions burned:
But languor weighed my limbs and eyes.

HONEY FROM THE LION ❧ 1942–1948

Now by my empty desert grot
The birds of desolation scream;
And when I sleep I seldom dream,
And what I knew I've long forgot.

The Fruit Uneaten

The fruit was in my hand:
"Take, eat," he said.
But I would only stand
And look, and be afraid,

And look, and wish to sink
My teeth within
Those satin sides, and drink
Its cider sharp and thin.

Not that it was so fair
As apples go:
I have seen orchards where
Far finer grow!

But still its smell was sweet
And I was starved:
He said again, "Take, eat."
My fingers curved

About its russet waist,
I felt the flesh within;
My tongue crept out to taste
Its bitter skin.

One bite was all I took:
I never reached the core.
Its rind I barely broke
While craving more:

The Song of the Sun ❧ Leah Bodine Drake

I feared his slanting brow
And grinning mouth . . . . .
Now I am old and know
A burning drought

For want of perilous fruit
I would not eat,
Sensing its snaky root,
His cloven feet.

Gage to a Lover

I cannot give
Clear pale honey
From a neat hive
In orchard sunny:

Rich and dark
Is the comb I promise,
Ripped from an oak
And stung with malice.

O do not ask
For a meadow-pool
That lies at dusk
Serene and cool:

Mine is the brine
Of restless seas
Distilled in wine
To burn or freeze;

And I learned song
From a falcon's throat,

Honey from the Lion ~ 1942–1948

So do not long
For the stock-dove's note.

Do not demand
That I should wear
A halo bland
Upon my hair:

Pan kissed my brows
When I was born,
And each one wears
A graceless horn!

If you could choose
You'd have me be
A garden enclosed,
A symmetry

Of pleached green alleys
And statued walks,
With beds of lilies
On smooth meek stalks:

But I'm a tangle
Of nettle and briar
Whose flowers spangle
My boughs like fire;

And with the rose
Which you would gather
A sharp thorn grows:
One from the other

May not be torn
Or both you'll lose—
So dare my thorn
And wear my rose!

The Song of the Sun ~ Leah Bodine Drake

A Vase from Araby

Shaped like a tear-drop, pale as haze
Down where the mirage-cities stand,
Here is a blue enamel vase
Brought overseas from the fabled land.

Stoppered with turquoise, scribed around
With golden symbols that curve and flow
Like a guardian serpent, the flask is bound
In some secret spell of the long ago.

If curious fingers should break the seal,
What would be found in its narrow hold:
Poison to murder or herbs to heal,
Attar of roses or dust of gold?

Beware! .... In a cloud as black as shame,
Amazed eyes might see a Form appear,
With furious wings and hair of flame ....
The Jinni for ages imprisoned here!

The Window on the Stair

As I went up the small steep stair
    The sun was dipping low
And the little window's coloured panes
    Turned into jewels aglow:
Purple, golden and ruby-red,
    Emerald as Samarkand,
They twinkled against the last long rays
    Like the doors to Faërieland.

HONEY FROM THE LION ❧ 1942–1948

The house was hushed as the snow outside
    And time was still for a space,
Await for something to come to pass
    In that light, in that glamoured place;
Something—I knew not what or how—
    Would awake in that rainbow light . . . . .
I stood looking up from the midmost step
    And my throat felt small and tight.

Then a clock chimed, off in a distant room,
    The sun slipped under the rim:
Suddenly all of the little panes
    Were lusterless, cold and dim.
Disenchanted, they held the dusk;
    And I went on up the stair,
Never to know what magical thing
    Had almost happened there.

The Phoenix Egg

If trees should spread their roots in air
And fruit grow underground for worms:
If men should water weed and tare
And curse the wheat and praise the storms:

If fowls began to talk, and deer
Should mate with panthers in the wild
And wells turned salt as any tear
And lions tore the lion's child,

Then we could say: Come, let us weep,
For wrong has won and truth's denied;
The sun shall join the moon in sleep
And God again be crucified.

The Song of the Sun ❧ Leah Bodine Drake

But still the Spring-awakened tree
Translates her winter dream to peach;
The shell the waves sucked out to sea
Lies tossed upon another beach;

The fingers of the young grass grip
The hollow burrowed by the bomb;
The honey thickens in the skep,
The holy child stirs in the womb.

We will not weep: through all her pain
Earth neither hastes, nor holds, her breath:
The phoenix-egg cracks wide again
And life soars from the bones of death.

Changeling

I am out on the wind
    In the wild, black night,
On the wings of the owl
    I take my flight—
On the ghostly wings of the great white owl;
And whether the night be fair or foul,
Or the moon be up or the thunder growl,
    Happy I be,
    Happy I be
When the changeling blood runs green in me!

When meek folk sleep
    In their dull soft beds,
I creep over roots
    That the weasel treads,
Where the squat red lamps of the toadstools glow,
And only the fox knows the ways I go
And nobody knows the things I know!

HONEY FROM THE LION ❧ 1942–1948

Wise I be,
Wise I be
When the changeling blood runs green in me!

O Mother, slumber
    And do not wake!
Thin voices called
    From the rain-wet brake,
And the child you cradled against your breast
Is out in the night on the black wind's crest—
For only the wild can give me rest.
    O sad I be,
    Sad I be
When the changeling blood runs green in me!

Retrogression

"Subterranean cities will be man's only defense against the atom-bomb, says aerial armaments expert."
    .... NEWS ITEM, August, 1945.

The spent fox slinks along the hill
To win the refuge of his den:
From fury of the hounds and men
The earth gives sanctuary still.

The hare leaps from the sunny rock;
She slips beneath the naked land,
And in the bulwarks of the sand
Forgets the shadow of the hawk.

Now toward a sky turned strangely feral
Mankind must bend his rigid back,
And seek the scorned and ancient black
Womb of earth: from man-made peril

The Song of the Sun ~ Leah Bodine Drake

To crouch there in the dusty house
Where not for ages has he lain;
And death must look for him again
Beside the hedgehog and the mouse.

Bread of Solitude

I have a hunger hot and deep
To leave the world of men, and go
Where woods their cleansing lore impart
And rocks teach all that I would know.

I want large airs that are not thinned
By heavy breathings of the crowd,
Or shaped to rooms where men have sinned,
Sucked sapless by the dull and cowed.

I would drink water at its source
Upon a granite-breasted hill
Before it seeks the water-course
And marries with the forge and mill.

In some blue temple of the air,
Remote upon a sunburnt crest
I would recall the wise and fair,
I would remember all the best.

Then strengthened by the wine of space
And filled with bread of solitude,
I could meet once again my race
And call him friend and find him good.

Honey from the Lion ❧ 1942–1948

Music for Sun and Moon

All over Italy the chimes
Ring up the evening on the air,
And Eire's belfried music climbs
The sunset's old and ruined stair;

A shadow in the Kentish wood,
The nightingale salutes the moon,
The lovers murmur, and the flood
Of ocean trembles to the dune;

And by the Congo's muffled shore
The hoarse and painted drums resound;
The conch-shells by the Ganges roar,
And bays the Thessalonian hound;

The cock in triumph crows her out
With horn whereby he wakes the sun;
In Tartary the mountains shout,
The Mongols beat their leather gongs,

And pious Mecca's minarets
Fling fierce cries into the blue;
The lark ejects his crystal jets,
The whistles of the cities blow.

Around the bland clock-face of time
The hours set their ambuscades,
And tick by tick the fires dim
Within the sun's huge heart, and fades

His savage shadow on the weak
And hollow moon; as toward the Lyre
Our planet spins, foredoomed to wreck
Upon those siren-rocks of fire,

The Song of the Sun 🙢 Leah Bodine Drake

Yet still, with frail and transient breath,
Time's ancient markers still we hail,
And Earth goes singing to her death
With tongues of bells and nightingales.

Enchanted Honey

Under this low, root-raftered roof
I sit with heavy heart and head,
By order of a wicked troll
To spin harsh nettles into thread.

A dancing elf, I fluttered near
The dark wood where this evil house
Peers beneath mossy thatches, like
An old grimalkin at a mouse.

Like all my fairy clan, I knew
A troll-wife dwells within, who swore
To capture every elf who dared
Approach her squat, root-guarded door.

O foolish fay!—I flew to taste
That rich, gold-gleaming honeycomb
Set out in acorn cups—such sweets
Could lure Lord Oberon from home!

What trollish sorceries were cast
About that honey on her sill
My fairy powers could not unwind
By magic wand. Bound by her will,

I toil at wicked spinning-wheel
Far, far from shining sun and star;

Honey from the Lion ⁓ 1942–1948

In cellar deep within her tree,—
The mole and toad my neighbours are.

My fairy kin seek everywhere,
Calling through fields of twilight dew—
I hear their lovely voices fade,
I hear the witch-wife's chuckles, too!

Never again the moonlit dance,
Never again my flower-home—
My wand is broken, and my wings bound
With dark, enchanted honeycomb.

Luna

The sun, impartial host,
Upon nine great globes showers
His charity. A ghost,
The moon is solely ours;

Only the burnt-out moon
Is still unique to Earth,
And shines for us alone,
And then with echoed worth.

In all the house of space
No ray from Luna spills
On any planet's face
But on these little hills;

And in this shallow air
Her singular wine is vialed
That wakes the hound's despair
And drives the poet wild.

The Song of the Sun ❧ Leah Bodine Drake

Ballad of the Seal-Woman's Daughter

I am half of the land
    And half of the water,
For my dam was a seal
    And I am her daughter.

I am sib to the land
    And kin to the sea,
For my dam was a seal,
    But a king sired me.

My father has built me
    A tapestried bower
Where twelve duke's daughters
    Serve, hour by hour.

Heroes and princes
    Come wooing me—
But there's never a one
    Who smells of the sea.

My old nurse tells me
    I must beware
When I walk on the shore
    With my unbound hair,

For out of the cold sea
    A lover may rise,
Dark, sleek and furry,
    With brown seal-eyes.

So I walk on the sands
    When the grey winds blow,
Afraid of the waves
    And what's below.

HONEY FROM THE LION ❧ 1942–1948

I sit with my maidens
    And weave at the loom—
And my flesh rebels
    At the fire-warm room:

For I'm not all beast
    And I'm not quite human,
Who have eyes of a seal
    In the face of a woman.

And how can I rest,
    A brown seal's daughter,
Who hates the land
    And fears the water?

Fairy Cider

A fairy made cider
    One blue autumn day,
From little crab-apples
    She'd stolen away

From a tangled old orchard,
    Forgotten and lorn.
Not a soul saw that fairy,
    Busy all morn

Filling her basket
    With tart little fruits,
Flitting back to her house
    In an oak-tree's roots.

Not a soul saw that fairy,
    In her tattered fern dress,
Turning apples to cider
    In her wee cider-press.

The Song of the Sun ❧ Leah Bodine Drake

Not a soul in the forest,—
    Fox, rabbit or elf,—
Saw her little stone jugs
    In a row on the shelf.

All alone lived the fairy,
    Far under the oak;
On her house dim and quiet
    The snow spread its cloak.

Howled wind in the branches;
    Froze river and pond;
Crouched hare in the bracken
    Deep under the ground.

The fairy, sly-smiling
    And snug in the gloom,
Emptied jug after jug,
    Grew drowsy and warm,

Curled up in the oak-leaves,
    And all Winter through
Dozed, tippled and dreamed
    On her sweet golden brew.

King Solomon

Solomon, old and worn and wise,
    Walked through his splendid halls;
Cedar were the beams thereof
    And linen hung the walls.

Wine gleamed in a golden cup,
    Fruit, on a golden tray:
Solomon bit into a plum,
    Tossed the half away.

And snug in the gloom, emptied jug after jug,

The Song of the Sun 🙢 Leah Bodine Drake

In small rooms screened with ivory,
    Like cells in honey-hives,
There smiled through spangled gauzery
    His thousand flawless wives.

And some were camphor-white, and some
    Were dark as Egypt's sky,
And all were skilled in arts of love:
    Solomon hurried by.

He came into a secret room
    Whose floor was purple tile
Traced with a golden pentagram.
    Here Solomon, long while

After strange gods had briskly strayed,
    Or raised the terrible Jinn;
Solomon yawned, and thought how stale
    Were all the crusts of sin.

Was there no new thing beneath the sun?—
    He sought his carven bed.
Two golden seraphs watched the foot,
    Two cherubim the head.

He took a parchment and a quill,
    Struck with a sudden thought:
There was a great truth he must tell,
    A poem to be wrought!

"*Vanity, vanity,*" he scrawled;
    A sigh welled from his throat.
(How comfortable bed was!) "*All
    Is vanity,*" he wrote.

HONEY FROM THE LION ⁊ 1942–1948

Turning Point

Nowhere foretold,
This could be true:
That God, grown old,
May turn and view

The whole crazed scheme
Of life and fate,
Love's murdered dream,
The thrones of hate,

The endless terror
That orders us:
And cry, in horror,
"Did *I* do thus?"

Nativities

"If life exists on other worlds what is Christ to them?"—(*Anon.*)

Not only here may magian eyes
Read dazzling portents on the black
Pages of night: to other skies,
Where swings a wilder zodiac,

The shepherds and the kings may kneel
Among fantastic beasts, and see
A strange *star*, where the old stars wheel,
Blazon their hopes' Nativity.

Not only here on Earth the thorn
May blossom, and the heavenly seed
Wing down choiring clouds to burn
Some chosen womb for mortals' need.

The Song of the Sun ~ Leah Bodine Drake

Wherever creatures with each breath
Draw in their heritage of pain,
Wherever life contends with death,
The Word descends to flesh again.

What Eden's fade, what falls from grace
Wither life's fruit in alien air
Upon some planet out in space,
Is mystery. But Love walks there.

And brings the mercy of His crook
To fields no Adam's son beholds,—
And leads at last to one sweet brook
The sheep of all His folds!

The Comet

With his turbulent golden hair
Flung out behind him
This strange, compassionless angel takes his way
Across the roof of midnight.
Beyond all knowing is where or why he goes:

We, of stranger clay,
Can only gaze with wonder at his passing.
Is it curse or prayer
That hurries him on while his mane
Scatters sparks behind him?
He does not tarry at Earth,
We are not his desire.

What shall we be, and where, when this busy hero
Burns through the sky again on his secret quest?
Cold be our fires
And Earth herself an ember,
While the unappeasable flames still burn in his breast.

HONEY FROM THE LION ↬ 1942–1948

Bird's-Eye View

It is not well for man to see
Earth from too high an altitude:
Into one green obscurity
Submerge the evil and the good.

The airman looks down depths of space
And sees events as shadows pass:
Man seems a grub without a face,
Grief but a cricket in the grass.

The world shrinks to a painted toy,
The towns sink level with the dust;
Limbs pain-contorted mimic joy
And love takes attitudes of lust.

The lonely arrogance of height
Distills a power sweet to taste:
It gave to Lucifer delight
And tempted Jesus in the waste.

Oh, it is perilous to stay
Too long above these anguished clods!—
Too high to feel man's charity,
Not high enough to fathom God's.

December Stars

The Great Bear thrusts a bright paw forth
To rip cold honey from the Hive
Where hum the white bees of the North.
The sky-track sees Auriga drive

The Song of the Sun ~ Leah Bodine Drake

His jeweled chariot through space
On wheels that burn with frozen fire.
Across dark depths the Twins embrace;
Crackling with ice the Chair rolls higher.

Orion, toreador of heaven,
Now flings his cape against the Bull
Pierced with the banderillas Seven:
The tide of winter is at the full!

Again the stelliscripts combine
Above the wounded fields of Earth
To form the old, familiar sign
That once shone on a holy birth;

And once again men raise their eyes
In a wild hope that even now
Some saviour-star will rise and blaze
Between the Lion and the Plough.

Cold Orchard

She walks always in her intimate, own
Season, dreaming of past summer's wealth
On winter hills. The fruits are picked and gone.
Wandering under naked trees, her breath
Clouds as she cries, "There are rich fruits
Still on these branches—winter has not come!"
And shakes bare boughs or fumbles at the roots
For some forgotten apple, a blackened plum.

HONEY FROM THE LION ❧ 1942–1948

Bats

Against a leaf-green twilight sky
The little bats in rapture fly,
Circling in couples or alone
To some still music of their own.

By day, each like a shabby mouse,
Skulks in the crannies of the house,
A timid, frail and alien thing.
But dusk sees spread each velvet wing
In sudden pride. Their right-of-way
Lies on the edge of dying day.

Then up the clover-scented stairs
Of night they chase the plodding Bears,
Wheel to Antares and are gone,
To brush the white wings of the Swan,
Swoop where the Dogs relentless roam,
And back to Spica's harvest-home.

No longer cousin to the mole,
Within their darkling lands they rule,
Kin to the stars and welcome there,
These dusky princes of the air!

The Unclimbed Hill

There is a hill I shall not climb:
Too high its pinnacle, too steep
The stony, strong flanks, where like slim
White flames the birches skyward leap.

But I can see it from below,
Looming above the crouching hills,

The Song of the Sun ❧ Leah Bodine Drake

Wrapped in a mystery of snow
Or purpled when October spills

Her dark, enchanted dwale. At night
Polaris kindles on its crest—
Great neighbour!—always in my sight,
Guarding what glens of leafy rest,

What fountains for the spirit's cup,
What unstained havens from our pain,
What honey-hives for us to sup,
Unknown to bees of any plain?

It is too high—I shall not go
Up on those slopes of brighter air,
But it is happiness to know
Such height, such lordliness is there.

The House in the Hollow

When we take the long way
    Home from school,
(Down along the hollow,
    By the froggy pool)

We pass a little house
    Half way across,
Hidden among hollies
    And green with moss.

Whoever lived there
    Moved long ago:
It's lonesome and scary
    When the sun is low.

HONEY FROM THE LION ❧ 1942–1948

Wonder what it looks like
    In the rooms inside?
Bold Johnny Johnson
    Says he nearly died,—

He crept past the hollies,
    Through the broken gate,
And it seemed like the chimney
    Was made of chocolate!

There was a cookie roof
    And gingerbread door.
And the door began to open . . . . .
    He didn't stay for more!

So we all pass quickly
    And keep very still—
For a Witch might step out
    On her peppermint sill!

And if she beckoned
    We would have to follow,
Like Hansel and Gretel,
    To her house in the hollow!

The Black Peacock

When the peaks of Kâf receive the dawn,
And the doe seeks water with her fawn,
Down in the gardens of the Khan
    Wakes the one black peacock.

An alien in the feathered herd
Of peacocks indigo and verde,
He is the sole obsidian bird,
    The proud black peacock.

The Song of the Sun ❧ Leah Bodine Drake

In what strange jungle did he nest?
Beneath what peri's burning breast?—
This darkling prince, shunned by the rest,—
    The lone black peacock?

Beside the marble-prisoned lakes
He cries his grief. His screaming wakes
The close, night-drenched acacia-brakes,
    The sad black peacock.

And humbler birds, grown silent there,
Thrill to the anger and despair
Of one too splendid and too rare:
    The proud lone sad black peacock.

Snowy Night

Somewhere sinks the hidden sun;
Earth and sky are strangely one,
Blurred with whiteness, field and town,
As hush on hush the snow comes down.

Now the cedar's arms are bowed
With a load of frozen cloud,
And the corn-shocks weirdly stand
Like ghost-tepees in the land.
Now will chipmunk families sleep
In their leaf-lined burrows deep.
On the hillside, in a rock
Swept by sheltering hemlocks,
Bright-eyed foxes in a nest
Huddle to each other's breasts.
In his hole fat woodchuck drouses,
Fairies sleep in tree-root houses;
And children cuddle in their beds,

HONEY FROM THE LION ❧ 1942–1948

As over all the dreaming heads
The kindly blanket of the air
Holds the round world in its care,
Guarding from Space above, below,
Colder, colder than any snow.

Cinder-Jewels

Old Giant Grimly Gore, club on shoulder,
Clumps down the hill as the night grows colder.

His big boots bore great holes in the snow,
His one eye reddens like a forge a-glow.

Muttering and grumbling he stalks toward the home
In the Wuthering Wood, of the Cinder-Gnome.

Old Grimly Gore, thump thump thump,
Sees the warm smoke from the chimney stump,

Sees the casement shine like a fiery rose
(While the cold creeps in and nibbles his toes).

There sits the Cinder-Gnome supping his gruel,
And feeding his fire, jewel by jewel:

That fire of marvel, of which they tell
From Land of Cockaigne to Hy Braseil,

For its coals are rubies out of the sun,
Radioactive, every one!

Oh, the giant longs for the burning jools!
His one eye weeps, his wide mouth drools.

The Song of the Sun ❧ Leah Bodine Drake

Small good it does him, as he knows well—
The gnome will neither lend nor sell.

Grimly Gore thinks of his castle cold,
Of the frozen emeralds in his hold,—

Gems of Earth, giving out no heat—
Oh, how will he warm his poor old feet?

He stands and shivers, old Grimly Gore,
On the weather-side of the gnome's wee door,

Looking and longing, all by his lone,
(And the cold creeps in and cracks a bone.)

Birds in a Barn

Birds are the heirs
of all deserted barns.
Long, long after
men and their beasts are gone
the birds remain.
Swallows nest in the rafters,
sparrows peck at the corn
scattered from harvest-years,
and through sun and rain
there is the flutter and stir
of pigeon wings.

Old barns die slowly:
life like a tide runs out
from manger and mow.
One day the cows are gone,
and the soft-eyed mares.
There are no sounds of hooves

HONEY FROM THE LION ~ 1942–1948

on the rotting floor
or the clank of plough,
nor the scent of hay on the air.
Time has drained all away—
the creak of harness, the calls
of men at their labor.
The worn beams fall from the roof,
and the walls have the wind for neighbour.

Build as high and as firm as he will,
man passes
and the others come into their own,
the bright-winged masses
that had the land at the first:
the sparrows swarm,
the swallows mate and are born and die,
and the pigeons fly
from the stalls to the musty loft.

This is ever the way with a farm
whose life is past:
only the birds are left,
only the birds have the barn at the very last.

A Country Grave

Under this final stone
    Lies one whose life took form
From change: the seasons' round,
    Star risings, drouth, and storm;

Who scanned the skies for rain
    In fall, could prophesy
How soon the snows would come
    From watching the wild geese fly.

The Song of the Sun ~ Leah Bodine Drake

The ordered turnabout
    Of bud and bloom and fruit
Gave wonder and delight
    To him whose being's root

Took hold on ancient things:
    The young green shoots of corn
Seemed the fresh miracles
    They were in Eden's morn.

How can he sleep thus, when
    Once more above him now
Arcturus climbs the hill,
    His fields await his plow?

No Refuge

Over the sodden fields through which I pass
there comes a sullen wind that smells of snow.
Quail run like blown brown leaves
in the sere grass.
The year slopes down to death,
The light fades.
Slow,

and slower yet, my steps. Beyond grey hills
mourns the sluggish freight's long whistle.
Only the west's
false fires burn farm-windows.
Thin mist fills
wet hollows, clots the hedge, the deserted nests.

Closer the old house crouches to the earth:
here is the body's haven—
shut the door on the dark wind!

HONEY FROM THE LION ❧ 1942–1948

But from more secret storms there is no roof:
no refuge from the cold wastes of the mind.

Earth: Atomic Age

In the galactic swirl
A flake, minute in girth;
Of water more than soil—
How humble is the Earth!

How frail her glowworm spark
Against Antares' blaze!
In the surrounding dark
How brief her brightest days!

Trailing her outcast moon
She bears her swarming life,
Breeding a mote called man
Given to noise and strife,

An ape-like, angry folk:
From many a milder race—
The antelope, the oak—
He steals her living space.

And if he lifts his arm
Against his mother, Earth,
In one last, senseless storm
And kindles her to death,

What star would shine the less?
What world would cease to turn
In all the universe,
To watch one morsel burn?

The Song of the Sun ❧ Leah Bodine Drake

Yet in this grain of sand
Beset, beperiled now,
Is Leonardo's hand,
And Keats, and Helen's brow.

And if Earth dies, dies all
Of Greece . . . . the Parthenon,
The Trojans on their wall . . . .
And Rome, and Avalon:

Lost in the shock that kills
Her Alps, her legend'd sea,
Crumbling with all her hills,
And one called Calvary.

Daphne

I, who turned into a tree
when the god's passion flamed on me,

See come to my dark-shining tent
ere the hot noons are spent,

Lovers, laughing and afraid,
who seek the honeyed shade
of Daphne, laurel-maid.

Lovers, who kiss and clip
and lie beneath my flowers lip to lip,

And little know their innocent jeweled bower
was born in a far hour

HONEY FROM THE LION ~ 1942–1948

From one girl's fear of love!
And on their faces from the boughs above

Rain down my pearl, my coral-spangled tears
for those lost girl-years.

To an Atheist

You map for me your personal space:
A close, unpeopled emptiness
Around your ego . . . . nothing else.
What an unappetizing place!

Now mine is filled with glittering towers,
And wonderful wheeled and burning things,
And wide enough for angels' wings
And Oh, such Thrones, such fiery Powers!

Cold Comfort

Death, who binds with tighter jess
The hawk, and folds the wren in earth,
Shall find a place for me no less
Than for his guests of greater worth.

With all the legended dead I'll lie,
As deep as Sheba in her tomb,
My stilled song one with Roland's cry,
His comrade in death's ample room.

Companion of the least and best:
Though no bronze tablets tell my tale,
What man shall say whose is the dust,
Caesar's or mine, blown down the gale?

The Song of the Sun ~ Leah Bodine Drake

Then, heart, take comfort in the word
That death can even every score.
(*Ah, let me live—a worm, a weed,
But living!* the heart cries evermore.)

The Beaches Beyond Oblivion

Down the long beaches of the past
they shine among sea-wrack and broken shells:
the face of Helen, Roland's horn
and Khayyam's scattered rose.

Somehow they still survive the ebb and pull
of oblivion's dark tide:
High Tara clanging with its shields and harps,
Penelope's torn web
and Jason's silvering oar
stuck upright in the sand.

Here is the sword Excalibur
still sweaty with the mark of Arthur's hand,
and that small rocketing bird
is Shelley's lark.

And my hope it is, that something I may say,
some verse or rhyme,
might wash up on that shore like a drifted spar
from the drowned ship that was I.

     *   *   *

What was the vessel's name?
        No matter.

Honey from the Lion ⁂ 1942–1948

Ballad of the Jabberwock

(*A Tale of Squankom*)

My grandmother tells me,
    When the lights are low,
How the Jabberwock appeared
    In Squankom, long ago.

First a frightened farmer,
    Tearing into town,
Told how his wife had seen
    Something big and brown,

Horned like a billy-goat
    And scaled like a dragon
Perched cross-legged
    On their brand-new wagon.

It leaped into the barn
    And hid in the hay.
She screeched blue murder
    And fainted away!

The Timmermans saw It,
    Coming from Cross Keys:
It crept through Corkray's Woods
    And peered 'round the trees.

Footprints were found in fields
    Clawed like a bird's;
It clumped over Marsh's roof,
    Gibbering words.

Then folk began to see it
    Here and everywhere,

Then folk began to see it . . . clinging to the steeple

HONEY FROM THE LION ~ 1942–1948

Clinging to the steeple,
   Winging through the air

With vans of a mighty bat;
   Or walking in a pasture
Upright as any man
   And cocky as a master!

Squankom locked all its doors,
   And bright lamps were lit
In chilly front-parlors
   Where folk seldom sit

Except for a funeral
   Or the minister's call . . . . .
But what lurks in darkness?
   They lighted up all.

Some few were skeptical
   And would only smile . . . . .
But the path to the barn at night
   Seemed like a mile!

Reverend Walsey preached of sin,
   And most folk agreed
The *Thing* was a warning
   They had better heed.

They named It the "Jabberwock,"
   For want of another;
But some shook their heads: "It's
   The Devil's own brother."

Then people came to church
   Who'd never been yet;
Some patched up a quarrel,
   And some paid a debt.

The Song of the Sun ~ Leah Bodine Drake

Cousin Jo and Cousin Kate
    Forgot they didn't speak,
And Old Man Jones stayed sober
    For one amazing week.

Wives left off nagging,
    And husbands kissed their wives;
The Claybrook brothers went to work
    For once in their lives.

No one watered any milk
    Or cut the measures down;
And Tillie got religion,
    And all her girls left town!

. . . .

Then one day the town awoke
    To find It had fled;
No one saw It squatting
    On his barn or shed,

No one saw those footprints
    Huge upon his lawn.—
As suddenly as It had come
    The Jabberwock had gone!

The church held a meeting
    And great thanks were given
That Satan had done his worst
    And left them scared but shriven.

Satan had ramped about
    Like a roaring lion!
But Squankom held firm, and now
    Was a little Zion.

HONEY FROM THE LION ⇼ 1942–1948

We were the wonder-town
   Of the countryside,—
They had driven Evil out!
   We let Good abide

For almost a fortnight—
   Then someone stole a sack
Of flour out of Barker's store,
   And Tillie's girls came back.

To One Who Fears Poetry Is Useless

Bless the unearthly flame!
Not till the poets sing
Does history win a name
Nor legend crown a king.

Song can revive the stone:
Forgotten and forlorn,
Troy would have burned unknown
Had Homer not been born!

Design for a Tapestry: 14th Century

Weave here a dame in Flanders cloth,
A tall, unlimber lady, blonde,
Horned with a headdress grandly Goth,
And thin as an enchanter's wand.

Set on her left a falcon'd knight
In dagged and parti-coloured clothes;
From a crisp arbour on her right
She offers him a damask-rose.

The Song of the Sun ❧ Leah Bodine Drake

Around them web a garden, small,
Where gentle hares and dormice hide;
Four candle-snuffer towers wall
Them from the hunters' wood outside

Where the white unicorn is slain,
And faintly silver bugles cry.
Thickly among the dogs and men
Scatter bluets and fleurs-de-lys.

Outside our weaving-loft the snow
Slants down, and wolves prowl by the gate.
All ironclad our lovers go
To distant lands of war and hate.

Oh, let our shuttles guide the wool
To scenes where grace and order walk,
A cloistered summer-land of crewel
Whose foes are only hind and hawk,

Where death is but a hound that goes
Through greenwoods to the sound of horns,
And love is but a crimson rose
Plucked from a thicket without thorns.

To Elinor Wylie

So at last you did
What your poem vows:
Went away and hid
In your secret house

That lies too deep
For the mangrove's root,

HONEY FROM THE LION ⁂ 1942–1948

In a wood where sleep
Is the final fruit.

O do not waken
And break the spell!
For the years have taken
What you loved well:

The foxes grin
By the ravished vine;
Down jowl and chin
Drips the golden wine.

The king's third son
Snores in a ditch,
And Rapunzel turns
Into the witch.

The last white hind
By the hounds is torn
And hunters blind
The unicorn.

O, you were blessed
Who could slip away
Before the burst
Of our dreadful day,

When mankind fumbles
A forbidden lock,
And the hurt world stumbles
Toward Ragnarok!

The Song of the Sun ~ Leah Bodine Drake

Legend

They always knew their doom would come
from the white-lipped sea below.
Their city was built high on cliffs
for it was told their doom would come

In legions from the angry sea.
So they built galleys, tier on tier
of benches for the blond-haired slaves.
Their gull-descended captains spied

A stranger-ship almost before
it left its home-port! There were gongs
hung in the hills where watchers gazed
forever seaward for the doom.

The sibyl cried within in her cave
at last: Woe, woe! And guts of gulls
portended now disaster, signs
that fail not. And the young men bragged,
mending armor in the fire-lit rooms.

The king asked merchants from afar:
What alien ships saw you at sea
ringed furiously about with shields?
What gossip have you heard of war?

One day a ship with ragged sails
lingered for water at the marble wharf,
and from its stinking hold went forth
a secret cargo on the heedless shore.

And the rats entered through the gates,
through every crack and gape and door,
slipping between the people's feet
in a black-brown unlovely spate.

HONEY FROM THE LION ☙ 1942–1948

And that city sickened till it died.
Those few who still lived stumbled up
and wandered in the hungry hills
and died, and all the dogs went mad
and the gulls picked out their shell-cold eyes.
The city was a hollow shell.

And all along the harbored seas
men told of how that city fell.

Beyond Eden

When Adam and Eve awoke
In the thin light
After the first night in their desert bed,
For one heart-beat it must have seemed
That they had dreamed
A blurred nightmare of sin and sudden loss—
Of that swift-turning sword,
The unpitying angel, and the hard
Irrevocable closing of a gate.

They would look back towards Eden, across
The flat unprofitable land
With its barbed plants, glister of mica, flinty stone,
Its salt wells, and the lion-tracks in the sand,
And seen afar
The Garden shining like a tiny star
Green, green in its own luminous air,
Remote as a mirage and Oh, how fair!

It must have been then humanity's despair
Awoke: their hearts broke
And the first tears sprung;
And to man's astonished tongue

The Song of the Sun ❧ Leah Bodine Drake

Came, bitter beyond belief,
The incredible taste of grief.

Heard on the Roof at Midnight

As I sat by my fire one night
Witches I heard on the roof alight.
I heard their broomsticks whinny and neigh;
And then I heard one beldame say:

"Well met in darkness, Tess, my lass!
Have you seen our coven comrades pass?"

"Aye, Lib! the Kelpie from her tarn,
And half the cats from miller's barn
Tore through the air with fiery eyes,
Each one grown to twice his size!
The hen-wife passed in a weasel's habit—
Oh, the coven gathers for the Sabbat!"

Then my blood ran cold, and hot again,
As I heard the witches (heard them plain),
Cry, "You who doze by the dullard hearth,
Open your soul to the ancient mirth!
Chain no longer your secret self;
Take down the besom from its shelf!
The owl's cried twice, the night wind moans,
The moon grins over the Sarsen Stones,
Fling wide the casement, mount and ride,—
Walpurgis Night is all outside!"

Then I barred the window, I said a prayer;
(To listen longer I didn't dare!)
I clasped the Book and I closed my eyes:
I heard them rush through the midnight skies.

HONEY FROM THE LION 1942–1948

So I looked out the window: all was bare,
Roof and ridgepole and milky air,
And only two bats, who vanished soon,
Were winging their way across the moon.

Help Wanted

Folk in the Old World
    Have in their homes
Wee men to help them—
    Brownies or gnomes.

We'd like a Brownie,
    In a cap of red,
Who'd keep the mice from thieving,
    And put Puss to bed;

To keep sweet the butter,
    And mend all our socks,
To find our lost pennies
    And wind up the clocks.

We *need* a Brownie
    To guard the house from ill,
To shoo away the nightmare
    From our Jack and Jill.

There will be no harsh words
    To make him take affright,
And he'll find a sugar-bun
    On the hearth at night!

We know a little hole
    Half-way up the stair,
Just made for a Brownie!—
    He could cuddle there

The Song of the Sun ❧ Leah Bodine Drake

And sleep away the daytime
    As snug as a mouse . . . . .
Oh, who knows of a Brownie
    Who'll come to our house?

A Likely Story!

Up the dragon's rocky glen
The young knight crept.
The dragon, lonely in his den,
Unheedful, slept.

The young knight felt no numbing fright,
But pride and awe:
No living eyes had seen such might
As his now saw!

This was the Ancient of the land,
The primal wonder
Told of in legend, grimly grand
With wings of thunder

And coil on coil of body scaled
And pavonine,
Crusted with gold and lapis, mailed
In tourmaline.

Was this the maiden-thief, the bane
Of kings and courts?
This old aristocrat would scorn
Such childish sports!

The young knight felt a sudden ruth:
How did he know

HONEY FROM THE LION ❧ 1942–1948

Those fearsome rumors were the truth
And this a foe?

Why should he bring this gorgeous worm
To death and dolour
To gratify a princess's whim
And prove his valour?

A wild thought hurtled through his brain
Like blazing light:
Perhaps in dragons as in men
God took delight.

The hero sheathed his sword once more . . . . .
"The Devil take
The princess, then!" he softly swore;
And through the murk

Went down to jibe and ridicule,
Dishonour-clad,
Feeling a little like a fool
But fiercely glad.

Leonardo Before His Canvas

When setting to work in paint, it was as if he were mastered by fear.
—GIOVANNI PAOLO LOMAZZO

Within my brain lies, pure and clear,
A land of unfabled rocks and screes,
Crags cut from jasper rising sheer
From the slow waves of sunken seas,

Mountainous isles like dragons' spines
Cloisoned on glacial waters, and deep

❧ 281

The Song of the Sun ~ Leah Bodine Drake

Grottoes of hollowed tourmalines
Where the unloving sirens sleep.

There cities domed, unpeopled, plunge
Down spiraling stairways to the shore.
There, like a kestrel, thought can range;
And at that country's secret core—

Her feet upon shards of agate rent
By iris and brooding columbine—
Sits my Enigma, innocent
And, like her flowers, androgyne.

Closed in a cone of emerald light
Is Leda, Narcissus, Anne the Blest,
Saint, ephebus and water-sprite:
Synthesis of my soul's unrest.

Now the angelic pinions stir,
Troubling my fountain! Now my hand,
Charged with the feared, familiar fire,
Waits my ambivalent command.

The light, the perilous fires fade,
The emerald is unbroken still:
The god in me yet hangs betrayed
By the old Judas of my will.

Dark Memory

Along the edges of my mind
A dreadful memory runs
Four-foot, through forests black and blind
That meditation shuns.

HONEY FROM THE LION ✤ 1942–1948

I know that sly beast-shape that prowls
Beyond my guarded wall!—
An exiled grief, as dark and cruel
As wolf in fairy-tale!

Beside these hinterlands, like deer
My thoughts move, quick to leap
At rustlings perilously near!
But sometimes deep in sleep

When the worn brain lets down its bars
And is by dreams unmanned,
From out that wood the beast-eyes peer
Of something banished, banned.

It springs, its great claws rip my heart!
And I wake to the old pain
Of a wound re-opened, and the smart
Of styptic tears again.

Snow Crystals

Now from thick skies descend
Six-sided motes, their mold
Cast in the forge of cold.
Rays of the double-three,
Ubiquitous trinity,
Criss-cross and blend.

The multitudinous flakes!
Rose-windows, narcissi,
Gothic grotesquerie
In diamond and white sapphire,
Wheels of sidereal fire
Which the great Craftsman makes!

The Song of the Sun ❧ Leah Bodine Drake

Here settles on the glass
One jewel, fine, unique:
I would have far to seek
To find the transient twin
Of this frail frost-sequin
Whose pattern soon must pass.

But in its tiny thews,
Precisely weighed and strained,
Creation's ardour burned
As if this mignon star
Were destined to endure
No less than Betelgeuze!

The Vision

I saw a city on a hill
Where city there was none:
It rose with crescent-crested domes
Between me and the sun.

The bare, familiar hillside bore
A swaying camel-train:
The scent of sandalwood and spice
Blew in my face like rain.

I saw the cloaked and fierce men
Ride through the dazzling light . . . .
One turned and waved a hand to me . . . . .
Then vanished out of sight.

HONEY FROM THE LION ⁊ 1942–1948

Minor Poet

An unheroic hunter, I
Enter the sacred wood of words,
Gun at the ready should I see
The velvet cats, the golden prides

Of which the mighty hunters boast.
The daphne and acanthus-brake
Rustle—but loose no fiery beast
As met the master-arms of Blake.

Somewhere within these thickets nests
The phoenix on the incense-tree,
But not one feather from his breast
Has drifted flame-like down to me.

On mornings when no withered leaf
Rattled a branch, I've watched the strange
Dance of the lonely hippogriff,
Wings folded—still beyond the range

Of my crude weapon! Random-shot,
Home of an evening I may bring
A fox-brush, pigeons for the pot—
Only some small unepic thing.

My walls are not without their heads
Of deer; there's meat upon the board.
But still I seek the golden prides,
The burning lions of the Lord!

The Song of the Sun ❧ Leah Bodine Drake

Old Daphne

Here water-music makes a low lament
Around my chilly roots,
And in my coral-gemmed, dark-shining tent
Wind-whisperings, bird-flutes
Tell me of Spring again. No other sound:
And yet I seem to hear
The god's feet throbbing on the ground
As in that lost young year.

And a sigh that green blood hardly understands
Makes my branches quiver,
Feeling my flowers, like love,
Slip from my hands
To the hurrying river.

Wild Geese in Spring

Once more the wild geese leave the cypress bayous
And seek the wuthering north where the glaciers breed.
Their beaks point to the Pole, they scorn the summer,
They will not be held by sun and the lavish seed.

The shores they seek are in latitudes of hunger,
Water stiffened with cold in the desolate marsh,
Rock under the breast and wind in the gullet,
And berries that grow in the bogs, bitter and harsh.

Something is there that the wild geese have a need for:
I hear them cry down the sinking Pleiades,
Fly the old roads with the old longing
To the rim of the world and the lands of little ease.

HONEY FROM THE LION ❧ 1942–1948

Moment at Sunset

The sun in a grave of gold;
The moon on a sapphire stair:
To think that one sky can hold
Two lights so great and fair!

The earth in a lilac glow
Where the twin rays meet and merge,
And Venus glittering low
On the crumbling sunset's verge.

We walk a dangerous star,
Perils lie left and right—
Hunger and hate and war—
But oh! in what splendid light!

Poplar-Wind

Liveliest of trees, the poplars always find
the hidden wind.
On the stillest day
when there's no wind to play
with sycamore or pear,
and the catalpas are too weary to rouse
from their repose,
wakeful in sleepy air the poplar trees
dance in their personal breeze.

Somewhere among their glittering boughs
the poplars house
a small, blithe gale
that neither sleeps nor grieves.
When all the large winds fail,

The Song of the Sun ~ Leah Bodine Drake

then through the poplar rows
a quicksilver quiver goes,
and all their leaves
twinkle and frolic in the day's dull stare,
as if a secret laughter shook them there.

The Fur Coat

I had a queer thing happen once;
   (The girl in beaver said)
I had this coat on—it was new—
   When I felt a sudden dread,

A wild despair, there on the street,
   And pangs shot through my wrist
Like burning pincers . . . . I smelled blood,
   My mouth was dry with thirst.

And then I screamed! . . . . but no one stopped
   To turn a startled face;
And yet I seemed to scream and scream
   Alone in some dark place!

But the worst part of this strange affair—
   Just as it passed (she said),
Was that I felt *I* was this fur
   And I was dying . . . . dead!

Honey from the Lion

I came upon it unaware.
First there was sand and silence there,
Blue-burning haze and scorching rock,
Short, daggered grass . . . and then the shock

HONEY FROM THE LION ⁓ 1942–1948

Of great limbs stretched before a lair:

The old brave body, stiff and prone,
Of some king-lion done to death
Upon the threshold of his earth,
All that huge ardour still as stone.

Wild bees had built their honeycomb
In his bright carcase, thunder-maned.
Through brow and jaw the nectar strained:
What Pharaoh in his spicy tomb
Had such rich amber seal his mouth?
I dipped my finger in the sweet—
And O, the fiery savage meat
Bred from the lands of lack and drouth,
Tanged with wild joy and deep unrest
And desolate courage, and the strength
Of loneliness: I knew at length
What fury burned in Samson's breast!

Now garden honey's over-mild
To satisfy the sharpened taste
Of one who's eaten of the Waste.
I know a hunger never filled
Since that strange banquet long ago,
That dark and bitter sweetness grown
Out of the lion's blood and bone,
Out of the desert's pride and woe.

The Heads on Easter Island

We know that human hands carved these lean faces
And set them on the dark volcanic hill,
Not fiends or Titans!—only brown Earth-races,
Mysterious, unknown, but mortal still.

The Song of the Sun ～ Leah Bodine Drake

Whoever made these gods they gave them homage,
Brought yams and sweet green cane at dusk or dawn,
Danced to the shaking drums in sea-birds' plumage
And cried their names, and loved them, and are gone.

Yet to what men have worshipped always clings
A sense of life unearthly—and there lies
A spell of power and of timeless things
In these sardonic lips and hooded eyes;
And awe takes hold of every traveler there
Who feels these stones are sleeping, but aware!

The Return

In stripped and shaken trees
Last summer's birds'-nests can be seen,
Clinging like withered fruit to the high-flung boughs
That arch the empty house.
Life's tide of green
Has ebbed, the inconstant birds are blown
Over the seas to remembered fiery lands.
And in the autumn dusk the old house stands
Lonely and bare as a forsaken tree,
Its nestlings flown,
The laughter gone,
The lights out, one by one,
And the panes blind.

What do I think to find
In this grey place where happiness turned dust?

Nothing is here.
Yet I come back, year after fading year,
Hoping to see on some dim, creaking stair,
The shadow of a darling head,

HONEY FROM THE LION ❧ 1942–1948

To feel a stir of air
Made by one pitying ghost,
Or hear an echo still unfled
Of a voice long loved and O! so long, long lost.

Song against Smallness

Pity the great!
Yes, for a change of mood,
Let us now speak with something less than hate
Of those not meek or crude,
Who in this age in little breasts awake
A raging envy masked as scorn.
Giants are suspect and forlorn.
Sniggering pygmies stone blind Samson's brow:
The dwarf's the fashion now.

Lost, lost is love for all the fine and fair,
The unique and the rare,
Peacocks and ivory.
The world can only see
Beauty in apes.

Come, let us be unpopular and praise
Aristocratic shapes—
Not cabbages but kings.
Let us say kindly things
Of lions and their ways
And birds-of-paradise:
Enough's been made of mice.

I heard the name
Of one who was a giant in his day
Made mock of by the mangy pack
Wild with their own lack.

The Song of the Sun 🙵 Leah Bodine Drake

They cocked their legs against his princely height
And fouled his fame.

And then I knew
If Lot's guests came again our way
Walking, as angels do, in light,
How they'd be hounded out for being bright!

Willow-Women

Why are you weeping, shepherd boy,
    Lying in the sedge
Among the roots of willows
    By the water's edge?

I weep for willow-women—
    That they come no more
From the pool at twilight,
    Calling 'round my door.

My love she was a willow,
    A woman from the pool:
For the willows turned to women
    When the dusk was cool.

The farmer in the lowland,
    No willow-love had he;
He feared the faëry women,
    He cursed them tree by tree.

The farmer in the lowland,
    He trampled down the sedge,
He cut the haunted willows down
    By the water's edge.

HONEY FROM THE LION ☙ 1942–1948

Cut down my true-love's willow!
    O dead and gone is she
Who came to me at twilight
    And gave her love to me!

Thus cried that lonely shepherd
    Beside the water's edge,
Weeping for willow-women,
The thin green willow-women,
The lost loved willow-women
    Who called from the sedge.

Mad Woman's Song

I know that the black dog crouches beyond the door,
I can hear him whimper over the whistle of wind.
The willows down by the brook are wringing their hands
And the clock is telling time that is frayed and thin.

I say to myself: if I let the black dog in
He will master the house,—but his whining will drive me mad!
I know that he wants me to follow him down to the brook—
I can hear him snuff at the sill and slouch and pad.

The willows and he have a pact—I've heard them talk
Together, on midnights without a moon or star,
When they thought I was sleeping under the dripping eaves.
I know how they plot! I've caught all their words in a jar

And hid it away on a shelf! Now I'm going to rock
And I'm not going to open my door to the willowy dark
And that damned black hound—let him howl all night!
I will stay indoors and talk to my grouchy clock.

The Song of the Sun ❧ Leah Bodine Drake

But the moon comes up with a rush through the window-pane
And looks at me as I rock, with a huge dog-eye . . . . .
O, I'll have to follow that moon and that crazy hound
Down, down to the brook and throw myself in, and die!

Song of the Sun

Set in the streaming void
By the Hands that made the night,
The sun with a mighty voice
Shouts for his own delight.

With body and breath of fire,
Hung beyond hope or blame,
Nothing is his desire
But to roar with a living flame.

Ere the first planet spun
Tilt-wise around his throne
He sang the song of the sun
For the sake of the song alone.

An earth or two may bask
In his warmth—he does not care,
He is conscious of no task
Burdened upon him there.

And let who will employ
His powers for wrong or right:
He sings in his boundless joy
And the song of the sun is light.

And worlds may totter and fall
And all man's grief be done
Before the rapture fails
In the huge heart of the sun.

HONEY FROM THE LION ❧ 1942–1948

The Old World of Green

We are so near to you,
   (I heard the Wild Folk say)
Only a meadow or two,
   A field and a farm away.

Up in the pine-sweet air,
   Up where the blue haze lies,
More than the fox or hare
   Whispers and creeps and cries!

We are so near, so near,
   To the roofs and hearths of man—
Strange that you never hear
   The clattering hooves of Pan!

Only the heron sees
   The undines in water-falls;
Only the wild kildees
   Answer the satyrs' calls.

But there are eyes in the sedge,
   There are hands in the thorn—
Waiting just over the edge
   Are we who are wilderness-born.

Maiden wandering late
   Where the hills' long shadows lean,
Come where the Wild Things wait
   In the old world of green!

The Song of the Sun ❧ Leah Bodine Drake

Currier and Ives Prints

This is the country that our grandsires knew,—
A land that rolls enormous to the West
Where pony-riders dash, and braves pursue
The buffalo that rock the prairie's breast.

Here stands the blacksmith, with small boys who crowd
To watch him at his old, heroic trade;
And here across this scene, superb and proud
The fire-horses gallop, unafraid.

Here, arm in arm with their bewhiskered beaus,
Bell-skirted beauties skate in Central Park,
And sleighs go jingling through nostalgic snows
Where mansions blaze a welcome through the dark.

This is a land of harvest-homes and fairs,
Of holidays with Grandma on the farm;
These landscapes gleam in mellow golden airs
With none from over-seas to blow alarm.

Now in a season when no air is calm
And skies fill with the thunder-heads of fear,
We find in these old prints a poignant balm:
Bright, happy, safe, our brave young land is here.

The False Messiah

They promised a redeemer of their own,—
Our modern magi—who would cure each ill,
Science his name, triumphant son of man,
No hurt myth hung on some small Asian hill!
Messiah-jinni from a chemic jar

HONEY FROM THE LION ❧ 1942–1948

Who'd bring bonanzas and (of course) world peace:
They split our temple's veil from roof to floor
And set their nursling in the holy place.

But that dark star they followed was the rot
Of fox-fire smoldering on a boggy heath.
They see their saviour now: Iscariot,
Pressing upon the Earth his kiss of death;

And while they watch, bewildered, it is he
Who hammers mankind to the ultimate Tree.

The Unknown Land

There is a strange, recurring dream
That haunts my sleep: do what I will
To steer to other shores, I seem
To drift to one, remote and chill,

Unknown to any map. Here run
Rivers of living pearls and jades
Beneath a sky where moon nor sun
Shines on the centaur-cavalcades.

Here I wander, unarmed, alone,
Through glens whose guards are giant toads,
To some half-guessed, half-memoried throne,
Longing and fright my master-goads.

Down from the Leonardesque scars
And spurs come bands of hunting-sphinx,
To pools like secret emerald stars
Where the great golden peacock drinks.

And the giraffe and white baboons
Feed among stiff, funereal trees,

The Song of the Sun ～ Leah Bodine Drake

On fruits like little silver moons
Which the green glow-worms suck like bees.

Here the sands quiver with the shock
Of furiously-passing unicorns,
And silens stamp from rock to rock,
And in the hills sound ominous horns

Blown from some thunder-smitten spur:
But what may mean those curious notes
I know not—or whether flesh or fur
Covers those unseen monstrous throats.

Challenge or plea: what is their call?
What city builded of ice or flame,
Lorded by fairy or by troll,
Forsees my coming and knows my name?

Shall I be hero or victim there?
Wrestle what dragon or minotaur?
Peri's palace or gorgon's lair
Lies beyond what adamant door?

Some night my dream will bid me climb
The last high slope where my doom awaits;
And my soul, enchained beyond space and time,
Will hear the clang of the closing gates!

The Green Door

I can't remember
    Where I'd been,
But once I came
    To a door of green.

Honey from the Lion ☙ 1942–1948

I was five at the time—
    It was early fall,
And I'd gone with Grandma
    To pay a call

In a queer high house
    On an unknown street
Where the smell of cooking pears
    Was sweet.

There was a lawn
    And an old red wall.
(It all comes back
    In the early fall!)

I played on the lawn,
    While the talk inside
Rose and fell
    Like a gentle tide.

A-jar in the wall
    Was a low green door
That seemed to beg me
    To explore.

Who knows what wonders
    Were close at hand?
At five, all doors lead to
    Fairyland!

My hand reached out
    To pull it wide,
When voices called me
    To come inside

For cookies and jam—
    So I turned away,

The Song of the Sun ❧ Leah Bodine Drake

Half glad, half sorry,
    I needn't stay.

What lay beyond
    To startle or bless
I never will know
    And I'll always guess.

The door was green . . . .
    The month was September . . . .
Where was it? . . . . and why
    Do I still remember?

After the Green Star Dies

After the day of doom
    Fades from the fields of slain;
After the last great bomb
    Has taken God's name in vain;

When Earth, betrayed and lost,
    With one heart-stricken cry
Crumbles to atom-dust
    Down an affronted sky—

Still like a ghost will shine
    Her light through the abyss,
Lovely and Oh! serene
    As from the home of bliss!

And somewhere among the worlds
    May sigh one in despair:
"How bright the Green Star burns!
    Life must be happy there!"

HONEY FROM THE LION ❧ 1942–1948

"Like Breath upon a Glass"

In dream I saw a world
star-luminous, all pearled
with rivers, seas,
and rapturous-green with trees.
And one with wings nearby,
sensed more than seen,
said, "Look on the Earth
and all her billion years."

Then out across her face
swiftly a shadow ran—
turbulent, alive,
swarming like dark bees in a hive
and with a sound of tears.
I watched it pass
like breath upon a glass,
blurring the green.

In one sigh's span
it came and fled.
Once more the planet shone
pearl-pure, serene;
and the winged creature said
"That was the age of man."

The Pool

The child came to a pool in the heart of a thicket,
Close-hung with alders speckled amber and brown;
Leaves floated like gems on the hazel water.
Shaken with shade, the pool went down and down
'Till vision was lost in a gently-moving mirror

❧ 301

The Song of the Sun ❧ Leah Bodine Drake

To a water-world too strange for a human's sight!
Roots of a beech writhed down like guardian serpents . . . . .
Over the pool she leaned in the slanting light.

Slowly a face took shape in the dusky water,
Pale and still and curtained with ferny hair.
Round green eyes gazed up from a flurry of ripples,
Fixed themselves on the child's in a long grave stare.

Breathless, balanced between delight and terror,
Caught in a dream-come-true that she'd dreamed alone—
Of meeting someday a thing from the world of Faërie—
The child still knelt . . . .

                        Faintly, the first star shone
Over the tapestried trees and the leaf-sweet hollow,
And slowly, slyly, awoke the life of the wild
While they gazed, one over and one under water,
Each held spell-bound by the other, nixie and child!

Precarious Ground

1949–1952

PRECARIOUS GROUND ❧ 1949–1952

The Windows of Chartres

Piercing dark stone they gleam
Where moth nor rust
Corrupts: the Gothic dream
Outlasting dust.

In the high glass saints stand,
Purple and blue,
Heart-red: halo and hand,
The sky shines through.

Prismatic crowns and staffs:
Not glass but air
The bodiless light itself
Seems painted here,

A filtering-screen, jewel-stained,
Held up to space
Where eternity is strained
Through Christ's own face.

The Lariat: 6000 B.C.

From the black woods and sad Siberian marshes,
Pounding green miles under their unshod feet
Come the wild herds, the proud unmastered horses!
Free as the cold deep rivers and as fleet,
Southward they gallop, screaming against the wind!—
Khans of the wastes and demon-haunted passes,

It is thought that the first horses to be tamed by man were those of the plains of High Asia, around the above date.

The Song of the Sun ~ Leah Bodine Drake

Leaving the ice-lipped bogs for the sighing land,
The rippled steppes, the wide unlegend'd grasses.

Under the nameless stars their princes race
Down to pale sleeping pools. Wild lord and lady
Nuzzle the sweet . . . while from its hiding-place
Slips the long Scythian rope, coiled and ready:

And in that primitive lasso as it springs
Are ploughs without number and the thighs of kings.

Gifts for Christ

Gold, frankincense and myrrh
The wise kings brought to You;
Most precious and most rare
Those first love-offerings were.

I too would bring You gifts
To lay before Your feet:
Here, torn from my dark heart,
Is all my less than good,
Old scorns, deep-gutted lusts,
Anger, and greed's ungrace,
The shabby commonplace
Of all our sensate clay.
With what long-last relief
At Your hurt feet I lay
My pride, my unbelief!

With love and joy You lift
From me each dreadful gift,
Against Your side to hold
My arrogance and fear,
Turning my heart's unsweet

PRECARIOUS GROUND ∂ 1949–1952

To frankincense and myrrh
And my long dark to gold.

The Darkened Glass

Think of the eye of man, that gem
Cut to less facets than the fly's,
Through which he catches but one gleam
From the vast prism of his skies.

Trusting his two dim mirrors he
Must view the world through seven veils,
Build on surmises and rely
On symbols and on fairy-tales.

He dares to judge the stars, whose light
Strains through a personal lens, to name
The atom and the germ, though sight
Betrays him with a candle-flame.

He walks through private landscapes where
Phantoms and legended beasts abound.
Beyond, the very-world lies clear,
The actual tiger laps the pond,

The sunset's secret colours glow,
And on the turning planet falls
The absolute glory he can know
Only in broken intervals.

Yet in his darkened glass there moves—
Behind the eye, within the heart—
A vision of the Earth he loves
Cleansed of her last befouling spot.

The Song of the Sun ❧ Leah Bodine Drake

A world without end that glimpsed or guessed
Shines with no light of land or sea:
By his imagination blessed
Beyond the ranges of the bee.

Atavism

I remember well . . . . .
I was a deer
Chased up a hill
And fleet with fear.

I was a horse
And I felt the crack
Of the heavy lash
On my laden back.

An elephant-king
Of valiant heart,
I died in the ring
For Roman sport.

In an otter's shape
I gnawed me raw
To leave in a trap
My bloody paw.

To the cornered fox,
The baited bear,
The seal on the rocks
With the sealers there,

My blood responds
With a secret cry:
I feel their wounds
And daily die.

PRECARIOUS GROUND ❧ 1949–1952

Dirge for a Doomed Planet

Braced with an iron heart
And equipoised with sea,
How carefully the Earth
Was planned and told to be!

Whirled from the father-star
And spun about his face
Neither too near or far,
And given one special grace:

A subtle web of air,
Well-tempered to her clay,
That holds good powers here
And keeps the ill at bay.

But now man turns the key
In the forbidden gate:
Out of dark spaces, he
Summons to serve his hate

Wild forces that unbless
The light that shapes us so,
Answering Heaven's yes
With an infernal no

That rips the silken mesh,
Pollutes the purest well,
And burrows in the flesh
To shatter cell from cell,

While all Hell waits a-grin
For Earth to perish, lost
By unredeemable sin
Against life's Holy Ghost.

The Song of the Sun ❧ Leah Bodine Drake

To Certain Poetry Critics

They say we shouldn't praise the violet
Purpling the secret hollows of the Spring,
Avoid the plough, the seasons ancient ring!
As for the moon—she mustn't rise or set
For any poet now! We must forget
Archaic words like beauty when we sing,
Deny the rose, and out to limbo fling
All that pre-dates the dynamo or jet!

But Nature still refuses to suppress
One ripening apple or one harvest-row
To please a critic! In a trite re-birth
Each year they come again, and men will bless
Hackneyed creation, and his songs will show
A love as old as Adam for the earth.

The Undine

They go down deep O deep beyond all telling,
The mind's cold under-seas: a secret tide
Sets bells of drowned forgotten temples tolling
For gods whom long ago the shore denied.

Here rust treasure-chests bulwarked by supple
Red octopi, and coral towns of death,
And pirates' bones that bloom with white and purple
Anemones' soft feral funeral-wreath.

Shining and blue the surface! None surmises
What hides below, what filled some innocent shell
Cast on the beach. Only when undine rises
Green-haired, web-fingered, on the wave's long swell,
Do alien eyes beneath our eyelids stare,
And those who love us see a stranger there.

PRECARIOUS GROUND ❧ 1949–1952

Sunset Apocalypse

For a terrible moment the sky fierced and throbbed
with the gold and purple wings of seraphim!
Plume against plume, they arched from west to east
lifting long swords of fire;
and the sea, an awakened angel, shone
with sudden peacock colours, raised his voice and billowed:
                      Holy   Holy   Holy.
Miracle threatened the Earth.

And we, going home across the dunes, turned startled faces
to those prophetic hosts
and cried in half-belief: It is the end of the world!

Then somewhere beyond the light
God must have said: Not Yet.
His Hand drew darkness over the sky, the sea,
and the Earth was saved once more from intolerable glory.

Kingfisher Lake

A place that I know
    lies low in a hollow,
Low, low in a hollow
    lies Kingfisher lake.
The water is dark
    with the shadow of willow,
        the willow that weeps
where the long ripples break.

Blue, blue are the reaches
    of whispering water
where sleep the great bass

The Song of the Sun   Leah Bodine Drake

    in the heat of the noon,
where the kingfisher dives
    from his willowy shelter,
        and the whippoorwill waits
        for the rise of the moon.

Once as a child,
    I crossed somebody's pasture,
        went down a blackberry-
        lane and a hill—,
and there was the lake
    in the summer's gold luster,
        as blue as the light
        on a kingfisher's quill!

Long, long by the lake,
    with my dog curled beside me,
        I dreamed through the hush
        of the hot afternoon,
of perils and joys
    which the future's denied me,
        wild, innocent visions
        that faded too soon.

Low, low lies the lake
    with its water sun-lighted
        and shadowed with dream,
        where a new child will play;
but for me it is lost
    like the dreams it invited,
        for the years have all brambled
        and hid it away.

PRECARIOUS GROUND ~ 1949–1952

The Revenant

Now up the shore
    The ripples slide,
The full moon pulls
    The haunted tide,

The lamp leaps up
    In the cottage pane
And I am up
    From the depths again.

Wild with sorrow
    My spirit beats
Up-wind to where
    The sea-sand meets

The darker soil
    Of furrowed land,
Where the little church
    And the gravestones stand.

I know one headstone,
    White and cold,
Whose carven lie
    Stares through the mold:

"God rest our darling
    Drowned at sea." . . . .
The calm earth-grave
    Holds none of me!

Even my spirit
    Cannot stay
Where the graveyard grasses
    Bend like spray.

The Song of the Sun ~ Leah Bodine Drake

For the jealous sea
    Calls back its own,
'Though the warm earth calls
    To the sea-held bone,

And there is no rest
    In the old, kind ground
For the bones unblest
    Of one self-drowned!

Cave Paintings, Altamira

Across the secret walls they rush
In their tremendous hush:
The totems of the cave, reindeer and boar,
The stag, the bear, the newly-mythic bull,
Coloured dim orange, indigo and brown—
Quarry and god in one,
Epic and beautiful.

Who would pronounce these walls the groping shoot
Of the great green tree of art?
Here is no cotyledon just uncurled
Like a child's fist from the deep-buried root,
But for that day
The culmination of the artist's way,
The rich the final fruit.
This boar is very-boar:
All China's done no more!

In carbon, in red clay, in blackened bone
The hairy priest set down
His vision of the world,
The sacred beasts, the hieratic hunters,
And his breast

Stirred with the bright unrest
That gnawed at Leonardo's heart
And ripped Van Gogh apart.

The Unploughed Field

In my one field the grass
Grows unconfined and sweet.
Green is my meadow with grass,
Not white with wheat.

Careless and sweet and warm,
Green blade and clover-head—
Yet not as sweet to Him
Who hopes for bread
As rows of wheat would be
Strong in the sun!
A thrifty Granger, He
Will send his Ploughman down
Whose terrible shares demand
Furrows from featureless plain,
And whose resistless hand
Casts the undying grain.

Then will my ransomed field
Stand blessèd with His corn,
White with a richer yield
Through which on harvest-morn
The Husbandman shall pass
And say, "Behold my gain!
This field of fruitless grass
Turned to My darling grain
On which the nations build,
On which My lovers feed."

The Song of the Sun ~ Leah Bodine Drake

O, Ploughman, plough my field!
O Sower, sow Thy seed!

We Come Out of the Forest, Fearing Stars

We come out of the forest, fearing stars,
bowed by going forever under branches.
How lost, how low are laid our girdling trees!

It was safe in those dim woods,
our bodies were shaped to the forest, heavy and shy.
The guardians of the tribe, thick wooden lords,
blessed us with painted eyes beneath moss-curls,
water fell broken and kind from the rustling heavens
whose green held rumours of another sky.
We knew that lions prowled the wood's edge, for their eyes
torched terribly the darkness,
their threats flattered us where we huddled
warm and unseen among the totem leaves.

Now in a tempest-year the wood betrays us,
our leafy castles are thrown, the bark-gods dead,
and we go walking warily in this bare landscape
fearing stars.
Still bowed by going forever under branches
our spines rebel at the vertical:
to be proud in the tall wind is to be naked
to lions' eyes.
How lost, how low are laid our girdling trees!

O unknown Powers of this empty land,
temper your lions to the little spears
of tree-men suddenly bared to the perilous stars,
walking tall in a world without totems
far from trees!

PRECARIOUS GROUND ～ 1949–1952

The Vision of Jenghiz-Khan

They say he saw a vision, a mirage
Once in his youth, a valley green with grass,
A hidden place beyond a mountain-pass
As musical with waters as Shiraz.

There all his people and their herds could rest
From wandering, secure from wind and war:
He saw it waiting like a secret star
Beyond the steppes, somewhere along the west.

It lightened the horizons of his dreams.
So to and fro he rode with sword and fire,
Walled city after city to harass

That stood between him and that land of streams,
Burning the world away in his desire,
Forever in his eyes a dream of grass.

Precarious Ground

On the volcanic hill
The small brave village clings
And the rich grapevine swings.

In wheat foredoomed to fall
Beneath the reaper's blade,
Meekly and undismayed
The fieldmouse makes her nest,
And down to the sea's false arms
The harbour alleys run,
And farmhouse windows burn
Each with its tiny sun
Against the tremendous night

～ 317

The Song of the Sun ❧ Leah Bodine Drake

Arching this tilting dust
That is a world in flight.

On such precarious ground
Life rears its endless house
For meadowlark and mouse
And fiery-rooted flowers,
And love itself must shape
Its vulnerable towers
On the uncertain sand
Of the wild human heart,
Raising its reckless port
Beside an unknown sea,
Building with desperate trust,
Building because it must
Only upon the slope
Of old catastrophe.

Love Song

From the dark bracken of my personal wood,
From undine-haunted pool and fierce thorn
That only bends to jealous unicorn,
I have been whistled up. Been caught by a word

Flung like a net to hang a silly hare
Over your careless shoulder, when you strayed
Close to my secret oak, whose leaves betrayed
Their hamadryad crouched and peering there!

What could I do but hunger for and follow
One who bore love as lightly as a pelt
Of some limp, delicate vixen at his belt?
Insouciance witched me from my solemn hollow

PRECARIOUS GROUND ❧ 1949–1952

Up to your arms' gay city, to delight
In the miraculous towers of your flesh!
Now from your trophied walls I glimpse the flash
Of lyric fountain brimming desolate

Among forsaken trees, and hear the stamp
Of that lost friend, my outraged unicorn,
Searching for me along these gaudy lanes
And squares wherein your laughing tigers ramp.

The Mermaid

Flashing through facets of her glassy world,
The many-chambered sea, cold mermaid rises—
For a lean shadow now obliquely moves
Across her rippled roof.
Up, up, from her hollowed water-land,
Up convoluted stairways of her restless house
The mermaid mounts, shaking her dangerous hair;
And see! she spreads before the vessel's bow
Her gold-green locks and scarlet seaweed crown,
Her pearly-pale half-body of a girl
Cupped in its husk of opalescent scales.

Who flushes red, and leaps, and in her arms
Sinks with a bubbled cry of fear and joy,
But he the youngest of the gaping crew?
Call in vain to your lost brother, fling the net,
Tough, powerless fishers straining desperate-eyed
Against the dripping side!
Then bid the women on the hungry shore
Raise the wild keen and wring their empty hands!

Far out the mermaid, tired of her play,
Lets her chill toy drift weathercock, supine,

❧ 319

A lean shadow now obliquely moves across her rippled roof.

PRECARIOUS GROUND ~ 1949–1952

In hammocks of the swinging tides, while she
Flicks a bright fin and darts to comb her curls
Among rough water-rocks off Brittany.

Cobra

"Cobras . . . are fond of both music and milk."
—V. B. METTA in *International Studio*

Is this the classic fiend,
The shape of sin,
The primary unfriend
Of beast and man?

A slithering length of spite
And hooded hate
Born to betray, affright,
To lie in wait

For the symbolic sheep,
The pious dove,
And, bent on mischief, creep
Through sacred grove—

This creature who, though filled
With icy venom,
Is fond of milk? A mild
Drink for a demon!

Not poppy-juice nor sap
Of nightshade berry,
But an impeccable cup
From an honest dairy.

Yes, though he hisses death
He loves the notes

The Song of the Sun ~ Leah Bodine Drake

From reedy pipes, the breath
Of lyric flutes.

Such delicate tastes imply
A gentle soul
Who wouldn't hurt a fly,
Damned with his role

Of Hell's original boy—
Incarnate Wrong—
Who wants but to enjoy
Plain milk and song.

But see those glacial eyes . . .
Make no mistake,
Back of his meek disguise
Still rears the Snake!

Six Merry Farmers

(A Cumberland Mountain Tale)

Six merry farmers
    lurching from a tavern,
swaying down a village street
    at midnight, arm in arm.
One tried to kiss the moon
    shining in a puddle,
went to sleep and snored there
    miles from his farm.

Five merry farmers!
    Two got to fighting,
the sheriff came by and
    hauled them off to jail. The

PRECARIOUS GROUND ❧ 1949–1952

fourth roared a gospel-hymn
    and went to look for women;
the fifth thought of little lambs
    and sat down to wail.

The last merry farmer
    weaving up the hill-road
met an old witch-woman who
    was anything but fair.
When he gravely cursed her
    she up and be-spelled him,
and what had been a farmer
    was a wild buck hare!

Two merry farmers
    Riding home in dawn-light;
one sees a big buck hare
    and lets off his gun!
Five merry farmers
    sleeping off their merriment—
and one not so merry
    lying dead in the sun.

The Wind in the Chimney

Nothing moved in the old house,
    Nothing crept up the stair;
Only the wind in the chimney
    Spoke to the silence there.

Nothing darkened the mirror,
    Blank as the face of Fate;
Only the wind in the chimney
    Stirred the ash in the grate.

The Song of the Sun ❧ Leah Bodine Drake

Nothing stooped to the cold bed
    Nothing shadowed the sheet;
Only the wind in the chimney
    Moaned to the ghostly sleet.

Nothing stirred in the old house;
    The clock had stopped at eleven;
But Something had come and departed
    With never a greeting given.

Something had quietly entered
    And touched what lay on the bed,—
And only the wind in the chimney
    Wept for the newly-dead.

Out!

That was the night I ran
Out of the house for good!
Airy as loosened leaf
From a bird-forsaken tree
I sped through the moonlit grass—
I was finished with love and grief
And the wilful ways of man.
Oh, I was gay and free!
Oh but my step was light!
Never a blade of grass
Trembled beneath my foot,
A mink on a rabbit's track
Never paused to let me pass;
A vixen with cubs at play
In a beech tree's twisted roots
Didn't bother to hide away;

PRECARIOUS GROUND ❧ 1949–1952

A spider-web hung with dew
Neither wavered nor broke
As I went softly through,
And not a dewdrop shook.

But when I came to the pond,
Wading through lily and reed,
And not a ripple stirred
Over its silver and black—
When gazing within its glass
I saw no face looking back
Nor the shadow of bending head—
Then, then I knew I was dead!

Bookworm

Under the quiet lamp his darling page
Glows with the Trojan flames, Achilles' rage:
Half a world and half of time away
He breathes the glittering air of yesterday.

Down the dark street beyond his placid room
A fire-engine shrieks of neighboring doom:
Upon his ears its urgent anguish falls
Not half so loud as the crash of Ilium's walls.

A Warning to Skeptics

Don't boast your unbelief in woods!
The dark leaves hide an ancient folk,
And it's unwise to say aloud
That there's no dryad in the oak.

The Song of the Sun ❧ Leah Bodine Drake

Mock, if you will, the troll and faun
When safe in fire-guarded house
Or on the tamed turf of your lawn—
There no strange Powers will arouse

From ferny sleep in all their wrath
To numb your modern soul with fright:
This side man's wall we name them myth—
The wilderness reveals their might.

Hush! Do not call the old gods "lies"
When under oak or ash or thorn,
Lest you be taken by surprise
Between the twilight and the morn,

And we could seek you everywhere
And never see, by moon or star,
One glimpse of hand or flash of hair
In any fields where mortals are.

The Final Green

This is of green, unclassic shade
Of which the Greek tongue was afraid:
Symbolic of the distance, where
Pure form melts into formless air.
A Saracenic colour, green,
From lands beyond the Byzantine,
Soul of the emerald, the dye
Of mermaid's hair and tiger's eye,
Of Persian tile and peacock's tail,
The Prophet's flag, the Holy Grail.

Green, the moon's proverbial cheese,
The blood within the veins of trees,

PRECARIOUS GROUND ❧ 1949–1952

The famous hue of envy's face,
Our planet's little light in space:
Earth's colour to which her peoples pass
Under the final green of grass.

The Foam-Born

Men try to hold her in enamelled crowns
of Gothic kings,
in terra cotta horses of the T'angs:
she the intangible, the swift, we dare
to follow and to snare.

Echoes of her voice ring down
from belfries belled in bronze,
and skeins of her hair in tapestry are wound,
in Persian rug and Byzantine brocade.
Phidias touched her robe and Homer heard
her footfalls. For a while
Da Vinci drew the shadow of her smile.

The feathered Aztec cloak,
the Cretan jar
bear witness that she travels far,
and no one knows when she will pass:
workmen in Chartres saw her mirror break
and jewel their window-glass!

Power and wisdom are not enough,
the apple goes
to the Foam-Born down the ages:
emperor's armour, bishop's crook
burst into pearls, gold binds the missal-book
And reverent Islam paints the Koran's pages.

Skeins of her hair in tapestry are wound, in Persian rug and Byzantine brocade

PRECARIOUS GROUND ❧ 1949–1952

* * *

The armour rusts, the parchment fades
but still we rhyme
weave tint carve hammer mold,
hoping to fasten down in Time
with hands of clay
that goddess timeless fleeting as the spray.

Red Ghosts in Kentucky

As I went home through the thirsty fields
Dark storm-clouds massed.
The heat-waves danced above the wheat
Where long ago sly doe-skinned feet
Of redmen passed.

And suddenly, over Tatum's Hill,
Redmen appeared!
Shawnee braves, who had made their stand
A century back in this river-land—
For a century unfeared.

Tawny-brown as the johnson-grass,
With wildcat grace
Walked the proud bucks. From war-belts swung
Scalps where the bloody drops still clung.
Paint masked each face.

Then I saw captives, stumbling and tied,
Herded in their wake,—
Pale-faced women with babes in arms,
Grim-eyed men from the clearing farms
Bound for the torture-stake.

The Song of the Sun ❧ Leah Bodine Drake

All around were the vanished trees,
Forest before, behind.
Faint cries came on the heavy air,
The brown limbs shone, the bloody hair
Rippled . . . . . I saw them wind

All in a bright, impossible line
Through the ghostly wood!
I watched the last plumed warrior go
Bearing his tomahawk and bow . . . . .
Rigid I stood

With the age-old terror awake in me
At the old name . . . .
Shawnee! . . . . the wolfish howls at morn,
The painted faces in the corn,
The cabin roofs aflame.

I shut my eyes and cried aloud!
Then with a roaring sound
The rainstorm broke on the fields long dry . . . .
But was it thunder that shook the sky,
Or drums on a stamping-ground?

An Unlikely Noah's Ark

Wyvern

The Wyvern is a little dragon,
His ears stick up, his tail is saggin'.
With rage his wings are always quivernin',
He's mean and spiteful, is the Wyvern.
You never see his tail a-waggin':
He wants to be a great, *big* dragon.

PRECARIOUS GROUND ❧ 1949–1952

Satyr

Goat-men roamed the classic hills
    Wooing nymphs by classic rills.
Goats and men are enterprising.
    Mixed, they must have been surprising.

Centaur

Buckety, buckety, over the plain
Of Thessaly tore the centaur train.

Horses and riders in one, they made
A highly compact cavalcade.

Buckety, buckety, back they tore,
With nobody nursing a saddle-sore.

Pooka

The Pooka lives down in the deeps
Of Killarney's lakes. Up he leaps
Like a little black horse
To run a wild course,—
Glory be, what he'd do in the Sweeps!

Minotaur

King Minos once thought it a lark
To lay out an underground park
    Where his bull-pated pal
    Wrestled Greeks. What a hell
Of a thing to have met in the dark!

The Song of the Sun ~ Leah Bodine Drake

Werewolf

The Werewolf's a bit of a tough,
His ways are uncommonly rough.
Of all men-into-beasts,
He's admired the least, s–
O he's never made into a muff.

Fury

A Fury looked a lot like woman,
Though snakes for hair is hardly human.
She hounded wicked men like crazy—
You must admit she wasn't lazy.
As if one Fury wasn't trouble enough,
There were three of these dolls doing their stuff.
Although Athenians bragged about them
They felt more comfortable without them.

Cockatrice

The Cockatrice is a telescoped economy-
size snake scorpion rooster this character
can kill by just glaring at you with one
good hard glare he's never been anybody's
pet and nobody has ever met the Cockatrice
Twice.

Chimaera

Chimaera was a triple threat—
Serpent, goat and lion yet!
When you saw Chimaera, you
Told yourself it wasn't true.
When you told your friends they frank-
ly said they thought you drank.

Precarious Ground ~ 1949–1952

Spirit-Fox

At sunset over Nippon's snow
Little fairy Fox-Maids go,
Out to ruin all they see
Of the male sex Japanee.

Man takes home a pretty doxy,
Sunup shows her pretty foxy.
Japanee boy get nasty shocks
To find he's necking with a fox.

Salamander

The Salamander is a lizard
Who isn't partial to a blizzard.
In leaping flames he makes his home;
He much prefers Mobile to Nome.
An impudent young Salamander
Can always raise his old man's dander
By whimpering, "I don't care *what*
I ought to like—it's too damn hot!"

Ghoul

Four-foot 'round the cemetery
Pad the Ghouls, dog-faced and hairy.
They feed on corpses full to busting,
Their table manners are disgusting.
Ghouling is a sort of dining-
Out a decent fiend's declining.
Too, one looks an awful fool
Hind end upmost, like a Ghoul.

The Song of the Sun ~ Leah Bodine Drake

Roc

The Roc
Never comes in a flock
Or a herd.
A buster of a bird,
He's unlike geese or oxen—
There's only one Roc, no reese or roxen.
He lives in the Arabian Nights
And one of his chief delights
Is collecting diamonds for decoration.
He is the envy of every nation.

Sphinx

Nobody knows if the Sphinx at Giza
Is positively a she, or if she's a
he. The Sphinx won't say what she (he) thinks
for that would make her (him) un-Sphinx.

It's hard to judge the lay of the land
With most of her (him) hidden by all that sand.

So the guessing goes on without restraint:
Is she is, or is she ain't?

Overheard in Baghdad

That man was prisoner on the isle of Lab!
She was a witch: they say that she could cast
Sorceries, spells, on merchants of good birth
Whose ships were wrecked upon her perilous coasts.
Beneath her evil gaze their souls would pass
Into the close pelts of beasts.

* * *

Precarious Ground ⇒ 1949–1952

That man
(Listen . . . . . I heard this in the mosque,)
Has worn the body of a sable pard!
(As Allah is my Witness, I speak truth,—
I heard it in the markets and bazaars.)
Within a panther's skin he knew her love.
He was the slave of Lab,
Sinning, and sinned against, (grant him that).
Until most terribly came
The fish-scaled, green, and finny-winged Sea-Djinn
Up from the under-seas,
Seeking their lost prince Badr.
All men know of the vengeance which they took,
Drowning the city in their cold sea-flame,
Banishing Lab and breaking the spells of Lab,
Till all the men were free
To find their homeward way across the inclement sea.

Now this man, as you see, gives thanks to God
(The Merciful, the Compassionate,)
That he is once more as men are,
Walking upright as a man walks,
Turbaned and shod.

And yet . . . . .
He lived a long time as a beast, you know;
Sorcelled or not, what a man has done, he's done . . . .
Allah!
You'll see his shadow beside him run,
Four-foot and sinuous, in a blaze of sun!

The Song of the Sun ❧ Leah Bodine Drake

Atlantis

Somewhere off shore
Beyond these grey-green swells,
Below the restless rooms
Of sea-anemone and jellyfish
Atlantis is,
Lie the lost harbours,
Rust the harps, the bells.

Half-legendary dream of all our kind,
Atlantis sleeps, we say.
Drowned deep in sea and time:
Not Paradise, but mankind's ageless boast
Of paradisial life that lay
Closer to what we name the best—
Of a purer, lordlier race
That moved, more loving and more wise,
Than under Grecian skies,
Called memory, myth or vision—
What you will—
But cherished still against all mock and reason.

And see! cast on this shore, a shell
Stained with the violet light
Of under-seas—
Mute witness that beyond our sight
Beyond our groping hands,
Far, far
Are water-lands too deep for diving-bell,—
Deep as the longing in the human heart—
Where the lost towers of Atlantis are.

PRECARIOUS GROUND ☙ 1949–1952

The Four

Four elements of which man regards the ways,
Of which he brags he is master,
Defeat him yet and deal him out disaster:
Earth stifles, water drowns, fire burns, air betrays.

Dwarf, undine, sylph and salamander
Personify his envy and desire. He's not content
With less than total rule of each element:
Not nursling, guest, invader or bystander.

He cannot move in air by himself as gull or hawk
But in metal only and then in fear of the fall.
Water receives him, remembering his lost gills,
But is ready to sink, flood, strangle and wreck.

Earth, most his own, can take as well as give:
Bury in minepit, choke his nostrils with dust.
Fire's a friend he cannot completely trust,
Landlords her house but within is unable to live.

So he invents, pries, dreams, lets his mind revel
In the spheres of flame, sky, rock and under-seas
Which he'd compel, inhabit, comprehend and use,
But can never decide whether like angel or devil!

The Birth of Beauty

In the gilt morning air
birds wheeled and dipped,
gull, tern and peewit circling
above her,
her long smooth yellow hair darkened with sea-water
and her long flanks unsheathed from their watery husk.

The Song of the Sun ~ Leah Bodine Drake

*   *   *

And gross-handed fishers all along the shore,
seeing her only as a curling wave
a shaft of sun
an eddy of wind-tossed sand,
felt a swift pang shoot through them,
pain and hard joy;
and their youngest, a boy,
clutched in his dirty fist a cast-up shell,
a coil of rose and pearl, and cried,
"Look, look! This shell!"
and cried again
"O look! the colours of this shell!"
knowing as yet no sudden word for beauty.

But he knew
    that it was beautiful.

We Move on Turning Stone
1953–1956

WE MOVE ON TURNING STONE ❧ 1953–1956

Powers of the Air

Upon the kingdoms of the air
Man's shadow falls. In regions where
The angels war with evil jinn
The sons of Adam bustle in

Noisy with atom-blast and jet—
A race that's not decided yet
Which party's squadrons it will swell:
Those of Heaven or those of Hell.

The Web

Sir Launcelot was bad cess to his sweethearts.
From his courtship they suffered a loss of crown
Or death by drowning. Didn't he have one sweetheart
More hardy of heart than most, who refused to pine

At the top of the house when he left? In all
His ladied landscape surely there had to be
Some tower snugged by a marsh, a sea-stung hall
Holding a love-light missed by Malory.

Some unrecorded damsel—perhaps a clever
Changeling skilled at weaving (they always were)—
No lily-maid to seek doom in the river,
No queen to take the veil in her despair.

An artist, one to whom no farewell angers
Came with the dawn, nor tears. She wouldn't have waited
For him to be up and off, before her fingers
Would fly to her wools to get the affair translated

The Song of the Sun ~ Leah Bodine Drake

To tapestry! Over the loom her shuttle
Would weave the sparkling pattern of her thought
Into mailed saints, and unicorns a-battle:
The heart's brisk interlude sublimed to art.

And the web would grow larger than life, enormous,
Till it left no place for anything else in her room—
Not that she would have wanted anything else!
But that, of course, in itself was a kind of doom.

Fool's Paradise

It is a landscape where the gauzy foliage
Silently fountains from the mortal waste,
Trees where peacocks nest among hard, savage
Fruits which ravish the eye but slake no thirst.

It is the eden of the heat-mirage, the phantom
Garden the caravan sees. Its painted grove
Sways without whisper of leaves, a dry kingdom
Where only blue shadows of water gleam and move.

Lovers dreaming they're loved wander its vineyards,
Invalids hopeful still with treacherous lungs,
Nations at perilous peace, and barnyard ganders
Held to the scattered corn by their crippled wings.

One can live for years among these palm-plantations
Blind to their flimsiness, to the rootless grass!
But under them all the while are the bleak damnations
Of terrible sand and the bones of the wilderness!

WE MOVE ON TURNING STONE ❧ 1953–1956

The Enchanted Swans

(From Grimm)

The bad queen waved her wand, and the brothers rose
Into the air as swans and flew the tower—
Six lordly cobs. Old winds and waters
Sent forth a call that raced their blood like fire.
Urging their wings. In sudden shirts of feathers
They circled above their sister, wild with wonder.

II.
The weeping maiden saw, with a sad wonder,
How their necks stretched north where the great rose
Of the aurora burned, and swan-girls' feathers
Gleamed like the snow where waters fell from towers
Of rock in the high glens. The wilderness fire
Sped them to webfoot wives by the tall waters.

III.
A savage innocence like hidden waters
Flooded their thought, they wondered, as birds wonder,
At roofs below, smoke-plumed with their tame fires,
At minster windows glowing blue and rose.
Man's world where good and evil stood like towers—
All less to them than the lightest pinion feather!

IV.
But the king's sons stirred beneath the magic feathers
And royal blood runs deeper than sweet water:
They dreamed, all six, one night of a wicker tower
With their sister bound, whose hands still shaped a wonder—
A cloth of nettles—her needle fell and rose
Even while toward her feet crept naked fire!

The Song of the Sun ⁊ Leah Bodine Drake

V.

Often their hearts awoke to forgotten fires
Of kindred love!—in a whillilew of feathers
The great birds headed south—old memories rose
To point them toward familiar fields and waters
And a royal square where gaping townsmen wondered
To see white wings fall with a noise of towers!

VI.

Six loving hearts that ringed the fagot tower
Twelve angry wings that beat the witch's fire,
And court and burghers saw a work of wonder:
The mute girls weep and throw on their singed feathers
Those stinging sarks wet with the holy water
Of human tears . . . and six young princes rose.

How we arise by loving! The dark towers
Fall like water, their magic frail as feathers
Before that mutual fire—O, the wonder!

Gipsies

Horses they knew, and the fates in cards, and thieving,
The side roads of the world and the maps in hands.
They wore many rings. Their women had skirts by the dozen
Like dirty rainbows. Their days were hounds
With yellow, mistrustful eyes. Their leaf-brown children
Scattered like quail when you neared their trundled house,
But tore the fruit from the trees when no one was looking,
Set snares for birds and frightened the farmer's cows.

You never see gipsies now with their gaudy wagons,
The fire-lit faces, the dogs, and the stolen hay:
They went from our lanes one night with their fiddles crying,
Like smoke that was drifting farther, farther away.

WE MOVE ON TURNING STONE ❧ 1953–1956

Solar

Imagine the sun in his strength,
The tongues the trumpets of fire,
The roaring chorals of heat
The adorations of fire!

In furious solitude,
With body and breath of flame
He shouts one living word
In syllables of flame!

His rapture is never done!
In ever-renewed delight
He sings the song of the sun,
And the song is Light!

Cat Mummy

Valley of the Kings, Egypt

The royal hands that tied
These bells about your throat
And stroked your supple side
Are dust; their spirit's boat

Has beached on other sands
Where your small ghost has gone.
The painted palace stands
Roofless beneath the sun,

And all that coloured court,
The gorgeous to-and-fro
Through which you softly went,
Seems like legend now,

You walked softly once to little bells

WE MOVE ON TURNING STONE ~ 1953–1956

A world too strange to sense!
Yet a thin jingle tells
That you walked softly once
To little bells.

The Jannigogs

Jannigogs came from the Moon, (and they should have stayed there).
On a mountain-top they landed their flying-ball;
They hung their talking-bells in a cosy cave there
And buried their happy-wine by a waterfall.

Furry and fat and small are Jannigogs. It was charming,
The grey fox grinned to himself, the way they'd make
Polite little bows when they met him—downright charming!
The fox dined often and well on Jannigog steak.

Jannigogs danced at night on the lonesome mountain,
And drummed on their little drums to salute the Moon
And made a hell of a noise. Far down the mountain
The Johnson hounds gave tongue—and not for 'coon.

And "What on airth's that racket?" cried the Johnsons;
They got their guns and they whistled up their dogs . . . . .
There were whoops and shots and "Fer-goshsakes—look!" from the
    Johnsons,
And squeals and scuttlings and blood from the Jannigogs.

Came dawn. The Jannigogs rolled out their space-ball
And sadly took each bell from its talky-place,
And counted noses, and wept, and left this Earth-ball
Where horror hides behind such a pretty face.

The Song of the Sun ~ Leah Bodine Drake

Jannigogs crouch again in the snug Moon-caverns
And whisper about this terrible world of Men,
And mothers threaten their cubs in the cubby-caverns,
"If you aren't good you'll be taken to Earth again!"

The Middle Ages: Two Views

I. Con

The wicked barons laid the landscape waste
With their two obsessions, hunting and battle.
They were always riding down something, man or beast,
And they placed the peasant on a par with cattle.

Castles were lordly prisons, ladies found life a bore
With their men forever away on feud or crusade.
They kept such open-house for the troubadour
That Holy Church anathemized his trade.

Their vices burned them spindleshanked and white,
(The tapestry-people prove this, says Michelet.)
Even crowned kings could seldom read or write
And villeins slept in sties and ploughed all day.

They had schools for magic, and the *droit du seigneur*,
And a low taste in fun, like the Feast of Fools.
There were racks, and covens of witches. They baited bears
And they had Gilles de Rais and plague and ducking-stools.

They ate with their fingers, and quite learned scholars
Debated how many angels could dance on a pin.
They thought the Earth was flat, and serfs wore collars
Of iron, and Hell was neatly circled in.

WE MOVE ON TURNING STONE ❧ 1953–1956

II. Pro

They enjoyed their times so much they pictured Paradise
As a little compact city with walls and spires,
With the Blessèd walking about in pointed shoes
And stylish liripipes, among rose-thorn and pears.

They worshipped courtesy and chastity and courage
And Woman: there was always a knight on the road
Glittering off to rescue a lady. The woods' foliage
Rustled with faïry hinds and Robin Hood.

They liked the beasts: the pious, fantastic towers
Prickled with pointed stone ears. They were subtle in love,
Craft-proud, ardent. Saints sprang up like flowers,
And that life was merry enough the *fabliaux* prove.

The lands glowed like a painted tabard with tourneys;
They had exquisite ivories, Dante and Joan of Arc.
They were always jogging about on exciting journeys
To Canterbury (see Chaucer), the Grail or the Holy Rock,

And they lived cheek by jowl with surprise and miracle!
They believed in mermen and elves and the Judgement Horn;
The Queen of Heaven might appear at some sacred well
And any thicket hide the unicorn!

Semele

She would wander the sun-struck hills about Thebes,
A tanned, long-legged girl thinking of lovers.
In the thundery afternoons she would leave the others,
Her chattering handmaids busy at their webs

In the palace, and the queen-mother's dos-and-don'ts,
To lie in some water-voiced cyclamen hollow

The Song of the Sun ❧ Leah Bodine Drake

On crushed mint leaves, looking up at the yellow
Sunlight sharpening the poplars into spear-points

Carried by heroes, plumed strangers in bronzed greaves.
They came wooing her, having heard of her dark tresses,
Offering hearts and princely deeds and smooth caresses—
She would tremble with innocent lust, hoping such loves!

But when Divinity descends to a mortal's bed
It is with no courting-speeches or if-you-please:
The bolt fell from the blue between her knees
And in one lightning moment she was wooed and wed!

Still half asleep, dazed with the sky-god's rape,
Semele thought she had dreamed of being held
In that brief, terrible embrace. Later she felt the child
Swell in her womb like wine within a grape.

Childhood Summers

Something, those summers, seemed to lie curled like a fern
In the blue heart of day, something we might find
Suddenly, anywhere—by the twisted stump at the turn
Of the wood-path, or beside the frog-loud pond.

We lived with imminent marvel! In some little room
Of the sumac, secret, hushed with sun, the more-than-real
Might appear: a talking beast out of Grimm
Or the toad with the green gem blazing in his skull.

In noon orchards, with each tree pooled in its own small
Shade, where wasps shrilled defiance from paper castles,
We would pause, listening . . . now, now the awaited call
Would come from the hot sky or the clumped thistles

We Move on Turning Stone ❧ 1953–1956

Where the Painted Ladies clung!—the fortunate rune
That opens the door into the true country. The bark might swing
Out from an apple-bole and show the steps leading down
To the jeweled cave, the hall of the sleeping king!

It is never wholly lost, that hope, nor quite outgrown:
Old children, we still half expect to see
In one form or another the crowned swan
Alight on the lake, the keyhole shine in a tree.

Railroad Tracks

Always the tracks lead onward blue as the distance
that they can never quite reach, or coldly grey

Under a roving moon, for they have one longing:
to be going going going forever away.

They pass through the town but they never linger in it;
trains rush over them in a fury of speed

crying out in their hollow mournful voices
that ever beyond beyond beyond is the place they need.

I would follow the tracks if I thought they had an ending
in some far fabulous city where men are kind.

I would go where the charging engines go in their headlong hurry,
leaving horizons forever forever forever lost and behind.

But the tracks are never the Here they are always the Yonder,
and I see them shine in the sun and their word is clear:

"Beyond the towns the hills and the lazy lonely valleys
we seek a city not here not here not here."

The Song of the Sun ❧ Leah Bodine Drake

The Web of Living

How delicately we should move
Through living's web! How circumspect
Must be our touch on all we love
Caught between cause and sure effect!

Cast a stone seaward . . . . from the shore
Go ripples, and far-off tides advance
Up the cold sands of Labrador
To start a glacier's avalanche.

Air

Adaptable element, fluid to all things' will
yet by its lack their master,
air is the matrix where we hollow out
our personal Merlin-towers of glass
to live marvelously castled.

Moving askew as wind
air unwinds the crossed ribbons of its maypole-dance,
blowing ships and seeds,
breaking the backs of trees,
keeping the globe that travels widdershins
still spinning with its tugging Westerlies.
Quiet, it holds up butterflies,
spreads traffic-lanes for hummingbirds and bombers
but betrays acrobats and apples.

Cambered roof against the rays of space,
the yonder with its vanishing iris,
theater of fire and mirages,
keyboard of sound:

WE MOVE ON TURNING STONE ☙ 1953–1956

how may we speak sufficiently of air
by whose presence in our bagpipe-breasts
we make our passionate music?

Yet this inseparable companion is never seen
in its purest state:
immaculate spirit must embrace the clay
to be made visible to earthy eyes.
So air collects salt, sand, dust,
sublimes to ice and snow,
turns cloud and piles up sunsets and thunder,
and like the pity of a god made flesh
lays on just tree and unjust, thirsting man
    the fingers of its catholic rain.

Flemish Artists

Fifteenth Century

What they loved, what their brushes proudly caressed
Was their rich, immediate North. They delighted to portray
The tapestried room with its mirrored *dinanderie,*
The fur on the burgher's coat, the chain on his breast.

Piety insisted only the holy, the past was worth
Rare powdered lapis lazuli or ground gold.
This problem faced each member of the painters' guild:
How to honour both God and His sparkling Earth.

So their subjects are Martyrs, Flights into Egypt, Views of Canaan;
But Sodom, say, is a pepper-pot town in the rear
Where Lot's wife tinily stiffens, while hugely at prayer
Down front is the patron's wife in a horned hennin.

The Song of the Sun ❧ Leah Bodine Drake

Angels are courtly *mignons* with crimped hair.
Paul suffers conversion near Damascus-gate
In full tilting-armour. The Baptist's head on a plate
Watches Salome fiddle some Flemish air.

Sometimes they concede slightly to the real East,
And then we'll get a Magus in a purple turban—
But his sleeves, as like as not, will be dagged and urban,
His squire a blond Flanderkin, hawk on wrist.

Look at any Virgin's Chamber, Annunciation . . . or rather, look
Through the room's usual little window . . . what
Do you find there? Palms? Orient domes? . . . you do not,
But steepled market-squares or Dutch seas pale as milk

Hemming green thrifty polders where the haywains pass,
Bringing the harvest home to the castle's Dame,
God's Mother, who may sit by a Gothic chimney's flame
In a halo that's part of an elegant screen of brass!

Through-Train

That night we hurtled through a little town,
one of the many where we didn't stop—
it wasn't, after all, much of a place,
some tank-town clustered close like a child's toy
under a courthouse clock. In the square
a public dance was going on, or carnival—
some sort of fiesta. Coloured lights were strung
over the very street our tracks cut through.

Out of the crowds, the flashing lights, one face
shone briefly, never known yet somehow known,
and it was the face that I was born to love!

Then it was whirled away, while the crossing-bell
clanged and clanged to the onward-rushing dark.

I never even learned that station's name.

The Unicorn Wounded

The beautiful, trusting beast that trotted out of the wood
To lay his head on the treacherous maiden's knees
Lies bleeding now, astonished at his quick wound,
In a hiding-place among the tapestry trees.

His elegant white hide rubies with his blood
Where the huntsman's spear struck but glanced aside.
Tears well in his blue eyes, fall. Bitterness feeds
On that heart so hot, so heavy with love and so betrayed!

The hunters snore in the pepperpot castle on the hill,
The spears are crossed on the walls, the maiden in bed
Crosses demure hands over sheets scented with dill:
The unicorn nurses his double hurt in the wood.

At dawn he'll waken, wound healed but with heart turned savage
With its overload of love too rich to bear
That love so delicately offered. Rage
Will make him paw earth—panthers will tremble. Then beware,

Castle folk, when walking your neatly-flowered swards:
The unicorn's hooves are sharper than unfaith or scorn.
He will stamp your needlework lilies to muddy shreds
And impale your choicest virgins on his horn!

The Song of the Sun ~ Leah Bodine Drake

Incoming Tide

The Dixie-cups, the orange peel, the lost spade,
Somebody's knitting clutched in a ravel of kelp,
Are being hurried away by watery brooms.

Going, going, the castle built out of sand,
Yesterday's news, the letter soddened to pulp—
They're on their way to the ocean's cluttered hells.

Even that length of sand we signed together
Where the dune-grasses bend their backs stiff with brine,
Is being scoured, smoothed, to never-was.

Who would know now where love was foe and friend
Or that your footprints ran awhile beside mine?
Our past drowns with the starfish, torn crab-claws

And the outline of the shore. The tide besoms
The shore's histories, as one clears summer's shells
From a mantel-piece. See, I have saved

This coil of fluted pearl from the rushing smother!
Take it, shelve it safe—as beyond seasons
The hour is stored in my heart's remembering rooms.

Drone

Gay burly beau, his life is summer only.
He lives in riot-time of green—jeweled summer
When golden odours rise from swamp and meadow
Of mint and clethra. O the lime's gold shadow
Falls on a world all one warm smell of honey
To this rich brummel in his banded gold!

We Move on Turning Stone ⁓ 1953–1956

He wings through mornings flower-sweet and gold,
Fit-as-a-fiddle velvet boy, fit only
To buzz in lazy joy and suck the honey
From honey-suckle swags, gold bells of summer
That chime so richly in the swamp's warm shadow
With clover-balls of sweetness in the meadow,

And he's the booming fop of the honey-meadow,
A swaggerer in velvet, boy of gold,
Upon whose useless head there falls no shadow
Of humming work: such haunts the virgins only,
Those fierce nuns who carry off the summer
To opulent cloisters dark with thrifty honey.

The warm days hum with their brisk song of honey,
Pure, hurried maidens in the lazy meadow!
Their tongues will seal away the happy summer
When riotous fields are wasted of their gold.
Proud amazons, their little hearts feel only
Scorn for the drone whose riches know no shadow.

Gourmand of grapes, the wild vine wears his shadow,
Rose and raspberry tangles cup him honey.
He thinks the goldenrod's sweet waters only
Distill for his delight and jewel the meadow!
He rinses his wings in odours rich as gold,
His heart is humming a song of always-summer.

But when October cools the gold of summer
On the poor clown falls the relentless shadow
Of thrifty virgin wings. O his splendid gold
Does not protect him from those nuns of honey!
He lumbers, stung to death, to the dark meadow
Where once he knew green days and riches only.

The Song of the Sun 🙵 Leah Bodine Drake

The swaggerer in gold lays on the meadow
His jeweled heart whose only song was summer;
And on him honey-dark falls the hive's shadow.

We Move on Turning Stone

We move on turning stone
Through the dark-bright of space,
Lighted by lonely sun
And the moon's known face.

We turn up every stone
Hoping to find some bright-
ness in dark. Alone
We seek an unknown light.

Darkly we turn our face
To suns and moons unknown,
We seek through lonely space
For brightness not in stone.

Lonely in unknown space,
Hopeful of dark or bright,
We seek in every face,
We turn towards any light.

The Gods of the Dana

The gods of the Dana are lords of one small green island.
They are tall, they have yellow hair, their brows are wide;
They have magical golden harps swung from their shoulders,
Their eyes are grey and look not to either side.

We Move on Turning Stone ~ 1953–1956

They go forth at dusk on fiery faëry horses
Through flowering thorn and over the peaty streams,
Kings of the ruined raths and the gull-loud places,
Of the fisherman's song and the lonely herd-girl's dreams:

Mider the Green, bearing the spiralling alder,
And sun-gold Lugh in a nimbus of feathered light,
Brighet the Horned scattering pale moon-fire
And Angus the Young circled with birds of white.

They are gods of this island only, narrow their kingdom
Bounded on every side by the screaming seas.
No one prays to them now in the windy mornings—
To Him on the Rood the wild Gael bend their knees.

Yet they ride from the hills at dusk, the gods of the Dana!
They guard the gates of the island east and west.
From the foe without and within they shield her beauty,
Against their terrible hearts her head is pressed.

For they have no other love, the gods of the Dana,
And they gave her long ago the gifts of the Shee:
The eyes of youth, the tongue of a linnet singing,
And the hunger and pride and grief of the restless sea.

Ark

Within the stable-smelling dark
Of Noah's pious, puissant Ark
The lion and the ram reclined,
Each mated after his own kind.
While the great gales around them tore
The lion hushed his hunting-roar,
And trembling in each trembling limb,
He cowered by the trembling ram.

The Song of the Sun ~ Leah Bodine Drake

Peace was the pact they gladly kept
While chaos through their landscape swept.

Land rose . . . . the married doves went free;
The forty days when earth was sea
Were over . . . . on the heathy ground
Stepped ram and ewe. With joyous bound,
The lion and the lioness
Roared with recaptured fierceness!
And off across the dripping hill
Fled sheep, raced lions for the kill.

Rock and Bramble

We're taught by rock and bramble
When flesh is young and tender,
By poison leaf, green apple
And yellow-jacket's stinger.
We touch and taste and suffer
And soon learn sweet from bitter.
By stern and stormy weathers
Flesh is made wiser, tougher.

On sharper stones and briars
We tear our hearts and stumble,
We eat forbidden apples
And late learn sweet from bitter.
The heart grows tougher, wiser,
As flesh grows old and knows it:
We're weathered grey with wisdom
When it's too late to use it.

WE MOVE ON TURNING STONE ❧ 1953–1956

Fairy-Tale: Twentieth Century

And now that he has climbed the stair
Beyond the last spell-guarded door
And slain the ogre in his lair
And laid him headless on the floor,

The king's son, bloody from endeavor,
Attains the maiden in the tower,
The princess of the Land of Never.

The castle clocks all strike the hour.

(The hour is a little late,
The princess is a little old.
She had a good long time to wait
And loves him not, if all were told.)

Under a streaming twilight sky
The hero leads his battered bride
Down from that fortress grim and sly
To his impatient charger's side.

Speak they, sing they, tell they so:

The prince, a simple-minded lout,
Forgets the dungeons far below,
Neglects to let the chained knights out.

Nor knows that in the castle's breast
Among the stone roots of the hold
The dragon and her children nest
Coil on coil, bright and cold.

The king's son and his lady strain
Through the dark wood about the place.
The princes once had scattered grain

The Song of the Sun ~ Leah Bodine Drake

Along the way to leave a trace
By which to find the long way back.

But owls and rats have gulped the clue.
The happy couple now, alack
Have no idea what to do.

The rain drips from the rusty trees
Upon a helmed, a braided head.
The princess, stifling back a sneeze,
Recalls the ogre's shaggy bed.

The prince, a talker, babbles on
About his horse, his sword, his spurs
And wonders where the path has gone.

(Remotely now the dragon stirs.)

Sardonic ravens, circling, say
In raven, What a place to spend
A honeymoon!

        (O what a way
For any fairy-tale to end!)

The Lazy Prince

I know the enchanted castle lies over the hill
Where the barley ends and those gloomy thornwoods thicken.
From my turret I've watched its weathercocks glitter and fail
To turn in any wind, its people and banners stricken

By the faëry sleep that has gripped it, ever since
The Princess (a beauty, they say) was pricked by the spindle
Of some old witch or another. A kiss from a prince
Takes, I believe, the place of bell, book and candle

We Move on Turning Stone ⁊ 1953–1956

In breaking the spell. I'd attempt the rescue myself
Being her neighbour, if only that confounded brier
Weren't so tough! .... and my armour's somewhere on a shelf.
And I've heard the stairs are steep that lead to her bower.

If I woke her, great gods! of course we'd have to wed!
I'd find myself with a bride whose tastes were passé,
For a century's a damned long time to be socially dead—
Oh, the time it would take to teach her our world's way!

But they say she's extremely pretty, and I'm a king's son,
And her castle lies practically on my own door-sill:
Maybe I'll ride over tomorrow ..... well, it's pleasant to plan
High daring to do, knowing I never will.

The Storks

They say the storks are leaving Europe, growing rare.
Those long-shanked gentlemen-fishers, farmers' friends,
Are leaving the Danish swangs and the Baltic mosses,
There are empty nests upon the stepped Dutch gables,
The Jutland thatch, the sloping Flemish roofs
And high, windy wheels poled above German cabbages.

The kindly burgher of Freiburg's chimney-pots,
Delft's water-wader in red galligaskins,
Ribe's grandfather-bird, Old Clappercraw.
Who flies the spring up from lands of sun and prayer
And blesses the house that wears his gawky nest—
Where has he flown? To marshes east of the sun?

More ancient than the phoenix, he is painted
On paleolithic caves, already aristocratic
Yet neighbourly, soon to step into fairytale
And to take under his wing men's newborn souls.

The Song of the Sun ❧ Leah Bodine Drake

Faithful and tender mate, provident sire—
The Arabs wrote, "Who kills a stork is an Unbeliever."

Most merciful bird, he spiraled the Gallows-Tree
Crying, "Be strong, be strong!" to the Crucified;
And having heartened Love's heart with these few words
Never spoke again; but his big, clumsy beak
Can clash a courteous greeting to his lady:
They tell this beside the tiled stoves of Sweden.

But soon blond children will lift little cold faces
To gusty Gothic skies, hoping for, not seeing
Clatterwings their kind fairy, their roof-angel,
Flapping up from Tunis bringing good luck and tulips.
To brood again on the brick stack, the ruined tower.
(Where does he go? To castles west of the moon?)

And Freiburg under the Schwarzwald, whose pines
Pad darkly down the slopes like a sloth of bears,
Will ring her great bells over the Munsterplatz—
Maria, Konrad, Michael, mighty *Christ*—
Calling the birds home to the steep ridge-poles,
And see no storks in their lordly sunset musters.

Perhaps the storks are weary of lands where pylons
String hangmen's-widdies across their froggy fens,
Of pumps that drink their bogs and watery kingdoms,
Of climbing wars that usurp their haughty flyways;
And though Ribe pray for storks, and Delft raise welcoming wheels,
The beloved birds are going. But where do they go?

We Move on Turning Stone ⊱ 1953–1956

Old Man on the Seashore

Morning

An old man in a greenish, too-long coat
shiny with wet sand
scrabbles among the kelp and mussel-shells
at the sea's edge, under a brindled sky.

What is he hunting for so furiously among the tide's rummage,
fumbling the slimy weed with knarred, red hands,
casting here and there like an eager old hound
along the ripple-marks
made by the tide's hellos and well-aways?
Are you searching for treasure from jeweled under-caves
that the ocean promised once,—
a mermaid's looking-glass, a living star, a lost crown?
Or something you as a child possessed,
some toy, a castle of sand that the tide swept out?

The gulls at dawn's edge wheel and scream,
the sky silvers, the water silvers, laps at his heels.
He still bends to his task, busy with the shore's trash,
picks up a soggy basket, a bottle, a torn shoe,
a few sticks of driftwood for a fire,
then shuffles on,
clasping to his breast the sea's riches, the precious gifts
given him by the sea at his life's edge
that his life's fires may burn for one more day.

Zanzibar

I know words that are fun to say:
Armadillo, and Mandalay,
Jericho, calico and balloon,

The Song of the Sun ❧ Leah Bodine Drake

Jabberwock, jitterbug, pantaloon,
Minaret, miniver, samovar—
And one that zings like a falling star—
   Zanzibar.

I know words that cast a spell:
Sorceress, amethyst, Tinker-Bell,
Coromandel and Timbuctoo,
High cockalorum and cockatoo,
Wuthering, willowy, and bazaar,
But what has the plink of a light guitar?
   Zanzibar!

There are tinkling words like Kinnikinnick,
And twinkling words like candlewick,
Words that are silly, like fiddle-dee-dee,
Words that are happy, like jamboree;
But what makes you think of things afar
Where lions and spices and palm-trees are?
   Zanzibar!

The Woods Grow Darker

We feared the incubus, the hex.
Passing a pond, we crossed two sticks
Against the green-haired water-nix.

Once woods were dark with goblin forms,
But boughs of oak and ash were charms
Against the witch, the nightmare swarms.

We are much wiser now—such fears
Have been an old wives' tale for years.
We have more modern fears these years:

We Move on Turning Stone ~ 1953–1956

We fear the mind's rank Freudian fen,
The death unleashed from cyclotron,
The Iron Curtain closing down,

The spy, the ships from space . . . we scurry
Through mental woods grown dark and eerie,
With not even twigs of ash to carry.

The Crows

I shortcut home between Wade's tipsy shocks,
And lookout crows alert in the bare elm
Ask each other about this form that walks
Stubbled mud they consider their own farm.
They know there's sometimes death where such shapes go.
I have no gun—I even feel akin
To these rude, lively birds. But to a crow
Kinship means Crow, and I'm not of his clan.

Off they flap to the wood with a hoarse curse,
And though the cornfield's greyer with them gone
I'm glad they're skeptics: someday someone else
Trudging these ruts may raise a sudden gun.

Distrust me, crow!—the not-as-crow, the other.
Croak "Damn your eyes!" and call no man your brother.

The Rain on the Stone

Abelard argued, Augustine wrote,
Plato and all the pride of Greece
Pondered and sifted wrong from right—
Their words to me are gabble of geese.

To a crow kinship means Crow,

WE MOVE ON TURNING STONE ❧ 1953–1956

What is wisdom when love has gone
And the rain falls on the cold stone?

Phidias carved and Rembrandt drew,
Van Gogh splintered the heart of light,
And never breaking and always blue
Hokusai's wave is the eye's delight!
But what is beauty when love has gone
And the rain falls on the cold stone?

Buddha mastered the wheel of life,
Moses thundered and Jesus taught
And martyrs died for their dear belief . . .
I know, I know, and the knowledge is naught—
And gods and beauty and wisdom's gone
When the rain falls on a cold stone.

The Weeds and the Wilderness

> *O let them be left, wildness and wet,*
> *Long live the weeds and the wilderness yet.*
> —GERARD MANLEY HOPKINS: *Inversnaid*

After you pass Owl's Candle and Pickporridge the lane tilts
to Marry-in-the-Up, where a stone barn burrows
into the steep side of the Pickpack lording the Waver valley.

Follow the cranky path and you come out upon Pickpack Heath,
magenta with heather in flower or coppered with bracken,
squatting like a gipsy in rainbow rags above the tidy hedges of the vale.
Here the track walks by itself
between abrupt pools of ancient clay-pits,
their cobalt water cloddy with cloud-shadow,
and ends at Brock's Clump where the old barrow humps in the ling
and five haggard pines, their orange trunks rooted in giants' bones,

The Song of the Sun ❧ Leah Bodine Drake

knuckle together against the huffles of wind.
This is the high place, the house of hare and whimbrel.
No one comes or goes.
Only at dusk a fox will slip like a rusty ghost among the thistles and
    broken stones
or a badger lumber from his sandy holt under a snarl of bramble.
From here you can overlook the brooky lands from Hern Plash to
    Puddleswick
where the Waver loses itself in marshes, and the basket-willows
drown their Ophelia-hair in little sly streams.
There the lanky heron feeds among the sedges and bayard moss
or flaps silently, like a thought through an unfretted mind,
over Rockinglass and its quaking sands to the hidden ponds of
    Dragonsholm and Pendragon,
far as The Slake itself where the mud wears tidewater like a silver skin.
This is the wet kingdom, the house of ooze and rush.

Heath and gorse, marsh and moss, the sandy, the sodden....
these are the uncouth places that planners of garden-cities do not love.
They are not concerned with man and his notions.
They exist only for themselves, and for that human few
who need the earth's tart as well as honeysweet
and feel most at home in such unhomely wastes.
They will go some day, I suppose,
the heather uprooted, the badger killed with his kindle,
even the flats drained for corn and emptied of hern.

So let me hold in my mind a day
when summer burned to autumn, when I walked
from Owl's Candle over the umber ling of the Pickpack to Brock's Clump
in a warm, gusty drizzle, with a sky of smoky pearl.
In wild air that smelled of pine and fern
I stood to my knees in burnt-gold brake that dripped with pendles of rain,
and saw below me

We Move on Turning Stone ~ 1953–1956

a swan rise from the wickers of Hern Plash with a squeak and brattle of wings,
to fly over to Rockinglass through a sudden spangle of sun.

The Well

The well in the field is bitter,
Only the spider
Lairs by that sullen glass,
Only the dry leaves sink
To its scummed face:
All other things
Pass on to fresher springs.
Not even the tramp in summer's drouth
Stops at that place.

Just once there was one who came,
Furtive, by night, and drank,
Being crazy with thirst
Wilder than he could bear;
Then wiped the rank
Taste from his mouth
On a ragged sleeve, and cursed
The well, despising in his shame
That water and himself for drinking there.

Under Funereal Lilies

Under funereal lilies here lies one
Of subtle lip and glittering, false tongue,
Whose words too deeply prized so flowered my mind
That even now, great tigerish blooms, they burn
Long after words of truer men have been
Scattered and lost, dry petals down the wind.

The Song of the Sun ❧ Leah Bodine Drake

The Good-Advisors

"Give him the back of your hand!"
was their advice,
"For he's empty of all but lies
And he'll take no woman to wife—
Don't waste your life
Waiting for him," they said.

Ah, how can they understand,
Bring richly fed.
How to the starved even half
A loaf, though bitter, is better
Than no bread?

The Crying of the Grass

When I press your head to mine
A voice cries from the grass:
"This head you hold so dear
Under the grass shall lie.
Far beyond wood and wave,
Where your feet will never pass,
His hushed, forgetful heart
Will nourish the wild rye
And the beating of his heart
Pass into the wind's sighs."

O with your mouth of love
And your heart's beat close to mine,
Silence the crying grass!
Speak, that I may not hear
The grass and its terrible lies!

WE MOVE ON TURNING STONE ☙ 1953–1956

Noon Light

Motionless hang the pears
Carved golden on the bough;
The pool is pewter now
Unstirred by torpid airs.

And hidden in the grass
The orchard's shadows sleep
Drowned in the noon's blue deep
That seems will never pass.

Invisible with light
The sun at zenith stands;
Time's vertical thin hands
Halt folded out of sight.

Time is and never was;
Time is and will not come;
The heart sleeps in a womb
Of light like globèd glass.

Beneath these flooded skies
The harrowed heart grows calm
And golden in our palm
Peace like a ripe fruit lies,—

Until the crystal walls
Shake in the evening's breath,
And life awakes to death
And the first pear falls.

The Song of the Sun ❧ Leah Bodine Drake

High Wire

Balanced upon a shining wire
Between the poles Need and Desire
I dance decisions sharp as fire.

Backward, forward, see me go!
My spangled feet now quick, now slow—
No safety net is spread below.

I hold my heart's bright parasol
And bounce as lightly as a ball
Above each day's steep waterfall,

Taking the wire's shining dare
In almost-joy and near-despair
O how my spangles fire the air!

My nimble leaps, my bold sashays,
Spectators watch them with amaze—
O how my peril lights their days!

And as I dance in spangled light
The twin poles hold the wire tight
Almost to breaking, left and right,

Straining Need against Desire
To balance life's amazing wire
Where the quick soul can dance its fire!

The Word of Willow

Older than Eden's planting, older than elves,
Willows remember a grand world of wet
Whose map was webbed by feathery, walking groves.

We Move on Turning Stone ≈ 1953–1956

They dream of that rich mud, they whisper yet
Of hazy, rindled valleys, the hush and drip,
Where willows strode about on yellow feet:

A race not human although somewhat, with green harps,
Masters of poems and small magics, who could make
Water-spells and runes for roots and sap.

Then Adam woke and named things: the willow-folk
Became all tree because he called them so,
Became sleeping princesses in towers of bark

And pollarded princes—all lost, the lore they knew.
Now their children shade sad lovers, burial-grounds
And haunted houses. Some are resigned. A few

Still weep into streams and wring grey, gnarled hands
Over wild feet knotted and held tight
In man's tamed earth, the power gone from their wands.

Others grow crabbed from straining against fate,
Are racked into Rackham-crones, hags and grutchers
Huddled in tattered shawls, awry with spite,

Wicked old wicker wizards propped on crutches,
And hobnobs of witches clutching besoms in bogs,
Hatching plots against man under their twiggy thatches.

But all sing "Willow, willow!" In shallow quag,
By dyke and ditch, from osier-holt to holt
A question sighs along their yellow rags:

"What is the master-rune of our leaf-alphabet—
The old Word of the Willow that could free us yet
To be trees as men walking?"
                    They forget, forget . . . .

The Song of the Sun ❧ Leah Bodine Drake

The Harvest

"Who is this one who strides
    Over your fallow field?"
    Mutter the watching skies.
"Adam the sower hides
  Seed in my empty field,"
    The fallow earth replies,
    "And great will be my yield."

"What will your harvest bear?"
    Murmurs the seeking wind.
    "Trouble," replies the earth,
"Crosses and thorns and war,
Terror and lust and death—
    Oh, trouble of every kind!
    But mercy, too, I'll bear."

"But who will eat such bread?"
    Whisper the careless rains.
"His sons will reap my wheat,"
The earth replies. "His sons
Will live by my black bread,
    Having none else to eat,
    And sometimes find it sweet."

The Fawn

God wearied of the world. He watched its strife,
Its senseless shouts and cruelties and kings,
And wondered if He had created life
To evil ends. He mused upon these things,
Then stretched His hand to pluck the noisy star
From the vast silence of His firmament,

The tiny creature . . . gave a little bound, frantic with joy,

The Song of the Sun ~ Leah Bodine Drake

When through His tears He saw a wood afar
Where a red fawn beside its mother went.
The tiny creature tottered on its feet,
Fell, staggered up and gave a little bound,
Frantic with joy, with life so new and sweet,
The sun so warm, so calm the woods around!
God smiled, and stayed His hand. "Earth may abide,—
Some things I made are good," God said, and sighed.

Moment in Paradise

Forever in God's eye the scene is fixed:
Eve, with the Snake beside her ear,
The apple on its bough unplucked,
As all was meant to be,
And Himself waiting in His heaven of Now.

The apple hangs, its core
Is richness turned to rot:
A bad world that may be.
God waits, the angels wait,
The creatures of the Garden wait,
Lion and lamb.
The moment waits on Eve.
Eve hesitates . . . . .
And then she takes the apple in her hand,
And all the rest is what has come to be,
And all the rest is what we weep about.

But in God's eye forever she will stand—
Eve, with not-lifted hand,
And the apple whole and round,
As was first meant to be,
    Alas, and
   Still on His tree.

We Move on Turning Stone ❧ 1953–1956

Comment on Man

We gaze up at the stars and say:
One of those blazing beacons may
Well be a world of bliss,
A country where
Dwell beings kind and fair
Moving in brighter air—
Far happier than this!

Ingenious mankind,
Dreaming, ambitious, blind,
In some not-distant age may find
The certain means
To reach whatever world he choose—
Mars, Mercury, Betelgeuse—
By his inventive wit,
His intricate machines.

O, if there is a heaven there—
The blossoming place
Of some wise, happy, helpless race—
Be sure that man will spoil it,
Bringing to the most serene of stars
His terrible toys:
His lust and cruelty, dirt and noise,
His billboards and his wars.

A Memory

A garden of old trees,
and the scent of pear;
a fence half tumbled down
where the thin ferns grew;

The Song of the Sun ~ Leah Bodine Drake

and the child that once was I
crouched in the grass
watching a drop of dew
silently tremble and fall
from a tip of the curving fern,
seeing a drop of dew
for the very first time at all!

After the lifelong years
I can smell the blossoming pear,
Back in the long lost years
Still trembles a drop of dew . . . . .

Why does this memory start?
Why does it shake my heart?

The Forerunner

In the scorched places between Kedron and the Dead Sea,
in the birdless land hummocked with pallid clay like the heads of lepers,
satyrs blinked at him from orange rocks,
ghouls spat at him from the carcasses of camels
when that scarecrow man Jokhannon
wandered the gritty waste.

He too met the Tempter.
When he roamed pitted hillocks seeking honey in the grey towers
      of the bees,
little imps—coneys with faces of pale girls—
lisped at his heels.
When he prayed voices assailed him, hissed from the dust-whirls,
roared blasphemies from the corrugated mountains, the bitter
      pink ravines
where the bad Jinn have their spectral castles,
doors opened in the air, spinning vortices of negation.

We Move on Turning Stone ~ 1953–1956

Sometimes mirages promised palaces and lakes,
flimsy gardens falsifying sand.
Sweet whisperings, sweet odours, rose and spice, stole through his sleep;
and worst of all Hell's lures,
would often come tripping towards him, two by two,
twelve ingratiating devils in the appearance
of young men and old, who cried
"Hail, Master! Hail, Messiah!"

But powers of the air cannot prevail with one
who hears the horn of judgement in his secret ear,
who feels the feet of the expected One
walking along the jordans of his blood.

So John saw the appointed day rise over the horns of the mountains.
Light danced like angels along their crests
as the Forerunner went striding cityward through the waste—
a dry wind shaped like a man, a walking voice,
a lion who cleared a pathway for the Lamb,
a thorn who knew he only foretold the Rose,
great cock of God who warned of the rising Sun
lest men should wither by its sudden fire,
lest men should perish from the shock
          of unprecedented Love.

The Nail

I sinned a sin today
That hurt myself and Heaven.
Oh yes, I know full well
The deed I did was sin!
For faintly, far away,
I heard a hammer's din—
Steady, relentless, even—
Back over time's abyss,

The Song of the Sun ❧ Leah Bodine Drake

Hammering one more nail
Into a burdened cross.

Multiple Clay

What strangeness forms my flesh, my intimate bone?
What brittle dust blown east off China's hills
Spumed into cloud above cold salmon-shoals
To fall as rain upon Kentucky stone?

Some druid oak shrank to this finger's length,
Amethyst-matrix split to line this skull,
These thighs are pedestaled on some beautiful
Mediterranean column's crumbled plinth.

And who lay down and gave his precious head
To earth that I might lift mine in the sun?
Whose iris greys my eye? Whose hair, unbound
By roots of plum and pear, is mine to braid?

What multiple clay fused to the single grain
That is myself, no family-tree can tell,
Or what fires lit my senses' heaven and hell.
These limbs are but a momentary loan

That I'll repay before I even know
What ends they've served. But while they walk the world
They move with wonder, thankfulness and pride—
O you who'll wear them after, wear them so!

WE MOVE ON TURNING STONE ❧ 1953–1956

The Hand

I.
The X-ray's eye that sees into the sheep
Sees the wombed lamb, the five-fold calcium stream
Of a foetal hand that ancient choice must shape
Into the animal hoof: these digits seem
Pathetic copies of our own proud five!
And by the lion's blunted paw is shown
Some old remote wrong-turning, which only gave
This great gold hammer to the lion line.

One creature chose the hand. In one alone
The Adam furied underneath the fur,
Aspiring spirit fought with brutal bone,
Furied and fought!—and rayed out like a star
To stroke a leaf, lift a stick at will,
Making a longer arm with which to kill.

II.
There were cold seas, and woods with the sea's moan,
And caves with fires at bay against the night;
And there were terrible choices: speed or brawn,
Instinct or mind, and later, love or hate,
Hand over hand, the earth saw Adam climb
From hole to tower, from slime to ledge to crest:
Some four-foot craft was lost to gain a thumb,
Some furry joy to earn a rich unrest.

Now at the moon he shakes his fisted five,
He tampers with the engines of the sun.
Pollutes the waters: will his hand engrave
HIC JACET on the planet's breast of stone
And hang all life to cross that final Tau?
Better the bestial wood, the primal paw.

The Song of the Sun ❧ Leah Bodine Drake

The Prisoner

Someday I'll hold a mirror to my face
And marvel then to see a captive there,
Peering at me beneath the greying hair
With shocked bewildered eyes set in a lace
Of delicate fine lines that slow days trace
Implacably, with infinite cruel care;
And find a self that once stood proud and fair
Turned to a stranger with a crone's grimace.

This is the prison that a jesting Fate
Slyly builds up within the traitor flesh
To snare the spirit . . . and no tear nor cry
Will smash these walls, nor ravel out the mesh
Of cob-web years, where, wild and passionate,
Fierce with life, there beats the Judas'd I.

The Face in the Water
1957–1964

THE FACE IN THE WATER ~ 1957–1964

The Rider

It is the East we dream of: there
We'd find the answer to despair,
The waters sweet, the women fair.

Seekers of truth ride through our land.
They scorn our commonplace and wend
Eastward: this we can understand.

There came a rider reined his beast
Beside our fountain, cried "At last
I've reached the waters of the East!"

The East our shabby countryside
And nothing more? "You lie!" we cried,
And so we stoned him till he died.

The Robin

The year half gone,
And the low sun
Sending long lights through darkening trees,
And a robin singing his good-night song
Somewhere among the leaves,
The music spilling like water from cool springs.
Limpid and clear,
As he sang last year
In gold light slanted and long.

With the old summer joy he sings and sings! . . . .
O Mother dead, I cannot bear his song!

The Song of the Sun ❧ Leah Bodine Drake

The Hellenic World

The Hellenic world emerges in our dream half history, half fable.
How the great names rise, passionless as marble, bathed in cloudless noon!
Helen and Homer, Plato, Pericles,
Phidias, Agamemnon, Leonidas—strained by time
of all colour and turmoil into the white simplicity of stone.

The Hellenic world . . . . the Helios-hour of man,
when man lived in the here-and-now,
and heart and mind meeting in equilibrium
drew order out of chaos,
giving the western world its darling dream:
We are the heirs, we boast, of marble men.

And the men were shaped by their land and its marvelous light,
a land saturated with light,
where the rocks give light back in floods of laurel, myrtle, ilex, pine,
and the sea tosses light back into the wind as if blue wells of fire
fountained beneath the waves.
A country defined by its own form and texture—
horizons intimate and lacking mystery, bony hills,
dry plains sparkling like goldstone, savage brooks
whose little journeys the eye follows in a glance,
thrusting headlands whose naked stones make pedestals
for the column of natural man.
That earth blossomed in man's image:
rivers tangled the pale hair of naiads among their cresses,
bay leaves rustled on the feet of dryads, goats played on pipes.
Even the gods were hardly more than men,
coming down from their accessible heavens
to mate with herdboys and kings' daughters in water-gap and fuming cave,
amazed and ravished as any mortal by their world's wonder!
The gods' houses stayed close to their worshippers, rooted like trees
in the common soil—even the Parthenon, synthesis

The Face in the Water ❧ 1957–1964

of body and mind made visible,
keeps in its marble posts the shape and sturdiness of oaks.

We forget now that the marble cast a shadow: we forget
the painted boys, the treadmill slaves, the oracles
with their glib puns and shoddy miracles.
We remember only the cities blond as honey among holy olives,
caryatids poised like jonquils on the shrines,
calm foreheads of philosophers.
We forget the haggling on the wharves, the quicksilver lying.
We remember only the horse-wild helms of heroes.

But how can we claim descent from these people of high noon?
They turned their backs on all that dazzle us:
antiquity, the faraway, the sky, the dissonances of personality.
We are soul-probers, star-mappers, wood-walkers, scalers of Everests,
pursuers of tomorrow and tomorrow and tomorrow:
how can we understand a people without clocks?

They were sailors, but of narrow seas,
poets, for ages without an alphabet,
artists, whose pigments had no green,
seekers of truth, to whom the mask was all the man,
masters of numbers, without zero—
    (for how could Nothing take a sculptured shape?)

How can we know them, whose word for *slave* was *thing*?

O lost Hellenic world,
small steady sun around which civilizations circle!
Your way was not our way, nor your day our past.
To us, the children of the gothic woods, cold fogs and yearning spires,
you are our darling dream, our marble fable!
And from this raveling age, when the ground you stood so firm upon
trembles in all its atoms at our feet,
we send our thanks to you,

The Song of the Sun ~ Leah Bodine Drake

for what we never could create and barely understand:
the white honey of your broken comb
caught in the bronze fingers of a charioteer,
in the rondure of a cup unearthed at Delos,
in scattered Sapphic lines . . . . .

We are not your sons, only your lovers.

"In the Night I Awoke"

(To Mother.)

In the night I awoke, and I was weeping.
I dreamed you had died, and fell at my feet and cried
Some agonized word.
I could hear it as I woke—
And O, the relief that arose in me like a wave
When I heard the rain,
And knew I had been sleeping
And had only dreamed you had died!

And then the wave broke,
And the old knowledge flooded my brain
That the summer rain
Was falling upon your grave
           where you had lain
                     seven months dead.

The Face in the Water ⁓ 1957–1964

"Brightness Falls from the Air"

(To Mother)

She who was here, who took her place
In the world's space,
With her body's splendid tower,
Who lived her mortal hour,
Is gone, is gone,
And the song her loving made
Is still, and flowers not anywhere
In this world's air.

Now where she stood no love is,
Where her heart beat no song is,
The stones of her tower fell apart,
And the music of her heart
Went away somewhere.
But in some lovelier air
A place is splendoured by her soul's strong tower
And her life's great triumphing flower.

Alone

When I opened the door, the wind
Blew into the hall with me.
That was all there was in the house with a voice,
And the voice a moan.
I was alone, and it was dark November.
And I remembered how it used to be
When I opened the door—
Someone would call to me,
Somebody there,
Early and late to care

The Song of the Sun ❧ Leah Bodine Drake

If I came into the house at all
Or went out of it.

"I Dreamed That You Took My Arm." . . .

I dreamed that you took my arm;
I cried, "I thought you were dead!"
And you smiled, and shook your head:
"I'm alive," you said.
And we walked side by side:
"Oh, is this Heaven?" I cried,
And you nodded your head.
And the place where we walked was the road
Under the oaks to the farm:
"But it looks like the farm!" I said;
"There's the orchard-lot, and I see the barn
And the lilacs by the shed—
Why, we're home again!"
          and you smiled—
"Of course," you said.

Uncle Jay

Eccentrics, characters. . . . those off-beat ones
every town has a spicing of,
who exasperate and embarrass solid citizens, but in the long run
        come to be cherished and bragged-on:
   "We had a fellow where I lived—a real character". . . .

What city hasn't its old ladies in awful hats and dragging hems,
who walk side-streets replacing manhole-covers
       so stray dogs won't fall into them?—
men, youngish sometimes, living in river-shacks all broken out
with umbrellas and goats and empty cereal boxes,

The Face in the Water ❧ 1957–1964

    who locate water with a doodlebug
        and can quote you Greek?

We had a character in our clan, one of my uncles on my father's side—
    Uncle Jay—
a stout man with prominent mournful teeth,
who never married and got religion late.
How he fretted his mother with his lamp going till all hours in the attic,
while he studied Scripture at the top of his voice!
    "Nobody at our house has slept much since Jay found Jesus", she
        used to say.
At last my uncle, primed with golden rules,
took to haunting the depot when the trains came in.
He'd hail the traveling-men like they were long-lost sheep,
sometimes climb a pile of crates or trunks,
    shouting he'd come to save them damn their guts.

    (The station-master didn't like it, but what could he do?
        Uncle Jay was one of the Old Families.)
Drummers or visiting mayors—it made no never-mind to my uncle.
He meant to shout salvation into every pore of them
until breath or inspiration ran out
    or a porter wanted to move the boxes.
Some of them listened, briefly enchanted, I guess,
by the unexpected oaths, the big sad teeth
the pious saliva spraying them, and all that murderous love
    he sweated through his shirt.
We children, hanging about the edges, would giggle in wonderful joy
and a proud shame in our uncle, the family scandal.

Years after, in another city, and long since the death of Uncle Jay,
I met a man whose only memory of our town
    was that holy yelling.
He had changed trains there and could hardly recall the place,
only the name and that big, toothy figure under the station light
    shaking a Bible in his face

The Song of the Sun ❧ Leah Bodine Drake

while the train backed and clanked and let off steam.
He remembered Uncle Jay.
He said he'd never seen such sorrowful teeth or heard such bossy cussing.
    "I learned a couple of whiz-bang cuss-words
        that night from that uncle of yours",
he told me, with a kind of gratitude forty years removed.

Folk-Tale

There was a land where all the toys were made,
The clockwork-men, the painted tops, the drums,
The tiny cradles carved for tiny dolls,
The jumping-jacks, the balls of coloured glass
To swing from all the wide world's Christmas trees.

There was a land of green, dwarf-haunted heights
Where happy homesteads nestled.
                      There would be
An old grandfather seated by the door,
His stein of beer beside him on the bench,
A china pipe with roses on the bowl
Waiting his leisure.
                Still the good old man
Must carve an arm just-so, or put the last
Fine eyelash upon some small Gretel's doll.
Around the open door the air was warm
With spicy cooking-smells; and up the hill
Came Hansel with his merry violin
To make the old man glad with that new waltz
His teacher said he'd mastered.
                    Over all
The golden light of evening spread its wings,
And Peace walked through the town on unseen feet.

THE FACE IN THE WATER ~ 1957–1964

    *   *   *

There was a land—remember?—where these things
Were part of every day . . . . .
        How strange it seems
To hear the old folk tell of ancient times
When Germany was the land where men made toys!

The Tale of Tannhauser

The tale says Rome refused him. The aging rake
In sackcloth, on arrival in pardon's city,
Found that salvation was a hard nut to crack
For one whose change of heart was seven years tardy.

At the Holy Father's feet Tannhauser wept.
Stammering out a story about the cave
In the belly of the Höraelburg, where he had kept
High court with the queen of bawdy and knew her love.

The Pope and the pilgrims were profoundly shocked,
For seven fat years in that randy faëryland
Was really pigging it! The Pontiff shook
His jeweled stave and named Tannhauser damned.

He said his crook would blossom like the rose
Before such a lengthy lecher be forgiven.
With Gothic pride the knight dusted his knees
And turned his back on that stony-hearted haven:

He would seek the old hot mountain of his youth
Up in the German pines. As he trudged North
Tannhauser sighed: what was repentance worth?
He gave up his plans to marry Elizabeth.

The Song of the Sun ~ Leah Bodine Drake

Now the Venus-rock is always easy to find. Back at
The familiar wicket he gave the usual rap.
Before they opened the door he could hear the racket,
The drums and laughter. But he just wanted to sleep,

With a place to hang his harp out of the rain.
He was dead on his feet and in no gamesome mood.
Then Venus herself came downstairs at the din,
And hushed the noise, and took his hands and shooed

Her girls away, the kind good trull, and said
"You're home, now, dearie, come sit by the hearth,"
Stroking the icy raindrops from his beard
Crooning "There, there," as she fed him warm broth.

And Tannhauser slept and dreamed that Elizabeth,
Winged like an angel, with special orders from Heaven,
Crowned him before all Rome with a rose wreath
Whose buds were picked from the amazed staff of Urban.

Lullaby After Death

Now the mole in downward tower,
Now the bee in cupped flower,
Fish in pool and bird in tree,
All, all are sleeping—
As you, belovèd, with heavy head
Sleep tonight in a green bed,
Beyond what was or is to be
That sets the dark world weeping.

While the old slow planet turns,
While the star of summer burns—
Hot Antares in the south—
You will know the keeping

THE FACE IN THE WATER ❧ 1957–1964

Of the dark forgetful earth.
All the tale of sorrow told,
Never lover, friend or child,
Now may kiss or bruise your mouth,
Never sound of weeping wild
Wake your deep sleeping.

All the world could do is done:
You are safely sleeping
Where the roots of silence are:
All the cities of earth may fall,
You will hear not—let them fall!
Nothing on our troubled star
Breaks your slumber—no, not one
Sound of your child weeping.

With Her Death

Within her eye the wild world moved and shone,
Within her ear the sea-bell rang its song,
And on her tongue the grape grown dark with wine
Savoured its own sweetness, and the strong
Bones of the earth she walked on at her touch
Shifted to lift the jeweled hills in place;
Lilac and lily realized their rich-
Breathing hearts when she pressed them to her face.

Now the grape hangs unripened, and the sea's
Great clapper is dumb without an echoing shell
And rocks are locked in sleep: one of the ways
In which life looks at itself and knows its soul
Passed with her passing. The world's gleam and shine
Died with her eyes—and shows how dark in mine!

The Song of the Sun ~ Leah Bodine Drake

To Mother

When you were here
I hardly knew
You were the air
I daily drew,

The solid world
On which I stood,
The water and bread
My common food.

Now for that life
Whose breath was love,—
That water, that loaf—
I daily starve.

Ariadne on Naxos

(New Wine in an Old Bottle)

Theseus left Ariadne flat:
She never quite got over that.

She married Bacchus? Oh, I think
That simply means she took to drink.

A Voice

Out of the vast
I entered time
And a circling place.

I had a form.

THE FACE IN THE WATER ~ 1957–1964

* * *

I breathed an air.

I loved, I wept,
But why or how
I remember not.

One name I spoke,
One face I kissed.
Now I've gone back
Into the vast.

Somewhere in time
Is a circling place:
What was that name?
Where was that face?

The Convent Bell

Before dawn, in night's worst hour, alone,
I awoke and thought of my dead, and wept.
There was none to comfort me. I wept.
It was night's deadliest hour, I was alone.

Then out of the frozen dark the sound of a bell
From the house of the Poor Clares—a single voice
Lifting heavenward those holy voices of peace
That spoke for us, asking that all be well.

On chilly stones nuns knelt and told their beads
For those who weep, for the newly-buried dead.
The silent town turned over in its bed,
Orion tilted down. And still they prayed,
And rang their bell—voice of unsleeping love
Through night's worst hour, when the great griefs move.

The Song of the Sun ❧ Leah Bodine Drake

"Only a Little Dust"

I shall cry out "Unjust!"
Against your death that made
So small, so brief a stir
Among the world's affairs.
Anger instead of tears
Rise within my breast,
That when you were borne away
Over the road from town,
Only a little dust
Rose on the winter air
To mark the passage there
Of beauty and wit and pride
That never will come again
In the same blood and bone.
I shall cry out "Unfair!"
That the world you had put away
Went on its own affairs.
Went on and did not care
What light went darkened there.
With only a little dust
Rising, settling down
On the common road from town.

That Summer

That summer everyone said they had never
Seen such a summer: the sun burned
Just enough, and when we needed a shower
A shower came, and a perfect rainbow shone.

The Face in the Water ❧ 1957–1964

The hay got in before the storm furied;
Blackberries burst their wine-skins: nature's palm
Cupped the earth gently, gently. The river flowed
Silky and green at the bend when we whooped and swam.

And the sky was blue as God, and the corn ears
Filled and richened; and at the river's bend
The mockers sang all night in the sycamores!
That was the summer when my brother drowned.

Lying Awake

Lying awake in bed
I feel the planet turn,
Heavy with tears and sin,
Heavy with all its dead.

There was a time I drew
Close to a darling form
Beside me, loving and warm,
There was a voice I knew

Calming the darkest air,
Saying, "O do not fear—
We have each other near!"

That voice is now nowhere.

In the long dark I lie
And count the heavy years.
Red in my window, Mars
Burns like a baleful eye.

The Song of the Sun ❧ Leah Bodine Drake

What the Devil Said

I.

Come to me, all you who burn and are complex-laden,
        And I will give you lust.
My couches bid your most lewd dreams from hiding,
        Fantastically fleshed,
And when you couple coldly in my name,
Lo! there in the belly-midst of you I am!

II.

For the poor in spirit who find this universe
        Too rich to look upon
I've spectacles of artfully blemished glass
        That can soot the sun,
Show Earth a sty and men like walking turds:
Wear these, all you who paint or work with words.

III.

How often I do bless the Christian meek
        Who tempt the passionate strong
To strike, and strike again, their forgiving cheek!
        Some virtues change
Mild anger into murder, even war—
And the lion's led by the lamb to my trap-door.

IV.

However, pride's still double meekness' worth,
        So slay the lordly trees,
Conquer the grass with concrete, kill all life
        That's odd or does not please.
Creation's varied, but the world has space
Only for one breed—yours, the monkey's race.

The Song of the Sun ❧ Leah Bodine Drake

I hear at the window the same silly tune
Of desperation, and find he's crawled once more

Through some hole he's never able to find from this
Side. I repeat the performance: raise the screen,
Prod him out . . . oh, to stay hard, serene,
Against these tiny plights like everyone else!

I'm getting bored with his fix. I know he would
Not lift a wing to help me. I say
Suffering is natural and so on—who am I
To question the laws of life, holy and good?

But here he is back, bumping himself about,
Bruising his wings against the laws of life;
And I decide that they aren't quite good enough,
And I open the damned screen and let him out.

The Witches

Across the tapestry-lands of the Middle Ages
Like a murky skirl of clouds the witches ride,
Glooming the hunting-woods and the proud churches.

We picture them: the taggles of hags astride
Boar-pigs and withy-besoms in peaked hats,
Red-cloaked or lewdly nude, under a burred

Moon, flying to Lapland for their Sabbats,
Or hopping hobby-horse to the Druid Stones
To skip to the Devil's loo with prancing goats,

The Song of the Sun ~ Leah Bodine Drake

And the cry grew wild,
"Lover, where are you—where?"
But the winter air
Answered never a word.
But I heard the cry.
And it echoed my own despair
And the voice was my own that cried.

[Untitled]

Good Pope Urban
Wrapt his head in a turban.
He knew it was Mohammedan
But said he didn't give a damn.

The Spray

I have danced with berries in my hair
and torn my flesh on their briars.
I joyed in the berry,
I wept at the briar,
but I still hold out my hand for the whole spray.

On the Night-Wind

O Mother,
is that your voice I hear
sighing among the willows?

THE FACE IN THE WATER ❧ 1957–1964

The Growing Tree

A growing tree scratched fingers on the screen
and beat a tiny torment on my brain.
It was my study window, and the sound
pushed like a busy meddler through my thoughts.

I broke the branch that beckoned, 'though the wound
my fingers made defaced the little thing:
I didn't like to look too closely then
upon that stump of tree. But nature went
about her silent cure. It wasn't long
before new leaves shot from the crippled stalk
and brushed against my window, just as though
I'd never tried to twist its life to mine,—
So ruddy-green, so desperate to be!—
I felt almost a villain for my act.

I don't know why I'd ever thought that I
was any more important than a tree,
or why it was my right alone to say
which way a bough should go.
                              I've let it be.
A tree knows best the place that it should grow,
and I know mine a little better now.

The Wasp in the Window

A wasp for his own reasons has crept here
This side the screen. Now he wants to get back.
His panic frets me, keeps me from my book,
So I raise the screen and give him a slight steer.

Off he buzzes into the summer air!
My peace of mind returns, but all too soon

The Song of the Sun ~ Leah Bodine Drake

I hear at the window the same silly tune
Of desperation, and find he's crawled once more

Through some hole he's never able to find from this
Side. I repeat the performance: raise the screen,
Prod him out . . . oh, to stay hard, serene,
Against these tiny plights like everyone else!

I'm getting bored with his fix. I know he would
Not lift a wing to help me. I say
Suffering is natural and so on—who am I
To question the laws of life, holy and good?

But here he is back, bumping himself about,
Bruising his wings against the laws of life;
And I decide that they aren't quite good enough,
And I open the damned screen and let him out.

The Witches

Across the tapestry-lands of the Middle Ages
Like a murky skirl of clouds the witches ride,
Glooming the hunting-woods and the proud churches.

We picture them: the taggles of hags astride
Boar-pigs and withy-besoms in peaked hats,
Red-cloaked or lewdly nude, under a burred

Moon, flying to Lapland for their Sabbats,
Or hopping hobby-horse to the Druid Stones
To skip to the Devil's loo with prancing goats,

The Face in the Water ❧ 1957–1964

All circling to a drum's beat widdershins;
Or maybe a coven brewing a hurricane
With conjurings of cats and dead men's bones!

We see an old crone humping a brambly lane,
Her hair snarly with imps, or in willow-wicks
Cutting a broom-size nicky; or a bad queen

Turning people to swans by stirring a black
Kettle, or rolled down-hill in a spiked cask.
For all their skill they never had any luck.

What was it she wanted, the witch? we ask.
What was the vision she chased up the chimney-hole
And over the cuckoo's nest at the double risk

Of fire for her body and rackety soul?
Was it just to do somebody a bad turn?
To find a short-cut to wealth by the grace of Hell?

Was it to worship some outlawed holy horn,
Or to finger the criss-cross threads of nature's loom
That she'd slip like a weasel through the midnight fern?

She alone could have told us her dark dream . . . .
And whatever became of witchcraft? for they say
No woman goes in for witching in these times.

And yet . . . . when the moon shines in a certain way
The most unlikely of wives will sense a humming
Along the blood of something deeper than joy,

Older than love, beyond blessing or damning.
Oh, she'll knit beside the hearth, but it's all shamming—
Her soul is off with the owls to a muffled drumming!

"Who are you, flimsy ghost on a ghost-horse riding the night-wind?"

THE FACE IN THE WATER ⁊ 1957–1964

A Meeting on a Northern Moor

"Who are you, flimsy ghost on a ghost-horse
Riding the night-wind?"
                        "Bugaboo my name,
Wild Huntsman, bogle, goblin—only words
To frighten ploughboys. Once my temples rose
All over Scandia and the Germanies,
My hand sent forth the lightning. I was called
Wotan then, All-Father . . . and you,
Thin lank-haired crone on the broom-stick?"
                        "People call me now
Old Mother Holle, midnight witch, and hag,
Terror of nurseries! But I have been
High Lady of Heaven, giver of bread and life,
Frigga the loved and beautiful. Alas!
Old lord and husband, know you not your wife?"

Tarascon

  Ste. Martha, patroness of housewives, saved the Rhone Valley from a great dragon by charming him with her piety, and leading him by her sash to the river, where the townsfolk stoned him to death.

I think of that poor dragon Tarascon
 Who, innocent of hate,
Ravaged the towns of Arles and Avignon,
 Fashioned by God and fate

To be a scourge to men for their souls' health.
 I am sad for him, beguiled
By Holy Martha's womanhood and worth,
 Docile as a child,

The Song of the Sun ~ Leah Bodine Drake

Lurching in happy trust at her apron-strings,
    As the tale runs—quite tame!
They slew him in the river-flats with slings,
    Then gave the place his name.

Say Tarasconus terrified the good
    Folk of Avignon and Arles;
Say monsters really have to be destroyed:
    Perhaps. My quarrel

Is less with the deed than with the one who wove
    A fowler's net
Out of a fellow creature's humble love—
    That thrifty Saint!

And I suppose her face was tender and bright
    And her hand on the halter
Gentle . . . In Tarascon I will never light
    A candle on Martha's altar.

Little Song

(To C. B. D.)

Out of the fragments of an urn
We try to guess what measures flowed
From harps tuned to the Dorian mode:
How can we guess at harps unheard?

From brown papyrus can we learn
What magic moved Salome's thigh
Or breathed in Cleopatra's sigh?
What script embalms a living sigh?

THE FACE IN THE WATER ⁊ 1957–1964

And Sappho's friends alone could say
What songs she sang, on what note
The thrushes wakened in her throat,
And they can tell us not a jot.

And you, gone into yesterday—
When I am gone, then who will know
That once you walked like rivers flow,
And how you held your head just so?

Orchids

How sad that Orchid is the human symbol
For everything magnificent and idle!
We call them parasites, those purple spangles
On jungle trees: we say their beauty strangles
The jungle trees from Amazon to Malay.
But it's all in the point of view: the orchids say
"Only for us to purple in and dangle
Did God pronounce the words Let There Be Jungle."

The Snake

On a hill's side, in a place where no one came,
They lay—until then friends only—face to face,
And felt along their blood the hot tides race
And felt their friendship take a darker name.

But moved apart and went down in the old wise,
Hand cool in hand; and only one looked back
And saw, where they had lain, the cleft in the rock,
The unsuspected coils, the fangs, the eyes.

The Song of the Sun ~ Leah Bodine Drake

In the Night

Lie on my breast a moment, so—
As gently as the moon's cool glow
Lies on the sleeping poplar-lands.
Touch me with undemanding hands
As softly as a windless shower
Touches the petals of a flower—
Oh, lie still, lie so—
Before the winds of passion start
And the great storms shake the heart.

The Terrible Meek

How terrible are those meek
Tempting the strong,
Who strike their forgiving cheek,
To strike again!

There is a meekness knows
Its power, alas.
And seems to beg for blows.
How Hell must bless

That kind of pious game!
I know a wife
Who plays such tricks on him
Who shares her life—

A man whose rage would fade
If she would give
Back word for furious word—
But she'll forgive,

THE FACE IN THE WATER ❧ 1957–1964

And show him she forgives . . . .
She knows so well
How martyred sweetness drives
Him wilder still!

And we who match her game
Learn by what net
The lion is led by the lamb
To the ultimate pit.

The Morning

In pulse upon pulse of joy
Day wakes beyond the hill.
Darkness yet clings to leaves,
But on an upland farm
A cock crows, faint and far,
And into the cedar's night
The last late owl goes home.
Only the loving light
Weighs on the innocent air.
This is the moment, soon
Gone, of untouched joy,
When the earth half believes
She is the Garden still
And all her days are joy
With no dark deeds to come
And all her children kind;
And the pet bird on the sill,
Forgetting his caged wings,
Feels the fresh light between
His tiny bars, and turns
To the bright sky his blind-
ed eyes and sings, and sings.

The Song of the Sun ~ Leah Bodine Drake

All-Hallows

Hands that caressed move now
in the yellowing plumes of bristle-fern,
lips that sang lullabies, lips that ardently kissed,
redden the fence-row bittersweet,
darling dust richens the pawpaw thicket
               where the mockers nested.

Some part of those we mourn returns
in leaf and wind and water:
O whose is the beloved voice I hear
               sighing among the cedars?

Royal

I met a lady walking in the snow
    barefoot, with a crown on her head.
"Queen, it is cold, you should not walk so,
    you will die," to the queen I said.

"There is no snow," that lady answered me,
    "and my feet are handsomely shod," that lady said,
"though I thank you for your love and courtesy."
    And she proudly passed, and her tracks in the snow were red.

Circe

Always they turn into brutes,
Though I hope for nobler shapes
From the crews of royal ships
The winds bring to my straits.

THE FACE IN THE WATER ~ 1957–1964

Under my wand and wine
Their innermost selves appear;
And always, just as I fear,
They're panthers and apes and swine.

Among these wandering kings
Isn't there one my rod
Will magic into a god,
Or even a horse with wings?

Ah! There's a sail on the sky
And the shore's a-swarm with men!
Wand, to your work again,
Hogs, make room in your sty.

The Presence

The night her spirit came to me
I awoke and sat up in bed,
Listening . . . . . "Mother," I said.
There was no word from her.
I saw nothing, the dark was still as still could be.
But on the air
The smell of flowers, where no flowers were,
Was there.

The Face in the Water

That afternoon you bent
Over the skiff's side
To pick a water-plant
Where willows' wimpled shade
Made a green looking-glass.

The Song of the Sun ~ Leah Bodine Drake

There, I could see your head
Darkling, the eyes blind,
The childish hair drowned
In willow-skein and cress.

"I wonder what I'd find
On the pond's floor?" you said.
"If I could just sink down!"
"Just mud." "Oh, no!—a place
Like in a fairy tale,
Enchanted castles, queer
People—I know it's there!"

A little sudden squall
Ruffled the water then
And blurred your dreaming face;
And blew across my heart,
Chill, on a day of heat.

And that was long ago.
Dear friend, I hope you found
Your dreamed-of water-door,
And what it had to show
Was well worth sinking for,
That day, years after, when
They found your drifting boat—
And the scrawled note.

The Eve of St. Tib

On the Eve of St. Tib time is not, nor any space we know, and it is there that all dimensions meet.

It was chill in the withered wood and still,
But the stillness deepened and there the dull

The Face in the Water ～ 1957–1964

Air glittered in an unseen, stronger sun
As veil by veil the voids of space were torn.

And I was gazing at a face, at eyes
That looked at me across great galaxies—
Looking with love, and galaxies between—
He in his world, and I, O I in mine!

At Alise Sainte-Reine

The hill is green where Vercingetorix paced his tent,
and thorn and hornbeam huddle
where the last stand was made.
Below, roofs rise, and freight-trains rattle
where Caesar camped his host.

No one hails Caesar at Alesia now!
and though Rome marches through the words
of grey-eyed farmers, carting cabbages to town,
sometimes from the deep loam of their speech
barbaric spear-heads thrust—
after two thousand years
still keen with the Celtic edge.

Fairy Tale

He climbs up glimmering water-stairs to poise
On a lily-pad, the sad enchanted frog,
And bagpipe love-songs through the twilit bog
Where the fat females squat and gulp at flies.

He sings to her, the flaxen-haired, compassionate king's daughter

THE FACE IN THE WATER 🙰 1957–1964

Such clammy brides repel him—he knows well
He is no common frog! He sings to her,
The flaxen-haired, compassionate king's daughter
Whose kiss of innocent magic breaks the spell

And frees his princely self from this uncouth shape,
Revealing proud hawk nose and elegant limbs . . .
"Princess and saviour, come O come," he booms,
"My frogginess is only skin-deep, skin-deep!"

Down to the pond she wanders, bare of foot,
Tattered, the girl who tends the castle geese,
And she sings to herself of a lady in disguise
Royally blonde beneath the barnyard dirt.

And so they meet, briefly, and neither deems
The other worth even a glance—she in her rags,
He with his yellow throat and bandy legs—
Princess and prince, lost in their separate dreams.

Ask the Trees

Ask the butternut trees, ask the beech and hickory
where the Shawnees went.
Here where the subdivision sprawls
Shawnees passed once, painted for war and death—
and where did they go?
The trees might have told us but the trees are gone.

Ask the buffalo herds where the Cheyenne rode to
on their little ponies over the prairie
where the jets now roar—
Cheyenne going somewhere, going away, gone.
The buffalo might have told us but the herds are gone.

The Song of the Sun ❧ Leah Bodine Drake

A Back-Country Road in God's Country

Here where the road bumps to a dip by Tipton's woods
The pond lay. In spring its clean muck
Was plushy with pussy-willows, and frogs made
Water-noises among new lily-pads.
Hot days brought Tipton's old mare
Down to the sycamore shade where mallows glowed.
In autumn the rag-tag leaves ambered the water
Under the bittersweet loops. One winter dusk
I saw a dog-fox lope from the pawpaw patch
To break a hole in the shallow ice and drink.

This is the place now where the wreckers dump
Carcases of cars, where a Yellow Cab,
All doors swinging, leans on a stump
That used to be the sycamore, and the huge husk
Of a schoolbus topples down the dried bank
Where, springs ago, kingfishers had their nest . . . . .
Goodby, goodby.

The Gossip

Apple-blossom, poppy-petal,
Spray of lilac, leaf of maple,
Lily from a neighbour's plot,
All goes into her busy pot.
All that's innocent and fair
Withers, blackens, changes there
To a brew that's past belief—
One that tastes of shame and grief.
You'd never think a fragrant flower
Could make a tea so dark and sour!

* * *

And if you pass her witch's hut
You'll find her stirring her foul pot;
And if you're foolish enough to stop
She'll press on you her witch's cup;
Or all alone, with a secret glee,
She'll sip and savour her terrible tea.

Okio's Geese

Japan, 18th Century

From the dappled east, stretching their long throats
Toward the paddy-fields, the skeins of wild geese
Come over silvering pools of the tidal flats
For their day's first bout with hunger. In the ice-

Hard mud of the marsh, hidden among sedges,
A crouched man feels the familiar breath-catch,
The old need to capture those savage wedges
In nets of his skill, and thereby ease the ache

Of a different hunger. He can never cease
Marveling at beaks sharpened by desire,
Bones balanced for flight—at how the commonplace
Rhythms of brute lives can somehow fire

The human spirit to a rage of love!
They pass, and he wrenches up from the cold slime,
Legs half frozen, head abuzz like a hive
With beautiful geese, and hobbles happily home

To scalding tea and his brushes.
     Well, Okio
Painted the scroll we know as "Geese and Sea."
The real birds were presumably filled; and so,
In his own way, was Okio, and so are we.

Alternate Readings and Unfinished Poems

Alternate Readings and Unfinished Poems

Evening in Late Summer

The sky is coloured like a peacock's breast;
There lingers yet one thin, chill line of gold
Down where the woods their somber branches hold
In silhouette against the haunted west.
Dark leaves, dark earth, slow-breathing and at rest,
Whence frail scents rise of dew-wet grass and mold;
A single star gleams diamond-clear and cold,
Like one sharp note from elfland viol wrest.
In such a gloaming did the lorn knight meet
The faery woman in the river-mead;
Such secret woods young Tristram's madness knew,
And Merlin harping at white Nimue's feet . . . .
And 'neath such lonely star a deep-spurred steed
Reared at the Dark Tower, while a slughorn blew!

Unicorn

Among the straight, stiff-flowered trees
    Of that Botticellian wood,
Under a peachbloom-porcelain sky
Where clouds like golden wool puffed by,
Beside the lily-lashed, deep eye
    Of that small pool I stood.

Poised between terror and delight,
    Seeing, as in a glass
(Stepping through lilies soundlessly,
Mane curling foam-like to white knee,
Tossing proud horn of ivory)
    The faëry creature pass.

The Song of the Sun ❧ Leah Bodine Drake

Under the pastel trees he came,
    Mirrored in waters still . . . .
I saw him pause, the Unicorn,
The lonely one, the elfin-born!
And dipping heraldic, twisted horn
    He drank his lovely fill.

But not among lilies by my side
    Did that bright fable gleam . . . . .
Only within those waters deep
Did white horn shine and pearl hooves leap.
When, for one moment in its sleep,
    The pool disclosed its dream.

Coming Back to the House

Over the sodden fields through which I pass
There comes a sullen wind that smells of snow;
Quails run like blown brown leaves in the thin grass.
November. The light fades. Slow, slow

My steps. I walk alone. Beyond grey hills
Mourns the sluggish freight's long whistle. From the west
False fires burn the windows. Thick dusk fills
Wet hollows, clots the hedge, the deserted nests.

Closer the old house crouches to the earth.
Empty. Why should I enter? No one is here.
The one who warmed it died with the leaves' death.
It is cold, cold inside,—more hushed and drear

Than the vacant fields, the imminent snow,
More desolate O than the night's wide gloom!
No use to huddle over the hearth's glow;
It is winter, winter forever in this room.

Alternate Readings and Unfinished Poems

Nativities

Not here alone may longing eyes
Read starry tidings on the black
Pages of night: to other skies,
Where burns a wilder Zodiac,

The shepherds on their hills may kneel
Among fantastic flocks, and see
A new star, where the old stars wheel,
Presage some strange nativity.

Not here alone love buds the thorn
And gilds the manger's straw with grace:
Each far world has its holy morn
And Christ is born with many a face.

Wherever creatures with each breath
Draw in their heritage of pain,
Wherever life contends with death,
The Living God descends again.

And in the heart's unique, dim earth
(Remoter than the planets are!)
He sends the rumor of His birth
And hangs within our night a star.

Gothic

When from this age I seek escape
I search the past's transfigured nooks,
And fancy takes archaic shape
From tapestries and missal-books:

The Song of the Sun ~ Leah Bodine Drake

I am a dame in Flanders cloth,
A tall unlimber lady, blonde,
Horned with a headdress grandly Goth
And thin as a magician's wand.

Upon my left a falcon'd knight
Approaches in parti-coloured hose;
From the crisp hedges on my right
I offer him a damask-rose.

Around us is a garden, small,
With fish ponds where the slow carp slide;
Four candle-snuffer towers wall
Us from the hunters' wood outside

Where the faint silver bugles ring
And the white unicorn is slain
Beside his disenchanted spring,
Dying in beauty, without pain.

And high on pointed hill-tops loom
The little compact castles, set
Each like a thimble on a thumb,
Above the peasants in the wheat.

O let imagination free
A mind that fear and pity stalk,
To never-lands of tapestry
Beside the unicorn and hawk,

Where death is but a hound that goes
Through greenwoods to the sound of horns,
And love is but a crimson rose
Plucked from a thicket without thorns!

Alternate Readings and Unfinished Poems

Cold Orchard

Like one in orchards stripped and chill
who seeks for fruit no longer there
is she who's loved no more, but still
loves against hope: with wild despair,

She says: "The winter's snows are lies—
these boughs are rich with fruit!" And she
gropes for the vanished sweets and cries
and shakes a black and barren tree.

Unlikely Story

Down to the dragon's house of stone
The young knight came.
The dragon, sleeping on his throne,
Blazed like a flame

With coil on coil of body scaled
And pavonine,
Crested with gold and turquoise, mailed
With tourmaline.

And must he slay this bane of kings,—
This mosaic'd wonder,—
Robber of princesses,—whose wings
Were folded thunder?

A beast so perilous and bright
Gave earth a glory:
It seemed a counteract of right
To end its story.

The Song of the Sun ❧ Leah Bodine Drake

More ancient than the mountained land
Or primal wood
The great worm slept. With sword in hand
The young knight stood

Irresolute. The kings he knew
Were cruel, and all
The princesses were dull. He'd rue
Beyond recall

This deed! And yet he knew he had
High precedent . . . .
"The devil take tradition!" said
The knight, and went.

Poplar Wind

Somehow the poplars always find
the hidden wind.
On the stillest day
when there is no wind to sway
the sycamore or pear,
and fallen leaves lie in a sullen drift,
gaily in the tired air,
the poplar trees
blow in their personal breeze.

Somewhere among their glittering boughs
the poplars house
a small, blithe gale!
When all the large winds fail,
then through the poplar rows
a quiver goes,
and all the light leaves lift

ALTERNATE READINGS AND UNFINISHED POEMS

against the day's dull stare,
as if a secret laughter shook them there.

Landscape with Horses: 6000 B.C.

Over the grassy steppes,
swift as the cold sweet streams
threading the frozen marshes,
down from Siberian woods
race the wild herds,
the proud, undisciplined horses!

Lords of the wastes,
with eyes like the ice-blue water
and terrible hooves of thunder,
they gallop over the hills
to the wide green miles,
pounding horizons under.

Beside the lost black lakes,
under tremendous skies
where the nameless stars wheel over,
stallion with stallion wars,
screaming against the wind,
for the crisp-maned mare, his lover.

Under the fading stars
wild horses go by, unhaltered,
khans of the passes!
While, waiting in the chill dawn
with the first noose in his hands,
a Scythian boy hides in the grasses.

O the last gay stampede,
the spontaneous coursing

The Song of the Sun ❧ Leah Bodine Drake

of horses hooved with wild wings!
The rope curls . . . and in its length
are whips and innumerable ploughs
and the thighs of kings.

Dirge for a Doomed Planet

(To Gerald Heard)

Braced with an iron heart
And equipoised with sea,
A garden called the Earth
Was planned and told to be.

Set in a special space
Made empty star by star,
And spun around the face
Of Sun, not near, not far,

Closed in an airy ring
Well-tempered to her clay,
That bids good powers in
And holds the ill at bay:

Down through tremendous time
The Earth matured her crust,
Perfecting scene and clime
For the beast erect at last.

And where but here may gleam
That one peculiar spark,
Lit by the Very-Flame,
That leaps against the dark?

ALTERNATE READINGS AND UNFINISHED POEMS

How private to this pale
The forms it came to wear—
The lilac and the quail—
How private and how dear!

But now man turns the key
In the forbidden door:
Out of the outer he
Brings, by an evil lore,

Wild forces that unbless
The light that shapes us so,
Changing creation's Yes
To an infernal No

That slacks the silver cord,
That breaks the golden bowl,—
The unconstructive word
That shatters cell from cell.

And all Hell waits a-grin
For Earth to perish, lost
Through irredeemable sin
Against the Holy Ghost.

Reincarnation

I remember well . . . . .
I was a deer
Chased up a hill
And fleet with fear.

I was a fox
And the hounds were running;
They lost my tracks
For I had cunning.

The Song of the Sun   Leah Bodine Drake

A lion-king
Of valiant heart,
I died in a ring
For Roman sport.

I led the wedge
In my wild-goose days.
I was horse—and drudge
To go men's ways.

In a weasel's skin
I killed and killed:
I reveled in
The blood I spilled!

A timid mole,
I kept to the dark;
But joy filled my soul
And I soared as lark!

A clownish ape,
The woods I ran
In the piteous shape
Of the almost-man.

Human at last,
What should I be
But what my past
Lives made of me?—

Cruel and mild,
Brave and shy,
Tame and wild,
Noble, sly,

ALTERNATE READINGS AND UNFINISHED POEMS

Tragic, gay . . . .
This is no surmise!
What soul can say
It is otherwise?

This Side of Oblivion

Along the long beaches of the dark
Time strews his lovely things,
The face of Helen, Shelley's lark,
The swords of fabled kings.

Far down the past, like pale sea-shells,
They glimmer,—Sappho's lyre,
Drowned Lyonnesse with all its bells,
And Ilium on fire,

Surviving yet oblivion's deep.
O may it be my lot
To have one song such company keep!—
Though the singer be forgot.

The Under-Seas

They go down deep, O deep beyond all telling,
Those shadowy green under-seas of mind
Where lie forbidden things: with faint bells tolling,
Rise old unholy temples drowned and blind;
Pirates' bones, and uncharted reefs of coral
Building their scarlet deaths within the brain;
The groves of rainbowed polyps stung with peril,
The sly anemone whose soul is pain.

The Song of the Sun ❧ Leah Bodine Drake

Shining and blue, the waves. No one surmises
What hides below, save when some curious shell
Washes upon the shore, or undine rises
Pale haired, pale-handed on the dark tide's swell.

Then cold green eyes beneath our eyelids stare,
And those who love us see a stranger there.

The Under-Seas

They go down deep O deep beyond all telling,
Those under-seas of mind that lie below
The combers of our thought.
With clear bells tolling,
White towers rise, Hesperian gardens bow
Their golden fruit, immortal leaves of beryl,
Above pure fountains of wisdom. fed by love,
And on drowned islands scened with bliss and peril
The guardian serpents and the undines move.

O desolate swimmer in the day's harsh reefs!
Plunge the submissive will to deeper seas!
Find the lost landscapes where the Tree of Life
Whispers hosannas in the tidal breeze,

Enter the cavern of the holy well
Where Deity wakens on the fluted shell!

The Cytherean

In metals men pursue her: in the crowns
    Of Mycenaean kings,
    In mirrors of the T'angs;
Her voice rings down an evening belled in bronze.

Alternate Readings and Unfinished Poems

Skeins of her hair in tapestries are woven,
    In chasubles and albs,
    In laces' spider-webs,
In temple-flags as gold as China's Heaven.

Da Vinci glimpsed her image in a shoal
    Among the river-reeds;
    His testimony fades
Yet still it bears a glimmer of her smile.

The marble frieze, the cameo, are charms
    With which we hope to snare
    The goddess risen here
And pin her fugitive wing-beats fast to Time.

But who has ever bound with stone or glaze
    Her pure intolerable grace
    Or cast her burning face?
Well-served is he who once has known her pause,

Invisible with light, upon an urn,
    A rhyme, a portico,
    Shed her inconstant glow,
Then pass beyond brush or pen, beyond return.

Air

Blue goblet of water, dust and gas
with Earth curled inside like a dark pearl undissolved
in vital wine,
the element of air surrounds, pervades us.

Adaptable essence, fluid to all things' will
yet by its lack their master,
air is the matrix where we hollow

The Song of the Sun ~ Leah Bodine Drake

our personal Merlin-towers of glass
in which we live, marvelously castled.

Moving aslant as wind
air unwinds the crossed ribbons of its maypole-dance,
blowing ships and seeds,
breaking the backs of hemlocks,
keeping the globe, that travels widdershins,
still spinning with its tugging Westerlies.

With transparent hands it holds up butterflies,
spreads traffic-lanes for hummingbirds and bombers
but betrays acrobats and apples.

Cambered roof against the radiance of space,
the yonder with its vanishing iris,
the theater of fire and mirages,
the keyboard of sound:
how can we speak sufficiently of air
by whose presence in our bagpipe-breasts
we make our passionate music?

Yet this inseparable companion's never seen
in its purest state:
immaculate spirit must embrace the clay
to be made visible to earthly eyes.
So air sublimes to ice, crystals to snow,
turns cloud and piles up sunsets and thunder,
and like the pity of a god made flesh
lays on just tree and unjust, thirsting man
    the fingers of its catholic rain.

Alternate Readings and Unfinished Poems

Adam's Hand

Warm seas and fins, and then the landward leap
Into fur, and terrible choices: should he move
Toward speed or brawn, or cunning of the ape?
And which should be his pole-star, hate or love?
Hand over paw, the Earth saw Adam climb
From cave to tower, from slime to ledge to crest.
Some four-foot craft was lost to gain a thumb,
Some furry joy, to earn a rich unrest.

Now at the moon he shakes his fisted five,
He tampers with the engines of the sun
And fouls the waters: will his hand engrave
HIC JACET on the planet's breast of stone
And hang all life to cross that final Tau?
Better the sea, the fin, the wood, the bestial paw!

With Every Death

Within her eyes shone the wild world,
In her shell of ear the sea rang its song;
Now is the shining gone and the song done.
When she died there ended
One way in which life looked at itself.
A part of the world dies with every death.

———

Within her eyes the wild world lived and shone.
In the shell of her ear the sea rang its deep bells,
And on her tongue the grape made known its wine;
Now is the wine untasted, and the sea
To emptiness rings its bell—for she is gone.
Gone, buried and lost, for whom the world
Existed in its glory for a while—

439

The Song of the Sun ❧ Leah Bodine Drake

With her there ended one of many ways
By which life looks at itself—with every death
Part of the world gives up its living breath.

That Summer

That summer the old folks said they had never
Seen such a perfect summer. The sun burned
Just enough, and when we needed a shower
A shower came and a double rainbow shone.

The hay got in before the storm furied.
Blackberries burst their wine-skins: Nature's palm
Cupped the earth gently, gently. The river flowed
Silky and green at the bend where we whooped and swam.

And the sky was blue as God, and the corn-ears
Filled and richened; and at the river's turn
The mockers sang all night in the sycamore,—
"Summer and life and joy!" the mockers sang.
Summer and joy . . . . . until the day we found
Your boat adrift and your young body, drowned.

From a destroyed early poem

. . . . . "The lofty tomb that lives of slaves once bought—
That Cheops might retain a hold on time."

. . . . "Men strive to touch infinity with stone,
Far-reaching laws, by carving with a sword
Some chip of history to be called their own,
By faiths that promise some delayed reward."

Alternate Readings and Unfinished Poems

"Hunter"

Animal, upright, forked
With gun for a longer arm,
Nosing the thickets, dumb,
What god have you involved?

What do you hope to find,
Hunter in what you kill?
What longing does it fill
Of spirit, deep and blind?

What is the inner lack
That only can be fed
By slaying if the dead
Be beautiful and quick?

How quick and beautiful
Is fox and mountain cat,
Panther and mountain-goat—
Not for a pot to fill

Not for their fur to hide
Our nakedness is slain
Again, again, again
The innocent, the wild.

Some need without a name
For shapes complete and pure
Brings up the gun, the spear,
Powers the deadly aim.

In beauty's blood and bone
The hunter dips his hands,
Imagines then he stands
In splendor not his own.

The Song of the Sun ❧ Leah Bodine Drake

Adam the First Poet

But to His (God's) child He gave the power
To clothe with syllables the bird;
And Earth, awake in beast and flower
Beheld the flesh become the word.

From a poem to Mother

Would I have kept your old heart beating
for one more cold season in its cage?
Dear wings, fly away,
                find your sun, your south,
Dark skies, dark seas, be merciful!

The Five Angels

Five angels stood about my bed (when I was born)
and blessed my body, feet and head
and gave me hearing, taste and smell, and vision and touch.

hearing—"larks in their exultations."

sight—"all falls of light all slanting rains"

sound—"the movements of great oceans, their comings and withdrawals"

smell—Christmas trees, cedar trees—smoky railroad stations long ago.

"Crows and their quaint notions" (sight)

"For these I live my praise,
    I open out my days."

Alternate Readings and Unfinished Poems

A Charm for the New Year

The new young year comes in
To waking bells and snow,
And once again I turn
To stars and spells to know

What road [is good] to take,
What star spells out my good;
Will love like flowers wake?
Will snow obscure my road?

The year ahead unwinds
As new untraveled snow[.]
What stars are foes or friends
In the country where I go?

The bells repeat their word
I walk into the year

I only know I face
A country

I walk into the year
Hopi[ng] to bear the snow,
My good will all be new—

My stars are what I do
My loving is my good—
I wake the road I go,
My going *is* the road.

The Song of the Sun ❦ Leah Bodine Drake

[Untitled]

Lying awake at night I hear the rain
Sobbing down gutters of tiled foreign roof,
In this old city where the speech is not my own.
Rain on the red tiles[,] rain against
                the closed wooden shutters,
rain dripping from poplar leaves down by the lake
                which every one knows
                    from postcards—
And the planet turning, turning heavy with all its dead—

There was a room I knew long ago in another house
in a land whose speech was my own.

Coral Reef at Calico Key

Here on our southern doorstep where
        the flaking Continent
           dips into shallow seas,
                the corals live,
a drowned kaleidoscope of busy jewels.

Dive down, dive down into a place less known
        to air-bound man
than the mapped craters of the moon
though Beebe filmed it and divers roam it.
Go down through shifting jades and tourmaline
        into your own dim past
where sunlight is everywhere at once,
as if it had been mixed with water at its birth
but by refraction
coming not down,
topsy turvey like all things[.]

Alternate Readings and Unfinished Poems

Move in a world with no precise horizon
as in a Japanese print
where background's a blurred pastel. Forever
these distances
seen through water _____
in gauzy [?]
extend no further than a yard away
and hold the swimmer in a globe of glass.
This is a world of silence,
    where you move
        as in an old-time film,
where all around among these lilac temples
& tanga__ taj mahals
of the coral-towers
    desperate dramas
    take place in utter calm.
What elfin tinklings may arise from fish
are played on strings too fine for human ears.
The very landscape lives—this golden rock
    is not a rock, but living, a sponge
    these lilac trees
    swaying in water-winds
are not trees but sentient creatures whose
    delicate lacy nets
    fish the warm currents
    for their tiny prey,
these bed nasturtiums these creamy blooms
    like lacy Flemish ruffs
are small vats of poison
sworded and spiked.
Danger's the drum to which these cold lives move.
So all go masked and armed—and wary
    here in this deadly fairyland—
    the rockfish wears a face
    like a Javanese nightmare

The Song of the Sun ❧ Leah Bodine Drake

    the jelly-fish
        drifts from nowhere to nowhere
under their white umbrellas
    like Asian kings
bear daggers under their traily silks
the sea-worm's orange tuft will sting
    like a hornet
        the sea-urchin
under his green coonskin cap,
carries a switch-blade like a corner tough.
Even the sponge—the one you thought a rock, is barbed.
And all are quick-change artists here,—
    When a hunting-fin
    goes over, and its shadow falls
        on the coral-towns
        the roses fade to ash
    in dome and gothic tower
    as the flower worms
    withdraw into their mignon caves
the azure of the angel fish tines of cobalt
    the red hind dulls to amber
        the squid pulses
        from black to brown to grey,
and in the green sea grasses
    the sea horse turns into the
        very blade he clings to
    till the peril passes.
Sea's exile now,
    we rove these waters clumsily,
        Out of place
        and yet we know
this magic one
When in some final cradle of a reef
    like this, along some under-shore,
we wandered, finned and scaled, and dreamed of land.

Alternate Readings and Unfinished Poems

Move carefully among these waving fans
    these bright metallic fins
    and nacreous lives—
for who knows what final magnificence
    watches you lumber by
        its tiny lair.
Something that on some moonless night
    will flop its way
        onto the mudflats of Calico Key.
And gasp, and taste the air, and gasp, but flap
    a little further up the muddy shore.
And like it there, and find a way to change
    again and stay?
For there are more things in the sea
    that ever came out of it—
Go back, go up, through gauzy greens golds
    to the old airs and sands.
This is not now your home.
This is the coral reef,
and no man knows it—
though Beebe filmed it
and divers roam it—
For there are things in the sea still coming out of it.
And where our past was, now a future waits,
unknown, unguessed,
not necessarily for us.

Switzerland

Switzerland is a big country
But the land goes up, not out—
There's a lot of land in Switzerland
But it's in heaps and piles—
More land than in France or the British Isles

The Song of the Sun ❧ Leah Bodine Drake

But the Switzer miles
Climb toward the sky.

If you want to go anywhere in the country
You either go down or up.

in the woods of the Vaud

. . . . . . "and two elves, gossiping on the highest branch of a beech
see me and are outraged at this walker in their woods.
They enchant themselves with feathers, and with a curse
flap suddenly off as crows."

Fiction

FICTION

Time and the Sphinx

(For Lord Dunsany)

Time was weary of the Sphinx. Age after age, eon after eon, the eyes of Time had looked upon the Sphinx where she crouches between the river and the sand, forever staring into the rising sun and smiling her ambiguous smile.

Time could remember when the Sphinx had been young and he had loved her. Before the Pyramids were built, stone upon careful stone; before the desert Djinn carved Petra from ruby star-dust shaken from Antares' rays; before the wall of the children of Han slithered like a dragon across the yellow hills where unicorns stamp; even before shaggy men raised Stonehenge to salute the dawn—even before these, nimble fingers had fashioned the young Sphinx, painted her cheeks and set her between the river and the sand. Her face had been fairer then, the centuries had not yet gnawed like rats at those stony excellences. But even then that sly and subtle smiling had troubled the soul of Time, for it hinted at a secret that he, the elder and with older lore, could not fathom.

And as the sand gathered, grain by grain, between her lion-paws, city after city had risen and gone down: proud Troy, burning with its double flame of beauty and death; Antioch, coloured like a peacock, peering through jeweled veils at Rome; Thebes, where the gods walked; Balkh, mother of cities high in Asia's heart; Carthage, so cruelly splendid, that had become less than an echo upon the wind; Baalbek, and Babylon, and Tara of the kings. All had had their hour, and all had been vanquished by the hand of Time. But between the river and the sand still crouched the Sphinx, enduring the dubious caresses of Time while she gazed just a little way beyond him into the rising sun.

Then Time grew tired of seeing that calm head which would not be humbled before him. His caresses turned to blows and his hand fell heavily upon her painted cheeks and the sand crept about her loins. But still the huge woman-monster continued to smile her secret smile and

451

The Song of the Sun ~ Leah Bodine Drake

gaze at something just beyond him.

Then Time set himself to devise ways of bringing her to heel, and he spent long ages—as with one hand he tumbled Ys back into the sea and with the other hand swept the Mayas from the map—dreaming of means by which he could rid himself of this disquieting foe. Nation after nation rose and were, for a while, and then were not. The Moors left Granada, hiding the keys of their ravished palaces in the folds of their cloaks. The jungle closed in upon Angkor, upon the coiled serpents and the little dancing queens. The riders of the steppes turned the heads of their small, wiry horses toward the cities of the West and terribly dreamed. And riding upon a whirlwind and vanishing within it, came and departed Bonaparte, but not before he had stood before the Sphinx and given her glance for glance.

And still Time chafed at the everlastingness of the Sphinx who endured while more lovable things perished: the eyes of Helen, the music of Atlantis, the great bronze horse of Leonardo: Time did not know how much longer he could spare "The Last Supper."

Then one morning, as he wrinkled the face of a harlot and watched the last of the Shawnees die, he thought of the one appalling way to overthrow the Sphinx.

Ever had the weapons with which man dreadfully amused himself become more complex and more evil. Time had seen the stone ax give way to the spear, and the arrow had passed from history even as had the knightly sword. He had seen gunpowder innocently born in a land of porcelain pagodas to flower horribly in the countries of the West. Now and again Time opened his treasure-chest and gave his beautiful or cruel gifts to man—those gifts which he had brought with him when, with his sister the Earth, Time had been cast from the heart of the sun. Now he bethought him of a gift which would indeed overthrow the Sphinx and place her among those things which had been and were not.

Then, not without sadness (for Time loved his sister Earth and the curious and dangerous and noble things upon her), he opened his treasure-chest and gave into the hands of man his last gift. And man took the gift, which had been born in the sun and had the sun's power, and man played dreadfully with it, and the gift was a perilous gift.

FICTION

And so Time went again into Egypt and stood before the Sphinx where she crouched between the river and the sand, and he said, "O woman-monster who persists in enduring while worthier things fail, O you of whom I am weary—your doom will come upon you at last and I shall conquer! A while and yet a while, and man will play one game too many with this new toy I have given him, and it shall get out of hand, being a perilous toy and not meant for his playing. And when it does, Earth and all things upon her, even you and your abominable smiling, will blaze up into one great cloud of flame. And all the things of Earth, yea, even the roots of the mountains, will drift away into space as cindery dust. And that which has been shall be as though it never were, and you, O Sphinx, shall be as the rest, and I will no longer have to endure your everlastingness and your smile."

Then the Sphinx spoke. Her thick lips moved as they had never moved since she first greeted her father Ra, as he rose all golden on the day of her birth.

"Time, old enemy and lover," said the Sphinx, "you have verily found the means of destroying me at last. This weapon which contains the sun's power and with which man now most dreadfully plays, shall send down to death this Earth he treads and all that his hands have made, and all that Hands greater than his have made, even the roots of the mountains. And even I, who am coeval with them, shall die."

Then yet again spoke the Sphinx. "But when Earth goes into oblivion in a burst of flame, you also, O Time, must perish. For you are of this world only, and the universes know you not, as do not the divine Hands that made us. And so, until that ending, I shall face you still, O Time."

And the lion-woman, smiling secretly, fixed her eyes on Ra, the rising sun her father, and she waited in unalterable grandeur for death.

Time spoke three words. "You have conquered." And brooding somberly on the end of Earth and on his own annihilation, Time saluted the Sphinx in farewell and departed for a peak of the Himalayas where a temple stood whose ruin was long overdue; and on the way there he stopped to wither the petals of a rose.

The Song of the Sun ❧ Leah Bodine Drake

Whisper Water

I always said there was something different about Dan Redwine.

The Redwines had the big farm down the pike a piece from us and Dan was the only boy. He was a little, wispy fellow, with big grey eyes that always seemed to see a sight more than anybody else and he never was a talker. But he was happy-hearted and a right clever lad, and just about the best friend I ever had. Dan was a hard worker, too, for all his puny frame. Old Mr. Redwine was poorly, and Miz' Redwine was a slipshod, oh-let-it-rest woman, who rocked more than she worked. There were two Redwine girls, but they married early and moved into foreign parts, two–three counties away.

So it was up to Dan to bear a man's burdens, even in his youthful days. Many's the time I've wanted him to go hunting or to a play-party over in Hurdsville, and he'd say No, he had to mend a fence, or look for a cow that had strayed, or hoe the burley, or what-all. Yessir boss, Dan was a drivin' boy.

Maybe I'd better say who I am, although I have little to do with the story. I'm Jed Clay Bullion, and it was my Uncle Wade Bullion who was Sheriff of Tatum county the time we had those terrible goings-on that I will try to tell of. Uncle Wade has it all writ down and signed, what was a real, sure-enough death-bed confession, and I saw some and heard a lot of what went on, my own self.

Like I said, Dan Redwine worked hard, but he was still just a tad, time my story begins. He liked to prank around like other young ones, and he liked to fish, I mind, better than anything else. When he had the time he'd get his dad's ol' fishing pole and go down to a pretty little branch that cuts through Redwine land, named Whisper Water.

Whisper Water is well-called. I don't just mean because it seems to whisper to you when you walk by its banks, 'specially at sundown when the nighthawks are flying and the breeze makes spooky rustlings in the willows. I mean, there's always been whispers *about* it—mostly among the old folks—how a man might see and hear more than ripples and wind and fish jumping or a 'coon washing its dinner in those deep, brown waters. There used to be Red Indians around here, they say, in the old days—Shawnee, and Kickapoo and Cherokee. I reckon that any place where *they've* been will always have queer tales told of it. They never camped here permanent, just used to come down here for hunting and their little wars, and then go back again across the river.

But they slipped in and out of the state enough to leave shadows, so to speak, of their outlandish spooks and spirits, and there was a kind of wispy idea that something from those old times, something heathen and powerful, lived in our branch. Nobody had ever described it, and 'twasn't known if it were good or bad, but whatever lived in Whisper Water never seemed to trouble its mind over humans. That is, never till once . . . but I'm 'way ahead of my story.

Dan liked to hang around Whisper Water, particularly where it bulged out into a kind of little pool near an enormous old willow-tree. Many's the swim we've had together in that-there little pool. Dan liked to sit under that tree and fish, and play on a mouth-harp that he always carried in his jeans. He could play right good, too—"Sourwood Mountain" and "Hand Me Down My Walking-Cane" and "Lord Lovell He Stood By His Castle Wall." But his favorite was the one that begins, "Have you seen my true-love with the coal-black hair?" Over and over, while the willow swayed in the summer wind and the catfish nibbled his line, he'd play that sweet, sad piece.

Dan took a kind of personal pride in that branch. Whisper Pool was just below the Redwine house a ways, and Redwine property so to speak. He used to keep it cleaned out good. You know how some folks in the country are—we incline towards using a branch-bed as a kind of dumpheap. It's against the law now, I reckon, but back when Dan and I were young lads there wasn't any such law, or if there was nobody in Tatum county had heard of it. But Dan saw to it that no old blowed-out tires or tin cans were cast into his part of Whisper, and he always tidied up after any picnickers who drove in here from foreign parts. Dan was fair silly about that stream, but whatever lived in it appreciated his care, because the way the fish bit for Dan was a pure wonder!

I asked him about his amazing luck, once.

Dan seemed kind of embarrassed. He muttered something about "an agreement with a brown lady."

The Song of the Sun ~ Leah Bodine Drake

"Brown lady?" I said scornful. I was at the scornful age then, around twelve or thirteen. "Boy, are you crazy? Don't nobody live around here except you-all and Old Man Tuttle up on the hill. *What* brown lady?"

Dan didn't answer and kept on fixing a worm on his line, pretending like he didn't hear me.

"Shoo," I went on, "she must have been one of those picnickers that worry you so. She was just a picnicker, having fun with you. Some of those foreign ladies are awful sassy."

But Dan shook his head and said No, wasn't any city-lady. That's all I could get out of him, because when it came to Whisper Water he always got mum-mouthed, for all we were friends.

Well, we got older and started going to the dances in Hurdsville and beauing the girls around and I guess Dan sort of forgot about "brown ladies," for pretty soon he was courting Honeybird Sanders.

Everyone to his own taste, is what I thought when Dan took to Honeybird. I'll admit she was a fair sight in those days—tumbled red hair, snappy blue eyes and smart and sassy. But man, was she a tartar! She could flare up over a trifle, and then her blue eyes would spark and her mouth tighten up, and she'd look like she could kill you. Besides that, she had too much of a roving eye to suit me. But Dan married up with her. Or rather, Honeybird married *him*, being a mighty purposeful woman when she wanted something. At that time she wanted Dan Redwine, and the Redwine land, maybe, it belonging to him now that his dad and ma had died.

A funny thing happened at the wedding. There was a right smart lot turned out for it, and I thought I knew most everybody present. But there seemed to be one person I couldn't quite place. It looked like a woman, but I never could see her real plain. She was always just slipping away behind somebody, or just beyond the corner of my eye, and when I'd turn to look at her she'd be a little way out of my range still. It was the aggravatingest thing! I got the idea that she was small and dark and dressed kind of odd, in what looked like old-fashioned, but handsome greeny stuff—like fine, store-bought velvet, maybe. I also thought she was barefoot, and I recall saying to myself, "Well, Missy, seems like you could have wore your shoes to a wedding!"

Don't nobody live around here except you-all and Old Man Tuttle

The Song of the Sun ~ Leah Bodine Drake

Nobody else seemed to notice her, and as she didn't go into the church with the rest, I forgot about her. I thought I saw Dan look around kind of sharp-like, once or twice, like you'll do when someone comes up behind and speaks suddenly to you. But who it was, if anybody, I never did see.

The wedding party went off fine and dandy, and Dan and Honeybird settled down at his place and for a while things went along peaceable enough.

Peaceable for Honeybird, that is, but maybe not so much for Dan. Honeybird's temper didn't quiet down any, and her tongue was still razor-sharp. She had a rough hand with beasts, too. I mind one time Dan brought home a baby muskrat whose mother had died in a trap. He cared for it and petted it, just like he did all small, helpless things. Honeybird got the rifle down when he was over in Hurdsville, and killed it. But instead of being merciful and shooting it, she beat its head in with the butt! She told Dan it had bit her, but I don't think he believed her, because he never again brought any young creatures to the house.

The worse she got, the more he took to going off by himself to Whisper Water and sitting by the willow to fish or just play his mouth-harp and brood, where it was quiet and peaceful. He had to practically sneak off, though, as Honeybird had a powerful dislike for that branch. It got to be more—it was a kind of nameless fear with her.

She showed this one day when the Redwines were walking home from church with me and my Sally. When we turned off the pike to take the short cut through the field by Whisper Water she stopped dead.

"You-all can go back along the branch," she said, "but I'm staying on the pike."

"Whatever for, Birdie?" said my Sally. "It's a sight hotter and dustier."

"Hot or dusty or not—the last time I come along Whisper that big willow hit me in the face. All right, *laugh!*" she snaps, although nobody had. "A great, long willow-wand reared back and smacked me right square across my face and left a big red welt. My laws, it felt just like some living person had slapped me!"

"All right, Birdie girl, we'll go with you along the pike," said Dan, looking, I thought, a little worried.

FICTION

We ought to have seen that—here was a token, but human beings are funny. They hate to admit that there are things in this world that are more, or less, than human, with powers for good or ill, according to whether it's good or ill that's done them by men. Honeybird never would walk by the branch again, though, and knowing what I do now, I can't blame her.

She and Dan had been married now about ten years. I reckon it got lonely for her up at the Redwine place, Dan being such a quiet man, and there never being any children. If she'd had a passel of young ones to busy her mind things might have been different. But she never did, and sometimes I wonder if Whisper Water was to blame—but maybe I'm fanciful.

Anyway, things perked up when some oilmen came down here and leased some of Dan's land. Pretty soon they moved in a big rig, with cable-tools, and the contractor—Mr. Bill Brady, his name was—brought in a crew and they started drilling. Two of the boys located themselves in Hurdsville and drove to work every day around noon. But Mr. Brady, who helped drill, and his tooldresser got themselves fixed at the house for room and board. They were going to run tower (as they called it) at night, and it was a sight handier to live on the place.

Mr. Brady was a youngish man, pleasant-spoken if a mite school teacherish, and no great shakes for looks. But his tooldresser, that Foley, was a humdinger!

Big, black-eyed and rowdydow, always laughing and pranking and shining up to the girls! He was the sweet-talkingest man I ever did see, poor soul! He just naturally made a set for Honeybird, and she was smitten with him from the start. After living alone with slow-spoken Dan for ten years, she was pleased and flattered to have such a big, good-looking man like Foley Mathers shine up to her. That was the toolie's name—Foley Mathers. Lard, how can I forget it?

Right away Honeybird smartened up like she hadn't since her wedding. She put herself out to cook better than since the honeymoon. Sweet potato pie and her best peach preserves on the table every day! She even took to curling her hair again and pinning on a ribbon or two, and when Honeybird set her mind to it, she was a right taking woman.

Foley just ate it up. Lots of time when I was there, around noon,

459

The Song of the Sun ⁊ Leah Bodine Drake

when Mr. Brady and him would come off tower, Foley'd come busting in the kitchen roaring, "Where Miss Honeybird? Where's that good-looking landlady of mine?" and she'd giggle and prime herself like a girl.

Working half the night like they did, Mr. Brady and Mathers slept a good piece of the afternoon. I hate to scandalize anybody's name, especially when they're dead and gone, but seems like Foley wasn't sleeping all that time.

Mr. Brady had the spare room to himself, and he was a little hard of hearing, so what went on when Dan was down in the low ground at the corn, or hoeing the burley by the woodlot will never now be rightly known to man. But it's certain there was enough between Foley and Dan's wife to make her jealous of other women.

One noon I was over at Redwines' returning a harrow I'd borrowed. Mr. Brady was in the kitchen unlacing his field-boots, when Mathers came in the back shed. He started washing up, but pretty soon he stuck his head around the door and said, "Who's that cute little black-eyed gal around here, wears her hair in two big braids over her chest?"

"No *grown* woman'd be silly enough to wear her hair like that," snaps Honeybird, "nobody but a Red Indian, that is, and there've been none of them kind around here for many enduring years, that's certain."

"Say!" bawls Foley. "Come to think of it, that's just what she looked like—a cute little Indian squaw, like I've seen out in Oklahoma, time I was working on a well near Nowata."

He stepped into the kitchen. "Mean, too, like an Indian woman can get. Man, did she give me a dirty look as she passed me! Like she's ready to scalp my hair off. Br-r-r!"

"What had you done, Mathers?" asked Mr. Brady, in a casual way. "Make a pass at her?"

"Why, Mr. Brady, you know I'm as innocent as a lamb around women!" Foley answered, big-eyed and mock-solemn. "Anyway," he went on, half to himself, "I don't think she cared much for me, because she made some kind of a funny movement with her hand—like she was pushing me away, or gesturing me off or something."

"Where did all this take place, Mr. Mathers?" I asked him.

"Down by Whisper creek, Mr. Bullion," Foley answered. "It was kind of funny—I met this good-looking gal just before I come up to that big willow. You know, that real, big one by the bend, where the creek is kind of a pool. She was walking towards me, big as life and mad, like I said, when all-a sudden—whoosh! she wasn't there! Wham! Gone—just like that!" He snapped his fingers. Then he sort of studied a minute. "It looked mad, too, shaking all over," he added. "That tree, I mean."

Mr. Brady was interested by now. He leaned back in his chair and said in that school-book way of his, for all he was a young fellow, "I understand that this used to be Shawnee camping-ground once. Is that so, Mr. Redwine?"

Dan, who had kept his head turned aside during these speeches, muttered, "I reckon so," and I could tell by Honeybird's back, where she stood over the stove, that she was all ears.

Brady went on, "That's interesting what Foley said about an Indian girl, or someone who looked like one. Now if we were superstitious redmen we'd say that Foley'd met the guardian spirit or goddess of something around here, most likely something along the creek, what you folks here call the branch. Our red brothers believed that all things had their good or bad spirits, and they could take any shape or size they wanted. Indian legend is full of bear-women and tree-lovers and buffalo-girls, who sometimes fell in love with human beings. Sometimes I guess they fell into *hate,* too, if I may put it that way." He turned to Foley smiling. "Looks like the mysterious lady of the creek didn't take to Foley here."

Foley opened his mouth like he was going to say something, then shut up and sat heavily down to the table. Honeybird was setting the biscuits in front of him, and as she passed me I could tell she was shaking. I had the queerest feeling, my own self, that I'd heard something like this talk before, but I couldn't figure out why it seemed familiar.

Then Dan spoke up all of a sudden. "If I was you, Mr. Mathers, I'd not walk that part of the branch."

"Why not?" says Foley.

"Well," says Dan, "that bank's treacherous. Even in a dry spell like we're having now it's always muddy along Whisper Water, and when we have a big rain the bank crumbles fast.

"As for that . . . woman you met," he went on slowly, "I reckon that

The Song of the Sun ~ Leah Bodine Drake

was old man Tuttle's granddaughter, come from Hurdsville to visit with him. Yes, sir," he added briskly, "I'd say that—there was Willie Pearl Wakefield."

I had to smile to myself, because Willie Pearl is a tubby little towhead about eleven years old.

Honeybird wasn't smiling. All of a sudden she slapped the greens down and bust out with, "I hate that branch! I hate that Whisper Water, so dark and slimy! And I hate that big old willow most of all! Dan Redwine, I've told you and *told* you all these enduring years, to cut down that nasty old willow! It's bad—bad!"

She was just about screaming, and as we all stared at her she started to cry, ran out of the room and banged the bedroom door.

I made my fareyouwells right soon, as I was embarrassed for Dan's sake. I went home along the branch, like I always did, anyway, but this time with all my senses alert and my ears pricked, so to speak. When I got near the big old willow something dashed out from the brush and I almost yelled my head off. It was nothing but a little old rabbit, but I was taking no chances: I called after it, "Howdy, Mister Rabbit!" the way we boys used to, for good luck. Yes, sir, boss, I was feeling very polite towards *any* creature I met down by Whisper Water right then!

Like Dan had said, it hadn't rained for weeks. August was slipping into September, and the weather held—hot, dry and terrible hard on the corn and only less so on the burley. The Joe-pye weed's purple looked rusty, and the pasture grass was a sorry sight. The earth was hard as a rock. The only soft spot around was the branch-bed and banks, because even in the driest weather Whisper Water always was full. Queer, come to think of it.

I was so busy hauling water and tending to my crops that I didn't go over to Redwines' for a couple of weeks. I heard bits of news, how the oil crews were hard put to it for water; how Dan's tobacco seemed to be doing a sight better than anyone else's; and how the goings-on between Mrs. R. and Foley Mathers was getting to be a scandal and a shame. Don't ask how those things get around, but I supposed the daylight crew noticed things, coming on and off tower, and talked about it in town. It worried me, on Dan's account, but I reckon I spent more time worrying about my corn and my tobacco than I did anything else.

One evening, as I finished milking, Dan came slowly around the side of the barn. He looked unhappy and mad and worried, all at once. In the bitterest voice I've ever heard from him, he said, "Jed Clay, it's true. It's damn true, and I've been a tomfool not to guessed it before this."

"Boy, what you talking about?" I said, though I feared to hear—because I reckoned I knew what was coming.

"Honeybird and that Foley Mathers," said Dan. "Honeybird's been disgracing her and my name with that loud-mouthed tooldresser, that I ought to have knowed better than to take in my own house." He smashed his fist against the barn wall. "Damn these foreigners, Jed Clay! I wish I'd never leased my land to 'em. I wish they'd never come around here looking for oil."

"Hold on, Dan," Jed said. "What makes you so sure?" I put my arm over his shoulder. "People just naturally talk about a good-looking man or woman, and they're both that. Mathers is a big-talking fellow, but I doubt that it's any more than just sweet-talk and compliments, and such."

"It's more than that, Jed Clay," he answered. "That's all I'm going to say about it, but I'm facing them both with it tonight, and if he or she gets the least bit of a guilty expression, I'm going to light into that Foley and I don't know where I'll stop at."

"Take it easy, Dan—you're admitting right now you ain't really sure. Sleep on it tonight, boy, and don't be so hasty in your anger." I was really scared that Dan *would* jump Foley, and considering the difference in their sizes, Dan was liable to be the worst-used one in *that* ruckus.

I talked and jollied him and thought I'd quieted him down some, because he promised to think it over during the night. But when he turned away to head for home, I had the feeling that I'd never see him again. I started to call him back and ask him to stay the night with Sally and me, and I wish to glory, now, I had.

I worried so about Dan that a couple of days after that I went over to Redwines'. The house looked quiet, and I figured the night-crew were still asleep, it being around four in the evening. I knocked softly on the porch floor, and after a long while Honeybird came to the door. She looked kinda wild and sick. "Dan's not here," she said. "Dan's gone on a trip."

The Song of the Sun ~ Leah Bodine Drake

"Gone on a trip?" I said. "Where to?"

"Down to Memphis," she said, in a defiant, you'd-better-believe-me way.

"Memphis?" I guess I yelled it. "*Memphis?* Whatever for? What's Dan doing in Memphis?"

"He's a-visiting some of his kinfolk," she answered. "He's been away couple of days now, visiting his kin down in Memphis."

I was stumped. "I never knew Dan had any kinfolk in Tennessee. He never mentioned any to me, that I recollect."

"Well, he has, and that's where he's went," she snaps back and starts to close the door.

"He's picked a fine time to take a trip," I said. "Right when the burley needs cutting, he goes to *Memphis*—to visit his *kin!*"

"Don't you yell at me, Jed Clay Bullion!" Honeybird's temper was rising. "Can I help it if Dan Redwine's a fool? Always *was* a fool, to my mind."

"That's enough, Miss Honeybird," I said, very mannerly, because I was getting mad myself. "Dan's my friend, and if he wants to take a trip to Memphis, I reckon he knows what he's doing. Funny, though—nobody in town said anything about it when I went in yesterday. Seems like somebody would have seen him take the train, or something." Then just to end the conversation on a pleasanter note, I asked, "How's the oil-well coming? Struck oil yet?"

That did it. She just blew up. "That Foley! That big, drunken ox of a man!"

"Why, what's Foley done?" I asked. "I thought he was your star boarder, Birdie."

"You shut up!" she began, when we heard a sound which most of us had been honing* to hear for weeks—a crack of thunder. Whilst we were talking the sky had begun to clabber up with big purplish clouds, and as we stood there a wind sprang up that smelled of rain not far distant. Lightning split the purple masses, thunder banged away, and the first warm drops fell. Then more of them, and faster, and cooler.

* *"honing"*—Kentucky dialect for longing, fervently wishing.

FICTION

I felt like dancing. "Fare-thee-well, Miz Redwine my bonny-o!" I sang out. "I'm fixing to get home before she busts open and Whisper starts to spill over. Don't want to be caught in the low ground when Whisper starts to flood."

At that I thought she'd gone crazy. She staggered back against the screen door and put her hand to her mouth. "The branch!" she said, like to herself. "O my Lord, the branch!" and slammed both doors shut and I heard her lock the inner one.

Well, I'll swanny, I thought to myself, what a woman! No more manners than backwoods trash. But I forgot about Honeybird, because it was now raining buckets, and our Tatum county clay was already turning slippery under my boots and I had to set my mind on getting home in a hurry. The sky was now one big bruise with white forks of lightning playing over it every few minutes and the rain seemed to come down harder every step. When I passed the rig I saw the daylight crew, Collins and Mack, huddled up in their "dog-house" away from the storm. That made me think of the other crew at the house, and I thought, they won't get much sleep with all this racket. Then another thought struck me— something Honeybird had said. How she'd called Foley a drunken ox ... "*drunken*"? Mathers was kind of a blow and sweet on the ladies, but he never drank anything stronger than buttermilk!

What had made him a "drunken ox" all of a sudden?

That night's storm was the worst I ever did see. Sally and I and the youngones bunched up together in the kitchen, and Sally prayed a little, and I thought about Dan and Honeybird and Foley, and how troublous life can be. I said to Sally, "I'd sure hate to have to go out in *this* tonight! Don't reckon the boys will do any more drilling till it's over. It's not a fit night for a hound dog to be out in," little knowing it wouldn't be many hours before I'd be clumping around in the wind and rain and thunder, looking for a murderer!

Now comes that part which even now seems mighty hard to credit, even though I saw some things with my own two eyes that no man could rightly disbelieve. But what with the confused and wild way in which Foley told his part of the doings, and the noise and fury of the storm that kept up while he was telling it, together with the downright

465

The Song of the Sun ❧ Leah Bodine Drake

unnaturalness of the whole business—well, that last part is none too clear after all these years.

Needless to say, Dan hadn't gone to Memphis. Seems that when he left me that evening and went home, he found Honeybird and Mathers talking in the kitchen. Dan walked up to him and asked him what Foley later said was "a very personal question," and one word led to another, and they started belting each other.

I'd always been afraid to see Dan get into a fight with big Foley Mathers, but it seems like he made a fair showing. He was mad and he was hurt, and righteous wrath hath its own strength. Anyway, Honeybird thought her sweetheart was getting the worst of it. Foley said all of a sudden he heard a funny, dull sound, like a squash had been cracked open, and Dan slumped down on the floor, with his head busted wide open—and Honeybird standing over him with a bloody poker in her hands.

She was like a woman made of stone. She told Foley to get Dan out of sight before Mr. Brady got back, and forbade him to go get a doctor, as Foley swears he wanted to do. She said Dan was dead, and she wasn't going to hang for it, and if Foley had any sense he'd help her bury him and pretend he'd gone out of town. They could think up what to do later, she said, and Foley was so dazed with fighting and fear of that awful woman he'd been fool enough to admire, that he followed her like a whipped dog. He slung poor Dan's corpse over his shoulder, and Honeybird got a shovel from the toolshed and they stole out of the house in the dusk.

Hard and dry as the ground was, Honeybird had presence of mind enough to know there wasn't much use digging anywhere but the one spot where the earth was always soft—by Whisper Water. Much as she hated and feared that branch-side, she realized that there was the only place to hide away her husband's poor, broken body. The two of them stole around by way of the wood-lot; and down by the branch, where he used to fish and play his mouth-harp, they buried what was left of Dan Redwine. A makeshift grave it was, too, but they were in a mighty hurry and dizzy with fear and, I hope, remorse.

Those next few days must have been plain hell for her and Foley—him having to dress tools and her cooking for him and Mr. Brady, as though nothing had happened and her husband had sure-enough gone on a little trip and would be coming back soon! That was when Foley started drinking, and nobody—almost—knew why.

Then the worst happened. It rained. That downpour that everyone welcomed so was doom and destruction for the guilty pair. No wonder Honeybird mighty near fainted when I mentioned the branch flooding—she had a clear picture of that shallow grave and the way the banks crumbled in a storm!

She rushed into the house and woke Foley, and let him have the news. If he were drunk then, it sobered him up good. He could hear the rain swishing down, and knew that pretty soon the water would uncover what they wanted desperately to stay hidden from the sight of man. I don't reckon they knew what they'd do when they got there, but they couldn't sit around the house in a plight like that—they had to make a stab at covering Dan up better somehow. They crept out of the house, hoping against hope Mr. Brady wouldn't hear them, and through the wind and the lightning and the wild wet they made their way down to Whisper Water. With all that clay pulling at their feet Foley said they ran all the way as if the devil was after them, and maybe he was.

Now here's the part where Foley shook so with pain and fright, and where he'd stop so often to pray or to curse, that it's pretty much of a blur in all our minds, mine and Uncle Wade's and the others who stood around his bed there in the Redwine leanto that night. He says that as they got to the branch, they could hear Whisper Water rushing away between her banks, like something strong and big and angry, and somehow alive. In the semi-darkness they saw that the willow was bending and shaking all over like a woe-begone woman, and the banks were flaking rapidly. The lightning flashes showed that they'd come none too soon! Two stiff, helpless boots and a stretch of blue jeans stuck out from the clay. The earth they'd heaped so hasty over poor Dan's body was washing away, and the husband Honeybird Redwine had murdered was silently condemning her.

The branch was boiling and churning and the trees were tossing in the wind, as they grabbed and dug in the mud with their bare hands, when a terrible glare of lightning lit up the whole place. By its wild light

The Song of the Sun ❧ Leah Bodine Drake

Foley saw the big willow, that had been bending and thrashing like the others, sort of straighten up and hold itself rigid.

Then, before their eyes it seemed to tower into the dark, wild sky, higher and higher like a horrible, huge green fountain, before it swooped down on them like a thing alive! Foley fell over backward before its rush, and in the darkness beside him he felt Honeybird go down, too. He heard her give a fearful scream, and then a kind of awful gurgling noise. Another lightning glare came, and Foley saw what no human being ought to ever see—instead of a willow tree, it was a huge, angry Indian woman, brown-skinned, black-braids and all, bending over them—but it wasn't a human woman.

"Then, O my God!" Foley'd cry, as he told and retold that awful scene. "She was reaching down for Honeybird, and choking the life out of her with her long, thin hands!"

But the worst is yet to tell. Foley's shrieks brought the crew from the well and Mr. Brady, and together they got him up to the house as best they could—what with his leg hanging broke, where it had caught in a root when he fell. Collins said afterwards that it was caught so tight they could hardly get him loose, "just like it was hands holding him down," he said.

There wasn't a sign of Honeybird. They laid Foley on his bed in the leanto, and Collins got out the Ford and slid and slithered into town for Doc Luttrell. From what he'd seen and heard Collins figured he'd best get the Sheriff, too. Uncle Wade rounded some of us up, and in the wind and rain we went out to look for Honeybird. The storm had died down some, but we still had trouble with our lanterns, and I don't reckon we'd have come across her when we did if it hadn't been for Coleman Tate's old dog Luby. It was really Luby that found Honeybird.

Away down stream, caught among the brush that overhung the bank, was what looked like an old ragbag. Coleman's hound nosed it and let out a howl. It was Honeybird. Wrapped around her throat, coil on coil, so tight that it cut 'way into the skin, was what looked like a thin green rope. Luby set up another howl, and when Coleman and I picked her up, we almost did our own selves.

Not because she was dead. I guess we'd kind of expected that all along. But because that wasn't any rope that had strangled the life out of Honeybird Redwine—it was a long, green willow-wand!

Poor Foley died the next day. Doc Luttrell took off what was left of his leg, but he had a bad fever and what with the pain and the awful fright and . . . other things, like remorse, maybe . . . he just couldn't pull through. Dan was dug up and buried proper in the churchyard, with what was left of Honeybird—Lord pity her—along side him, although I recall there was some sentiment against it. Dan's widowed sister came over from Logan county to run the property. The drillers finished the hole with a new tooldresser Mr. Brady brought down, but they didn't get oil, so pretty soon they shut down and plugged the hole and went away. Things quieted down again, and after a while people sort of forgot about the Redwines, like you do forget things, even the worst.

But Foley had muttered something that night when he was raving and groaning—something that nobody else but me seemed to hear, and which never got into the statement my Uncle Wade writ out and had Foley sign. Yes, Foley seems to think he saw something else when that tree turned into that tall, goblin woman. He seems to have seen her bend down, after she'd cast away poor Honeybird, and sort of scoop up what looked like Dan's body out of his pitiful grave. Only it wasn't the blue-jeaned, dead body of Dan Redwine that Foley had helped bury. It was Dan, all right, but whole and unharmed, like he used to be, and naked as a new-born child! And in his hand he was holding on hard to something, some little object.

I could have told Foley what that was, and the tears come to my eyes to think on it. It was Dan's little old mouth-harp. Yes, sir, that little old mouth-harp that he was never without. And his ghost still held on to it!

Down by Whisper Water of a summer's evening, when the nighthawks are out and the fish are splashing, I've heard a sad, pretty little tune curling and creeping through the willow-wands: "Have you seen my true-love with the coal-black hair?" and the breeze in the big willow by the pool is sort of humming along with it, like a happy woman whose lover's come to her at last.

The Song of the Sun ~ Leah Bodine Drake

Foxy's Hollow

Burke Bennett was out with the Peddingham one wet day in autumn when his mare took a fence in the worst possible manner and threw her rider seven feet away.

When Burke tried to rise he found he had a sprained ankle and that the mare was nowhere to be seen.

Now isn't this dandy? thought Burke. Isn't this just dandy?

He didn't know where he was or how to get to Bewley Hall where he was staying, from here or how he'd walk there if he knew. Why couldn't he have stayed with the field instead of streaking off by himself in strange country?

Burke Bennett was a large young American with a red face and bad manners who wrote fiction of a sort about tanned young men who met beautiful young women on beaches. He was much beloved by bookies and loan-sharks and was a great hand with the girls, none of whom he intended to marry. Lord Bewley, who collected Americans, Irishmen and Toby jugs, had asked him down for the hunting in a part of England that Burke didn't know very well, and here he was in the middle of Hawkshire with a sprained ankle. He was sitting in the mud, cursing splendidly, when he saw a little wooded hollow nearby from which smoke was curling lazily. Now to Burke, who was no Boy Scout, smoke in the woods meant just one thing—a house. He hoisted himself painfully to his feet and limped off towards the trees.

When he got closer he saw he'd guessed right. There was a house there—big, half-timbered job, all sloping eaves, dormer windows and little leaded panes. It was set in a formal garden of rose arbors, dark yews, and privet trimmed in the shapes of ships and peacocks. For a minute Burke had the idea that there was something odd about it. Then he realized what it was: the day had been misty, but now the sun was shining brightly on the golden beeches and glossy holly-trees. Must have cleared up in a hurry, he thought briefly. The house had a great many little twisty chimneys, two of which stood up on each side of the main building like the ears of some animal. Quaint as hell.

Thud! Thud! . . . Burke at the door-knocker, which was a fox's head in brass, and grinning. Nobody answered. Burke hadn't known he could swear so colourfully. He gave the door a kick and it swung open, so he walked in. There was low-ceilinged hall with the usual things found in English country houses—good, heavy, old-fashioned furniture, crossed hunting-crops on the walls under foxes' masks, a stuffed otter (very dusty) on a side-board, and a fire blazing away on the hearth. Burke yelled, "Hey! Anybody home?" . . . Nobody. So he made himself cozy before the fire, pulled off his boot and decided to wait it out. Someone was bound to show up sometime.

The day waned. Dusk fell. Burke was nearly asleep when there was a noise at the front door, it was flung open and slammed shut, and a loud feminine voice said, "Beat 'em again, by gad!"

Burke took one look at the owner of the voice and forgot about his ankle. She was a slim, red-headed girl as beautiful as any of his own heroines. Instead of a bathing-suit, she wore russet tweeds, and she was breathing hard, which did interesting things to her chest. She didn't seem surprised to see Burke, and as she came over to the fire observed pleasantly, "What a run! Jolly good, though that last bullfinch is all that saved me! Please don't get up—I know you've hurt your foot." She added, "I'm Clarinda Foxer."

Burke, wondering how she knew about his ankle, explained who he was, and so on, and so forth, and said, "I'll have to ask your hospitality, Miss Foxer, until word can be gotten to Bewley Hall for somebody to drive over here and pick me up."

He really had no intention of leaving yet, and he turned on the charm that had devastated blonde Hungarian countesses. He was pleased to see that it worked here, as the young woman said, "Oh, not so fast! I haven't enjoyed a good-looking man's company for ages and I'm not giving you up so soon! Old Bewley can wait a bit. I like you—even if you *were* out with the Peddingham, blast 'em."

"Oh, you've been watching the hunt?" asked Burke.

The girl gave a sharp laugh. "Watching, hell! I'm the fox."

Ha ha to you, too, thought Burke, think you're funny, don't you? Aloud he said, "Well, that's a new way of seeing hounds work, I guess," which his hostess seemed to find unaccountably funny, for she gave a

The Song of the Sun ❧ Leah Bodine Drake

series of short, sharp laughs. Burke joined in, and soon they were chummy as all get out, with Miss Foxer bringing in a bottle of champagne and some cold chicken. Burke outdid himself in charm and whatnot, and it wasn't long before the two of them were making love together, and Clarinda told him (they'd gotten to "Clarinda" and "Burke" by this time, as well they might) that he was at Foxy's Hollow. The estate had originally been called Faux Air, the same as her own name, the family having come over from France a long while back.

"Faux Air . . . that means a kind of make-believe, doesn't it?" said Burke, and Clarinda told him not to get personal, and bit him playfully on the neck.

The morning came, and Burke said he didn't feel up to moving about on that ankle, and Clarinda said she should think not, and for him to lie up at Foxy's Hollow until it improved. Burke wondered aloud feebly what his host would think of his absence and Clarinda replied that he'd probably suspect the worst, and Burke was too sleepy to try to figure that one out. In mid-morning Miss Foxer told him she was going out for a while, and that there was a cold rabbit pie in the boot-cupboard if he got hungry. Burke lolled about the big empty house all day, wondering where the servants were, if any. He examined the portraits of former red-haired Foxers, peering at the signatures to see if they'd been painted by anybody worthwhile; poked around the dining hall and calculated how much, at a pinch, could be raised on the plate, and finally resigned himself to reading some poems of his hostess's which she'd dug out of an old hat box and left for his perusal, after learning he was a writer. They were terrible.

About three o'clock Clarinda came in, very sweaty and with twigs in her hair. She threw herself in a chair before the fire, and said briskly, "Saw some of your friends today. I'll bet they're wondering where you've got to! This is Saturday country for the Peddingham, you know."

"Good Lord, I almost forgot about Bewley! What did you tell 'em, baby?"

"Tell them! I can't talk to anyone when I'm out! I've told you, Burke—I'm a fox."

"Oh, sure," nodded the American. "O.K., you're a fox. How could I have forgotten?" (Could this babe be a looney? But a gorgeous job, at that!)

"I am, too, a fox," insisted his hostess, facing him suddenly and looking so alert that Burke almost expected her ears to prick up. "Quite likely you find that hard to believe, but I've *been* a fox, confound it, since 1789! I've been running before Peddingham hounds and old Bewley and his ancestors for two hundred years, almost. And though it's been devilish close at times I've never been caught yet—and won't be, as long as I can get back to this house. Not that it looks like a house now to 'em," she added oddly.

"Why don't they ever chase a real fox?" (This was crazy talk, but kind of cute.)

"Why, they do! Been a good many tods around here that haven't gotten clean away like myself. Friends of mine, too." She sighed. "Poor little devils."

"Well, why do you let 'em run you? Should think you'd just hole up here." (If she wanted to keep up this screwy conversation Burke was her boy.)

Clarinda carefully pulled a thorn from her right thumb. "Can't—against Rules. You see, sweetheart, it's my Doom. Have to let 'em chase me. And I get a kind of kick out of it." She giggled. "And I *do* rob their roosts."

She grew solemn. "You see, Burke, I used to dabble in witchcraft when I was a girl. Runs in my family. And I got mixed up with a wizard. Big, black-eyed fellow from Sligo. We got into a bit of a hum one night at a Sabbat. He claimed I kicked him while we were dancing—maybe I did—God knows I was stinking drunk. Anyway, he was furious! Black Irish temper. He turned me into a fox. On account of my red hair and my name, naturally." She stared dreamily into the fire. "He was a romantic old beggar."

When she found out she was a fox (she continued) she hid out in the woods. She was ashamed of letting the servants and her father see her. She had hung around the house at night and old Mr. Foxer used to put out dead pheasants and small animals for her until she got accustomed to foxy ways. But he died soon afterwards—"I'd ruined his huntin', you see. He never knew if he were chasing his own daughter. Deuced awkward."

The Song of the Sun ❧ Leah Bodine Drake

Then it seemed that the servants started leaving, Faux Air was empty, so she moved in. But the country people claimed it was haunted and one night they burned it down. . . .

"*What?*" shouted Burke at this point. For a minute he'd gotten quite a shock, she sounded so serious!

"Oh, yes! They said it was a very mischancey place," she went on cheerfully. "So I just moved what had *been* the house into another dimension, bag and baggage. I can always move it back—temporarily—for various reasons." She leaned over to Burke, smiled and patted his knee. "And it hasn't been at all bad, being a fox. I get exercise with the Peddingham, and I've kept up with current styles and all that sort of thing, by sneaking around Bewley Hall during week ends. Bewley always has had a very *tonish* crowd. And of course that wizard permits me to keep my own shape while I'm in here. Has to—in the Rules, you know. He even keeps an eye on me to see I don't really come to any harm. Always was a bit of a cake about me."

"After two hundred years that guy still gets about? Some wizard!"

"Oh, yes! Dashed good one. Sociable fellow, too. Likes huntin' and all that."

"You're nuts, baby, but I love you," said Burke. (She was a screwball, all right! Might be able to use some of this in a story, though.)

Crazy or not (Burke forbore to say "crazy like a fox") Clarinda was a gorgeous job and he stayed on at Foxy's Hollow. The days passed, all pretty much alike. When Clarinda wasn't out in the hunting-field they'd doze together in front of the fire. At dusk his companion would rouse herself and get lively as anything. They'd drink champagne and snap wishbones, or play piquet, or argue about breeds of foxhounds, or make love, and then Clarinda would slip out of the house and stay for all hours. The next day they'd have chicken for dinner.

It was after Burke had been at Foxy's Hollow for about a week (as he reckoned it) that he began to notice things. Although he seemed to be as drowsy as Clarinda in the daytime now, he still spent less time in bed than she did, and in his prowls about the silent house he noticed quite a lot. Item: the little leaded windows with their painted panes of purple, red and amber cast a peculiar light in the room that was exactly like that in an autumn wood when the sun is shining. Item: although nobody came to the house and neither his hostess nor himself lifted a hand to clean the place, the beds were made up daily and the dishes washed. Item: one of the Foxer portraits, a young woman in lilac lutestring and patches, bore a remarkable resemblance to Clarinda and the date on it was 1786. Item: however freely he could walk in the house, he couldn't seem to open any doors to go *out* of it, although its owner popped in and out at will. Item: its owner's nose was really very pointed and her teeth very white and sharp, and she cracked goose-bones with them. She also had a damned foxy laugh. Could it be possible . . . ? Was she really a . . . ? Burke began to wonder.

One night he had a disturbing experience. He'd gotten up for a perfectly natural reason and happened to glance out of the bedroom window. Instead of the formal garden with its well-trimmed shrubbery and autumn-brown lawns, he saw something quite different. There were no lawns, only wet leaves, and brambles and docks growing all over. The privet peacocks were indistinguishable, and there certainly were a lot more hollies and yew-trees about than he'd thought. And what was that heap of rocks doing over where the stables should be?

Burke was thoughtful as he went back to bed.

The next morning he looked at Clarinda, who'd come in about dawn, lying curled up in a ball amid a tangle of red hair, and uncommonly foxy she looked too. I'm getting out of here, he said to himself.

But he didn't. He wouldn't admit it, but the poor fellow was spellbound. Doors wouldn't open to let him out. Those curious little windows seemed to be glued fast. Of course there was no telephone. It looked as if he really *was* stuck in the fourth dimension or whatever it was, ha, ha, ha, ha, with this awful doll, this witch, this . . . this . . . *fox!* Burke now spent all his time, while his companion was asleep or outside, in roaming the house looking for a way out.

The Peddingham was due around again one day and Clarinda left about noon—"to have another go at the little bastards," she told him—and Burke roved about in desperation. First, however, he locked the front door against her sudden return, muttering bitterly as he did so, "I can shut myself in, all right, but I can't get out."

All at once he heard a terrible baying and barking and yapping com-

The Song of the Sun ❧ Leah Bodine Drake

ing nearer and nearer, and then a wild scrabbling at the door. He knew what *that* was—it was Clarinda. There was a frenzied squalling and vixenish squawking. He knew what *that* was, too. It was Clarinda saying, "Let me in, Burke, and be devilish quick about it!"

Burke stood a moment pulling at his jaw and listening to the noises. Then he walked to the door and drew down the big old-fashioned bolt. Now the door was locked and bolted.

"Just try to get in now, Miss Foxy Foxer," he gritted.

There was more scrabbling and fumbling, then a regular pandemonium of sounds—doggy noises, hooves, and the high, hoarse note of a horn. Then some more hubbub, a cheer, and the sounds moved away. All was quiet.

Very quiet. Burke felt cold and a little dizzy. He thought he heard a small voice, high above him and growing fainter, say, "All right for you, Burke Bennett!" Then the walls of the house gave a shake, and then they weren't there. He was standing in a wooded hollow, full of wet leaves and brambles. There was no house. There was some crumbled masonry, a great many hollies and beeches and overgrown privet, but no house.

At his back was a hole in the stones of what had probably once been a cellar, almost hidden by nettles and vines. In front of it were some bones and reddish fur, or hair, with blood on them. The hole had been neatly stopped up with stones—from the inside.

Burke shuddered. Man, what a dream he'd had! Must have knocked himself out when he took that spill in the morning! And still in the middle of Hawkshire with this damned ankle. . . . He heard hooves and, looked up. A man on a big hunter was looking down at him. With a sigh of relief, Burke recognized him as one of Lord Bewley's house guests.

"Gillegan! Am I glad to see you!" Burke lifted a hand in greeting. He felt an unpleasant shock go through him. He looked at his hand.

Hand! It was a paw. He looked down at himself. He was a large red fox.

He heard Gillegan give a whistle, and then a whole pack of hounds could be heard coming towards them, giving tongue happily.

He looked up. Gillegan was smiling down at him in a very nasty way. His eyes were black and shining.

"Start running," said the Irish wizard.

Fiction

Mop-Head

In abandoned cisterns and old wells, in moldy heaps of straw forgotten in the corners of deserted barns, in reedy pools deep in the woods, in fungied hollows of dead trees, in all such secret places apart from man, strange life engenders, drifts in and takes root and form.

In a place called Yancey's Meadow such a thing grew and waxed and made itself a shape, listened and dozed and waited.

"Dorothy, where are you and Harry Todd going?"

"Just over the Yancey's Meadow to play, Mrs. Trevyllian."

"Not Mrs. Trevyllian, honey—*mother*."

"Yes . . . mother."

"Well, don't you all stay long. Daddy'll be home from Court early today."

"Yes'm . . . . *mother*."

Oh, dear, thought Aline Loveless, will I ever make a dent in that child's affections? Won't she ever forget that I was Mrs. Trevyllian and not her natural-born mother? Little Harry Todd accepts me—at least, he tolerates me. But Dorothy, no.

The stout, pretty red-haired woman watched the two little figures, seven-year-old girl and five-year-old brother, as they moved off towards the fields that lay close by, for the home of Jeff Loveless stood on the edge of the small county seat of Elkford.

I declare, she thought bitterly, if I'd known what a chore it would turn out to be, trying to mother a dead woman's children, I might have thought twice about leaving Bardstown to marry Jeff! That's a fine way for a little girl to address her mother—"Mrs. Trevyllian"—all right, *"stepmother"*! But even Harry Todd says, "Aline." Why doesn't Dorothy go one step more and call me the Widow Trevyllian?

Six months ago Aline had married the lonely young lawyer with the two motherless children, and for six months she had tried, with all her store of natural warmth and kindness, to take the dead Reba's place. She knew she had succeeded with Jeff, and to a degree with his little son. But with the girl she had failed. The child seemed almost to hate her. Nobody had ever hated Aline in her life and the tears welled as she gave

477

The Song of the Sun ~ Leah Bodine Drake

rein to her thoughts. The stitches in the apron she was hemming grew dim and she threw down her work with disgust.

"I'm such a softie!" she said aloud, and bent down to lift Mudge to her lap.

Mudge, a chunky Maltese, was the last living link with her former life, and the feel of the heavy little body gave her comfort. "Mudge loves me, at any rate—don't you, fellow?" she muttered to the purring cat as she rocked in the well-worn chair in the dining-room's bay window. "I reckon I shouldn't even sit here, in Reba's chair, if Dorothy had her way."

The noise of hoofs and a rattling wagon coming to a halt at the back gate made Aline wipe her eyes hastily, and by the time a discreet knock sounded on the boards of the kitchen steps, country fashion, she was once more to all appearances her happy, pleasant self. The knock was followed by a rich baritone calling softly, "Miz Loveless? Ah's heah with de fryahs."

"Oh, it's you, Ben! Come in," and Aline moved to open the kitchen door. Ben Pondy, the coloured man who owned a small farm on the outskirts of town, had brought in his weekly order of frying chickens.

"What nice, fat hens you raise, Ben," she said as she took the two limp bodies and rummaged in the broken teapot for change.

"Yes'm, thank you, ma'am." The old man took the money but lingered.

"What is it, Ben?"

"Well'm, Miz Loveless, Ah don't want you to figger Ah'm buttin' in wheah ain't got no call to—but them two li'l chilluns of Mistah Jeff's—they shouldn't be out yondah in that theah field so much. No'm."

"You mean somebody keeps a bull over there? My goodness, Ben, I'm glad you told me!"

"Well, no'm . . . not 'xactly bull. But they's that ol' well in de field yondah. Ol' dried-up well wheah they ain't been no house for de Lawd know *how* long."

"Of course they shouldn't play near a well!" cried Aline. "Why, they might fall in! I'll see that they stay away from there from now on."

"Yes'm . . . 'Course, they *might* fall in, though it done got coupla planks laid 'cross it. But Miz Loveless ma'm, it's kind of a funny place, that Yancey's field. Ah come by theah once, right smack in de middle of de evening, sun shinin' with all his might, ever' thing nice and peaceful, and Ah heah a noise like somebody chucklin' and awhistlin' to hisself over by that ol' well. Man, Ah never *did* stop to heah no more! An' Ah ain't never go through that field again—no *ma'm!*"

"How queer! Do you reckon there might be snakes there?" Aline was half alarmed, half amused at the old man's tale. "I'm grateful to you for telling me, Ben."

"Yes'm. Sho' wouldn't want nothin' to happen to Mistah Jeff's and Miss Reba's chillun. Sho' wouldn't go theah my own self."

As she heard the clatter and clop of Pondy's decrepit outfit move away Aline took a yard-rake and went across the narrow lane into Yancey's Meadow. The sun was hot and the strong musty smell of drying grasses filled the August air. Funny, she thought, ever since I've lived in Elkford I can't remember ever seeing any people in this field, not even any cows. Nobody ever seems to come here except Jeff's young ones.

She trudged across the meadow, her short sturdy young body plowing through the long Johnson grass. Jimsonweeds caught at her skirt and stick-tights to her stockings. Grasshoppers leaped up in alarm as she brushed by their green hideyholes. A faint breeze wandering aimlessly towards her brought the sound of children's voices talking excitedly and, she thought, a little stealthily. There seemed to be a third voice, with something thick and unnatural about it. It was vaguely unpleasant, she thought.

She could see no one. The insects whirred, Joe-pye weed nodded its purpling plumes, the sun beat down. A quick little chill ran over Aline. "Dorothy! Harry Todd!" she called, her voice skittering away across the field like a scared rabbit.

Some way off, where there had been no one, the heads of the two children suddenly popped up from the grass. As they got to their feet the little girl had a sullen look on her pretty face, and the boy looked frightened. They came slowly towards Aline, and she said sharply, "What were you two doing near that old well?" For now as she moved forward she could see the dark opening in the long weeds, the ancient grey boards that covered it haphazardly pushed aside.

There was a moment of silence, then Dorothy said, looking anywhere

The Song of the Sun ~ Leah Bodine Drake

but at her stepmother, "We were just foolin' round. Just sorta walkin' by."

"Walking by? But I couldn't see you—you must have been leaning right over it! Don't you know that you might have fallen in? Dorothy, you ought to look after your little brother better than this!"

As neither answered her, Aline's impatience, always near the surface, got the best of her. "What on earth do you two find so fascinating, anyway, about this place? You and Harry Todd have been kitin' off here all summer! And Ben Pondy thinks there's snakes around."

"Ben Pondy!" Dorothy looked at her stepmother, suddenly scornful. "That ol' cowardly custand! That ol' scairdy-cat! Ain't any snakes in that well."

"Well, you might fall in. . . . And who were you talking to? I'm sure I heard three voices."

Dorothy hesitated, then she replied, "Nobody. Nobody at all."

"Wasn't nobody, Aline," Harry Todd's treble piped up brightly. "Just ol' Mop-Head. He talks to us all the time and—*ouch!*"

"Why, Dorothy Loveless, you kicked your brother!" Aline, shocked, stooped to comfort the boy whose small shin had been given a surreptitious warning by his sister. "And you *were* talking to someone," she went on. "I heard you, and Harry Todd just said so. Who's Old Mop-Head, and why do you tell me stories?"

"He's just somebody we made up, Mrs. Trevyllian. He's just a play-somebody, honest—mother."

Her manner changed. She was all smiles and sweetness as she took her stepmother's hand.

"Harry Todd and I just stopped to peek down that ol' well for a teeny weeny little ol' second—didn't we, Harry Todd?"

"Uh-huh, I reckon so," mumbled the boy as he took Aline's other hand. As the trio moved off towards home the little girl looked up sideways at Aline in an appealing way she had, and said, "Now that Queen Esther's got the misery again and can't come around tonight, can I wipe the dishes for you, mother?"

To have you call me mother, Aline thought, I'd let you break every one of them, including my big Spode platter. Aloud she said, "Certainly, honey, that'll be a help."

As the little party entered the back yard Jeff's car turned into the drive. Not even the fact that the two children tore their hands from hers to fling themselves on their father, leaving her for a moment outside the family group, could spoil her happy mood that the feel of those small hands had induced. Even Ben Pondy's warnings dimmed in the sudden rush of well-being.

This pleasant state lasted through a hilarious if rather scrappy supper, result of the absence of the imperious Queen Esther whose reign in the Loveless kitchen was frequently interrupted by her "misery in de back." Not until brother and sister were in bed (after a washing-up marked by only one broken cup) and Aline was sitting with Jeff on the screened-in side porch, did she remember Ben's story about Yancey's Meadow.

"Jeff, do you know anything about an old well over there in that field—the one they call Yancey's Meadow?"

"What, honey?" He lifted his head from the radio's glowing dials. "Oh, that place. Yes, there's a well there. Been there since the Year One. Why?"

"The children have taken to playing there all the time, and I'm afraid they may fall in, or get bitten by a snake, or something. Ben Pondy hinted they might, when he brought the fryers today. He said he wouldn't go through that field himself for love or money. What's wrong with it, Jeff? Outside of snakes, I mean?"

Jeff studied his pipe a moment. "I don't rightly know, Aline," he said slowly. "I never much liked to go through that field as a kid, but I couldn't have told you why. That well's been boarded over, though, as long as I remember."

He stopped to light up. "Tom Bell tried to pasture some horses there once, but they got skittish about something, and one jumped the fence and took off for the woods, and it was two days before they found her. Funny...."

"Well, I want you to forbid them playing there, dear. And Jeff, do you know anybody named Mop-Head? The children seem to know somebody by that name. I never heard of 'em."

"Mop-Head?" laughed Jeff. "I should hope not! What a handle! There's some Moreheads, live up by Tyewhoppety, but that's a sight too

The Song of the Sun Leah Bodine Drake

far for their kids to come down here visiting of an evening. But about that well—I'll tell the little huzzybugs to stay away from it."

The radio crackled and sang, the smoke from the pipe mingled with the cloying scent of clematis in the warm Kentucky night. Where the street straggled off into the fields a lonely arc-light swung, its pale glow like a guardian posted against all things that crept or padded or cried in the rustling woods and ferny hollows, and were not of man. And off in its own place, amid the scummy water and crumbling stones, the dead leaves and moldering bones of field-mice, the thing called Mop-Head was awake, ears up in the quiet.

And the children, awake in their beds, watched a yellow half-moon sail up from the dark woods and send a long ray across the floor. The house was still. The big folks had gone to bed. A whispering began: "Harry Todd, you awake?" "Uh-huh." "Well, get up! We gotta go to the field. We promised ol' Mop-Head."

"I'm scared. He's ugly. He's uglier'n a scarecrow."

"I know—but he's our friend, and he'll do what we want about—*you know*—if we get him things. He promised us, that time we woke him up. He can't do everything by himself—he *told* us that! Hurry up!"

Quietly, as if with much practice, the two children got out of bed and stole downstairs to the dark kitchen. The girl took a large covered plate from the refrigerator, and as carefully as two little animals on the prowl, brother and sister left the house and headed for Yancey's Meadow. Through the milky river-mist that lay in long veils over the grass, they went straight to the well in the far corner. Pulling and tugging, they removed the rotting planks to one side, and tipped over the plate's contents into the darkly gleaming depths.

A wind ruffled the fair hair of the two young heads. A hunting owl called from the hedge, and a fox, passing on some private business of his own, stopped and lifted a startled paw. And that which lived and had its curious being in the well chuckled with pleasure, and all its small mouths slobbered as it noisily feasted.

When Aline discovered her loss next morning she was only annoyed and puzzled at first.

"Who took those chickens out of the ice-box?" she asked at breakfast.

"Not guilty. Don't look at me!" said Jeff, busy with ham and eggs.

"Well, somebody did. Those hens couldn't walk off by themselves. And Queen Esther hasn't been here for almost a week—and I doubt if even she would make off with two whole dressed chickens, although I'm well aware of her small-scale pilfering from the larder." Aline turned to the children. "Do you youngsters know anything about it?"

Downcast eyes and absorption in their breakfast of brother and sister told the young woman that she was getting warm. "Come to think of it," she went on, "seems like a lot of food has been disappearing around here lately. Half a coconut cake that vanished over night—just like those fryers—and other things. Come on, kids, 'fess up. Which one did it, and what for?"

"Didn't take 'em," muttered the girl, while the little boy buried his nose still deeper in his milk mug.

"I'm sorry to say this—but, Dorothy, I don't believe you," said Aline, hoping desperately that she didn't sound like the mean stepmother of fiction. Her fear was realized as her husband said quickly, "Oh, come now, Aline! If Dolly says she didn't take them, I'm sure she didn't. Dolly, baby, speak up and tell the truth, the whole truth and nothing but the truth, so help you Moses."

Harry Todd laughed, but his sister burst into tears. Jumping from the chair she ran to her father and clung to him, sobbing, "I didn't, I didn't, I didn't! Oh, Daddy, I want Mommy! I want my *real* Mommy!"

Jeff Loveless turned worried eyes to his wife. "Don't you reckon some tramp may have stolen those hens? What would Doll here want with them, anyway? Tell you what," he added, "I'll go by Pondy's and have him bring you two more. O.K.?"

"Oh, all right," Aline agreed weakly, angry at herself for letting the matter drop so casually. Her thoughts were far from happy as she saw Jeff off to his law-office and heard his last orders to the children to "stay out of Yancey's Meadow." Dispiritedly she turned to the usual chores of the day.

Outside, under the big sycamore Dorothy pushed her brother back and forth in the swing and whispered fiercely, "Old Mop-Head doesn't want any more dead stuff. He wants somethin' alive next time, he said.

The Song of the Sun ❧ Leah Bodine Drake

Then pretty soon he'll get strong and powerful and can give us our wish . . . *you* know what."

"Ain't got any live stuff," said the boy.

"Well, then we'll have to find some. That's what *he* wants . . . and you want Mommy back, don't you?"

"Mommy's dead. They put her in a box," he answered, swinging himself vigorously.

"Silly! I know *that*, Harry Todd Loveless! But Mop-Head can get her back, like we asked him, and then that Mrs. Trevyllian, that ol' red-headed woman, will have to go home."

Her young mind scurried about the house and yard like an invisible mouse, considering all the prospects of living food for their peculiar friend. He had said if he had live food he could bring Mommy back. . . . She tiptoed to the side porch. Mudge was busily washing himself on the step.

When the potato sack swooped down over him the big Maltese was so taken by surprise that neither clawing nor writhing helped him. With the spitting, moving sack bumping along between them, his captors hurried over to the forbidden field. They pulled aside the boards and looked down. Something glistened a little far below. Dorothy set the sack on the well's lip and pushed it over.

"Yoo-hoo!" she called softly. Mudge made a fine splash.

The sun shone and westered. Insects hummed and chirred in the warm grass. The shadows lengthened and dusk fell on trees and vines and hedges. Bats stole out of their secret places and field-mice ran through their tiny alleys in the weeds. And that which was at the bottom of the well in the meadow felt strong currents pass through its crazy veins, felt the living blood it had tasted nourish the rackety body.

The thing called Mop-Head was not animal or plant or rock, although, by now, it was a little of each. It had no definite body, and it longed for one. A scrap of elemental force that had drifted down over the field from far-off places, and settled long ago in the forgotten well, it had gradually built itself a body and a consciousness over the years. From darkness and silence and damp, out of earth-mold and wet leaves and blown dandelions, of scum and spiders' legs and ants' mandibles and the brittle bones of moles it formed a shape and a sentience. From the thin laughter of children and the far calls of men, from the haunting songs that the winds blew towards it from the Negro church in the woods, from fox's bark and owl's cry and rain's patter, the creature had made itself a clumsy mockery of speech.

It was not good, not evil, and it had one desire: to acquire a solid body. Being an elemental, it had vigor far beyond its size. Now that it had eaten, it felt strong, capable of anything. It clambered up the sides of the well and slipped over. The rising moon glistened on its fuzzy greyness, glittered in its many eyes. Its antennae waved in the warm air and the thing whimpered a little. And in Ben Pondy's henhouse the hens awoke and protested against the strangeness in the air, and along the countryside, from yard to yard and from farm to farm, the dogs set up a barking.

The thing gathered its gimcrack body together and its feelers tested the wind. Finding the direction it wanted, it stood rigid a moment. Then it wobbled off toward the town. And the dogs barked at its passing, telling their masters of what was abroad in the night, and their masters slept.

As the Loveless family sat at lunch the next day, Jeff talking gaily of a case he had handled that morning, Ben Pondy's old horse came down the alley at a clattering pace and stopped at the gate.

"Mistah Jeff! Mistah Jeff!" The coloured man came in the yard at a run. "Come heah quick!"

When the young lawyer let him in the old man grabbed his arm and clung to it, moaning, "Oh, Mistah Jeff, suh! Somebody been at Mizz Reba's grave and mess it all up!"

"In Heaven's name, Ben, what are you talking about? Talk sense!"

"Yessuh, am talkin' sense. Somebody got into you all's lot in the grave yard and dig up Miss Reba. I come by theah jest now, and de grave all open, an'—" He groaned again and clung tighter to the other's arm. "Oh, Mistah Jeff, somebody break open that theah coffin and done stole Miss Reba!"

Drawn by the uproar, Aline and the children stood in an amazed group on the steps. Harry Todd started to cry, but Dorothy, her hands pressed tightly together, grew stiff with some inward emotion. Jeff, without a word and not even stopping to get his car, ran to Ben's wag-

The Song of the Sun ~ Leah Bodine Drake

on. With its owner scrambling up beside him, he sent the ancient horse to a feeble gallop in the direction of the cemetery.

Left alone, Aline felt she couldn't sit home and puzzle herself over the outrageous news. A heavy feeling of unease invaded her. Old Miss Crittenden was a near neighbor, and the young woman decided she wanted the companionship of someone besides the strangely excited children.

"Wash your hands, babies, we'll go over to Miss Sarah's a while."

"Isn't Mommy in that ol' box any more?" asked Harry Todd brightly.

"Hush, sugar—don't talk about it. Your Mommy's in Heaven," said Aline. But she thought she heard Dorothy say to her brother in a low tone, "Mommy'll be back," although such a remark certainly made no sense!

As they passed the side steps she wondered where Mudge was. Her pet hadn't shown up for his usual breakfast of fish-heads. Probably out on the tiles last night and hasn't gotten home yet, she decided with a slight smile.

It was a far from smiling group of men who assembled later at the Loveless family plot in the cemetery. Before the incredulous eyes of Jeff, Sheriff Helm and the posse which the latter had hastily gotten together, the grave of the first Mrs. Loveless lay open. The earth was thrown up as if a huge mole had burrowed under it, and the wooden casket, its lid ripped open, and with long scratches on its polished surface, was exposed. Except for the stained silk of the lining, still pitifully impressed with the dead woman's shape, the casket was empty.

Who had taken Reba Loveless from her grave, and why? As the news went around, and the baffled posse explored cellars and alleys and the nearby woods, the question was on every tongue in Elkford. Nobody reported having seen any strangers in town, and there hadn't been a tramp lying-up in a culvert for weeks. And nobody in these parts had any rhyme or reason to do such a thing! By twilight, Sheriff Helm owned himself stumped, and declared it a day until other plans could be made.

"I'll run you home, Jeff," said Deputy Joe Barndollar as the weary men straggled back, in threes and fours, to the courthouse. "We'll start out again tonight, if you say so, but you ought to get something to eat first."

"Eat! . . . Hell, Joe, I can't eat anything! But thanks for the lift—guess I *will* go home for a while," Jeff said in a tight voice, groaning inwardly. My God, who can have done this to poor Reba? He longed suddenly for Aline's calm good sense and practical, affectionate concern.

Aline herself was feeling anything but calm or sensible. Miss Sarah had a taste in conversation for rather grisly gossip and speculations. Then, as the word spread from the old lady to her many acquaintances via the phone, with the circle widening as they passed the news along, the jangling of that instrument got to be more than Aline could bear. Several calls to the Sheriff's office had brought no fresh word, and as the afternoon wore on she felt that she'd be better off at home. If Jeff came back he'd be tired and unhappy. Yes, she'd much better go home.

"But I'll leave the children here, if you don't mind," she told Miss Sarah as she prepared to leave. "I don't want them to hear about that grave and Jeff's bound to talk about it."

Old Miss Crittenden was delighted to have company for supper and pressed Aline to stay, too. "You don't want to be in that house alone with Jeff gone, and all the menfolks off in the woods and all," protested the old lady. "Anybody who'd make off with a dead woman must be a nasty kind of crook, and there's no telling what he'd do to a *live* one."

But Aline had made up her mind to be home when Jeff returned. As she went into the empty street she was surprised to see how far the sun had westered. It's later than I knew, she mused, glancing towards Yancey's Meadow, which was a glory of golden light. For a minute she thought she saw a figure coming across the field towards her, dark against the sunset. It moved quickly, and there was something odd about it. But the light was in her eyes and she could not see it distinctly. By the time she had walked the short way up the street to her house and turned into the driveway she'd forgotten it.

The clematis vines made an early dusk on the screened-in porch and the air was growing cool. She shivered a little, and as she entered the house she heard the back gate click. She thought the children must have come home after all. Then a foul smell, unbearably rank and loathsome, assailed her. Rapid, shuffling footsteps sounded on the kitchen floor and

The Song of the Sun ~ Leah Bodine Drake

a shadow darkened the doorway. Aline looked up . . . and screamed, and screamed again at what she saw before her.

In its most recent dress, Mop-Head was there.

It leaped towards her, thin arms wound themselves around her neck and pressed. Her senses reeled as she fought the thing with every ounce of strength in her short, solid young body, while the filthy odor sickened her and the wild horror of it dazed her mind. The pressure on her throat grew harder, waves of pain rolled over her, until one wave, more powerful than the rest, swallowed her up in merciful unconsciousness, and she fell heavily to the floor.

Through the still evening air, down the shady street went a peculiar whistling call. The horses in Tom Bell's stable heard it and whinnied. The town dogs heard it and challenged it fiercely. The Loveless children, playing on the Crittenden veranda, heard it and knew what it was. They looked at each other, and Dorothy said excitedly, "Mop-Head's awake! Come on, Harry Todd, let's go find Mommy!"

The sun was sinking behind the sycamores as the boy and girl ran down the street towards home. A car passed them, and the little boy cried, "There's Daddy!"

Joe Barndollar slowed down and the children piled in, Dorothy crying happily, "Daddy, we're going to see Mommy pretty soon! Our real Mommy, I mean!"

"What? . . . Good Lord, no, baby!" said her father, horrified.

"Yes, we will—somebody we know is going to bring her back to us—from Heaven, I reckon. He *promised* us!"

"I don't know what you're talking about, Doll," said poor Jeff wearily. "Come in, Joe, I'll ask Aline to fix you a bite to eat. I just want some coffee, my own self."

As the car slowed down in the driveway a repulsive odor met them. Could Aline have left a gas-jet on? Jeff wondered, although it smelled a lot worse than gas. There was no light in the house, but they could see somebody sitting in the rocking-chair by the bay window.

"Look! Look! There's Mommy!" cried Harry Todd, pointing.

Dorothy leaped from the car and tore into the house. The men heard her give a curious gasp and then a strangled cry. They raced in after her, to stumble over the unconscious body of Jeff's wife on the floor. But it wasn't this that made them fall back, holding their arms over their eyes to shut out the horror that met them.

From the rocking-chair in the bay window a figure rose to confront them in the twilight. With rotten silk crumbling away from the yellow flesh, with soil and twigs fouling the long, fair hair, with dead eyes upon them in an unseeing stare and dead lips smiling in terrible mockery of life, the body of Reba Loveless tottered towards them. The shredding arms stretched towards Dorothy and the grey mouth opened.

"Here I am!" said Reba.

With a sob of terror Jeff sprang forward to sweep the little girl out of the creature's reach. As he caught her to him, Joe Barndollar took one look at that shape, drew his gun and emptied its barrel in its chest.

A tremor passed over Reba's body. For one moment longer it stood erect. Then the parody of what had been Reba Loveless collapsed in a heap of decaying flesh and bones. As it fell, Barndollar thought he saw something run out of the dead mouth—"like a big curly-haired mole, or a kind of shaggy spider," as he described it later. It was making a chuckling noise as it scuttled across the floor and out the door into the warm darkness. Joe hurled his empty gun after it, but missed. He dashed out after it, only to see it disappear in the grass. Although there was a rustling in the mock-orange hedge that bordered Yancey's Meadow, he could see nothing.

The body of Jeff's first wife lay where it had fallen, in a gruesome little pile. The imitation life that had supported it briefly, that had raised it from the grave and had kept it hidden in the abandoned well until its moment had come to present itself to Dorothy—that life had gone with its alien guest.

But Aline's still-living body moved feebly, and Jeff was down on his knees, his brain whirling while his hands helped her to sit up. Her hands moved feebly at her mauled throat. As remembrance of the horror flooded back she began to cry silently, with long shuddering sobs. Then she saw Dorothy.

Her step-daughter stood like a small statue, her eyes round with fright, but no sound, other than that first faint gasp, had come from her.

The Song of the Sun ❧ Leah Bodine Drake

"Dorothy... Harry Todd?" Aline managed to say.

"They're all right, Darling—don't try to talk," Jeff cried, while the boy threw himself upon her, sobbing, "Don't die, Aline! Don't die!"

Aline still looked at the little girl. She had such a queer, frozen appearance....

"Dorothy?" she said again.

Dorothy wanted to answer, wanted to cry out as her brother had, "Don't die, Aline—Mother!" She wanted to say many things to the woman she had resented for so long—like, "I know I was bad ... I wanted you to go away and for Mommy to come back ... but I didn't want all *this*! I didn't want Mommy like *that* ... and I'm sorry for what I did to Mudge ... and oh, Mother, I'm scared! I'm scared!"

But nothing of this would come out. Her throat felt funny and she couldn't make the words sound like they ought to—only a kind of choked gurgle.

Jeff's jaw dropped. "My God, she can't talk! Aline! Dolly—she can't *talk!* Oh, my poor baby!" And Jeff suddenly knew that the horror had been too much for one small girl to face, as she had alone, in a dark room, and that it had struck her dumb.

Yet, as the deputy dialed Doctor Oldham with a shaking hand, a faint, half-bitter hope crept into Aline's mind. She'll need me now, she thought. Until the fountains of her speech can be unlocked again, Dolly will need me now.

Farther and farther away, over the darkling fields in and out among the misty trees, along the reedy banks of creeks and down into damp hollows, the thing which the children had called Old Mop-Head hurried and danced and tumbled.

It felt light and gay, but its strength was fading. The fierce but transient power which had filled its makeshift body, which had spurred it to burrow and rip and choke and reanimate was leaving it. Its essential being had not been harmed by the bullets, but its ramshackle body was coming apart. Here fell away a giant mandible, there a long shred of borrowed possum-fur, there again a beetle's wing and a spider's leg. It was getting sleepy, too. It wanted to find a place that was deep and dark and hidden, and wet with an ancient wetness, where it could rest until it had assembled a new shape. This world it had stumbled into had all sorts of exciting possibilities, all kinds of shapes, and materials for shapes, and other beings to talk to and do things for and make friends of!

But right now all it wanted was to sleep and sleep. . . .

It began to look about for a forgotten cistern or an old well.

Nonfiction

NONFICTION

Frederic Prokosch

The ancients believed that words have a power of their own, an ability to create life, which is illustrated in one instance by the story of the City of Ys, whose walls were raised totally without aid of human hands and by the chanting of magic runes alone. The magic that lies in words is nowhere better shown than in the poems of one of today's finest lyricists, Frederic Prokosch.

Prokosch's range of themes is perhaps narrow, for love and death almost entirely comprise it. Of course, love and death are paramount in human experience, and may be unique in the universe. As far as we know, other star-systems know not these experiences. Prokosch realizes this, when he states:

"This is our world: whose creatures nightly bless
Their pure and singular power to love and die."

Intensely subjective, his verse might be likened to a diamond, for each poem is chiseled, precise and brilliant. One may not agree with Gertrude Stein that the sounds of words alone make poetry, but one is tempted to sympathize with her views after reading Prokosch. He is often obscure, involved and has a passion, seemingly, for the indirect approach, as do so many moderns. But he has a feeling for phonetics relations bordering on the marvelous, bringing together words whose syllables make a haunting music. Take this instance:

"Music, the lion, the legendary day" . . . . . .

This glittering line standing alone without the rest of the poem, is pure poetry.

His expert use of cognates is shown in such phrases as the following: "Sun-girdled Heliogabalus",

"Go South, they said, beyond the torrential islands"

Prokosch has a rich, an almost Byzantine splendour of imagery:

The Song of the Sun ❧ Leah Bodine Drake

"Single-flamed humanity
   Shines in a mirror.
The whole star-littered lake is but another heaven,
   and Portugal
Only another cloud."

"Angelic shapes delight
Only the perpetual child.
The murderer plans his night
And the green hunter's horn
   Drives the unwanted wild."

   "Love with his lyre-horned anger".

". . . . . . the happy day at last lies hidden,
   An agate among rocks."
". . . . . . wolves, wolves, wolves,
Deep in the brain, deep in some old Siberia."

"The leafy evening rings her bells
   All over Italy".

. . . . . "the dry dome-scattered East".

It is the East that has fascinated Prokosch. The Wisconsin-born young poet (he was born in 1909 [*sic*]) says in one of his most highly-praised efforts, the "Ode" from *Carnival*:

"Asia once held me: the visual leap through the limitless, a world all covered with hungers, the threatening
   swarms of the past, migrations,
   And a belief in the dangerous magic of human memory."

All men seek their spiritual homes, and these are not always that of the land which gave them birth. James Branch Cabell found that the comedy of Man was made more luminous for him when set against the tapestried background of the Middle Ages, and his work is not less faithful to life for that setting. Prokosch has evidently received a heightened sense of values, man's hates, loves and terrors, from the vast and mournful reaches of High Asia and their forgotten peoples. His descriptions of these lands are colorful and haunting:

"Black and still under the Siberian heaven
Lies the lake: rise the weeds: sleep the herons, and the sands still."

"Soon they came to the salty sands, and stones by the sands
Bitten to statues."

In many of these lyrics the poet tells us that the beauty of the world is deceitful: not in any religious sense ("the . . . flesh and the devil") but in a natural sense, that of its transience and its independence of man. Prokosch's complaint is that pain underlies all things, and that mankind even worships pain and hate, that "the woods where the centaurs roamed" are empty of those old and kindly myths, and now cover a more hideous legend. Men desire a god, but a terrible one who slays, and the earth has become a theater for his bloody rages. Be not deceived by the loveliness of the earth, he repeats; it has become a danger and a snare.

Frederic Prokosch's lament seems to be that the opportunities for amorous dalliance are becoming fewer and fewer, as the century's need of more drastic experiences becomes more imperative. He regrets the past with its leisure for the subtleties of love and pleasure, and fears the swift and deadly impact of contemporary events upon the human spirit, with its danger of stifling the springs of tenderness and romance. That this is a real danger we all know, not only by simply reading the daily newspapers, but by watching the progress of all the arts.

Yet to look back upon more mellow times simply because in them one's self was happy is a rather selfish, and rather narrow attitude. Bemoan the past if you will, but do not pin down the history of man with the needle of one's own desires, saying: "The past was better, for in it *I* had time to love."

But he is adept in putting into words the horror of the present:

"What once was real is now degrading. Lost
Utterly lie the onanistic, the lazy, in an age of falsehood:
For certainly this is the age of lies: we stare, we listen;
The phrase, the photograph., weave their deceptions, nor is history
The eventual voice of truth and justice."

The Song of the Sun ~ Leah Bodine Drake

> "The frightful crystal of the present
> Records what we knew yet dared not whisper."

Recently Prokosch has taken even more to heart the despair and fear of man; his consciousness has opened more fully onto the wider range of contemporary misery untinged by that personal implication which we have criticized. Likewise, his technique has changed a little: he favors a more direct approach, is less obscure. But in becoming more comprehensible he has lost some of that music, that magical glamour which his earlier poems cast. Many poets when writing of the world's present state seem to feel so deeply its woe that they lose their sense of poetry. The urge to express immediately what they feel overrides their craftsmanship and need to condense and polish, with the result that more sloppy poetry is being turned out now than ever before. Edna Millay is a horrible example of what too-fervent emotion does to a poet.

Mr. Prokosch is guilty of such sinning against his muse, but in a far less degree. That all these poets will go back to their original purity of technique when the world is in a calmer state, and there is time to prune and polish, is not to be doubted.

With the sensitive spirit with which Frederic Prokosch is blessed (or cursed!) and with the plethora of emotion and beauty with which his poetic genius is burdened, it seems that he could easily be in the forefront of a new movement in poetry: that of a more robust, positive school of faith and interest in the future. Too much poetical water has already gone under our modern Bridge of Sighs. It is time for a reaffirmation of the glories of life, not despair of them. They never pass or change. Now, if ever, we need messages of faith, not of doubt.

It would be heartening if Frederic Prokosch should reaffirm his own belief in the goodness of the earth and the men upon it by his future verse. He is a young man, and of course the young are always bitter when their world crashes around them. But poets must be ageless.

Prokosch has the genius, the sense of beauty and marvel from which alone pure poetry is born. Also, he has a full-bodied love of the aspects of nature and the beauties of earth, both natural and man-made, which all modern poets by no means possess. This quality would seem to make him feel more at home among the positive values of life than the negative. Many moderns seem emasculated in their sense of frustration and despair. "Their fathers have eaten bitter fruit and the children's teeth are set on edge." The result has been a very sickly verse.

Prokosch seems to me to be in the wrong galère when he voices their weak regrets. No one who sees beauty in earthly things such as he does can by nature be a pessimist! We who admire his work would like to see him giving his gifts to reaffirming the world's unconquerable glory. Let the lutes of lost love be stilled in the bugle-cry of an advancing faith in the eternal values.

[Untitled judge's report]

Acting as judge of the K. Quarterly Contest for April–May–June, Leah Bodine Drake wrote as follows:

It was with the greatest difficulty that I made my final decision as to the winning poem in this contest. I started with over a dozen excellent poems marked for consideration, narrowed them down to three, and finally to "Separation Center," by Walter Mann. Although this poem contains several faulty lines, and one word—in the last stanza—which, for clumsiness and brash expediency, stands out like the proverbial sore thumb,

"And with a farewell *clever*,"

the poem miraculously survives. It is a genuine lyric, simple in style yet universal in thought and emotion, expressing all that many soldiers must feel when taking last leave of companions who have been so much a part of their lives. The last two lines moved me profoundly,

"Simply reached and shook my hand
And walked away forever."

I do not think comparison with Housman is unwarranted,—Mr. Mann's poem has some of that poet's brevity, force, controlled grief, and resigned acceptance of life's stark indifference. But oh, I do wish he had used another word besides "clever"!

Running Walter Mann a close second and third were Byron Herbert

The Song of the Sun ~ Leah Bodine Drake

Reece's "O Heart Take Care" and "Storm" by Leila Jones. I also particularly liked these other poems:

"Sea-Change," by Ruth Morehouse.
"Unchanging Void," by Winifred Adams Burr.
"Horoscope," by Frances Angevine Gray.
"This World," by Nat C. Hunnicutt.
"The Warning," by Hibbard Gustav Gumpert.
"The Man From Spain," by Beulah May.
"Victor," by Judi Warne.
"Reflections in the Water," by August Derleth.
"Words," by John Gallinari Whidding.
"The Refrigerator," by Mollie Ruth Bottoms.

This last I thought rather remarkable in that an abysmally prosaic object was successfully made into a subject for poetry!

It was a pleasure, although no easy one, to judge these poems.

Gremlins

SOMETIME NEVER, by Roald Dahl. Charles Scribner's Sons, New York. 244 pages, $2.75.

When you begin to read *Sometime Never*, you think that Roald Dahl has written just a delightful fantasy of the R. A. F. and those high-flying pests the Irish fliers imported from the Ould Sod—the Gremlins. The description of the Battle of Britain waged by the airmen, not only against the Messerschmitts, but also against the little inhuman creatures that liked to drill holes in their planes, is told with colour and wit. One is amused rather than alarmed by hero Peternip's first sight of a Gremlin, even though the green bowler hat worn by the imp gives the pilot the shakes! But reading further, you sense more than a pleasant drollery in this book. It begins to shape up as a bitter, hard-bitten satire, in places as devastatingly unflattering as Swift's, of man and his incredible appetite for war. The Gremlins, who loathe man, are just waiting, in their underground burrows and tunnels, for man to knock himself out in the next war, after which, their dictatorial leader tells them, they will take over the Earth—what's left of it. They do not have long to wait, for World War III kills off most of the human race by atomic bombing, and then comes World War IV which, waged with a weapon that drives men insane, really finishes mankind. On a world reduced to cinders, the Gremlins emerge, only to mysteriously disappear themselves before they have had time to settle down and start ruling.

The author has not troubled to tell us why the Gremlins, too, vanish from the world. Like old soldiers, they fade away, quite possibly because of what mankind managed to do to Earth before passing into history. This intriguing omission, however, does not detract from the book's worth. Dahl's savage descriptions of what an atomic and/or a bacteriological war would be like shadows John Hersey's report from Hiroshima. Nothing I have ever read of the effects of atom-bombing can touch these ferociously dreadful passages on the plane of fiction. They should be required reading for every statesman, dictator, and president in the world—while we still have a world.

Whimsy and Whamsy

". . . AND SOME WERE HUMAN," by Lester del Rey. The Prime Press, Philadelphia. 331 pp., $3.00.
MOONFOAM AND SORCERIES, by Stanley Mullen. The Gorgon Press, Denver, Col. 364 pp., $3.00.

Lester del Rey's first collection, ". . . *And Some Were Human,"* will interest those readers who, like this reviewer, prefer their fantasy with more whimsy than terror. Dealing with dryads, gnomes, the Great God Pan (in his gentler aspect), and kind-hearted ape-men rather oftener than with rockets to Venus and such usual props of the science-fictioner, the author has culled, he says, the best of his publishing in *Unknown* and *Astounding Science-Fiction*. While slight of plot and too often falling flat at the very last, these tales have tenderness and a respect for moral values too often lacking in this sort of literature. His unhuman creatures are far from being hideous or inimical to man,—too often it is man who is the villain. Pure villainy, however, is not too much in evidence in del Rey's kindly-disposed universe, his imagination being a fresh, happy and amiable one. With more application to his plot-development and the rounding-out of a more mature style this young man may some day offer serious competition to H. F. Heard, the writer with whom his attitude of mind has the most in common. Someday—but not yet. Sol Levin has drawn appropriate chapter-headings for the volume.

The handsomely gotten-up collection of Stanley Mullen's stories has two strikes on it from the first,—a title, *Moonfoam and Sorceries,* that is on the lavender-and-old-lace side, and a scattering of very long poems in very free verse bridging the hiatus between each tale. Unlike the book just reviewed above, this one goes in a little more for the terrible and the malign, but its author, too, prefers good to evil, and his horrendous creatures always get their come-uppance at the hands of the forces of light. Some of these stories, too, fail to come off, but in "The Queen Bee," "The Ophidians," and "The Gods of Shipapu," Mr. Mullen has combined original conception with really powerful description. But his imagination, while able to conceive grand, even lofty images, is not equalled by a technique able to present them quite adequately to the reader. Too often he seems to be hurrying to get his story finished and over with. This is a pity, for he has a real talent for this kind of fiction. Full-page illustrations by Roy Hunt are striking and add a great deal to the appearance of this volume.

The Devil and Miss Barker

PEACE, MY DAUGHTERS, by Shirley Barker. Crown Publishers, New York. 248 pp., $3.00.

The Devil, the witch, and the whole problem of evil seem to have an undying fascination for people of New England heritage. Their consciences, too, seem to bother them, every so often, about the Salem witch-trials. They justify them, condemn them, or just explain them away, but they are often on their minds.

Seldom, however, have they been handled in novel form as well as in Shirley Barker's *Peace, My Daughters*. The writer, herself a descendant of that pious, nail-hard, courageous and often mean-minded race who settled New England, has attempted to answer the old questions—just what *did* take place in Salem back in 1692? Was the Devil really abroad, or was it mass-hysteria? Who really were the culprits—the "afflicted children" or the good wives they accused? And what part *did* the self-righteous judges play in the trials?

Miss Barker claims that while much of the witch-scare can be laid to the vicious craving for excitement of adolescent girls and weak-minded women bored half-crazy by the long Puritan winter evenings, not all that happened can be so easily explained. There was, she holds, something more. So she gives to Evil the shape of a man, a shoemaker, decorous, plain (even if, from his description, he must have looked like Gregory Peck) who walks to and fro upon the lanes of Salem, intent on destroying as many of Adam's race as he can. Few suspect him to be more than man. To Remember Winster he seems both man and friend, and she falls passionately in love with the one, as she abhors the other aspect of John Horne. All through his strange sojourn among the citizens of Salem, she never quite makes up her mind as to what he is—although when John Horne leaves, it is noticeable that peace, more or less, descends upon the sons and daughters of the town.

This is a first novel of distinction, with a fine, restrained mood, a vividly presented atmosphere of horror and fear, and a lovely, lyric style, which is that of a writer who is first of all a poet. (Her *The Dark Hills Under* was one of the Yale Series of Younger Poets.) So deft is her evocation of the period, and so clean-cut the characterizations of both the historical and fictional people concerned, that the book reads like a genuine experience of the writer's among the events she describes. (Does Miss Barker by any chance own some sort of astral broomstick that lets her hop back and forth in time?) If some readers will not see eye to eye with all her conclusions in the realm of metaphysics, they will admit that hers are ingenious and sincerely offered. She has seemed to endeavor earnestly to reach a just balance between jeering disbelief and superstitious credulity. The one thing this reviewer found difficult to swallow was the ease with which her heroine contemplated marriage with a man she is pretty sure is Old Horny himself. Tall, dark and handsome as the fellow was, surely a sensible girl like Remember would have run from him like—well, like the Devil!

Abracadabra

When the stage-magician cries "Abracadabra!"[1] and flings up a flock of pigeons from his hat, or whips back the veil from the magic cabinet and produces a beautiful young lady instead of the tottering crone who entered, he probably does not know that he is calling upon the dreadful name of a very old, very puissant god of almost unimaginable antiquity.

Abracadabra was the name of a deity worshipped in Sumeria [*sic*] by a people who had already passed into history when Abraham left Ur of the Chaldees. What Abracadabra was lord of is not known, but he must have been a kindly power, as his name, worn as a charm, was a protection from evil. It had to be written in the form of a triangle, as below, worn for nine days, then thrown backward over the shoulder into the waters of an east-flowing brook. Here is how it should look, written correctly:

```
A B R A C A D A B R A
 A B R A C A D A B R
  A B R A C A D A B
   A B R A C A D A
    A B R A C A D
     A B R A C A
      A B R A C
       A B R A
        A B R
         A B
          A
```

Although Sumer had become a dead language long before the conquering of the land by the Babylonians, the latter were so impressed by its literature that they had tablets made of the Sumerian religion, legal, commercial and scientific writings. These were divided into two columns of cuneiform script, the first being the old Sumerian, the second the "modern" Babylonian. Consequently, when archaeologists discovered (and uncovered) the civilizations of Babylonia and Chaldea, the extinct tongue of the Sumers lay open before them.

How the name of this one divinity, however, traveled down nearly seven thousand years to our own day, is an intriguing bit of speculation. Still part of the small-change of modern "magic", it is as old as the art of genuine magic itself. Although it has come to be merely the "Presto change!" of the clever prestidigitator and the cheap faker, its essential majesty and awesomeness has not quite left it. Perhaps someday a too-glib Blackstone will pronounce this hoary word in just the right way, and with the ancient accent, of the Sumerian sorcerer, and then something quite surprising may happen to him! Even a long-forgotten deity does not like his name taken in vain. Better let sleeping dogs lie!

Notes
1. See S5.6: "Where does our modern stage magician get his '*Abracadabra*'?" / From the ancient name of a Sumerian god. We don't know what of, but his name was used as a charm against evil. [¶] It had to be written in the form of a triangle. It came down as a great word of power through the Babylonians, went north with the Medes and Persians, and west into Europe. It is now the typical word of magic, to the man in the street: 'Abracadabra, zem, zem, zem! (sum, dum, dum!)'" (pp. 61–62).

Miscellaneous Reviews

SHELLS BY A STREAM. By Edmund Blunden. New York, The Macmillan Company. $1.75.

Edmund Blunden has always seemed to me one of the most truly representative of living English poets, as much a part of the country scene he loves as one of its early inhabitants,—some shaggy old brock, that most British of British beasts, knowledgeable in the ways of England's dark and ancient soil.

Shells by a Stream, his first book of poems since 1940, is a robust re-

The Song of the Sun ~ Leah Bodine Drake

affirmation of his belief in the goodness of the countryside, that oldest, most traditional England. There is something very heart-warming and reassuring about these grave, lovely poems, these close-packed lines, sometimes rough as an English moor in texture, and rich as a plum-cake with the names of Britain's birds, plants and animals. The man-made war which has left the actual land largely unscarred has also touched his work but lightly. That more enduring world of the fields,

> Where Nature's war is news,

provides him with themes that never turn stale. Sunny-hearted as these poems are, there shows in some of them a certain mistrust of his fellow-man's good intentions toward the things of Nature. In "To Teise, a Stream in Kent," he says,

> May no man end
> With shore-seen plan or powerful greed
> The centuries of your joy. . . .

One of the finest poems in the book is "Thoughts of Thomas Hardy," which in a few short, but amazingly deft lines, sums up the whole philosophy, mood and personality of the great "Wessexman."

But it is to the classic rural types that his poems turn oftenest:

> The scythesman and the thatcher are not dead,
>   Or else their ghosts are walking with a will;
> Old England's farms are shrewdly husbanded,
>   And up from all the hamlets jumps old skill. . . .

And it is Blunden's poetry which helps to keep alive, in the world of the spirit, that homelier, nobler England of hay-field and manor, water-mill and grange, whose passing would be somewhat in the nature of a major catastrophe.

FORTY SHILLINGS. By Ruth Crary. The Press of James A. Decker, Prairie City, Illinois. $2.

Gentle in mood, but with a pronounced undercurrent of strong, even passionate feeling running through them, these seventy-odd verses are the evidence of a sensitive, proud, intensely devout personality.

NONFICTION

Sometimes banal in theme,—gardens, old houses, gipsies,—there are few that are not characterized by a sharp sense of irony and an exactitude of observation that lift them out of the "women's magazines" class of verse. At least once this reviewer felt that clutch at the throat and chill around the knees that are said to be infallible signs that what one has just read was poetry!

It is in the poem called "Definition" that Ruth Crary reaches the heights of her craft. In its beauty of idea, clarity of expression and almost startling rightness of imagery,—so that one gasps, "Why, of course, that's how it will be!"—the author has created that rare thing, a perfect poem and a perfect sonnet, worthy of preservation by some future Palgrave:

> I stand upon the seashore. With the tide,
> A ship is spreading eager-winging sails
> To greet the morning breeze. I watch her ride
> Voluptuous waves, until at last she pales
> And hangs a moment poised triumphantly—
> A tiny fleck, just where the lambent dawn
> Flares forth to mingle with the sky and sea.
> Then some one at my side breathes, "She is gone!"
>
> Gone where? Gone from our sight and that is all;
> For she is just as brave in hull and mast
> As when she left port at her captain's call.
> And in that moment when one says, "At last,
> She's gone!" there are expectant voices crying,
> "A ship! a ship ahoy!" . . . And that is dying.

THE SHIMMERING DISK. By Martha Salonen. The Wings Press. $1.75
FAR HILLS ARE BLUE. By Blanche Whiting Keysner. The Wings Press. $2.00.
DOWN QUIET LANES. By Anobel Armour. Brochure. The Wings Press. $1.00.

Martha Salonen's *The Shimmering Disk* is the inclusive title of a sonnet-sequence which makes up fully one-third of this first volume of poems from a poet whose work has appeared in *Wings*. "The Shimmering Disk" is

> the dream we call awareness,

The Song of the Sun ❧ Leah Bodine Drake

and the poem concerns itself with man's interpretation of his world and his goal of finding his true place in it. This is an ambitious theme, and while at times the author seems as much at sea as her hero, Man, the work as a whole is rather impressive, and curiously provocative. There is in places a striving after effect,—"in answers too precise to flatter fire,"—which meant absolutely nothing to this reviewer. But there is also a kind of tough, wry beauty about the turn of phrase, the images, that make these sonnets well worth a re-reading. In them, as in the various lyrics and sonnets which constitute the rest of the book, the author has something to say and says it well. More we can hardly ask of a poet. Miss Salonen will bear watching.

Dealing with simpler themes, but with a sure and delightful touch, is the author of *Far Hills Are Blue*. Blanche Whiting Keysner has chosen Blue Ridge Mountain subjects for many of her poems in ballad-form, while others treat of orchards, such as the one planted by hands now dead, where "The apple blossoms drift and spill, Far lovelier than a marble tomb."

These delicate lyrics do not probe very deeply into momentous affairs of the soul, although in the poem called "In The Beginning," the author decries the fact that in all the universe,

> Puny man alone rebels
> Proudly building little hells,

with a peculiarly apt choice of words.

Anabel Armour in her brochure strolls *Down Quiet Lanes* taking pleasure in country things, small boys, ducklings and spring flowers. She is that rarity in these days, a happy-hearted poet, for whom

> Each dawn is such a special dawn,
> As if each newly-minted sun
> Had scattered coins of life to spend. . . .

Slightly reminiscent of Robert P. Tristram Coffin, these poems are as wholesome as brown bread and as crystal-clear as a country brook.

None of these volumes have any "social significance" whatsoever, for which we should be profoundly grateful!

NONFICTION

POEMS AND SONGS. By E. N. Da C. Andrade. The Macmillan Co., New York. $1.50.

Someone (I think a character in a Thurber cartoon) once said, "Why has everyone stopped writing about rich people?"

Readers of modern poetry often feel like paraphrasing that question: "Why have the poets stopped writing about love?" Who nowadays writes love poetry in the grand tradition of Shakespeare, Donne, Suckling, Lovelace or Browning? Taken up by social themes, with prophecies of doom and anathema against war, it's a brave poet who will write a sonnet to his lady's eyebrow. If he does, it is more than likely to be addressed to her moldy bones or empty eye-sockets, for even the lovers these days wander bewildered through a Dali-esque landscape of the heart.

Not so E. N. Da C. Andrade! In his recently issued *Poems and Songs,* which combine the best of his early and latest work, Prof. Andrade writes love-poems that shine in an almost Elizabethan sunlight. Gravely-gay, unsentimental, with that certain masculinity of tone and implacability of purpose that distinguishes Elizabethan or Jacobean passion, his clean-cut, compact verses, perfect in their craftsmanship, could stand up well against some of Crashaw's or Waller's. This is "The Hawk," given in full:

> "What can you do, my dear?
> Give me nothing, give me all,
> Say, gainsay, dismiss, recall,
> I am master here.
> Wish me well or ill,
> I can feign you kist,
> Call your image as I list,
> Praise you how I will.
>
> The hawk so high above
> Scorning all pursuer
> May let no man mew her:
> But I'm the air in which you move—
> Through little you perceive me,
> Neither can you leave me."

An Elizabethan poet could not, however, have written "The Body of Light." In this long, beautiful poem the scientist speaks, yet a scientist who has a poet's soul. If Henry Vaughan had known as much of physics as Prof. Andrade, he might have written of light the same way, and drawn the same conclusion, that not through science alone can anything be understood.

This is a volume of exquisite lyrics, fresh, musical, and oh, so gloriously healthy!

TESTIMONY OF TIME. By Helen Nivens. The Wings Press. $2.50.

This is the first book-length collection of poems by a writer whose work, appearing in various poetry magazines, has shown great promise. That the total effect of this volume is one of promise rather than of realization is due partly to the fact that, like most first volumes, it contains too many poems and not all of them good.

Characterized by a deep mysticism, some of these poems just miss "coming off" by an inclination to obscure the meaning in a cloudy blur of fine phrases and by a seeming attempt to combine two or three ideas in one poem. But for a first book, *Testimony of Time,* shows brilliant promise, a bright and soaring imagination and a background of strong philosophical convictions. When the poet has learned to assemble her thoughts more coherently the reader will find some worthwhile messages waiting for him.

Many of the poems are about the sea, and these have sweep and beauty. There is one in particular, "Storm at Sea," which graphically underlines the littleness of man's proudest inventions against the might of Nature. One third of the book is devoted to sonnets, and here the poet's most powerful expression meets her most serious defects, which are of communication rather than of technique. But her imagery is always fresh and vivid in both the sonnets and the lyrics, among which latter form "A Metaphor of the Old and the New Year" stands out:

> Hours, yelping at the heels of each stag year,
> Yield not their prey the pastime of new fear;
> But find his foaming flank and sink their fangs
> Just where his sire received his fatal pangs.
> The leader bays the hunter; the hunter hangs
> His horn, and wipes his brow, and rests his sear.
> The proud, impatient pack whine round the deer—

> Each brindled brace alert. The hunter's ear,
> Attuned to conquest, knew the old stag hung
> When first a wolf within a hound gave tongue.
> A fawn, begotten by this stag, is young.
> Another winter, yelpers after blood,
> Another stag will wallow in this flood;
> Then hang upon this hunter's wooden stud.

THE CHARITY OF THE STARS. By John Heath-Stubbs. William Sloane Associates, New York. $2.50.

To open a book by a new, and unknown poet, and to read, with increasing excitement and delight, page after page of magnificent, breathtakingly-beautiful poetry, is surely one of life's major adventures. I had this experience with John Heath-Stubbs' *The Charity of the Stars*.

Heath-Stubbs, a young Englishman, is one of that gradually enlarging group of modern writers who are returning to the traditional well-springs of poetry from which to draw their imagery and their themes. The symbols of Christian and pagan faith, the Greek myth and the fairy-tale, contribute to the glittering tapestry of his poetic thought; and these are handled with such fresh emotion and sharp insight, such original turn of phrase and slant of vision, that the old becomes startlingly new. Like Yeats who advised it and Robert Graves who almost commands it, this poet has saturated himself in the great traditions of mysticism. He knows that the finest poetry is that which has its roots in the fundamental beliefs and hopes and fears of mankind, that the older an idea, the more familiar a symbol, the more it conveys to us in memories, emotions and imaginative vision,. Poem after poem is luminous with the angelic, the demonic and the magical: this, from "Ballata,"

> In northern woods the buried emperors stir
>   Deep in their gem-lit chambers underground,
> Hearing the huntsman through the groves of fir
>   Winding his horn, and dreaming at that sound
> (As in their sleep reopens the old wound)
> Of queens who tricked them in the years before.

Or this, from "Saint Cecilia,"

The Song of the Sun ❧ Leah Bodine Drake

> ... And three nights in the shadow he has stood
> Erect, yet with bowed head, and six wings furled
> About his bare and splendid body;
> Long hair like small blue flames swept back above
> His lucid brows, and great eyes deep with love ...

The longest poems in the book are written in a kind of irregular blank-verse, of which "Through the Dear Might of Him Who Walked the Waves" and "Epithalamium" seem to this reviewer the finest. "Epithalamium" is a synthesis of Christian faith and far older Corn-King and Spring-Queen beliefs,—lovely, lyrical, reverent and joyous:

> Take this cup,
> The honey and milk of the initiate,
> And sing a wedding-song
> For Him, our youthful vine-god, coming up
> From Jordan's waters ...

RENDEZVOUS IN A LANDSCAPE, by August Derleth. The Fine Editions Press. $2.50.

August Derleth, the young Sage of Sauk City, is easily the Thoreau of our present day. Living in self-imposed semi-isolation at his house on the great Wisconsin prairie, he gets about as close to nature as man can get in this age, when even the haunts of coot and heron are invaded by the passing airplane. Thoreau, too, had his mechanical monster, the iron horse, which however he felt less despoiled than enhanced the sylvan solitude,—a feeling shared by many nature-lovers, among them this reviewer.

One of the most enchanting little poems in this book (they're almost all little, and they're all enchanting) is "The Moving Landscape", which fits good old Mechanical Dobbin neatly within the framework of the wildwood:

> "... a bird, a wild creature sped through the wood's heart
>   so long every day, it has become a part
>   of landscape, an integer with bush and tree..."

Like Thoreau, to whom he pays his debt, as he does to Robert Frost and Edgar Lee Masters, Mr. Derleth finds more to be learned from "wind's talk, hawk's talk" than from man's. His poems are clear, concise, starting out simply enough with some minutely-observed bit of local wild-lore, and then hitting the reader right between the eyes with a good, sound, root-deep observation of human life and feeling that is philosophy in the true American vein. If the style and flavor of many of these poems remind you of Frost, that will surprise no one, the poet least of all. He acknowledges his admiration for the New England poet at the beginning of his book, and even his long tribute to Thoreau shows that if Derleth's philosophy stems from the latter, it is the former whose poetic manner intrigues him.

The book is a quartet, three sections dedicated to the poet's three masters, the fourth to a beloved whom he identifies only as "Psyche."

A sensitive feeling for animals, an ever-fresh capacity for wonder, a highly-developed sense of beauty of homely things (hay-barns, two birds bathing, a familiar star grown unfamiliar as a street-lamp, woodpiles and bonfires) give this book an appeal often lacking in those of so-called major poets. As August Derleth has said about his own work, "There is room for minor voices, too."

When they are as communicative and lyrically lovely as this one, the minor voices are probably those which most of us are going to remember longest.

DIRECTIONS IN THE SUN, by Eric Barker. The Merle Armitage Press, 1956. $3.00.

A certain wild, rugged strip of California coastline—that which runs from Carmel to Point Lobos—has inspired some of the finest poetry being written today by two American poets, one already world-famous, the other surely destined to become so: Robinson Jeffers and Eric Barker.

Jeffers' poetry draws its inspiration from the same roots as Barker's, the rocks, trees and seashore of this comparatively untouched country, and so it is just an fitting that the elder poetry should have written a foreword to the younger poet's new book, *Directions in the Sun*. This Merle Armitage publication, an example of handsome book-making as well as impressive poetry, is Barker's second book. His first, a Wings publication, was *The Planetary Heart,* and came out about fourteen years ago. Many of the poems in the current volume have appeared in the bet-

The Song of the Sun ❧ Leah Bodine Drake

ter magazines over the intervening years: the *Atlantic, Saturday Review, Yale Review, Poetry,* among them.

I have said that Jeffers' and Barker's poetry have the same roots. True, but there is a difference in their viewpoint. Where Jeffers sees only tragedy and shows an sublime resignation to the impersonal forces of life, Barker takes a view—not resigned exactly, but more objective, less despairing because fundamentally less interested in man's fate on earth, less concerned with the destinies of either hawks or man than Jeffers. In fact, in one of his poems, Barker plainly states he is far less interested in man than in nature:

> "Praise deserts, not hermits;
> Mountains, not dweller in caves,
> Not hawks, but the flowing sky . . .
>
> . . . "do not praise mortality in the bone."

His poems celebrate nature almost to the exclusion of Man—indeed, all animal life plays far less large a part in his poems than trees, rocks, the sea and the sky. His landscape becomes, at times, the landscape of a stage-setting, in which we wait for the actors to appear, and wait in vain. Say that man is a passing phenomenon on earth's face; say he is a mere sojourner, and a less lovely one, among timeless rocks and cypresses: still for the time being, he is here. He is a part of creation's web and cannot be ignored.

Yet in other poems Barker fits animal life tenderly and perfectly into his timeless nature-world, as in "Something Once Beautiful as a Wave," where the death of some sea-creature inspires these haunting lines:

> "Dry bones will speak
> Nostalgic as the lips of emptied shells
> Of all the motions of the changing sea
> When the scoured graveyard of this death
> Restores again the lost reminiscent flower,
> And the bare structure of the skeleton
> Shows through the arches how the wave was bent
> To clasp a creature molded to its form."

And man himself is made the pivot of a handful of lovely poems such as "The Owls," "My Barefoot Girl," "Night Swim," "Lost Heritage" and "Night Watch."

Barker's ear is flawless: read "Full Moon, West Coast," for proof, with its strong beginning:

> "Blotched with its unattainable mountains
> This was that yellow half-wheel rolled above Bald Hill."

To the exquisite "dying fall" of its end:

> "A poet wherein the heaviest stone may fall
> And write its weight of nothing on the glass."

Again, read "Birds" for its colour and sound:

> "Struck on the wing by night's enormous bird,
> Black-breasted with Antares-colored eye."

And completely unhuman but a perfect summoning-up of the strange, insentient (but is it? how do we know?) Being of nature's phenomena is "On a Piece of Driftwood." You can feel the rough texture, you can taste the salt crust, you can see the silver bones of that piece of wood as few poets can make you feel, taste or see. Not for nothing has the Welsh writer, John Cowper Powys (a personal friend of the poet's) stated in his preface to the book, "Barker moves in and throughout his favorite subject until he seems to become almost synonymous at times with the particular element that he writes about."

I think that *Directions in the Sun* is a book of promise rather than completion—tremendous promise, which will lead to . . . tremendous completion? Never say the word! For a poet to reach completion is a fate worse than death indeed, it is a kind of death! Either in actual poetic Creation, or in critical estimation, for a poet to have finally "arrived" often means his finish as a poet. I think that Eric Barker is one of this century's greatest poets, or rather on his way to becoming so. He has affinities with Dylan Thomas (to whom he has written one of the best poems in the volume) through his exact and vivid choice of images. For sheer beauty of words and an uncanny sense of pace, Barker need bow to none. To me, this little book is of enormous significance in Modern

The Song of the Sun ~ Leah Bodine Drake

English poetry (English in a language sense, and not in a national, although the poet is indeed a native of England). The bardic quality of verse has not died with Dylan: it survives strong, assured, and with infinite promises for the future, in the poems of Eric Barker, who has more poetry in his little finger than many of the craft's so-called masters have in their whole frames.

This book won its author the Borestone Mt. Poetry Award (shared with David Morton) in 1955, in its manuscript form.

[On "We Come Out of the Forest..."]

And now we turn to the discussion announced in the March Letter, of Leah Bodine Drake's poem: "We Come Out of the Forest, Fearing Stars":

Twenty three interpretations were received and sent to Miss Drake for checking. No names appeared on the copies sent to her, which were designated by the letters A to W. She cited ten of these as especially good, and of these ten only parts of three or four can be reproduced here, owing to limitations of space. However, I have four or five carbon copies of the entire twenty-three interpretations. I shall copy Miss Drake's marginal comments on these, and send the whole of all the texts to members who wish to make a detailed comparison of them. No names will appear on these. First consideration (in order of rotation, for of course there are but a few copies to go around) will of course go to those who wrote interpretations, and second to Contributing members who did not, and then the order of mailing will depend on order of receiving requests.

I now quote from a few of the papers especially mentioned by Miss Drake:

E. To the least discerning reader, "We Come out of the Forest, Fearing Stars" is merely the story of a primitive tribe of tree-dwellers, stooped by years of creeping through the safe woods, and ignorant of anything beyond their shelter. Suddenly they find their sanctuary destroyed by a storm. They now dread the lions beyond the wood, which they have heard but never seen. They bewail their plight, but are powerless to exchange the stars and the tall wind and the new experience of walking erect for their previous safe yet animal-like existence. Even their faith must be revised; they appeal to the unknown Powers of the new land rather than to the dead totems.

The broader interpretation, left to the reader, suggests man's eternal unwillingness to be driven from the safe and comfortable to a life where peril and opportunity loom large. That man finally becomes the master rather than the victim is foreshadowed in his prayer that his spears may be adequate, and his walking tall . . . .

F. In the first line, with the use of the word "we," Leah Drake establishes her poem as both personal and universal in sharing an experience which is common to us all, and yet is varied as are the characters of the individuals who read it.

For me, this poem is a telling commentary, in the form of a parable, on how man has lost the privilege and art of being the best and truest self, encircled by the trees of conformity, bent out of his intended stature by the thinking of others, and by the rules and regulations of the society in which he finds himself. He depends on forces outside of himself for safer and easier living until he has, as Eric Manners expresses it, become a "Thing" (this little spear of a tree-man) rather than "the unique and incalculable reality that is the human soul."

This poem is in truth complex: it may be interpreted in a material or in a spiritual sense or in a combination of both. The trees of the forest may be of as many varieties as there are influences which keep a man from seeking or reaching his highest point of mental, physical, or spiritual development; seemingly kind in their protective functions, their branches hide the illuminating pattern of the celestial heavens or obscure the eternal verities. The lions may well represent all the dread terrors of warfare, the loss of wealth, prestige or power among nations, or, for the individual in his own sphere of life, may be the fear of losing that measure of security and power which he or his loved ones now enjoy. The "thick wooden lords" or "bark-gods" are as numerous as those false idols of material satisfactions that we worship until they are laid low by the tempest, which might be a hurricane of earthly events or the turmoil of our own souls; we are stripped and exposed and left to walk "warily in this

The Song of the Sun ~ Leah Bodine Drake

bare landscape, fearing stars," so warped by our way of life and habit of thought that we lack the ability to change or to straighten our attitudes, are unable to face the "tall winds" of high adventure unafraid. The stars, long unseen and forgotten offer but perilous hope to the man who exchanged the glory of their guiding light for the dimness of the forest. . . .

P. . . . We have become such slaves to a mode of living ("How low are laid our girdling trees") and to conventionality ("bodies were shaped to the forest") that we are uncomfortable and even afraid to throw off these shackles and to become free spirits, guided by our own desires and beliefs.

Our lives have been shaped by a certain pattern—we are born in it, raised in it, and live in it for years, contented with our way of life, partly because it was the way of our forefathers ("waters fell broken"—"rumors of another sky") and partly because it was the path of least resistance ("huddled warm and unseen").

Some unforeseen upheaval ("tempest year") changes the course of our lives and we enter into the new way with uncertainty ("walking warily") and fear ("fearing stars"). We are afraid of the difficulties we must meet and overcome ("Lions") and fearful of adverse public opinion ("stars"—the eyes of the world). It takes courage to stand on our own two feet ("walking tall") and alone ("without totems").

T. . . . Actually this is the tale of growth; consequently it is as universally true as it is painful. We love being the ignorant sheltered creatures which our prejudices, our "idols of the tribe," our intellectual mores have made us. We are comforted by the proximity of our horizons, beyond which lie the terrifyingly radical thoughts (the "lions" whose "eyes torched terribly") of our neighbors—to us, our enemies. We are satisfied with the physical well-being ("the water from the rustling heavens") which these unthinking guardians, "thick wooden lords," promise us if we submit to their overlordship despite the fact that we have crippled ourselves in the attempt to confine our spirits to their dimensions. But suddenly our own ineffectuality betrays us, the year of decision exposes us and our assurances are found wanting—"our leafy castles thrown," "our bark gods dead." We are ashamed and distressed by our new liberty (although it is a native state), "our spines rebel at the vertical," we are fearful of beauty, and we call upon the unseen to save us from the disillusion of this dreadful moment.

U. There is no feeling of terror akin to the one where an entire group has lost its protection, whether that protection by [*sic*] physical or spiritual. Leah Bodine Drake highlights this terror. I liken it to a primitive race's search for some power to stand between them and the savagery of their world. Forced by circumstances into a new world which they did not understand, beset with dangers with which they were unable (or unwilling) to cope, and lacking the flexibility necessary in the face of such extreme change, they are overwhelmed by the mystery of their broadened existence.

The individual of today who goes beyond his segment of the universe, either through choice or cold necessity, faces the same situation. Man is forced into an over-expanding consciousness of that which composes his world, and the more he explores (or is forced to explore) the less benevolent becomes that world until he, too, can only pray.

V. . . . The forest's womb-like security, its trees with their bole-bark, dull, wooden gods, branches and "totem leaves" is an aspect of primordial ignorance and superstition from which man emerged.

The "rumors," via "rustling leaves and broken water" aroused his curiosity. He became timorous, "wary" in the "star"-light of knowledge, yet the Human Spirit within him spurred him onward. The refrain, Lines 3 and 22, emphasizes the stifling inadequacy of the "lost and low girdling trees" beyond which he is flattered by "torched," watching eyes, to advance.

Now in historical and modern "tempest"-driven years, man senses that all too long he was betrayed by the slow groveling of immaturity so that he is still hampered by aeon-long confinement in the "dark forest," and mind rebels at change.

The Human Spirit, in danger of "wind" (a biblical synonym signifying conflict), ignorance and negations versus truth, delving, probing and expanding is "proud" and determined.

The poem's core is its celebration of the Human Spirit's supremacy over inertia.

The Song of the Sun ~ Leah Bodine Drake

And now we turn to Leah Bodine Drake's own analysis of her poem, written after reading the 23 critiques from the *Poetry Public* members. Miss Drake has done more than simply give her interpretations; she has traced the development of her poem from its inception. I quote her remarks in full. I don't care if this month's letter runs to 15 pages, but I think this material is too good and too important to deny a single word of it to our members. A devoted study of all these remarks can be of incalculable value to both readers and writers of poetry. It can open up whole new worlds of imaginative insight:

To read twenty-three different interpretations of one's own poem is quite an experience! It could be a shattering one, if the analyses hadn't been so almost entirely correct, in their judging of what the author had in mind.

Almost to a man, their various interpretations agreed, which gratified me, for "We Come Out of the Forest" is, I suppose, a rather complex poem.

The genesis of the thing is rather interesting: it shows how some poems come into being. In fact, it rather proves the rightness of the theory of "inspiration," as against the theory of mechanical deliberation.

I was reading a book of poems by Josephine Case, and a certain line or two fired me:

> "Not in the darkest shade
> That night and leaves have made
> Is anything to fear;
> No man is here." .... (and so forth. ...)
> (From "Forest: Night," in *Freedom's Farm*.)[1]

Who can really tell why a certain set of words will suddenly touch off the spark that develops [*sic*] into a poem? Why these few lines? I don't know—I really don't know. But this verse, from a poem in no way akin to what I was going to write, started the poetic wheels aturning.

I thought how the animals must have rejoiced when our early ancestors left the woods and left them alone. Then out of the deep subconscious mind came memories of what I'd read about primitive man—how he once lived in trees (or some races did), how safe he must have felt, and how, if those trees were suddenly blown down, or some other catastrophe drove him out, he must have been scared half to death at the wide, bleak wilderness, the beasts (from which he couldn't run and climb a tree!) and the utterly new, unknown and far, far away skies with terrible watching eyes in them.

In my mind's eye I could see a prehistoric tribe, stooped, as early men *were* stooped, still bestial, but having weapons, of a sort, and gods, of a sort. They trooped out of their familiar woods, hugging their short spears (although I doubt that such early man had spears—more likely slingshots—or maybe clubs with spikes on them! But hell, "spears" is a nicer word! So let's give 'em long clubs with sharp flint or bone splinters in the tip—and jump the gun a little and call 'em spears!) frightened at the desert and the lions, amazed at the stars, which they hadn't looked at through the covering of leaves, and with their pitiful, helpless gods of carved tree trunk and painted upright log blown down.

Then the subconscious got to work, and from intending to merely write a poem about a tree-living tribe of early man, the poem took its own way and kept getting more and more complex and with deeper and deeper meanings as I went on writing. When I saw the line it insisted on taking, I then deliberately elaborated on it, and of course in the revisions (not many, believe it or not) I added a bit here and there of deliberate symbolism.

But the symbols, from the very first, seemed to appear of themselves, so that I had little actual work to do looking for them. Some, of course, are not symbols—"moss curls," "painted eyes" are literal descriptions of early tree-idols. Maybe their eyes were made of shells, and then painted,—I don't know. There is no hidden meaning in these words, or in "thick" lords: all logs are thick—except that the word "painted" gives a feeling of falseness.

Then from the travels of one tribe, the poem began to describe the travel of Mankind himself, up from a bestial state to that of real Adamness, full-fledged man.

But as I wrote on, I saw where I really was describing the travels of the individual *person,* in the *world,* and the individual *soul* in the *spiritual* realm.

The Song of the Sun ❧ Leah Bodine Drake

Almost all the P.P. saw this—that some went farther and saw a *national* angle to it just proves that all can read in a poem what they bring to it. While I didn't have the nation in mind, exactly—more the individual—the poem certainly can be interpreted to mean our country's emergence onto a wider world stage.

But primarily the poem deals with man, and individual man. He hugs his safe traditions, ways of life, modes of thought. He's afraid (and too lazy) to shed them even if it means a higher life, both physically and spiritually, for him. He is afraid to accept the challenges of a wider life (actual life, soul's life) even though he knows it would make him greater and more heroic, and he's rather flattered that life (and God) considers him worthy of such attention, but still he intends to do nothing about it—until some catastrophe, some devastating experience of life in time, or life of the soul, literally forces him out of his complacency and inertia and sin and smugness.

His accepted standards and false values now stand him in no good stead—in fact, he sees them as the weak things they are—perhaps to one person his idol is wealth, or race-prejudice, or dependence on his own family or clan or teacher, etc. (The idols are legion!)

Faced with real life, with genuine demands on him, he is frightened, and his little spears of accepted rays of thought and resources seem inadequate.

The lions are not symbols of evil, only of challenge. I could have used another symbol, but lions to me combine so perfectly the dangerous and the noble. The experiences of life may be perilous, but they are challenges to us that give us a chance to be heroic. (The "darkness" is used merely to carry out the surface-meaning of the environment of early man: lions hunt at night.) But of course, it can be our ignorance and sin, as well.

The stars are evidence of a higher destiny, both spiritual and emotional and physical: as I said, this poem is on four or five levels. We've heard of such, we know they are there, but we've been too lazy and cowardly to look at them, and in their unobstructed glory they frighten us.

But faced with the necessity to really look about us and meet life with courage and honor and some kind of worthwhile response, we

NONFICTION

have to stand up. We *have* to be "men." And we feel proud standing upright. We are not so beastly, now; we are nearing real Adam-ness, as God intended.

The use of the plural—"Powers"—is not to imply a multiplicity of Divinity. While I actually myself believe in superhuman powers of good and evil—angels and devils, if you will—I believe in one God. But early man—and remember, this poem, on the surface, is about him—had a whole slew of deities. Every locality had its god, and when he came out onto the desert, and saw all these eyes looking at him, he must have thought this new land he'd come to had many gods and great Powers, and he needed their help against the lions and the possibly dangerous stars.

Of course, in a deeper sense, the "Powers" mean God and the hosts of Heaven. The stars only *seem* perilous—they are God's eye upon Adam—remember how he and Eve "covered their nakedness with leaves"? God, to one who has ignored, denied, or placidly accepted the knowledge of Him without really trying to know Him, can seem terrible, for he seems to demand that we come out of our sloth and ignorance and false pride, and we are really rather comfortable in them! But when we do, and become real men, we know a good pride. But we also know that we need His help more than ever as we walk upright to meet the challenges that he sends us.

So the levels of meaning in this poem are six:
1. A prehistoric tribe.
2. The race of Man from semi-beasthood to real manhood.
3. The individual person in the world, in life.
4. The soul in its spiritual world and life.
5. Our nation in the modern world.
6. Mankind himself as he stands today.

I was particularly struck by the letters from E, F, M, N, O, P, T, U, V and W.* Even those who read things in it that I hadn't intended—like the one who thought I was taking a poke at religion in favor of science!—got the general drift.

The Song of the Sun ❧ Leah Bodine Drake

The interpretations were excellent, and showed a pretty sound knowledge of what to look for in a poem. Evidently the intentions of P.P.'s Director are paying off!

—Leah Bodine Drake. April 10, 1953.

*E—Ruth De Long Peterson F—Marion Crites M—Marie Townsend N—Vernon Westmoreland O—Mabel Bankes Piper P—Jessie C—Thompson T—Sister Dorothy Mercedes U—William Z. Iron V—Lillian Dirkson W—Bertha Palmer

Notes
1. Josephine Young Case (1907–1990), *Freedom's Farm* (Boston: Houghton Mifflin, 1946): 9.

New Voices in Poetry

There is an idea popular with non-poets that every man is a poet in his youth, and in his youth only. After that, his poetic arteries harden and he gives up verses and devotes himself to prose. If the Victorian poets are pointed out in rebuttal, the answer is that they only *looked* elderly on account of those beards. Two current books by poets well past their salad days, who are not only writing poetry but better poetry than before, should give the final blow to that old chestnut. Edwin Muir did not start writing until he was thirty-five years old. John Hall Wheelock has just published his first book of verse in twenty years; and although its title is *Poems Old and New,* many of the poems in it were written as late as 1955.

Orkneyman Edwin Muir has only recently begun to acquire the audience his poetry deserves—at least in the United States. With his latest book, *One Foot in Eden* (Grove Press, Evergreen Books, $1.00), this semi-neglect should become one with Babylon and Tyre. For here are grand poems, in the true sense of the word, built around the themes of good and evil, man's lost innocence and hard-won experience, his refuge in dreams and memory from a world he never made, but which his original fall from grace undoubtedly influenced for the worse. In Muir's interpretation of sin and its consequences he seems to be the poet counterpart of

NONFICTION

theologian novelist C. S. Lewis. Here are moral poems by a profoundly Christian poet, and in them the old religious ideas are given new vigor.

Muir often uses the classic myths, as well as Biblical themes, to point up the human situation. Prometheus and Helen move through his verse, their stories freshened by the poet's insight and keen intelligence; and although the poems in *One Foot in Eden* certainly have a "message," they are never preachy or platitudinous. Deceptively simple in style, they are miracles of organization. Often a line will seem headed straight for a cliché; then—like the garden path in *Through the Looking-Glass*—it will give itself a twist and end unexpectedly. In "Milton" comes such a twist:

> Shut in Isis darkness, these [fiends] he could not see,
> But heard the steely clamour known too well
> On Saturday nights in every street in Hell.

Muir's diction is stripped of fashionable embroidery and the brokenbacked syntax by which some modern poets hope to appear original and profound. He is direct because he is profound; his poems are plain in texture because he has so much to say that he won't waste time on gilt and gewgaws. In "Outside Eden" we find this plainness:

> Guiltiest and least guilty, they
> In innocence discovered sin
> Round a lost corner of the day,
> And fell and fell through all the fall
> That hurled them headlong over the wall.
> Their children live where then they lay.

Man in these poems looks backward to lost splendor, lost simplicity, to a time when the Absolutes of courtesy, kindness, wisdom, and purity of heart were his crowns and royal vestments. "The Young Princes" say:

> There was a time: we were young princelings then
> In artless state, with brows as bright and clear
> As morning light on a new morning land.

Yet even in his exile man can still hope, and this poem ends:

> . . . And yet sometimes
> We still, as through a dream that comes and goes,
> Know what we are, remembering what we were.

The Song of the Sun 〜 Leah Bodine Drake

In his title poem, too, the poet sees light in our spiritual dark. With C. S. Lewis, Muir says that God can make use of Satan to further His good, although the new good may be different from His original plan. Not all is lost:

> But famished field and blackened tree
> Bear flowers in Eden never known.
> Blossoms of grief and charity
> Bloom in these darkened fields alone.
> What had Eden ever to say
> Of hope and faith and pity and love
> Until was buried all its day
> And memory found its treasure trove?

These are completely realized poems, hard-cut as gems, where each facet is worked to its own particular meaning and has its own flash of understanding. Muir has looked at our state of ungrace and found it not too bad, as long as we can, by memory and hope, experience and dream,

> . . . bring
> From the dull mass each separate splendour out.

In my opinion Edwin Muir's book is one of the year's most important literary events.

In *Poems Old and New* (Scribner's, $3.50), John Hall Wheelock has brought together some of his most felicitous early poems—such as "The Fish-Hawk," "De Coelo," "The Lion-House," "The Black Panther," "The Undiscovered Country"—and at least forty poems which have been written in the past two or three years. It might be feared that his turn-of-the-century pieces, written at a time when American poetry was bathed in a warm goo of sentimentality, would reflect the prevailing and less than felicitous mannerisms of their period. But except for one or two poeticisms sprinkled here and there, these earlier poems stand up well. For these are the work of an ardent, sensitive nature combined with a disciplined craftsmanship.

In much of Wheelock's verse there is the same sense of resignation and bafflement before life's "inexplicable will" that we get from Hardy's, the same deep compassion for the human and animal victims of it. Poem

NONFICTION

after poem reflects this somber wonder—"Reconciliation," "Herring-Gull," "The Two Societies," and that recently written poem, "The Abandoned Nestling," which ends:

> Out of nothing there came a need, a mouth, a cry,
> Out of peace, a suffering,
> Drawn back into it now.

In the section called "Scherzo," Wheelock indulges in a flurry of light verse. But oftener he is the man who lives "in an old house on a dark star," who sees—as in "Bonac" and "Amagansett Beach"—the old night that surrounds the globe and its beauties, outward symbol of man's personal dark, through which he walks to unknown ends:

> And in the road are prints of hoof and foot:
> Along the surface of this lonely planet,
> Now naked to the hunger of the stars,
> Man and beast—on the old pilgrimage—
> They passed together here, not long ago.

Thus Wheelock spoke thirty-odd years ago, but today he is more hopeful that the total of life is somehow good:

> Suddenly the morning sun looks out at me
> And I start up from sombre reverie,
> The light of a god upon me from afar—
> Pierced by great light, the glory of a star.
> Out of a cloud, in kindness, suddenly
> A god has looked at me.

2

In Peter Viereck's new book, *The Persimmon Tree* (Scribner's, $3.00), the poet displays a more mellow mood than in his former volumes of verse. His technical virtuosity is still here; some of the poems pop with surprises as fantastic and absurd as any in a Bosch canvas. But there is a sensuousness, a gentleness, developed—if I guess correctly—in Italy, where Mr. Viereck was recently Visiting Professor at the University of Florence. Gone is that vague unease, that preoccupation with nightmare and fugue, that haunted his earlier work, along with his slight posturing of being a

The Song of the Sun ~ Leah Bodine Drake

devil of a fellow. Under Italy's hard blue skies the poet seemed to find reality as being quite good enough. In "Etruria," the earth herself says:

> Your yearned abstractions cannot live where sol lives;
> And even luna's half-lights, clinging, contour
> My several greens exultantly specific.
> My vines are vines; each tangible full rondure
> Is just itself, no symbol and no dream.
> That dust is three-dimensional. The olives
> Are really there. I am the land I seem.

This is one of the best poems in the book, but what a clumsy rhyme—"sol lives" with "olives"!

In what to me is the book's loveliest poem, "Frutta Di Stagione," there is the same warmth, acceptance of reality, and a new-found tenderness. In this poem he half sadly, half whimsically advises some young girl—an innkeeper's daughter, perhaps—to savor all her seasons,

> You of a season, Valerie Sophia.

He tells her not only to gather her rosebuds while she may, but to welcome her autumn, too, with all the fruits of "the menu . . . you never wrote"; and the poem ends:

> And each husk, destined to its own true waning,
> Pales vulnerably perfect, Valerie.
> Believe the menu, fruits were always so.
> Say: "Of the season,"
>   voice as kind as rain;
> Believe no branches,
>   eyes as sad as spray.
> When destined, tears are seasonable wines.
> And each one gentle, Valerie Sophia.

For a poet of Viereck's stature, some of the things in this book are pretty thin stuff, seemingly little more than notes for poems. Yet even here we find the sharp phrase, the arresting imagery. And "I Am an Old Town Square" demonstrates anew that nobody can pick odd subjects for poems like Viereck!

NONFICTION

Norman MacCaig blends insight with craftsmanship, a daring use of words with traditional form, and lyric warmth with a wry, shrewd humor, all of which make his new book, *Riding Lights* (Macmillan, $1.75), a pleasure to read. Mr. MacCaig, like Muir a Scotsman, has the same sure sense of structure, and often opens with the same dramatic punch:

> Bury my name in the ground and watch it grow.

He is a master of the pungent phrase and the exact if startling image. How aptly he can write of the early morning!

> The window whitens; stars back into the sky;
> A wind picks up the argument it had lost:
> The horizon like a train of gunpowder
> Smoulders from east to west.
> Night sluices off the roofs, dives into drains;
> And day dries on the stones.

MacCaig's world, like that of the Georgians he resembles, is a morning world in which simple, familiar things—haystacks, hedges, horse troughs, and herring gulls—are seen in a clear light, not transcendental, but that of common day:

> Here is the hand with flowers for chessmen.
> Here's the light coming that will make
> Another move towards the moment when
> Over the fields he'll stoop and whisper "Check".

Perhaps MacCaig seems overoccupied with death—actual death, no spiritual defeat as is Muir's concern—but he isn't bitter about it and means to make full use of his time upon earth. So do all the creatures in his poems:

> Round clouds of glory change no creeping mouse:
> No dark diminishes the lion. Each
> Inhabits his own moment and his house
> Leans on a shelving and a dangerous beach,
> And time will be when mouse and lion can,
> Being dispossessed, fall heir to all of man.

Being a Celt, MacCaig has the faculty of identifying himself with the natural world around him, as in that fine lyric "Summer Farm":

The Song of the Sun ❧ Leah Bodine Drake

> Self under self, a pile of selves I stand
> Threaded on time, and with metaphysic hand
> Lift the farm like a lid and see
> Farm within farm, and in the centre, me.

Loving the natural world, it follows that MacCaig has no soft illusions about it. "Birds All Singing" is honest and funny and delightful:

> Something to do with territory makes them sing,
> Or so we are told—they woo no sweet and fair,
> But tantalize and transfigure the morning air
> With coarse descriptions of any other cock bird
> That dare intrude a wing
> In their half acre—bumptious and absurd.
> Come out and fight, they cry, and roulades of
> Tumbling-down sweetness and ascending bliss
> Elaborate unrepeatable ancestries. . . .

Not all the poems in *Riding Lights* are as good as this. Many of them, underneath their nimble, gift-o'-the-gab richness of imagery, ring rather hollow. Some of the sophistication seems posed. But they are evidences of a subtle mind and of a capacity for transmitting experience.

3

Another celebrant of nature, although of her less human aspects, is Eric Barker, whose *Directions in the Sun* (Armitage Press–Gotham Book Mart, $3.00) won for its author three of this country's most princely prizes—the $1250 Borestone Mt. Award for the manuscript, the same amount for the published book, from the same group, and recently their $300 prize for the "best poem": his "In Memory of Dylan Thomas," which first appeared in the *Atlantic*. With forewords by Robinson Jeffers and John Cowper Powys, Mr. Barker's book is one of the most stimulating and unusual of the current offerings.

I use the word "unusual" not because the structure or diction of the poems is bizarre—quite the opposite! This book is unusual in that it is by a younger poet yet it is *not* an attempt to be bizarre, complex, and incomprehensible. Here is poetry in the rich, romantic tradition, with a basic elemental quality that gives it virility and truth. Barker's deep-rooted empathy with the wild country in which he lives—near Point Lobos, California—gives his verse almost a religious tone, if only in the pagan sense. Like MacCaig, he too is as often the seen as the seer. Barker has identified himself with his subjects—the old, wind-twisted trees, the defiant rocks of that stormy coast, the gulls and seals:

> In the sea-smelling darkness
> I stand and listen,
> Perhaps as crabs and sea-urchins listen,
> All creatures christened with salty names.
> The sea moves through me, what I feel
> Drenches the dark, and my sea-lost name,
> Whatever it was, is named again
> In the name of the deep baptismal mother. . . .

He employs a style midway between traditional and modern, toward which most of the younger poets seem to be working. And he has a fine ear:

> Hear how the heart makes memory sad,
> Beating like a calling bell
> Or the wings of the sunset rooks in the fired trees
> My legs would follow to the steeple's view
> And the gilded cock with the four winds in his tail.

Some of these poems seem a little hazy in concept, and a few display more frosting than cake. Yet in the total effect we have an authentic poet, one with a deep if narrow vision, and with his own voice, his own music:

> Something once beautiful as a wave
> And in its element embathed as gulls in air
> Has gone beyond all mourning by the sea,
> Is nothing even of what in blindness breeds,
> A rage in nature and an eating fire. . . .

Richard Wilbur's *Things of This World* (Harcourt, Brace, $3.00) contains only thirty-two poems, but enough to win its author the coveted National Book Award for poetry. (This year the award, for the first time, consisted of $1000 as well as a gold medal.) In his latest volume there is evidence of the same mellowing effect of Italy on a poet's work as we find in Viereck's. Mr. Wilbur used to be a kind of backward-

The Song of the Sun ❧ Leah Bodine Drake

looking, forward-aspiring fellow. If it were a spring day, he perversely wanted it to be an autumn one. If it were the elegy season, then his poetic desires panted after the water-brooks of spring. Like the invalid in *Pollyanna,* if he were brought calf's-foot jelly, he wanted soup; if presented with soup, he wanted calf's-foot jelly.

But all is changed now. In his newest work he stands squarely in the midst of the things of this world and likes all of what he sees, smells, hears, touches, and tastes. He accepts, as they come, the fruits of the season, and he, like Viereck, seems to have shed some of his gothic distrust of the flesh. He says, in "A Voice from under the Table":

> I take this world for better or for worse. . . .

If *Things of This World* is marked by Wilbur's new-found sense of reality, it still exhibits what have come to be the trademarks of his work—formal elegance, unusual although never grotesque imagery, control, quiet gaiety, and an agile imagination. Now that Wallace Stevens is dead, Wilbur seems headed toward being the dandy of American verse. He has been accused of loving a poem's fine clothes a little too much, of overloading his lines with qualifiers, and he still does this at times, as in "Altitudes":

> With the gold-rosetted white
> Wainscot, the oval windows and the fault-
> Less figures of the painted vault.
> Strolling, conversing in that precious light. . . .

But he can be as stripped to the buff as Muir or Yeats, as in "John Chrysostom":

> He who had gone a beast
> Down on his knees and hands
> Remembering lust and murder
> Felt now a gust of grace,
> Lifted his burnished face
> From the psalter of the sands
> And found his thoughts in order
> And cleared his throat at last.

Yet who would do without those adjectives so aptly, so precisely chosen, that sparkle through his poems, as in "A Plain Song for Comadre"?

> Sometimes the early sun
> Shines as she flings the scrubwater out, with a crash
> Of grimy rainbows, and the stained suds flash
> Like angel-feathers.

"The Mill" is a curiously haunting poem, teasing the reader's mind with hinted-at significance, a vague but pronounced sense of mystery almost, but never quite, resolved. In "Digging for China," too, is this feeling for the strangeness in everyday things, although the mood here is playful. In this same poem he sums up, so to speak, his discovery of the things of this world:

> I stood up in a place I had forgotten,
> Blinking and staggering while the earth went round
> And showed me silver barns, the fields dozing
> In palls of brightness, patens growing and gone
> In the tides of leaves, and the whole sky china blue.
> All that I saw was China, China, China.

The digger for China in the poem is a child, and Wilbur the man has gone full circle and come back to that lost sense of delight in the actual world which a child knows, and which every poet carries inside him, however he may have thought he had mislaid it for a time.

The New Poetry

Nothing brings home more strikingly how far poetry in America and in Britain has traveled in the last decade from its former complexity than leafing through one of the "advance guard" anthologies of the forties. Here are the structural distortions, the private symbols, the complicated imagery, the *outré* frames of reference that have been familiar features of our serious poetry since the twenties.

But pick up any of the books by the younger poets, and you'll be amazed at the difference between poetry then and now. Here we have the theme clearly expressed instead of obliquely hinted at, the natural instead of the surrealist metaphor, the conservatism of form. "Public speech" and Marxism are out, and religion is in. The machine as an image has been

The Song of the Sun ❧ Leah Bodine Drake

gently put in its place: the poets seem able to take it or leave it. With this New Conservatism, however, there are all kinds of interesting things going on in diction, pattern, and rhythm. The new poetry is by no means simple, but it is not "difficult," and nobody seems to be trying deliberately to make it so. Whatever or whoever turned poetry back into the main highway of the English poetic tradition, one thing seems certain: the cult of obscurity is old hat. Name any one of the better-known younger poets—Richard Wilbur, W. S. Merwin, Adrienne Rich, Eric Barker, Joseph Langland, Alastair Reid, William Meredith, Philip Booth, and Philip Murray—there isn't a surrealist or a clenched fist among them.

On the debit side, some of today's verse shows a lack of the vigor which characterized much of the older school. The emotional tone is cool, there seems little inclination to get very much excited over anything. But although some hard purposefulness has been lost, urbanity and grace have been acquired. Among the Americans, the work of William Meredith is typical of the trend. Mr. Meredith's first book, *Love Letter from an Impossible Land,* was published in 1944 in the Yale Series of Younger Poets. His third and current volume is *The Open Sea and Other Poems* (Knopf, $3.50). One of Meredith's attractive features is his interest in practically everything. He has a wide range of subject matter, and he uses a variety of patterns which gives sparkle to the appearance of his book. (Nothing can *look* so dull as poem after poem in the same form and meter.) He has the knack of choosing the right form for his subject: "Notre Dame de Chartres" is written in the medieval sestina. In this poem's envoi he has rather neatly summed up the temper of the French Gothic world, whose "genius" was religious architecture:

> *Sancta Camisa,* the blessed shirt of the Mother,
> Because it had not burned, required a house
> And spoke to the stone that slept in the groin of France.

He is essentially a Romantic, although often his viewpoint is anything but. The title poem says:

> Nor does it signify that people who stay
> Very long, bereaved or not, at the edge of the sea
> Hear the drowned folk call: that is mere fancy,

NONFICTION

> They are speechless. And the famous noise of sea,
> Which a poet has beautifully told us in our day,
> Is hardly a sound to speak comfort to the lonely.

His observations are ingenious and piquant. He sees an espaliered tree branching all over a wall like the many-armed dancing Hindu god, Siva. Sometimes a conceit becomes a little arch:

> A beast in a human dream must go in dread
> Of the chance awakening on which he dies.

But in "To Absent Friends" we get the kind of witty remark which this poet seems so well able to make:

> Like Irishmen, we only think the best
> Of people, once inside the smoky bar
> Of our regard.

He is debonair, but he is also compassionate, with the insight that only compassion can give. In "A Korean Woman Seated by a Wall" he shows what war can mean to the innocent and humble. Mr. Meredith has vivacity and intelligence, a feeling for language, and a good humor that infects the reader. At the back of the book there is a huddle of notes on the poems. Why?

Although the poets are rediscovering God as a subject for poetry, not many poets are writing devotional poems. This may be due to any number of psychological factors, but it can also be due to a purely technical one: the fact that in unsure hands a poem in this genre is apt to turn into jogtrot hymnbook verse or a glimmering mist of words.

But Daniel Berrigan in *Time Without Number* (Macmillan, $2.75) side-steps both these perils. This is Father Berrigan's first collection, and the poems are skilled, the work of a subtle, finely tempered mind. On the ardently conceived vision he has imposed a firm intellectual control. I almost said "the ardently *perceived*," for some of these poems have the effect of things seen, not imagined—seen in the older, supernatural meaning of the word "vision." In "Little Hours" he describes the Incarnation:

> Like a waterfall, from what height falling
> he came to her; falling, filling her body . . .

The Song of the Sun ~ Leah Bodine Drake

> As tongue to her bells; O from that shaken
> and living tower, what music flies! . . .
>
> or came in a tide, riding her pure lands under.

He writes a tightly knit, sinewy, unrhymed line, with varying rhythm and with an economy of phrase that often has a Greek conciseness: in "Pentecost," when the gift of tongues descends on Peter and John,

> All their lives rounded in a backcountry brogue
> now to see, at crowd's edge, the fine Athenian profiles
> agape as bumpkins, scenting their delicate language like
> odor of muscatel or honey.

Father Berrigan can turn off a Chestertonian paradox. Of a dead priest he writes:

> The white Christ of the altar
> broke him apart; that Wine he raised
> desired and drank him to Its hungry heart.

In "Loneliness" St. Joseph's private anguish is vividly expressed:

> I had even less to do with the stars
> that having led her to me, bring her still face to me
> evening and dawn, snaking of evening and dawn
> one tranquil ecstasy.
>   Blade, hoe, manhood—
> what have my tools to do with What wakes in her?

Not all the poems are religious in theme, although they are in essence. Many present aspects of nature, for the greater heaven does not prevent this poet from seeing the lesser heaven. For him, both are integrated. "Lightning Struck Here," "Some Young God," "Its Perfect Heart" show this dual perception. Father Berrigan's book is the 1957 Lamont Poetry Selection by the Academy of American Poets, and should take its place among those which illuminate for us both the outer and the inner worlds.

A new volume by British poet Cecil Day Lewis is a literary event. An established poet in the thirties and associated, rightly or wrongly, in the public's mind with the Auden Circle, Mr. Lewis's work always showed a deeper lyrical strain than that of most of his contemporaries, together with a quality which can only be called heart. The façade might be hard-boiled in the then popular manner ("Love is the big boss, at whose side forever slouches the shadow of the gunman"), but passion and sensitivity infused all he wrote. Now, in *Pegasus and Other Poems* (Harper, $3.00), we get the impression that Mr. Lewis is writing at last just as he has always wanted to.

An expert craftsman, urbane, salty (Mr. Lewis is Anglo-Irish), with experience of situation and character, and with his lyricism even more pronounced, he is at his best in his latest book. The journalistic metaphor has been dropped in favor of metaphors drawn from the countryside, the religious ritual, and the legend. Complex in emotion but never in expression, these poems point up the current change-over in high-style poetry better, perhaps, than any others reviewed here. The four narrative poems which open the book are the Greek myths of Psyche, Ariadne, Pegasus, and Baucis and Philemon, retold in a style of great beauty and elegance. Mr. Lewis has let the myth speak for itself, without any recourse to Freud—a temptation that not all poets would have the strength to resist. In "Pegasus," how all of Helicon watches and waits as the attempt is made to catch poetry's winged horse:

> The cyclamen bow their heads, the cicadas pause.
> The mountain shivers from flank to snowy top,
> Shaking off eagles as a pastured horse
> Shakes off a cloud of flies. The faint airs drop.
> Pegasus, with a movement of light on water,
> Shimmers aside, is elsewhere, mocking the halter.

The polished lines are laced with a quaint, homely idiom. When Pegasus taps a spring, the water runs

> through thyme and grasses down-along.

In "Baucis and Philemon" the setting has almost a County Queens atmosphere. The copper pans shine in the cottage; when the gods come to the door they seem, to the old wife and husband,

> only a couple of tramps or tinkers . . .

Baucis's hands are "palmed thin as a saint's relics." She lays her finger on her husband's lips "Like a holy wafer." As Bronze Age Greeks

The Song of the Sun ❧ Leah Bodine Drake

had no saints, this interpolation of Christian imagery gives the poem a timelessness, an immediacy that is very moving. Baucis and Philemon could be any aging, loving couple anywhere.

This turning back to ancient sources for subject and image shows a distrust of the present which is underscored in the book's following sections. Here, Mr. Lewis gives the back of his hand to the cult of the Machine, of Intellectualism, and of Science, that triad once so adored by the poets of his youth. In "Sheepdog Trials in Hyde Park" he picks up the machine image and throws it away:

> ... The guided missiles,
> The black-and-white angels follow each quirk and jink of
> The evasive sheep, play grandmother's-steps behind them,
> Freeze to the ground, or leap to head off a straggler
> Almost before it knows that it wants to stray,
> As if radar-controlled. But they are not machines—
> You can feel them feeling mastery, doubt, chagrin:
> Machines don't frolic when their job is done.

"The Great Magicians" have taken from man more than they have given him; maybe they can "fish for pearls in Lethe,"

> But the hollow in the breast
> Where a God should be—
> This is the fault they may not
> Absolve nor remedy.

More personal poems are found in the last section, including a grand tour de force called "Moods of Love." Others, nostalgic in mood, have a whole web of fibers branching downward to our deepest longings and regrets. In "Christmas Eve" hope wins out, by ever so little, and is highly qualified:

> "Yet would it not make those carolling angels weep
> To think how incarnate Love
> Means such trivial joys to us children of unbelief?"
> No. It's a miracle great enough
> If through centuries, clouded and dingy, this Day can keep
> Expectation alive.

Nonfiction

The poetry of May Sarton has always been distinguished by a spiritual refinement which, with her technical excellence, intellectual keenness, and verbal music, makes her work a delight. Miss Sarton has never been one to trim her sails to the prevailing winds in poetry fashions; hence her work has a feeling of integrity which gives it stature and authority. If her poems are conservative in structure, they are wholly modern in temper and have a warmth not always found in modern verse. Yet unlike so many women poets, she does not wear her heart on her pen point. Miss Sarton's new volume, *In Time Like Air* (Rinehart, $2.75), again shows what a first-class poet she is.

One characteristic feature is her sharp sense of the past—not only the past *as* the past, but the past as part of the present. Her historic sense is quickly touched by old buildings, Gothic churches. Old houses and cathedrals, heaven knows, have been the subjects of many poems, good and bad. But in Miss Sarton's hands (as in Meredith's) they emerge newly charged with meaning. In "Lifting Stone" the stonecutter's craft is the frame around which the poem is built:

> Below a solitary figure stands
> To gentle the long bundle from its bed;
> Athens and Troy are leaning from his hands;
> The Roman arch, then perilous Chartres ascends
> Out of the empty spacious world where he
> Nudges rich burdens toward history.

Occasionally she seems to take the easy way out. "The Return" has the poet coming back to her "home of gloom and light," and all she can do is "stand and stare"—leaving the reader pretty much where he was at the beginning. This slackening of the imagination leads, for instance, to a use of such overworked words as *peace* to clinch a last line, giving us vagueness where we expected concreteness. But among fifty-odd lyrics these flaws show up small. The title poem, with its fusing of idea and image, beautifully fulfills its intentions. Miss Sarton's elegies are memorable, rich with a haunting music. "All Souls" moves to the rhythm of its emotion and so re-creates for us that emotion:

> Did someone say that there would be an end,
> An end, Oh an end to love and mourning?

The Song of the Sun ~ Leah Bodine Drake

> Such voices speak when sleep and waking blend,
> The cold bleak voices of the early morning
> When all the birds are dumb in dark November,
> Remember and forget, forget, remember.

Not the least fine in this group is "Lament for Toby, a French Poodle"—the great Toby of the "Remote and tragic air," who was not only "Courteous and discreet," but became famous in New Hampshire for killing a porcupine:

> If we were brave as he,
> Who'd ask to be wise?
> We shall remember Toby:
> When human courage fails,
> Be dogged in just cause
> As he before the quills.

In its lack of bathos, its tenderness and wit, this could well have been signed "Andrew Marvell."

Not many people today write plays in verse. Name T. S. Eliot, Christopher Fry, and you have named all. There seems to be the feeling that verse drama does not allow for the emotional sweep or the realism of prose drama. Yet, as Mr. Eliot himself has said, "the human soul in intense emotion strives to express itself in verse." So when a play in verse comes along, by a much-honored poet, it causes a flutter among the critics.

Archibald MacLeish is the poet who has just crashed the verse-play barrier with his paraphrase in modern dress of the world's oldest sob story, the Book of Job. *J. B.* (Houghton Mifflin, $3.50) is a play within a play, with an acted prologue, approximating the structure of the original poem. As poetry, much of *J. B.* ranks high. As drama, it has force and inventiveness. As philosophical statement, it is wide open for some lively debate. To take the ancient Jobian idea of God—an Oriental tyrant laying bets with Satan for a human soul—and to place this kind of deity in the setting of a twentieth-century and (nominally) Christian civilization is to make for a pretty state of confusion. That is not our idea of God these days, was not the prevailing one in Job's time. The Voice that huffed and puffed some bombastic, rhetorical questions (to avoid giving Job a direct answer) was a poetic device by an unknown Hebrew poet. As a poetic device, then, we will have to consider Mr. MacLeish's Voice in the whirlwind, also.

The setting is a big top at night, deserted except for two seedy circus venders, Mr. Zuss and Nickles. These are, of course, Zeus and the Old Nick—man-made conceptions of Good and Evil—fallen on hard times. More or less casually, they begin a burlesque of the tragedy of Job, wearing masks that represent, respectively, God and the Devil. The action of J. B. and his family takes place on a sideshow stage in the tent's corner. As the show proceeds, the shabby godlings find that their masks have a life of their own: says Nickles, "Those eyes *see*." They begin to realize that they themselves are no longer acting, that something beyond them has taken the show over, is turning it into the real thing:

> Mr. Zuss: At least we're actors. They're not actors.
> Never acted anything.
> Nickles: That's right.
> They only own the show.

These scenes with Godmask and Satanmask have an intensity, a magic that is positively eerie in its implications of strange powers, impending terrible revelations. In comparison, the J. B. scenes are a letdown. Our hero is too self-satisfied by half to be very endearing, and his family at Thanksgiving dinner may remind you of that appallingly perfect group in the old-time children's classic, *The Fairchild Family*. The Three Comforters are current types who claim to have all the answers, a soapbox radical, a psychiatrist, and a clergyman—the latter an ambiguous character that the author handles rather gingerly. That windy bore, Elihu, has been jettisoned in favor of a gaggle of hags, who comment, half pityingly, half gloatingly, on the misfortunes of their betters.

The ending of the play is, naturally, inevitable, with J. B. himself getting no more satisfactory an answer in America A.D. than his namesake did in Uz B.C. Yet MacLeish has attempted an answer of a sort: only in man's love for man is there hope. We need not expect any from heaven.

> Sarah: You wanted justice and there was none—
> Only love.
> J. B.: He does not love. He
> Is.

The Song of the Sun ~ Leah Bodine Drake

Sarah: But we do. That's the wonder.

Some readers will feel that for the author to deny the Creator a quality which he gives to the creature is to make the part greater than the whole. Many will still agree with an earlier poet whose God was not only one of power but of that "love which moves the sun and the other stars."

Books and Pictures Which Influenced My Poems

1. "The Wind in the Willows"
2. "The Princess & the Goblin" and
3. "The Princess and Curdie"
4. "Back of the North Wind"
5. Oscar Wilde's "Fairy Tales."
6. Walter de la Mare's Poems with *Dorothy Lathrop's* pictures
7. "King Arthur" Series of Howard Pyle
8. Grimm's Fairy Tales illustrated by *Arthur Rackham.*
9. Hans Andersen with Edmund *Dulac's* pictures.
10. "Arabian Nights"—Dulac.
11. All Andrew Lang's "Fairy Book" series—the "Red Fairy Book," etc. with *H. J. Ford's* enchanting illustrations.
12. "Mopsa the Fairy"
13. "The Sleepy King."
14. Lord Dunsany's wonder-tales

Magic Casements

There are certain passages in the books of our childhood that immediately cast a spell over us—a spell, incident[al]ly, that never quite loses its power in after-years, for they can always still evoke something of that first thrill.

These passages—lines of poems, paragraphs of fairy-tales—sometimes a mere sentence or two—have a peculiar enchantment, which their authors perhaps hardly realized in the act of creating them. They are literally Keats'

NONFICTION

> . . . magic casements, opening on the foam
> Of perilous seas, in faëry lands forlorn—

itself one of the world's most magical phrases! One of the most evocative passages in all literature!

(Incident[al]ly, why is it that the word *"faërie,"* spelt with the "e" instead of the "i" and with the umlaut over the i, is so much more magical and unearthly and elfin than the usual spelling: "f-a-i-ry"? Who knows the full power of each letter of the alphabet?)

Remembering my own particular spell-binders, I find one element common to them all, from which stems so much of their power to ensorcel: *the hint, the promise of something wonderful to come.*

Recalling some of these passages, I find in all of them this mystical anticipation, this power of making me feel as if I stood tiptoe before an half-open door. Consider these extracts from famous tales, and see how they arouse your sense of *something about to happen:*

1. . . . "When she came to the foot of the old staircase, there was the moon shining down from some window high up, making the worm-eaten oak look very strange and delicate and lovely.

   "'What if I *should really* find my grand beautiful old grandmother up there after all?' Irene said to herself, and put her foot on the first stair. Yes, that was a humming-sound she heard behind the door—the sound of a spinning wheel!"*

2. . . . "It was a very great thorn-tree and the hollow was so large that two or three boys could have stood upright in it; and when he got used to the light in that brown, still place he saw a good way above his head, there was a nest. Just then he thought he heard some little voice cry, 'Jack! Jack!'"†

3. And in "The Water-Babies"‡ this line occurs over and over in one chapter, in which the little hero, a chimney-sweep, runs away from

---

*Geo. MacDonald—*The Princess and the Goblin.*
†Jean Ingelow—*Mopsa the Fairy.*
‡[By] Charles Kingsley.

The Song of the Sun ❧ Leah Bodine Drake

his master and goes over a dreadful, never-before-climbed fell . . .
. . . "And all the while he never saw the Irishwoman coming down behind him."
(The "Irishwoman" was the Good Fairy of the book.)

4. And then there is this tremendous moment—one of the most tremendous in all literature with its promise of things-to-come:
. . . "It happened one day about noon going towards my boat, I was surprised with the print of a man's naked foot on the shore. . . . I stood as if thunder-struck!"*—and so does the reader!

A Poem Should Have

A Poem Should Have:
1. Beauty of words: the "fall" of the sounds.
2. Beauty of vision: the picture.
3. A reading of life: some discovery.
4. Fresh imagery & expression: some memorable phrase.
5. The lyric cry.
   (John L[ivingston]. Lowes)
"It is necessary for a poet to be steeped in some great tradition of mysticism."

To Be a Poet

To be a poet you must be able to enter into things by more than one door—not with one sense only in each department of sense, but with all five *in* all fire: you must be able to not only *see* a star—you must be able to *hear* them; they are like long glissandos on the piano, or they tinkle like sistrums.

You must *feel* moonlight, *see* the wind, *taste* sunlight and *smell* colour.

*Daniel Defoe—*Robinson Crusoe*.

Unless all of your senses can play the role by each sense (at least in a metaphysical way) you cannot comprehend all sides of a thing or reach its heart.

Life in These United States

Several years ago I went from Indiana to New York on a business trip, and on a self-imposed budget. Having some time to fill before my plane left, I went into a restaurant in the upper Fifties and ordered dinner. I was in the first stage of using eyeglasses and hated to wear them in public, but to my dim sight the price of the meal seemed surprisingly low. I was wrong—it wasn't. When the bill was brought to me I had the horrible sensation of realizing I hardly had enough cash left to pay for it. A quick look at the menu—with [sic] time with my glasses—proved the waitress right and myself embarrassingly wrong.

The manager was sent for. A courteous Frenchman, he looked and listened in silence while I scrabbled in my handbag, dragging out various cards in proof of my stainless reputation "back home"—my press-card, D. A. R. membership card, voter's registration, and so on and on and on. Surely the man could see I was just a newspaper gal with bum eyesight and no bum!

He examined all my desperate offerings carefully. Then he said, "Madame, I believe you. Let me suggest what to do. Go on back to Indiana, and send me the money when you get home. And, he added, smiling "don't be so upset. It could happen to anyone."

Well, I did just that—and never did I pay a bill with greater delight. And now, when I hear anyone complain that New Yorkers are hardhearted, rude and unfeeling, I want to yell, "Don't you believe it! Tain't necessarily so!"

The Song of the Sun ~ Leah Bodine Drake

[For *The Living Voice*]

Thomas Edward Francis, The Hun School of Princeton (New Jersey), Co-director of The National Library of Spoken Literature and the Living Voice Anthology, accepted six poems from Drake for his project: "The Web," "Precarious Ground," Old Man on the Sea Shore: Morning," "The Birth of Beauty," "The Undine," and "The Final Green." The book was to be published by Prentice-Hall. William Carlos Williams and Langston Hughes were other participants. He wrote Drake: "I will need written commentaries on each of these poems, approx. 1–3 typed pages as you see fit (Double spaced pages) plus a theory of poetry—a prose statement on what you think poetry is or how you wrote poetry etc." (10 March 1961, TLS University of Kentucky). Carbons of Drake's comments are among her papers. The book was not published.

What Poetry Means to Me

I can't do better than to quote George MacDonald: "A poet is someone who is glad of something, and tries to make other people glad of it too."

Poetry is a continual hymn of praise to life, earth and God, and therefore a full-time job. Nothing so infuriates me as to hear poetry spoken of as "therapy"—like a kind of liver-pill—or worse, as a "hobby"—as if writing poems was something you do on a rainy afternoon, like tatting. A true poet knows only too well that poetry is a poet's life-blood.

Anything less is greeting-card verse.

The Web

"The Web" is one of those poems in which the last lines come into the mind first. Since a child, I have been fascinated by that little picture, by one of the Pre-Raphaelites, which illustrates "The Lady of Shalott" [*sic*] in some editions of Tennyson, and shows the Lily-Maid tangled up in the skeins of her web. The loom seems to crowd her tower-room, and looking at the picture again several years ago I thought, "That web is enormous—it leaves no space for anything else in her room." That thought was the catalyst that started the familiar "chain of reaction."

NONFICTION

I began the poem sometime in 1953, but the first versions didn't satisfy me. In the autumn of 1957 I sat down at my desk, determined to bring order out of chaos from several unfinished poems, and pulled out the sheets on "The Web." That was one of my lucky days, for the poem practically wrote itself, with the whole thing building up backward, so to speak, from the last verse. The last line of all . . . "But that of course in itself was a kind of doom". . . . hit me like the well-known bolt from the blue, and capped the whole piece.

The poem's metre is a kind of free-wheeling iambic pentametre, with prose cadences strung along the basic metre. A friend of mine said once: "I can always tell one of your poems—you write like you talk".

I like to vary so-called "perfect" rhymes with slant rhymes, for these give an element of surprise to the lines. This is a poetic trick that's popular just now, and when it is over-done it can be affected as all get out! But it's such fun to do!

I also like to use the figures from myth, legend and fairytale as poetic subjects, for these have built themselves into the very backbone of man's emotional response. They endured as realities for so many thousands of years that they are part of man's Unconscious, even when not accepted intellectually any longer. An object such as a loom, for instance, has accumulated countless associations in the mind of the human race, for it was in daily use all over the world for heaven knows how long. It went out of general household use only about two hundred years ago, and is still used in many parts of the earth.

The older symbols still carry more of an emotional impact than modern ones, because in ancient times man credited inanimate objects with a kind of life. It was not for nothing that the knights gave names to their swords: "Durandal," "Excalibur"—just as they named their horses. We can see the beginnings of a new legend, so to speak, right now, with the passing steam-locomotive, which is already taking on the characteristics of a live thing—a kind of clumsy, faithful and beloved beast. Given enough time, perhaps the impersonal unloved diesel may go through the same metamorphosis.

The Song of the Sun ❧ Leah Bodine Drake

Precarious Ground

"Precarious Ground" had its genesis in a newspaper account of a volcanic eruption somewhere in Italy a few years ago. I thought at the time "Why do people persist in building their homes on the sides of volcanoes, on the very slope of catastrophe?"

Again, the last lines came first—the poem was built up from, and towards, the last lines. . . . "only upon the slope / Of old catastrophe."

All the lines of the poem rhyme, although the rhyme scheme is irregular.

Some lines in the second stanza owe their life to an observation often made by myself, during the many trips my parents and I used to take in our car, through southern Indiana, where we lived, or over in Kentucky—where we also lived off and on for several years. Coming home after dark, I'd see the little, widely-scattered farms, with their tiny lighted windows, set under such a huge black sky that it seemed it would overwhelm them some night. It gave me a proud feeling, that little man, so helpless really, could build with so much trust in the face of night, space and the uncertainty of all tidings. This experience was repeated over a period of years. I suppose it awaited a catalyst—as most ideas do—to become a part of a poem. This was furnished by the account of the eruption, and the idea—which had lain dormant in the part of the mind which holds our creative imagination—what June Downey calls "that region back of the North Wind"—fused into the new idea, and took its predestined place in my poem.

Old Man on the Sea Shore: Morning

As a child, I spent all my summers at Ocean City, N.J., where my mother's parents had a summer home. The sea moved through my young years like a living presence, and has coloured my poetry.

The poem is written in free verse for no esoteric reason: the first lines simply came to me that way. Every poem has its own idea of what it wants to be, its own plans for development. Unless the poet begins it as a set piece, a poem follows the lines of its own being. I find that a poem usually comes with its form built-in with the idea. If it's forced into a different form, as in the bed of Procrustes, the result is a mangled poem, and therefore a bad poem.

I have used one form (*knarred*) of the word *gnarled*, because the double r in the first and the hard k give the impression I want, of hardness, roughness and age. The *l* in the commoner word gives a softer feeling. I like old words with German–Norse roots. They have a burry, knotty feel to them which gives sinew and vigour to the lines. Words of Romance origin are more limpid with their many vowels and syllables. Consonants pepper the Anglo-Saxon words—their z's, w's, m's and d's are brisk, tough. They *explode,* they don't murmur, and you can use more of them in a line, giving a feeling of density. I once spent a winter week going through Webster, picking out wonderfully plummy, rough-textured words rooted in solid British earth!

The Undine

Some readers find the hand of Freud in this poem, and others of Jung. The first would have found only pirates' bones, the second would have gone deeper and found the lost gold. Both are here.

I'm guilty in this poem of one or two instances of poetic license—something I rarely avail myself of, as I think it is a form of cheating. But in "The Undine" I have put corals and anemones in cold depths of ocean where they never live. Both are creatures of off-shore reefs and warm, shallow seas.

I like to break up the sonnet form (and incidentally, I don't write many sonnets) to follow the outline of the sentence structure, and also because the huge bulk of the octave gives an impression of heaviness and ponderousness—the octave overhangs the poor little sestet like those topheavy Elizabethan houses!

The Birth of Beauty

The poem speaks for itself.

Man must have found the world beautiful long before he had any words to express his feelings, or before he even knew *what* he was feeling.

The Song of the Sun ❧ Leah Bodine Drake

Aphrodite must have risen from the waves in many places, and at many times, before her beholders could say or even know what they had seen.

Using a Greek myth for my symbol, I of necessity had to keep the poem spare, clean-cut and without the frills of emotional emphasis or too-bright tonal colour. I wrote the lines very swiftly, and then, as is my usual practice, read them over to start revision. But the poem needed no working over—it stood complete as it was! And so I let it stand, and here it is.

Final Green

This poem is merely a little hymn of praise to green, my favorite colour.

In regards to some of the references: green is an "unclassic shade," or the Greeks, who are reported to have had a word for everything, seem to have had none for this. They had no green in their dyes and pigments. They just didn't like the colour. One reason was their profound antipathy to anything symbolic of space, the distance, timelessness, eternity—anything formless and vague and vast. As such conceptions couldn't take sculptured shapes, they were not only bored with them, but a little afraid of them. Green seemed to them to be the colour of endless stretches of nature, of the faraway, the eternal. As a colour to be admired and used, green came to us from the Near East and the Arabs, who loved it because they saw so little of it.

The Holy Grail is supposed to have been made of green glass.

Our planet gives out a greenish light from the seas and plant-life, although before plant-life evolved, our light must have been reddish, like that of Mars, from the vast wastes of sand which covered the earth. But that, as the man said, is another story.

NONFICTION

Foreword [to *The Various Light*]

The publication of *The Various Light* fulfills a long-held desire of the editors to make a collection of outstanding poems, whether written by some as yet unknown or signed with the most dazzling contemporary name. It was also our wish to show through these poems the happier balance with lyricism during the past ten years or so, as well as the rediscovery of the natural world, love (and not simply sex on the one hand or procreation on the other), the sense of the divine and the importance of the individual.

Too many collections have either included trivia or else have trotted out the humorless rhetoricians of former decades with their contrived semantics, their often precious "social consciousness," their prevailing concern with man only as a part of the masses, and the shying away from anything suggesting a soul. Far too many readers of modern poetry, we found, knew these poets only; and all their conceptions of today's verse were coloured by yesterday's dreary wastelands. The names of many serious newer poets, and much less their work, are comparatively unknown, by and large.

The idea of an anthology of this kind was first discussed by the editors in 1960. In 1960–61 we went over the huge mass of submitted manuscripts (from some ninety poets), making successive selections and eliminations. The book attained its final form at Lausanne, Switzerland, in January 1964. For the few typesetter's errors, uncaught, that will probably be found we apologize.

No anthology is ever complete. Several poets we wished to include we could not contact. Others had to be foregone because of reaching us too late. Yet the lines that are here bid well to stand the test of time, and to constitute an enduring reference anthology of distinguished modern poetry in English. May they afford the reader as much pleasure in reading them as the editors enjoyed in assembling them.

We note with deep regret that C. S. Lewis and Richard Hertz will not see this book.

THE EDITORS
Lausanne,
1964

Letters

Published Letters

To the *Chicago Sunday Tribune*

On a Hypothetical Island

Henderson, Ky., March 19—To the Editor: My list of the 10 favorite books which I would take on that hypothetical Island: *The Wind in the Willows*, by Kenneth Graham; *Walden*, by Henry David Thoreau; *Essays* by Ralph Waldo Emerson; *Jurgen*, by James Branch Cabell; *Perelandra*, by C. S. Lewis; *Leonardo the Florentine* by Rachel A. Taylor; the poems of Elinor Wylie; *Alice in Wonderland* and *Through the Looking-glass* [in one volume], by Lewis Carroll; *Beyond Sing the Woods*, by Trygve Gulbrans[s]en; *The Decline of the West*, by Oswald Spengler [this last would occupy me for at least three years]. LEAH BODINE DRAKE

Some Good Novels

Henderson, Ky., June 17—To the Editor: I agree with Aldia Symington that modern novelists are, generally speaking a pretty shabby lot. But with his flat statement that there hasn't been "one novel of the last four years which can properly be considered of the first rank," I must take exception. I think that *David the King*, by Gladys Schmitt, almost reaches the first rank, and *A Lion Is in the Streets*, by Adria Langley, is a first-rate novel within certain limits.

But definitely of the first rank are those three novels of C. S. Lewis, *Out of the Silent Planet, Perelandra,* and *That Hideous Strength*. Perhaps Reader Symington overlooked these books.

LEAH BODINE DRAKE

To *Hearst's International*

Evansville, Ind.

Anyone who doesn't like Mary Margaret McBride does not like the fine, wholesome things of American life. As a newspaper woman myself, I say, "Hurrah for Mary Margaret McBride—long may she rave!"

The Song of the Sun ✤ Leah Bodine Drake

To *Photoplay*, "Brickbats & Bouquets"

More Talkies for Tots

[c. December 1930], Coleman, Texas

Why can't we have more moving pictures for children? "Tom Sawyer" is the first "kids" picture that has been made in a long time.

What with drawing room dramas dripping with English Accents and epigrams, musical comedies with undressed chorines and murder mysteries, I should imagine the kids have a poor time of it.

LEAH BODINE DRAKE

To *Weird Tales*

Reprint "The Wendigo"

[c. August 1935, Fort Worth, Texas]

This is just a note to suggest that for one of your weird story reprints you use "The Wendigo" by Algernon Blackwood. This is one of the most haunting and poetic ghost stories ever written. A "sho'-nuff" weird tale. I read it as a child ten years ago, and it has stuck in my memory ever since. It is unforgettable, really. I am enclosing the coupon from the last issue to let you know the stories I liked best. I like Clark Ashton Smith, especially his poetry. One of the best and most unusual tales I ever read was in your April number—"Out of the Eons" by Hazel Heald. It was great! Did she get her idea from Easter Island? They found an undecipherable script there too, you know. I've seen pictures of it and it looks like nothing human! As for the Brundage-cover controversy—let them *all* be of lovely ladies. I hate pictures of doctors among their apparatus, and funny test-tubes, and so on. Makes the magazine look like a science monthly. Ugh! Another tip—did you ever consider having a department of weird information? About magic, and old legends and religious spells, and so on? Or would that be unveiling the mysteries too much and sort of take the kick from too many stories? It's just an idea, anyway.

PUBLISHED LETTERS

An Old Howard Masterpiece

[c. April 1937, Dallas, Texas]

I tried yesterday to buy some back numbers of WT at the second-hand magazine stores. I finally succeeded in running a few copies to earth in one store—issues from way back in 1930 and '31. The clerk said old WTs were hard to get, and harder to keep—and they cost more than other magazines, too—even such publications as *House and Garden* and *Harper's Baza[a]r!* In one of the numbers was a story I liked very much—"The Black Stone" by Robert E. Howard in the November, 1931 number. It ought to be good for a reprint someday for the benefit of WT readers who can't secure back copies . . . Here is a bouquet for WT—there is never anything in your mag that is over-sexy, improper or nasty. The greatest prude could read one of your numbers from cover to cover, and never blush or feel the gorge rise. That's more than can be said for the other mystery mags—some are horrible, and one cannot even finish the stories in them. I couldn't. But I know when I buy WT I won't be compelled to consign it to the furnace. So what? So I buy *only* WT in the mystery line.

Concise Comments

[c. July 1938, Shreveport, Louisiana]

"Fortune's Fools" is grand!—truly exciting and poetic. Each instalment of "The Black Drama" gets better. "Mother of Toads" reminded me of Dunsany. Your contents get better every month.

Changed

[c. November 1938, Owensboro, Kentucky]

Where is the One-And-Only Mrs Brundage? I missed her luscious maiden on the cover, and I'm mad! And where is our Virgil? He has no poem-picture this month (November), and that is one feature that I particularly liked and watched for. I liked Jim Mooney's picture, too, for "Beyond the Phoenix" last month, although I do not really think mystery stories should have illustrations, as a rule. And where is Clark Ashton Smith? And how come you've cut down on the letter department? I

557

The Song of the Sun ~ Leah Bodine Drake

always enjoyed reading the readers' opinions so much, as they were all of interest, and written evidently by highly educated people. As for the stories this month, I like "Fothergill's Jug" the best; "Lynne Foster Is Dead" the next; and "The Hound of Pedro" third best. I imagine that the serial about Cleopatra is going to be fine; but I am going to read it all in one piece, as it were—keep the instalments until I have them all. I'm through reading serials as such—they leave me too excited at the end of an instalment, and having to wait a whole month before you know whether the train runs over the heroine, as it were, is too much! Now please bring back Finlay, C. A. Smith and a longer letter-department, more poems—and please oh please reprint "The Woman of the Wood" by A. Merritt. I've asked it once, I've asked it twice—I'll keep on asking until I've had a chance to read this famous tale!"

But We Did Reprint It

[c. January 1939, Owensboro, Kentucky]

What would you think if you had wanted something for quite a long time—a very small something, but wanted passionately, all the same!—and all of a sudden, out of the blue, you get it, and from a perfect stranger? Wouldn't you believe (especially at this time of the year) that there was a Santa Claus? This is what happened: for long months, letter after letter, I've asked the editor of WT to pul-*leaze* reprint Merritt's "The Woman of the Wood." Nothing ever happened; the story didn't appear; the editor, cruel tyrant, would publish my letters, would even publish my own feeble attempts at literature in the form of poetry—but never, oh never, the "W. of the W." But a good fairy was listening, and the result was that a complete stranger, male or female I know not, but one of the most kind-hearted humans this globe has even seen (and now I mean *you*, W. Shedlow of Chicago!) took it upon him (her) -self to send me that story, *completely and elegantly typewritten from his or her own copy of it!* Now what do you-all think of anyone so kind, so doggone swell, as to type and send a long manuscript like "The Woman of the Wood" to an utter stranger? I've already sent a letter of thanks to my own private Santa Claus, alias W. Shedlow, but this is an open letter to all the WT readers and its editor, to tell you all what a grand somebody The Shed-

Published Letters

low is! Thanks again, right out in public, friend Shedlow! Now as for the stories in the January number—I liked "Medusa's Coil" best, "Waxworks" next, "These Doth the Lord Hate" third. The poetry this month was especially good, the Ansley quatrain in particular. It takes genius to put so much of magic and eeriness in four little lines. I am keeping all three of them for my scrap-book, the Ansley, the Petaja and the Starrett poems. Now, as I have gotten my wish in regard to the Merritt story, I'm going to pester poor Editor Wright some more, and ask, "Please, dear Editor, use Blackwood's 'The Willows' for a reprint sometime?"

A Horse Race
[c. June 1939, Owensboro, Kentucky]

I wouldn't have believed it possible if I hadn't seen it happen, but WT keeps right on doing it. Doing what? Not the "Turkey Trot," but putting out a better magazine every month, every one of those 160 pages! The last issue was a dilly! First honors go to Seabury Quinn. I don't see how he does it, but he crashes through every so often with a story so fine, so beautifully written, so sincere, that I think the man must be inhuman. "Washington Nocturne" was a bit off the beaten track for WT, being less of a weird tale than a timely piece of propaganda, and "pointing a moral." It is hard to pick out the show and place horses (it's race-time down in "Old Kaintuck"!), but my money went on "Almuric" for place, with "Watcher at the Door" and "The Face of Death Corner" tying in to a dead heat for third. The others were all thrilling and intriguing tales, especially "The Dark Isle"; and if the others had to be, of necessity, also-rans, it was a stake-race and not a claiming one. (To get back into English, they were all good, even if they didn't make first, second and third places in my judgment.) The poetry, as is usual in WT, was good. How Virgil Finlay's inventive powers keep going at full stride I cannot imagine. He rings the bell every time with his eery picturizations of famous weird poems . . . That man surely uses a quill of the Ruhk, or a feather from the wing of a Marid—no earthly pen could ever limn such scenes.

The Song of the Sun ~ Leah Bodine Drake

A New Writing Technique

[c. August 1939, Owensboro, Kentucky]

The August WT was remarkable for two features which your writers have been working towards for some time: character-study, and a superlative style of writing. I'll take my stand (in Dixie and elsewhere) that for distinguished writing, WT authors can give cards and spades to any of their brotherhood in the "slicks." Take "Spawn," for example: here is a completely new style of writing. Reminiscent of Charles Fort's, the peculiarly gripping style of this story was something new in the work of putting words together—not an easy feat! Mr. Miller has read his Bible to considerable advantage, for certain sentences, and groupings of words, are Old Testament if I ever read it (which I certainly have!) Then take "Apprentice Magician," which was humorous in style, and yet none the less weird and thrilling for that. A comic ghost-story is usually very dull, and certainly not thrilling—yet this story was a true weird tale and the dry drollery of its "Li'l Abner" hero did not detract from its grotesquery. Mr. Price in some strange way managed to blend two usually irreconcilable elements. Let's hear more about that cute li'l old country boy! "Giants in the Sky" reveals yet a third new idea in WT stories: the entirely logical notion that all unearthly and alien beings are *not* evil and hostile to man. Long's creatures were outré and unhuman, but in them, as in those of our own race, were the elements of pity and tenderness, and a not-unkind curiosity resembling those of our own scientists. The story was touching, poignant—and so sane! For certainly the denizens of other spheres have the same emotions as we do, seeing that one Creator designed us all! Perhaps the best example of the first two elements of writing that I mentioned—character-study and distinguished style—is the story "The Valley Was Still." That was a perfect piece of writing! There was not only the necessary weird element in it—there was an ideal portrait of a Southern soldier; there was the eternal conflict between honor and—the easiest way. And honor won. It was a story that I would place among the great short stories of the world. It had more than a pure style (all Wellman's stories have that)—it had beauty . . . For these new features of WT stories—for the issues that get better and better each month—let us all give a hurrah, banzai, and viva, while making a deep salaam!

PUBLISHED LETTERS

Howdy, Mr. Rabbit!

[c. January 1941, Evansville, Indiana]

[An open letter to Francis X. Moriarity, in reply to his comment in *Weird Tales* 35, No. 5 (September 1940): 124, in which he wrote: "Is greeting a rabbit some real superstition somewhere, say in the Catskills? From now on I can see where I'll be tipping my hat every time one crosses my path. Which doesn't seem likely!"]

You may be interested, among other WT readers, to learn that the superstition around which Gans T. Field's superb story, "The Dreadful Rabbits," (July issue) was written, it is a sure-enough real one. The locale is not the Catskills, however, but a section of the "Green River" country of my own state, Kentucky. Although it is really a custom of farm-folk in Daviess County to salute every rabbit seen with the greeting, "Howdy, Mr. Rabbit!", other near-by counties do not observe it, nor have they all heard of it. Yet in Daviess a farmer will bring his car to a dead stop in the road if some member of the party neglects to say the time-honored words, and he will "stay stopped" until the omission has been remedied! How or when or why the habit started is not known—at least not by me, who hail from the Blue Grass section, where, alas, there are few superstitions left.

During a correspondence with the author, I happened to mention this quaint custom; and he wrote back what a good idea for a story it would make. Not long afterwards he wrote the tale you all read in WT, and a dilly of a story it was! If his explanation of the custom's beginnings do not tally with the unknown real one, it should have been as he wrote it, anyway!

P.S.—Thanks for the kind things you said about my "pomes." The editor has several in WT's poetry bin now, awaiting the light!

Letter to Sight and Sound

[. . .] Lea Bodine Drake, of the "Courier", Evansville, Indiana, points out: "British pictures, when well done, beat ours all hollow. French films, I fear, would be over the heads of Evansville Ind. crowds. The more intelligent people here like English films."

Letter to *American Mercury*

Pity Among Animals

SIR: Being a long-time admirer of Alan Devoe, I hate like the deuce to have to take him up on anything—but I must beg to differ with him on his statement, in the June "Down to Earth," that animals know nothing of compassion.

In this article he claims time and again that only Man can know pity and tenderness, and that the beasts act through instinct and a kind of unconscious wisdom, but never through compassion. While I can't claim anything like the nature-knowledge that he has, I have heard and read of too many instances where animals, particularly dogs, have shown all the earmarks of the emotion of mercy. Irvin S. Cobb and Albert P. Terhune have told of dogs who carried their own food to a trapped or wounded fellow. I have an article from an old *Good Housekeeping* which tells of a coon-dog in Virginia who kept a companion-collie alive for days, when the latter was caught in an abandoned mine-pit, by taking his own dog-biscuits to her, going hungry himself that his friend might be fed. If that isn't self-sacrifice and mercy, what is it?

I read in *Nature*, in an article by Ivan T. Sanderson, of a captured cow-elephant who was "rescued" by two males of her herd, and, being wounded in her legs, was supported between them exactly as a wounded human would be supported by two compassionate and helpful companions.

Perhaps such instances of the emotion of pity are rare in the animal world, and perhaps they are more frequent than we know. But to make the sweeping claim that only Man knows mercy, in the face of the evidence to the contrary, IS BEING SOMETHING LESS THAN JUST TO OUR ANIMAL KIN. IF THE Earth must depend only on Man's mercy—then Heaven have mercy on us!

LEAH BODINE DRAKE

Evansville, Ind.

Unpublished Letters

To August Derleth

[1] [TLS]
Leah Bodine Drake,
Motion Picture Editor.
[THE EVANSVILLE COURIER
EVANSVILLE, INDIANA]

Evansville, Indiana,
September 13, 1943.

Dear August Derleth:
    Perhaps you have seen some of my poetry in our mutual friend, WEIRD TALES's pages, and also in POETRY CHAP-BOOK, POETRY: A MAG. OF VERSE, VOICES, etc.

I am writing to inquire if your publishing firm, Arkham House, would consider putting out a volume of fantastic poetry of mine? Many poems which I would include in the collection would be re-prints from WT, THE SOUTHERN LITERARY MESSENGER, TALARIA, and other mags. Ted Malone has recently re-printed two of my "Spookies" in his "Between the Book-Ends Vol 5".[1]

I realize that the audience for such a volumn [sic] would be small, but possibly the same readers who buy your Lovecraft and Smith volumns would like my poems. You understand I do not intend to include all the poems which I have had published,—just those which come under the heading of "weird"? Many poems in the book would be hitherto unprinted as yet.[2]

Will you let me know what you think of such a venture? I rather think such a book would sell. "A HORN-BOOK FOR WITCHES",— you see, I've already named it!
    Sincerely ours,
    Leah Bodine Drake.

The Song of the Sun ❧ Leah Bodine Drake

Notes
1. "All-Saint's Eve" and "The Tenants." Ted Malone (1908–1989), born Frank Alden Russell, was an American radio broadcaster. See Benét letter 3.
2. Ten poems in *HW* were previously unpublished.

[2]   [TLS, in private hands]
                    [Leah Bodine Drake]
                                                Henderson, Kentucky,
                                                    Jan. 15th, 1946.
Dear August Derleth:

You know they say that great minds run in the same channels....

About two weeks ago I made out a long list of poems of the grotesque and weird, with the vague idea of some day writing to you all of Arkham House, and suggesting that a book of such verse be published,—you the publishers, I the editor. I had two titles that I was undecided between: "THE WIND IN THE CHIMNEY", and—believe it or not!—"FROM THE DARK SIDE OF THE MOON".

Don't tell *me* there isn't something in mental telepathy!

Surely, you may use my poems,—any you wish. I'm delighted with the whole idea, and really believe that there will be a market for such an anthology. As far as I know, there never has been any anthology of weird verse. Hence my own idea,—doggone you up there for stealing a march on me!

I am inclosing three other spooky poems of mine which were published in the now-defunct (again!) "SOUTHERN LITERARY MESSENGER". The Dietzes started this famous old Virginia mag. again, about eight years ago. You know, it had once been edited by Edgar Allan Poe, died the death during the War between the States, and was revived for a few years, (alas so few!) by Mrs. F. Meredith Dietz and her son.[1] The Dietzes now run the DIETZ PRESS, of Richmond, Virginia, and if you should like these poems of mine enough to want also include them in your anthology, you would, of course, have to get their permission. I know they would freely give it, as they are special friends of mine. Their address is 109 East Cary Street in that city.

All of these have been broadcast over the radio,—Richmond, Evansville, Ind., and New York, the latter by Ted Malone on his program.

Two of them appeared in Ted Malone's last anthology, "BETWEEN THE BOOKENDS, Vol. 5",—"THE TENANTS", and "ALL-SAINTS' EVE."[2]

If you don't care to use them, will you send them back? Just the printed copies,—I don't want the typewritten one, of course.

By the way, I just sent in an order to ARKHAM HOUSE yesterday, —for the new Blackwood book, "THE DOLL AND ONE OTHER".

If you'll notice, I live over the river (Ohio) in my old home state of "Kaintuck" once more. Still traipse over to Evansville, though, same as ever, as I am still Movie Editor on the Evansville "COURIER",—the enormous distance of seven miles. Our original home was Lexington, Ky.

We came through your town last summer. I had to go to the Mayo Clinic at Rochester for a rather serious operation, and will have to go back again this summer for a check-up. We motor up, so perhaps I'll stop in and see you all of the "Spooky House" next July or August!

Thank you for wanting my poems in your anthology, and I'll be looking forward to it with interest.

Cordially yours,
L. B. D.
1041 South Main Street.

Notes
1. Frieda Meredith Dietz (1897–1965), journalist, author and travel lecturer, revived *Southern Literary Messenger* (August 1834 to June 1864; 1939–1945).
2. The third poem LBD submitted was "Figures in a Nightmare."

[3] [TLS, in private hands]

Jan. 25th [1946]

Dear August Derleth:

It was nice of you to take two more of my "spookers". I look forward to the publication of your book with a very great interest. I hope the title,—"Dark of the Moon",—won't confuse buyers with the current play of that name,[1]—far be it from me to suggest another, but two titles in the same season can be confusing to the public. In the Carnegie Library in Evansville is one shelf (only one!) reserved for the new books of poetry and plays, and just the other day I saw the above-mentioned "Dark of the

The Song of the Sun ~ Leah Bodine Drake

Moon", in book form, on it. Placed right next to your own forthcoming book of poetry, it might look simply like two copies of one book.

As to ME. . . . . .

As you can see from my name, I am of British and French-Huguenot stock, with a dash of Welsh and Irish. (My paternal great-great-great-etc., etc.-uncle was Sir Francis Drake.) My people have been in this country from before the Revolution, on both sides,—and fought on both sides! That goes for the War between the States, also!

Although I call Lexington, Kentucky, my home, and attended Hamilton College there, (also the Kendrick School for Girls, in Cincinnati) I have lived in about fifteen different states,—father's an oil-man! I think it is having lived in places, mostly in the South and South-West, where Nature is manifested in her greatest aspects,—such as the ocean, the mountains, the deserts and the swamps,—that early gave me a feeling of kinship with elemental forces. This fact, superimposed upon a partly Celtic heritage and a background of negro "mammy-tales", is probably why my poetic stream flows in the channels of the fabulous and eerie.

I've published in the ATLANTIC MONTHLY,—THE CORNHILL MAGAZINE (London)—NATURE MAGAZINE—KALEIDOGRAPH —POETRY: A Magazine of Verse,—POETRY CHAPBOOK—The SOUTHERN LITERARY MESSENGER—TALARIA—WINGS—VOICES,—WEIRD TALES, THE SATURDAY EVENING POST—EVE'S JOURNAL (London)—COUNTRY BARD, etc. etc. I've been re-printed in the English anthology, Thomas Moult's "BEST POEMS OF 1941" ("Fantasy in a Forest" from Wings being the poem) in the Ted Malone anthology "BETWEEN THE BOOKENDS VOL. 5," and in the current anthology, edited by Stanton A. Coblentz, "THE MUSIC MAKERS".

I have been a show-girl for Billy Rose, and the "Spirit of Dallas" in that city's Centennial Day parade of 1936. At present I am the Movie Editor of the "Evansville (Ind.) COURIER". My ambition? To go on writing poetry!

Whew!—I see where you'll have to chop *this* down considerably! And Lawsy, man, I haven't told you a *thing* about my short but hectic married life and divorce in Mississippi (I resumed my maiden name, in case you are curious) or about how I am related (distantly!) to Winston Churchill and the Duke of Alba. Or about the time mother and I were robbed of all *her* rings in a train hold-up in Louisiana. (This last sounds, I know, as though I must have lived 'way back in the time of the James boys, at least,—but you just look in the southwestern papers for 1928, and you'll read about it.

To wind things up: you have probably noticed that I make no mention of my birth-date. Well, sir, I don't intend to. . . . . .!
                Yours Cordially,
                Leah Bodine Drake
1041 South Main Street.

[P.S.] I'm *ashamed* of this paper being bob-tailed like this—I ran out!

Notes
1. Written in 1946 by Howard Richardson and William Berne.

[4] [TLS]
         [Leah Bodine Drake]
                              July 14th, 1946

Dear August Derleth:

I don't know if it's too late for you to include any more poems in your anthology,—it may be on the presses right now,—but I couldn't resist sending this of mine to you, on the off-chance that (1) there was time, (2) you liked it.¹

My "Jabberwock" recently won the 1946 "Stephen Vincent Benét Ballad Contest", which is conducted by the "Word Weavers" of Los Angeles. From over a hundred contestants, too! Whoops! It's never been published anywhere, and the Word Weavers give me my rights of publication,—I don't think they have a magazine, for Mrs. Crockett, the Pres., simply spoke of keeping my manuscript for their *files*. She also said that all rights of publication were mine.

It definately [*sic*] should go into some publication that wants weird stuff,—it's far too long for WEIRD TALES, so I haven't even considered sending it there,—I sent it to the "ATLANTIC MONTHLY", which has published some of my poetry, and they said it was funny as all

The Song of the Sun ~ Leah Bodine Drake

get out, but so long for them, and could I cut it down to fit into their "Design for Living" section? As I definately *could, and would* **not***,* that was THAT. SO I never sent it anywhere else, until I submitted it to this contest. It won, and so here I go again, for it must be pretty good to come out ahead of the field!

It's based on a real American legend,—one of the few bits of genuine folklore that we have, I think, that is *white* man's and not Negro or Indian. Maybe you will recall your parents talking about a scare this country had,—at least the Eastern part,* [sic] around the turn of the century, when people in South Jersey, and even in Philadelphia, saw a weird beast that flew through the air on enormous wings, had goat feet, and talked in some "unknown tongue". Some called it the "Jabberwock" (from "Alice's" creature in the looking-glass world) but it seems to have come down in legend as "the Jersey Devil".[2] I never have heard just what it was,—my source is my mother, who came from Williamstown, N. Jersey, and whose Mother claimed it was the Devil himself. (Grandma Bodine,[3] married to a "yankee" but born on a Maryland plantation, was just full of "mammy-tales".)

There really was quite a lot in the Camden and Phillie newspapers about this creature, and was a nine-days-wonder, it seems. As far as I know, there has been absolutely nothing about it in poetry or prose: if there ever WAS a subject for both, this is it, too! So I can claim, I believe, to be the first person who has used this truly American folk-tale in a poem.

My poem is not entirely fanciful as to the effects of the visitation, either: Grandma said that a lot of people in Williamstown got religion in a hurry! By the way, the town's old name really WAS "Squankom",—it's an Indian name, and means "Place of the Evil God". I used that designation in one other poem, "THE PATH THROUGH THE MARSH",[4] which you are using,—remember? Well, that poem stems from the country around Williamstown, which is marshy and cranberry-boggy. My grandfather owned a lot of bogs.

If you use both of these "Squankom" poems, you might give them a footnote as to the literal translation of the name.

We're going to be up around your way about the first of next month. I have an appointment at the Mayo Clinic for a check-up on the

9th of August, and as we are driving up, we will leave Henderson about the 5th, I reckon. I admit that by-passing Wis. is the shortest way,—we found that out on our return last year!—but I'm going to persu[a]de my Dad to cut over into your state, and as the route goes right through your fair city, the natural thing would be for us to stop and say "Howdy".

Best Regards,
L B D.

[*Enclosure:*] "The Ballad of the Jabberwock: (A True Tale of Squankom Town.)"

Notes
1. LBD had previously submitted seven poems for *DM*.
2. During the week of 16 through 23 January 1909, newspapers of the time published hundreds of claimed encounters with the Jersey Devil.
3. M. Virginia Slocum Bodine (1833–1913) of Dorchester County, MD, wife of William H. Bodine (1823?–1908) of Philadelphia, whom she married in 1857.
4. Actually *Squankum*. LBD uses the epithet "place of the evil god" (l. 27) but not "Squankom."

[5] [TLS]
[Leah Bodine Drake]
[Henderson, KY]
July 19th, 1946.

Dear August Derleth:
I'm mighty glad you like ol' Jabberwock, and are going to include him.

Here's the footnote,—you may have to cut it down some, but I've tried to keep it short but explicit:

Squankom, which in Indian means 'the place of the evil god', was the early name of the little South Jersey village of Williamstown. Located near the cranberry country, this was one of the many places where the famous and mysterious creature called "the Jersey Devil" or "Jab[b]erwock" was seen around the turn of the century. The above poem, based on this legend, won the first prize in the 1946 "Stephen Vincent Benet Ballad Contest", held annually by the "Word Weavers".

The Song of the Sun ~ Leah Bodine Drake

I felt that some mention should be made of the contest, either in the footnote or in the front of the book with the other credits, as they are, if not the first publishers of the poem, its first sponsors, so to speak. I really believe it should be with the other credits,—it looks awkward in the footnote, don't you think?

I'll be seein' you,—at Coenen's counter, come the fifth or sixth of August, and probably, if the weather's like this God forbid, ready for an ice-cream soda . . . . . .

As Ever, L B D.

[6] [ALS]

[HENDERSON, KY.]

August 12 [1946]

Dear August Derleth:

Well, we didn't get away when we thought we would—expect to be up around your way next week, sometime—but don't hang around that ice-cream counter for me!

Looks like (from the cold weather we're having) that I'll need a bowl of hot soup instead of ice cream.

Look for me when you see me!

Yours,

L. B D.

[7] [ALS]

[Leah Bodine Drake]

Tuesday,
October 8th [1946]

Dear August Derleth—

Well, I'm actually leaving for Rochester tomorrow—only two months off schedule!

I hope to come thru' your city en route, & I'll page you at Coenen's—right?

Hope you haven't grown a long gray beard in the meantime—I think *I* have!

Yours,

L. B. D.

Unpublished Letters

[8] [ANS]

Henderson
October 20 [1946]

Dear August D.—
 I want to tell you how much we all enjoyed meeting you in your "enchanted cottage".[1] For an outrageously busy man, you were mighty gracious to bother with a car full of strangers.
 You were just as I'd thought of your too—big and lusty, & looking like a figure from a mural titled "Spirit of Wisconsin" or bearing a sickle, as the earth-spirit of Sac Prairie!
 Did I thank you for using another of my poems in "Dark o' the Moon"? Every one talked at once, and time was a-wastin'!
 I'm trying to get my hands on "Evening in Spring",[2] but my Mother won't put it down long enough. Both you & your work made kind of a hit with the Drakes!
       Yours,
        L. B. D.

Notes
1. The Drakes stopped in Sauk City on 11 October. AD notes this in his journal.
2. AD, *Evening in Spring* (New York: Scribner's, 1941), a novel of young love.

[9] [ANS]

Feb. 28th [1947]

Dear August Derleth:
 We're moving back over to Evansville so I'll give you my new address:
  1219 S.E. 1st St.,
   Evansville,
    Indiana.
 So send all communications in the future to that address.
 How's the anthology of spooky poems coming along?
 Stanton Coblentz of "Wings" is getting up one similar to it.—the difference is that his poems deal with psychical experiences: dreams, etc. He's using three poems of mine—none you are using, however.[1]
       As Always,
        Leah B. Drake.

The Song of the Sun ~ Leah Bodine Drake

Notes
1. Coblentz used "Figures in a Nightmare," "On a Night of Stars," and "Terror by Night" in *Unseen Wings: The Living Poetry of Man's Immortality*.

[10] [TLS]

[LEAH BODINE DRAKE]

March 17th. [1947]

Dear August Derleth:

The top o' the marnin' to ye! (Every year at this time, I remember that I had an Irish great-grandmother.)

The books and the check came today. I am delighted with both, and many thanks to you. The book is lovely, and the paper is so nice! I like it, too, because it's not leaf-thin, as so many books are now. It certainly is a treasury of good, scary poetry!

As Ever,

L B D.

1219 S. E. First Street,
Evansville, Indiana

[P.S.] Don't forget—I want a copy of *Carnacki the Ghost-Finder* by Hodgson,[1] when it's ready.

Notes
1. AD published the book by William Hope Hodgson (1877–1918) under his Mycroft & Moran imprint.

[11] [TLS]

[Leah Bodine Drake]

Sept. 5th, 1947.

Dear August Derleth:

Your proposed ARKHAM SAMPLAR[1] [*sic*] sounds interesting—I know I'm going to have to take it. Do you intend to publish poems in it, of the spooky sort? Why don't you think about that? I know that I'd LOVE to send you some! I've LOTS AND LOTS of weirdies!

We plan to come up to Rochester around the first of October, and may drive by way of Wisconsin, as before. If we do, I'll stop by and say 'Howdy' again,—I want to see that new addition to ARKHAM HOUSE that you were a-buildin' when we were there last year. (And buy some new books!)

By the way, I've finally quit the paper and the movie job,[2]—six years of seeing five and six movies in two days['] time just about ruined my eyes.

As Ever,
L B D.

Notes
1. A quarterly journal of fiction, verse, and nonfiction. It ran for two years.
2. LBD was soon back at the paper. The *Who's Who Supplement* states that she was "Drama editor Evansville (Ind.) Courier, 1941–51."

[12] [TLS]
[Lean Bodine Drake]
1219 Southeast 1st Street
Evansville, Indiana

Sept. 26th. [1947]

Dear August Derleth:

I'll admit that I sent "A Hornbook for Witches" to WEIRD TALES, and they sent it back, said it was too long. Also, (although they didn't say so) I suspect that the rather tongue-in-the-cheek attitude toward my subject put them off: WT allows no ironic attitude towards magic, witchcraft and spooks! Well, there's no other place to send it—I'd like to see any editor's face when he opened such a poetic manuscript, as the subject simply isn't used by anybody BUT WEIRD TALES. I often wonder just where Edgar Allan Poe would have published his things, if he'd lived now? So if you think you can use it, and that it rates a subscription to the SAMPLAR,—it's yours.

Did I ever get around to telling you that I thoroughly enjoyed your book "Evening in Spring"? I think it's one of the most poignant, lyrical love-stories I ever read, extremely moving and rooted in such earthy realism. I take it that it is autobiographical,—but you needn't answer that one. I don't want to be nosey.

We "allow" to start up to Rochester around the sixth,—we may come through Sauk City, and if we do we'll surely stop by for a few minutes.

I finally broke away from the COURIER—if I'd stayed there seeing six and seven movies a week for *another* six years I'd have gone blind. I'm now

The Song of the Sun ❧ Leah Bodine Drake

at what is classically called a loose end. Writing lots of poetry, though.
    Yours, as ever,
        L B D.

[*Note by AD:*] Enter for 1 yr of SAMPLER: Gratis

[13] [ALS]

[Leah Bodine Drake]

Dec. 7th. [1947]

Dear August—
    We are starting for Rochester the first of the coming week—(of all times of year!—everyone else we know is heading *South*!) We'll stop off for a look in at Arkham House on our way up there. Hope you are going to be home. I'll wire you definately.
    As Ever,
        L B D.

[14] [ANS]

Jan. 31st [1948]

Dear August:
    Your baby, the Samplar, came yesterday. I like it *so* much—and gosh, you use purty paper! My poems looked attractive printed, didn't they? The word "could" in the first line ought to have been "*would*"—maybe *I* made the mistake—I don't remember. Anyway, I'm so used to seeing my movie write-ups in the Courier misspelled after going thru' the hands of the copy-readers that I've become resigned to misprinting![1] I do hope you continue the mag.—it is unique in its field. Also, I have some more poems to unload on you!—as inclosed![2]
    Best of luck,
        Leah.

P.S. When will the "Web of Easter Island"[3] be out? I *loved* "Carnacki".

Notes
1. Oddly, she said nothing about the omission of the entire fourth stanza.
2. "Unhappy Ending."
3. A novel by Donald Wandrei, published in 1947.

UNPUBLISHED LETTERS

[15] [TLS]

April 17th. [1948]

Dear August:

Well, here's another poem for which I'll never be able to find a market except the ARKHAM SAMPLER![1] I've never even tried to send it anywhere.—too long for WT, and just TRY to sell it to any other magazine!

How about sending me a book to review sometime? I've reviewed books for the WINGS PRESS,—poetry, of course,—and used to regularly review current books of all sorts for the paper when we had a decent art-literature section. (It had to make way for an enlarged sports-page! The March of Progress.) At any rate, I'd try not to make the blunder which one of your reviewers did, when he spoke of one of H. F. Heard's stories in "THE LOST CAVERN", as about "a horrible ritual cup"[2] .... it happened to have been the Holy Grail, or something very close! Anyway, it was just bursting with holy power and routed the forces of evil very effectively,—not exactly *horrible,* in my estimation. I like Heard,— he's almost, but not quite, as good as C. S. Lewis. Did I tell you I've had about six letters from Lewis. I sent him a Christmas box, and we've corresponded ever since. In his last letter he wrote a poem for me, and to me.[3]

Something very odd has come up in poetry circles. . . . Did you notice in the LYRIC for Winter, in which you have a (very fine) poem,[4] that the group of four poems at the front of the book were supposed to be by a certain Helen Petrofsky? Well, the first poem, "Hiatus", is by Lionel Wiggam and appears in his book, "LANDSCAPE WITH FIGURES" (Viking 1936), and the last one, a sonnet, is by Elsa Barker, a member of the Poetry Society of America, (which I belong to), and appears on Page 6 of the "POETRY SOCIETY OF AMERICA ANTHOLOGY" (Fine Editions Press 1946.)[5]

The other two I can't place,—but I reckon they are by some other poet than this Petrofsky![6] She had had a poem published in the Feb. KALEIDOGRAPH, and it turned out to be one of Wiggam's! My friends and yours, Clark Ashton Smith and Eric Wilson Barker,[7] spotted the plag[i]arism and told K. about it, and "K." had to apologize in their March issue. Vaida Montgomery of K. wrote me that the Petrofsky girl wrote them a very pathetic letter of apology, and said she had been men-

The Song of the Sun ~ Leah Bodine Drake

tally ill for years. Maybe,—but that's always the accused criminal's first line of defense! They never seem too mentally ill to commit their crimes.) In the LYRIC I notice where she says she's engaged in "library work". All I can say is, the librarians I know are completely sane. I think her library work consists of leafing through poetry books and copying down other poets' work wholesale! She also claims to be writing a novel ..... "GONE WITH THE WIND", I presume?

None of the editors seem to have spotted her thefts. The Wiggam poem in the LYRIC was re-printed in the "Poets' Column" of the N. Y. TIMES Book Review last week. Wonder what Wiggam (an Indianan, by the way) and Elsa Barker would feel, to see their work staring up at them over the fine old Anglo-Saxon (sic) name of *Petrofsky*? I'm expecting to see some of my early things pop up with her name attached someday,—or maybe she doesn't like mine! I hope she doesn't for I think I'd have a cat-fit. The poor thing must really be batty, though—such boldness could stem only from a deranged mind.

We haven't been up to Rochester yet, but will sometime this summer. There's no great need for me to go, but they like to check up on all their patients; and of course with what I had, it's the best thing.

    As Ever,
    L B D.

Notes
1. "Old Wives' Tale."
2. John Haley had reviewed *The Lost Cavern and Other Stories of the Fantastic* by H. F. Heard (1889–1971). LBD refers specifically to Haley's comment on "The Cup." In 1948 LBD read Heard's *Is God Evident?: An Essay Toward a Natural Theology*.
3. Unidentified, probably unpublished.
4. "Bonfire in the Evening Wood."
5. The book contained two poems by AD, none by LBD.
6. See "Helen Petrofsky, Plagiarist," *Lyric* 208, No. 1 (Spring 1948): "We regret to have to record that all four of the poems printed by us in our winter number, 1948, over the name of Helen Petrofsky were stolen. The first of the group, 'Hiatus,' is the work of Lionel Wiggam, and may be found in his book *Landscape with Figures* (p. 20), published by The Viking Press in 1936. The second and third poems, 'Farewell Call' and 'Tristesse', were written by Edith Lent, a young high school student and prize-winner in an inter-high school poetry contest . . . The fourth poem, a sonnet entitled 'When I am Dead,' is the

work of the well-known poet Elsa Barker" (108). Petrofsky was about twenty-six at the time. *Kaleidograph* 19, No. 1 (March 1948) also made note of the affair, noting that Clark Ashton Smith was among those who spotted the plagiarism. See "Plagiarism" (15).

7. AD does not seem to have corresponded with Barker. Smith's papers do not include letters from LBD and he does not mention her as a correspondent in his letters to others. LBD and Smith had poems on the same page of *Wings* for Autumn 1943.

[16] [TLS]

July 24th. [1948]

Dear August:

As long as you'll take 'em, I reckon I'll send 'em!

This is too long for WT, but maybe not for the SAMPLER.[1]

Looky here, boy, you done spelled one of my words wrong,—or your printer did. (Having been on a newspaper for years, how well I know the infuriating ways of proof-readers, type-setters and printers!) Could you make a little note to this effect in the next issue?

Anyway, whoever is guilty my poem "Old Wives' Tale" had in it the word "silen": i.e., a satyrish being, one of the followers of Silenus,—called "sileni",—which were more man-like than satyrs, however, having only the hoofs & long pointed ears of a horse, and the tail of a horse, to give them their unhuman look. James Branch Cabell spelled it, "sylan",—but you know Cabell,—always recherche! Not to say rococo! Webster gives it "silen", and in articles on Greek vase painting it's spelled Silen.

It came out in the poem, "siren",—an inexcusable mistake, but I never heard of *sirens* living on Scottish moors! (Well, I never heard of Greek silens on Scottish moors, either.) Anyway, I'm using it again in this new poem, so tell your printer to get it right next time, in case you take the poem,—or I'll come up there and stretch him on the rack.

Did you notice that Eric Barker, you and I were all in the Spring CHAP BOOK?[2] You know, I think that magazine is the best poetry magazine being published. I sent a copy to C. S. Lewis, with whom I've been corresponding for over a year. Are you one of the Lewis Cult? I've converted several near-atheists with Lewis![3] Lordy, what a mind! Personally, I think he is really and literally inspired. The world needs a hundred more like him, as Manly Wade Wellman puts it. (He's another

The Song of the Sun ❧ Leah Bodine Drake

Lewisite.) I stumbled on Lewis quite by accident,—and he really changed my whole viewpoint.

We plan to get up your way in August or early Sept. I'll warn you in time!

Yours, as ever,

L B D.

Notes
1. "The Unknown Land."
2. LBD actually refers to the Summer 1948 issue of the *Poetry Chap-Book*, which contained AD's "Chickadee," her "Minor Poet," and Barker's "Two Poems": "The Stream" and "Before the Chanticleer."
3. Lewis himself had been an atheist who then became a Christian (Anglican). LBD had probably read some of his apologetic treatises, such as *Mere Christianity* (1943).

[17] [ALS]

[LEAH BODINE DRAKE]

Saturday
Sept. 4. [1948]

Dear August—

I think your proposition about a book of my "spookers" sounds fine—and I'll be *delighted* to get together that first and well-known "slim volumn". I think, with you, that a whole book of weird poems *should* be on the thin side, as too many weirdies are a little hard to take.

I'll look over my published and unpublished stuff, & get a list compiled, and see how large a book-manuscript it would make. I should think thirty-five to forty poems should be enough, don't you? Anyway, I'll get busy & type them off in the next few weeks.

As for a tentative title: how about the name of that group of my poems that you published—"*A Horn-Book for Witches*"? It's odd, eye-catching, & certainly indicates the unearthly!

Thanks awfully for your offer—I'm honored to be one of the *Arkham House* gang.

Yours, as ever,

L B D.

PS. I may see you before long.

[18] [TLS]
[LEAH BODINE DRAKE]
1219 S. E. First Street
Evansville,
Oct. 7, 1948.

Dear August:

I'm sending the manuscript of "A HORNBOOK FOR WITCHES" off today.

There are 46 poems in it,—I've tried to include only those that I like, and which I think are good. You may not care as much as I do for a few of them, and will want to take them out. But try to leave the *order* of the poems as I have them listed in the table of contents. I've placed them that way for several reasons (1) lighter things first; (2) poems that use the same words, such as "fabulous" or the like, I don't want close together lest it become monotonous and (3) poems on the same subjects I want spaced far apart (as *Goat-Song* and "*Last Faun*" and "*Old World of Green*" for instance.)

Most of these were in Wt, [sic]—but "The Centaurs" was in the CORNHILL MAGAZINE, "Goat-Song" took a prize from WINGS, "The Queen of Sheba" was in SO. LIT. MESS., as were several others,—"The Fur Coat" is from NATURE, and "Mouse Heaven" from COUNTRY BARD. TALARIA first published "Terror by Night", and "Rabbit Dance" and both took prizes. "Heads on E. Island" and "Vision" are due to come out in WT.

I've been invited by Gustav Davidson[,][1] of the Poetry Society of America, to come to New York in December and take part in a WEEK OF POETRY he is gettung [sic] up. He is going to group the poets, and I believe I'm to be among what he calls the "younger poet[s]". (He didn't say whether in years or poetic achievement!) We will read from our published work at the Public Library the week of Dec. 6 through the 10th.[2]

I hope I will be able to go, for I had such a marvelous time in Virginia last Spring a year ago when I did the same thing in Richmond.[3]

How will MY BOOK be bound—in the regulation Arkham House black and gold affair? I hope it comes out looking like "Carnacki the Ghost Finder",—gold stripes and all! I have that, and "House on the

Border-land" by Hodgson in that binding and they are sensational on a book-shelf! Catch the firelight like nobody's business[.]

As Ever,

L B D

Notes

1. Gustav Davidson (1895–1971) was a poet, writer, and publisher, best remembered as the author of *A Dictionary of Angels*. He attempted to get LBD's *MC* published posthumously.
2. Davidson's "week of poetry" was held 14–18 January 1952.
3. Letters 26 and 27 list poets in the Richmond area, whom LBD presumably met in 1947 when she read her poems before the Richmond Poetry Society.

[19] [ALS]

Thursday.
[c. 7 October 1948]

Dear August—

Somehow this dedication-page got left out of my manuscript. So please see that it is included.

I was interested to read in the current *Time* about this very ancestor![1] They even mentioned one of his most famous books—"The Demonomania of Sorcerers". It is odd, isn't it, that this penchant for witchcraft should come down in the Bodine family after four centuries & pop forth in me! (Maybe I'm a reincarnation of the learned Jean—he, too, was crazy over *politics*[2]—which I'm afraid is one of *my* besetting vices.)

Yours,

Leah B.

P.S. "Bodin" is the original spelling of our name—it got Anglicized when a descendant of old Jean, another Jean Bodine[,] settled in Staten Island in 1682.[3]

Notes

1. [Unsigned], "*Suverenitet! Suverenitet!*" *Time* 52, No. 15 (11 October 1948): 29.
2. According to the Internet Encyclopedia of Philosophy, Jean Bodin (c. 1529–1596) "was one of the most prominent political thinkers of the sixteenth century. His reputation is largely based on his account of sovereignty which he formulated in the *Six Books of the Commonwealth*. Bodin lived at a time of great upheaval, when France was ravaged by the wars of religion between the Catho-

lics and the Huguenots. . . . Bodin believed that different religions could coexist within the commonwealth . . . He was also one of the first men to have opposed slavery."
3. Jean Bodine (c. 1620, Hiers-Brouage, Saintonge, France–c. 1694, Staten Island, Richmond, Province, New York).

[20] [ALS]

Oct. 11, 1948

Dear August:

You can take out the "Queen of Sheba" or leave her in just as you like. It doesn't make any difference to me. Come to think of it, that really isn't so *very* spooky—altho' it does border on the fantastical: her method of traveling, for instance. But if you'd rather it came out—then give the old gal the heave-ho.

If you eliminate the poem, then of course the credit to that artist, John Duncan, should come out. (I really owe some of my ideas to that picture.)

You may notice a few little, bitty changes in the "Jabberwock"—names, & what-not. I thought, as long as the town is a real place, & all those people real (some are my kinsfolk *and* still living) I'd better not make it to[o] obvious.[1]

Most of the other names are just disguised enough to render recognition possible but not definitely so.

Glad you liked the poems.

As Ever,

L B D.

LEAH BODINE DRAKE
1219 SOUTHEAST FIRST STREET
EVANSVILLE
INDIANA.

(There!)

P.S. Always—but *always*—write out "Southeast First *Street*". There's also a first *Avenue* here—and it's the red-light district!

Notes
1. LBD changed the names *Marsh* to *Karsh* (l. 23) and *Jo* to *Flo* (l. 57).

The Song of the Sun ~ Leah Bodine Drake

[21] [ALS]

Evansville, Indiana,
Oct. 24th, 48.

Dear August—

I'm getting up a radio poetry program on a new station (WJPS) which is opening here in November. I'd like your permission to read any of your poems, wherever I find them. I plan to read "*Bonfire in an Evening Wood*"[1] on the first program. How about it?

I'm going to have a marvelous spot—we intend to carry the Met Opera, (we are linked up with Mutual & ABC) Saturday afternoons, & I'll be on just before. Isn't that a nice, cultured bit of billing for Saturday matinees?

Did you want my "Acknowledgements" in "*Hornbook*" any more detailed? I can send you an itemized list of poem & publisher, if you like. Myself I favor the blanket-method—shorter and neater.

As Ever, Leah.

1219 S.E. First Street.

Notes

1. From *Lyric* 27, No. 4 (Winter 1948): 104. The plan did not proceed. See Benét letter 3.

[22] [TLS]

[Leah Bodine Drake]

Friday, Oct. 29th [1948]

Dear August:

Thanks for the nice little build-up you gave me in the ARKHAM SAMPLER this month!. [*sic*] But "Indiana-born"?[1]. . . . oh, August, August! How could you? I know that there are far worse places to be born in than Ind., but it so happens I just wasn't.

You'll say that Kansas, my real birth-state, is no better,—I can't dispute you there, as I know nothing about it, having left there at the ripe old age of three months. I'm Kentucky-reared and Kentucky-schooled, boy, and don't you ever forget it! The back of me hand to you for this unkindest cut of all!

Unpublished Letters

       Selah.
       LBD
1219 S. E. First St.,
  Evansville, Ind.

Notes
1. *Arkham Sampler* 1, No. 4 (Autumn 1948): 98.

[23] [TLS]

               November 1st, '48.
Dear August:

  As you announced in the last *Sampler* that there would be forthcoming poems in the A.S. by "Clark Ashton Smith["] and "Leah Bodine Drake", I can't let you stand a liar in your beard, can I? I just *had* to send you another poem![1]

  About the "Journey of the Quuen [*sic*] Of Sheba": I think I want it taken out of the Book. It isn't really fantastic. Will you return it,—or anyway, tear the pages of it out of the manuscript.[2]

  I just wrote to Lord Dunsany, for permission to read some of his poems over my radio program,—sent the letter to Dunsany Castle, County Meath, Eire. Is that the right address? Or should I have sent it to his Cadogan Square house in London?

  As Ever, LBD

Notes
1. Presumably "The Saints of Four-Mile Water." The poem was written in 1934.
2. The poem was not used. The T.Ms. survives with the T.Ms. of *HW*.

[24] [TN]

            [Postmarked Evansville, Ind.
               4 November 1948]
               Evansville, Ind., Nov. 4.

Dear August: Thanks for taking the poem. The head librarian at Willard Library here wants you to send her your booklets of new publications of Arkham House. I've had her order several A.H. titles for me, but she doesn't know all your titles, and Willard (a large and well-endowed semi-private one) buys a great many mysteries and thrillers,—more than the Carnegie L. here. The address of Willard Library is:

        21 First *Avenue,* Mrs. Gray Williams, Librarian.
            As ever, LBD.
1219 Southeast First St.

[25] [TLS, Brigham Young University]

                                        November 6th, 1948.
Dear August:

Instead of the "SHEBA" poem, I'm going to ask you to include these two in the HORNBOOK FOR WITCHES. I was trying to work them over when I sent the manuscript off, and they just WOULDN'T come out right. Well, today I did, and here they are. I want them in the table of contents thisaway: "Encounter in Broceliande" in-between [*sic*] "The-Stranger" [*sic*] and "The Window on the Stair", and the madwoman in between "Old Daphne" and "Griffon's Gold".

That makes, all told, forty-seven poems in the book. I promise I won't keep this sort of thing up, to confuse you and make you more work. But I really did want these poems to go in the book, in the first place, but they were so fractious!

    Good-by now!
           LBD.
1219 S. E. First St.,
    Evansville, Ind.

[26] [TLS]

                    [Leah Bodine Drake]

                                        Feb. 21st, 1949.
Dear August:

I'll be glad to review the Barker book for you, and I appreciate your thinking of me in regards to it. I just ploughed through Robert Graves' "The White Goddess", a book about the origins of poetic myth (the man says). I can go along with him on some of his conclusions, but when he reduces Sarah, Abraham's wife, to a water-goddess and Ulysses' wife, Penelope, to a *purple duck,*—then I quit.

UNPUBLISHED LETTERS

I'm sending you a list of people[1] to whom I'd like you to mail your March catalog, with the announcement in it about MY BOOK.
1. Manly Wade Wellman—Pinebluff, N.C.
2. Archibald Rutledge....Hampton Plantation, McClellanville, S.C.
3. (Hold your breath on this one)—Mrs. Steven Boljanich....Ord. Village, Fremont Circle 16 A, Monteray, [sic] Calif. (Her husband teaches Serbian at the Army Language School,—they are both Yugo-Slavs)
4. Mrs. Harold Cook....6512 Fortieth Ave., University Park, Hyattsville, Maryland.
5. Lord Dunsany....Dunstall Priory, Sevenoaks, Kent. (I had an interesting letter from him.)
6. J. Franklin [sic] Dew....1300 West Main St., Richmond, Virginia.
7. Miss Maryrose Roach.....814¼ N. Detroit, Los Angeles, Calif.
8. Mrs. Florence Dickinson Stearns....501 N. Allen Ave., Richmond, Va.
9. Mrs. Mary Willis Shelburne....915-19th St., N.W., Suite 504, Washington, D.C.
10. Mrs. H. S. Saunders....103 N. Colonial Ave., Richmond, Va.
11. Boyce House....1410 Hurley St.,—Ft. Worth, Texas.
12. Mrs. Maurine H. McGee.....1316 S. Newport, Tulsa, Okla.
13. Carnegie Public Library....Lexington, Ky. (I don't know the librarian there now.)
14. Mrs. Grey [sic] Williams....Willard Library, Evansville
15. Mrs. James Rich.....1855 McDonald Road, Lexington, Ky.
16. Benham Sims....236 Woodspoint Road, Lexington, Ky.
17. "Buddie" Treacy....375 Transylvania Park, Lexington.
18. Mrs. Julian Foard.....Middletown, Delaware.
18. [sic] Eric Wilson Barker....56 Telegraph Place, San Francisco, Cal.
19. W. J. Kennedy....P.O. Box 869, St. John's, Newfoundland.
20. William Rose Benet.....SAT. Review of LIT.
21. Miss Sylvia Sherborne Pedder....Sherborne, New Lawn, Tasmania.
22. Miss Lynn Hamilton....819 N. Gordon, St., Pomona, Cal.
23. Charles Collins...."A LINE O' TYPE OR TWO", you know where.

24. Geoffrey Johnson...11 Orchard Estate, Ely, Cambs., England
25. Dr. C. S. Lewis....Magdalen College, Oxford, Eng.
26. Mrs. Mary Sinton Leitch....Lynnhaven, Va.
27. Ernest Emerling....LOEW'S THEATERS, Loew Bldg., Publicity Director....Broadway at 45th St., New York 19.
28. Mrs. Fletcher Stewart....70 Beechwood Ave., Manhasset, Long Island, N.Y.
29. Arthur J. Wiley....321 Millburn Ave., Millburn, N. Jersey.
30. William Bell....Dept. of English, Indiana U., Bloomington, Ind.
30. [sic] Miss Mary Drake....1704 Oak St., Parkersburg, W. Va.

I will send you a LOT more when publication time nears . . . these are just put down at random.
    As Ever,
    L B D.

    Afterthoughts

31. Ruth Morehouse——Crystal Springs, Deerbrook, Wisconsin.
32. Herbert W. Simpson....106 S. Alvard Boulevard, Evansville, Ind.
33. Miss Ruth Espenlaub....East Side Library, Evansville.
34. Central Libraray [sic]....Evansville.
35. Tessa Sweazy Webb....251 West 8th Ave., Columbus 1, Ohio.
36. Peggy Dowst....Poetry Ed., SATEVEPOST.
37. John Gallinari Whidding....740 N. Ardmore Ave., Los Angeles 27, Calif.
38. Miss Barbara Ely....William Sloane Associates, 119 West 57th St., N.Y.
39. Richard W. Westwood, NATURE MAG., 1214 Sixteenth St. N.W., Washington 6, D.C.
40. Mrs. Clarence Wise....108 North St., Allegan, Mich.
41. Dr. Louise Osborne....Newburgh, Ind.
42. Joseph Joel Keith.... 3845 Ingraham St, Los Angeles
43. S. A. McElfresh....317 Cedar St., Lexington, Ky.
44. Ralph Collins...(In[d]iana U. Writers' Conference Director, Indiana U., Bloomington.

UNPUBLISHED LETTERS

I think I'll call it a day!
L B D.

Notes
1. Not all can be identified; most are friends, coworkers, and associates from places where LBD had lived. Manly Wade Wellman (1903–1986), American writer of science fiction and fantasy; Archibald Rutledge (1883–1973), American poet and educator, the first South Carolina poet laureate (1934–73); Steve "Teacher" Boljanich (1899–1998), a Serbian Language Teacher at Defense Language Institute in Monterey, married to Ljubica (Violet) Grkovich-Boljanich, author of *The Swan's Songs* (1961); Martha Ellen Cook (1915–1997) wife of Harold Cook (1913–1996); John Franklyn Dew (1901–1984), a poet; Maryrose Roach, a reporter for the *Evansville Crescent*, the weekly newspaper for Evansville College, in the 1940s; Florence Dickinson Stearns (1883–1958), Virginia poet, reviewer for the *Richmond Times-Dispatch;* Mary Willis Shelburne (1895–1975), a widow, a journalist, poet, critic, correspondent of C. S. Lewis, who sent her a monthly stipend; Carolyn St. Clair Saunders (1909–2000), wife of Homer Stuart Saunders (1905–1976); Boyce House (1896–1961), editor for the *Fort Worth Star-Telegram,* technical advisor for *Boom Town* (1940), a movie about oil wildcatters (like LBD's father) starring Clark Gable, Spencer Tracy, Hedy Lamarr, and Claudette Colbert; Maurine Halliburton McGee (1898–1977), a minor Oklahoma poet; Gray Davis Williams, first academically trained librarian at the Willard Library (served 1941–56); Benham J. Sims (1904–1962), otherwise unidentified; Eric Wilson Barker (1905–1973), poet, friend of both LBD and Clark Ashton Smith; Lynn Hamilton, editor of *Sophisti-Cats: Poems for Cat Lovers;* Charles Collins (1880–1964), editor, *Chicago Tribune;* Geoffrey Johnson (1893–1966), a poet; Mary Sinton (Lewis) Leitch (1876–1954), contributing editor to *Harper's Monthly, New York Herald,* and *New York Evening Post,* a founding member of the Poetry Society of Virginia, president in 1933, co-president in 1944–45; Ernest Emerling (1904–1979), a vice-president of Lowes Theaters; Arthur J. Wiley (1901–1978), otherwise unidentified; Mary Gale Drake (1878–1962), LBD's aunt; Ruth Morehouse, editor of *Northern Spring* by the Wisconsin Fellowship of Poets; Herbert W. Simpson (1904–1970), advertising executive who ran a mail advertising firm; Tessa Sweazy Webb (1886–1979), poet and founder of Ohio Poetry Day; Peggy Dowst Redman associate editor of the *Saturday Evening Post*; John Gallinari Whidding (1908–1984), poet; Richard W. Westwood (1896–1961), editor of *Nature;* Lucy M. Wise (1905–2003), wife of Clarence S. Wise (1906–1970), otherwise unidentified; Louise Osborne (1909–1983); Joseph "Joel Keith" Biesenkamp (1901–1967), prolific poet, member Poetry Society of America, president of the Los Angeles branch of P.E.N., and managing editor of the Borestone Mountain Poetry Awards; S. Allen McElfresh, science fiction fan and poet who attempted to edit (1942) an anthology of science fiction poetry; Ralph L. Collins (1907–1963), teacher and scholar, primarily interested in theatre and drama.

The Song of the Sun ~ Leah Bodine Drake

[27] [TLS]

March 1, 1949.

Dear August:

I'll give you some more names[1] as long as the book will be available for orders soon:

1. Miss ANNIE H. BODINE....408 North Second St., Camden, N.J.
2. MRS. ED DRAKE.....2422 Inwood Drive, Houston, Tex.
3. Mrs. GEORGE HELLER.....1967 Grand Ave., St. Paul, Minn.
4. Mr. Earl C. Ward....1387 Clearview Road, Cleveland 2, Ohio.
5. Miss HELEN GARWOOD....Williamstown, New Jersey.
6. Mr. William Earl[e] Bodine...8135 Cedar Ave., Elkins Park, Pa.
7. Mr. Gordon Belle....123 Rice's Mill Road, Wyncote, Pa.
8. Mr. William M. Harris...5281 Independence Ave, Riverdale-On-Hudson, New York City 63.
9. Mrs. RUDY NUNN....1041 South Main St., Henderson, Ky.
10. CARNEGIE PUBLIC LIBRARY....Henderson, Ky.
11. VAIDA STEWART MONTGOMERY...("KALEIDOGRAPH") 624 N. Vernon Ave., Dallas, Tex.
12. Ft. WORTH CENTRAL LIBRARY....Ft. Worth, Texas.
13. DALLAS PUBLIC LIBRARY....Dallas, Tex.
14. Miss EMMA GRAY TRIGG....Prestwould Apts., Richmond, Virginia.
15. MR. BRODIE HERNDON....4524 W. Seminary Ave., Richmond, Va.
16. B. Y. Williams...500 Palace Theater Bldg., Cincinnati, Ohio. (TALARIA)
17. Stanton A. Coblentz...."Wings"..Box 332, Mill Valley, Cal.
18. Miss Katharine [sic] Feldmeyer....194 Prince George St., Annapolis, Maryland.
19. Central Public Library....22 S.E. Fifth St., Evansville, Ind. (Mr. Roseaen, [sic] Librarian.)
20. KARL KAY KNECHT....Evansville COURIER, Evansville, Ind.
21. Mr. DON SCISM, Editor....Evansville COURIER,   "   "
22. Mr. Ed J. Fehn, Publisher....Evansville COURIER.
23. MARIE HORTON WOODS.....Evansville COURIER "   "

UNPUBLISHED LETTERS

24. Mrs. Edna Paul, Book Dept., Butterfield's, Evansville, Ind.
25. Miss Flora Clements....1615 Harmony Way, Evansville, Ind.
26. Mrs. Philip Anderson....2118 E. Chandler, Evansville
27. Mrs. A. B. Brown, 1420 Akin Drive, Evansville
28. Miss Constance Frick....219 Washington, Ave.,
29. Mrs. Harold Weeks....628 E. Mulberry, Evansville, Ind.
30. Dr. G. B. Underwood....1408 Lincoln Ave., Evansville
31. Mrs. Jessie Torrance....215 S.E. First St., Evansville
32. Miss Salibelle Royster....643 E. Blackford, " "
33. Miss Louise Helm....1500 W. Florida St., " "
34. Mrs. Julia Merritt....848 Washington Ave., " "
35. Miss Wahnita De Long....2226 Bellemeade, " "
36. Mrs. Russell Kelso....400 S.E. First St., " "
37. Mrs. Charles Boyles....1614 S. Bedford Ave., Evansville,
38. Mrs. Mary Margaret Calvert....2601 Adams Ave., " "
39. Mrs. Herbert Henderson....820 East Blackford, Evansville
40. Mr. Robert Bruce Moore....520 Roosevelt Drive, " "
41. Mrs. James Kirschgessner [sic]....1309 S. Kentucky Ave., Evansville
42. Mrs. Richard Rosencranz....844 East Powell, Evansville, Ind.
43. Miss Virginia Fly....701 S. Norman, Evansville
44. Mrs. William Stone....2117 E. Mulberry, Evansville,
45. Mrs. Allen Von Behren....621 S.E. Riverside, Evansville, Ind.
46. Mrs. A. K. Swann....3113 E. Blackford, " "
47. Miss Helen Foote....415 S.E. First St., Evansville,
48. Mr. James Carey....LOEW'S MAJESTIC THEATER, 17 S.E. Fifth, Evansville.
49. Mrs. Mary Oschmann....1630 Shadewood Ave., Evansville
50. Miss Alma Oberst....626 S. Norman, Evansville
51. Mr. Kenneth McCutcheon....McCutcheonville, Ind.
52. J. Clarence Kerlin....258 Washington Ave., Evansville
53. Mrs. Julia Neville...420 S.E. Second St., Apt. B. Evansville
54. Miss Florita Eichel....Evansville Museum of Fine Arts, 216 N.W. Second. Evan[s]ville
55. Mrs. Helen Odell....1501 Glendale Ave., Howell, Evansville, Ind.
56. Mrs. Sol Brentano.....Newburg[h], Ind.

The Song of the Sun ~ Leah Bodine Drake

57. Mrs. Grace Gentry....520 S.E. First St., Evansville,

My hand's numb,—I can't type any more! I'm sedning [sic] the book review herewith,[2]—it was GOOD!

LBD

Notes

1. Not all can be identified; most are friends, coworkers, and associates from places where LBD had lived. Annie H. Bodine (1869–1964), LBD's aunt; Louise E[mma] Drake (1893–1977), second wife of Edward J. Drake (1867–1935), Thomas H. Drake's brother and also an oilman, whose first wife was Nannie Clara Johnson (1869–1891); Helen Garwood (1876–1952), daughter of Joanna Boucher Bodine Garwood (1852–1944); William Earle Bodine (1893–1977), LBD's first cousin; Vaida Stewart Montgomery (1888–1959) and her husband, Whitney Maxwell Montgomery (1877–1966), editors of *Kaleidograph;* Emma Gray Trigg (1890–1976), artist and a prime mover behind the arts in Virginia; Brodie Herndon (1901–1977), president of the Poetry Society of Virginia and the Virginia Writers' Club; Bertye Young Williams (1876–1951), poet, editor of *Talaria;* Stanton A. Coblentz (1896–1982), science fiction writer and editor of *Wings;* Arnold Rosaaen (d. 1951), librarian who proceeded Herbert Goldhor (see letter to the Stuart Art Gallery); Karl Kae Knecht (1883–1972), cartoonist for the *Evansville Courier* from 1906 to 1960; Don Scism (1893–1954), longtime editor of the *Courier;* Ed J. Fehn (1884–1964), publisher and president of the *Courier;* Veneta Hahn Anderson (1913?–2017); Amy Vance Weeks (1905–1991), a local poet; Jessie Torrance (1868?–1953), worked at the *Evansville Journal News* and *Courier;* Salibelle Royster (1895–1975), English teacher at F. J. Reitz High School and Evansville College; Louise Bagley Helm (1887–1962); Wahnita De Long (1889–1987), associate professor of English at Evansville College; Mary Hedges Henderson (1899–?; wife of Herbert R. Henderson, 1899–1991); Robert Bruce Moore (1905–1958), whose wife, Vardine Russell Moore (1906–1993), poet, author, and director of a private nursery school, was a friend of LBD who once planned to write her biography; Lorene Spradley Kirchgessner (1910–1999); Margaret Eberle Rosencranz (1892–1954), a disk jockey on WGBF-AM in Evansville; Virginia Fly Carillo (1922–2006); Adrean Crockett Von Behren (1902–1991); Mary Missouri Dixon Oschmann (1893–1979); Alma Oberst, entertainment writer for the *Evansville Press;* J. Clarence Kerlin (1900–1992), reporter at the *Evansville Courier* and newscaster for WGBF Radio; Julia Hary Neville (1890–1955); Florita Eichel (1882–1983), artist and registrar of the art museum; Helen Heilman Odell (1886–1984).

2. Presumably "The Devil and Miss Barker."

UNPUBLISHED LETTERS

[28] [ALS]

July 26. [1949]

Dear August—
I thought this article on "Abracadabra" might come in handy for the *"Sampler"*. I found the information about it in an old notebook of mine (on folklore, etc,) that I haven't looked at for years![1]

Of course, I had to pad it out with bits of historical detail, but the speculations in it, so to speak, are my own ideas. Webster gives the charm but doesn't elaborate on the why & wherefore. I found the meaning of the word in an old book but where and when and what its name was, I don't recall.

The entire article, however, is my own work. I'm not plag[i]arizing anybody!

Yours, as ever,
L B D.

Notes
1. *Witchcraft—Notes by Leah Bodine Drake* (1956) contains such information.

[29] [TLS]

[Leah Bodine Drake]

Evansville, Ind.,
Oct. 10th, 1949.

Dear August:
There's two matters I want to write about. First, one of the poems in "HORNBOOK FOR WITCHES" is "The Old World of Green". "WEIRD TALES" accepted it long ago, but recently they wrote and said they were going to use it in another of their publications, "SHORT STORIES".[1]

So now I reckon you'll have to write in "SHORT STORIES" among the "acknowledgments["] in the front of the manuscript, just ahead of "SOUTHERN LITERARY MESSENGER", pribably [*sic*].

Second matter: to be very blunt, what do you charge to talk to an organization? The Assoc[i]ation of American University Women here wish to bring a poet to give a lecture at one of our big meetings later on in the season, and as a member of the Creative Poetry Section of this organization I suggested you. All the others are enthusiastic over the prospect of hearing you (and seeing, too, as I've told them you're good-

The Song of the Sun ~ Leah Bodine Drake

lookin',) and asked me to write and inquire what you are accustomed to receeive [sic] for a talk on poetry.

If your rate isn't too staggering, you'll hear from me again,—provided, of course, that you'd care to come down here. we really are a pretty nice bunch,—liberal, too,. . . . we've just taken a Negro girl into our own group, the first group here to do such a thing.

Let me hear from you as soon as possible,—I hope this interests you.

As Ever,

L B D.

Notes

1. Had *Weird Tales* published the poem, LBD would have had one more poem there than Dorothy Quick, and so the most poems by a woman in the magazine.

[30] [TLS]

[Leah Bodine Drake]

Evansville
Jan. 2, 1950.

Dear August: I'm inclosing a drawing of a wyvern. The description is: "The *wyvern* differs from the dragon in having only two legs, although it has the beast's head, the eagle's claws, and the serpent's tail."

I think a wyvern alternating with a centaur or a leaping Pan might make a good combination, don't you? Remind the artist[1] that *my* Pan is a beneficent deity, a real nice fellow to know,—not a devil! Most of my "monsters" are good rather than evil, anyway.

I'm going to have a photo made soon,—let me know what you think about it being on the jacket.

I hope 1950 is the best year yet for you and ARKHAM HOUSE,—for "A HORNBOOK FOR WITCHES", incidently [sic].

As ever,

L B D.

Notes

1. See 64n1. The dust jacket displays sixteen repeated pairs (some obscured) of a wyvern and Pan and lettering in white against a black background. The general design, using other images, was imitated on subsequent volumes of poetry issued by Arkham House.

UNPUBLISHED LETTERS

[31] [TL, carbon, but signed]
[Arkham House: Publishers
SAUK CITY, WISCONSIN]
23 January 1950

Dear Leah:
One of those annoying little problems which publishers often face has come up in connection with publication of A HORNBOOK FOR WITCHES. Even at the least expensive, the book is going to cost me approximately $1 a copy, maybe slightly more. Now, priced at $2—and we can hardly price it at more—that means that trade buyers who buy 5 or more, or just 1, with other orders totalling 5, get a discount to $1.20 the copy. If we were to pay royalty on top of that, of $.20 the copy, we would simply be out of pocket and selling at a loss. I have, therefore, a proposal to make. Your total royalties, if we sold all the books, would amount to $100.00. Would you be willing to take one half that amount in books at 50%, or 50 books at $1 the copy in place of royalties on the first 250 copies sold? You do already have 6 free copies coming, in accordance with the contract, and we will want to send you some extra copies for signature for some of our readers. We plan publication in May or June, and if this arrangement is satisfactory, I wish you would let us know, so that we can direct the plant to send books directly to you once they are ready. Also, the photograph you spoke of sending—we have not had it; and, if you have not already sent it (and you may, for I've not consulted my files at this hurried writing) the biographical data for the flap. The jacket design of wyverns and pans has been made, looks good, I think.
  Best always,
                August

[32] [TLS]
[Leah Bodine Drake]
Thursday, Jan. 26th, 1950

Dear August:
  Here is the flap-biography data. It's a bare outline, you can word it as you like. I left out a lot,—about being married and divorced, a show-

The Song of the Sun 🙰 Leah Bodine Drake

girl, Miss Dallas,—all that. It seemed irrelevant.

It's all right about taking part of the royalties in books. I never expect to make any money out of poetry anyway! Who does? I'm glad to have the book published,—any profit on it will just be lagniappe!

I had a picture made by our photographer on the paper,—it isn't bad, but it isn't good, either. I'm going down tomorrow to have another made. Will air-mail it to you if it turns out well. But if you want to use just the biog and NO picture, it's all right with me. Nobody cares what I look like. Frankly, I think I'd prefer just the biog. Let's leave it at that.

As Ever, Leah.

[Typed enclosure]

HORNBOOK FOR WITCHES......Leah Bodine Drake

Born, Chanute, Kansas, daughter of an oilman, moved to Lexington, Kentucky, as a child, lived all over the South and Southwest, summers spent on the Jersey coast. Earliest memories are of trains, the ocean, the tremendous silences of the Navajo country, the woods and swamps of the South, tales of han'ts [sic] by "Aunt Coopie", a Negro member of the household.

Attended Hamilton College for Women in Lexington.

Ancestral background is English, Irish, Welsh and French, and family-tree includes Sir Francis Drake, Davy Crocket and Jean Bodin. [OK = no final "e" at that date (1550)]

At present living in Evansville, Ind., where (she) is movie, dramatic and music critic for the *Evansville Courier*.

Main interests, beside poetry, are collecting books illustrated by Dulac and Rackham, walking in the woods, the works of C. S. Lewis, Dixieland jazz, D.A.R. work, and, as vice-president of the local humane society, rescuing dogs, cats and horses from what E. E. Cummings calls 'manunkind'.

[33] [ALS]

[LEAH BODINE DRAKE]

Wed., Oct. 13. [1950]

Dear August—

I read this over carefully, and everything seems to be O. K. little as I know of such matters—this being my maiden book. But I trust you and "Arkham House" to do right by Little Nell.[1]

I'm mighty pleased that you think enough of this book to venture *600* copies instead of the proposed 500.[2]

Golly, I hope you sell 'em all! I'd feel awfully sorry for you—and me—if A. H. got stuck with them!

I had to smile at the large wording of the contract at one place—those "first 5000 copies". Well, it'd␣be nice if there *would* turn out to be that much of a demand for *A Hornbook for Witches* . . . .

As ever, and with thanks (and I *do* mean many of them)
   Yours
    L B D.

Notes
1. A virtuous young girl in Dickens's *The Old Curiosity Shop.*
2. Five hundred fifty-three copies were printed.

[34] [TLS]
    [Leah Bodine Drake]
      Nov. 14, 1950.

Dear August:

I'm sending the proofs back tomorrow, with a very few corrections. There are remarkably few mistakes, I'm glad to say. I've marked them, and made a list, too.

The pages look wonderful, and I don't see why it won't sell. I think I can dispose of the 50 copies right here in town, and I have lots of interested friends elsewhere. My own paper, the COURIER, will give me a good write-up (even if I have to write it my ownself!) [*sic*] with a photo, and the head of the book department at our one and only bookstore, SMITH AND BUTTERFIELD'S, is a friend of mine, Enid [*sic*] Paul. She has already placed some orders with you, I think.

All the libraries here know me, and I know will order a copy, at least, from you.

I hope we both make a little money on it, but anyway, the book is it's [*sic*] own excuse for being. Thanks for all you've done, August. I can appreciate it enormously, and maybe someday I can do you a handsome turn!

The Song of the Sun ⁂ Leah Bodine Drake

We haven't yet gotten to Rochester this year. Now the weather is so bad, I doubt we'll attempt it until Spring.

  As Ever,
    Leah.

[35] [ALS]

    [Leah Bodine Drake]

      Thanksgiving
      [23 November 1950]

Dear August:

 I think I'll inform my Evansville friends that they can buy the Hornbook" from me—but an announcement from you, too, might deepen the impression! I think both libraries here are going to order from you, and Smith & Butterfield's, too.

 Will you send review copies to the following?—:[1]

1. "Poetry Chap-Book"
2. "New York *Times* Book Review" (J. Donald Adams)
3. "Wings".
4. "Voices".
5. Florence Dickinson Stearns 501 North Allen Ave., Richmond Virginia (she reviews for the *Times Dispatch*)
6. "Saturday Review of Literature"
7. "Kaleidograph"
8. "Talaria"
9. "*Time Magazine.*" (I had a letter from *Time* in 1948 about it—they were interested & wanted a copy to review when it came out.)
10. "The New Yorker."
11. "New York Herald Tribune"
12. "Chicago Tribune" (Edward Wagenknecht)

Well, here's to luck!

  As Ever,
    Leah.

Notes

1. Of the magazines and reviewers listed, AD checked off 1, 3–8, and 10 but crossed out 2, 9, and 11–12. The *Times* (not *New York Times Book Review*) published a review; see letter 41.

UNPUBLISHED LETTERS

[36] [ALS]
Nov. 27, '50.

Dear August—
I'll have some cards printed here, and send around town. So maybe you'd better skip Evansville & just send to the names on the list in other towns.
The libraries here, Willard, & Central, and Smith & Butterfield's Book Store, however, will most likely buy from you, so please send them one of *your* cards.
Then I'll just sit back and wait to get rich. (Loud laughter.)
I hope you'll soon pull out of that $18,000 debt you mentioned. Under the circumstances, I deeply appreciate your going ahead with my little book, because the Lord knows you can't really expect to make very much money on it! I mean, after all . . . . . poetry . . . . . Well, *you* know.
I'm glad to learn that Arkham H. is still doing business—I thought maybe you were planning to shut up shop.
We are buried in snow up to *hyar*—real Wisconsin weather!
'By now
LBD

[37] [ALS]
Nov. 29. [1950]

Dear August—
The flap material is awfully good—thanks for the nice things you said about my poetry!
Mrs. Paul of Smith & Butterfield's talked to me about the autograph party—the *store* sends out cards, & they advertise in the papers. I'll also see to it that a photo is used & a story in the *Courier*. (The *Press* will most likely copy it.)
She wants to be sure, though, that the books will arrive—what a bust to have an autograph party & nothing to autograph!
I think I have enough friends here to sell my own 50 books to & Butterfield 50—as the list I made out for myself totals 100. (I'm having a friend print me some cards.) Anyway, an autograph party is recognition, & that's important.

597

The Song of the Sun ❧ Leah Bodine Drake

> Adios,
> Leah

[38] [ALS]

Saturday,
Dec. 9. [1950]

Dear August—

The books came today—to me, and to Smith & B.

They look wonderful! The jacket—lettering & drawings—are superb. The Gothic script gives it that spooky look!

I've autographed your 14 copies & will ship them back to you Monday. The autograph party is Dec. 18—I'll write you all the details, & send you all newspaper clippings.

Thanks for everything—I'll never forget your kindness. Someday I maybe I can do something for you—brew you a love-potion or something. Mine are considered most effective!

> Yours,
> LBD.

[39] [ALS]

Thursday Dec. 14. [1950]

Dear August——

No—I only got the 70 copies[1] & have already sent the ones' [sic] back to you signed.

The book is arousing *lots* of interest, & S & B. is really doing me up proud, as is my paper—I'll send you clippings. Have already sold 18 of my own books, with orders for almost all the rest.

> Love and kisses,
> Leah.

Notes

1. I.e., LBD's six author copies, fourteen to autograph and return to AD, and the fifty additional copies as part of her payment.

Unpublished Letters

[40] [ALS]

Dec. 21—[1950]

Dear August——
 The autographing party was a Big Success!—we sold all the first 50 books, & had to draw on the second batch.[1] Mr. Butterfield was delighted. He had the store photographer take a picture, & when it's in the paper (Sunday) I'll send you one.
 People like the book. A local musician & composer, Pauline Fehn,[2] asked my permission to set "Witches On the Heath" to music.[3]
 The book is selling, & I've sold all but *ten* of my own stock, mostly to out-of-towners. Harold Vinal promises to review the book for *Voices* when you send him one. Sydney K. Russell of *Poetry Chap-Book* bought one from me.[4]
 Thanks again for everything & I hope your Xmas and New Year's is happy and successful—
  As Always,
   Leah.

Notes
1. It is unclear how many more copies of *HW* Butterfield obtained beyond the first fifty it had ordered. See Brennan letter 9.
2. Pauline Goad Fehn (1920–1999), flutist, composer, and poet.
3. Curiously, the guitarist Buckethead produced an instrumental work called "Witches on the Heath" (2002). The poem is narrated by Vincent Price on *A Hornbook for Witches*.
4. Harold Vinal (1891–1965), poet and editor of *Voices: A Journal of Poetry*, which published eight of LBD's poems. He was later a secretary of the PSA. Sydney King Russell (1897–1976), poet, composer, editor of *Poetry Chap-Book*, which published eleven of LBD's poems.

[41] [ALS]

Jan. 8, 1951.

Dear August—
 Everybody loves the book and the make-up (jacket, paper, etc.) is so much admired. I've sold all my 50 copies & can't fill orders!
 The book was reviewed in the Jan. 1st (daily) New York *Time's* [*sic*] (no less!) by Orville Prescott.[1] He *liked* it! I'd never hoped to land in the

good, grey *Times*—oh frabjous day, Calloo, Callay!² He quoted "They Run Again" in its entirety.

  More anon.
  As Ever,
    Leah.

Notes
1. Orville Prescott (1906–1996), main book reviewer for the *New York Times* for 24 years.
2. Lewis Carroll, "Jabberwocky" l. 23.

[42] [ALS]

Feb. 7, 1951.
Dear August—

 Thanks for the certificate of copyright registration. I'm glad the book is selling—S. & B have a few left. If you knew Sidney B. like Evansville knows him you wouldn't expect to get paid any too soon. He's slow as cold molasses! Perfectly honest, & all that—just slow.

 I went to New York for the P S A dinner, at which I read my poem: "*Lariat: 6000 B.C.*", which took the second prize in the yearly contest. I never *had* such a marvelous time! Met all kinds of interesting people, royalty included.¹ I had myself a whirl. The body's back in E-town, but the spirit is still in New York!

 Harold Vinal is going blind—isn't that awful?

  As Always,
    Leah.

Notes
1. Prince Alexis A. Droutskoy (1897?–1976) and Princess Droutskoy (nee Maria Theresa Berry; 1923–2005) were present to bestow the Alexander [*sic*] Droutskoy Memorial Award on Gustav Davidson.

[43] [TLS]

Nov. 27th, 1951.
Dear August:

 I guess I'm a nuisance, but I still think *we* ought to get together a book of thrillers in which animals play a large part.

UNPUBLISHED LETTERS

You spoke in one letter about the public being uninterested in ghosts. Well, the idea of an anthology which I had in mind wouldn't exactly be ghost stories. I had thought of stories that could come under the heading of thriller, fantasties, [sic]—many of the stories I've had in mind are actual events, or at least, non-supernatural. I particularly thought of a tremendous story (which I'm sure you've read) called "*Leinisen Versus the Ants,*" [sic] which is NOT ghostly at all.[1]

I recently read a wonderful collection of short stories by an Englishman who takes the pen name of "Sarban". His book is called "RINGSTONES", and while some of the tales are downright supernatural, two at least are "natural" and about animals, one called "THE KHAN" being a dilly.[2] Walter Duranty's tale "THE PARROT" is another non-spooky thriller.[3]

I still think we could make a good thing out of such an anthology. Let me scour the world for the material, you check it and publish it. ?????

When do you want me to get a new weird poems book together?

As Ever,

Leah—

Notes
1. "Leiningen versus the Ants" by Carl Stephenson (*Esquire*, December 1938); a translation, probably by Stephenson himself, of "Leiningens Kampf mit den Ameisen," originally published in German in 1937.
2. John William Wall (1910–1989), British writer and diplomat who published under the pseudonym Sarban, author of *Ringstones and Other Curious Tales* (1951).
3. Walter Duranty (1884–1957), Anglo-American journalist who served as the Moscow Bureau Chief of the *New York Times* (1922–36). "The Parrot" won the O. Henry Award, First Prize, 1928.

[44] [ALS]

March 4 [1952?]

Dear August—

You mentioned something about getting out another collection of my weird poems sometime. Are you serious?[1] I don't know what I have enough of that type to fill another book—would have to begin to write some more! I can do it **if** I thought it worth my while and that you really planned to publish another of the type.

  As Ever Leah

Notes

1. In a letter to Anthony Boucher (8 April 1952), LBD wrote: "Derleth will publish my new spooker whenever I can get it ready,—maybe next year."

[45] [TLS]

               Evansville, Indiana,
               Nov. 6th, 1952.

Dear August:

  Thank you for the surprise check. I don't know why, but I'm always kinda surprised when I get a royalty check—I can't believe even yet that I actually have had a book published! After two years, that the "HORNBOOK" is still selling is a constant wonder to me.

  You'll be glad to know that I have made an attempt at fantasy fiction and that WEIRD TALES has taken my pristine effort—a tale of the Kentucky backwoods called "WHISPER WATER". It should be out in a Spring issue. I haven't even tried to write fiction since I was a child and wrote innumerable fairy-tales, illustrated beautifully by Rackham, Dulac and Pogany:[1] I tore their pictures out of my books, AND my family's. I remember a copy we had of Omar's RUBAIYAT illustrated by Dulac. Almost every picture in it came out, to illustrate my own almost-exclusively Oriental fairytales.

  Did you see the review I did of your latest book of poems in the POETRY CHAPBOOK? Gustav asked me to do it, knowing I liked your work.[2] Frankly, I like your poems better than Frost's.

  Did the election results please you? We are still shouting the jubilee! Each of my family is proud of the way their own state voted for Ike— Father for Virginia, Mother for New Jersey, and me for both Kansas and—well, ALMOST for Ike—Kentucky. (Up until now Ky. was still Democratic, but all in the hill-counties, who are Rep.[,] are not in.)

    Best to you,
      L. B. D.

UNPUBLISHED LETTERS

Notes
1. Arthur Rackham (1867–1939), English book illustrator. Edmund Dulac (1882–1953), French-born, British naturalized magazine and book illustrator; his illustrated *Rubaiyat* appeared in 1909. William Andrew Pogany (1882–1955), a prolific Hungarian illustrator of children's books and others.
2. Davidson was the director of the Fine Editions Press, which published AD's book.

[46] [TLS]

Evansville, Indiana,
Feb. 26, 1953.

Dear August:

How many HORNBOOKS are left now? The reason I ask, I've had at least a half dozen people write me, asking where they could buy one, from as widely seperated [*sic*] places as Kentucky (a man in the Mayor of Owensboro's office, of all prosaic places!), Kansas City and Los Angeles.

If this keeps up, you should get rid of the remaining copies and be in the market for a new collection? How about it?

I have a story—my very first—coming out in the next WEIRD TALES (May), about March 1st. Cover-picture illustrates it, too!—Success![1] Let me hear from you as to your opinion of Drake as a fictioneer. Title: "WHISPER WATER".

Did you hear of my wonderful award from POETRY AWARDS? A poem of mine, Precarious Ground, won the first prize of $300 in the "magazine-poetry of the English-speaking world" section of their contest. Their check came just before Xmas!

I also had another bit of luck, when Rolfe Humphries took two of my poems for an anthology he is editing for BALLANTINE BOOKS,—a 35-cent pocket-book of modern poetry.[2] The company pays ten dollars a page for the poems, then gives royalties besides. Good deal! The publicity from this will be invaluable for me. I should have an even better sale of any poetry collection I get out now. I wish I could pay Dorothy Lathrop[3] to illustrate a new weird collection—but imagine she'd charge a lot.

Let me hear from you about assembling some spookies for a new book.

The Song of the Sun ❧ Leah Bodine Drake

As Ever,
L B D.

Notes
1. The cover was by Joseph Eberle (1926–2006).
2. "The Final Green" and "Honey from the Lion." George Rolfe Humphries (1894–1969) was a poet, translator, and teacher.
3. Dorothy Pulis Lathrop (1891–1980), American writer and illustrator of children's books.

[47] [TLS]

1023 First St.,
Henderson, Ky.,
Feb. 10th. [1954]

Dear August:

The inclosed sheet will tell you what a terrific prize I won recently. I went to New York for the PSA dinner, and received the check personally. Had a simply terrific time!

By the way, Lawrence Thompson, Director of libraries at the U. of Ky., wants the typescript of HORNBOOK FOR WITCHES very much for the library's collection of Drake.[1] (Wow!) Could you dig it out of the attic and send it to him?

By the way, I've had two people ask me where they can buy the HORNBOOK—how many copies do you have left? If I can get one at bargain prices, I'd even buy another copy for my own self.

How are things with you?
As Ever,
L B D.

Notes
1. It is not known how or when Brigham Young University came to own the T.Ms. of *HW*. See LBD letter 1 to Thompson. The *Parkersburg News* for 27 September 1959 stated that "A collection of her 'poems in the rough' and work-sheets is in the Lockwood Memorial Library [*sic*] at the University of Kentucky." LBD once had papers on display at the Lockwood Memorial Library in Buffalo in 1948. LBD's scrapbooks, notebooks, typescripts, and photographs at the University of Kentucky–Lexington were deposited there in 1968 by John Herring, a distant cousin, but the library holds other mss. by LBD as well.

Unpublished Letters

[48] [ANS]

[Postmarked Henderson, KY,
1 December 1954]
Dec. 1st, 1954

Dear August:
Received the royalty yesterday. I was surprised to know any more copies had been sold at this late date! The book really went well, didn't it? Did you know Clark Ashton Smith had been married recently?[1] A widow with 3 children.
As Ever, LBD.

Notes
1. LBD probably learned this from Eric Barker, who had introduced Smith to Carol Jones Dorman. They married on 10 November 1954.

[49] [TLS]

Henderson, Ky.,
March 11, 1955.

Dear August:
Will you send me a copy of HORNBOOK FOR WITCHES,—that is, if you have any left—and bill me April 1st?[1]
Edward Davison,[2] who just became president of the Poetry Society of America, as you know, asked me for any book of my poems. So far, the HORNBOOK is the only book—although THIS TILTING DUST looks as though it would be out soon.[3] (I'll tell you the details later.) There's no copy of HORNBOOK around these parts, and I have only one for my own self.
What do you think I'm starting next month?—the silliest dam' job for a poet you ever heard of!—society editor, by gad, for the Henderson *Gleaner*. They need a new one, I need money—so . . . . . But I still think it's a waste of time for a poet!
How is the Derleth hope & pride? Has she begun to write yet?[4] She will, of course—with such a pappy!
As Ever,
Leah.

The Song of the Sun ❧ Leah Bodine Drake

Notes
1. On this letter, AD wrote "3/14 $1.31 due" or LBD's cost of $1.26 and postage.
2. Edward Lewis Davison (1898–1970), Scottish poet and critic, born in Glasgow, who later moved to the U.S. and served as President of the Poetry Society of America 1955–56.
3. It was not published until December.
4. April Rose Derleth (1954–2011), at the time only seven months old.

[50] [ALS]

Evansville, Indiana—

Nov. 30th [1955]

Dear August—Watch the T V program—*"The $64,000 Question"*—from now on—I'm to be on it very soon, my subject: Witch Craft!

Many people have asked me how to obtain a copy of "The Hornbook For Witches" as a result of some preceeding [sic] publicity. I have a book—*"This Tilting Dust"*—coming out in December,[1] & will get a wonderful send-off about it by being on the T V program!

I don't know if a new edition of the "Hornbook" is to *your* mind—but it bears thinking about.

Wish me luck!

As Always,
Leah
927 Lincoln Avenue.

[51] [TLS]

Evansville,
Dec. 7—'55.

Dear August—

If you need a good be-witching, just line me—I ought to be able to blast crops, kill hogs, and wreck [sic] general havoc from here to Oshkosh, by gosh! I've got magic coming out of my ears by now, and feel ready for $64,000 questions and then some!

August, I think the copyright of *The Hornbook* is mine now, isn't it? You may be right in feeling that a second edition might not pay you to print it—probably not. But anyway, some friends of mine are toying with the idea of printing some extra copies, and I want to make sure I own all rights to it now, and can give the printing and/or new publishing rights to whom I please (with of course, Arkham House's *imprimatur* on the title-page or wherever—[you know how I mean] in reprints.)

So let me have your answer as soon as possible. The iron won't stay hot long! (Incidently, I *loathe* T–V—wouldn't have one!)

As Ever,
L B D.

[52] [TLS]

Feb. 14, 1956.

Dear August:

What a fine review of my book you gave! I like it being in the Madison paper, as it is read by the University crowd. Thank you so very much for your high praise, and for the promptness—poetry usually has to wait and wait and wait for the reviewers to get around to it.

Incidently, I wasn't taking so-called poetic license with the line "Here IS rain", etc.—it was an oversight, and one which, strangely enough, no one has caught, except you, not even myself, and then I had to re-read the lines a couple of times until I realized (ten years too late) that the word should have been "are".[2] Not even editors noticed it—the poem appeared in an English magazine (I mean, a British, not an Eng. Lit.) and in two anthologies!

I'm going to try and get my publisher to rectify the line, in the new edition he is getting out.

And what have you got against lions? Whatever the real beast may be like (and I like him), I use him as an ancient symbol of royalty, nobility, and even godhead. (As does C. S. Lewis!)[3]

"Flemish Artists" is, I'll admit, more or less playful verse, even though it was published in the ATLANTIC Monthly.

I'm still waiting to be called to N.Y. for the quiz-show. But as Revlon has taken the show away from the man I talked to, Steve Carlin,[4] my hopes of being on it keep getting dimmer.

Thanks again, August, for a grand write-up,—your remarks should help me a lot. Did a copy go to Farrar[5] (the publisher)?

How's married life by now?
As Ever,
L B D.

Notes

1. Smith and Butterfields carried *TD* and had an autograph party, as it had in the case of *HW*.
2. In "'What Are Little Girls Made Of?'" LBD had written "Here is sun / And rain along the wind and azure air [. . .]" ll. 8–9.
3. See her comments on lions in "[On 'We Come out of the Forest . . .]." she refers to Aslan, a lion, the rightful King of Narnia in *The Lion, the Witch and the Wardrobe* (1950).
4. Steve Carlin (1919–2003), executive producer of *The $64,000 Question*, a television show that was part of the quiz show scandal of the 1950s.
5. Clarence E. Farrar, editor of the Golden Quill Press. The Press published AD's *West of Morning* (1960).

[53] [TNS]

[Postmarked Evansville, IN, 29 February 1956]

Feb. 28

Dear August:

C. Farrar, publisher of the Golden Quill Press, wants to quote from your fine review of my book for some publicity he's planning. Could you send him a copy soon?

How proud you must be of that blonde elfling whose snapshot you sent me! She's darling, and looks like her pappy, as I see it—not knowing her mother, I don't know if she resembles her, too. But A.D., very much.

You'll be quite the pater familias pretty soon.[1]

Best regards to you all,
L B D.

P.S. Did you read John Ciardi's review of F. Frost?[2] He spared her not at all. Merciless!

Notes

1. AD's son Walden William was born on 10 August.
2. Frances Frost (1905–1959), American poet, novelist, editor of *American Poetry Journal*. Poet and critic John Ciardi (1916–1986) harshly reviewed Frost's *This Rowdy Heart* (1954) in the *Nation* 179 (4 December 1954): 490–91.

Unpublished Letters

[54] [ALS]

May 7th—56.

Dear August—

How "thoughty" of you to send me the FSF. review. I hadn't seen it—but I don't buy the mag. every month as I used to: I am a little bored with science-fiction. Give me old-fashioned spooks and C. S. Lewis instead!

Tony Boucher is going to reprint a poem from my book in "F. &. S.F." ("*We Move on Turning Stone*".) One of his favorites was "*Flemish Artists*" but he can't reprint it as it certainly isn't fantasy! I don't think *any* of the poems in "*This Tilting Dust*" are really true fantasy—the "fantasy" in them is symbolic, not actual.

Incidently, the "*Atlantic M.*" carries a long poem of mine in this (May) issue.[1] Their editor has asked me to do a review now and then of books of poetry for the *Atlantic*—I'm so pleased about it! Now I can say nice things about my friends' books, in their pages! And the prestige is not to be taken lightly, of getting my by-line among those of the "A."'s reviewers stable!

      Best as always, Leah.

Notes
1. "The Weeds and the Wilderness."

[55] [ALS]

1801 Avery St.
Parkersburg, W. Va.
[late 1958 or early 1959]

Dear August:

The above address is permanent—well, as long as the address of an oil man's family *can* be!

We hope to move back to Indiana, however. I don't care much for W. Va.—no culture. It's beautiful, however—hills, woods, etc. And I'm glued to my desk at the paper & never see anything or do anything. I haven't written a line of poetry for 4 months. And just after I made "Who's Who in America" for the first time! (Well, the *Supplement* to it.)

My last book "This Tilting Dust" went fine—I suppose you read where it made list of nominations for the 1957 National Book Awards?

The Song of the Sun ⁊ Leah Bodine Drake

(Wilbur's book *won* it.)[1]

I have quite a few good poems for a third volume. I am thinking of applying for a Guggenheim so I can write more poems to warrant such a third publication. I write poetry reviews for the *Atlantic* each year—7 or 8 books at once. They ship me a dozen or more books & let me choose. It all helps—at $300 a review.

There is a small oil boom here in W. Va. & that is the reason we are here. Father has been fairly successful,[2] but my job helps out. Neither he nor I intend to remain here all our lives. I love the mid-West & the sleepy sloughs of southern Indiana & the bird-flocks going over fall & spring. And Mother's grave is there.

My best to you and yours for 1959—As Ever LBD.

Notes

1. There were fifteen finalists for the poetry award, won by Richard Wilbur for *Things of This World*.
2. An article (20 October 1957) in the *Parkersburg News* stated that LBD's father was retired and that at the time they were only visiting, intending to return to Indiana.

[56] [ALS]

Parkersburg-on-the-Little-Kanawha.

August 30—1959.

Leah Drake / 1801 Avery St / Parkersburg, W. Va.

Dear August—

I'm 'way behind on all my correspondence—but want to thank you for the natty-looking little book on *Arkham House*.[1] A collectors' item!

Yes I can send you some unanthologized weirdies—about 13. Most appeared in "*WT*" after the "*Hornbook*" was published, but several were in "*Fantasy & S F*" in recent years, and one, at least, in the "*Atlantic*". One or two, even, have never been published.[2]

I'll get them to you as promptly as I can type them—but this Society editor job is a rock-crusher—my *typing arm* aches, & when I get home I try to rest it as much as possible. We (the other society ed. & myself) do all our own editing & picture making, write heads & make the layouts. We get out the Sunday soc. pages on Thurs. & Fri. nights, from 2:30 in the afternoon until *3* **a.m.**! Last week we had **28** weddings to write, as

UNPUBLISHED LETTERS

well as accounts of club programs, homecomings, anniversary open houses, etc. etc, [sic] *ad infinitum*. No wonder the job is always open—it would break Hercules! Know anybody who wants a good scrubwoman?
Best as always,
poor ol' tired L B D.

Notes
1. *Arkham House: The First 20 Years* (1959).
2. LBD had only six poems in *FSC*, none from *Weird Tales*. Three were from *F&SF*, one from *Atlantic*, one from *Orb*, and one previously unpublished.

[57] [TNS, privately held]

[n.d.][1]

Data: Author of two books of poetry, A HORNBOOK FOR WITCHES, Arkham House, 1950; THIS TILTING DUST, Golden Quill Press, Francestown, N.H., 1956. (This volume in manuscript form won the $1250 Borestone Mt. Poetry Award in 1954.)
Wrote Poetry for THE ATLANTIC, 1957, 1958.
Poems published in many anthologies, including the Borestone Mt. Poetry Awards each year; Ballantine Boks "NEW POEMS BY AMERICAN POETS["] ed. by Rolfe Humphries, 1954, 1957; "JUBILEE", the anthology of ATLANTIC MONTHLY pieces over 100 years of the magazine's existence; Braithwaite's anthology 1959; etc. etc.
Listed in "Who's Who in World Poetry", and "Who's Who in America" (Spring supplement 1959.)
Am an assistant society editor on the Parkersburg NEWS, Parkersburg, W.Va.
Native of Kentucky, [sic] but call myself a Hoosier, after 20 years in Evansville, Ind.
Member of the Poetry Society of America, etc.
During one summer (1953) had a strange spurt of prose-writing: three fantasies, "WHISPER WATER", "MOP-HEAD" and "FOXY'S HOLLOW".[2] (Never before or since!) All published.
That's a-plenty,—who cares, anyway? The poem's the thing!
LBD

The Song of the Sun ~ Leah Bodine Drake

Notes
1. Presumably this was provided as personal information to be included in *FSC*. It may have been an enclosure to the previous letter. AD acknowledged receipt of it in a letter (TLS, University of Kentucky) dated 10 September 1959).
2. LBD must be in error as to the date or dates of composition. In November 1952, she wrote AD that "Whisper Water" had been accepted. Writing to Anthony Boucher in September 1952, she submits an untitled story, her "first SF attempt," though she told AD that "Whisper Water" was her first. The publication of it and "Foxy's Hollow" in the spring and summer of 1953 does not allow for the lag between publication and acceptance. It may be that she wrote the three stories in the summer of 1952.

[58] [TLS]

Leah Drake / 1801 Avery St / Parkersburg, W. Va.

Sept. 18 [1959]

Dear August:

Thank you, first, for your acceptance of the poems for your anthology. Then second, thank you for looking out for my interest, re the 'magic' anthology of the World Pub. Co.[1]

I wrote them to the effect you suggested, also told them I could submit other "fairy" poems if they were interested. (Interested or not, they're going to get copies from me) I think the 'Pool' you took would be acceptable, also 'Fantasy in a Forest', and a few from the HORNBOOK.

Had a request for a HORNBOOK recently—I don't suppose there are any left?[2] Do you think a special limited edition might pay? What I'd LIKE would be about 30 poems culled from it and illustrated with woodcuts by the man who did the book jacket. What's his name?

Best always. How's the growing family?
    Leah.

Notes
1. LBD refers to *Poems of Magic and Spells,* which used her poem "Changeling."
2. *Arkham House: The First 20 Years* listed the book as out of print.

UNPUBLISHED LETTERS

[59] [TLS]

1801 Avery St.,
Wednesday.
[23 or 30 September 1959]

Dear August:

Don't worry about a repetition of poems in the anthologies. I am not sending any of the ones I sent you to the Children's anthology: POOL, WORD OF WILLOW, etc.

I was surprised to learn of your divorce. But so glad you have the children.

The World Publ Co. agreed to my fee, but don't pay until the book is out. That's alright. I am sending them a few others, per their request.

Best, as ever,
LBD
Leah.

[60] [ANS]

Jan. 18—60

Dear August—
How's this?[1]

It's certainly man-and-nature! I would have sent it before this—but have had my hands full with sickness, both my own (flu) and Father's—(operation for cancer of the prostate) who is still a semi-invalid at home.

As Ever, L B D.

Notes
1. "The Crows."

[61] [ANS]

Jul 2—1960.

Dear August—I hoped you would see my news-item in the PSA Bulletin about an anthology I am helping edit for the Falcon's Wing Press & I would get some poems from you. Evidently, it passed your notice.[1]

Will you send me about 10 of your poems, old & new, published or not, for me to consider? The deadline is past, but as the book won't ap-

613

The Song of the Sun ❧ Leah Bodine Drake

pear until Spring, 1962, there is time. I spent June in Locarno, Switzerland. Yours LBD

Notes
1. LBD's notice appeared in *PSA Bulletin* (March 1960): 8.

[62] [ANS]

July 9 [1960]

Dear August—What lovely, lovely poems!

I am sending them to Dr. Muses, & will let you know which we choose.

I like them all, but we won't take a large group from each poet, as he did in "Prismatic Voices". We have a real first-class flight of talent—V. Watkins, Swenson, Merwin, Sarton, Wright, Rich, B. Deutsch, Lattimore,—all the *best!*

Thank you for being so prompt.
   As Ever, Leah.

[63] [TLS]

4006 Emerson Ave.
[c. 20 August 1960]

Dear August:

Note new address: we have at last found a house on the town's edge,—fields and swampy, shaded brook to look at, and in our back yard a huge weeping willow, sycamore, and holly tree covered with green budding berries, phlox, honeysuckle, roses, a pair of brown wild bunnies and a quail family who come quietly up to feed in the early mornings. I am never quite happy, away from woods and fields.

Attendez-vous! I've left the society desk, and am training for—you'd never guess—hat salon manager.[1] I take my training here, and in three or four months (if I'm smart and can learn) will be sent by the millinery company (a Chicago firm) to another of their salons in some other city—I put in my bid for the Lexington, Ky. one, as of course that is my old home.

I cannot say that I'm in love with my work: naturally, it leaves me little time for writing—perhaps a bit more than the newspaper did, although not much—and I'll never be happy not engaged in some sort of literary work. The poetry thing Muses & I worked on in Locarno was PERFECT—just the sort of work I can really put heart and soul into, and to hell with the salary. But as long as my poor dad remains broke, and I must work, I think the hat deal will be a better thing for me than society drivel—which drained my mental energies for any other *real* writing.

Perhaps this poem will be liked, for H. and W.[2] (Incidently, what a handsome magazine! And good poetry, too.)

As Ever,
Leah.

Notes
1. LBD had taken a position at Broida, Stone and Thomas to train for hat salon management, starting 29 July. The intent was for her to take over management of one of the Goldstein–O'Connor Millinery Company's salons.
2. *Hawk and Whippoorwill* (1960–63), a journal devoted to "poems of man and nature" edited by AD. This poem—not "written with my heart" (AD 64) is not identified, but may have been "That Summer."

[64] [TLS]

Sunday
Sept. 11 [1960]

Dear August:

Hope you like this poem—it was written with my heart, as the other one I sent you wasn't: I *had* a mother who died, I never had a brother or sister who even lived. (Only child.)

Incidently, where do you get your beautiful letterheads? Are they woodcuts by Lankes? Tell me where and how I can get some for my own stationary [*sic*].[1]

I liked the magazine very much, and think some of the poems are excellent. Am going to subscribe soon. (Not said as a bribe!)

This poem won a prize from the PSA but I've re-written it since then. In fact, completed it today, my one day at home from selling those damn hats.

I hope you at least break even on the H&W deal, for it is needed. There are so few *good* poetry publications.

The Song of the Sun ❧ Leah Bodine Drake

    Best ever—
        Leah.

[P.S.] What nice things you said about me! Thank you![2]

Notes

1. LBD refers to Julius John Lankes (1884–1960), illustrator and woodcut print artist. The artist was in fact Frank Utpatel (1905–1980), artist friend of AD who did many jackets and interiors for Arkham House and was also a woodcut artist. He also designed the dust jacket for *HW*. Utpatel's illustration for the just jacked of *Carnacki, the Ghost-Finder* is pasted in S1.1 for "The Path through the Marsh."
2. AD had written (to LBD, 24 August 1960; TLS, University of Kentucky): "I remember the thing most outstanding about you when you visited me here some years ago—transcending even your good looks—was your sense of presence . . ." Comments AD made in his journal (11 October 1946) about her looks were less complimentary.

[65] [TLS]

                                        Nov. 4, 1960

Dear August:

    Will you give me WRITTEN permission to use the poems—whichever they are—of yours, for our anthology, "THE VARIOUS LIGHT". (Definate title.)

    Dr. Muses has hired me as a kind of long-distance secretary, to do all the work of the anthology, and one of my first jobs is to get written permits from all the poets.

    What makes my work so hard is the fact that he simply WON'T send me the list of poems chosen for the book, so the permissions from all you guys must be a kind of over-all affair. I've asked him three times to send me his FINAL choices of all the poems to be used, also where to write for publishers' copyrights, as most were indicated on the separate [*sic*] manuscripts.

    I know he's busy, but confound him, he spent two months traveling around Morocco, of all places. In the meantime, the anthology just "rested". Now when he wants me to do all the work for him (pay or no pay)[,] he seems disinclined to help me do it right. I don't dig that cat at times.

    Anyway, please help me out by hand-writing your permission, and telling where the poems were first published and who owns the copyrights. Maybe someday I can inform you WHICH of your things we took!

Unpublished Letters

As Always,
   Leah

[66] [ALS]

Feb. 23—'61

Dear August—I made a few changes in this poem—please use the copy & throw out the former.

For a while it looked as if the poetry anthology I've been working on with Muses was going to go pft-t-t—some intra-mural war at Falcon's Wing Press. But he has succeeded in saving it—so maybe I can soon let you know which of your poems he's keeping. It's been long enough!

   Best, as ever
   LBD.

P.S. May I have your permission to use "*With Her Death*" and "The Crows" from "H.&W." in a book I'm planning of new & old poems of mine?[1] The project is still tenuous—I haven't even titled the collection yet.
   L B D.

Notes
1. LBD included only "The Crows" in the T.Ms. of *MC*.

[67] [TLS]

April 5. [1961]

Dear August—

Dr. Muses spent Easter with us here—en route from L.A. to Washington, and then on to Locarno. He wants me to get brief biogs. From all you guys,——*where* born (but not when), where most of life's been spent, where published, in what forms, occupations, hobbies. Keep it short, and write it in your own style. This is for THE VARIOUS LIGHT.

Man, what I could tell you about what went on, *re* the anthology! Sometime I will. Poor Charles! He has borne the brunt of the ruckus himself, and was in no wise to blame for the mess. They have treated him dreadfully.

The anthology is slated for next fall—sooner than first planned.

What poems of yours did he take?

The Song of the Sun ~ Leah Bodine Drake

Incidently, when is your own anthology of macabre poems coming out? Could you use another from me about witches? It's brand-new.)[1]

All kinds of things are cooking—I may have some big news to tell you, quite soon!! ***! (No, I am NOT getting married again!)[2]

I hope all is well with you. My father is much, much better, gets around rather briskly, and feels much less pain. I sometimes have my doubts that he HAS cancer—doctors can make mistakes, too. Wish we had the opportunity to have him looked over at Mayo's.

As Ever,
Leah

Notes
1. *FSC* contains "The Witches."
2. Perhaps LBD refers to taking a job with Charles A. Musès in Switzerland. See letter 69.

[68] [ANS]

[Postmarked Parkersburg, WV, 28 April 1961?]

Dear August: Dr. M. called me last night from Wash., D.C. to reassure me the *Various Light* **would** be published. He said to tell you he had taken six of your poems. There seems to be a terrible *contretemps* somewhere that I don't "dig". But I trust him.

Regards, Leah

[69] [TNS]

[Postmarked Parkersburg, WV, 27 June 1961]
June 26

Dear August—I sent you a P.O. card giving my address in Lausanne. I'm taking an editorial job with Muses—flying SAS on July 4th to Copenhagen, & onto Zurich. May be gone a year! I'll send you a nice corny post card of Lac Leman![1]

LBD

Notes
1. I.e., Lake Geneva.

UNPUBLISHED LETTERS

[70] [TLS]

July 15—1961

Dear August—
  I came over by SAS jet last week—it seems as though I'd been here forever!—Everything is so beautiful, and Dr. Muses & I are getting out the anthology with amazing rapidity, considering all the obstacles in the way.
  Here are the poems we are keeping, of yours:
  "Brook Talk"
  "A Lonely Place"
  "Haybarn in Winter"
  "Evening Train" and
  "Veery".[1]
  Charles insists on using *8* of my poems—I have *begged* him to use only 2 or 3—as I am one of the editors & it makes me look so *greedy*.[2] But he overrules me with the argument that he likes my work. Anyway, the book is shaping up grand—we have a goodly company of poets! When we finish this project, then I begin cataloging his enormous library—a kind of job I'll enjoy. Let me hear from you.
  As ever, L B D.

Notes
1. "Haybarn in Winter" and "Veery" were not included.
2. Four poems by LBD appeared in *VL,* three of which had appeared in Musès previous anthology.

[71] [ANS]

828 Murdoch Ave.
Parkesburg, W. Va.
[February? 1962]

Dear August—I flew back, by Swissair jet, on Jan. 25th, spent a week in New York, job-hunting (I landed *two*!) in the publishing line, & plan to return there in about 3 weeks. Depends on my Dad's health when I go.) I found your beautiful anthology here—it is in every way a fit shelf-companion to "Dark of the Moon".

619

The Song of the Sun ❧ Leah Bodine Drake

Our anthology is *finis,* & a gorgeous job it is, too. Will be out in March or April.

Incidently, those are beautiful youngsters of your—the boy is a chip off the old August!

>Best, as always,
>>Leah.

[P.S.] Please overlook the pin-holes in this card! I had it tacked to the wall & find I have no other writing-paper available at the moment. Will keep you posted as to my address in NYC.

>———Leah

[72] [TNS]

>[Postmarked Parkersburg, WV,
>9 June 1962]
>June 9.

Dear August: I have been wondering how you came out, with your operation,[1] which you told me was coming up in the near future? I do hope you are well.

Not long after I got back from Lausanne, my Aunt Mary (with whom my father and Aunt Nancy stayed while I was abroad) fell down the stairs and died a week later.[2] I am swamped—with all the red-tape of estate-settling, and looking after a ten-room house and two elderly sick people.[3] For my father goes from bad to worse, and there seems to be no cure for what he has. But oh, how glad I am I came home when I did! If ever I was needed, this is it!

The latest date set for The Various Light is next fall—I just heard from M. to that effect.

>Best, as ever, Leah

P.S. I don't know who the publisher will be—not Falcon's Wing, at any rate! Will keep you posted.

Notes
1. For adjustment of a bilateral hernia.
2. Mary Gale Drake (b. 26 December 1878) died 29 March.

3. Besides her father, LBD was caring for Anne Harriet Bodine, her mother's twin sister.

[73] [ANS]
[Postmarked Parkersburg, WV,
28 July 1962]

Dear August—Wade Wellman sent me your postal to him—No, I didn't go back to N.Y.C. as my Aunt Mary died and I have to stay here & settle her estate and look after my Father—he recently had half of his stomach removed & is bedfast—probably will never be too well, but is certainly in better shape than he was. At least he's out of pain. I'll be here for quite a while. Best L B D

To Anthony Boucher[1]

[1] [TL]
[Leah Bodine Drake]
Evansville, Ind.,
Dec. 4th, 1951.

FANTASY AND SCIENCE-FICTION,
The Editors;
Gentlemen:
    There's only one thing lacking in your bing-bang magazine, and that's a good weird poem or two. As an old (relatively) "WEIRD TALES" hand, I would like to correct this.[2]
    Incidently, the superstition of the witch-woman who can turn people into rabbits, foxes and other forms of wild life is a still-valid belief in many parts of my own state of Kentucky. Of all states (in the present day,) Kentucky has more witches and belief in witchcraft than any other.
    Hope you will want to see this and start a new trend in F-SF.
    Cordially,

Notes
1. Pseudonym of William Anthony Parker White (1911–1968).

The Song of the Sun ❧ Leah Bodine Drake

2. Verse began to be reprinted from other publications in *F&SF* in the June 1952 issue, but original poems soon began to appear thereafter. LBD's own verse first appeared there in April 1954.

[2] [TLS]

Evansville, Indiana,
April 8th, 1952.

Dear Mr. Boucher:

Here I come again, trying to corrupt you people with my scheme for getting "F. and SF." to publish original verse.

These ribald lines are from what will be my second book of fantasy verse for ARKHAM HOUSE. (No title, as yet.) You may take them all, or just a few. But I still say F. & SF. should use original spooky poetry—there isn't very much good weird verse at all, even among Old Masters, and that has been reprinted until most of it is a mere ghost of itself! (Pun.)

Derleth will publish my new spooker whenever I can get it ready,—maybe next year.

Yours,
L B D.

[3] [TLS]

Evansville, Indiana,
Sept. 21, 1952.

Dear F & SF:

Please be kind to this story—it's my first SF attempt,[1] and all but first attempt at short stories at all, at all!

I certainly haven't given up poetry, but fiction pays so darned much more!

I hope you like it, and keep it for S [*sic*] & SF, but if not—please, pul-leeze let me down aisy!

Yours,
L B D.

1219 S.E. First St.

UNPUBLISHED LETTERS

Notes
1. Unidentified, though possibly "Foxy's Hollow." Only LBD's "Time and the Sphinx" (a reprint) appeared, posthumously, in F&SF, although it was accepted while LBD was alive.

[4] [TNS]
Evansville, Ind.,
March 24, 1953.

Dear F. & S.F. Editors:

If this story looks familiar to you—it should. I sent you a much longer version some time back.

Now I've cut it, and changed the plot considerably. I hope this time you'll find it up your alley.

Yours,
    L B D

[5] [TN]
June 8, 1953.

Dear Editors of F. & S.F.—

I'm delighted to see where you've changed your policy about poetry! It's been good, too.

I'm sending you one which I think you may like. It will be included in my next book of weird verse which Arkham House has asked for. Title of book still unchosen (can't make up my mind) and date uncertain of publication, but it's on the fire.

Yours, LBD.

[Unidentified exchange between Boucher and J. Francis McComas:]
6/30: Thot you might look over. Like idea & many of the lines, but it's spoiled by too many crudities and tritenesses. Any hope in polish?

Jul 10 (where has this been? I just got it yesterday!)
I like this a lot, & (in view of LBD's best work elsewhere) think the polish can come off. But it offers other problems . . . See attached letter.

The Song of the Sun ~ Leah Bodine Drake

[6] [ALS]

July 13 [1953]

Dear Anthony Boucher—

I'll try and see what I can do about tightening up "*Jannigogs*", & shortening it enough to fit the mag. without impairing its sense. You'll hear from me within the week.

"Impatient Leah".

[7] [TLS]

Evansville, Ind.,
July 19, 1953.

Dear A.B.—

I've telescoped eight stanzas into six—not a mean feat! Also changed the wording hither and yon a bit—just a bit.

That IS "talky-place",—NOT talking-place.[1] Be sure and make the printers' [sic] see it my way. I've had enough experience with THAT sort of thing in newspaper work! Oh, the gaffes they used to make with my copy. . . .

Hope this version suits you-all. (Yes, I'm from Kentucky.)

Ever thine,

 L B D.

  Leah Bodine Drake,
   1219 S.E. First Street.

Notes
1. Line 18.

[8] [TNS]

[Postmarked Evansville, IN,
18 August 1953]
Evansville, Indiana
Aug 18, '53.

Dear Mr. Boucher—

I've moved to the address below, so please send all correspondence about "*The Jannigogs*" here. What did you decide about the poem?

 L B. Drake.
3115 E. Mulberry St.

Unpublished Letters

[9] [TLS]

1023 First Street
Henderson, Kentucky[1]
Feb. 11, 1954

Anthony Boucher & J. Francis McComas, Editors:
Gents:

'Tis a poem I'm after sendin' you that is all about the Ould Sod, glory be to God! Sure, and one of you boys is of the Gaelic, or his name wouldn't be McComas, at all, at all. Could you be usin' the poem now?

Suppose you saw the grand award I won recently—the Borestone Mt. Poetry Award of $1250! That's what I'm after callin' a broth of a prize!

Well, I can't keep THAT up—the Gaelic, I mean—any longer. In plain Kentuckian, howcome youall ain't never printed my JANNIGOGS yet? Youall done paid for the piece, and it's been a right smart time since you took it. What little ole hidey-hole you got it hid in? Been wearing out my two lookin' eyes every month for it.

Yours for the honor of the South, suh, AND the Ould Sod,

L B D.

The Hag of the Hollow.

P.S. Why, you even live on "Dana" Street![2]

Notes
1. LBD sent a change of address card indicating the change on 10 October 1953.
2. At 2643 Dana Street, Berkeley, CA. *F&SF* published LBD's poem "The Gods of the Dana."

[10] [TLS]

Henderson, Ky.,
Feb. 24, 1954.

Dear Anthony Boucher (one of the "gods of Dana Street"):

I've re-written the poem, and hope it now suits. Yes, the ending WAS sorta weak and arch.

The Borestone Mt. Poetry Award is given by a group of poetry-minded folks out your own way—shame on you for not knowing! The award I received was for my unpublished book-length typescript of poetry, "This Tilting Dust". A fellow Californian, Eric Barker, (incidently a

The Song of the Sun ~ Leah Bodine Drake

close friend of mine!) was runner-up. The inclosed photo, for which I will sing an Irish curse over the personnel for taking it, was in the N.Y. Post. I call it Howling Wolf, but my friends say it's a true, speaking likeness—i.e., my mouth's open as usual.[1] Please don't send it back.

   Yours, LBD.
   (The Shame of the Kirwins)[2]

Notes
1. "Proud Poets," *New York Post* (29 January 1954): 34. See photo p. 85.
2. Alluding to her maternal ancestors from Virginia, originally from Ireland.

[11] [ANS]

               March 23, 1954
Dear Anthony Boucher:
 What did you decide about my "Gods of the Dana"? I changed it, per request, and sent it back to F & SF a month ago.
 So much of our mail gets delayed because of our moving, that I'm afraid it (your letter) may have been lost.
   Yours,
    LBD.
   Leah B. Drake

[12] [TLS]

               Henderson, Ky.,
               April 24, 1954.
Dear Anthony Boucher:
 Your check for "The Gods of the Dana" received, and thank you, suh.
 Have you people at F. & S.F. ever given any thought to starting a department that would enlighten the public on sorcery, magic and legend? You may or may not be surprised to learn how ignorant even avid readers are, of myth and magic! (You opened up your pages to poetry—an innovation—and now look who've you've got writing for you!) I feel pretty competent to handle a series of articles,—short, and if you wish, slightly on the humorous side—of magical terms and the history, etc of diabolism and the black arts, and related stuff. Purely amateur, let me assure you!

UNPUBLISHED LETTERS

Of course, the man to really write such articles was Charles Williams! Also C. S. Lewis,—but I don't think he'd bother. Between you and me, I think there "is something to it"—so much so that I'd never go to a seance, or dabble in any way in such matters. I'm not wicked enough to enjoy them, and not good enough to expose myself to them and beat them!—the forces of Evil, I mean—spelled with a capitol [sic] E. (Did you ever hear Manly Wade Wellman on this subject? Wow!)
Let me know is [sic] this idea does anything to you.
        Sincerely,
    Leah B. Drake

[13] [TLS]

June 2 [1954]

Dear Anthony Boucher:
    Is this too childish for F & SF?[1]
    Thanks for the copies with my "Gods of the Dana".
    I wish you'd reprint some of the old Dunsany tales out of his "Book of Wonder". Did you ever read a wonderful collection of fantasy tales called "Ringstones", by a writer whose non [sic] de plume is just "Sarban"?[2] It came out about three years ago,—some English firm. "The Khan" is a dilly!
    Yours, LBD

Notes
1. The poem "Cinder-Jewels." It was never published.
2. See AD 43n2.

[14] [TLS]

Henderson, Ky.,
August 13, 1954.

Dear Anthony Boucher:
    First, congrats on your becoming sole First and Foremost of "F&SF".
    The extra work this entails must be the reason for your never telling me if you are keeping a poem I sent you over two months ago.
    I sent "Cinder Jewels" to F&SF on June 3rd. Kindly let me know its fate!

The Song of the Sun ❧ Leah Bodine Drake

> As Ever,
> LBDrake

1023 First Street.

[15] [TLS]

Oct. 14th. [1954]

Dear Tony Boucher:

The change of words from *hurry* to *scurry* is all right with me—in fact, I like it.[1]

Thanks mucho for accepting my poem.

My mother went to school at a "Miss Boucher's School for young Ladies" in Philadelphia—any kin to you?

> Yours,
> LBD.

Notes
1. "The Woods Grow Darker," l. 13.

[16] [ALS]

Feb. 16 [1956]

Dear Tony—

I'd be glad to have "We Move on T. Stone" reprinted in "F & S.F". by the way—it never appeared in any mag., so you don't have to bother about *that* angle. I wrote it just as an end-poem, a kind of summing-up, for "T T D". I like it myself. "Flemish Artists" is a favorite of mine—playful verse, but fun to write. (Augie Derleth called it "a poor poem" in his otherwise-grand review in the Madison (Wis.) *Times!*) Nuts to Augie!

The book is *selling*—not only here, among my friends, but everywhere. I'm delighted and amazed!

Why not reprint a poem or two from my old book, "*Hornbook For Witches*"? I own all copyrights, & I'm to be on the *$64,000 Question*, the T-V show, someday, on *Witch Craft!* A good tie-in.

> As Ever,
> L B D.

UNPUBLISHED LETTERS

[17] [TLS]
Evansville, Ind.
March 16, 1956

Dear Tony—

The possibility of me appearing on that goddam T-V show seems fading farther and farther into the wild blue yonder. And man, do I need that money! (I take it for granted I'd win—everyone else does.)

The worst part of it all is, that I sat in Steve Carlin's office, his secretary at hand, and heard him say right out and in perfect English, "I'm not going to give you the soft soap we give some of our prospects—"thank you for letter us talk to you and if we want you we will call you," and all that guff . . . . . I'm telling you that you are definately in, and we'll get in touch with you in say, two or three weeks". (It was then Nov. 20.)

Does that bear out the last report: "there is nothing definate" . . .? Hell, no.

I think they are weaseling out of it. I don't know why. I hear from another source that Carlin was quote, "Terribly impressed with Miss Drake". Well, what's he waiting for, and why is the time set so far ahead that it is practically in the 21st Century?

I am going to do an article for the MERCURY[1] on witch-hunts, then and now, and they may hold it for months. what I had in mind for F&SF was entirely different and I can take my time about it, then send it to you and if you want it, you can keep it until I appear. Or, if you'd rather wait until I actually DO appear, and heaven knows that may be not at all, from the way things seem to be shaping up—well, we'll just have to wait and see.

I had planned, for your mag., an article on survivals of witchcraft in modern times—more than you'd think. or we could just wait and I could do one on the program itself. Let me know.

I'm getting sick of the very word "witch". Guess I'll just buy a ticket on the Irish Sweeps and let nature take its course. The back of me hand to the $64000 ? !

Yours,
   The Witch of the Wabash,
      LBD.

The Song of the Sun ~ Leah Bodine Drake

P.S. You asked how to contact the Cowan office. Don't write to the address given on the Revlon show—send your letter direct to Steven Carlin, of Louis G. Cowan, Inc., N.Y.C

Tell them your business, your hobbies, and what subject—in your case, opera? They like a contrast between the prospect's work and his hobby.

lbd

Carlin is the director and manager of both the $64000 ? and "The Big Surprise".

Notes
1. LBD had nothing in the *American Mercury* except a letter.

[18] [ALS]

May 7th [1956]

Dear Tony——

How "thoughty" of you to give "This T. Dust" a mention in the pages of "F. & S.F."! I hope the people who buy it, on your recommendation, won't be disappointed when they find it isn't a second "Hornbook for Witches"!

August Derleth sent me the review, which was very considerate of him. (He's such a nice guy.)

Incidently, I've been asked by the *"Atlantic Monthly"* to do a review of poetry books for them, now & then—and I'm pleased as Punch about it! (*Was* Punch pleased—about anything?)

Have you read "Directions in the Sun" by Eric Barker? (Merle Armitage Press, Yucca, Calif. $3.00) He is a friend of mine & a very fine poet. You'd enjoy his work. One of the poems is a Fantasy, which you might like to reprint. (He surely could use the money—he's poor, like me!) It's called *"On the Possibility of Un-Earthly Visitors"*. (Flying S.'s) Also, *"Isaac Newton"*—a grand poem! The address of the Armitage Press is Manzanita Ranch, Yucca, Cal.

Robinson Jeffers has a foreword to it.

I am becoming less & less inclined to believe that other planets are trying to communicate with us. I've been re-reading C. S. Lewis, & I agree with him that *our Tellus* is the only bad apple in the barrel, & God protects His other worlds from man!

Tony, do you know if his (Lewis',—not God's) "Out of the Silent Planet" & "Perelandra" are available any more in the Avon Pocket Books? I have to get my copies from the Public library. (I have all Lewis' other books, even his fairytales.) Thanks again for your kind words.
  Ever Thine etc., LBD.

[19] [TNS]
Dec. 7th, 1956

Dear Tony:
  This is a long 'un[1]—but it may be called a fable in poetry, rather than prose.
  You'll be interested to know that one of your favorite poems, "FLEMISH ARTISTS", has been included in the latest Borestone Mt. Poetry Award anthology—"POETRY AWARDS: 1956".
  I think you would have liked the last poem of mine in the September ATLANTIC—"The WORD OF WILLOW". It is right up F&SF's alley.[2]
    Merry Christmas, etc.,
      from
       L B D.

Notes
1. "Peddler's Pack" remained unpublished.
2. *F&SF* reprinted the poem in the December 1957 issue.

[20] [TLS]
Evansville, Ind.,
Jan. 21, 1957.

Dear Tony:
  I wonder if you ever received a poem—a pretty long one—called "PEDDLER'S PACK", which I sent to F&SF on Dec. 7th?
  We've had trouble with our mail,—the ATLANTIC never got a poem I had sent them last November, and nobody seems able to find it. Will you look through your poetry files for this poem, and let me know if you got it or not? Then I'll take steps, and see what's up with the local P.O.
  Incidently, "*This Tilting Dust*" has been placed on the poetry list for the coming National Book Awards next March. There are 45 books all

The Song of the Sun ❧ Leah Bodine Drake

told nominated for these honors, 15 of them poetry. The people who make these nominations are 1700 book-reviewers, librarians and booksellers. I'd like to win it, but that's almost too much to hope for.

I received the latest F&SF anthology, and like it. Glad to see C. S. Lewis. Did you know he has a new book out?[1] He has been one of the molders of my thought since I discovered him.

    Sincerely,
     Leah

Notes

1. *The Best from Fantasy and Science Fiction, Sixth Series* contained both LBD's "The Woods Grow Darker" and Lewis's "The Shoddy Lands," *F&SF*, February 1956. The book was probably *Surprised by Joy: The Shape of My Early Life* (1955).

[21] [TNS]

        Evansville, Ind.,
        April 3rd, 1957.

Dear Tony:

Whatever happened to my poem, "Peddler's Pack"?

I sent it to you 'way back—Dec. 7, 1956. As I didn't hear from you, I wrote again asking if the manuscript had ever reached you, sometime in Feb. of this year. It's been 4 months ago that I sent it.

Will you look it up and let me know its fate?

  Sincerely,
   LBD.

[Note by Boucher:] returned May 27

[22] [TLS]

        Evansville, Indiana,
        May 30th, 1957.

Dear Tony:

My poem, THE WORD OF WILLOW, was published in the ATLANTIC MONTHLY, September 1956.

I need not tell you to be sure to get permission [Also a credit-line.] from Mr. Edward Weeks, the editor, if you care to reprint it. I inclose the poem.

Unpublished Letters

Tony, do you know the author and title of a book I am anxious to find out? (Boy, am I helpful!—don't know the title OR author!) The plot bordered on SF—I read it a good many years ago,—right after the war, or during it. This was the idea: astronomers discovered with horror that the Moon was off its track and was rapidly approaching the Earth. Warnings were issued, and the resulting book was about the odd things mankind did in the face of a total destruction of his planet—people dug themselves in, one woman raided the unguarded Lourve [sic] and used the "Mona Lisa" as one side of her makeshift little lean-to. It was a well-written book, English I'm sure. The title was something like this: "The Collyer Papers" or "The Collier Report", or the "Bennet Manuscript". . . . . does any of this ring a bell?[1] The library cannot help me, for naturally they don't know all the plots of their books and I can't remember author or name! BUT I *know* the author was British, and the book was one of those slim things gotten out during the war to save paper.

As Ever,

L.B.D.

Notes
1. LBD refers to *The Hopkins Manuscript* (London: Gollancz, 1939) by R[obert] C[edric] Sheriff (1896–1975).

[23] [TNS]

[Postmarked Evansville, Ind.
8 June 1957]

Dear Tony: Thank you for coming to my aid *re* the SF book I wanted. The library here had it in their stacks, and I've already checked it out and gulped it down—it reads just as good the second time! Why don't you reprint it as a serial in F&SF?

I'm glad you like my willowy poem. I think it's just right for F&SF.

Love and kisses,

LBD.

The Song of the Sun ~ Leah Bodine Drake

[24] [TLS]

Evansville, Jul 22. [1957]

Dear Tony:

After a year and a half, and after the poem was published, I make the amazing discovery that technically it is not perfect!

I refer to "THE WORD OF WILLOW",—which is, of course, in *terza rima*—aba, bcb, cdc, etc., etc., for as long as the poet can keep it up. Well, upon my using my own poem for a copy, while writing another terza rima,[1] I found to my own flabbergastion that in the square middle of the poem I have departed in no uncertain way from the pattern. Oh, unfrabjous day, boo-hoo, scudda-hay![2]

It's too late for the ATLANTIC, of course, to change it, and they never noticed the mistake, and evidently none of the readers did, for I've had several letters praising that poem,—I didn't even notice the error myself, until yesterday. So, when you reprint it, will you make the change, noted below, as it will appear in my next book (whenever that is.)[3]

I inclose a separate sheet with the poem written *as it should have been*. (I think the answer to my booboo is, that I shortened the poem before sending it to the Atlantic, and in doing so, of course upset the rhyme-sequences.)

Yours,

L. B. D.

Notes

1. Unidentified and possibly nonextant. "High Wire" was written before "The Word of Willow" and consists of rhymed tercets.
2. See AD 41n2.
3. In the *Atlantic*, ll. 13 and 15 read "And pollarded princes, their lore seeped out of mind," [. . .] "And haunted houses. Some of them are resigned." The end rhymes should have matched *so* in l. 11. LBD's other rhymes in the poem are far from perfect; e.g., *drip*, *harps*, and *sap*, to name just one example.

[25] [ANS]

Parkersburg, W. Va.
Dec. 27, 1957.

Dear Tony—

What have I done to deserve all these free monthly copies of

UNPUBLISHED LETTERS

"F&SF."? I don't subscribe, but each month, for the past three I've received a lovely copy of your spooky-book. Howcome? Also, why???
Of course I love it. I have no objections if you want to *force* them on me! Happy New Year & all that jazz.
   Yours,
    Leah

To William Rose Benét

[1] [TLS]
         Evansville, Ind.,
         June 7th, 1948.
Dear Mr. Benét:
   Knowing your wide humanitarian interests, I'm sending you some literature which I hope will impress you with the need for national legislation. I've written to all this states' congressmen and senators, and while they claim to be interested, you know what politicians are like! Cruelty to animals never seems to be a major crime,—not half as bad as cruelty to the dairy lobby, and the like! I've already bothered them with plans on behalf of the "Displaced Persons" Bill (the Stratton Bill), and I suppose I'll keep on bothering them as long as brutality and injustice walk this earth. (I'll admit that "our" Ed Mitchell, Evansville's own GOP Representative,[1] is very responsive and good-hearted.)
 I wonder if somehow the SRL couldn't plug this anti–steel trap campaign a little? These little booklets will give you only too vivid an idea of how badly action is needed in this affair.
 By the way, I hope you can use my poem, "CITY ZOO,"[2] in the SRL. The Evansville zoo is the "inspiration," shall I say?—of it. well-run zoos are bad enough—but a poorly-run zoo is a small hell.
      Cordially,
      L B D.

Notes
1. Edward Archibald Mitchell (1910–1979), U.S. Representative from Indiana.
2. Nonextant. Her poem "Gazelles in a Zoo" had been published by this time.

The Song of the Sun ~ Leah Bodine Drake

[2]   [TLS]

[Leah Bodine Drake]
1219 S.E. First St.,
Evansville, Indiana.
October 25th, 1948.

Dear William Rose Benét:

I am starting a radio poetry program over our new station here, next month. We will be affiliated with Mutual and ABC, and my program will be every Saturday afternoon, fifteen minutes, just before the Met Opera program, which we will carry. WJPS will serve Indiana, Kentucky and Illinois.

I plan to use poems of modern poets almost exclusively,—which gives me an elastic margin, for several, although now dead, surely come into that category. This includes the poems of Stephen Vincent Benét and Elinor Wylie (the latter being my personal idol.)[1]

Now I'd like your permission to use the poems of your late brother and of your late wife on my program, and also your own poems, whenever I wish. May I have your permission?

Also, may I read poems from the current SRLs, such as Eric Wilson Barker's, Sara Henderson Hay, etc., if I give credit to both poet and publication? (That's taken for granted, of course, in every case.)

I may see you in person this winter: Gustav Davidson of the PSA, is, as you very likely know, getting up a WEEK OF POETRY next December, and asked me to come on and read my poems, as a part of the group called "the younger poets." I'm not sure if *that* means "younger" in years,—or poetic achievement! Both, I reckon!

Very Truly Yours,
L. B. D.

Notes

1. Stephen Vincent Benét (1898–1943), American poet, short story writer, and novelist, was William's (1886–1950) brother. Elinor Wylie (1885–1928), American poet and novelist popular in the 1920s and 1930s, was William's second wife.

Unpublished Letters

[3] [TLS]
[Leah Bodine Drake]
1219 S.E. First St.,
Evansville, Ind.
November 24th, 1948.

Dear Mr. Benet:

Thank you for your long letter *re* the obstacles in the path of the radio poetry reader. It *does* seem to be in a snarl!

However, the program here has been shelved for the time being,—it seems they've hooked up with Ted Malone(!) and one poetry spot is about all, they feel, that the good burghers of Evansville would stand for.

I had hoped to meet many of you PSA members this winter, if I took up Gustav Davidson's invitation to participate in his POETRY WEEK, but it didn't work out that way.

You may be interested in knowing that August Derleth of ARKHAM HOUSE, (which as you know publishes only fantasy) is bringing out a book (my first!) of my weird poems. Not things like the one you all published),—HONEY FROM THE LION—but only my more spooky verse. It will be called "A HORNBOOK FOR WITCHES,["] and will be out in about two years,—massey, that's a long time to wait, when it's one's first book! It will be, I believe, ARKHAM H.'s second book of poetry, the first being the anthology "DARK OF THE MOON," you remember.[1] The best thing about MY BOOK (you can just hear me say it in capitals!) is, that August, whom I know personally (and a grand person he is, too) wrote me and suggested the whole idea to me, and is going to finance the job and pay me 10% royalties. I had a horrible idea that poets always had to put up the money for their own first book,—but I must have been wonderfully wrong!

Cordially,
L B D.
(Miss) Leah Bodine Drake.

Notes
1. Benét had two poems in *DM*: "Metropolitan Nightmare" (1927) and "Nightmare Number Three" (1942).

The Song of the Sun ❧ Leah Bodine Drake

[4] [ALS]

            Evansville
            Indiana
            May 5, 1950.

Dear SRL.—

 It was with shock and sorrow that I read in this morning's paper of the sudden death of William Rose Benét.[1]

 Please accept my deep sympathy for your loss—a double loss for WRB was not only a beloved feature of the Review but your friend as well, I know.

 Mr. Benét will not only be missed in the world of poetry, but in that of liberal thought whose issue he so vigorously championed. I did not always agree with WRB in all of his opinions or estimations, but I always admired him. I am sorry he is gone.

 Very Truly yours
 Leah Bodine Drake.

Notes
1. On 4 May.

To Joseph Payne Brennan

[1] [TNS]

[THE FALCON'S WING PRESS
INDIAN HILLS • COLORADO USA • FALCON'S WING PRESS BUILDING]
          [Postmarked Switzerland]
          June 13, 1960

Dear Mr. Brennan—Dr. Muses and I like your poems very much, and are keeping three—THE SERPENT WAITS, WASTE OF DUNES, THE MAN I MET. When we make our final selections, we may accept more. These first choices of all the poets are tentative. Reply to me at my address in the States; 801 Avery Street, Parkersburg, West Va. I leave Locarno the end of June.

UNPUBLISHED LETTERS

Be sure and indicate where these poems were first published, and be sure to obtain permits from the magazines, etc. Thank you for submitting such fine work.
   Cordially,
    L B D

[2] [ANS]
            Parkersburg, W. Va.
              July 12. [1960]
Dr. Mr. Brennan—I don't think the use of the chosen poems in the Derleth anthology[1] would rule them out for ours—but I will pass the word along to Dr. Muses. Didn't you once write a longish poem about a walker in the woods, describing the trees, plants, etc? "This is the place the walker(?) goes"—all my books are still in storage back in Evansville, Indiana. I can't check.
    L B D.
[P.S.] Thank you for your kind words!

Notes
1. *FSC*. The book contained fourteen poems by Brennan, none of which is in *VL*.

[3] [ANS]
              August 4—'60
Dear Joseph Payne Brennan—Thank you for your book—it was such a wonderful surprise to get it. I am copying "Strayer's Song",—"A Fable"—"Heart of Earth"—"Communions"—to send to Dr. Muses.[1] He leaves for Korea soon so it may be some time before I can let you know his decision. But I'm sure he'll like your things as well as I do. This card might be an illustration to "Strayer's"—![2] L B D.

Notes
1. The four poems named, from Brennan's book *Heart of Earth* (1949), a poetry collection, all appeared in *Various Light*. LBD had read "Strayer's Song" in *Poetry Chap-Book* (Summer 1948). See AD 16n2.
2. The card depicts "La forêt vivante" by the German artist Marianne Schneegans (1904–1997).

The Song of the Sun ~ Leah Bodine Drake

[4] [TNS]

Nov. 9 [1960]

Dear Mr. Brennan:

At the risk of repeating myself, may I ask for your written permission (per orders from Dr. Muses) for the use of these poems in our anthology THE VARIOUS LIGHT: "THE SERPENT WAITS," "THE MAN I MET", "WASTE OF DUNES",[1] "HEART OF EARTH", "COMMUNIONS", "STRAYER'S SONG", "A FABLE".

I haven't yet been told by my co-editor whether he has accepted the second batch of poems I sent him. He's been traveling and anyway, has all the manuscripts in Switzerland. He has asked me to do all the letter-work on the book, but as he has the stuff with him, it means I have to ask each poet all over again for copyright data, where each poem was published. Please bear with me and give me such information again! This book is really getting done—but the hard way!

  Cordially,
    L.B.D.

Notes

1. *VL* did not take "The Man I Met," "Waste of Dunes," or "Heart of Earth." "The Man I Met" and "The Serpent Waits" appeared in *FSC*.

[5] [TNS]

Feb. 22, 1961

Dear Joseph P. Brennan—I'm sending your letter of Jan. 26 on to Locarno, for Dr. Muses' files. Thanks for the permission to reprint, and congrats on having the 2 poems accepted. I don't know which poems of yours will eventually be accepted, as there was quite a hitch in the progress of the anthology (which we've titled, THE VARIOUS LIGHT.) It's too long a story to relate here, but it looked for a while this winter as if the book was not going to be published. Dr. Muses, however, fought a winning battle to continue it—I had a cable from him, from "La Suisse", last week, O.K.ing it—thank heavens!

  Best regards,
    LBDrake.

[6] [TNS]

Feb. 28 [1961?]

Dear Joseph Payne Brennan—Just a note to ask you to simply ignore any letters you might get from a C. M. Spicher at Indian Hills, Colo., saying that the anthology, "The Various Light" is off. IT IS NOT BEING DISCONTINUED. She has no authority to make any such statement, and Dr. Muses wishes me to write all our poets and tell them so. The book is going forward as planned. There's been misunderstanding there somehow, but just disregard any statement made to the effect that the anthology is abandoned.
                      Best regards,
                            LBD

[7] [TNS]

April 5, '61

Dear JPB—
    Please send me a short biog. of where you were born (not when), where lived most of your life, where published, what form, and hobbies.
    As we will use these biogs. In THE VARIOUS LIGHT written in each poet's own word, make it interesting!
    As planned now, the anthology will be out in the Fall of this year.
    Best,
        L B D

P.S. Did Dr. Muses accept any more poems?

[8] [ANS]

June 19, 1961

Dear Joseph—I'll give you my address *after* July 4th—
        17 av des Peupliers,
            La Rosiaz, Lausanne Vaud,
                Switzerland.
    Am taking a position as editorial assistant with Muses—*Not* with the Barth people, those nuts!
    Yours, LBD.

The Song of the Sun ~ Leah Bodine Drake

[9]   [ANS]

March 28 [1962]

Dear Joseph P.—Congratulations on your literary successes! I'll watch our TV for the thrillers.[1] As to the 200 "Hornbooks" sold—I had an autograph party, given me by the local bookstore in Evansville (Ind.) & sold over 150 copies. Then, too, I sent out cards to a great many people, & sold a lot that way. Augie D. had given me 50 copies extra. Also, the "Magazine of Fantasy & Science F." gave me a line or two. It's a rat-race!
Luck! LBD

Notes
1. The Lethal Ladies episode of *Thriller* (16 April 1962) aired television adaptations of two stories by Brennan, "Good-Bye, Mr. Bliss" (as "Good-Bye, Dr. Bliss") and "The Pool" (as "Murder on the Rocks").

[10]   [TNS]

June 21, 1963

Dear JPB—

I don't say the anthology is dead—let's just say it is lying dormant at the moment. Dr. M. isn't associated with the Barth group now, so their financial backing is off. They behaved rather badly on this, and other, projects. If the V.L. sees the light of publication, it will have to be with other financing. M. is working on this, and eventually the book may come out. I hope so.

My father died just a month ago. He had had bone cancer and kidney trouble for years and the past year he spent in bed, growing weaker all the time. His death was for him a blessed release, but for me, of course, it leaves a big hole in my life. I will go back to Switzerland someday, but right now I must stay here—an elderly aunt makes her home with me.
Best regards,
L B D.

UNPUBLISHED LETTERS

[11] [ANS]
[Postmarked Parkersburg, WV,
28 March 1964]

Just got back from three months in Lausanne. Dr. M. and I went over *The Various Light* without mercy, eliminating & substituting. It *should* be out next Fall—*let us devotley* [sic] *hope!* I have a new Parkersburg address—812½ W. Va. Ave.
Regards, LBD.

[12] [ANS]
[Postmarked Parkersburg, WV.
21 April 1964]

Dear J.P.B.—I left out "*Fable*" from the list of poems we are using from you. The list should read "*Communions*", "*Strayer's S.*", "*Fable*" & "*The S. Waits*". (We jettisoned *all* biogs.) I think creative activity comes in waves—great surges of power, then long troughs of barrenness—then the great swell again,—Oh joy!
Yours, L B D.

To Grace and Fletcher Stewart

[1]   [ALS, on printed card]
[With all good wishes for / Christmas / and the New Year]
[January 1955]
Dear Grace & Fletcher—
I don't see why you all persist in the living 'way off thar in California, when your friends around here want you back. I see where I'll be reduced to coming out there to see you. I have several friends in Cal. that I want to see some day, so maybe the Drakes will take a motor trip out there sometime. The "head office" of *Poetry Awards* (which bestowed that princely prize on me last January) is in L.A. (Occidental College) Dr. Robert Thomas Moore, a professor there, is the director of P. A.[1] He and Mrs. Moore attended the PSA dinner, & he presented the check for

The Song of the Sun ~ Leah Bodine Drake

$1250.00 to me personally,—as flashbulbs flashed and a national hook-up carried our (brilliant!) words over the national air! Mother went with me to New York, and she and the Moores discovered that they had many friends in common—Mother's father had known *his* father back in Jersey! They are grand people—if you go down to L.A. look them up. They live at 582 Meadow Grove Place, Pasadena. (This *is* near L.A.?)

I've just been invited to be an Advisory Editor on a new poetry magazine published at Chadron College, Chadron, Neb. "Poetry Public".[2] I'm the only *female* on the board—the rest are well-known (men) poets & English professors. I don't have to *move* to Nebraska as some of my friends here thought! Watch the Feb. "*Atlantic*"—I have 2 poems coming out.[3]

How are "old" and young Stewarts? How I'd love to see you all!
As Ever, Leah.

Notes
1. Robert Thomas Moore (1882–1958), American businessman, ornithologist, philanthropist, and founder and editor-in-chief of the Borestone Mountain Poetry Awards.
2. Lawrence R. Holmes (1906–1981), an instructor at Chadron State College in Nebraska (1956 to 1965), edited the *Poetry Public Letter*.
3. "Flemish Artists—Fifteenth Century" appeared in the *Atlantic* for February 1955; the other poem, "Drone," appeared in June.

[2] [TLS]

Evansville, Dec. 23,—56.

Dear Grace and Fletch:

As you can see by the inclosed envelope, I sent you people a card to the wrong address, the old one. Didn't know you all had moved.

I was so glad to get your Round Robin letter, and the note on the card (and what a beautiful card, too!) I can hardly believe Clark is so *old*! Your own studies sound exciting—the semantics especially. I love words!

To enlarge on the ATLANTIC bit: last summer the editor, Edward Weeks,[1] wrote to me and asked if I'd be interested in doing an article on the new poets, for them. They have a regular book reviewer, for novels, etc., but none for volums of poetry. They have been publishing quite a good many of my poems lately, and I suppose think that if I can write it,

Unpublished Letters

I can criticize it,—which isn't always the case, really. They've been shipping me packages of books ever since! Naturally, I said I'd enjoy writing the article for them!) Now, today, a couple more came—I have about 13 books already, and will be getting new ones, as they come out, up until March. Then I'm to write up the six or 7 poets I think most worthy of a review, and the article will appear, presumably, in a late Spring issue of the ATLANTIC. I'm proud as a peacock,—and for one reason: that *they* asked *me*, not vice versa!

Did I, or did I not, tell you last winter about having been interviewed, while in New York, for the "$64,000 Question", and being told definately that I'd be on the show—subject, Witchcraft—? Well, nothing so far has come of that interview or the promise. The "Big Surprise", (put on by the same outfit) called me last August, and wanted to know if I'd switch from the 64000? to *their* show. As they hand out even *more* money, I naturally agreed! Even sent them per request, a brief history of Witchcraft, and the books they could read on the subject[2]—almost wrote my own questions. Not a word from them since. I am so mad at both their houses, that I'd put a hex on [']em,—if I could. (No, I wouldn't—I've read enough about hexes, and magic, to know that it can kick back—if you believe in it,—which, frankly I do, a little.) (Don't tell Fletcher this—he'll think I'm nuts.)

Give me the lowdown about You Know Who, won't you? I had a card from her this year, and she bought one of my books, and yet I never write to her any more. I wish she didn't admire my work so much—it's embarrassing, as I don't care to keep up the acquaintance. Her letters are in[n]ocuous enough. (Is that spelled right? It hath an odd look.)

Love to all, and write,
Leah.

P.S. I just learned, via air-mail, that a poem of mine, "*The Hand*" (still unpublished, of course) had won the ($100) "*Arthur D. Ficke Sonnet Award*".[3] The prizes are $400—supposed to be all in one lump, but the PSA split it four ways. Well, we all probably can use $100 apiece—all poets being poor!

Notes
1. Edward A. Weeks (1898–1989), writer, essayist, and editor of *The Atlantic*.

The Song of the Sun ❧ Leah Bodine Drake

2. The second page of LBD's notebook, *Witchcraft: Notes by Leah Bodine Drake* (1956), is a list of nineteen "Books Read on the Subject" of witchcraft. The notebook likely was the source of what LBD would have spoken about on the television program.
3. Arthur Davison Ficke (1883–1945), American poet, playwright, and Japanese art expert. He had a national reputation as a "poet's poet" and an expert sonneteer. The award was established and funded by the poet Witter Bynner. The four winners were LBD, "The Hand"; Margaret Haley Carpenter, "Imminent Harvest"; Frances Minturn Howard, "The Meek Shall Inherit the Earth"; Ulrich Troubetzkoy, "The Diesel Horn."

[3] [ALS]

Evansville, Ind.
Aug 2—1957

Dear Grace—

This is a letter I've had in mind to write for months—I have the sad news for you of my Mother's sudden death—from a heart-attack—just three days after Christmas. We buried our precious one on New Year's Eve afternoon—and a part of me lies in that earth. Mother was more than just a beloved parent; she was a delightful companion to me. Life is strange and queer with her not in it.

I hope all is well with you and yours. Mrs. Rhinelander and I often talk of you—I see her at St. Paul's. Incidently, we have a *wonderful* new rector—Father Webb—the most popular priest we've had there, in my time at least.[1]

I have been writing quite a lot for the *Atlantic Monthly*—had an article (per their request) on poetry in the June issue & they will publish a long poem in their Oct. one—"The Hellenic World". My book, "This Tilting Dust" made the *list of nominations* for the last "National Book Awards" (but failed to win!) How proud *Mother* would have been! But I believe she knows . . . . . and helps me!

Do write soon
        Lovingly,
           Leah

Notes
1. W. Robert Webb (1910–1988) of St. Paul's Episcopal Church at 301 SE 1st Street in Evansville.

UNPUBLISHED LETTERS

With Lawrence S. Thompson

[1]   [ALS, University of Kentucky]

Henderson, Ky.,
Oct. 25th, 1953.

My dear Prof. Thompson:

Your flattering request for copies of some of my poems is, as you see, being answered "Yes" so quickly that I'm practically breathing down your neck.

I'm now living back in the Grand Old State (have just joined the staff of the Henderson GLEANER & JOURNAL as special features writer). Newspaper work and science-fiction are side-lines with me, though. Poetry is my heart's darling!

I am inclosing poems written both in type and longhand, as some collections prefer one, some the other. The U. of Buffalo, for instance, wanted some of my work-sheets, to show the "creative process at work".

I am writing out, therefor, "FINAL GREEN" "HONEY FROM THE LION" and "PRECARIOUS GROUND". The latter recently won the $300 First Prize from the Borestone Poetry Awards, as being "the best poem published in 1952 by a magazine of the English-speaking world."

I've typed "THE LARIAT: 6000 B.C.", which won second price from the Poetry Society of America, of which I'm a member. Also, "FANTASY IN A FOREST", which was one of Thomas Moult's "BEST POEMS" of 1941, and has since appeared in several editions of a text-book for British schools, published by Macmillan's of London, "Adventure into Poetry".

My manuscript for the HORNBOOK is at its publisher[']s, Arkham House. The original manuscripts of its 50-odd poems are mixed up in many notebooks. But perhaps August Derleth, the publisher of A. House, might give you the manuscript. He's a grand fellow!

Whenever I get up to Lexington again rest assured I shall drop in on the Margaret I. King Library, both to see your fine collection and to meet its director.

The Song of the Sun ❧ Leah Bodine Drake

> Cordially,
>
> Leah Bodine Drake.
>
> 1023 South First Street.

[2]   [TL (carbon), University of Kentucky]

> Mrs. [*sic*] Drake is a truly significant new poet, and we should watch her work carefully.
>
> LST

11 November 1953

Miss Leah Bodine Drake
1023 South First Street
Henderson
Kentucky

My dear Miss Drake:

When I returned to my desk after an absence of over two weeks I was delighted to find your good letter of 25 October and manuscripts you were kind enough to send. We are delighted to have them, for, as I have already written you, I have been greatly impressed by your creative work. The Commonwealth should be very proud of you.

I hope you will think of us as the regular repository for your manuscripts. We will be most grateful for anything that you excavate from your notebooks, particularly your work-sheets (for which I envy the University of Buffalo).

In a few days I will write to August Derleth and ask him to try to find the manuscript for *Hornbook* for us.[1] I will tell him that you referred me to him.

I shall look forward to meeting you some time soon, in Henderson if not in Lexington.

> Sincerely yours,
>
> Lawrence S. Thompson
> Director of Libraries

UNPUBLISHED LETTERS

Notes
1. See AD 47.

[3] [ALS, University of Kentucky]
Jan. 2, 1955
Dear Prof. Thompson—
Knowing of the interest you take in my work, I thought this recent clipping might interest you. (Lordy, am I repeating myself in one *sentence*?!!)
I'll have two poems in the next (Feb.) *Atlantic Monthly*. They asked me if I'd mind being included in their "Young Poets" issue?—"mind"? I'm *flattered*!
                    Cordially,
                    L. B. D.

[4] [ALS, University of Kentucky]
Henderson,
Jan. 10th, 1955
Dear Director Thompson——
Here are the hand-written copies of the poems recently accepted by "*The Atlantic*" which you asked for—hope you (and future students of Drake?!!) can read my handwriting—Nobody *else* can!
                    Yours,
                    Leah B. Drake

[Enclosures: "Drone" and "Flemish Artists—Fifteenth Century."]

[5] [ALS, University of Kentucky]
UNIVERSITY OF KENTUCKY
LEXINGTON, KENTUCKY
17 Nov. [1958]
UNIVERSITY OF KENTUCKY LIBRARIES
    MARGARET I. KING LIBRARY

My dear Miss Drake:
    I have just had an inquiry from the Guggenheim people about you. I

The Song of the Sun ~ Leah Bodine Drake

said everything favorable I could think of and concluded by saying that a grant to you would be a real contribution to American letters.

Best of luck!

Sincerely,

Lawrence S. Thompson

[6] [TLS, University of Kentucky]

Parkersburg, W. Va.
Jan. 1, 1959.

Dear Dr. Thompson:

Do you remember that, long ago, I promised to send you some work-sheets of poems?

Frankly, I hardly ever think about saving them, while I am writing—just throw them away. I don't know why this incident is an exception, but anyway I saved the drafts of this poem, which I wrote while in New Harmony, Ind., last summer.

I have a friend, Jane Blaffer Owens,[1] [sic] of Houston, who has bought up over a dozen old Rappite houses in this small town.[2] The Rappites were a Dutch religious sect who settled there in frontier times. They sold their village, lock, stock and barrel, to Robert Dale Owen, the English schoolmaster, idealist and—let's face it—screwball. He and his Utopians bought the houses, and all—the first and only instance known of a *town* being sold.

After their socialistic experiment failed (as of course it did), many of these well-built but primitive structures were allowed to fall into ruin. Jane, who is a Texas oil heiress (her father owned the Humble Oil Co., which in Texas is the equal of the Standard Oil elsewhere), and has twenty million in her own right, had married the great-grandson of Robert Dale Owen, Kenneth Dale Owen. He, too, is a multi-millionaire (oil).

Between them, they own pretty much of Posey Co., Indiana,—in a beautifully rural part of the state where the Wabash flows into the Ohio. Wild birds use the swamps around the rivers' juncture as a migration-stop. (That part of Ind., which includes Evansville, is what Audubon called the great bird-path of America. Every season, fall and spring, we could see the great flocks go over.)

Well, Jane has furnished many of these old houses, in a quaint style that preserves their frontier spirit, but with comfort added! She lets those of her friends who are writers (and most of her friends are) stay at these houses free of charge, with their grocery bills 'for free', to do their writing in peace and quiet. That's where I wrote over a dozen poems between July 1st and 21st last summer! It was wonderful. What added to the joy was that Dr. Walter Starkie,[3] the Irish writer and expert on Spanish gipsies and music, was staying there, with his wife, in another of June's houses. We all had dinner together almost every night and became firm friends. I will see them in New York this month, when I go there on business.

It's a good thing I wrote so many poems in a bunch, for heaven knows I've written NOTHING since getting this Society-editor job on the paper! By the way, Ronnie Butler, one of your bright young men at the University, is the son of our city editor here. Ronnie is dear!

This poem has been selected by Modern Age,[4] but not yet published. My best to you and yours for the new little ol' year.
                Cordially,
                L B D

[P.S.] Sorry I can't seem to keep up with my Library dues—too poor.

P.S.S. Would the U. of Ky. be interested in having Dr. Starkie talk to the students? He gives marvelous talks on Gipsy lore and magic, etc. Although he and his wife Augusta live in Madid, they are in New York for the winter.

Notes
1. Jane Blaffer Owen (1915–2010) of Houston, was the daughter of Robert Lee Blaffer and Sarah Campbell Blaffer and wife of Kenneth Dale Owen (1903–2002), a descendant of Robert Owen. Her father helped start the Humble Oil Company (now Exxon). Her mother was the daughter of William Thomas Campbell, founder of the Texas Oil Company (formally known as Texaco). The group of houses LBD refers to were known as the Blaffer Trust Foundation Center. The *PSA Bulletin* noted that one year another poet stayed there as "poet-in-residence," and so LBD may have stayed in New Harmony in a similar capacity.
2. I.e., New Harmony, IN, not Parkersburg. The Harmony Society established Harmony, IN, in 1814 under the leadership of George Rapp. The 20,000-acre

The Song of the Sun ~ Leah Bodine Drake

settlement initially was the home of Lutherans who had separated from the official church in the Duchy of Württemberg and immigrated to the US. The Harmonists built a new town in the wilderness, but in 1824 sold their property and went to Pennsylvania. Robert Owen, a Welsh industrialist and social reformer, purchased the town in 1825 intending to create a new utopian community and renamed it New Harmony.
3. Walter Fitzwilliam Starkie (1894–1976), Irish scholar, Hispanist, author, and musician. Known principally for his popular travel writing: *Raggle-Taggle* (1933), *Spanish Raggle-Taggle* (1934) and *Don Gypsy* (1936).
4. "With Her Death" did not appear in *Modern Age*.

[7]   [TL (carbon), University of Kentucky]

7 January 1959

Miss Leah Bodine Drake
1801 Avery Street
Parkersburg, W. Va.

My dear Miss Drake:

Thank you very much for sending us the work-sheets. This is the type of thing we are always eager to add to our collection of Kentucky authors. Please do try to remember to save them for us in the future.

I have long wanted to visit New Harmony, and I hope I will make it some day soon. It is one of the famous places of the Middle West, and I am chagrined that I have never managed to get there.

Dr. Starkie's work is well known here and in the world of scholarship in general. I shall talk to some of our people who arrange lectures about the possibility of bringing him here. I for one would like very much to hear him.

Ronnie Butler is well known here in the library, and favorably. I am glad to hear of this personal association with him.

Don't worry about contributions to the Associates. You will stay on the mailing list. We are primarily after people such as your friend from Houston, but we never reject any contribution from any sources.

Best wishes for 1959.
    Sincerely,
    Lawrence S. Thompson
    Director of Libraries

UNPUBLISHED LETTERS

[8] [TNS, University of Kentucky]
14 April 1960
UNIVERSITY OF KENTUCKY LIBRARIES
MARGARET I. KING LIBRARY
LEXINGTON, KENTUCKY

Delighted to hear about your good fortune. Bon voyage!
I am leaving week after next for three weeks in Spain and France.
Hang on to your working papers for us. It would be interesting to have drafts of your poems on Lausanne hotel stationery.
  Sincerely,
    Lawrence S. Thompson

[9] [TLS, University of Kentucky]
UNIVERSITY OF KENTUCKY
LEXINGTON, KENTUCKY
June 26, 1962
UNIVERSITY OF KENTUCKY LIBRARIES

Mr. [sic] Leah Bodine Drake
828 Murdoch Avenue
Parkersburg, West Virginia

My dear Mr. Drake:
 I am slowly putting together a little exhibit of manuscripts of modern poets. It will take a year or so, and I may well find that it will be necessary to have two or three series of exhibits when I get all the examples I want together.
 We have no manuscripts in your hand, and, indeed, I hope you have selected some appropriate depository for your manuscripts. I would, however, like to have an original manuscripts poem in your hand for the exhibit I am planning, and I would be most grateful if you could write out some piece, even a short one, for us.
  Sincerely,
    Lawrence S. Thompson
    Director of Libraries
LST:fg

The Song of the Sun ❧ Leah Bodine Drake

To the Stuart Art Gallery

[TLS, WHS]¹

Evansville, Indiana,
Nov. 25th, 1956.

Stuart Art Gallery, Inc.,
Boston, Mass;

Gentlemen:

 I have been laughing out loud at Mr. Shaw's deliciously caustic little book, "PRECIOUS RUBBISH".² It says so well what I have often thought myself about holier-than-thou critics. I blush to say it, but I was one of the Absolutist breed myself some years ago: as movie critic for the COURIER here, I lay down the law to about 130,000 local show-goers and goodness knows how many others in the country around. If I liked a picture, it was good, if I didn't like it, it got thumbs down for everybody. The self-styled intelligentsia here loved my column, for I was second to no one—no, not even Chicago's Claudia Cassidy³—in ripping the hide off of a movie that I didn't think came up to scratch. Many of the so-called morons must often have felt liked throwing rotten eggs at me—in fact, I used to get some pretty salty letters.

 I am mellower, now, I hope, and nothing irratates [sic] me more than to be told point-blank, that So-and[-]So is the "best poet writing in English today", or that Whosis is *not* one of the best poets writing in English today. I think differently, perhaps: I think So-and-So is an affected so-and[-]so, that Whosis is the darling of the Museis [sic].

 Shaw's book has pleased me so, that I am giving a couple of copies to friends who, I hope, will take him to heart. I am an Advisory Editor to a very highbrow little poetry explicator which, lately, has been getting more and more on the side of the obscurest poets. It seemed good to me to send a copy the other day to Prof. Holmes, the editor. (The magazine is POETRY PUBLIC, Hastings, Neb. where Holmes is an assistant professor of Eng.) There's place for both traditional and "modernist" in his mag.

 I have recently been made the poetry-book revi[e]wer for the AT-LANTIC—that is, they send me a batch of new books of verse, then I'll review them in a fairly long article—one that Mr. Weeks calls a poetry "round-up"—for an issue next Spring. I'm going to try and follow some of Shaw's hints for a critic—to remember that one man's meat is another man's poison. I WON'T put myself in the silly position of the two critics I now quote:

    Frederick Eckman, in POETRY, October 1956:
"(Robert) Creeley is, in my opinion, the best poet under forty now writing". (That lets *me* out.)[4]

Who's Creeley? Did you ever hear of him? I didn't. Eckman's quotes from this guy's new book have determined me never to open a book by him—not if I know it.

  Another abab: this one by *William Meredith* in the N.Y. Times: "Herbert Read is . . . one of the 4 or 5 best poets in England today."

  I think Read is fine, too—but why 4 or 5? Why not 3 or 7? How did Meredith get this number out of an island with more poets the square inch than most countries have in a thousand miles? (Gosh, have I abbacated [*sic*] here?)

  I inclose, for Mr. Shaw's delectation, a bingbang abab from a local pundit, the lovable, kissable, dictator of our Central Carnegie Library, Mr. Goldhor.[5] (Goldhor thinks so little of ANY novel, or poetry volumn, that this particular library has almost nothing, any more, but books on how to be your own plumber. We all go out to Willard.)[6]

  Zane Grey, whom I possibly couldn't read today, was a childish enthusiasm, and the man who first made me see beauty in lonely plains and sagebrush. "Riders of the Purple Sage", among Mr. Goldhor's dammned [*sic*] souls, early gave me a sense of magic and mystery about the west that isn't lost even now, after having lived for 8 horrible years in Texas. (New Mexico stands up well, even in actuality.)

  There must be many others for whom Zane Grey spells beauty and pleasure. But nope, Goldhor the big brain, Goldhor the self-appointed boss-o of Evansville readers, says, heave-ho and off to Limbo, to the Sage of the Purple West.

  And get that bit about mayhem and blood . . . Oh God! Oh Montreal![7] . . . . did he ever read Mailler, [*sic*] James Jones, Faulkner, Hemingway, Ruark, and so on and so on and so on? The library has these

The Song of the Sun ~ Leah Bodine Drake

gentle souls' books.

I hope "Precious Rubbish" gets the wide sale it deserves. It won't be reviewed in half the mags., though, for obvious reasons.

Thank you, Mr. T. L. Shaw, for tramping down hard on the critics, even though you unwittingly stepped on my own toes.

    Sincerely,
    Leah Bodine Drake

(Miss) Leah Bodine Drake,
927 Lincoln Avenue.

Notes

1. It is unknown why this signed letter (not a carbon) is among AD's papers.
2. Theodore L. Shaw (1925–1990?), *Precious Rubbish, as Raked out of Current Criticism and Commented On* (Boston: Stuart Art Gallery, 1956). Shaw wrote several books critical of criticism. LBD was one of twenty-two judges who evaluated unsigned critiques of the book for *Poetry Public Letter*. In her evaluation, LBD wrote:

  "'A' effectively explodes Shaw's naïve contention that the 'simple' is necessarily the 'low-brow'—('A' uses a good illustration: 'Stopping by Wood on a Snowy Evening' by Frost.)

  "'D' 's illustration of the unseen magnet is good: the Absolute (values) drawing us toward itself almost without our knowing it.

  "All contestants which I consider the *best* (I'm being an Absolutist!) discovered immediately Mr. Shaw's own brand of Absolutist laying-down-the-law—and *what* a law! The 'law' of Chaos!

  "Shaw, in his book exposes himself as a rank Absolutist—He is hoist with his own petard!

    "Leah Bodine Drake

  "P.S. These papers are *very* well done—penetrating, thoughtful, and at times quite witty.—L.B.D."

Under "Judging and Scoring the Papers," *Poetry Public Letter* 5, Nos. 2 and 3 (April–September 1957): 25.

3. Claudia Cassidy (1899–1996), music, dance, and drama critic in Chicago, known for harsh criticism but also enthusiasm.
4. "Six Poets, Young or Unknown," *Poetry* 89, No. 1 (October 1956): 60. LBD was 21 years older than Creeley.
5. Dr. Herbert Goldhor (1917–2011) became the third Chief Librarian of the Evansville Public Library in 1952 and served there until 1962.
6. I.e., the Willard Library in Evansville.
7. The expression "O God! O Montreal!" is a refrain found in the poem "A Psalm of Montreal" by Samuel Butler (1835–1902), first published in the *Spectator* (18 May 1878).

Appendix

Appendix

[Announcement of Award]

Lean Bodine Drake, whose poem, "No Refuge," was chosen by the judge, Eric Wilson Barker, to receive the K[aliedograph]. Quarterly Award of $25 for the first quarter of this year kindly gave this panorama of herself:
"I was born on a Thursday, and true to the old saying, 'Thursday's child has far to go,' I spent the early part of my life on pullmans tearing back and forth across the continent. I went from Kansas to Philadelphia when I was three months old, and have lived all over the South and Southwest and along the Atlantic seaboard. (Father is an oil man!) My grandparents (maternal) had a country home on the ocean near Atlantic City, and I used to spend all my childhood summers there. I've been held up by a bandit on a train coming through Louisiana, in several cyclones, seen two gangster mobs 'shoot it out' in Camden, New Jersey, back in the roaring '20s, been 'The Spirit of Dallas' in the Texas Centennial Parade, and a showgirl for Billy Rose in his 'Casa Manana' in Fort Worth (dare I mention the name?) in 1936. At present I'm the motion picture Editor of the Evansville, Indiana, *Courier,* just over the river from here."

Born in Lexington, Kentucky, [*sic*] Miss Drake attended Hamilton College for Women, also for a time, Sayre College, and spent one year at the Kendrick School for Girls in Cincinnati. Her poems have been in *Atlantic Monthly, Saturday Evening Post, Voices, Poetry Chap-Book, Nature Poetry: A Magazine of Verse, The Cornhill Magazine* (London), *Talaria, Weird Tales, Prairie Schooner,* etc., and in various anthologies, as Thomas Moult's *Best Poems of 1941,* Ted Malone's *Between the Bookends,* Coblentz's *The Music Makers,* and is to have six [*sic*] poems from *Weird Tales* in August Derleth's *the Dark of the Moon,* a collection of weird and macabre verse.

Leah Bodine Drake Writes Volume of "Macabre" Poems

Critic for The Courier to Autograph Copies of Her New Book at Party Monday

Evansville will doff its hat next Monday to a young local authoress whose first book of poems is rolling off the presses this week.

She is Miss Leah Bodine Drake, movie, drama, and music critic for *The Courier*, who will autograph copies of *A Hornbook for Witches* at a party in Smith & Butterfield's store from 3:30 to 5 p.m. and from 6:30 to 8 p.m. Monday.

Although *Hornbook* marks the first time Miss Drake's poems have taken a bow in a volume of their own, her verses have been attracting attention ever since she ticked off her first rhyme at the age of seven.

Four months ago, she won the Albert Ralph Corn lyric award for her piece of verse called "The Darkened Glass." And just this week, she took second honors in the Poetry Society of America's annual competition with "The Lariat: 6000 B.C."

To Be Guest Speaker

As a result, she'll appear as guest speaker at the society's annual dinner meeting at Sherry's Restaurant in New York Jan. 24.

Miss Drake's lyrics have appeared in the "Atlantic Monthly" and "Saturday Evening Post," among other magazines. Ted Malone and Stanton Coblentz have included her in poetry anthologies, and Thomas Moult, British anthologist, used her "Fantasy in a Forest" in his *Best Poems of 1941*.

"Fantasy in a Forest" is being used by MacMillan's of London in a textbook for English literature classes in British schools. And last summer, two of Miss Drake's lyrics appeared in the New Zealand magazine "Arena" as works of a representative American poet.

Examples of her "working manuscripts" are on display in Lockwood Memorial Library at the University of Buffalo.

APPENDIX

Fantastic and Macabre

Hornbook is a collection of half a hundred poems written in the vein of the fantastic and the macabre . . . poems "of ghosts and goblins, of witches and warlocks and things that go bump in the night."

They're being published by Arkham House of Sauk City, Wis., a firm established 10 years ago by August Derleth to cater to a new public taste for the weird and fantastic in literature.

A "horn-book," explains Miss Drake, "is a wooden frame with a thin sheet of horn covering a page with the alphabet and simple words. It was used in early American and European schools to protect the precious paper from children's smudgy little fingers.

"A horn-book for witches means a sort of primer, a text book on how to be a successful witch. Of course, these aren't serious poems. I just wrote them for fun and amusement for a special audience."

Native of Kansas

Brown-haired and vivacious, Miss Drake was born in Chanute, Kan., where her father was drilling an oil well. Since then, she's lived in Lexington, Ky., Shreveport, La., Dallas and Ft. Worth, Tex., Cincinnati, O., New Mexico, Jackson, Miss. and Philadelphia, Pa.

She attended Oakhurst School for Girls in Cincinnati, Hamilton College for Women and Sayre college in Lexington.

Although the bookish life is her first love, Leah took time out back in the 30's for a stint as a showgirl in Billy Rose's "Casa Manana Revue" at the Texas Centennial in Fr. Worth. On the festival's opening day, she donned a diamond crown to reign as "Miss Dallas."

Miss Drake's knack for the spooky is no accident. Her 16th century ancestor, Jean Bodin, who served as king's attorney to Henry III of France, penned a book on witchcraft, "Demonomanie Des Sorciers," which served as a guide for official witch-prosecutions. It's to him that she dedicates her own book.

Her father's family stems from a brother of Sir Francis Drake, who emigrated to Virginia. Her mother's include the Kirwins, also of Virginia, who came originally from Castle Hackett, Co. Sligo, Ireland.

She's a member of Vanderburgh county chapter, Daughters of the

The Song of the Sun ~ Leah Bodine Drake

American Revolution; vice-president of Evansville's Animal Refuge, Inc., and belongs to the Poetry Society of America.

Miss Drake's literary influences are the fantastic tales of Lord Dunsany, the Bible, and the poems of Walter de la Mare, Edith Sitwell and Elinor Wylie. She admires the work of Oxford don, C. S. (*Screwtape Letters*) Lewis, with whom she had corresponded for the past few years.

Possible Earnings on *A Hornbook for Witches*

Without proper documentation, it is impossible to say just how much money *A Hornbook for Witches* earned its author and publisher. August Derleth had estimated that the book would cost a dollar per copy to produce. He did not specify the print run, but because he said Drake would earn $100.00 in royalties at the standard royalty of ten percent, the print run was assumed to be five hundred. He felt customers would not spend more than $2.00 for the book. In the end he printed five hundred fifty-three copies and charged $2.10 a copy. A rough estimate of the costs to Arkham House and earnings is provided below.

	$2.00/copy	$2.10/copy
Cost to print	($553.00)	($553.00)
Royalties (on all 553 copies)	($110.60)	($116.13)
Total sales on 553 copies	$1,106.00	$1,161.30
Publisher's net	$442.40	$492.17
Earnings if all books sold at 40% discount	$663.60	$696.78*
Shortfall	($221.20)	($204.61)
Drake's loss of royalties on 250 copies	$50.00	$53.00
Drakes' royalties on only 303 copies	$60.60	$63.63
Drakes earnings if she sold her 50 copies	$100.00	$105.00
Drake's total earnings (royalties + direct sales)	$160.60	$168.63
Increased earnings over royalties only on all 553 copies	$50.00	$52.50

*Smith & Butterfield bought 50 copies at 40% discount, and so Arkham House received only $63.00 instead of $105.00 had those copies been sold at cover price. The store actually bought more books, though the quantity is uncertain.

Appendix

The numbers are mostly conjectural: we do not know the exact cost to print the book, what Arkham House paid Drake in royalties, whether Drake sold her copies at the cover price, or even if she sold all fifty copies. It is unknown whether Arkham House made money on the book, although Derleth's scheme to pay Drake in copies while reducing amount of royalties paid, and also increasing the cost of the book by ten cents, seems to have paid off, for Arkham House published another poetry book within a year, at $2.50 a copy. Thus, the test case of Drake's book showed that Arkham House could indeed publish poetry books without losing money.

A Hornbook for Witches [Jacket Blurb]

August Derleth

Few poets are as felicitous in their chosen medium as Leah Bodine Drake is in the genre of macabre poetry. Here are close to half a hundred of the best contemporary poems in the field of the fantastic—poems of ghosts and goblins, of whimsy and of terror, of witches and warlocks and curses, of visions and dreams.

From the title poem, which opens the collection, to the final "The Centaurs," the vein of the macabre never falters. Miss Drake writes with a sure hand and with an admirable restraint of subjects which are not dared by poets far better-known, and, whether she is concerned with the pathetic but credible creature of "Mad Woman's Song" or the fractious "Wood-Wife," with the malefic beings of "Unhappy Ending" or what was "Heard on the Roof at Midnight" she is equally effective in arousing doubts as to the proximity of ghoulies and beasties and things that go bump in the night.

Here are such remarkably effective poems as "The Path Through the Marsh," the prize-winning "Ballad of the Jabberwock," "All-Saints' Eve, "The Window on the Stair, "Goat-song," and many another outstanding example of the macabre in a medium all too seldom exploited by writers in the field.

The Song of the Sun ✣ Leah Bodine Drake

These poems will satisfy that all too human curiosity about the other side of darkness at the same time that they will afford a kind of entertainment which is becoming increasingly rare in our time.

The Lineaments of Faerie

Anonymous

The following poetical fragments were discovered as short manuscripts and marginalia penciled in a close male hand on and between the pages of a miscellaneous collection of legends purchased in London, the volumes of which had all evidently belonged to the same person.

Written down in chance moments, these fragments show a distinct talent in their anonymous author. Their depth of understanding the authentic bardic inspiration warrant their inclusion in *The Various Light*.

I
The Land of the West, the Land of Evermore,
In a sea that is not sailed and a cloud that does not lift,
Which none can penetrate without a call therefrom.
    It sees eternity welling up in glory like a still dawn:
    The Way of the Gates of Faerie: who knows, who knows?
    Many have said, I see; but few there are who enter, and few indeed return.
An island set in deep waters, an isle of luminous shadow cast from Paradise.
They say that the waters are amethyst, they say that the trees are emerald green,
That voices and music are there,
Music of voices, paeans of music sweet . . . .
Strange things unseen of normal mortal eyes
Which follow on certain baptisms and certain words of bewitching
At christening feasts.

Appendix

II
Folly goes fast to the well of wishing
    But prudence approaches slowly. . . .
Give me a wise heart
When the angel comes with gifts.

The hidden trades of Faerie—
    Slippers of glass
    And lasts of golden shoes.
Strange bookings for strange travels. . . .
O the house of exchange in Faerie
    And of what may be bought and bartered.

III
The primal sun of the mind is in Faerie:
O golden fleece of Faerie
    Which never a hunter won,
    For it cannot be got by killing,
The kingdom of this world
Warns away from the kingdom of Faerie.
    Give me the glass of vision
    That shows the world of Faerie,
    Give me the horse that carries the rider there.

IV
Of stars on the forehead in Faerie
And other wonders of vesture and high adornment.
There is a star on the forehead of a white roe
And it may lead from here to Ever-and-Ever.

V
The race of royalty in Faerie
Is other than that of earth:
    It is good will only
    That truly reigns in Faerie,
    And eternity is the path of crowns.

The Song of the Sun ~ Leah Bodine Drake

The Mystery of Seven in Faerie—
>Seven words, powers, graces
>Lead to the hidden truths;
>And among these is the crown.

VI
Hell is a kingdom like Faerie
But all against the grain—
A world at cross-purposes seen from Faerie:
The Devil is a fool in Faerie!

VII
The key of the church in Faerie:
Faerie is a place of the word
>And the word is never broken.
Every wicked spell in Faerie
>Is the result of a false word
>>Spoken in action or by mouth.

But there is always a counterword in truth. . . .
Shadows cast in Faerie,
And some shadows are luminous;
But the shadows of true words
>Are shadows of glory.

A prayer is a work in Faerie
And a moonbeam may carry it.

VIII
The music of trees in Faerie
>And what the shadowing leaves may write
>>On the sward in moonlight. . . .
Who reads this tongue?
It is like a soft wind in the pipes
>When no one touches the stops,

APPENDIX

It is like the colloquy of pattering rain
   With the wind-harp in a solitude.

All is man in Faerie,
   And this is one of its secrets.
The forest is a great nation
   And the still pool is a soul.

IX
Thou Land of End-Attained,
Thy Law gives me talents of gold
   —a heap, a heap, and a half of one heap of talents.
The talents of Faerie are tablets
   —within, about, and around:
Tales of wonder in Faerie.

The new tales, the old tales,
The same tales everywhere.
The old tales I heard yesterday,
And over and over again
They will tell the new tales tomorrow. . . .

X
Now I have told the heads of Faerie.

[From *The International Who's Who in Poetry*]

DRAKE, Leah Bodine, born 22nd December, 1904. *Educated:* Miss Kendrick's School for Girls, Cincinnati, Ohio; Hamilton College for Women, Lexington, Kentucky. Poetry books reviewer, The Atlantic Monthly. An advisory editor to "Poetry Public." Member, Poetry Soc. of America; The Wilderness Society; Daughters of the American Revolution; the University of Kentucky Library Associates, etc. Winner of Borestone Mt. Award, 1954, etc. *Publications:* A Hornbook for Witches, This Tilting Dust. *Contributor:* Atlantic Monthly, Poetry (Chicago), Sat.

The Song of the Sun ❧ Leah Bodine Drake

Review, Beloit Poetry Journal, Commonweal, The New Yorker; Contemporary Poetry, etc., and various anthologies. *Recreations:* Reading, dancing, walking in the country, conversation with friends, listening to music, eating, living in general. *Clubs:* Evansville Philharmonic, Assoc. of American University Women. *Address:* 828 Murdoch Avenue, Parkersburg, West Virginia, U.S.A.

[From *The Supplement to Who's Who*, March–May 1959]

DRAKE, Leah Bodine, poet; b. Chanute, Kan., Dec. 22, 1904; d. Thomas Hulbert and Cornelia (Bodine) Drake; student Miss Kendrick's Sch. for Girls, 1920–22, Hamilton Coll. for Girls, 1923–24; m. Lewis Leslie MacAllister [sic]. Nov. 29, 1928 (div. 1930). Drama editor Evansville (Ind.) Courier, 1941–51; poetry reviewer Atlantic Monthly, 1957–58; asst. society editor Parkersburg (W. Va.) News, 1958–. Vice pres. Vanderburgh County (Ind.) Humane Soc., 1950–54; mem. bd. women's assn. for Evansville (Ind.) Philharmonic Orchestral Soc. Recipient Borestone Mt. award for best poem in English-speaking world, 1952; Borestone Mt. award for book-length manuscript (poetry), 1953; prizes Poetry Soc. Am., others. Mem. D.A.R. (radio chmn. Vanderburgh County chpt. 1948–49), Poetry Soc. Am., Wilderness Soc., Kentucky Library Assn., Wood County Humane Soc. Episcopalian. Club: Womens Civic (Parkersburg). Author: A Hornbook for Witches, 1950; This Tilting Dust, 1956; poems pub. numerous mags. Address: 1801 Avery St., Parkersburg, W. Va.

[Death Announcement]

To Whom It May Concern:

As friends of Leah Bodine Drake and on her behalf, we thank all who have written to her and in other ways helped to brighten her days during her illness. For some who receive this letter, this will be the first report of her death[,] which occurred November 21, 1964.

Appendix

Many of you have long been aware of the fine work Leah has produced through many years of writing as well as collecting poetry. We wish we might have known her earlier and longer!

About six years ago, she came to Parkersburg with her father. His sister, Mary Drake, was still living here. For a while she worked on a local newspaper, and was in Switzerland with the Barth Foundation for a time. She returned to care for her father in his final illness, and her mother's twin sister "Nana"* (Anne) Bodine came to stay with them. In the summer of 1963, following Mr. Drake's death, Leah underwent surgery for gastric malignancy. In the fall she was well enough to return to Switzerland to help with the completion of *The Various Light,* an anthology of modern poetry, including some of her best, in which she collaborated with Dr. C. A. Muses. (This book is now being printed in Portugal and may be ordered from the Aurora Press, 17 Av. des Peupliers, Lausanne, Switzerland.)

She was forced to return in the spring of 1964 to care for her Aunt. Nana had a lingering illness and Leah's own health began to fail. Following her aunt's death she entered the hospital where her condition was diagnosed as terminal cancer. Leah did not know how serious her condition was, and after her doctor sent her home, she remained alone with no telephone for a number of weeks nursing herself. Her neighbor, Mrs. R. U. Cariens, looked in on her every day, doing many kind and generous services, and a variety of Parkersburg landlords cut the rent or charged none during times of her greatest financial stress.

We finally persuaded Leah to let us bring her to our home where we could give her constant care and love. Shortly after she came to the rectory her doctor told her that she was going to die. She was very brave and wise in her response to the shocking news and we have very gratifying memories of her stay with us. Letters and gifts from friends and family meant so very much to her.

One last project was completed. Leah had been working for months to compile the best poems she had published through the years and some new unpublished ones. These were ready for publication and we hurried

*LBD rendered her aunt's name as "Nanna."—ED.

The Song of the Sun ~ Leah Bodine Drake

to ask the help of the Poetry Society of America. Mr. Gustav Davidson complied at once in seeking a publisher. Two days before her death the manuscript was mailed to a publisher who had agreed to read it. The title poem, "Multiple Clay" was read at her funeral in Trinity Church.

Until the end none of us knew how much suffering and poverty Leah had faced. As the bills come in we realized her loneliness and frustration. Her father had experienced the run of bad luck familiar to many in oil well drilling and all he left Leah was an accumulation of debts. She wished to work and meet the bills but could not do so and look after Mr. Drake. The small income of Miss Bodine ($75.00 a month, interest on a trust fund left Miss Bodine by a friend in Philadelphia) was not enough to feed them and meet the rent. In addition to her father's debts, when her Aunt Mary died that legacy was absorbed by the debts; Nana died and left Leah one half of the trust fund, (the other half going to her cousin, Mrs. C. E. Downs.) Leah's share was used immediately to pay another portion of the debts. She once laughed and said "The only thing I ever got to spend on myself was a bed-armchair cushion!" After Nana died, Leah was faced with complete poverty, too ill to work, but writing at home. She has left a wealth of wonderful creative writing. We have just begun to discover how great a quantity of her published poems Leah has collected in scrapbooks, and in the hand written illustrated manuscripts which she has kept of all her poems. What a lot of good reading! We keep asking ourselves why we had not known of Leah and her poems long before this! Here is the real Leah. It is our hope her work will be used and shared by many.

Perhaps a greater spirit has walked among us than any realized. A letter came yesterday from a student in England asking where to buy her books. Wouldn't she be pleased? In many ways we are sorry you who knew her could not have seen how lovely she was . . . a kind of reality came to her personality that she had tended to hide . . . her beautiful eyes . . . her fine bone structure . . . her really lovely mouth without make-up . . . She was in no pain until the last few hours . . . narcotics gave relief and she slept away . . . this was her wish. Leah Bodine Drake was buried November 23, 1964, near her father in Parkersburg. Her cousin, John Herring from Charlottesville, Virginia, came to attend the

Appendix

funeral. You gave her real comfort and joy with your thoughts and prayers and loving messages in these last days. Thank you.

 Leah Bodine Drake had a kind of mystery. Her ability to inspire attracted all who have the slightest shred of mystic understanding . . . especially men! We found in her a soaring kindred spirit.

Griffin & Betty Callahan

Bibliography

Poetry Collections

A Hornbook for Witches: Poems of Fantasy. Sauk City, WI: Arkham House, December 1950. n.p.: Archadic Press, 2017. viii, 70 pp. *Contains:* A HORNBOOK FOR WITCHES: I. The Besom; II. The Familiar; III. The Magic Circle; IV. Enchanted Sleep; V. Magician's Hat; VI. Witch's-Wheel; VII. The Spells; VIII. The Coven; IX. The Covenant. Unhappy Ending; Witches on the Heath; The Tenants; The Ballad of the Jabberwock; Bad Company; Mouse Heaven; Rabbit-Dance; Wood-Wife; *A Likely Story!; The Man Who Married a Swan-Maiden; All-Saints' Eve; *The Last Faun; Changeling; In the Shadows; Figures in a Nightmare; The Witch Walks in Her Garden; The Seal-Woman's Daughter; They Run Again; The Path through the Marsh; Old Wives' Tale; A Vase from Araby; The Fur Coat; *House Accurst; The Vision; Sea-Shell; *Willow-Women; *The Girl in the Glass; Heard on the Roof at Midnight; Terror by Night; *Legend; The Heads on Easter Island; Haunted Hour; Goat-Song; The Nixie's Pool; The Stranger; *Encounter in Broceliande; The Window on the Stair; The Old World of Green; Curious Story; The Steps in the Field; Midsummer Night; *Old Daphne; *Mad Woman's Song; *Griffon's Gold; Black Peacock; The Centaurs.

Dedicated "To My Sixteenth Century Ancestor / JEAN BODIN / Who Also Concerned Himself / With Witches." In her presentation copy to the publisher, Drake wrote: "To August Derleth, one of the best friends a witch could have!—Leah Bodine Drake. 1950."

*Indicates that the first appearance of the poem was in the book.

The Song of the Sun ❧ Leah Bodine Drake

T.Ms., L. Tom Perry Special Collections, Harold B. Lee Library, Brigham Young University. The T.Ms. includes as the concluding poem the five-page "The Journey of the Queen of Sheba." Drake withdrew the poem at the publisher's request and sent as a substitute "Encounter in Broceliande" and "Mad Woman's Song," both of which reside with the T.Ms.; both, unlike the other pages in the T.Ms. and like the late supplied dedicatory page, have the header "A Hornbook for Witches," whereas the other pages do not. In a letter to Derleth of 10 February [1954], Drake requested that he send the typescript of her book to Lawrence S. Thompson, director of libraries at the University of Kentucky, for the library's collection of her papers. It is unknown how the T.Ms. instead came to Brigham Young University. WHS box 104 holds the corrected galley proofs and Drake's separate handwritten list of corrections

Reviews: Orville Prescott, "Books of the Times: Stirred in a Cauldron of Verse," *New York Times* (1 January 1951): 15. Stanton A. Coblentz, "The Reviewer's Quill," *Wings: A Quarterly of Verse* 10, No. 1 (Spring 1951): 23–24. August Derleth, "Minority Report." [Madison, WI] *Capital Times* (15 March 1951): 8. Anthony Boucher and J. Francis McComas, "Recommended Reading," *Magazine of Fantasy and Science Fiction* 2, No. 6 (June 1951): 84. [Dorothy McIlwraith], *Weird Tales* 43, No. 4 (May 1951): 10. [Harold Vinal], "Briefer Comment," *Voices* No. 145 (July–August 1951): 55.

This Tilting Dust. Francestown, NH: Golden Quill Press, December 1955. 61 pp. *Contains:* Precarious Ground; Air; Solar; Luna; The Final Green; Rock and Bramble; Fantasy in a Forest; Drone; Cat Mummy; The Storks; Cobra; Wild Geese in Spring; Flemish Artists, Fifteenth Century; The Lazy Prince; Childhood Summers; "What Are Little Girls Made Of?"; The Undine; Semele; The Birth of Beauty; The Foam-Born; Cave Paintings, Altamira; Windows of Chartres; Beyond Eden; The Lariat: 6000 B.C.; Honey from the Lion; Atavism; The Well; Man in Winter; Minor Poet; The Beaches Beyond Oblivion; Song against Smallness; Leonardo Before His Canvas; Vestal; Fool's Paradise; Love Song; The Fruit Uneaten; *Incoming

*Indicates that the first appearance of the poem was in the book.

Tide; Through-Train; *Old Man on the Seashore: Morning; I Met a Lion; Descent of Angels; We Come Out of the Forest, Fearing Stars; The Darkened Glass; The False Messiah; Dirge for a Doomed Planet; We Move on Turning Stone.

Dedicated "*To my Parents* / Thomas Hulbert Drake / *and* / Cornelia Bodine Drake." Winner of the $1250 Borestone Mountain Poetry Award (1954) and finalist (1957) for the National Book Foundation poetry award. The title derives from "Precarious Ground," l. 13.

T.Ms., University of Kentucky. The surviving T.Ms. apparently is neither the original nor a carbon copy, but perhaps a first draft or file copy, made on assorted types and sizes of paper, including pages removed from an "Amateur Radio Station Log." The poem "The Well" therein is incomplete; "Old Man on the Seashore: Morning" is heavily revised by hand.

Reviews: Judson Jerome, "Among the Nightingales," *Antioch Review* 16, No. 1 (Spring 1956): 118–19. August Derleth, "Minority Report." [Madison, WI] *Capital Times* (10 February 1956): 7. Anthony Boucher, "Recommended Reading," *Magazine of Fantasy and Science Fiction* 10, No. 6 (June 1956): 104. Stanton A. Coblentz, *Wings: A Quarterly of Verse* 12, No. 6 (Summer 1956): 25–26. George Abbe, "Reviews," *Poetry Public Letter* 4, No. 4 (October–December 1956): 16–17. Alonzo Gibbs, "Ladies' Day," *Voices* No. 162 (January–April 1957): 42–44.

Anthologies

The Various Light: An Anthology of Modern Poetry in English. Edited by Leah Bodine Drake and Charles Arthur Musès. [Lausanne, Switzerland]: Aurora Press, 1964. *Contains:* Foreword [by the editors]; George Abbe: Horizon Thong; Mint; Heron and Child. Dannie Abse: From "Looking at a Map"; Epithalmion [*sic*]. Bernice Ames: On the Island of Sleep; When You Kneel. Howard Ant: The Were-Wind's Lover. Eric Barker: In Easy Dark; In Thames Ditton; Lost Heritage; Deserted. Kate Barnes: Swimming Horses; A Mare; The Pinto. Gene Baro: The Ladder; The Image; Thirst After Sweetness; The Well. Daniel Berrigan: From "St. Joseph"; Love Is a Difference; Some Young God; The Castle. Earle Birney: Mappemounde; Gulf of Georgia; From the Hazel Bough. Louise Bogan: Last Hill in a Vista; From "After the Persian." Philip Booth: The Islanders; Gresham's Law; Convoy; Jake's Wharf. Kate Brackett: Something Has to Burn. Joseph Payne Brennan: Strayer's Song; A Fable; The Serpent Waits; Communions. Edwin Brock: An Attempt at Exorcism. Jean Burden: First Communion; Dayspring. Fred Cogswell: Tame Goose. Thomas Cole: When All Standards Are Changing; The Impossible Is Only Imagined; Portrait of a Lady. Robert Cooke: Manger Scene. Henry Dalton: Apple Tree; Dry Branches; Autumnal Equinox; Cold Perfection. Irene Dayton: Age Along the Seine. Kyril Demys [pseudonym of Charles A. Musès]: Matrix Manipulation; The Birth Song of Myrahi; Zenigmatic Dialogue; Meaning of Blackness. August Derleth: Brook Talk; Lonely Place; Evening Train. Babette Deutsch: Damnation; Natural Law; Fountain and Unicorn. Dorothy Donnelly: Snowflakes; Spider Compared to Star. Alfred Dorn: Snowflake; Age of Automatons; Afterimages. *Leah Bodine Drake:* Fantasy in a Forest; The Storks; The Word of Willow; Precarious Ground. Peter Kane Dufault: Glimpse of Three Children on a Picnic; Logos; Jet-Vapor-Trail; Farm Animals at Evening. David Duncan: I Myself. Mary Ballard Duryee: Prelude in Denmark. Charles Edward Eaton: The Greenhouse; Sea Trauma. Loren C. Eiseley: Dusk Interval; Incident in the Zoo. Abbie Huston Evans: Fact of Crystal; On the Curve-Edge. Norma Farber: Lullaby for an Æsop Lionet. Patrick Galvin: Ballad for My Mother; My Lover to Market; An Caisideach Ban; This Brotherhood. Robert Graves: A Lost Jewel; In the Wilderness; Advocates; The Song of Blodeuwedd. Donald Hall: O Flodden Field; On the Third Anniversary. John Heath-Stubbs: Footnote on Epic Diction; Quatrains; Lament for the "Old Swan," Notting Hill Gate. Leslie Wolff Hedley: Headlines, Headlines, Headlines; Somewhere Men Read Poetry with Their Lives. Moss Herbert: The Single Tree. Richard Hertz: The Dragon Bowls of the Yi Dynasty; The Curio Vendress in the Bando Hotel. Katherine Hoskins: When Snow Falls; A Kind of Progress; Temple. Barbara Howes: On a Bougainvillæa Vine at the Summer Palace. Robert Huff: Quail;

BIBLIOGRAPHY

King Salmon; Traditional Red. Ted Hughes: Snowdrop; Fourth of July; Pike. Donald Justice: Sonnet; Love's Map; Speaking of Islands. Joseph Joel Keith: Flogged Child; Return to Hawley. Joseph Langland: Hunters in the Snows: Brueghel; Evergreen; Winter Juniper. Richmond Lattimore: Poussin's World: Two Paintings; New Homes; Epigraphical Note. C. S. Lewis: The Meteorite; The Sunrise. Othelia Lilly: A Child Dreams. Warren S. McCulloch: Sang Real. Audrey McGaffin: The Imagined Country. Lenore G. Marshall: Love Poem. Anne Marx: No Cages. W. S. Merwin: Low Fields and Light; Deception Island; Bell Buoy; The Drunk in the Furnace. Ewart Milne: The Fifth Wind; A Song My Mother Taught Me; The Poet; The Martyred Earth. Howard Moss: A Portrait; Dreams. Lisel Mueller: I Knew an Ancient Woman; The Mermaid. Philip Murray: The Turning; De Arte Illuminandi. Howard Nemerov: The Quarry; Angel and Stone; Moment. Anthony Ostroff: In Small Things; The Zoo. Jennie M. Palen: Knowledge of Sassafras; Eden: Prologue. J. Phoenice: I Am of Glass. William Pillin: Essay; A Winter Night Poem. Dorothy Cowles Pinkney: Certainty; Full Circle. Kenneth Pitchford: The Wheatfield; Heraklion. Sylvia Plath: The Hermit at Outermost House; Snakecharmer. Alastair Reid: Ghosts. Adrienne Rich: The Explorers; The Roadway. Paul Roche: The Dessert Spoon; The Cheap Teaspoon. Rose Rosberg: Formula; Guide. A. L. Rowse: Late Spring at Trenarren; Buckinghamshire. Archibald Rutledge: Insight; Lion in the Night. May Sarton: After Four Years; Sonnet. George Scarbrough: The Field; Lines for an Early Returning Home; The Cicada; Story. R. J. Schoeck: Lake Twilight. Henry Seitz: Antique. Howard Sergeant: The Inland Sea; Sandcastle Days; Lyric by the River; High Kingdom. Ruth Forbes Sherry: Fling Finite Against Infinite; The Last God. Louis Simpson: Against the Age; The Legend of Success, the Salesman's Story; To the Western World. Libby Stopple: Joy. Jon Swan: In Her Song, She Is Alone. Thomas Burnett Swann: The Blue Dolphin: A Tanka. May Swenson: Was Worm; The Poplar's Shadow. John Tangen: From "Epic in Progress." Sydney Tremayne: Wind Shakes the House; One Morning; Small Boy and Lighthouse; Legend. Vernon Watkins: The Forge of the Solstice;

677

The Song of the Sun 🙵 Leah Bodine Drake

Woodpecker and Lyre-Bird; The Shell; Great Nights Returning. Richard Wilbur: She; Two Voices in a Meadow: A Milkweed [/] A Stone; Fall in Corrales. Mary Woodlee: Sweet Grapes; Silent; The Secret. John Woods: When Senses Fled; The Elements. James Wright: Three Steps to the Graveyard; At Thomas Hardy's Birthplace, 1953. Anonymous: The Lineaments of Faerie.

Dedicated [by C. A. M.] to João e Janine / Maurice et Bénédicte / Henry and Alyce. The phrase "the various light" comes from Andrew Marvell's "The Garden" (l. 56). Three of Drake's four poems appeared in Musès's *Prismatic Voices*. She included all four poems in the T.Ms. of *Multiple Clay*. No reviews have been found.

Recordings

A Hornbook for Witches: Stories and Poems for Halloween. Edited by Eugene H. White. Narrated by Vincent Price. Caedmon CDL5 1497 (1976); Tangled Corpse (2017). *Contains:* A Hornbook for Witches (3:08); Witches on the Heath (0:57); The Ballad of the Jabberwock (3:14); All-Saints' Eve (1:20), and works by others.

Reviews: Josh Schafer and John DeSantis, "Tales from the Crate," *Lunchmeat* No. 5 (May 2010): 32–33.

Contents of Leah Bodine Drake's Scrapbooks and Notebooks

Drake's scrapbooks and notebooks are held by the University of Kentucky–Lexington. They were deposited there c. 1965 by John Herring, her cousin and the executor of her estate. Contents are listed below as the poems are titled and appear sequentially in the scrapbooks, not as they are listed in Drake's own tables of contents within them. Numbers indicate box number first followed by the folder number. Dates in brackets are assigned by the archive; otherwise, the dates are Drake's.

1.1 *Caravans from Paristan. Early Poems by Leah Bodine Drake. 1918–1935. Contains:* Table of Contents; ON A CHINESE SCREEN: I. Lady Writing a Letter; II. Moon Festival; III. The Deserted Courtyard; IV. By the River; V. A Lady of the Emperor's Palace; VI. One In-

BIBLIOGRAPHY

toxicated. Mombāsa; To a Lost Sweetheart; Song at Sunrise; Apple; The Land of the Japanese Prints; The Country Lover; Belle and Beau; Words After Wisdom; In the Shadows; The Man Who Married a Swan-Maiden; The Path Through the Marsh; The Sailorman (1690); High Renaissance; Unicorn [first version of "Fantasy in a Forest"]. Paristan is the name of a fairyland in the folklore of the Middle East, South Asia, and Central Asia. Drake does not use the word anywhere except in the title of this scrapbook.

1.2 *Domes and Minarets. Poems by Leah Bodine Drake. 1934–41. Contains:* Contents; A Dream of Samarkand (in Contents as "Samarkand"); Tiger; Crocodile; [the following are labeled THREE VIGNETTES in Contents:] India: In the Garden of Spice; Burma: Moulmein Bazaar; Japan: The Persimmon Gatherers; I Met a Lion; He Dreams of Barbary; The Old Khan and His Falcon; The Assyrian Lion; Born Under Capricorn; "My Help Cometh from the Hills"; The Bittern; A Sigh in Spring; The Centaurs; Our Lady's Song.

1.3 *Magic Casements. Children's Poems by Leah Bodine Drake. 1935–37. Contains:* Contents; The Nixie's Pool; The Wind and the Leaves; The Fairies in Autumn; All-Saints' Eve; Witches on the Heath; 'Round and 'Round; The Giant's Garden; Rabbit-Dance; The Pixy Fair; Enchanted Honey; The Old Granny's Story.

1.4 *The Haunted Hour. Poems by Leah Bodine Drake* [1938]. *Contains:* Contents; Unhappy Ending; Luna; Midsummer Night; Ballad of the Seal-Woman's Daughter; Full Moon, 1940; Willow-Women; Cold Comfort; Sea-Shell; Curious Story; The Stranger.

1.5 *The Search of the Soul. Poems by Leah Bodine Drake* [1946]. *Contains:* Contents; Earth: Atomic Age; To an Atheist; This Side of Oblivion [first version]; Gothic [not listed in Contents; first version of "Design for a Tapestry: 14th Century"]; To One Who Fears Poetry Is Useless; The Unclimbed Hill; No Refuge; Retrogression; Snow-Crystals; Turn of Year; Birds in a Barn; To Elinor Wylie; Nativities; WINTER HARVESTS [Contents gives numbered sequence; actual order in scrapbook differs, and the poems are not numbered]: [1.] Frozen Heart; [3.] Owl's Cry; [4.] "Peace on Earth"; [2.] Winter Harvest [table of contents in scrapbook lists poem as "Winter Harvests"].

☙ 679

The Song of the Sun ❧ Leah Bodine Drake

1.6 *The Singer from the Waste. By Leah Bodine Drake* [1942–49]. *Contains:* Contents; The Singer from the Waste; On a Night of Stars; Vestal; The Phoenix Egg; "What Are Little Girls Made Of?"; Man in Winter; Gage to a Lover; The Fruit Uneaten; Bread of Solitude [i.e., Solitude]; Dark Memory; Poplar-Wind; Kingfisher Lake.

2.1 *The Book of Elfin. Poems by Leah Bodine Drake* [1944]. *Contains:* Contents; The Croon of the Mer-Mother; Explanation; Ducks and Pigs; Fairy Cider; Snowy Night; Jilly and the Elf; Zanzibar; Puss-in-Boots and the Three Mice; The House in the Hollow; The Girl in the Glass.

2.2 *Troll-Women and Elfin-Maids. Poems by Leah Bodine Drake* [1940]. *Contains:* Table of Contents; The Wood-Wife; They Run Again; Heard on the Roof at Midnight; The Girl on the Saw-Backed Mountain; The Tenants; Bad Company; Figures in a Nightmare; Lost Heritage; The Witch Walks in Her Garden; "Run with the Fox."

2.3 *The Garden of Spices. Poems by Leah Bodine Drake* [1935–48]. *Contains:* Contents; The Journey of the Queen of Sheba; Descent of Angels; Goat-Song; Terror by Night; Serpent-Ring; The Youth of Circe (listed in Contents but omitted); A Vase from Araby; Music for Sun and Moon; House Accursed; Encounter in Broceliande.

2.4 *Mermaids' Combs and Witches' Brooms. Poems by Leah Bodine Drake. 1935–1948. Contains:* Contents; The Saints of Four-Mile-Water (An Irish Legend); The Mermaid; Mad Woman's Song; Ballad of the Jabberwock (*A Tale of Squankom*); The Old World of Green; A Star Came Out; The Haunted Hour; Old Wives' Tale; The Ballad of Fair Elspeth; Little Things.

2.5 *The Court of Oberon. Poems by Leah Bodine Drake* [1937–40]. *Contains:* Table of Contents; "There Are Fairies"; The Seven Sons of the King of Thule; The Daughter of the Grand Turk Loses Her Ball; "Apples and Apricots, Peaches and Plums"; King Gog and King Magog; The Hen-Wife's Chickens; Help Wanted; Gold from a Kettle; Conversation in an Oak-Tree.

2.6 *Black Peacocks. Poems by Leah Bodine Drake: 1944–46. Contains:* Contents; King Solomon; The Black Peacock; The Comet; Birds'-Eye View; December Stars; Moment at Sunset; The Fur Coat; Currier and Ives Prints; Gazelles in a Zoo; Bats; A Country Grave. "Cold Or-

BIBLIOGRAPHY

chard" is listed in the table of contents, but the title was later crossed out ("rewritten 1961") and the poem omitted; see S4.3.

3.1 *Fantasy in a Forest.* By Leah Bodine Drake [1947–53]. *Contains:* Contents; Fantasy in a Forest; Song against Smallness; The Final Green; Solar; Gipsies; Legend; Honey from the Lion; The Heads on Easter Island; Leonardo Before His Canvas; The Vision; Wild Geese in Spring; Minor Poet; Windows at Chartres; The False Messiah; Beyond Eden.

3.2 *Precarious Ground. Poems by Leah Bodine Drake* [1949–51]. *Contains:* Contents; Precarious Ground; The Lariat: 6000 B.C.; Love Song; Cobra; Dirge for a Doomed Planet; We Come out of the Forest, Fearing Stars; Cave-Paintings, Altamira; To Certain Poetry Critics; Gifts for Christ; The Darkened Glass.

3.3 *A Hornbook for Witches. Poems by Leah Bodine Drake* [1940–48]. *Contains:* Contents; A HORNBOOK FOR WITCHES: I. The Covenant; II. The Besom; III. The Coven; IV. The Hell-Broth; V. The Magic Circle; VI. The Conjuration; VII. The Pentagram; VIII. The Spells; IX. The Magician's Hat; X. Witch's-Wheel; XI. The Familiar; XII. Enchanted Sleep. A Likely Story!; A Warning to Skeptics; The Revenant; The Steps in the Field; The Unknown Land; The Window on the Stair; Old Daphne; Griffon's Gold.

3.4 *Design for a Tapestry. Poems by Leah Bodine Drake* [1952–53]. *Contains:* Contents; The Foam-Born; Atlantis; The Undine; The Birth of Beauty; Fools' Paradise; The Return; Design for a Tapestry [T.Ms. dating to c. 1961; the subtitle, "14th Century" appears to have been erased]; Design for a Tapestry; Air; Cat-Mummy (Valley of the Kings, Egypt).

3.5 *Toadstool Town. Poems by Leah Bodine Drake. 1952–1954. Contains:* Contents; The Gods of the Dana; Six Merry Farmers (A Cumberland Mountain Tale); The Wind in the Chimney; Red Ghosts in Kentucky; Out!; Cinder-Jewels; The Green Door; The Woods Grow Darker; The Minotaur; Nonsensical Rhymes ["The Minotaur" is intended to be among these]; The Sphinx; The Salamander; The Roc; "Good Pope Urban . . ."; The Jannigogs. *Note:* The scrapbook contains a number of poems that date to before 1952.

3.6 *The Middle Ages. Poems 1953–55. By Leah Bodine Drake. Contains:* Contents; The Middle Ages: Two Views; The Storks; We Move on Turning Stone; Drone; The Unicorn Wounded; Atavism; Flemish Artists (15th Century); Old Man on the Seashore: Morning.

3.7 *Candle, Last the Night. Poems 1955–56. By Leah Bodine Drake. Contains:* Contents; Rock and Bramble; The Beaches Beyond Oblivion; Semele; Childhood Summers; Beneath Funereal Lilies; The Weeds and the Wilderness; The Lazy Prince; Incoming Tide; The Good-Advisors; Through-Train; The Crying of the Grass; The Well.

4.1 *"The Fruit-Uneaten." Poems by Leah Bodine Drake. 1956. Contains:* Contents; The Harvest; The Forerunner; The Word of Willow; Moment in Paradise; [The Worth of It, listed in the table of contents but crossed out;] Adam's Hand; The Hand; Sunset Apocalypse; [The Dead Girl to Her Lover, listed in the table of contents but crossed out;] Multiple Clay; High Wire. *Note:* "Adam's Hand" is not listed in the table of contents. "The Hand" is a revised version of that poem.

4.2 *The Turn of the Year: Poems 1957–59 by Leah Bodine Drake. Contains:* Contents; The Hellenic World; The Nail; The Rider; The Crows; The Rain on the Stone; The Convent Bell; Lullaby After Death; With Her Death; Alone; "In the Night I Awoke"; To Mother; On the Night-Wind; "Only a Little Dust"; "I Dreamed That You Took My Arm." . . .; Lying Awake; "Brightness Falls from the Air"; That Summer [That summer the old folks said they had never]; The Robin; A Voice; A Memory.

4.3 *A "Cindering of Phoenixes." Poems by Leah Bodine Drake. 1959–1963. Contains:* The Poems [i.e., Contents]; The Web; Tarascon; The Spray; The Witches; Ariadne on Naxos; Cold Orchard; The Terrible Meek; Little Song (To C. B. D.); The Cry; A Meeting on a Northern Moor; The Presence; At All-Hallow's; The Morning; Orchids; The Snake; In the Night; The Wasp in the Window.

4.4 *Enchanted Sails. Poems for Children by Leah Bodine Drake* [1937–41]. *Contains:* Contents; The Little Piper; The Pool; Changeling; The Last Faun; The Naughty Fairy; Mouse-Heaven; Peddler's Pack; The Three Green Ladies of Greenwich.

BIBLIOGRAPHY

4.5/4.6 *A Record of Poetry—Poems Accepted, Newspaper Write-ups, Reviews, etc. From October 1957 to [   ]. Leah Bodine Drake.*

4.7 *Collected Published Magazine Poems. Leah Bodine Drake.* 1954–[1964].

5.1/5.2 *Published Poems by Leah Bodine Drake,* 1935–51. These folders contain a large scrapbook that was unbound so that the sheets could be more easily stored and handled. The scrapbook consists primarily of clippings of published poems from magazines, but it also contains clippings from the newspaper about Drake, letters to Drake, and other miscellany.

5.3 *The Woods Grow Darker. Poems by Leah Bodine Drake.* 1962–64. *Contains:* The Poems [i.e., Contents]; The Enchanted Swans; The Tale of Tannhauser; Royal; Circe; The Eve of St. Tib; At Alise Sainte-Reine; Poplar-Wind; Okio's Geese (Japan, 18th Century); Okio's Geese [T.Ms.]; History of America; The Gossip; A Back Country Road in God's Country; The Face in the Water; Fairy Tale. *Note:* John Herring removed the poem "The Face in the Water" (though replacing it with a copy) to present to Mrs. John. B. (Josephine) Elliott of New Harmony, Indiana, as a keepsake (TLS, 10 April [1965], David L. Rice Library). Elliott was a friend of Drake, who occasionally drove her home from work to Henderson. She and Herring purchased Drake's grave marker.

5.4 *Notes on Poetry.*

5.5 *Notes on Folklore and Art.*

5.6 *Witchcraft—Notes by Leah Bodine Drake, 1956.* A small binder with 74 typed, numbered loose-leaf pages (though there are handwritten notes on versos of some leaves, and three additional autograph pages) on various topics pertaining to witches and witchcraft.

5.7 Correspondence with Publishers, 1950–60. Among the correspondence, there are several fair copies of poems presented to the Margaret I. King library for its collection of poetry manuscripts, as requested by Lawrence S. Thompson of the University of Kentucky.

5.8 Correspondence with Publishers, July–October 1964.

5.9 Correspondence with Publishers, November–December 1964.

5.10 *This Tilting Dust.* T.Ms., c. 1955.

The Song of the Sun ~ Leah Bodine Drake

6.1 Published poems, clippings: 1935–59. Also contains mss. for Mad Jenny; Drake of Devon; With Every Death [eight different drafts with various titles]; letter to Dr. Lawrence S. Thompson, 10 January 1955, with enclosures: Drone; Flemish Artists—Fifteenth Century.

6.2 The Supplement to Who's Who, 1959 March–May.

6.3 *Multiple Clay: New and Selected Poems.* T.Ms., 1964: *I. New Poems:* The Weeds and the Wilderness; The Rider; The Morning; *Ask the Trees; Multiple Clay; Sunset Apocalypse; The Convent Bell; Gifts for Christ; The Forerunner; All-Hallows; In the Night; Cold Orchard; The Crying of the Grass; Under Funereal Lilies; The Word of Willow; Tarascon; The Web; The Middle Ages: Two Views; The Wasp in the Window; *Fairy Tale; The Crows; High Wire; The Woods Grow Darker; The Hellenic World; The Spray. *II. Selected Poems:* Fantasy in a Forest; Childhood Summers; Cat Mummy; Drone; We Come Out of the Forest, Fearing Stars; Air; Song against Smallness; The Storks; Semele; The Lariat: 6000 B.C.; Leonardo Before His Canvas; Old Man on the Seashore: Morning; Cave Paintings, Altamira; Love Song; Incoming Tide; Rock and Bramble; Cobra; Flemish Artists; "What Are Little Girls Made Of?"; Old Daphne; We Move on Turning Stone; Honey from the Lion; Precarious Ground; The Beaches Beyond Oblivion.

Dedicated "To the Memory of / Mother, Father, and Nanna / 1956, 1963, 1964." Drake also noted: "For several ideas expressed in 'The Hellenic World,' the author is indebted to Oswald Spengler and Elie Faure." The T.Ms. initially was titled *Airs, Waters, and Places,* from a work by Hippocrates. The title is recorded on a list of "Possible Titles for Books" in her notebook (S6.6), *Poems in Progress.* The poems in the section "Selected Poems" are all from *This Tilting Dust* except for "Old Daphne," which is from *A Hornbook for Witches.* The heading "Airs, Waters, and Places" appears on only ten pages of the typescript, all crossed out but only four of which were changed to say "Multiple Clay." None of the other pages bear the designation "Multiple Clay." Some pages have only the designation "Drake" at the top.

*Indicates the intended first appearance of the poem.

Griffin and Betty Callahan stated that Drake "had been working for months" on the manuscript just before her death in November 1964, but Drake had written to August Derleth 23 February 1961 that she was planning a book of new and old poems.

6.4 Photographs [1914–1947].
6.5 "Leah Bodine Drake." Student paper by Edelene Wood, University of West Virginia, 10 April 1968.
6.6 *Poems in Progress* [1964]. *Contains* (in part) drafts written in a composition book and also loose carbons: Switzerland; Hunter; From a destroyed early poem (1935); [untitled: "Lying awake at night I hear the rain"]; The Five Angels; A Charm for the New Year; What the Devil Said" [also "Says"]; Coral Reef at Calico Key; Life in These United States; FOR THE LIVING VOICE: What Poetry Means to Me; The Web; Precarious Ground; Old Man on the Seashore: Morning; The Birth of Beauty; The Undine; The Final Green.

Goblin Market: Selected Poems

Contains: The Undine; Changeling; Luna; The Web; Gage to a Lover; The World of Willow; The Old World of Green; Childhood Summers; The Woods Grow Darker; *There Are Fairies; He Dreams of Barbary [as "He Remembers Barbary"]; The Phoenix Egg; The Spray; The Rider; The Foam-Born; The Middle Ages; Old Daphne; A Warning to Skeptics; Hellenic World; Minor Poet; *The Croon of the Mer-Mother; Tarascon. The images are mostly by Arthur Rackham, Warwick Goble, and Edmund Dulac.

Drake prepared another scrapbook, auctioned on eBay in 2007 and now in private hands, called *Goblin Market: Selected Poems by Leah Bodine Drake,* dated in an unknown archivist's hand to "[1963–64]." The date range provided refers to the time when the scrapbook was prepared, not to the dates of the poems therein, which date from 1935 to 1961. The scrapbook, found in the library of Charles A. Musès, was a special presentation copy for him. The seller stated: "Loosely laid [in] is a leaf

*Indicates unpublished poems.

of paper in the hand of Dr. Charles A. Musès, listing the contents and stating "'GOBLIN MARKET—Leah Bodine Drake Rec'd. Feb 20, 1964 [sic], by Leah's Will.'" If the book was specified in Drake's will to go to Dr. Musès, he doubtless received it in 1965. The book resembles Drake's other scrapbooks in general makeup, but unlike those, the poems in *Goblin Market* are typed (although there are some handwritten corrections) and neatly pasted into the scrapbook, ornamented in Drake's typical fashion. The scrapbook is much tidier in assembly than Drake's other scrapbooks, although it, too, is a somewhat amateurish affair.

Of the twenty-two poems in the scrapbook, seven were not in a book (or in the *Multiple Clay* T.Ms.) and two of those were unpublished, five were in *A Hornbook for Witches,* five were in *This Tilting Dust,* and five (plus "Old Daphne") were earmarked for *Multiple Clay.* The scrapbook may contain texts that would serve as copy text for some poems (such as "The Croon of the Mer-Mother"), but it could not be consulted. *Goblin Market,* prepared late in life, covers a wide swath of Drake's poetic career and truly is a volume of "selected poems," whereas *Multiple Clay,* prepared at about the same time, is more of a "best of" collection, of which roughly half comes from *This Tilting Dust* and many of which were poems Musès had published in *Prismatic Voices.*

The title of the book derives from the poem "Goblin Market" by Christina Rossetti, in her book *Goblin Market and Other Poems* (1862), and in *DM,* which contained poems by Drake.

Leah Bodine Drake Papers, David L. Rice Library

1.1 AAUU Poetry: 1941–58. *Contains:* After The Green Star Dies; Air; Ark; "As in a Glass Darkly"; The Assyrian Lion; At All Hallows; Atavism; Atlantis; Ballad of The Jabberwock (A True Tale of Squamkum [*sic*] Town); Beyond Eden; The Black Peacock; Bookworm; By the River; Caution to a Lover; Cave-Paintings, Altamira; Celestial Visitant; Childhood Summers; Cobra; Coming Back to The House; Comment on Man; The Cytherean; Daphne; The Darkened Glass; December Stars; The Deserted Courtyard (China); Dirge for a Doomed Planet; Fairy-Tale: Twentieth Century; The

Bibliography

False Messiah; The Fawn; The Foam-Born; Folk-Tale; Fool's Paradise [three versions]; The Four; French Cathedral Windows; Gazelles in a Zoo; Gifts for Christ; Gothic; The Green Door; Griffin's Gold; The Growing Tree; The Heads on Easter Island; Honey from The Lion; John The Forerunner; King Solomon; Lady Writing a Letter (China); Landscape with Horses: 6000 B.C; The Lariat: 6000 B.C. [two copies]; Legend; Leonardo Before His Canvas; "Like Breath Upon a Glass"; Luna; Mad Woman's Song; Man in Winter; The Man Who Married a Swan-Maiden; The Merrow [two copies]; Minor Poet; The Moment; The Moment; Moment at Sunset; Multiple Clay; Music for Sun and Moon; Noon Light; The Old Khan and His Falcon; One Intoxicated (China); Overheard in Baghdad; The Path Through The Marsh; The Phoenix's Egg; The Pool; Powers of The Air; Precarious Ground; The Prisoner; Protective Coloring; Railroad Tracks; Red Ghosts in Kentucky; Reincarnation; Retrogression; Rhymes Without Reason; or, History Made Difficult; Semele; The Singer in The Waste; Snow-Crystals; Song against Smallness; The Song of The Sun; Terror by Night; This Side of Oblivion; To an Atheist; To Elinor Wylie; To One Who Fears Poetry May Be Useless; Turning Point; Uncle Jay; The Under-Seas; The Under-seas; An Unlikely Noah's Ark; Unlikely Story; The Unploughed Field; Vestal; The Vision of Jenghiz-Khan; The Web; The Web of Living; The Wild Geese Go Over. Frederic Prokosch [an essay]. Also an unnumbered page containing the concluding eight lines only of "We Come out of the Forest, Fearing Stars."

The list above is alphabetical. The T.Mss. in the file are organized numerically (save for the fragment cited) with numbers someone has written on the pages. Citation of the T.Mss. in the bibliography employs that numbering. (Note that the T.Mss. of "Atavism" and "Reincarnation"—the same poem with different titles—are both numbered "100.") The assorted T.Mss. seem to be file copies that Drake provided to the Evansville chapter of the American Association of University Women, to which she belonged. Some of the poems were submitted after Drake had moved to Parkersburg, West Virginia.

1.2 Newspaper Clippings 1950–65. Includes articles by and about Drake.

The Song of the Sun ~ Leah Bodine Drake

1.3 Published Poetry 1946–58. Consists of seven clippings from magazines.
1.4 Photograph of Drake and Dr. Alfred J. Niedermayer, 1958 (p. 88 in this volume).
1.5 An untitled drawing by Cornelia Bodine Drake, 1952.

Verse

The dates of composition given are LBD's as determined from her scrapbooks and manuscripts, and even from some publications, such as *PV*. As is evident, she sometimes gave conflicting dates. These may indicate misremembering the exact, or even approximate, date of composition, but may also indicate further revision of a poem over time, before she considered it to be final.

Adam the First Poet. S6.6. Lines from a destroyed poem, written c. 1950.

Adam's Hand. S4.1. Written December 1956, May 1963. An early version of "The Hand." A sonnet.

After the Green Star Dies. R3. Written November 1948. There are no truly green stars. The color of a star is more or less given by a black-body spectrum and thus never looks green.

Air. [1.] *Variegation: A Free Verse Quarterly* 9, No. 33 (Winter 1954): 3–4. *TD* 12. *PV* 386–87 (1954). *MC. S3.4, written 1953. In l. 30, LBD alludes to Matt 5:45: "your Father . . . sendeth rain on the just and on the unjust." [2.] *ªR27, written May 1953.

All-Hallows. *Magazine of Fantasy and Science Fiction* 27, No. 1 (July 1964): 79. *MC. S4.3 (as "At All Hallow's"). Written 31 October 1961, Lausanne. *Mockers* (l. 7) are mockingbirds.

All-Saints' Eve. *Southern Literary Messenger* 2, No. 10 (October 1940): 554. *DM* 410–11. In *Between the Bookends with Ted Malone: Volume Five*, ed. Ted Malone (New York: William Morrow, 1942), 324. *HW* 24. *HW* (recording). *S1.3. Written 1936. In many Christian churches, 1 November is All Saints' Day (All Hallows' Day, Hallowmas). Thus, 31 October is All-Saint's Eve, or Hallowe'en.

Alone. S4.2. Written November 1957.

BIBLIOGRAPHY

Apple. S1.1. Written 1934. A *dead sea apple* (l. 10) supposedly disintegrates into smoke or ashes when plucked. In ll. 13–14, LBD alludes to the Golden Apple of Discord in Greek mythology. The goddess Eris tossed the apple into the midst of a feast of the gods as a prize of beauty, initiating a vanity-fueled dispute among Hera, Athena, and Aphrodite that eventually led to the Trojan War.
"Apples and Apricots, Peaches and Plums." S2.5. Written 1938. *Hylas* (l. 2) is any tree frog of the genus *Hyla*.
Ariadne on Naxos. *Magazine of Fantasy and Science Fiction* 19, No. 2 (August 1960): 48 (as "New Wine in an Old Bottle: Ariadne"). *S4.3. Written May 1958. Ariadne, daughter of King Minos of Crete, helped Theseus defeat the Minotaur but was then abandoned by him. Later she became the bride of Dionysus (Bacchus in Roman mythology). The title as used in *F&SF* alludes to Lk 5:37: "And no man putteth new wine into old bottles; else the new wine will burst the bottles, and be spilled, and the bottles shall perish." The adage nowadays substitutes "wineskins" for "bottles."
Ark. R55. A retelling of the story of Noah from Genesis.
"As in a Glass Darkly." R52. See "The Darkened Glass."
Ask the Trees. *MC. In S5.3 as "History of America." Written April 1964.
The Assyrian Lion. *Wings: A Quarterly of Verse* 7, No. 1 (Autumn 1944): 1. In *The Music Makers: An Anthology of Recent American Poetry*, ed. Stanton A. Coblentz (New York: B. Ackerman, 1945; Great Neck, NY: Granger Book Co., 1978; Whitefish, MT: Kessinger Publishing, 2005), 55. *S1.2, written 1935; R70. A sonnet. In ancient Assyria, lion-hunting was the sport of kings, symbolic of the ruler's duty to protect and fight for his people. LBD refers specifically to the Lion Hunt of Ashurbanipal, a famous group of Assyrian palace reliefs from the North Palace of Nineveh on display at the British Museum.
At Alise Sainte-Reine. S5.3. Written January 1964, Lausanne, Suisse. Alise is the site of the decisive Battle of Alesia in 52 B.C.E. that marked the defeat of the Gauls under Vercingetorix by the Romans under Julius Caesar.

The Song of the Sun ❧ Leah Bodine Drake

At All-Hallow's. R37, written November 1961. See "All Hallows."
Atavism. *Nature Magazine* 42, No. 12 (December 1949): 468. *TD* 40. *PV* 401 (1949). *S3.6, written 1949; R100 (as "Reincarnation").
Atlantis. *Poetry Chap-Book* 11, No. 2 (Winter 1952–53): 32–33. *S3.4, written May 1952; R22, written June 1952. S3.4 and *Poetry Chap-Book* read *land* for *life*.
A Back-Country Road in God's Country. S5.3. Written April 1964.
Bad Company. *Weird Tales* 35, No. 8 (March 1941): 119; *Weird Tales* (Canadian) 37, No. 1 (September 1942): 91. *HW* 14. *S2.2. Written 1938.
The Ballad of Fair Elspeth. S2.4. Written 1933. *Elspeth* is the Scottish form of Elizabeth, meaning chosen or consecrated by God. A *beck* (l. 6) is a small stream. The *quicken* (l. 26) is the mountain ash (or rowantree) or the service tree. *Shoon* (l. 62) is an archaic plural of "shoe."
Ballad of the Jabberwock. *DM* 411–14. *HW* 10–13. *HW* (recording). *S2.4, as "Ballad of the Jabberwock (*A Tale of Squankom*)," written 1946; T.Ms., WHS (with letter to August Derleth dated 19 July 1946); R81, R81a, R81b. Winner of the Stephen Vincent Benét Ballad Contest of the Word Weavers of Los Angeles in 1946. In William S. Ward, *A Literary History of Kentucky* (Knoxville: University of Tennessee Press, 1988), 331 (ll. 1–12). In R, LBD used the epithet: "(A True Tale Of Squamkum [*sic*] Town.)" *DM* and *HW* contained the following note: "Squankom, the original Indian name of a certain little town in South Jersey, and which means 'the place of the evil god,' is one of the places where the mysterious creature variously called the 'Jersey Devil' or 'Jabberwock' was seen around the turn of the century." The poem deals with the sighting of the Jersey Devil in Williamstown (initially Squankum Town) during 1909. To *ramp* (l. 81) is to stand or advance menacingly with forelegs or arms raised. For the appearance in *HW*, LBD changed the names *Marsh* (l. 23) and *Jo* (l. 57) to *Karsh* and *Flo* so as not to cause offense to living persons.
Ballad of the Seal-Woman's Daughter. *Weird Tales* 39, No. 9 (January 1947): 85 (as "The Seal-Woman's Daughter"). *HW* 30–31 (as "The Seal-Woman's Daughter"). *S1.4, Written 1944. LBD's seal-

woman may be related to the selkie of Scottish mythology, a being capable of changing from seal to human form.

Bats. *Nature Magazine* 37, No. 9 (November 1944): 456. *S2.6. Written 1944. *The Bears* (l.12) refers to the constellations Ursa Major and Ursa Minor. *Cygnus* (l. 14 = the Swan) is a northern constellation that contains the asterism, the Northern Cross. *The Dogs* (l. 15) refers to the constellation Canes Venatici, the Dogs of Boötes. *Spica* (l. 16) is the brightest object in the constellation Virgo

The Beaches Beyond Oblivion. *TD* 44. *MC. S3.7. Written February 1953, as a longer version of "This Side of Oblivion" (q.v.). *Roland* (l. 3) (d. 778) was a Frankish military leader under Charlemagne and a principal figure in the literary cycle known as the Matter of France. He is poetically associated with his Oliphant, a signaling horn. *Tara* (l. 7) is a mysterious hilltop castle that was home to Irish high kings. It existed somewhere in what is now County Meath from very ancient times well before the time of St. Patrick (432) until its destruction, probably in the 6th century.

Belle and Beau. S1.1. Written 1934. By *Black Sambo* (l. 3), LBD is not using the modern racial slur, referring to any African American, or even to the main character in *Little Black Sambo* by Helen Bannerman, who was a Southern Indian boy who outsmarted a group of tigers, but perhaps to the black-skinned Indian servant of the Sedley family from Chapter One of Thackeray's *Vanity Fair,* or a similar person. *Good lack* (l. 16) is an archaic expression of surprise or objection. A *posset* (l. 21) was a hot British drink made of milk curdled with wine or ale, often spiced, used as a cold remedy.

Beneath Funereal Lilies. S3.7. Written 1955, rewritten January 1961. See "Under Funereal Lilies."

The Besom. See "A Hornbook for Witches."

Beyond Eden. *Recurrence: A Quarterly of Rhyme* 3, No. 9 (Summer 1952): 36. *TD* 37. *S3.1, written 1946, 1952; R23, written June 1952.

Bird's-Eye View. *Kaleidograph* 16, No. 9 (January 1945): 3. *New York Herald Tribune* (25 February 1945): A4. *S2.6. Written 1944.

The Song of the Sun ❧ Leah Bodine Drake

Birds in a Barn. *Prairie Schooner* 20, No. 1 (Spring 1946): 36–37. *S1.5. Written March 1945.

The Birth of Beauty. *Variegation: A Free Verse Quarterly* 7, No. 28 (Autumn 1952): 75. *TD* 33. *S3.4. Written August 1952.

The Bittern. *Country Bard* 7, No. 5 (Spring 1939): 11. *S1.2. Written 1938.

The Black Peacock. *Talaria: A Quarterly of Poetry* 11, No. 3–4 (Autumn–Winter 1946): 26. *HW* 69. *S2.6, written 1945; R64. For *Káf* (l. 1), see note on "King Gog and King Magog." In S2.6, l. 20 (not followed here), each word is written out on separate, staggered lines.

Bookworm. R18. Written June 1951.

Born Under Capricorn. *Kaleidograph* 16, No. 2 (June 1944): 3. *S1.2. Written 1938, 1943. LBD won the $10 Billy Chandler Memorial Award for the poem. LBD herself was a Capricorn.

Bread of Solitude. *Wings: A Quarterly of Verse* 6, No. 3 (Autumn 1943): 13 (as "Solitude"). *New York Herald Tribune* (17 October 1943): A6 (as "Solitude"). *S1.6. Written 1943.

"Brightness Falls from the Air." S4.2. Written 1957, 1964. The title is taken from l. 17 of "A Litany in Time of Plague" (1593) by Thomas Nashe (1567–1601?). LBD contemplated *Brightness Falls from the Air* as a possible book title. James Tiptree, Jr. used it as the title for a novel.

Burma: Moulmein Bazaar. S1.2. Written 1934. Mawlamyine (formerly Moulmein), is the fourth largest city of Burma.

By the River. R78. See "On a Chinese Screen" (S1.1).

Cat Mummy. *New Yorker* 30, No. 29 (4 September 1954): 66. *TD* 21. *PV* 398 (1955). **MC*. S3.4 (as "Cat-Mummy"). Written 1953.

Caution to a Lover. R99, R99a "(unfinished)." See "Gage to a Lover."

Cave Paintings, Altamira. *Epos* 2, No. 2 (Winter 1950): 14. *TD* 35. *Borestone Mountain Poetry Awards: 1951,* ed. Robert Thomas Moore (Philadelphia: University of Pennsylvania Press, 1951), 20. *The New Orlando Poetry Anthology,* ed. Richard Eberhart (New York: New Orlando Publications, 1963), 2.23. *PV* 407 (1955). **MC*. S3.2, written 1949–50; A.Ms., S5.7 MIK; R32. The Cave of Altamira in Cantabria, Spain, is famous for its cave paintings and drawings of wild mammals and human hands, created 18,500 to 14,000 years ago by early man during the Upper Paleolithic Period. It was discovered in 1879. A *cotyledon* (l. 10) is the first leaf or one of the first pair of leaves developed by the embryo of a seed plant or of some lower plants (such as ferns).

Celestial Visitant. R86. See "On a Night of Stars."
Centaur. See "An Unlikely Noah's Ark."
The Centaurs. *Cornhill Magazine* 160 (No. 958) (October 1939): 461 (under "Two Poems" [the other was "Himalayan Half-Wit" by Lt-Col J. D. Scale]). *HW* 70. *S1.2. Written 1938; revised 1943.
Changeling. *Weird Tales* 36, No. 7 (September 1942): 99; *Weird Tales* (Canadian) 36, No. 7 (January 1943): 3. *DM* 405–6. *HW* 26. In *Poems of Magic and Spells*, ed. William Cole (Cleveland: World Publishing Co., 1959), 52–53. *The Witches' Almanac* No. 33 (Spring 2014–Spring 2015): 9. *S4.4, written 1942; *GM*.
A Charm for the New Year. S6.6. An incomplete draft.
Childhood Summers. *Recurrence: A Quarterly of Rhyme* 4 (No. 15) (Winter 1954): 51. *TD* 29. *New York Times Book Review* (14 July 1957): 2. *MC. S3.7, written June 1953; R30, written November 1953; *GM*. "Won Second prize from Poetry Society of America for monthly meeting (Oct)." In l. 8, LBD refers to the *toadstone* (a.k.a. *bufonite*), a mythical stone or gem thought to be found in the head of a toad supposed to be an antidote to poison. *Painted ladies* (l. 13) are a migratory butterfly with predominantly orange-brown wings and darker markings.
Chimera. See "An Unlikely Noah's Ark."
Cinder-Jewels. S3.5. Written 1945, 1954. Submitted to the *Magazine of Fantasy and Science Fiction* but rejected. Cockaigne (l. 14) is a land of plenty in medieval myth, a place of luxury and ease. Hy Braseilis is a phantom island said to lie in the Atlantic Ocean west of Ireland.
Circe. S5.3. Written June 1963.
City Zoo. Nonextant? Submitted to *Saturday Review of Literature* in June 1948. Apparently not "Gazelles in a Zoo," published in early 1947.

Cobra. *New Yorker* 27, No. 36 (20 October 1951): 64. *TD* 24–25. **MC.* S3.2, written June 1951; R19, written 1951. The epigraph is by V. B. Metta, "Music Given Form in Hindu Painting," *International Studio* 79, No. 323 (April 1924): 48.

Cockatrice. See "An Unlikely Noah's Ark."

Cold Comfort. *Different* 2, No. 3 (July–August 1946): 6. *NecronomiCon Providence Memento Book*, ed. Victoria Dalpe and Justin Steele (Cranston, RI: Lovecraft Arts & Sciences Council Press, 2019), 68. **S1.4. Written spring 1946. In l. 7, *Roland* (d. 778) was a Frankish military leader under Charlemagne who became a principal figure in the literary cycle known as the Matter of France.

Cold Orchard. **ªThe Folio: A Magazine of Indiana Writing* 12, No. 3 (March 1947): 22. Listed in table of contents of S2.6, but crossed out with note "re-written 1961." *Fiddlehead* No. 57 (Summer 1963): 51 (under "Two Poems by Leah Bodine Drake"). **MC.* S4.3. Written 1944–54, rewritten 1961, Lausanne; 1962, West Virginia. Different from earlier poem and likely the rewritten version to which LBD alludes in S2.6.

The Comet. *Kaleidograph* 17, No. 4 (August 1945): 11. **S2.6. Written 1944, 1951. The comet van Gent–Peltier–Daimaca 1944a was discovered on 17 December 1943.

Coming Back to the House. R91. See "No Refuge."

Comment on Man. R62.

The Conjuration. See "A Hornbook for Witches."

The Convent Bell. *Commonweal* 69, No. 11 (12 December 1958): 290. **MC.* S4.2. Written 3 July 1958. A sonnet. In Evansville, the Drakes lived less than 6 miles east of the Franciscan Monastery of Saint Clare.

Conversation in an Oak-Tree. S2.5. Written 1937, 1956.

Coral Reef at Calico Key. S6.6. A very rough and unfinished draft, presented here only as a nascent poem. William Beebe (l. 8; 1877–1962), prolific science writer, made many deep dives in the Bathysphere.

A Country Grave. Under "A Line o' Type or Two," *Chicago Tribune* 104, No. 77 (30 March 1945): 12 (as "Country Grave"). **S2.6.

"Prophesy" (l. 6) reads "prophecy" in S2.6. *Chicago Tribune* is followed instead. The *plow* (l. 20) is the Big Dipper, also known as the Plow).

The Country Lover. S1.1. Written 1934. *Money Musk* (l. 13) is a Scottish fiddle tune that originated in the 18th century that takes its name from an Aberdeenshire, Scotland, baronial estate called Monymusk House. *Stance* (l. 20) = stanza (obs.).

The Coven. See "A Hornbook for Witches."

The Covenant. See "A Hornbook for Witches."

Crocodile. *Talaria: A Quarterly of Poetry* 6, No. 3 (Autumn 1941): 20–21 (under "Two Poems"). *New York Herald Tribune* (21 December 1941): A8. *S1.2. Written 1937, 1941. Line 5 alludes to Lk 12:27: "Consider the lilies how they grow: they toil not, they spin not . . ." *Memnon* (l. 16) presumably refers to the Colossi of Memnon, two massive stone statues of the Pharaoh Amenhotep III, who reigned in Egypt during the Dynasty XVIII. They have stood in the Theban Necropolis west of the River Nile from the modern city of Luxor since 1350 BCE. This may be a nod to Shelley's "Ozymandias," with its collosal ruined statue.

The Croon of the Mer-Mother. *S2.1; *GM*. Written 1934. *Faï* (l. 62) means of or resembling a fay (i.e., a fairy).

The Crows. *Hawk and Whippoorwill* 1, No. 2 (Autumn 1960): 9. *MC. In *Reflections on a Gift of Watermelon Pickle and Other Modern Verse*, ed. Stephen Dunning, Edward Lueders, and Hugh Smith (Glenview, IL: Scott, Foresman; New York: Lothrop Lee & Shepard, 1966), 24. In Stephen Dunning, *Teaching Literature to Adolescents* (Glenview, IL: Scott, Foresman, 1966), 84–85. In *Literature for Adolescents: Teaching Poems, Stories, Novels, and Plays*, ed. Stephen Dunning and Alan B. Howes (Glenview, IL: Scott, Foresman, 1975), 70. S4.2, written 1955, 1959; T.Ms., WHS.

The Cry. S4.3. Written December 1959.

The Crying of the Grass. *Recurrence: A Quarterly of Rhyme* 6, No. 23 (Winter 1956): 43. *PV* 388 (1956). *MC. S3.7. Ms. University at Buffalo Libraries (ten A.Ms. drafts). Written October 1955.

The Song of the Sun ❧ Leah Bodine Drake

Curious Story. *Silver Star* 1, No. 4 (Fall 1938): 3 (as "The Sirens"). *Wings: A Quarterly of Verse* 5, No. 5 (Spring 1942): 7. HW 62–63. *S1.4. Written 1936.

Currier and Ives Prints. Under "A Line o' Type or Two." *Chicago Tribune* (13 February 1948): 16. In *The Linebook 1948,* ed. Charles Collins (Chicago: The Tribune Co., 1948), 27. *S2.6. Written 1948.

The Cytherean. R49. LBD noted the poem as "to be in 'The Lyric,'" but such an appearance has not been found. Alternate of "The Foam-Born." An *alb* (l. 6) is a full-length white linen ecclesiastical vestment with long sleeves, gathered at the waist with a cincture. A *chasuble,* worn over the alb, is a sleeveless outer vestment an officiating priest wears when saying mass.

Daphne. R54. In Greek mythology, Daphne is a naiad whose beauty attracted the attention of Apollo, who pursued her. Just before being overtaken, Daphne pleaded to her father, the river god Ladon, for help, and so he transformed her into a laurel tree.

Dark Memory. *The Folio: A Magazine of Indiana Writing* 12, No. 3 (March 1947): 12. *S1.6. Written January 1947.

The Darkened Glass. *Poetry Chap-Book* 9, No. 1 (Autumn 1950): 12–13. TD 58. PV 383–84 (1950). *S3.2, written 1949; R.13, written 1949–50. Co-winner (with Alma Robison Higbee for "Hill Woman") of the $100 1st Prize Albert Ralph Lyric Award 1950. First title "'As in a Glass Darkly.'" The poem alludes to 1 Cor 13:12: "For now we see through a glass, darkly." Line 6 alludes to Salome's "dance of the seven veils" before Herod II, from Oscar Wilde's play *Salome* (1893).

The Daughter of the Grand Turk Loses Her Ball. S2.5. Written 1938, 1948. A *midden* (l. 43) is a refuse heap. *Aigrette* (l. 52) is a variant of *egret.* A *mameluke* (l. 59) is a member of a military class, originally composed of slaves, that seized control of the Egyptian sultanate in 1250, ruled until 1517, and remained powerful until massacred or dispersed by Mehemet Ali in 1811. For *pedlar's pack* (l. 61), see "Peddler's Pack."

The Dead Girl to Her Lover. Listed in contents of S4.1 but crossed out and omitted. Nonextant or retitled.

BIBLIOGRAPHY

December Stars. *Atlantic Monthly* 174, No. 6 (December 1944): 107–8. *S2.6, written 1944, 1952; R97; [R97a] "Re-written after publication. / Revised 1955." The poem is LBD's description of what had supposedly appeared as the Star of Bethlehem. The Beehive Cluster (l. 2) is in the constellation Cancer. The Twins (Castor and Pollux, l. 7) refers to the constellation Gemini. The Chair (l.8) is also known as Cassiopeia's Chair. The constellation Orion (l. 9) is named for a mythological huntsman, not usually regarded as a bull-fighter. The Bull (l. 10) is the constellation Taurus. A *banderilla* (l. 11) is a decorated dart thrust into a bull's neck or shoulders by the banderillero during a bullfight. LBD refers to the Pleiades (the Seven Sisters), an open star cluster. *Stelliscript* (l. 13) is that which is written in the stars. In l. 20, LBD refers to the constellation Leo and the asterism the Big Dipper, also known in the UK as the Plough and Charles' Wain (a part of the constellation Ursa Major).

Descent of Angels. *Kaleidograph: A National Magazine of Poetry* 14, No. 3 (July 1942): 6. *TD* 56. *S2.3. Written 1935, 1942. The epigraph is from the story of Noah.

The Deserted Courtyard. R77. See "On a Chinese Screen."

Design for a Tapestry: 14th Century. *Wings: A Quarterly of Verse* 7, No. 8 (Winter 1947): 8–9 as "Gothic." S3.4, "Revised Feb. 1953," also including *T.Ms. (c. January 1961) laid in. First version = "Gothic" (S1.5). *Dagged* (l. 6) means edged with decorative scallops or the like. The subject is *The Lady and the Unicorn* (*La Dame à la licorne*), the modern title given to a series of six tapestries woven in Flanders from wool and silk, from designs drawn in Paris around 1500.

Dirge for a Doomed Planet. *ᵃPoetry Chap-Book* 8, No. 2 (Winter 1949–50): 36–37; *TD* 60. *S3.2, written February 1949, rewritten January 1955; R10, written May 1949. In *Poetry Chap-Book*, dedicated "To Gerald Heard." Gerald [Henry FitzGerald] Heard (1889–1971) was a British-born American historian, science writer, lecturer, and philosopher

Drake of Devon. T.Ms. S6.1. Inscribed to her aunt, Anne Bodine, "For Nanna from L B D." (Written 1940?) The poem is largely about Sir

Francis Drake (1540?–1596), the renowned British sea captain. In 1573 he captured the Spanish Silver Train (20 tons of silver and gold) at Nombre de Dios, a port in Panama. In 1577 he began a circumnavigation of the earth, rounding Cape Horn (the southernmost point of South America) and returning to England in 1580. In 1588 he defeated the Spanish Armada in the English Channel as it was set to invade England. In May–June 1940, hundreds of private sailing vessels left England and reached Dunkirk, a town in northeast France on the English Channel, to evacuate more than 300,000 English soldiers trapped there by the Nazis.

A Dream of Samarkand. *Southern Literary Messenger* 3, No. 9 (September 1941): 442–43 (as "Samarkand (for Harold Lamb)." *S1.2. Written 1934, 1941. Samarkand is a city in modern-day Uzbekistan, one of the oldest inhabited cities in Central Asia. Harold Lamb (1892–1962) was an American historian, novelist, short story writer, and screenwriter. Timur the Lame (also Tamerlane) (1336–1405) was a Turco-Mongol conqueror, founder of the Timurid Empire in Persia and Central Asia. *Heart's Delight* (l. 24) is Dilkusha Kothi, an 18th-century house, now in ruins, built in the English baroque style in the Dilkusha area of Lucknow in India.

Drone. *Atlantic Monthly* 195, No. 6 (June 1955): 38. TD 19–20. In *Jubilee: One Hundred Years of the Atlantic,* ed. Edward Weeks and Emily Flint (Boston: Atlantic–Little, Brown Books, 1957), 603–4. In *New England Oracle: A Choice Selection from One Hundred Years of the Atlantic Monthly,* ed. Edward Weeks and Emily Flint (London: Collins, 1958), 457–58. *MC. S3.6, written April 1954; A.Ms, S6.1, written April 1954. A sestina. A *brummel* (l. 6) is a dandy.

Ducks and Pigs. S2.1. Written 1937.

Earth: Atomic Age. *Poetry Chap-Book* 5, No. 3 (Spring 1947): 54–55. *Kansas City Star* (23 March 1947): 96. *Greensboro* [NC] *Daily News* (29 July 1948): 6. *S1.5. Written 1946, 1957. Received runner-up acknowledgement award for *Poetry Chap-Book.*

Enchanted Honey. S1.3. Written 1944, 1956.

Enchanted Sleep. See "A Hornbook for Witches."

BIBLIOGRAPHY

The Enchanted Swans. S5.3. Written 1953, 1962. A sestina. The story of the Six Swans is no. 49 of the fairy tales collected by the Brothers Grimm. It tells of a king who married a witch who turned his six sons from a previous marriage into swans. A *minster* (l. 16) is a church founded by a missionary in ancient times. A *whillilew* (l. 26; var. of *whillaloo*) is a cry of lamentation, an outrcry, uproar. A *sark* (l. 35) is a shirt or chemise.

Encounter in Broceliande. *HW* 59. *S2.3. Written 1938, 1948. Brocéliande is a legendary forest in France that first appears in literature in 1160, in the *Roman de Rou,* a verse chronicle by Wace. *Helleborine* (l. 3) is the common name for a number of species of orchid. *Miniver* (l. 6) is an unspotted white fur derived from the winter coat of the ermine, frequently used in the robes of British peers.

The Eve of St. Tib. S5.3. Written December 1963, Lausanne. In Discordianism, 29 February is coterminus with St. Tib's day in the Discordian calendar. Discordianism is a parody religion founded in 1963 by Greg Hill with Kerry Wendell Thornley, working under the pseudonyms Malaclypse the Younger and Omar Khayyam Ravenhurst.

Evening in Late Summer. Published appearance (c. 1935?) from a clipping, as by Lea Bodine Drake (in S6.1), has not been determined. See "Haunted Hour." A sonnet. In l. 12, *Nimue* is one of several names for the sorceress known in folklore as "the Lady of the Lake."

Explanation. *Story Parade* 13, No. 10 (October 1948): 37. *S2.1. Written 1935; revised in the 1940s.

The Face in the Water. *S5.3: a photocopy of the A.Ms., which was removed and presented to Josephine Elliott in April 1965, now held at the David L. Rice Library. Written August 1963. A *wimple* (l. 4) is a covering worn over the head and around the neck and chin by women in the late medieval period, and also by some modern Catholic nuns.

The Fairies in Autumn. S1.3. Written 1935.

Fairy Cider. S2.1. Written 1944.

Fairy Tale. *MC.* S5.3. Written 1964. LBD apparently submitted the poem to *Fantasy and Science Fiction* under another title. Avram Davidson, the editor, wrote LBD: "I [...] would have taken 'Frog

699

Prince' if we had not already run Don White's prose treatment of the theme in the October [1962] F&SF" (ALS, University of Kentucky; n.d. but c. early 1964). He refers to White's "Twenty-Four Hours in a Princess's Life, With Frogs." *Skin-deep* (l. 12) is a parody of "knee-deep," the supposed croak of the frog.

Fairy-Tale: Twentieth Century. R58.

The False Messiah. *Wings: A Quarterly of Verse* 9, No. 1 (Spring 1949): [1]. *TD* 59. *S3.1, written 1948, rewritten January 1955; R5, written 1948. A sonnet. LBD said the poem was "to be in Stanton Coblentz's new book—a critique of the scientific viewpoint in modern literature" (R6), but no such book was published. Line 7 alludes to Matt 27:51: "And, behold, the veil of the temple was rent in twain from the top to the bottom . . ."

The Familiar. See "A Hornbook for Witches."

Fantasy in a Forest. *Wings: A Quarterly of Verse* 5, No. 1 (Spring 1941): 8–9. *TD* 17–8. In *Best Poems of 1941*, ed. Thomas Moult (New York: Harcourt, Brace, 1942), 105–6. In *The Music Makers: An Anthology of Recent American Poetry*, ed. Stanton A. Coblentz (New York: B. Ackerman, 1945; Kessinger Publishing, 2005), 53–55. In *Adventures into Poetry: Secondary Book IV*, ed. Mary Daunt (London: Macmillan, 1941–49, 1951, and many other reprints), 22–24. *PV* 405–6. *VL* 113–14. *MC*. S3.1, written 1940; T.Ms., S5.7 MIK. Amelius of Gault appears to be imaginary; the name may be a play on *Amadis de Gaula* (*Amadis of Gaul*), a chivalric romance dating to the early 16th century. A *bestiary* is a compendium of beasts, usually presented in the form of an illuminated manuscript. *Fell* (l. 6) is a leopard skin.

The Fawn. R90. A sonnet.

Figures in a Nightmare. *Southern Literary Messenger* 3, No. 5 (May 1941): 239. *HW* 28. In *Unseen Wings: The Living Poetry of Man's Immortality*, ed. Stanton A. Coblentz (New York: Beechhurst Press, 1949), 187. *S2.2. Written 1935, although LBD also notes on one leaf of the ms. "1935–40."

The Final Green. *Lyric* 31, No. 3 (Summer 1951): 67. [Montreal] *Gazette* (7 July 1951): 6. *Greensboro* [NC] *Daily News* (8 July 1951): 45. *Kansas City* [MO] *Times* (9 July 1951): 20. *Panama American*

BIBLIOGRAPHY

(15 July 1951): supplement, p. 4 (under "Poet's Corner"). *Lansing* [MI] *State Journal* (18 July 1951): 8. *TD* 15. In *New Poems by American Poets,* ed. Rolfe Humphries (New York: Ballantine, 1953), 49. *S3.1; A.Ms., S5.7 MIK. T.Ms. University at Buffalo Libraries. Written 1952. LBD alludes in ll. 1–2 to the fact that green was not counted among the four classic colors of Greek painting—red, yellow, black and white—and is rarely found in Greek art.

The Five Angels. S6.6.

Flemish Artists, Fifteenth Century. *Atlantic Monthly* 195, No. 2 (February 1955): 57. *TD* 27. *MC. In *Best Poems of 1955: Borestone Mountain Poetry Awards 1956,* ed. Robert Thomas Moore (Stanford, CA: Stanford University Press, 1957), 30. *PV* 408 (1955), as "*from* Flemish Artists, Fifteenth Century," but omitting ll. 21–28. S3.6, written November 1953; A.Ms. S6.1, June 1954. *Dinanderie* (l. 3) were decorative objects of brass, copper, or bronze such as made in the 13th to 15th centuries chiefly for ecclesiastical or domestic use. A *hennin* (l. 12) was a high cone-shaped headdress, usually with a thin veil pendent from the top, worn by European women in the 15th century. A *mignon* (l. 13) is something small and delicately pretty, referring in this case to a woman. The image in ll. 14–15 is a woodcut from Hartmann Schedel *Liber chronicarum mundi,* Nuremberg, 1493. *Dagging* (l. 19) is edging on a garment with decorative scallops or similar. A *polder* (l. 25) is a parcel of low-lying land reclaimed from the sea or a river and protected by dikes, especially in the Netherlands. S3.6 contains a clipping of Pieter the Elder Bruegel, *Massacre of the Innocents,* in a Dutch setting, in winter, depicting Walloon soldiers in the pay of Spain.

The Foam-Born. *Voices: A Journal of Poetry* No. 150 (January–April 1953): 38–39. *Greensboro* [NC] *Daily News* (10 April 1953): 8. *Charleston* [SC] *Daily Mail* (8 March 1953): 8 (as "Back-To-Nature Writer"). *TD* 34. *S3.4, written 1952; R24, written December 1952; *GM.* In Hesiod's *Theogony,* Aphrodite is born off the coast of Cythera from the foam (aphros) produced by Uranus's genitals, which his son Cronus severed and threw into the sea. The T'ang dynasty (l. 3) ruled China from 618 to 907. It was regarded as a

701

pinnacle of Chinese civilization and famous for the brightly coloured tomb figurines, known as *mingqui,* it modelled out of clay. The figurines included horses, camels, dancers, musicians, courtesans, civil officials, and servants. In l. 10, Phidias (480?–430 B.C.E.) was the preeminent sculptor and painter in ancient Greece.

Folk-Tale. R89.

Fool's Paradise. *Contemporary Poetry* No. 13 (Summer 1953): 23. *TD* 48. *PV* 392 (1953). *S3.4, written January 1953; R29, written October 1952; R29a, written June 1952; R29b, written May 1952 ("Subject to change").

The Forerunner. *Commonweal* 64, No. 20 (17 August 1956): 494. In *Best Poems of 1956: Borestone Mountain Poetry Awards 1957,* ed. Robert Thomas Moore (Stanford, CA: Stanford University Press, 1957), 26–27. *MC. S4.1. Written June 1956. In Eastern Christianity, the name for John the Baptist is John the Forerunner. *Kedron* (l. 1) is a valley between the Mount of Olives and Mount Moriah, east of Jerusalem. *Jokhannon* (l. 5) is LBD's spelling of Jokanaan, the name under which John the Baptist appears in Oscar Wilde's play *Salomé* (1891).

The Four. R21. Written June 1952.

French Cathedral Windows. R44. See "Windows of Chartres."

From a destroyed early poem (about 1935). S6.6. Written c. 1935. LBD noted: "(These ideas were original with,—I think—Elie Faure, not me.)" Jacques Élie Faure (1873–1937) was a French art historian and essayist. In *MC,* LBD had noted ""For several ideas expressed in 'The Hellenic World,' the author is indebted to . . . Elie Faure."

Frog Prince. See "Fairy Tale."

from a poem to Mother. S6.6. Written 1957.

Frozen Heart. S1.5, under "Winter Harvests." Written 1935.

The Fruit Uneaten. *Poetry Chap-Book* 1, No. 2 (December 1942–January 1943): 52–53. *TD* 50–51. *S1.6. Written 1942.

Full Moon, 1942. See "Full Moon, 1940."

Full Moon, 1940. *Wings: A Quarterly of Verse* 5, No. 7 (Autumn 1942): 12 (as "Full Moon 1942"). *S1.4. Written 1940.

The Fur Coat. *Nature Magazine* 41, No. 1 (January 1948): 23. *HW* 38. *S2.6. Written August 1947. LBD opposed the use of leghold traps.

Fury. See "An Unlikely Noah's Ark."

Gage to a Lover. *Kaleidograph* 14, No. 5 (September 1942): 8–9. *New York Herald Tribune* (20 September 1942): A10. In *Ted Malone's Adventures in Poetry*, ed. Ted Malone (New York: William Morrow, 1946), 125–27. *S1.6, written April 1942; *GM*. Alternate title: "Caution to a Lover" [R99, R99a]. A *gage* is something deposited as a pledge of performance.

Gazelles in a Zoo. *Lyric* 26, No. 4 (Winter 1947): 43–44. *S2.6, written 1933–45; R96. A *cloison* (l. 6, a noun) is a partition. For "Life" (l. 32) read "God" in *Lyric*.

Ghoul. See "An Unlikely Noah's Ark."

The Giant's Garden. S1.3 (on table of contents as "Giant's Garden"). Written 1935.

Gifts for Christ. *Poetry Chap-Book* 8, No. 2 (Winter 1949–50): 50. *MC*. S3.2, written 1949; R38 (A.Ms.), R42. Ten A.Ms. drafts, University at Buffalo Libraries, first title "Gifts of the Christ." A clipping in one of LBD's scrapbooks that identifies the poem as having appeared in *Poetry Chap-book* bears the printed name "Pearle Le Compte" at the bottom, followed by the written note "Used by her on her 1960 Xmas cards." Le Compte was the author of *Dramatics* (New York: A. S. Barnes, 1931). The poem refers to the story of the Magi in Matt 2:1–12.

Gipsies. S3.1. Written May 1953.

The Girl in the Glass. *HW* 45 (l. 20 has "Moony"). *S2.1. Written 1936, 1938.

The Girl on the Saw-Backed Mountain. *Saturday Evening Post* 213, No. 35 (1 March 1941): 33 (as "The Girl on the Sawbacked Mountain"). *S2.2. Written 1940. To *hone* (l. 29) is to yearn.

Goat-Song. *Wings: A Quarterly of Verse* 5, No. 8 (Winter 1943): 9–11. *HW* 53–55. *S2.3. Written 1936, 1942. "Took a prize from WINGS." *Fox-fire* (l. 27) is the bioluminescence created by some species of fungi present in decaying wood.

The Song of the Sun 🙢 Leah Bodine Drake

The Gods of the Dana. *Magazine of Fantasy and Science Fiction* 7, No. 1 (July 1954): 60. FSC 79–80. *S3.5, written in 1954; T.Ms., WHS. LBD referred to editors Anthony Boucher and Francis McComas as "gods of Dana Street" because their magazine was headquartered at 2643 Dana Street, Berkeley. Published versions of the poem contained the following headnote: "(The Tuatha dé Danaan, the race of the gods of Dana, are the elder gods of Erin, also known as the Shee.)" The Gods of Dana were Brian, Luchar, and Lucharba—the three druids for whom Tuatha Dé Danann are named. *Mider* (l. 9) is a variant spelling of Midir, a character in early Irish myth. *Lugh* (l. 10) is a warrior god; *Brighet* (l. 11) is a variant spelling of the goddess Brigid; *Angus* (l. 12) is a variant spelling of Aengus, god of love.

Gold from a Kettle. S2.5. Written 1940.

The Good-Advisors. S3.7. Written September 1955.

The Gossip. S5.3. Written May 1964.

Gothic. *S1.5 (but not listed in the table of contents), written 1946, "Revised after pub., 1953"; R94. Marianne Moore read the poem (as "Gothic Artists") at the PSA meeting held 30 December 1953. See "Design for a Tapestry: 14th Century."

The Green Door. *Saturday Evening Post* 222, No. 12 (17 September 1949): 53. In *Birthday Candles Burning Bright: A Treasury of Birthday Poetry*, ed. Sara Westbrook Brewton and John E. Brewton (New York: Macmillan, 1960), 155–56. *S3.5, written November 1948; R7, written January 1949.

Griffon's Gold. *HW* 68. *S3.3, written 1940, 1948; R87, as "Griffin's Gold."

The Growing Tree. R79. In l. 6, LBD cancelled "little" and wrote "cho[o]se other word" but did not supply one.

The Hand. S4.1. Written November 1956. A brace of sonnets. Winner of the 1956 Arthur Davison Ficke Memorial Award, sharing the $400 prize with three other poets. *Hic jacet* (l. 26) is Latin for "Here lies," a common epitaph on a tombstone. A *Tau* (l. 27) is a T-shaped (Greek alphabet) cross.

BIBLIOGRAPHY

The Harvest. *Kaleidograph* 28, No. 1 (July–August–September 1956): 7. *S4.1. Written May 1956.

The Haunted Hour. First publication (c. 1935?) as "Evening in Late Summer," as by Lea Bodine Drake, per an unidentified clipping in S6.1. *Weird Tales* 36, No. 2 (November 1941): 105 (as "Haunted Hour"). *HW* 52 (as "Haunted Hour"). *S2.4. Written 1934. A sonnet. *Dwale* (l. 10) is a soporific drink made from deadly nightshade or belladonna. Line 14 alludes to Robert Browning's poem *Childe Roland to the Dark Tower Came*. In the last stanza, the hero sees the ghosts of those who died trying to reach the Dark Tower before him:

> I saw them and I knew them all. And yet
> Dauntless the slug-horn to my lips I set,
> And blew. (xxxiv.4–6).

He Dreams of Barbary. *Southern Literary Messenger* 4, No. 3 (March 1942): 125. *S1.2, written 1935, 1953; *GM* as "He Remembers Barbary."

The Heads on Easter Island. *Weird Tales* 41, No. 2 (January 1949): 67. *HW* 51. *S3.1, written August 1947; R51. A sonnet.

Heard on the Roof at Midnight. *Weird Tales* 39, No. 8 (November 1946): 87. *Weird Tales* (Canadian) 38, No. 4 (January 1947): 102. *DM* 415. *HW* 46. *S2.2. Written [i.e., revised] 1949. A *kelpie* (l. 7) is in folklore a shape-shifting water spirit inhabiting the lochs and pools of Scotland, usually described as appearing as a horse but able to adopt human form. For *Sarsen Stones* (l. 20), see note on "A Hornbook for Witches." For *Walpurgis Night* (l. 22), see note on "Old Wives' Tale."

The Hell-Broth. See "A Hornbook for Witches."

The Hellenic World. *Atlantic Monthly* 200, No. 4 (October 1957): 44–45. In *Best Poems of 1957: Borestone Mountain Poetry Awards 1958*, ed. Robert Thomas Moore (Stanford, CA: Stanford University Press, 1959), 32–34. In *Anthology of Magazine Verse for 1958*, ed. William Stanley Braithwaite (New York: Schulte Publishing Co., 1959), 51–53. *MC. S4.2, written April 1957; *GM*. In l. 46, "tomorrow and tomorrow and tomorrow" is from *Macbeth* 5.5.18. In l. 53,

LBD alludes to the fact that the Greek word *skeuos* ("chattel") also meant "inanimate object," but the more common word for slave in Greek is *doulos*. For l. 56, cf. Is 55:8: "For my thoughts are not your thoughts, neither are your ways my ways, saith the Lord."

Help Wanted. *Child Life* 25, No. 10 (October 1946): 8. *S2.5. Written [i.e., revised] 1947.

The Hen-Wife's Chickens. S2.5. Written 1941. The henwife is not merely a "woman who keeps poultry," nor merely a witch. In folk and fairytales from Ireland and Scotland the henwife is often a herbalist or a healer, synonymous with the Wise Old Woman archetype.

Her Death. T.Ms. S6.1, A.Ms. Written 18 July 1958. See "With Her Death."

High Renaissance. S1.1. Written 1935. In l. 10, Lorenzo da Pavia (b. after 1450–1517) was an Italian musical instrument maker who worked in Venice.

High Wire. *Wisconsin Poetry Magazine* 2, No. 3 (January–February 1957): 4. *PV* 382 (1957). *MC. S4.1. Written March 1956.

History of America. S5.3. See "Ask the Trees." Written April 1964.

Honey from the Lion. *Saturday Review of Literature* 30, No. 49 (6 December 1947): 52. *Arena* (New Zealand) No. 23 (Summer 1950): 6–7. TD 39. In *New Poems by American Poets,* ed. Rolfe Humphries (New York: Ballantine, 1953), 50. *PV* 403 (1951). In *You and Contemporary Poetry: An Aid-to-Appreciation,* ed. George Abbe (Peterborough, NH: William L. Bauhan, 1965), 37. In *A Celebration of Cats: An Anthology of Poems,* ed. Jean Burden (New York: P. S. Eriksson, 1974), 180–81.*MC. S3.1, written August 1947; A.Ms., S5.7 MIK; R47. T.Ms., University at Buffalo Libraries. LBD alludes to "Samson's riddle" to thirty Philistine guests: "Out of the eater, something to eat; out of the strong, something sweet" (Jgs 14:14). The riddle was based on a private experience of Samson who killed a young lion and after a while found bees and honey in its corpse. The answer to his riddle is "What is sweeter than honey? What is stronger than a lion?" (Jgs 14:18). LBD contemplated *Honey from the Lion* as a possible book title. In 1951, LBD won a prize of $100 for an unpublished book manuscript submitted to a poetry contest conducted by the Midwestern Writers' Conference.

A Hornbook for Witches. *Arkham Sampler* 1, No. 1 (Winter 1948): 41–42. In *The Arkham Sampler: A Facsimile Edition*, ed. August Derleth (Sauk City, WI: Arkham House, 2010), 41–42. *Contains:* 1. The Besom; 2. The Familiar; 3. The Magic Circle; [item no. 4 was omitted;] 5. Magician's Hat; 6. Witch's-Wheel; 7. The Spells; 8. The Coven; 9 The Covenant. *HW* 3–5: *Contains:* I. The Besom; II. The Familiar; III. The Magic Circle; IV. Enchanted Sleep; V. Magician's Hat; VI. Witch's-Wheel; VII. The Spells; VIII. The Coven; IX The Covenant; and *HW* (recording). *S3.3: *Contains:* I. The Covenant; II. The Besom; III. The Coven; IV. The Hell-Broth; V. The Magic Circle; VI. The Conjuration; VII. The Pentagram; VIII. The Spells; IX. The Magician's Hat; X. Witch's-Wheel; XI. The Familiar; XII. Enchanted Sleep. Written 1935, 1947. In I.4, *Pamphiles* is apparently an erroneous rendering of Pamphile, a Greek woman on the island of Kos who was purportedly the first to spin silk; *Endor* refers to the Witch of Endor (see 1 Sm 28:3–25); *Bork* refers to Sidonia von Borcke (1548–1620), a Pomeranian noblewoman tried and executed for witchcraft. In posthumous legends, she is depicted as a femme fatale, and she has entered English literature as Sidonia the Sorceress. In III.1, *Sarsen stones* (= Saracen, or pagan) are sandstone blocks found in quantity in the United Kingdom, such as those used to make Stonehenge. Cf. "Round and 'Round" for a magic circle. *Aconite* (IV.4) can refer to either of two lethal plant species—monkshood and wolfsbane. In Jewish mythology, *Mazikeen* (VII.1) are invisible demons that create minor annoyances (or greater dangers). The "twin-triangles" mentioned [VII.2] would be a star of David (a hexagram), not a pentagram; however, illustrations in LBD's scrapbook for this poem depict both star shapes, and both have mystical significance. In XII.1, a *limmer* is a low, base person.

House Accursed. *HW* 39–40 (as "House Accurst"). *S2.3. Written 1939, 1949. *Newell* (l. 20) is a variant spelling of *newel*, a post that supports a handrail at the bottom or landing of a staircase.

The House in the Hollow. S2.1. Written 1945.

"Hunter." S6.6.

The Song of the Sun ❧ Leah Bodine Drake

"I Dreamed That You Took My Arm." S4.2. Written November 1957.

I Met a Lion. *Wings: A Quarterly of Verse* 5, No. 3 (Autumn 1941): 15 (as "'I Met a Lion,'" alluding to Shakespeare, *Julius Caesar* 1.3.441). *TD* 55. *S1.2. Written 1940, 1954.

In the Night. *Fiddlehead* No. 57 (Summer 1963): 51 (under "Two Poems by Leah Bodine Drake"). **MC.* S4.3. Written September 1961, Lausanne.

"In the Night I Awoke." S4.2. Written August 1957, "(a true dream)."

In the Shadows. *Weird Tales* 26, No. 4 (October 1935): 476, as by Lea Bodine Drake. *DM* 407–8. *HW* 27. In *La casa della Strega: Il Meglio di* Weird Tales *2* (Fanucci Editore Traduzione: Daniela Galdo e Gianni Pilo, 1987) as "Tra le ombre," p. 91, as by Lea Bodine Drake. *S1.1. Written 1935.

in the woods of the Vaud. S6.6. Written near Lausanne January or February 1964. Lausanne is in the canton of Vaud.

Incoming Tide. *TD* 52. **MC.* S3.7. Written March 1954, January 1955.

India: In the Garden of Spices. S1.2. Written 1935.

The Jannigogs. *Magazine of Fantasy and Science Fiction* 6, No. 4 (April 1954): 74. *S3.5. Written June–July 1953. LBD informed Anthony Boucher that she had rewritten the poem from eight stanzas to six. The longer, original version is nonextant.

Japan: The Persimmon Gatherers. S1.2. Written 1937. In l. 19, LBD refers to Kitagawa Utamaro (1753?–1806), a Japanese artist best known for his woodblock prints and paintings.

Jilly and the Elf. S2.1. Written 1934. A *snood* (l. 23) is a type of headgear worn by women to keep their hair in place, usually taking the form of a cloth or yarn bag.

John the Forerunner. R28. Written May 1953. Alternate version of "The Forerunner" (q.v.).

The Journey of the Queen of Sheba. *Southern Literary Messenger* 4, No. 1 (December 1942): 440–42. *S2.3. Written 1937, 1942. Inspired by *The Queen of Sheba* by the Scottish painter John Duncan (1866–1945). A clipping of Duncan's painting faces the poem in the scrapbook. *HW* T.Ms. The queen of Sheba came to Jerusalem "with a very great train, with camels that bare spices, and very much gold, and precious stones" (1 Kgs 10:2). In *Southern Literary Messenger* LBD noted that "Haile Selassie, Emperor of Ethiopia, claims descent from Solomon and Balkis' son," Menelik. In *The Book of the Thousand Nights and a Night,* Cheheristani is a jinniyah, who is pursued by the King, under the form of a white doe (l.6). She marries him, and becomes the mother of Balkis, the Queen of Sheba. *Khem* (l. 41) is the Egyptian name for Letopolis, an ancient Egyptian city, the capital of the second nome of Lower Egypt. The term was often used to refer to the entirety of Egypt. An *ambassade* (l. 61) is the mission of one sent on a mission.

King Gog and King Magog. S2.5. Written 1940. In the Hebrew Bible Gog and Magog may be individuals, peoples, or lands. LBD seems to refer instead to the giants Gog and Magog, who were defeated by Brutus and chained to the gates of his palace on the site of Guildhall in London. *Hind* (l. 19) or al-Hind, is the Persian and Arabic name for the Indian subcontinent. *Kâf* (l. 22) or Mount Qaf, is a mythical place in medieval Islamic cosmology.

King Solomon. *S2.6, written 1944; R61. In S2.6, LBD states the poem was accepted by *Talaria,* but such an appearance has not been found. In l. 24, cf. "crusts of sin" to Alfred, Lord Tennyson, "St. Simeon Stylites": "Altho' I be the basest of mankind, / From scalp to sole one slough and crust of sin" (ll. 1–2). Line 25 is from Eccl 1:9, the quotation in the final stanza is from Eccl 1:2. Solomon is the purported author of Ecclesiastes.

Kingfisher Lake. *Lyric* 32, No. 3 (Summer 1952): 104. *S1.6. Written October 1949, June 1951. In *Lyric,* the poem is cast in five quatrains.

A Lady of the Emperor's Palace. See "On a Chinese Screen" (S1.1).

Lady Writing a Letter. R76. See "On a Chinese Screen" (S1.1).

The Land of the Japanese Prints. S1.1. Written 1934.

Landscape with Horses: 6000 B.C. R6. Written January 1949. First version of "The Lariat: 6000 B.C."

The Lariat: 6000 B.C. *Voices: A Journal of Poetry* No. 141 (Spring

1950): 4. *TD* 38. In *Borestone Mountain Poetry Awards: 1951*, ed. Robert Thomas Moore (Philadelphia: University of Pennsylvania Press, 1951), 19. *MC. S3.2, written 1949, PSA second prize 1951; T.Ms., S5.7 MIK; R12, written 14 November 1949, "Read at AAUW General Meeting November 12, 1951 / Won second price, annual contest 1950 of Poetry Society of America / accepted by 'Voices'—Nov. 14th, '49"); R14, written spring 1950. A sonnet.

The Last Faun. *HW* 25. *S4.4. Written 1937.

The Lazy Prince. *Recurrence: A Quarterly of Rhyme* 5, No. 17 (Summer 1954): 14. *TD* 28. *S3.7. Written 1954. LBD reimagines the classic story of Sleeping Beauty (*La Belle au bois dormant*) by Charles Perrault. In Roman Catholicism, *bell, book, and candle* (l. 8) is a ceremony formerly used in pronouncing "major excommunication" or "anathema." It dates to the late 9th century.

Legend. *HW* 49–50. *S3.1, written 1946; R56. Stanza breaks vary among all states, with only R56 being entirely in quatrains.

Leonardo Before His Canvas. *Poetry* 74, No. 4 (July 1949): 208–9. *TD* 46. In Manly Wade Wellman, *Twice in Time* (New York: Baen, 1988), 5. *PV* 380–81 (1955). *MC. S3.1, written 1947, 1954–61; R48. The Wellman book notes that a typescript of the poem given to him (with a letter dated 1 March 1949) had been dedicated to him (presumably it was merely inscribed) and states incorrectly that the poem was previously unpublished. The epigraph cites Gian [or Giovanni] Paolo Lomazzo (1538–1592), an Italian painter and art critic. His comment on Leonardo is from his *Trattato dell'arte della pittura, scoltura et architettura* (1584). LBD may have found it in Jean Paul Richter's *Leonardo* (London: Sampson Low, Marston, Searle & Livingston, 1880), 74. *Ephebus* (l. 19) is a youth of ancient Greece, especially an Athenian of 18 or 19 in training for full citizenship.

"Like Breath upon a Glass." R53. It is uncertain what LBD was quoting in selecting her title, but perhaps it was Edmund Gosse (1849–1928), "In Memoriam: Miss A. Clough," l. 16, a poem about the poet's deceased sister.

The Lineaments of Faerie. *VL* 373, 375–77. The "anonymous" poem may have been a collaboration between LBD and Charles A. Musès.

See late letter (12 October 1964) by Musès to LBD (ALS, University of Kentucky): "I wanted you to see [. . .] our beloved 'Anonymous' in page proof form." It is not clear what "our beloved 'Anonymous'" means. Perhaps the two composed the poem as a sort of inside joke between them. *VL* was "an anthology of modern poetry in English," though the note on the poem makes it sound as though the poem was much older—that is, unless it were a modern composition by them both. The poem contains images found throughout LBD's own poetry.

A Likely Story! *HW* 20–21. *S3.3. Written 1947. A variant of "An Unlikely Story." *Pavonine* (l. 14) means of or like a peacock. *Ruth* (l. 21) is a feeling of pity, distress, or grief.

The Little Piper. In *Contemporary American Woman Poets: An Anthology of Verse by 1311 Living Poets,* ed. Tooni Gordi (New York: Henry Harrison, 1936), 72, as by Lea Bodine Drake. *S4.4. Written 1934. LBD's first appearance in a book.

Little Song. S4.3. Written May 1961–November 1962. The dedicatee "C. B. D." is LBD's mother.

Little Things. *S2.4. Its supposed appearance in *L'Alouette* has not been found. Written 1934.

Lost Heritage. *Saturday Evening Post* 213, No. 10 (7 September 1940): 70. *S2.2. Written 1940.

Love Song. *Poetry Chap-Book* 10, No. 1 (Fall 1951): 5. In *Borestone Mountain Poetry Awards: 1952,* ed. Robert Thomas Moore (Philadelphia: University of Pennsylvania Press, 1952), 18. *Poetry Public Letter* 2, No. 5 (September–October 1954): 6. *Poetry Society of America Bulletin* (December 1955): 5. *TD* 49. *PV* 402 (1951). *MC. S3.2. Written February 1951.

Lullaby After Death. S4.2. Written 1958. Between ll. 11 and 12, LBD cancelled the lines "When the stars of winter rise / And Orion strides the skies".

Luna. *Poetry* 64, No. 6 (September 1944): 305. Unspecified Evansville paper c. September 1944, under "Local Poet Has Work Printed." *New York Herald Tribune* (15 October 1944): A4. *Daily Press* [Newport News, VA] (26 October 1944): 3. *TD* 14. *S1.4, written 1944; A.Ms., S5.7 MIK; R41; *GM*.

Lying Awake. S4.2. Written 1959, 1964.

Mad Jenny. *S6.1, T.Ms., as by Lea Bodine Drake. Written 1934. "To be published in *L'Alouette.*" Such an appearance has not been found.

Mad Woman's Song. *HW* 67. *S2.4, written 1948; R74.

The Magic Circle. See "A Hornbook for Witches."

The Magician's Hat. See "A Hornbook for Witches."

Man in Winter. *Voices: A Quarterly of Poetry* No. 110 (Summer 1942): 23. *TD* 42. *S1.6, written 1941; R1 written 1941–42.

The Man Who Married a Swan-Maiden. *HW* 22–23. *Weird Tales* 43, No. 4 (May 1951): 51 (as "Swan Maiden"); *Weird Tales* (UK) No. 11 (1951): 51 (as "Swan Maiden"). *S1.1, written 1935, 1948; R75.

A Meeting on a Northern Moor. *Magazine of Fantasy and Science Fiction* 21, No. 2 (August 1961): 72. *S4.3 (on table of contents as "A Meeting on a Gothic Moor"). Written April 1961. Wotan (l. 7) is the supreme Teutonic god, counterpart of Norse Odin. Frigga (l. 13), is wife of Odin, so LBD has mixed mythologies; Fricka would be her Teutonic counterpart. "Mother Holle" is a German fairy tale that comes from the book *Kinder- und Hausmärchen* (*Children's and Household Tales*) collected by Jacob and Wilhelm Grimm.

A Memory. S4.2. Written May 1956, August 1958.

The Mermaid. *Weird Tales* 44, No. 7 (November 1952): 75. *Weird Tales* (UK) No. 20 (April 1953): 75. *S2.4. Written 1951. In British folklore, mermaids appear as unlucky omens, both foretelling and provoking disaster.

The Merrow. R9, R9a. Written March 1949. First version of "The Mermaid." On the T.Mss., LBD notes that *merrow* is Celtic for *mermaid*.

The Middle Ages: Two Views. *Recurrence: A Quarterly of Rhyme*. 5 (No. 18) (Autumn 1954): 26–27. In *New Poems by American Poets No. 2*, ed. Rolfe Humphries (New York: Ballantine Books, 1957), 42–43. *MC. S3.6, written June 1953, August 1954; *GM*. In l. 10, Jules Michelet (1798–1874) was a French historian who abhorred the Middle Ages. *Droit du seigneur* (l. 13), also known as *jus primae noctis* ("right of the first night"), refers to a supposed legal right in medieval Europe allowing feudal lords to have sexual relations with subordinate women ("on the wedding night" is specific to some variants). *Feast of Fools* (l. 14) was a festival popular during the Middle Ages, held on or about 1 January, particularly in France, in which low and high officials changed places, a mock bishop or pope was elected, and ecclesiastical ritual parodied. Dante describes the nine circles of Hell (l. 20) in *The Inferno*. A *liripipe* (l. 24) is an element of clothing: the tail of a hood or cloak, or a long-tailed hood. *Fabliaux* (l. 32) were comic tales written by jongleurs in northeast France between c. 1150 and 1400, generally characterized by sexual and scatological obscenity, and by attitudes contrary to the church and the nobility. The angel Gabriel will blow his horn (l. 38) to announce the Last Judgment. Cf. 1 Thes 4:16: "For the Lord himself shall descend from heaven with a shout, with the voice of the archangel, and with the trump of God: and the dead in Christ shall rise first."

Midsummer Night. *Southern Literary Messenger* 6, No. 3 (July–August 1944): 272 (as "Summer Night"). *HW* 65. *S1.4. Written 1937, 1943.

Minor Poet. *Poetry Chap-Book* 6, No. 4 (Summer 1948): 84–85. *Anniston* [AL] *Star* (4 January 1952): 5. *Greensboro* [NC] *Daily News* (10 July 1948): 4. *Arena* (New Zealand) No. 23 (Summer 1950): 7. *New York Herald Tribune* (6 August 1950): A4. *Gazette* (Montreal) (11 August 1950): 6. *TD* 43. *S3.1, labeled both "Re-written" and written 1947, revised 1954; R46; *GM*. The "fiery beast . . . of Blake" (ll. 7–8) alludes to "The Tyger" ("burning bright / In the forests of the night") by William Blake (1757–1827); cf. "burning lions in l. 23). A *foxbrush* (l. 9) is a fox's tail, a trifle compared to the trophy head of a lion.

Minotaur. See "An Unlikely Noah's Ark."

The Minotaur. S3.5. See also "An Unlikely Noah's Ark."

Mombāsa. S1.1. Written 1920 (LBD appears to have erased a notation "1921" from the first page of the ms.). "Modeled after Talbot Mundy's poem 'Zanzibar'." "Zanzibar" by Mundy (1879–1940) has not been found, but his novel *The Ivory Trail* (1919) mentions Zanzibar in "The Njo Hapa Song." Mombasa is a city on the southeast coast of Kenya. It was founded around 900 C.E., purportedly by the African queen Mwana Mkisi. From the late 16th to the mid-20th century it was governed successively by Portugal, Oman, and Great Britain. The Ouled Naïl (l. 31) are a tribe and tribal confederation living in the Ouled Naïl Range, Algeria. In belly dancing, the term refers to a style of dance originated by the Ouled Naïl.

The Moment. R33, written May 1956; R34, written May 1956. See "Moment in Paradise."

Moment at Sunset. *Talaria: A Quarterly of Poetry* 12, No. 2 (Summer 1947): 12. *S2.6; R92. In S2.6, l. 1 has "red" for "gold," but "gold is retained here.

Moment in Paradise. S4.1. Written May 1956.

Moon Festival. See "On a Chinese Screen" (S1.1).

The Morning. *Fiddlehead* No. 58 (Fall 1963): 62. *MC. S4.3. Written October 1961, Lausanne; October 1962, Parkersburg.

Mouse Heaven. *Country Bard* 8, No. 2 (Summer 1941): 28. *Cameron* [Missouri] *Sun* (6 November 1941): 2. *HW* 15–16. In *Mice Are Rather Nice: Poems about Mice,* ed. Vardine Moore (New York: Atheneum, 1981), 54–55. *S4.4. Written 1938.

Multiple Clay. *Voices: A Journal of Poetry* No. 162 (January–April 1957): 36. *PV* 389 (1957).*MC. Gustav Davidson intended to publish the poem in the February 1965 number of the *Poetry Society of America Bulletin,* but the poem did not appear. S4.1, written August 1956; R40, on which the name Vardine Moore is written; T.Ms, S5.7 MIK. Moore (1906–1993), just as LBD, was a member of the American Association of University Women. In April 1974 she was considering writing a biography of LBD. Griffin Callahan read the poem at LBD's funeral.

Music for Sun and Moon. *S2.3, written 1943; R69, where in l. 1 reads "Mexico" for "Italy" and the last two stanzas are replaced by "His fiery shadow on the white / And hollow moon: time spins towards death, / And earth that hails and speeds each light / Hymns her destruction with each breath."

"My Help Cometh from the Hills." *Louisville Courier-Journal* (6 May 1935): 4, as by Lea Bodine Drake. *S1.2. Written 1934 or 1935. A

sonnet. The title comes from Ps 121:1: "I will lift up mine eyes unto the hills, from whence cometh my help."
The Nail. S4.2. Written July 1956.
Nativities. *ªPoetry Chap-Book* 4, No. 2 (Winter 1945): 40. *S1.5. "Rewritten *after* public." 1946, 1956.
The Naughty Fairy. S4.4. Written 1937. The scrapbook contains a print of "The Spindle Berry Fairy" by Cicely Mary Barker (1895–1973).
New Wine in an Old Bottle: Ariadne. See "Ariadne on Naxos."
The Nixie's Pool. *Weird Tales* 39, No. 5 (May 1946): 66. *Weird Tales* (Canadian) 38, No. 4 (September 1946): 49. *HW* 56. *S1.3. Written 1936.
No Refuge. *Kaleidograph* 17, No. 9 (January 1946): 2. *S1.5. Written August 1945. Contest judge Eric Wilson Barker selected the poem for the magazine's quarterly award of $25 (covering the January, February, and March 1946 issues). Alternate version: "Coming Back to the House."
Nonsensical Rhymes. S3.5. Written 1939. Comprises eleven clerihews, seven of which are included in "Rhymes without Reason" (q.v.). In l. 1, *berserkers* (or *berserks*) were champion Vikings reported in Icclandic sagas to have fought in a trance-like fury, a characteristic which gave rise to the English word *berserk*. In l. 5, Hereward the Wake (1035?–1072?) was an Anglo-Saxon nobleman who led the resistance to the Norman Conquest of England. In l. 9, LBD refers to Babur (Zahir-ud-din Muhammad, 1483–1530), sometimes spelled Baber, the founder of the Mughal dynasty in India.
Noon Light. R67.
Okio's Geese. S5.3, with *TMs laid in. June 1964. In S6.5, LBD wrote "Okio (d. 1795) 'powerful portrayer of great wild birds'—prints appeared around (1650–1711)."
Old Daphne. *HW* 66. *MC. S3.3; GM. Written 1947. See note to "Daphne."
The Old Granny's Story. S1.3. Written 1938. A *settle* (l.2) is a wooden bench, usually with arms and a high back, long enough to accommodate three or four sitters. For *limmer* (l. 25), see note to "A

Hornbook for Witches" XII.1. For "Fox's Hollow" (l. 33) see LBD's story "Foxy's Hollow."

The Old Khan and His Falcon. *Talaria: A Quarterly of Poetry* 10, No. 4 (Winter 1945): 13 (where Khan is misprinted *Kahn* throughout.) *S1.2, written 1937, 1959; R65. A *culgee* (l. 4) is a jeweled plume, as worn on turbans in India. LBD defines *Shaykhah* (l. 6) as the "'Chieftess' (Persian)" in S1.2; as "Chieftaness" [*sic*] in R65. A *stoop* is the descent of a bird of prey. The *Roc* (l. 13) is an enormous bird of prey in the popular mythology of the Middle East. The *Simurgh* (l. 15) is a benevolent, mythical bird in Iranian mythology and literature, sometimes equated with such mythological birds as the phoenix. A *varvel* (l. 17) is a metal ring attached to a hawk's *jess* (a short strap fastened around the leg of a bird) bearing the owner's name or coat of arms.

Old Man on the Seashore. *TD* 54. *PV* 390–91 (1955). *MC. S3.6 as "Old Man on the Seashore: *Morning*." Written January 1955.

Old Wives' Tale. *Arkham Sampler* 1, No. 3 (Summer 1948): 39. HW 35–36. In *The Arkham Sampler: A Facsimile Edition*, ed. August Derleth (Sauk City, WI: Arkham House, 2010), 39. *S2.4. Written 1935, 1948. *Walburga's Eve* (l. 20) is May Eve (April 30), referring to Saint Walpurga or Walburga (710?–779?), an English nun who evangelized among the pagan Germans. In Germany, Walpurgisnacht is the night when witches appear. A *silen* (l. 21) is a follower of the Greek god Silenus, believed to be the tutor of Dionysus. See LBD's letter to August Derleth of 24 July 1948, in which she chides him for the word appearing misspelled in *Arkham Sampler* as *siren*.

The Old World of Green. *Short Stories: A Man's Magazine* 208, No. 6 (December 1949): 87. HW 61. *S2.4, written 1948; GM. Originally accepted for *Weird Tales*. *Kildees* (l. 15) is a variant of *killdeer*, a large plover of the Americas.

On a Chinese Screen. S1.1. *Contains:* I. Lady Writing a Letter; II. Moon Festival; III. The Deserted Courtyard [alternate title: "The Deserted Courtyard"]; IV. By the River; V. A Lady of the Emperor's Palace; VI. One Intoxicated. Of "The Deserted Courtyard," LBD wrote: "My first poem written at 14" (i.e., in 1919 if LBD was not fudging her age). "Lady Writing a Letter" (R.76) contains the following notes: "'washer-girls' in Chinese and Japanese poetic imagery denotes the approach of Autumn." and "'Those-Who-Sleep, etc.' means the insects, who aw[a]ken in Spring." *Small wives* (l. 7) were sisters of the *chief wife* (or High Wife in l. 10), or concubines.

On a Night of Stars. *Wings: A Quarterly of Verse* 6, No. 5 (Spring 1944): 8–9. In *Unseen Wings: The Living Poetry of Man's Immortality*, ed. Stanton A. Coblentz (New York: Beechhurst Press, 1949), 232–33. *S1.6. Written 1941, 1943. Variant title: "Celestial Visitant."

On the Fast Express. See "Through-Train."

On the Night-Wind. S4.2. Written May 1960.

One Intoxicated. R78. See "On a Chinese Screen."

"Only a Little Dust." S4.2. Written November 1957, January 1958. The title is the first line of "Fallen Asleep" by Frank Lilly Stanton (1857–1927), another poem about a death, in *Songs of the Soil* (New York: D. Appleton, 1894), 35.

Orchids. *Green World* 1, No. 2 (May–August 1963): 22. *S4.3. Written May 1961.

Our Lady's Song. S1.2. Written 1934. The first stanza alludes to the story of Herod, king of Judea, who, according to Matt 2:16–18, ordered the Massacre of the Innocents (the killing of all male infants age two or under) in an attempt to foil the Magi's news of the newborn king of the Jews (i.e., Jesus) whom they were seeking. LBD cancelled the following lines between the second and third stanzas: "Oh, Thou art so small, so sweet. / There are times when I forget / That long road that waits Thy feet, / And the task that Thou art set."

Out! *Weird Tales* 46, No. 1 (March 1954): 107. *Fantasy Macabre* No. 16 (January 1994): 16. *S3.5. Written June 1951.

Overheard in Baghdad. R88. *Badr* (l. 18), a king, and *Lab* (l. 21), a sorceress, are characters in the *Arabian Nights*.

Owl's Cry. *Country Bard* 7, No. 8 (Winter 1939–1940): 9. *S1.5, under "Winter Harvests." Written 1935.

The Path through the Marsh. *Weird Tales* 38, No. 1 (September 1944): 51. *Weird Tales* (Canadian) 38, No. 1 (January 1945): 51.

The Song of the Sun ~ Leah Bodine Drake

DM 408–9. *HW* 33–34. *S1.1, written 1937, 1943; R71.

"Peace on Earth." *Southern Literary Messenger* 2, No. 2 (February 1940): 86. *S1.5, under "Winter Harvests." Written 1935. The title derives from Lk 2:14: "Glory to God in the highest, and on earth peace, good will toward men."

Peddler's Pack. S4.4. Written 1934, 1956. Suggested perhaps by "The Pedlar's Pack" (1886), a fairy tale written by Mary de Morgan (1850–1907), in which the protagonist is a traveller and salesman who meets three animals on a journey to a nearby town; the story concludes with the four travellers bitterly vowing never to trust one another again. In l. 12, a *Pleiad* is a group of usually seven illustrious or brilliant persons or things, in this case the *Pleiades*. *Bedlam* (l. 59) refers to any insane asylum, but specifically to the Hospital of St. Mary of Bethlehem in London. For *Jael* (l. 51), see Judg. 4.21: "Then Jael Heber's wife took a nail of the tent, and took an hammer in her hand, and went softly unto him, and smote the nail into his temples, and fastened it into the ground: for he was fast asleep and weary. So he died." *Widder-shin* (l. 53) means in a left-handed, wrong, or contrary direction; counter-clockwise. It was considered unlucky in Britain to travel in an anti-clockwise (not sunwise) direction around a church. LBD submitted the poem to *Magazine of Fantasy and Science Fiction*, but it was rejected.

The Pentagram. See "A Hornbook for Witches."

The Phoenix Egg. *Poetry Chap-Book* 2, No. 3 (Spring 1944): 74. *New York Herald Tribune* (16 April 1944): A6 (as "The Phoenix' Egg"). *New York Times* (23 April 1944): BR2 (as "The Phoenix' Egg"). In *Ted Malone's Adventures in Poetry*, ed. Ted Malone (New York: William Morrow, 1946), 218. *S1.6 (as "The Phoenix Egg"; on table of contents as "The Phoenix Eggs"), written January 1943; R45 as "The Phoenix's Egg"; *GM*. In published appearances the poem was cast in two twelve-line stanzas. The common *tare* (l. 3) is a kind of vetch. In S1.6, *thickens* (l. 19) is erroneously given as *thickets*. A *skep* (l. 19) is a straw or wicker beehive.

The Pixy Fair. S1.3; on table of contents as "Pixy Fair." Written 1934.

Pooka. See "An Unlikely Noah's Ark."

The Pool. *Talaria: A Quarterly of Poetry* 14, No. 1 (Spring 1949): 6.

FSC 77-78. *S4.4, written November 1948; R4, written 6 December 1948; T.Ms., WHS.

Poplar Wind. Alternate version of "Poplar-Wind."

Poplar-Wind. *ᵃChicago Daily Tribune* 106, No. 232 (27 September 1947): 10 (as "Poplar Wind"). S1.6, written August 1947; *S5.3, "Rewritten May 1964." In S.5, LBD capped each line in only the second stanza. The capping in the *Tribune* is followed instead.

Powers of the Air. R25. Written January 1953.

Precarious Ground. *Kaleidograph* 23, No. 4 (August 1951): 4. *Poetry Public Letter* 1, No. 9 (September 1953): 15. *TD* 11. *PV* 399–400 (1951). *VL* 118. In *The Golden Year: The Poetry Society of America Anthology 1910–1960,* ed. Melville Cane, John Farrar, and Louise Townsend Nicholl (New York, Fine Editions Press, 1960), 78–79. Winner of the $300 Borestone Mountain Poetry Award in 1952 for best poem published in 1952 by a magazine in the English-speaking world. In *Anthology of Contemporary American Poetry,* compiled/narrated by George Abbe. Folkways Records FW09735 / SL 9735 (1961). *MC. S3.2, written February 1951; A.Ms., S5.7 MIK; R17, written March 1951; T.Ms., West Virginia University, West Virginia and Regional History Center. "'Precarious Ground' had its genesis in a newspaper account of a volcanic eruption somewhere in Italy a few years ago." The eruption of Mt. Etna from 25 November 1950 to 2 December 1951 was one of the largest eruptions of the century. Lines 19–22 allude to Math 7:26: "And every one that heareth these sayings of mine, and doeth them not, shall be likened unto a foolish man, which built his house upon the sand."

The Presfence. S4.3. Written July 1963.

The Prisoner. R98. A sonnet.

Protective Colouring. R68. First title: "Protective Colouration."

Puss-in-Boots and the Three Mice. S2.1. "Puss in Boots" is a European fairy tale about a cat that uses trickery and deceit to gain power, wealth, and the hand of a princess in marriage for his penniless, low-born master, the fictional Marquis of Carabas. In English, the story appears in editions of *Mother Goose's Tales.*

Rabbit-Dance. *Talaria: A Quarterly of Poetry* 7, No. 4 (Winter 1942): 16. Won the "popularity prize" in the spring issue. *HW* 17. *S1.3. Written 1938.

Railroad Tracks. R57.

The Rain on the Stone. S4.2. Written 1955, 1960.

Red Ghosts in Kentucky. *Weird Tales* 44, No. 8 (January 1953): 66; *Weird Tales* (UK) No. 21 (May 1953): 66–67. *Spectral Realms* No. 6 (Winter 2017): 118–19. *S3.5, written 1952; R20, written March 1952.

Reincarnation. R100[a]. See "Atavism."

Retrogression. *Nature Magazine* 39, No. 7 (August–September 1946): 374. *S1.5, written "1943–45"; R59. The news item, which quoted Louis Bruchiss (1907–1988), appeared in newspapers on 21 August 1945.

The Return. *Lyric* 32, No. 4 (Autumn 1952): 135 (as "Return in Autumn"). *S3.4 Written August 1947, July 1952.

The Revenant. *Weird Tales* 43, No. 3 (March 1951): 24. *Weird Tales* (UK) No. 10 (May 1951): 24 (as "Revenant"). *S3.3. Written April 1950. A *revenant* is a visible ghost or animated corpse revived from death to haunt the living.

Rhymes without Reason; or History Made Difficult. The pieces about da Vinci, Catherine, and Shakespeare appeared as "Three Clerihews," *Chicago Tribune* (3 May 1956): 20. *R43. See also "Nonsensical-Rhymes." "*Macushla*" (l. 13) is an Irish song (1910) with music by Dermot MacMurrough and lyrics by Josephine V. Rowe. The title is a transliteration of the Irish *mo chuisle*, "my pulse," as in the phrase *a chuisle mo chroí*, "pulse of my heart"; thus *mo chuisle* means "darling" or "sweetheart." In l. 42, LBD refers to James Francis Edward Stuart (1688–1766), nicknamed the Old Pretender, the son of King James II of England (r. 1685–88), who was overthrown by William of Orange, who became William III. James continued to claim the British throne until his death. In l. 47, LBD refers to George Villiers, 1st Duke of Buckingham (1592–1628), a British courtier under James I and Charles I.

BIBLIOGRAPHY

The Rider. In *New Poems by American Poets No. 2*, ed. Rolfe Humphries (New York: Ballantine, 1957), 42. *MC. S4.2, written March 1957; GM.
The Robin. S4.2. Written March 1957, 20 July 1958.
The Roc. S3.5. Written 1952. See "An Unlikely Noah's Ark."
Rock and Bramble. *Lyric* 35, No. 2 (Spring 1955): 44. TD 16. *MC. S3.7. Written 1954.
'Round and 'Round. S1.3. Written 1937.
Royal. S5.3. Written January 1963.
"Run with the Fox." *Our Dumb Animals* 71, No. 10 (October 1938): 148. *Junior Red Cross Journal* 17, No. 2, Part 1 (October 1940): 55. *S2.2. Written 1938. An old proverb reads "you can't run with the fox and hunt with the hounds"—i.e., you can't have it both ways. In a fox hunt, a *thruster* (l. 18) is one who rides too close to the hounds.
The Sailorman (1690). *Southern Literary Messenger* 4, No. 3 (March 1942): 125–26 (as "The Sailorman (17th Century)"). *S1.1. Written 1934. Salé, or Sallee (l. 16), is a city in northwestern Morocco, founded c. 1030 by Arabic-speaking Berbers that later became a haven for pirates.
The Saints of Four-Mile-Water. *Arkham Sampler* 2, No. 2 (Spring 1949): 32–33. In *The Arkham Sampler: A Facsimile Edition*, ed. August Derleth (Sauk City, WI: Arkham House, 2010), 32–33. *S2.4, written 1934, 1946. Based on an actual legend. See *Fairy and Folk Tales of the Irish Peasantry*, ed. William Butler Yeats (New York: Thomas Whittaker, 1888), p. [214].
The Salamander. S3.5. See "An Unlikely Noah's Ark."
Samarkand. See "A Dream of Samarkand."
Satyr. See "An Unlikely Noah's Ark."
Sea-Shell. *Weird Tales* 37, No. 1 (September 1943): 87. HW 42. In Yaszek 252. *S1.4. Written 1938.
The Seal-Woman's Daughter. See "The Ballad of the Seal-Woman's Daughter."
Semele. *Poetry* 83, No. 4 (January 1954): 202 (under "Legendary Tapestries: Semele"). TD 32. *MC. S3.7 (though reading *dos* [l. 5], as

in *Poetry* and S5.7, rather than *does*), written June 1953; T.Ms, S5.7 MIK, written June 1953; R31, written November 1953. In Greek mythology, Semele, the daughter of Cadmus and Harmonia, was the mortal mother of Dionysus by Zeus. In the account of the legend as related by Ovid (*Metamorphoses* 3.253–315) and others, after her seduction by Zeus in the guise of an eagle, she demanded that he show himself in his true form. He did so reluctantly by showing the smallest of his thunderbolts, but she still perished by incineration. The last line alludes to the birth of Dionysus, god of wine.

Serpent-Ring. *Talaria* 8, No. 1 (Spring 1943): 9 (as "Serpent Ring"). *S2.3. Written 1937, 1941. The table of contents of the scrapbook gives the title as "Serpent-Ring," but the title above the poem is mutilated. It is assumed LBD wished there to be a hyphen in the title.

The Seven Sons of the King of Thule. S2.5. Written 1937. *Thule* is the farthest north location mentioned in ancient Greek and Roman literature. LBD's *Thule* is pronounced with only one syllable, but the word typically is pronounced with two. Cf. Poe, "Dream-Land": "I have reached these lands but newly / From an ultimate dim Thule—" [*TOO-lee*]. Heathenry (l. 6) is no particular place; the term merely applies to any non-Christian countries. A *yataghan* (l. 23) is a type of Ottoman knife or short sabre used from the mid-16th to late 19th centuries.

A Sigh in Spring. *New York American* No. 18,891 (8 April 1935): 13, as by Lea Bodine Drake. Her first published poem. *S1.2. Written 1935.

The Singer from the Waste. *Kaleidograph* 14, No. 10 (February 1943): 8–9. *S1.6, written 1942, "Slightly altered" January 1949; R82 as "The Singer in the Waste." (First title of R82a = "The Singer in the Waste-Land.") In S1.6, LBD offers two lines, described as "optional" for l. 11: "The Presence of the Lord was known" and "The head of God by me was known." The reading in *Kaleidograph* is retained here.

The Sirens. See "Curious Story."

Six Merry Farmers. *Weird Tales* 45, No. 4 (September 1953): 95; (UK) 3, No. 1 (1953): 95. *S3.5. Written June 1951. Line indents follow appearance in *Weird Tales*.

The Snake. *Green World* 1, No. 1 (Spring 1963): 3. *S4.3. Written September 1961, Lausanne.
Snow Crystals. *Kaleidograph* 22, No. 6 (October 1950): 7. *S1.5, written spring 1947; R8, written January 1949. S6.6 contains a brief note: "To rewrite 'Snow Crystals' use the first person singular: [¶] I am a snowflake—I am the only one of my kind, my pattern is unique to me. [¶] (The individual soul is unique in God's plan.)"
Snowy Night. S2.1. Written 1945.
Solar. Original to *TD* 13. *S3.1. Written May 1953.
Solitude. S1.6. Written 1943. See "Bread of Solitude."
Song against Smallness. *Voices: A Journal of Poetry* No. 134 (Summer 1948): 27–28. *TD* 45. *MC. S3.1, written January 1948; R50. Presented anonymously at the February 1946 meeting of the PSA; it won no award. In Gen. 19, Lot invited as guests to his house, two angels that had come to Sodom. Then men from town came to Lot's house, asking him to allow them to have sex with his guests. Line 17 quotes Lewis Carroll, "The Walrus and the Carpenter" (1871): "'The time has come,' the Walrus said, / 'To talk of many things: / Of shoes—and ships and sealing-wax— / Of cabbages—and kings—'" (ll. 61–64).
Song at Sunrise. S1.1. Written 1924–[33]. The latter date appears to be erased.
Song of the Sun. *Wings: A Quarterly of Verse* 8, No. 5 (Spring 1948): 9. R85, as "The Song of the Sun."
The Spells. See "A Hornbook for Witches."
The Sphinx. S3.5. See "An Unlikely Noah's Ark."
Spirit Fox. See "An Unlikely Noah's Ark."
The Spray. *Voices: A Journal of Poetry* No. 175 (May–August 1961): 30. *MC. S4.3, written May 1960; GM.
A Star Came Out. S2.4. Written "about 1938," 1959.
The Steps in the Field. *Weird Tales* 40, No. 1 (November 1947): 85. *Weird Tales* (Canadian) [40, No. 1] (January 1948): 91. *HW* 64. *S3.3. Written 1938, 1946.

The Song of the Sun ☙ Leah Bodine Drake

The Storks. *TD* 22–23. *VL* 115–16. *MC. In *Violets and Vinegar: An Anthology of Women's Writings and Sayings,* ed. Jilly Cooper and Tom Hartman (London: George Allen & Unwin, 1980), 115; rpt. as *Beyond Bartlett: Quotations by and about Women* (New York: Stein & Day, 1983), 115. Both appearances omit stanzas two and seven. S3.6. Written January 1955. A *swang* (l. 3) is a boggy depression, a swamp. *Galligaskins* (l. 8) are loosely fitting breeches. *Ribe* (l. 9) is a Danish town in southwest Jutland, the oldest extant town in Denmark (est. in the early 8th century). To *clapperclaw* (l. 9) is to claw with the hands and nails; to revile. *Sloth* (l. 32; or *sleuth*) is a term of vernery for a group of bears, just as *muster* (l. 36) refers to a group of storks. *Widdies* (l. 38) are hangman's nooses. In l. 42, LBD refers to the practice in Holland of setting old cart wheels in willow trees sawed off a few feet above the ground to attract storks.

The Stranger. *Weird Tales* 39, No. 12 (September 1947): 71. *Weird Tales* (Canadian) 38, No. 4 (November 1947): 63. *HW* 57–58. **S1.4*. Written 1938.

Summer Night. See "Midsummer Night."

Sunset Apocalypse. *Beloit Poetry Journal* 8, No. 1 (Fall 1957): 38. *MC. S4.1. Written 1949, 1956.

Swan Maiden. See "The Man Who Married a Swan Maiden."

Switzerland. S6.6. Written c. 1964.

The Tale of Tannhauser. S5.3. Written winter 1957, Christmas, 1962. Tannhäuser was a knight and poet who found the Venusberg, the subterranean home of Venus, and spent a year there worshipping the goddess. (To enter the Venusberg was to court eternal perdition.) After leaving he is filled with remorse and travels to Rome to ask Pope Urban IV (d. 1264) to be absolved of his sins. Urban replied that forgiveness is as impossible as it would be for his papal staff to blossom. Three days after Tannhäuser's departure, Urban's staff bloomed with flowers.

Tarascon. *Voices: A Journal of Poetry* No. 177 (January–April 1962): 34–35. *MC. S4.3, written May 1961; *GM*. In S4.3, the epigraph reads thus: ". . . . Ste. Martha saved the Rhone Valley from the fury of a great dragon by charming him with her piety and leading him by her girdle to the river . . . . ." Tarascon is a commune situated at the extreme west of the Bouches-du-Rhône department of France in the Provence–Alpes–Côte d'Azur region. It is still associated with fairy tales and legends dating back to prehistory. According to tradition, Saint Martha of Bethany, who came from Judea, landed at Tarascon where an amphibious dragon (the Tarasque) was destroying the river traffic. She tamed the beast, only for it to be butchered by the townspeople.

The Tenants. *Southern Literary Messenger* 2, No. 6 (June 1940): 380. *DM* 409–10. *HW* 9. *Fantasy & Terror* No. 13 (1992): 22. In *Between the Bookends with Ted Malone: Volume Five*, ed. Ted Malone (New York: William Morrow, 1942), 329. Malone read the poem on his radio program in July 1940. *S2.2. Written 1938.

The Terrible Meek. *S4.3. Written Lausanne, October 1961. Submitted to *Green World* but not published there.

Terror by Night. *Talaria* 9, No. 3 (Autumn 1944): 6. "Took prize." *HW* 47–48. In *Unseen Wings: The Living Poetry of Man's Immortality*, ed. Stanton A. Coblentz (New York: Beechhurst Press, 1949), 188–89. *S2.3, written 1935, 1942; R83. The *ounce* (l. 15) is the snow leopard. A *jess* (l. 26) is a short leather strap fastened around each leg of a hawk, usually having a ring or swivel to which a leash may be attached.

That Summer ("That summer everyone said they had never"). *ᵃ*Prize Winning Poems, 1959–1960* [Poetry Society of America, 1960], 5 (without attribution because of anonymity for judging in poetry contest). S5.1/2, T.Ms. "Won a PSA monthly prize [of $10]—Second place" at the Society's meeting on 19 November 1959. Comments on the poem, by Howard Ant and Eugene Maleska, were reported in the *Poetry Society of America Bulletin* (December 1959–January 1990): 8.

That Summer ("That summer the old folks said they had never"). S4.2. Written June 1959–July 1964. A sonnet and a variation of the previous.

"There Are Fairies." *S2.5, written 1934, March 1956; *GM*. The title may derive from the poem "There Are Fairies" by Madison Cawein

The Song of the Sun 🙞 Leah Bodine Drake

(1865–1914), in which the phrase is repeated several times. *Lob* (l. 10) refers to the lubber fiend or Lob Lie-by-the-Fire, a legendary creature of English folklore. He typically is described as a large, hairy man with a tail, who performs housework in exchange for a saucer of milk and a place in front of the fire. A *nixie* (l. 28) is a shapeshifting water spirit in Germanic folklore.

They Run Again. *Weird Tales* 34, No. 1 (June/July 1939): 36. *HW* 32. Quoted in its entirety in Orville Prescott, "Books of the Times: Stirred in a Cauldron of Verse," *New York Times* (1 January 1951): 15. In *Weird Tales*, ed. Peter Haining (St. Helier, UK: Neville Spearman, 1976), 128. In *Weird Tales: A Facsimile of the World's Most Famous Fantasy Magazine: Volume 1*, ed. Peter Haining (London: Sphere, 1978), 227. In *Weird Tales*[. *La mitica rivista di fantasy e fantascienza (parte prima 1923–1939)*] (Roma: Fanucci, 1982), ed. Peter Haining, as "I lupi mannari," p. 429, as by Lea Bodine Drake. In Yaszek 250–51. *S2.2. Written October 1938. In *Weird Tales*, LBD identifies *howe* (l. 6) as "a hollow."

This Side of Oblivion. *Wings: A Quarterly of Verse* 7, No. 6 (Summer 1946): [1], which "Won 4th prize." *New York Herald Tribune* (21 July 1946): A6. *Daily Press* [Newport News, VA] (24 July 1946): 3. *Oakland Tribune* (26 July 1946): 24. *Greensboro* [NC] *Daily News* (28 July 1946): 17. *ᵃS1.5, written 1946, "First Version"; R73 (first title "Survivors"). See "The Beaches Beyond Oblivion."

The Three Green Ladies of Greenwich. S4.4. Written 1937, 1947. A *band box* (l. 5) is a round hatbox. *Louis Quinze* (l. 14) refers to a style of decorative arts that appeared during the reign of Louis XV of France. *Bohea* (l. 21) is the former brand name of wuyi tea, a category of black and oolong teas grown in the Wuyi Mountains of northern Fujian, China. *Bon ton* (l. 31) refers to sophisticated manners or breeding.

Three Clerihews. See "Rhymes without Reason."

Three Vignettes. S1.2, where the table of contents lists these as "India: In the Garden of Spice"; "Burma: Moulmein Bazaar"; and "Japan: The Persimmon Gatherers" (q.v.).

BIBLIOGRAPHY

Through-Train. *Kaleidograph* 26, No. 2 (June 1954): 10 (as "On the Fast Express"). *TD* 53. In *The Poetry of Railways: An Anthology*, ed. Kenneth Hopkins (London: Leslie Frewin, 1966), 123. *S3.7. Written January 1954, August 1954. A sonnet.

Tiger. *Talaria: A Quarterly of Poetry* 6, No. 3 (Autumn 1941): 21 (under "Two Poems"). *S1.2. Written 1937, 1941. *Jungli* (l. 20) is an adjective meaning wild, uncultured.

To a Lost Sweetheart. *Cycle* 1, No. 1 (March 1935): 4, as by Lea Bodine Drake. *S1.1. Written 1924.

To an Atheist. *Lyric* 28, No. 3 (Autumn 1948): 137. *New York Herald Tribune* (23 January 1949): A6. *Lansing* [MI] *State Journal* (12 February 1949): 4. *St. Louis Post-Dispatch* (30 January 1949): 50. *Greenville* [NC] *News* (13 February 1949): 4. *S1.5, written 1946, "Revised after publication 1961"; R95. In the angelic hierarchy (l. 8), Thrones are third in the First Sphere (after Seraphim and Cherubim) and Powers are third in the Second Sphere (after Dominions and Virtues).

To Certain Poetry Critics. *Lyric* 30, No. 2 (Spring 1950): 252 (as "To the Critics of Poetry"). *S3.2. Written February 1949. A sonnet.

To Elinor Wylie. *Kaleidograph* 18, No. 7 (November 1946): 4. *New York Herald Tribune* (8 December 1946): A6. *Kansas City Star* (30 December 1946): 14. *S1.5, written 1946, 1954; R60. The published appearances omit lines 1–4 from Wylie's "Escape," included by LBD as an epigraph in R60: "When foxes eat the last gold grape / And the last white antelope is killed, / I shall stop fighting and escape / Into a little house I'll build." Elinor Morton Wylie (1885–1928) was an American poet and novelist popular in the 1920s and 1930s, and a favorite of LBD. The seventh stanza alludes to "To an Athlete Dying Young" by A. E. Housman (1859–1936).

To Mother. S4.2. Written 1958, 1961.

To One Who Fears Poetry Is Useless. *Lyric* 28, No. 3 (Autumn 1948): 137. *New York Herald Tribune* (6 February 1949): A6. *Greensboro* [NC] *Daily News* (22 February 1949): 17. *Charleston* [SC] *Daily Mail* 17 April 1949): 8. *S1.5, written 1946; R93.

Turn of Year. S1.5. Written 1934. In ll. 8–10, Pegasus, the Chair (i.e., Cassiopeia, once known as "Cassiopeia's Chair"), and the Water Carrier (Aquarius) are all constellations. Fomalhaut (Alpha Piscis Austrini) is the brightest star in the constellation of Piscis Austrinus and one of the brightest stars in the sky.

Turning Point. R63.

Two Poems. See "Crocodile" and "Tiger."

Two Poems. See "In the Night and "Cold Orchard" [She walks always in her intimate, own].

Uncle Jay. R35. Written November 1957. A *doodlebug* (l. 11) is a divining rod or similar device supposedly useful in locating underground water, oil, and minerals.

The Unclimbed Hill. *Kaleidograph* 18, No. 1 (May 1946): 5. *S1.5. Written 1945. "Won Quarterly Award."

Under Funereal Lilies. *Recurrence: A Quarterly of Rhyme* 6, No. 21 (Summer 1955): 13. *MC. S3.7 as "Beneath Funereal Lilies." Written 1955, rewritten January 1961.

The Under-Seas. *R2, written April 1948; *ᵃR11, written May 1949. See "The Undine."

The Undine. *Kaleidograph* 21, No. 4 (August 1949): 1 (as "The Under-Seas"). *Recurrence: A Quarterly of Rhyme* 3 (No. 12) (Spring 1953): 88. In *Borestone Mountain Poetry Awards 1954,* ed. Robert Thomas Moore (Stanford, CA: Stanford University Press, 1954), 25. *TD* 31. *PV* 409 (1953). *S3.4, written (i.e., revised) January 1952; *GM*. A sonnet.

Unhappy Ending. *Arkham Sampler* 1, No. 2 (Spring 1948): 41–42. *HW* 6–7. In *The Arkham Sampler: A Facsimile Edition*, ed. August Derleth (Sauk City, WI: Arkham House, 2010), 41–42. *S1.4 (but ignoring LBD's reading of "slit" in l. 20). Written 1935, 1942.

Unicorn. S1.1. Written 1937. "First version of what turned out to be (1940) 'Fantasy in a Forest.'"

The Unicorn Wounded. *Sparrow Magazine* No. 1 (June 1954): 12. *S3.6. Written 2 January 1954. LBD describes various scenes in the seven "The Hunt of the Unicorn" tapestries, dating to 1495–1505 and now in the Metropolitan Museum of Art, New York. A picture of tapestry no. 4 ("The Unicorn Is Attacked") is in her scrapbook.

The Unknown Land. *Arkham Sampler* 1, No. 4 (Autumn 1948): 50–51. In *The Arkham Sampler: A Facsimile Edition*, ed. August Derleth (Sauk City, WI: Arkham House, 2010), 50–51. *S3.3. Written 1948. The penultimate stanza is omitted in *Arkham Sampler*.

An Unlikely Noah's Ark. *R80, *R80a, *R80b. In S3.5, LBD dates "The Roc" to 1952, and so all are given that approximate date. "Pooka," "Minotaur," and "Werewolf" are limericks. The *pooka* (or púca) of Celtic folklore are bringers of both good and bad fortune, and could either help or hinder rural and marine communities. The *Furies* (or Erinyes) are crones and described variously as having snakes for hair, dog's heads, bat's wings, coal black bodies, and blood-shot eyes. The *cockatrice* is also known as the basilisk. LBD's "spirit fox" is known in Japanese folklore as *kitsune*, intelligent beings possessing paranormal abilities that increase with age and wisdom. According to Yōkai folklore, all foxes have the ability to shapeshift into human form. LBD makes reference to this in the poem "Spirit Fox" and the short story "Foxy's Hollow." In "The Sphinx," l. 8, LBD alludes to the song "Is You Is or Is You Ain't My Baby" (recorded 4 October 1943) by Louis Jordan.

Unlikely Story. R.72. See "A Likely Story."

The Unploughed Field. R15. Written 5 June 1950.

[Untitled.] "Good Pope Urban . . ." S3.5. Written 1960. Pope Urban VIII is frequently depicted in paintings and sculpture as wearing not a turban but a *camauro,* a cap made from red wool or velvet with white ermine trim, usually worn during the winter in place of the zucchetto. The papal headwear was not common to him alone.

[Untitled.] "Lying awake at night I hear the rain"]. S6.6

A Vase from Araby. *Weird Tales* 36, No. 10 (March 1943): 69. *Weird Tales* (Canadian) 36, No. 10 (July 1943): 3. *HW* 37. *S2.3. Written 1942.

Vestal. *Poetry* 62, No. 4 (July 1943): 188–89. *TD* 47. Undated appearance c. July 1943 in the *Evansville Courier* under "Local Writer Has New

Poem Published." *S1.6, written January 1942, revised 1954; R66. For *mignon* (l. 10), see note to "Flemish Artists, Fifteenth Century."

The Vision. *Weird Tales* 42, No. 2 (January 1950): 67. *Weird Tales* (UK) No. 3 (January 1950): 67. *HW* 41. *Arkham Sampler* 1, No. 1 (new series) (September 1983): 27. *S3.1. Written April 1947.

The Vision of Jenghiz Khan. R16. Written January 1951. A sonnet. Genghis Khan (1162?–1227), the Great Khan, was founder of the Mongol Empire. After his death, became the largest contiguous empire in history.

A Voice. S4.2. Written July 1958.

A Warning to Skeptics. *Orb* 2, No. 3 (Summer 1951): 6–7. *FSC* 76–77. S3.3, written 1951; *T.Ms., WHS; *GM*. LBD typed l. 13 over "Walk delicately, Agag-wise," the reading in S3.3 and *Orb*. *Agag* refers to 1 Sm 15:8 "And he took Agag the king of the Amalekites alive, and utterly destroyed all the people with the edge of the sword." The appearance in *Orb* bears the note "I Samuel—XV." In *Orb*, there are no stanza breaks.

The Wasp in the Window. *Voices: A Journal of Poetry* No. 177 (January–April 1962): 35. *MC. S4.3. Written autumn 1960.

We Come Out of the Forest, Fearing Stars. *Epos* 3, No. 2 (Winter 1951): 13. *Poetry Public Letter* 1, No. 3 (March 1953): [1]; "my own idea of my meaning is complex: the poem is actually on two levels" (p. 2). In *Borestone Mountain Poetry Awards 1952*, ed. Robert Thomas Moore (Philadelphia: University of Pennsylvania Press, 1952), 19. *TD* 57. *MC. PV* 393–94 (1955). S3.2, written 1950–1951; T.Ms., S5.7 MIK; R (unnumbered), second page only, written 1950.

We Move on Turning Stone. *TD* 61. *Magazine of Fantasy and Science Fiction* 12, No. 4 (April 1957): 32. *MC. S3.6. Written July 1954, "as . . . a kind of summing-up" for *TD* (Boucher 16).

The Web. *Atlantic Monthly* 201, No. 5 (May 1958): 65. In *Anthology of Magazine Verse for 1958*, ed. William Stanley Braithwaite (New York: Schulte Publishing Co., 1959), 54. *MC. S4.3, written 1953, 1957; R36, written March 1958; *GM. Bad cess* (l. 1) is bad luck. In l. 8, Sir Thomas Malory (1415?–1471) was a British writer, the author or compiler of *Le Morte d'Arthur*. The inspiration for the poem is the painting *I Am Half-Sick of Shadows, said the Lady of Shalott* (1915), one of three paintings of the Lady of Shallott by John William Waterhouse (1849–1917), illustrating Tennyson's poem.

The Web of Living. R26. Written January 1953.

The Weeds and the Wilderness. *Atlantic Monthly* 197, No. 5 (May 1956): 66. In *Best Poems of 1956: Borestone Mountain Poetry Awards*, ed. Robert Thomas Moore (Stanford, CA: Stanford University Press, 1957), 28–29. *PV* 395–97. *MC. S3.7. Written March 1955. The lines from Hopkins (1844–1889) are ll. 15–16. LBD's poem abounds with obscure terms, as might be found in Hopkins. *Ling* (l. 10) is common heather. To *huffle* (l.12) is to blow in gusts. *Whimbrel* (l. 13) is another name for the curlew. *Holt* (l. 16) is a small woods, a copse. *Bayard* (l. 20) is colored bay, reddish brown, notably said of equines. *Kindle* (l. 32) is the young of any animal; a brood or litter. *Hern* (l. 33) is an archaic term for *heron*. A *pendle* (l. 39) is a hanging ornament. *Wickers* (l. 41) are pliable twigs, typically of willow; *brattle* is a rattling sound. Several of the coined place names are found in S5.4 under "Made-Up Names (My Invention)."

The Well. *Recurrence: A Quarterly of Rhyme*. 5 (No. 20) (Spring 1955): 63. *TD* 41. *S3.7. Written March 1955. Cf. LBD's story "Mop-Head."

Werewolf. See "An Unlikely Noah's Ark."

"What Are Little Girls Made Of?" *Eve's Journal* (February 1939): 38. *TD* 30. *PV* 385. *MC. S1.6. Written 1938. In *Best Poems: 1948*, ed. Robert Thomas Moore (Stanford, CA: Stanford University Press, 1949), 41. The title derives from an old children's nursery rhyme (the answer being "Sugar and spice / And all things nice"). LBD agreed with AD that *are* was the correct verb to use in l. 8. (previous appearances, and also *MC*, prepared after hearing from AD, had *is*), and so it is applied here.

What the Devil Said. *S5.2; draft, S6.6. Written in Lausanne, Switzerland, 1959. The poem was one of several read anonymously for judging at the PSA meeting on 7 January 1960. Typed copies were circulated to a few poets for judging. The copy among LBD's papers is headed: "These poems are the private property of their authors and may not be used in any way without explicit permission from the authors." It also bears the note "Send to Leah B. D." Comments on the poem were read at the meeting by Hamilton Warren. The poem is about the Seven Deadly Sins. For ll. 1–2, cf. Matt 11:28: "Come unto me, all ye that labour and are heavy laden, and I will give you rest." For l. 7, cf. Matt 5:3: "Blessed are the poor in spirit: for theirs is the kingdom of heaven." For l. 13, cf. Matt 5:5: "Blessed are the meek: for they shall inherit the earth."

Wild Geese in Spring. *Kaleidograph* 19, No. 11 (March 1948): 3, "Won quarterly award." *TD* 26. *S3.1, written June 1947, 1953; R84 as "The Wild Geese Go Over." S3.1 omits the second stanza from *Kaleidograph*: "Winter was kind in the warm and fertile waters. / In swamps where the sky sleeps in a long blue dream. / There were succulent roots to eat in the lazy bayous, / rice in the fields and fish in the shallow streams.)" In R84 this stanza reads as follows: "Their days were sweet in the warm and fertile waters, / In the swamps where the sky sleeps in its long blue dreams. / There were succulent roots to eat in the lazy bayous, / Rice in the fields and flies in the lilied streams."

Willow-Women. *HW* 43–44. *S1.4. Written 1948.

The Wind and the Leaves. *Southern Literary Messenger* 1, No. 11 (November 1939): 769 (which changed the last line to read "Up, up to the heavens, alone and free!"). *S1.3. Written 1936. In S1.3, LBD has clearly written "rabble" (l. 11), and a clipping of the poem restores "rubble" to "rabble." This is an example of what LBD referred to as a "slant rhyme," which she liked to use to give "an element of surprise."

The Wind in the Chimney. S3.5. Written June 1951, 1952.

The Window on the Stair. *HW* 60. *S3.3. Written 1942. LBD suggests in her scrapbook that the poem appeared in *Southern Literary Messenger*, but no such appearance has been found.

The Windows of Chartres. *Poetry Chap-Book* 7, No. 2 (Winter 1948–49): 34 (as "French Cathedral Windows"). *TD* 36 (as "Windows at Chartres"). *S3.1. Written 1949, "Revised after pub., 1953." Lines 2–3 allude to Matt 6:19: "Lay not up for yourselves treasures upon earth, where moth and rust doth corrupt."

BIBLIOGRAPHY

Winter Harvest. *Driftwind* 10, No. 9 (March 1936): 250, as by Lea Bodine Drake. *S1.5, under "Winter Harvests." Written 1935.
Winter Harvests. S1.5. Written 1935. *Contains:* 1. Frozen Heart; 2. Winter Harvest [*sic*]; 3. Owl's Cry; 4. "Peace on Earth." (See entries for individual poems.) The poems are ordered differently between the table of contents and the actual text.
The Witch Walks in Her Garden. *Weird Tales* 29, No. 4 (April 1937): 412, as by Lea Bodine Drake. HW 29. *S2.2. Written 1935, 1948. A *bailie* (l. 6) is, in Scotland, a municipal officer and magistrate. *Jimp* (l. 26) means slender, trim, delicate.
Witch's-Wheel. See "A Hornbook for Witches."
The Witches. *FSC* 80–81. S4.3, written December 1960, April 1961; *T.Ms., WHS. *Skirl* (l. 2) usually refers to the sound of bagpipes, but LBD may have meant by it a scream or screech. In l. 9, LBD refers to the game of stealing partners (or swapping partners as in square dancing), called "Skip to My Lou." (Note that *loo* is Scottish for *love*.) A *besom* (l. 5) is a broom of twigs tied to a stout pole, in this case using a *withy* or *withe*, a strong flexible willow stem. A *burred moon* (ll. 6–7) is one with a burr or halo around it, said to be a sign of rain. A *burr* is the the prickly seed pod of the burdock. A *nicky* (l. 15) is a bundle of wood. Rolling a person downhill inside a cask with spikes (l. 17) on the inside was a form of punishment.
Witches on the Heath. *Weird Tales* 32, No. 4 (October 1938): 492. *Weird Tales* (Canadian) 38, No. 3 (March 1945): 62. HW 8. HW (recording). *S1.3. Written 1936. Pauline Goad Fehn had planned to set the poem to music but apparently never did. In early 1960, Alfred Dorn requested the poem for an "anthology of dance poems," but no such book appeared. The guitarist Buckethead (Brian Patrick Carroll) plays an instrumental piece titled "Witches on the Heath," on his album *Electric Tears* (2002).
With Every Death. S6.1, eight A.Ms. drafts, and one T.Ms., begun March 1958 (the first six lines are an incomplete "First Draft") and revised through 18 July 1958. Some drafts titled "Her Death" and "The Shining Dies." See "With Her Death."

The Song of the Sun ~ Leah Bodine Drake

With Her Death. *Poetry Society of America Bulletin* (March 1960): 2 (as "With Each Death"). *Hawk and Whippoorwill* 3, No. 1 (Spring 1962): 37. S4.2. Written March 1958, 1961; T.Ms., S.6 (along with numerous drafts of various titles: "With Every Death," "Her Death," "The Shining Dies"), written in New Harmony, Indiana, July 1958, as "Her Death"; *T.Ms., WHS, marked "revised version to be used / Revised copy as of Feb. 23 1961." The poem underwent many drafts and bore a variety of titles. A sonnet. In S4.2, the final two lines are "The world dies with each death. Oh, it will flame / For others, even for me, but not the same." LBD stated more than once that the poem was, or was to be, published in *Modern Age*. Russell Kirk, the editor, wrote LBD 23 March 1959 saying he still intended to publish the poem, but it did not appear there.

The Woods Grow Darker. *Magazine of Fantasy and Science Fiction* 9, No. 5 (November 1955): 38. FSC 75–76. In *The Best from Fantasy and Science Fiction: Sixth Series,* ed. Anthony Boucher (New York: Doubleday/Science Fiction Book Club, 1957): 44; (New York: Ace, 1962), 251. *MC. S3.5, written 1955; T.Ms., WHS; GM. *Iron Curtain* (l. 12) was the name for the boundary dividing Europe into two areas following World War II in 1945. The ash tree (l. 15), in British folklore, was credited with protective and healing properties.

The Wood-Wife. *Weird Tales* 36, No. 4 (March 1942): 59. *Weird Tales* (Canadian) 36, No. 4 (July 1942): 106 (as "Wood-Wife"). *DM* 406–7. *HW* 18–19. In Yaszek 251–52. *S2.2. Written 1939. *Weird Tales* and *DM* omit ll. 9–12 conflate ll. 26–30 as follows: "He dreams in a spell; / But not of golden curlylocks / Of Parson Jones' Nell—".

The Word of Willow. *Atlantic Monthly* 198, No. 3 (September 1956): 50. *Magazine of Fantasy and Science Fiction* 13, No. 6 (December 1957): 19. FSC 78–79. PV 410–11. VL 117. *MC. S4.1, written April 1956; T.Ms., WHS; GM. To *pollard* (l. 13) is to cut a tree back nearly to the trunk so as to produce a dense mass of branches. Arthur Rackham (1867–1939; l. 20) was an English book illustrator much favored by LBD. A *grutcher* (l. 20) is a murmurer, a complainer. An *osier-holt* (l. 26) is a place where osiers are grown for basket-making.

BIBLIOGRAPHY

Words After Wisdom. *Cycle* 3, No. 4 (December 1937): 4. *S1.1. Written 1926.
The Worth of It. Nonextant? S4.1; listed in table of contents but crossed out and omitted. 1 Kgs 21.2: "If it seem good to thee, I will give thee the worth of it in money." The phrase appears in Seabury Quinn's "As 'Twas Told to Me," *Weird Tales* 32, No. 3 (September 1938): 267; that issue published a letter by LBD. LBD read the poem aloud at the 17 November 1955 meeting of the PSA, but no poem of this title has been found. The December 1955 *Poetry Society of America Bulletin* said that at the time the poem was unpublished.
Wyvern. See "An Unlikely Noah's Ark."
The Youth of Circe. S2.3. Listed in table of contents but omitted. Nonextant. "Rewritten elsewhere," presumably as "Circe" in S5.3.
Zanzibar. S2.1. Written 1955.

Fiction

Foxy's Hollow. *Fantasy Fiction* 1, No. 3 (August 1953): 120–27.
Mop-Head. *Weird Tales* 45, No. 6 (January 1954): 2–16. *Weird Tales* (UK) 1, No. 3 (1954): 2–16. In *Horror Gems, Volume Two* (n.p.: Armchair Fiction & Music, 2011), 111–27. *Mop-Head* (n.p.: Start Publishing Company, 2015 [ebook]). In *Fantastic Stories Presents the Weird Tales Super Pack #1* (n.p.: Positronic Publishing, 2016 [ebook]).
Time and the Sphinx. *Different* 3, No. 4 (September–October 1947): 32. *Magazine of Fantasy and Science Fiction* 28, No. 2 (February 1965): 77–79, where the dedication reads "In Memory of Lord Dunsany," who died in 1957. The original dedication is retained here. LBD herself died before the story was reprinted.
Whisper Water. *Weird Tales* 45, No. 2 (May 1953): 6–15. *Weird Tales* (UK) No. 22 (June 1953): 6–15. In *Exklusive Alpträume*, ed. Heinz Flossmann (Rastatt [Baden]: Erich Pabel Verlag, 1974), 142–59 (as "Der flüsternde Bach"; tr. Christiane Nogly and Elisabeth Simon). In *Horror Gems, Volume One* (n.p.: Armchair Fiction & Music, 2011), 126–40.

The Song of the Sun ❧ Leah Bodine Drake

Nonfiction

LBD worked as a movie and drama critic and as a society reporter for various papers beginning in 1941. This bibliography does not attempt to list those appearances.

Abracadabra. *Arkham Sampler* 2, No. 4 (Autumn 1949): 97–98. In *The Arkham Sampler: A Facsimile Edition*, ed. August Derleth (Sauk City, WI: Arkham House, 2010), 97–98.

[Announcement of Award.] Brief article containing a quotation from LBD. *Kaleidograph* 18, No. 1 (May 1946): 16–17.

Books and Pictures Which Influenced My Poems. S5.4. 1. By Kenneth Grahame; 2–4. By George Macdonald; 12. By Jean Ingelow; 13. By Aubrey Hopwood.

The Devil and Miss Barker. *Arkham Sampler* 2, No. 2 (Spring 1949): 85–87. In *The Arkham Sampler: A Facsimile Edition*, ed. August Derleth (Sauk City, WI: Arkham House, 2010): 85–87. Review of *Peace, My Daughters* by Shirley Barker.

Foreword. With Charles A. Musès. *VL* iii. Both C. S. Lewis (1898–1963) and Richard Hertz (1898–1961) had poems in the book. LBD herself did not live to see the finished book.

[For *The Living Voice*.] Assorted T.Mss. (carbon copies), S6.6. The titles of the seven items other than "What Poetry Means to Me" are those of LBD's poems under discussion. *Includes:* What Poetry Means to Me; The Web; Precarious Ground; Old Man on the Seashore: Morning; The Birth of Beauty; The Undine; The Final Green. Written c. March 1961. The quotation by George MacDonald (1824–1905) is from *At the Back of the North Wind* (1871). June E. Downey (1875–1932), *Creative Imagination: Studies in the Psychology of Literature* (New York: Harcourt, Brace, 1929): "that realm back of the North Wind, the poetic imagination" (p. vii). LBD copied passages (including this one) from Downey in S5.4.

Frederic Prokosch. R39. Written September 1941. Frederic Prokosch (1906–1989) was an American writer of poetry, novels, memoirs, and criticism, and also a distinguished translator. LBD refers to his book *The Carnival: Poems by Frederic Prokosch* (New York, London:

Harper & Bros., 1938).

Gremlins. *Arkham Sampler* 1, No. 3 (Summer 1948): 91–92. In *The Arkham Sampler: A Facsimile Edition*, ed. August Derleth (Sauk City, WI: Arkham House, 2010), 91–92. Review of *Sometime Never* by Roald Dahl.

Judging and Scoring the Papers. *Poetry Public Letter* 5, Nos. 2 and 3 (April–September 1957): 35.

Leah Bodine Drake Writes Volume of "Macabre" Poems. *Evansville Courier?* A clipping in LBD's papers has date of 15 November 1950 written on it, but the probable date is 13 December. Unsigned, but probably by LBD. See Appendix.

Life in These United States. T.Ms. (carbon), S6.6. Presumably written for the continuing monthly feature of that name in *Reader's Digest*. It is not known if the piece was published. Written after January 1961 (ms. bears Murdoch Avenue address in Parkersburg).

Magic Casements. S5.4. The piece is titled after a line in "Ode to a Nightingale" (l. 69) by John Keats.

The New Poetry. *Atlantic Monthly* 202, No. 1 (July 1958): 77–80.

New Voices in Poetry. *Atlantic Monthly* 199, No. 6 (June 1957): 75–78. LBD's paragraph on Richard Wilbur appears in *A Library of Literary Criticism: Modern American Literature*, ed. Dorothy Nyren (New York: Frederick Ungar Publishing Co., 1960), 527. Her review of Norman MacCaig appears in *Contemporary Literary Criticism*, ed. Daniel G. Marowski (Detroit: Gale Research Co., 1986), 280.

[On "We Come Out of the Forest, Fearing Stars."] *Poetry Public Letter* 1, No. 4 (April 1953): 8–10. LBD's responses to select, anonymous comments on her poem in the previous issue.

A Poem Should Have. S5.5.

[Review of *Directions in the Sun* by Eric Barker.] *Poetry Public Letter* 4, No. 4 (October–December 1956): 19–20.

[Review of *Forty Shillings* by Ruth Crary.] *Wings* 7, No. 7 (Autumn 1946): 23–24.

[Review of *Rendezvous in a Landscape* by August Derleth.] *Poetry Chap-Book* 10, No. 4 (Summer 1952): [100–101].

The Song of the Sun ~ Leah Bodine Drake

[Review of *Shells by a Stream* by Edmund Blunden.] *Wings: A Quarterly of Verse* 7, No. 6 (Summer 1946): 23–24.
[Review of *The Shimmering Disk* by Martha Salonen, and others.] *Wings: A Quarterly of Verse* 8, No. 6 (Summer 1948): 27–28.
[Review of *Testimony of Time* by Helen Nivens.] *Wings: A Quarterly of Verse* 8, No. 4 (Winter 1948): 26–27.
The Reviewer's Quill. *Wings: A Quarterly of Verse* 9, No. 2 (Summer 1949): 24–25. Review of *The Charity of the Stars* by John Heath-Stubbs.
The Reviewer's Quill. *Wings: A Quarterly of Verse* 9, No. 6 (Summer 1950): 22–23. Review of *Poems and Songs* by E. N. Da C. Andrade.
To Be a Poet. S5.4. Written 6 January 1941. LBD describes the perceptual phenomenon known as synesthesia, in which stimulation of one sensory pathway leads to automatic, involuntary experiences in another. She discusses the phenomenon at length in her notebook.
[Untitled judge's report.] *Kaleidograph* 18, No. 4. (August 1946): 14–15.
Whimsy and Whamsy. *Arkham Sampler* 2, No. 1 (Winter 1949): 88. In *The Arkham Sampler: A Facsimile Edition*, ed. August Derleth (Sauk City, WI: Arkham House, 2010), 88. Review of "... And Some Were Human" by Lester del Rey and *Moonfoam and Sorceries* by Stanley Mullen.

Published Letters

British Films Overseas by H. H. Wollenburg. *Sight and Sound* 15, No. 60 (Winter 1946–1947). Contains snippet of letter by Drake on p. 147.
Defending Mary Margaret. *Hearst's International Combined with Cosmopolitan* 110 (April 1941): 142. (under "Letters"). Mary Margaret McBride (1899–1976) was an American radio interview host and writer, known as "The First Lady of Radio." Her popular radio shows ran more than 40 years, with daily listeners for her housewife-oriented program numbering six to eight million in the 1940s.
More Talkies for Tots. *Photoplay* 39, No. 3 (February 1931): 10 (under "Brickbats & Bouquets").
On a Hypothetical Island. *Chicago Sunday Tribune* (7 April 1946): C17 (under "The Voice of the Reader"). Rpt. in part *Baltimore Sun*

BIBLIOGRAPHY

(15 April 1946): 14 (as "Those Desert Island Books Again" under "Good Morning!").
Pity among Animals. *American Mercury* No. 297 (September 1948): 380. LBD discusses Alan Devoe's "Down to Earth: Tropisms," *American Mercury* No. 294 (June 1948): 742–45. She also cites Ivan T. Sanderson, "Teamwork in Nature," *Nature Magazine* 37, No. 6 (June–July 1944): 302–4.
Some Good Novels. *Chicago Sunday Tribune* (30 June 1946): C10 (under "Voice of the Reader").
[Untitled.] *Newsweek* (2 December 1957).

Letters to *Weird Tales*
But We Did Reprint It. *Weird Tales* 33, No. 3 (March 1939): 157. As the assigned title to LBD's letter suggests, *Weird Tales* had reprinted A. Merritt's "The Woman of the Wood" (orig. August 1926) in the January 1934 issue—apparently before LBD began reading the magazine. "Medusa's Coil" by Zealia Bishop (revised by H. P. Lovecraft), "Waxworks" by Robert Bloch, and "These Doth the Lord Hate" by Gans T. Field appeared in the issue for January 1939. The poems were "The Warrior" by Emil Petaja, "Othello Time" by Vincent Starrett, and "And Thus I Knew" by Dorothy Agard Ansley.
Concise Comments. *Weird Tales* 32, No. 3 (September 1938): 384. "Fortune's Fools" by Seabury Quinn and "Mother of Toads" by Clark Ashton Smith appeared in the July 1938 issue; "The Black Drama" by Gans T. Field was serialized in the issues of June, July, and August 1938.
Changed. *Weird Tales* 33, No. 1 (January 1939): 127–28. Margaret Brundage (1900–1976) illustrated no covers in *Weird Tales* between the issues of October 1938 and July 1940. "Virgil" refers to Virgil Finlay (1914–1971), who was illustrating classic poems in various issues at this time. "Fothergill's Jug" by Thorp McClusky, "Lynne Foster Is Dead" by Seabury Quinn, and "The Hound of Pedro" by Robert Bloch all appeared in the November 1938 issue. The "serial

about Cleopatra" is "I Found Cleopatra" by Thomas P. Kelley (November 1938–February 1939).

A Horse Race. *Weird Tales* 34, No. 2 (August 1939): 155. LBD discusses stories in the May 1939 issue: "Washington Nocturne" by Seabury Quinn; "Almuric" by Robert E. Howard (the first installment of three); "The Watcher at the Door" by Henry Kuttner; "The Face at Death Corner" by Paul Ernst; and "The Dark Isle" by Everil Worrell.

Howdy, Mr. Rabbit! *Weird Tales* 35, No. 8 (March 1941): 123. LBD used the pleasantry in "Whisper Water."

A New Writing Technique. *Weird Tales* 34, No. 4 (October 1939): 120–21, as by Leah Drake. LBD discusses stories in the August 1939 issue: "Spawn" by P. Schuyler Miller; "Apprentice Magician" by E. Hoffmann Price; "Giants in the Sky" by Frank Belknap Long; and "The Valley Was Still" by Manly Wade Wellman.

An Old Howard Masterpiece. *Weird Tales* 29, No. 6 (June 1937): 768, as by Lea Bodine Drake. "The Black Stone" appeared in the November 1931 issue.

Reprint "The Wendigo." *Weird Tales* 26, No. 4 (October 1935): 526–27, as by Miss Lea Bodine Drake. *Weird Tales* did not reprint "The Wendigo." "Out of the Eons" by Hazel Heald (revised by H. P. Lovecraft) appeared in the April 1935 issue.

Unpublished Letters

To Anthony Boucher (pseudonym of William Anthony Parker White, 1911–1968)/*The Magazine of Fantasy and Science Fiction*. Syracuse University Libraries. 25 letters and postcards.

To August Derleth. Wisconsin Historical Society, 68 letters, cards, and postcards; another 3 letters are held privately.

To August Derleth. L. Tom Perry Special Collections, Harold B. Lee Library, Brigham Young University. 1 letter.

To Dorothy Hobson, director of The League to Support Poetry, Lockwood Library, University of Buffalo.

To Eugene Magner, Curator of the Poetry Collection, Lockwood Library, University of Buffalo.

BIBLIOGRAPHY

To Fletcher and Grace Stewart. Manuscripts and Folklife Archives Library, Special Collections, Western Kentucky University. 3 letters.
To Joseph Payne Brennan. John Hay Library, Brown University. 12 cards and postcards.
To Lawrence S. Thompson. University of Kentucky–Lexington. 7 letters.
To May Swenson. Washington University in St. Louis. 6 letters.
To the Stuart Art Gallery. Wisconsin Historical Society. One letter among Drake's letters to August Derleth.
To William Rose Benét. Yale Collection of American Literature, Beinecke Rare Book and Manuscript Library, Yale University. 3 letters to Benét and one to *Saturday Review of Literature*.

General

Arnheim, Rudolf, [and others]. *Poets at Work; Essays Based on the Modern Poetry Collection at the Lockwood Memorial Library, University of Buffalo*. Introduction by Charles D. Abbott. New York: Harcourt, Brace, 1948.
Barker, Eric. *Directions in the Sun*. New York: Gotham Book Mart, 1956.
Blackmore, Leigh. "'Figures in a Nightmare': The Poetry of Leah Bodine Drake." *Spectral Realms* No. 2 (Winter 2015): 133–46 (Part 1); No. 3 (Summer 2016): 129–35 (Part 2).
Callahan, Griffin and Betty. "[Death Announcement.]" Mimeograph form letter, c. December 1964. Wisconsin Historical Society and University of Kentucky–Lexington.
Chalker, Jack L., and Mark Owings. *The Science-Fantasy Publishers: A Critical and Bibliographic History, 1923–1999*. Westminster, MD: Mirage, 1999. *HW* is discussed on p. 27.
Davin, Eric L. *Partners in Wonder: Women and the Birth of Science Fiction 1926–1965*. New York: Lexington Books, 2006.
Derleth, August. *Arkham House: The First 20 Years: 1939–1959*. Sauk City, WI: Arkham House, 1959.
———. "The Future of Arkham House." *Outré* No. 3 ([mid- to late] 1956): [16–18]. Rpt. in S. T. Joshi, *80 Years of Arkham House*. Seattle: Sarnath Press, 2019. 208–10.

———. Letters to Leah Bodine Drake. LBD papers, University of Kentucky–Lexington.

———. Letter (carbon) to Leah Bodine Drake. AD papers, Wisconsin Historical Society.

———, ed. *Dark of the Moon: Poems of Fantasy and the Macabre*. Sauk City, WI: Arkham House, 1947. Freeport, NY: Books for Libraries Press, 1969. Miami, FL: Granger, 1976.

———, ed. *Fire and Sleet and Candlelight*. Sauk City, WI: Arkham House, 1961; Freeport, NY: Books for Libraries Press, 1973. Author mss. WHS box 102.

———, ed. *Hawk and Whippoorwill*. Author mss. WHS box 102.

Dziemianowicz, Stefan. "Drake, Leah Bodine." In *Supernatural Literature of the World: An Encyclopedia*, ed. S. T. Joshi and Stefan Dziemianowicz. Westport, CT: Greenwood Press, 2005. 1.357–58.

Eng, Steve. "Supernatural Verse in English." in Marshall B. Tymn, ed. *Horror Literature: A Core Collection and Reference Guide*. New York: R. R. Bowker Company 1981. pp. 401–54.

Handley-Taylor, Geoffrey, ed. *The International Who's Who in Poetry*. London: Cranbrook Tower Press, 1958. 2 vols. Entry on Leah Bodine Drake, 1.34.

Hanley, Terence E. "Leah Bodine Drake." In *Tellers of Weird Tales: Writers and Artists of the Unique Magazine*. 28 April 2011. tellersofweirdtales.blogspot.com/2011/04/leah-bodine-drake-1914-1964.html

Jaffery, Sheldon. *The Arkham House Companion: Fifty Years of Arkham House*. Mercer Island, WA: Starmont House, 1989. *HW* is discussed on pp. 38–39.

Jones, Jan. *Billy Rose Presents . . . Casa Manana*. Fort Worth, TX: Texas Christian University Press, 1999.

Joshi, S. T. *Sixty Years of Arkham House*. Sauk City, WI: Arkham House, 1999. Rev. ed. as *Eighty Years of Arkham House*. Seattle: Sarnath Press, 2019. Brief entry on *HW* (pp. 56–57 [1999 ed.]; pp. 51–52 [2019 ed.]).

McLaughlin, William J., and Frederick B. Bevis. *Indian Hills Environmental Inventory—A Citizens Tool for Planning*. [Fort Collins, CO]:

BIBLIOGRAPHY

Colorado State University, [Department of Recreation Resources and Landscape Architecture], 1975.

Musès, C. A., ed. *Prismatic Voices: An International Anthology of Distinctive New Poets / Voix Prismatiques: Une anthologie international de Poètes neufs et distinctifs.* Indian Hill, CO: Falcon's Wing Press/Éditions L'aile du Faucon, 1958.

Nielsen, Leon. *Arkham House Books: A Collector's Guide.* Jefferson, NC: McFarland, 2004. HW is discussed on pp. 72–73.

Reid, Robin Anne, ed. *Women in Science Fiction and Fantasy.* Westport, CT: Greenwood Press, 2009 (2 vols.): 1.91. Brief mention of Drake.

Smith, Clark Ashton, and August Derleth. *Eccentric, Impractical Devils: The Letters of Clark Ashton Smith and August Derleth.* Ed. David E. Schultz and S. T. Joshi. New York: Hippocampus Press, 2020.

The joey Zone. "A Dark Muse: Leah Bodine Drake." *NecronomiCon Providence Memento Book,* ed. Victoria Dalpe and Justin Steele (Cranston, RI: Lovecraft Arts & Sciences Council Press, 2019), pp. 67–68.

The Supplement to Who's Who. Chicago: Marquis Publications, March–May 1959. Entry on Leah Bodine Drake, p. 2380.

Ward, William S. *A Literary History of Kentucky.* Knoxville: University of Tennessee Press, 1988. Drake is discussed on pp. 330–31.

Wood, Edelene. "Leah Bodine Drake." 10 April 1968. S6.5. Course paper for English and Rhetoric, West Virginia University.

Yaszek, Lisa, and Patrick B. Sharp. *Sisters of Tomorrow: The First Women of Science Fiction.* Middletown, CT: Wesleyan University Press, 2016.

Index of Titles of Poems

Adam the First Poet	442
Adam's Hand	439
After the Green Star Dies	300
Air [Adaptable element, fluid to all things' will]	352
Air [Blue goblet of water, dust and gas]	437
All-Hallows	414
All-Saints' Eve	161
Alone	391
Apple	109
"Apples and Apricots, Peaches and Plums"	206
Ariadne on Naxos	398
Ark	359
Ask the Trees	419
Assyrian Lion, The	141
At Alise Sainte-Reine	417
Atavism	308
Atlantis	336
Back-Country Road in God's Country, A	420
Bad Company	199
Ballad of Fair Elspeth, The	105
Ballad of the Jabberwock	269
Ballad of the Seal-Woman's Daughter	248
Bats	257
Beaches Beyond Oblivion, The	268
Belle and Beau	113
Besom, The	157
Beyond Eden	277

The Song of the Sun ❧ Leah Bodine Drake

Bird's-Eye View	255
Birds in a Barn	262
Birth of Beauty, The	337
Bittern, The	192
Black Peacock, The	259
Bookworm	325
Born under Capricorn	192
Bread of Solitude	244
"Brightness Falls from the Air"	391
Burma: Moulmein Bazaar	111
By the River	100
Cat Mummy	345
Cave Paintings, Altamira	314
Centaur	331
Centaurs, The	193
Changeling	242
Charm for the New Year, A	443
Childhood Summers	350
Chimaera	332
Cinder-Jewels	261
Circe	414
Cobra	321
Cockatrice	332
Cold Comfort	267
Cold Orchard [She walks always in her intimate, own]	256
Cold Orchard [Like one in orchards stripped and chill]	429
Comet, The	254
Coming Back to the House	426
Comment on Man	379
Conjuration, The	158
Convent Bell, The	399
Conversation in an Oak-Tree	186
Coral Reef at Calico Key	444
Country Grave, A	263
Country Lover, The	112

Index of Titles of Poems

Coven, The	157
Covenant, The	157
Crocodile	173
Croon of the Mer-Mother, The	120
Crows, The	367
Cry, The	403
Crying of the Grass, The	372
Curious Story	163
Currier and Ives Prints	296
Cytherean, The	436
Daphne	266
Dark Memory	282
Darkened Glass, The	307
Daughter of the Grand Turk Loses Her Ball, The	204
December Stars	255
Descent of Angels	152
The Deserted Courtyard	100
Design for a Tapestry: 14th Century	273
Dirge for a Doomed Planet	309
Dirge for a Doomed Planet	432
Drake of Devon	226
Dream of Samarkand, The	116
Drone	356
Ducks and Pigs	178
Earth: Atomic Age	265
Enchanted Honey	246
Enchanted Sleep	159
Enchanted Swans, The	343
Encounter in Broceliande	202
Eve of St. Tib, The	416
Evening in Late Summer	425
Explanation	150
Face in the Water, The	415
Fairies in Autumn, The	142
Fairy Cider	249

The Song of the Sun ❧ Leah Bodine Drake

Fairy Tale	417
Fairy-Tale: Twentieth Century	361
False Messiah, The	296
Familiar, The	159
Fantasy in a Forest	219
Fawn, The	376
Figures in a Nightmare	150
Final Green, The	326
Five Angels, The	442
Flemish Artists	353
Foam-Born, The	327
Folk-Tale	394
Fool's Paradise	342
Forerunner, The	380
Four, The	337
From a destroyed early poem	440
From a poem to Mother	442
From Nonsensical Rhymes	217
Frozen Heart	146
Fruit Uneaten, The	237
Full Moon, 1940	220
Fur Coat, The	288
Fury	332
Gage to a Lover	238
Gazelles in a Zoo	108
Ghoul	333
Giant's Garden, The	143
Gifts for Christ	306
Gipsies	344
Girl in the Glass, The	164
Girl on the Saw-Backed Mountain, The	221
Goat-Song	165
Gods of the Dana, The	358
Gold from a Kettle	224
Good-Advisors, The	372

Index of Titles of Poems

Gossip, The	420
Gothic	427
Green Door, The	298
Griffon's Gold	227
Growing Tree, The	405
Hand, The	383
Harvest, The	376
Haunted Hour, The	125
He Dreams of Barbary	140
Heads on Easter Island, The	289
Heard on the Roof at Midnight	278
Hell-Broth, The	157
Hellenic World, The	388
Help Wanted	279
Hen-Wife's Chickens, The	230
High Renaissance	138
High Wire	374
Honey from the Lion	288
Hornbook for Witches, A	157
House Accursed	214
House in the Hollow, The	258
"Hunter"	441
"I Dreamed That You Took My Arm." . . .	392
I Met a Lion	218
In the Night	412
"In the Night I Awoke"	390
In the Shadows	137
in the woods of the Vaud	448
Incoming Tide	356
India: In the Garden of Spices	139
Jannigogs, The	347
Japan: The Persimmon Gatherers	174
Jilly and the Elf	123
Journey of the Queen of Sheba, The	181
King Gog and King Magog	223

King Solomon	250
Kingfisher Lake	311
Lady of the Emperor's Palace, A	101
Lady Writing a Letter	99
Land of the Japanese Prints, The	110
Landscape with Horses: 6000 B.C.	431
Lariat: 6000 B.C., The	305
Last Faun, The	187
Lazy Prince, The	362
Legend	276
Leonardo Before His Canvas	281
"Like Breath upon a Glass"	301
Likely Story!, A	280
Little Piper, The	130
Little Song	410
Little Things	129
Lost Heritage	222
Love Song	318
Lullaby After Death	396
Luna	247
Lying Awake	401
Mad Jenny	126
Mad Woman's Song	293
Magic Circle, The	158
Magician's Hat	159
Man in Winter	229
Man Who Married a Swan-Maiden, The	137
Meeting on a Northern Moor, A	409
Memory, A	379
Mermaid, The	319
Middle Ages: Two Views, The	348
Midsummer Night	177
Minor Poet	285
Minotaur	331
Minotaur, The	215

Index of Titles of Poems

Mombāsa	101
Moment at Sunset	287
Moment in Paradise	378
Moon Festival	99
Morning, The	413
Mouse Heaven	208
Multiple Clay	382
Music for Sun and Moon	245
"My Help Cometh from the Hills"	134
Nail, The	381
Nativities [Not only here may magian eyes]	253
Nativities [Not here alone may longing eyes]	427
Naughty Fairy, The	188
Nixie's Pool, The	160
No Refuge	264
Noon Light	373
Okio's Geese	421
Old Daphne	286
Old Granny's Story, The	195
Old Khan and His Falcon, The	175
Old Man on the Seashore	365
Old Wives' Tale	155
Old World of Green, The	295
On a Chinese Screen	99
On a Night of Stars	228
On the Night-Wind	404
One Intoxicated	101
"Only a Little Dust"	400
Orchids	411
Our Lady's Song	118
Out!	324
Overheard in Baghdad	334
Owl's Cry	147
Path through the Marsh, The	171
"Peace on Earth"	147

ও 751

Peddler's Pack	131
Pentagram, The	158
Phoenix Egg, The	241
Pixy Fair, The	119
Pooka	331
Pool, The	301
Poplar Wind	430
Poplar-Wind	287
Powers of the Air	341
Precarious Ground	317
Presence, The	415
Prisoner, The	384
Protective Colouring	210
Puss-in-Boots and the Three Mice	179
Rabbit-Dance	194
Railroad Tracks	351
Rain on the Stone, The	367
Red Ghosts in Kentucky	329
Reincarnation	433
Retrogression	243
Return, The	290
Revenant, The	313
Rhymes without Reason; or, History Made Difficult	215
Rider, The	387
Robin, The	387
Roc	334
Rock and Bramble	360
'Round and 'Round	176
Royal	414
"Run with the Fox"	201
Sailorman (1690), The	115
Saints of Four-Mile-Water, The	124
Salamander	333
Satyr	331
Sea-Shell	196

INDEX OF TITLES OF POEMS

Semele	349
Serpent-Ring	184
Seven Sons of the King of Thule, The	185
Sigh in Spring, A	142
Singer from the Waste, The	236
Six Merry Farmers	322
Snake, The	411
Snow Crystals	283
Snowy Night	260
Solar	345
Song against Smallness	291
Song at Sunrise	103
Song of the Sun	294
Spells, The	158
Sphinx	334
Spirit-Fox	333
Spray, The	404
Star Came Out, A	203
Steps in the Field, The	207
Storks, The	363
Stranger, The	197
Sunset Apocalypse	311
Switzerland	447
Tale of Tannhauser, The	395
Tarascon	409
Tenants, The	199
Terrible Meek, The	412
Terror by Night	153
That Summer [That summer everyone said they had never]	400
That Summer [That summer the old folks said they had never]	440
"There Are Fairies"	129
They Run Again	210
This Side of Oblivion	435
Three Green Ladies of Greenwich, The	190
Through-Train	354

ঌ 753

The Song of the Sun ❧ Leah Bodine Drake

Tiger	172
To a Lost Sweetheart	103
To an Atheist	267
To Certain Poetry Critics	310
To Elinor Wylie	274
To Mother	398
To One Who Fears Poetry Is Useless	273
Turn of Year	119
Turning Point	253
Uncle Jay	392
Unclimbed Hill, The	257
Under Funereal Lilies	371
Under-Seas, The	435
Under-Seas, The	436
Undine, The	310
Unhappy Ending	145
Unicorn Wounded, The	355
Unicorn	425
Unknown Land, The	297
Unlikely Noah's Ark, An	330
Unlikely Story	429
Unploughed Field, The	315
[Untitled] [Good Pope Urban]	404
[Untitled] [Lying awake at night I hear the rain]	444
Vase from Araby, A	240
Vestal	235
Vision of Jenghiz-Khan, The	317
Vision, The	284
Voice, A	398
Warning to Skeptics, A	325
Wasp in the Window, The	405
We Come Out of the Forest, Fearing Stars	316
We Move on Turning Stone	358
Web, The	341
Web of Living, The	352

Index of Titles of Poems

Weeds and the Wilderness, The	369
Well, The	371
Werewolf	332
"What Are Little Girls Made Of?"	198
What the Devil Said	402
Wild Geese in Spring	286
Willow-Women	292
Wind and the Leaves, The	161
Wind in the Chimney, The	323
Window on the Stair, The	240
Windows of Chartres, The	305
Winter Harvest	149
Winter Harvests	146
Witch Walks in Her Garden, The	151
Witch's Wheel	159
Witches on the Heath	162
Witches, The	406
With Every Death	439
With Her Death	397
Woods Grow Darker, The	366
Wood-Wife, The	211
Word of Willow, The	374
Words After Wisdom	104
Wyvern	330
Zanzibar	365

Index of First Lines of Poems

A bersark was one	217
"A curse upon this house!" cried he,	214
A fairy made cider	249
A Fury looked a lot like woman,	332
A garden of old trees,	379
A growing tree scratched fingers on the screen	405
A peddling fellow came our way.	131
A place that I know	311
A star came out, the first!—so small	203
A wasp for his own reasons has crept here	405
Abelard argued, Augustine wrote,	367
Across the secret walls they rush	314
Across the tapestry-lands of the Middle Ages	406
Adam sitting at his ease	222
Adaptable element, fluid to all things' will	352
After the day of doom	300
After the storm of sorrow with its wrack,	146
After you pass Owl's Candle and Pickporridge the lane tilts	369
Against a leaf-green twilight sky	257
All over Italy the chimes	245
Along the edges of my mind	282
Along the long beaches of the dark	435
Always the tracks lead onward blue as the distance	351
Always they turn into brutes,	414
Among the black trees spider-webbed	199
Among the straight, stiff-flowered trees	425
An old man in a greenish, too-long coat	365

↝ 757

The Song of the Sun ~ Leah Bodine Drake

An unheroic hunter, I	285
And now that he has climbed the stair	361
. . . . . . "and two elves, gossiping on the highest branch of a beech	448
Animal, upright, forked	441
Apple-blossom, poppy-petal,	420
As I sat by my fire one night	278
As I went home through the thirsty fields	329
As I went up the small steep stair	240
As we went up the narrow stair,	137
Ask the butternut trees, ask the beech and hickory	419
At Four-Mile-Water down Wexford way	124
At sunset over Nippon's snow	333
Away down on the River Nile	173
Balanced upon a shining wire	374
Balkis the Wise, the Ethiops' Queen,	181
Before dawn, in night's worst hour, alone,	399
Between two unknown trees I stood	219
Beyond the black and naked wood	210
Birds are the heirs	262
Bless the unearthly flame!	273
Blue goblet of water, dust and gas	437
Braced with an iron heart	309
Braced with an iron heart	432
Bride of small, humble orchards,	109
Bring the black cock and the knife,	158
Buckety, buckety, over the plain	331
But to His (God's) child He gave the power	442
By the turning of this wheel,	159
By-low, little mer-babe,	120
Chimaera was a triple threat—	332
Come to me, all you who burn and are complex-laden,	402
Confess that in your secret wood	235
Cross-legged on the Sarsen Stone	157
Death, who binds with tighter jess	267
Deep in the gold forests of that dream,	153

INDEX OF FIRST LINES OF POEMS

Don't boast your unbelief in woods!	325
Down the long beaches of the past	268
Down to the dragon's house of stone	429
Eccentrics, characters. . . . those off-beat ones	392
Egypt's king, the Pharaoh,	215
Five angels stood about my bed (when I was born)	442
Flashing through facets of her glassy world,	319
Flatland fields grow tall tobacco,	221
Folk in the Old World	279
For a terrible moment the sky fierced and throbbed	311
Forever in God's eye the scene is fixed:	378
Four elements of which man regards the ways,	337
Four-foot 'round the cemetery	333
From the black woods and sad Siberian marshes,	305
From the damp earth rise the scents of Spring;	100
From the dappled east, stretching their long throats	421
From the dark bracken of my personal wood,	318
Gay burly beau, his life is summer only.	356
"Give him the back of your hand!"	372
Goat-men roamed the classic hills	331
God wearied of the world. He watched its strife,	376
Gog, he was a heathen king and Magog was his brother;	223
Gold, frankincense and myrrh	306
Good Pope Urban	404
"Hai-ai! Uu-aah-ai!"	116
Hands that caressed move now	414
Have ye seen the old witch-woman who lives on the edge o' town?	126
He climbs up glimmering water-stairs to poise	417
Heaven is a great House	208
Here in their man-made dells	108
Here on our southern doorstep where	444
Here water-music makes a low lament	286
Here where the road bumps to a dip by Tipton's woods	420
Here within this potent round,	158
Hereward the Wake	217

The Song of the Sun ❧ Leah Bodine Drake

High on the wires across the land	150
"Ho! Hob-in-the-Oak! Are you there?"	186
Horses they knew, and the fates in cards, and thieving,	344
Hosts of Mazikeen and Djinn	158
How delicately we should move	352
How sad that Orchid is the human symbol	411
How terrible are those meek	412
I am half of the land	248
I am out on the wind	242
I came upon it unaware.	288
I can't remember	298
I cannot give	238
I dreamed that you took my arm;	392
I found a curious looking-glass	164
I had a queer thing happen once;	288
I have a hunger hot and deep	244
I have danced with berries in my hair	404
"I have spells to cast tomorrow," says the witch,	151
I knew that shape the instant seen	202
I know that the black dog crouches beyond the door,	293
I know the enchanted castle lies over the hill	362
I know words that are fun to say:	365
I like little, fragile things,	129
I made the wilderness my home	236
I met a lady walking in the snow	414
I met a lion in the sands.	218
I met an old woman down in a valley	178
I remember well	308
I remember well	433
I saw a city on a hill	284
I saw him! I saw him!—just yesterday,	187
I shall cry out "Unjust!"	400
I shortcut home between Wade's tipsy shocks,	367
I sinned a sin today	381
I started with the hunt,	201

INDEX OF FIRST LINES OF POEMS

I think of that poor dragon Tarascon	409
I, who turned into a tree	266
If trees should spread their roots in air	241
Imagine the sun in his strength,	345
In a hollow oak-tree	211
In dream I saw a world	301
In metals men pursue her: in the crowns	436
In my one field the grass	315
In or out of dream, in the winter dark,	403
In pulse upon pulse of joy	413
In stripped and shaken trees	290
In the galactic swirl	265
In the gilt morning air	337
In the hot shadows of the old bazaar	111
In the night I awoke, and I was weeping.	390
In the scorched places between Kedron and the Dead Sea,	380
In the thin light	277
Is this the classic fiend,	321
"Is this the road to the City?" I said	150
It is a landscape where the gauzy foliage	342
It is not well for man to see	255
It is the East we dream of: there	387
It was chill in the withered wood and still,	416
Jannigogs came from the Moon, (and they should have stayed there).	347
King Minos once thought it a lark	331
Lie on my breast a moment, so—	412
Like a steeple to the skies	159
Like one in orchards stripped and chill	429
Like stately ship upon the Main	113
Listen!.	147
Little Babe, how strange a thing:	118
Liveliest of trees, the poplars always find	287
Look!	161
Lord, when will you return to us?	99
Lying awake at night I hear the rain	444

☙ 761

The Song of the Sun 🙵 Leah Bodine Drake

Lying awake in bed	401
Mangy, lean, of evil fame,	159
Men told him:	227
Men try to hold her in enamelled crowns	327
Motionless hang the pears	373
My grandmother tells me,	269
My young Lord walks with Lady Anne	112
Never let them tell you	129
Nobody knows if the Sphinx at Giza	334
Not here alone may longing eyes	427
Not only here may magian eyes	253
Nothing moved in the old house,	323
Now from the spray of the branching briar	177
Now from thick skies descend	283
Now in the slyly-lengthening dark	119
Now that the tumult of the Spring has fled,	147
Now the mole in downward tower,	396
Now this is the way of the tiger . . . . . He goes	172
Now up from Hades creeps the moon:	220
Now up the shore	313
Now with flute and little drum my skilled musicians	139
Nowhere foretold,	253
O Mother,	404
O what do they sell at the Pixy Fair	119
O, when I walked abroad with you	103
Oh, go not to the Nixie's pool!	160
Oh, me!	143
Oh, take me to my native hills again!	134
Old Giant Grimly Gore, club on shoulder,	261
Older than Eden's planting, older than elves,	374
On a hill's side, in a place where no one came,	411
On the volcanic hill	317
Once in my youth I saw the centaurs drinking	193
Once more the wild geese leave the cypress bayous	286
Out in a field that no one weeds	207

INDEX OF FIRST LINES OF POEMS

Out in the woods where the snow lies white	194
Out of the fragments of an urn	410
Out of the vast	398
Over the grassy steppes,	431
Over the sodden fields through which I pass	264
Over the sodden fields through which I pass	426
Piercing dark stone they gleam	305
Pity the great!	291
'Round and 'round an elder-tree	176
Say what more, what more can I do, O wild swan's daughter,	137
Set in the streaming void	294
Shaped like a tear-drop, pale as haze	240
She walks always in her intimate, own	256
She went to the moor in the honey-coloured twilight	155
She who was here, who took her place	391
She would wander the sun-struck hills about Thebes,	349
Since beholding your peach-bloom countenance	99
Sir Launcelot was bad cess to his sweethearts.	341
Six merry farmers	322
So at last you did	274
Solomon, old and worn and wise,	250
Someday I'll hold a mirror to my face	384
Somehow the poplars always find	430
Something, those summers, seemed to lie curled like a fern	350
Somewhere off shore	336
Somewhere sinks the hidden sun;	260
Stranded upon the sand,	196
Sunk deep in night Mombāsa lies.	101
Switzerland is a big country	447
That afternoon you bent	415
That man was prisoner on the isle of Lab!	334
That night we hurtled through a little town,	354
That summer everyone said they had never	400
That summer the old folks said they had never	440
That was the night I ran	324

෴ 763

The Song of the Sun ❧ Leah Bodine Drake

The air revealed a glimmering form	228
The bad queen waved her wand, and the brothers rose	343
The beautiful, trusting beast that trotted out of the wood	355
The child came to a pool in the heart of a thicket,	301
The Cockatrice is a telescoped economy-	332
The Dixie-cups, the orange peel, the lost spade,	356
The Emperor Baber	217
The Fairy who lives	188
The fruit was in my hand:	237
The gods of the Dana are lords of one small green island.	358
The Great Bear thrusts a bright paw forth	255
The hare in the stubbled meadow	210
The Hellenic world emerges in our dream half history, half fable.	388
The Hen-Wife in the valley	230
The hill is green where Vercingetorix paced his tent,	417
The Land of the West, the Land of Evermore,	666
..... "The lofty tomb that lives of slaves once bought—	440
The Minotaur	215
The new young year comes in	443
The night her spirit came to me	415
The orchard has been invaded	174
The owl, the bat, and the twisted tree:	199
The Pooka lives down in the deeps	331
The Princess of Turkey has lost her ball!	204
The Roc	334
The royal hands that tied	345
The Salamander is a lizard	333
The seven sons of the King of Thule,	185
The sky grows pale with the morning light,	103
The sky is coloured like a peacock's breast;	125
The sky is coloured like a peacock's breast;	425
The spent fox slinks along the hill	243
The stranger, the proud-headed man who sat	197
The sun in a grave of gold;	287
The sun, impartial host,	247

Index of First Lines of Poems

The tale says Rome refused him. The aging rake	395
"The terns that feed among these dunes	140
The Three Green Ladies of Greenwich	190
The well in the field is bitter,	371
The Werewolf's a bit of a tough,	332
The wicked barons laid the landscape waste	348
The wood was lonely and grey,	145
The Wyvern is a little dragon,	330
The X-ray's eye that sees into the sheep	383
The year comes 'round to Spring again,	142
The year half gone,	387
There are words of awful might	158
There is a hill I shall not climb:	257
There is a path through a marsh	171
There is a strange, recurring dream	297
There was a land where all the toys were made,	394
There was an old wizard who tried	224
There's a curious land in a faïrytale clime	110
There's a warm wind rustling my green-gauze canopy;	101
Theseus left Ariadne flat:	398
They always knew their doom would come	276
They go down deep O deep beyond all telling,	310
They promised a redeemer of their own,—	296
They say he saw a vision, a mirage	317
They say the storks are leaving Europe, growing rare.	363
They say we shouldn't praise the violet	310
Think of the eye of man, that gem	307
This block of hexagons carved out of topaz comes	198
This flexible, bright, foolish thing	184
This is of green, unclassic shade	326
This is the country that our grandsires knew,—	296
This is the season when the earth grows small	229
Three little mice sat down to spin,	179
Three witches danced on the heath last night,	162
Through the rusty brambles,	142

☙ 765

The Song of the Sun 〜 Leah Bodine Drake

Time was when maidens in the Lebanon groves	152
Under funereal lilies here lies one	371
Under the quiet lamp his darling page	325
Under this final stone	263
Under this low, root-raftered roof	246
Up the dragon's rocky glen	280
Upon his ivory throne the old Khan is weeping;	175
Upon the grey flags of the courtyard	100
Upon the kingdoms of the air	341
Valentine's took to his bed,	114
Vervain, henbane, lizard's leg,	157
Vivien, the limmer lass,	159
Warm seas and fins, and then the landward leap	439
We are so near to you,	295
We come out of the forest, fearing stars,	316
We feared the incubus, the hex.	366
We gaze up at the stars and say:	379
We know that human hands carved these lean faces	289
We move on turning stone	358
We see him sculptured in each ruined hall,	141
We're taught by rock and bramble	360
Weave here a dame in Flanders cloth,	273
What are Earth's gifts to a child of Spring?	206
What strangeness forms my flesh, my intimate bone?	382
What they loved, what their brushes proudly caressed	353
When Adam and Eve awoke	277
When from this age I seek escape	427
When full gallop they would speed	157
When I am dead, when I am still	192
When I gaze into my wine-cup	101
When I opened the door, the wind	391
When I press your head to mine	372
When I was but a young thing	104
When the peaks of Kâf receive the dawn,	259
When we take the long way	258

Index of First Lines of Poems

When you were here	398
Where apple-trees drift down a hill	149
Where have you been, O Sailorman,	115
Where is the place that the wind is going	161
Where is the tune we heard one day	130
Where red cranberries light the dusk	192
"Who are you, flimsy ghost on a ghost-horse	409
Who calls beyond the garden?	105
"Who is this one who strides	376
"Who is this sailing on our Main?" the ruffled Señors say,	226
Why are you weeping, shepherd boy,	292
"Will you come away with me?" said the Elf,	123
William Shakespeare	218
With his turbulent golden hair	254
Within her eye the wild world moved and shone,	397
Within her eyes shone the wild world,	439
Within my brain lies, pure and clear,	281
Within the stable-smelling dark	359
Would I have kept your old heart beating	442
Writ on scroll of felon's skin	157
"Yes . . . yes . . . I saw the sirens once,"	163
Yes, madonna! I have some curious treasures!	138
Yestere'en, as ever was,	195
You map for me your personal space:	267
Young wives and blossoming maidens	165

www.ingramcontent.com/pod-product-compliance
Lightning Source LLC
Chambersburg PA
CBHW060356230426
43663CB00008B/1293